We  **losions, and** far away.

My heart was pounding in my throat as I realized that any second I would be in the mouth of the beast....

I glanced back at the CO, then moved my eyes quickly back to our exposed flank as my peripheral vision noticed that the bushes were moving toward me. I stared harder; they were definitely moving toward me. My heart leapt into my mouth and froze. Things began to happen in slow motion as I started to turn my head slowly to warn Captain Federline of the danger while my body started to lower itself in self-preservation.

"We've got movement—enemy—on the right!" I yelled the warning as I dived to the ground, but halfway through my words the advancing, camouflaged NVA soldiers began firing....

RITES OF PASSAGE

Odyssey of a Grunt

Robert Peterson

BALLANTINE BOOKS • NEW YORK

A Ballantine Book
Published by The Ballantine Publishing Group
Copyright © 1997 by Joni Peterson

www.ballantinebooks.com

ISBN 0-345-44694-1

Manufactured in the United States of America

First Ballantine Books Edition: September 2001

10 9 8 7 6 5 4 3 2 1

Introduction

"Joni, I think I'm going." My husband winced with pain, squeezing shut his eyes as the labored breathing was taking its toll on him. I tried once more to ease his physical discomfort by cradling him in my arms, when the realization hit me. Like earlier times in our marriage, he had absolutely no fear as he faced death squarely. But this time, he really was dead of a heart attack.

The take-charge part of my personality wanted to begin CPR immediately while the spiritual and loving aspects of Joni, the wife, seemed detached, not wanting to disturb death's gentle encompassing serenity. Finally, his tortured body would no longer be racked with pain. The physical and emotional trauma were over. The Vietnam War finally was over.

His life had been a paradox. Nicknamed Bullet in high school because he loved to run fast, the name took on an ironic twist after he was wounded in 1967. Outwardly, he learned to cope with his paralysis by leading a highly productive public life. Inwardly, the effects of post-traumatic stress disorder continued to kill his spirit, much like the snipers he had faced in Southeast Asia. He had written: "Courage is not the absence of fear, but is the ability to carry on with dignity in spite of the fear you feel."

The days after his death on April 23, 1994, were full of a growing numbness that allowed me to witness the love and respect of the Soldiers Grove community for their former village president, while allowing me to push aside my rising fears and panic in facing a future without him. For me, he had been the source of stability, intelligence, romance and humor since 1969. But it hadn't been easy.

Two years after Bullet returned from Vietnam, I fell in love with a romantic poet who showered me with bouquets of roses while I was a college freshman. He surprised me with a diamond necklace and earrings, but first handed me a note:

For as much as virtue begets honor—
then beauty deserves beauty:
If I could pluck the brightest star from the heavens
And place it in your hands,
'Twould still not suffice.
So I give to you these,
As tokens of my esteem.
For you already have my love.

Early in our marriage, Bullet told me in a candid and very vulnerable moment that he was closer to the men who had served with him in combat than any marriage vows could ever bind him to me. I was crushed. I knew he loved me. I heard it in my head, but I had to ponder it in my heart for years. I remained threatened by the statement and strangely jealous of these men. I was too young and unworldly to even grasp what he was trying to express. And like most of America at the time, I was unable, unwilling or not ready to listen to the truth.

We continued to share many character-building experiences that left me wondering if the legacy of the Vietnam War would ever allow us to have a "normal" marriage. One dawn in 1972, a woodpecker started hammering on the metal roof of our home. Bullet bolted out of a deep sleep with instant beads of sweat on his body as he tried to shove me down in protection while he hollered: "Incoming!"

In 1979 he was accidentally locked out of the house. Because it was a chilly, rainy evening and he was too far away from the nearest neighbor, he decided to go around the house to the back porch doors and break the glass to get inside. About twenty feet onto the freshly seeded lawn, his wheelchair became completely mired in the mud. Somehow he dropped himself onto his belly. He folded the chair and grabbed the handle of the cumbersome, heavy silicone sitting pad. He propelled himself by the elbows, dragging his chair and the pad, and crawled until he reached the sidewalk. With sheer grit and determination he managed to become upright in his chair again and entered the house leaving a trail of blood, mud and torn clothing. When I arrived home after a three-hour visit with a friend, he had only just crawled into bed.

As I began my teaching career in 1980 he became more and more remote. It was as if he looked right through me and couldn't speak. Our beautiful intimacy was becoming a memory as I struggled to figure out this stranger housed in my husband's body. After many tears were shed by both of us, he was able to express that he had been having nonstop flashbacks during his waking hours. I had already known for years that when sleep didn't elude him, it was filled with haunting nightmares and garbled speech. I was beginning to comprehend the enormity of the situation.

When the Wall in Washington, D.C., was dedicated, veterans across the country were interviewed. I stood near the television and said rather smugly, "You know, it's those lunatic fringe elements that give the rest of you Vietnam veterans a bad name." A great silence followed my statement and then I heard the quiet gulps and the unmistakable sound of crying as he responded: "I identify more with those men that you call the lunatic fringe than I do with other veterans. These men are my brothers." I went humbly to him and held him as we both wept and knew the war would never be over for Bullet.

I enrolled in a multicultural grad class in the early 90s and I casually asked Bullet to name two black heroes. Without any hesitation, he replied: "Sergeants Watley and Underhill. They carried me to the chopper when I got shot."

We both grew in compassion for each other as well as compassion for other struggling veterans and their families. Bullet bought me a book for my birthday in 1993 about how to survive living with a Vietnam vet. The symptoms that I knew haunted Bullet were all there: night sweats, sleeplessness, flashbacks and nightmares. As I gently asked Bullet if he ever experienced any of the other symptoms listed, he took my hand and said: "Yes, I struggle with all of them, including an impending sense of doom."

My eyes filled with tears as he described hypervigilance: how he still constantly scanned tree lines for snipers while driving and checked fresh dirt piles for trip wires; why he insisted on the same earth tones for our roof shingles as well as the cedar siding because he could better protect us from an ambush with those colors. He continued to tell me in a halting voice how he had insisted on the earth berming to be just exactly the way he wanted because he could launch an attack if he ever needed to. He found freedom in the telling of his pain, but how could healing continue when the situation seemed so incredibly overwhelming?

Although we didn't have children of our own, we hosted six foreign exchange students until Bullet's death. Our first, Fabio

Sergio, proved to be a godsend when it came to healing many of Bullet's war memories. He asked in a straightforward manner countless questions about the war and its effects. His quest for truth forced Bullet to patiently examine various aspects of his experiences there. As Bullet explained in detail the horrors as well as the everyday humor that helped him to survive, Fabio and I witnessed a subtle change—a sense of peace and a beginning of coming to terms with his disabled situation. A renewed interest in living life to the fullest took place.

Bullet began to feel a sense of pride in the fact that he was a Vietnam veteran. He participated in a Chicago welcome home parade. When Wisconsin held a similar event in Madison, it coincided with his birthday and became a turning point in healing old emotional scars. The Highground, Wisconsin's memorial plaza in Neillsville, became a safe and sacred place for healing. It was in this place of incredible natural beauty that he could be at peace in dealing with the human cost of things that had plagued him and his fellow veterans. It was here that he wanted his ashes scattered.

Five weeks before he died I found out he had been shot by friendly fire. He always thought that I had known, and it was the one thing we had never discussed in our twenty-three years together. We spent the entire night holding each other as we talked through my rage and misunderstanding and how we could still believe that life was worth living. We talked like newlyweds, and everything seemed incredibly clear and in perspective. We had come full circle.

When he died in my arms, I couldn't wish him back. On another scrap of paper I found this last piece of his writing:

> *I took an hour*
> *to examine a flower;*
> *a day to examine*
> *a shell;*
> *a week went by*
> *as I looked at the sky;*
> *O Life has*
> *treated me well.*

—*JONI PETERSON*
March 1997

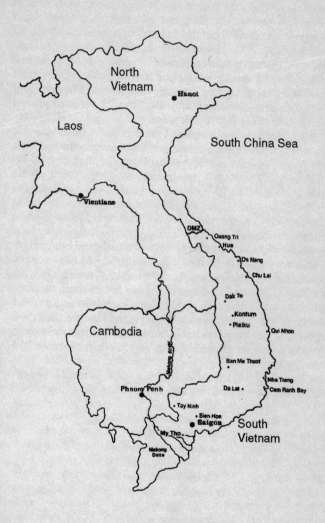

Prologue

The earliest childhood memories I have of my mother show her at the stove, at the sink, or staring at the refrigerator waiting for an idea, or a full meal, to jump out at her. In the summer she was in the garden, then back to the kitchen sink, then stove. While we were outside playing, or even occasionally working, the floors were somehow cleaned. Certainly, Ma must have wandered from the kitchen as the Peterson children numbered eleven—still do today though some of us are rather in ill repair.

Further proof resides in the memory of Sunday summer picnics and, almost without fail, Wednesday night and Saturday night trips to town to stock up on supplies in all forms. Town was usually always Soldiers Grove, but just about the time a kid could think he had his parents all figured out, Dad would pile us in the car (I remember a black 40s Olds, a maroon '47 Ford, a gray '49 Plymouth, a bronze '53 Ford—one of my favorites—a green '55 Plymouth, and a white and gold '57 Plymouth with push-button automatic transmission and tail fins) and head for another small town—Gays Mills or Boscobel. Summers would bring Wednesday night (or some other weeknight) and free movies at the Rolling Ground Store & Tavern or the Orchard Pump Tavern & Store. It's important to note the order: Rolling Ground was a store with a bar, Orchard Pump vice versa.

These were great times for kids. Instead of watching the movies, we would wander through the orchards, throw apples at one another, or the movie screen, and experience relationships with other children of our age who were not siblings: the rites of prepubescence. I have no recollection of anything "special" happening at these movies.

I recall the Fourth of July fireworks at Soldiers Grove. First, however, and foremost in my mind was the ball game. I loved baseball, and at a certain age—over ten, I guess—I looked forward to chasing foul balls. A retrieved ball was worth a nickel, then the price of a soda for a few years of my youth.

I remember the wonderful teams Soldiers Grove always had, composed of local boys and a few players hired to drive from Madison. Some of the names of imports still linger: Chick Lowe–2b, Gene Calhoun–C, Jim Thompson–outfield, great players. One of the things that differentiated Soldiers Grove from the other teams was the import of two black players who played in the early 50s: a pitcher whose last name was Shephard (Shep to all) and a catcher. Shep played and stayed (summers) in town for a couple of years. He was a fine pitcher with a fluid, stylish motion on the mound. He'd wind up, a long stride after a windmill, then pump two or three times, stretch, raise his arms high, and wriggle them downward. Soldiers Grove rarely lost and the games drew hundreds of fans to the ballpark, before TV, and many dollars to merchants—mostly the six tavern keepers and the four restaurant operators.

I recall a game with LaCrosse for the league title. LaCrosse had beaten Soldiers Grove at their park and led by one game. If Soldiers Grove won this one, the teams would have a playoff at the end of the season on the field of the team with the most fans attending. LaCrosse had drawn 1,200—to beat this was a mighty tall order, considering the population gap. The second game was advertised throughout the Kickapoo Valley and, on the fateful day, nearly 1,400 persons paid for the right to sit, stand, or squat along the foul lines. They covered the bleachers and the dike, a premier viewing area a few feet behind the bleachers at home and slanting down and away to right field, before standing along the lines on both sides. Soldiers Grove won, 3–2 and a LaCrosse player was thrown out at the plate late in the contest. In an anticlimactic playoff before over 1,000 fans, LaCrosse returned the favor and celebrated joyously before a subdued throng.

At one of the summer contests, I recall a foul tip getting stuck in the screen behind home plate which the batboy and several players tried to knock down without success. I formulated a plan. I had a pretty accurate arm and there were some small rocks handy. After the teams began to leave the field but while the lights were still on, I took a spot that would afford a clear shot and the best retrieval vantage point. I thought if I hit it squarely it would pop out, roll down to a hole and drop in front of me where I would grab it. I fired, hitting it perfectly with the first rock. The ball popped up but hit a bracket and went off the screen. On the other side a smiling, leering kid waited, grabbed it, waved, and ran off. The moral for me: You never know how the ball will bounce; or, life is full of bad hops.

We were young men in search of our destiny, our kismet; filled with the piss and vinegar of our years. We bragged about feeling no fear, yet all the while hoped silently, but fervently, that we might get assigned a soft job when we arrived. We were ready to be tested, if the test wasn't too severe. I wondered— how tough could it be? This was just a little pissant country that nobody could find on their map. This wasn't a real war—this was just Vietnam.

PART ONE

THE BORDER

1

I had emerged from a drunken and emotion-filled thirty-day leave at home, nursing a hangover but ready for the next step in my journey through life. After planing from Madison, Wisconsin, to O'Hare to San Francisco, I took a helicopter from the airport across the bay to Oakland. The Golden Gate Bridge was shining in the warm California sun as we passed over it. Once on the ground I counted my money, then flagged down a cab and told him to get me to Army Replacement Depot, wherever it was.

"Goin' to 'Nam, huh, soldier? All ones on your profile, I bet."

I nodded and grinned. "Eleven B Ten. Light infantry, headed for 'Nam."

"You look like an intelligent young fella. You know you don't have to go. There are lots of ways around it, even now. You could disappear to Canada."

"Desertion—that's a capital crime. I could face a firing squad. Not much future in that."

"Not if you never come back. Oh well, I'm just making conversation. Just something to think about."

"I know, and I have thought about the options, but I was raised to face things, so here I am."

As we pulled into the main gate I spotted some of the guys I had spent the summer with in Fort Polk, Louisiana.

"You can let me out here, man." I gave him a five and told him to keep the change, but he said, "Nah. Have yourself a couple of beers before you leave and keep your head down. Good luck, son."

I hefted my duffel bag onto my shoulder and got into line with the others. Mock, Miller, Doolittle, and I had endured advanced individual training in the same company at Fort Polk and now would be shipping out together. We exchanged hand-shakes and insults as the line moved into the building and processing began. Two days later, after numerous injections and in-doctrinations, hours of hurrying, then waiting, we were called into yet another formation.

"Group Three, grab your bags and head for the bus. You are shipping out. Move!"

My heart quickened, but I was glad the damned waiting was over and ready to get started.

The sleek Braniff 747 lifted off the runway at Travis Air Force Base a few hours later. The pilot pointed the jetliner west and we began to chase the sunset across the sky on the first leg of our journey—a journey to a different world.

We landed in Honolulu during the most beautiful sunset I had ever seen and headed into the terminal for a two-hour lay-over. There we sniffed out a cocktail lounge and quaffed more than a few drinks, toasting John Wayne, Audie Murphy, and America until it was time to go. We staggered back onto the plane, then began opening the small airport booze bottles we had procured and mixing it with the pineapple juice being served. A few drunken hours later, I began to fade and fell into a stupor. When I came back to reality we were descending into Clark Air Base in the Philippines.

After refueling, we reboarded. As the plane taxied to the run-way, smoke began billowing out of the right engine, forcing the pilot to turn back to the hangar where we got out quickly. No great damage was done but the repairs took several hours. I spent the time trying to sleep in the dilapidated terminal while my head throbbed and my stomach churned. Finally we boarded once more and began the final leg of our quest. Next stop—Tan Son Nhut Airport, Saigon, Republic of Vietnam.

As we began to descend and circle, I noticed that the land seemed to be covered with water. Must be the Delta, I mused. We came in fairly high, then dropped quickly and hit the tar-mac hard, bouncing and shuddering our way down the runway. The plane finally stopped about seventy-five yards from the nearest metal hangar and the troops began stirring, reaching for their bags and hats.

"Welcome to Vietnam. Make sure you get all your bags and personal belongings. Good luck."

The flight attendant sounded like she meant it. She smiled

forlornly at us as we headed out the door—into Vietnam. I felt like Alice stepping through the looking glass.

As I stepped out onto the portable stairs I was in a sauna—a very smelly sauna. Sweat beads formed immediately on my face and arms and I stopped to get a breath. Heat waves were shimmering off the tarmac and the acrid smell of jet fuel and smoke from distant fires filled my nostrils and overwhelmed my senses. Welcome to Vietnam, indeed. I flashed one last look back at the flight attendant, who gave me a worldly look and mouthed, "Good luck."

I turned back to the task at hand. I knew my life would never be the same from this moment on. This was the initiation into my Rites of Passage. Miller moved past me quickly, panting and half-dragging his bag.

"Oh, come on, Pete, let's get into the hangar. Maybe they've got air-conditioning." I hoisted my bag and we headed to the warehouse-style terminal where the others were gathering. By the time we reached the shade I was panting and sweat was running off my body.

"It's gotta be a hundred degrees or more. I thought Louisiana was bad, but I've never seen anything like this," I said to a drooping Mock while Miller nodded. "Fuckin' place doesn't have air. How do they work here?"

A specialist, 4th class (Spec 4) began yelling at us, "All right men, form up here and move out the rear door. We've got buses waiting to take you to Bien Hoa. Move out."

We loaded onto the olive-drab Army buses (circa 1945) and headed out of the main gate and into Saigon. Heavy screens covered the open windows, and as none of the troops had planned to throw anything from the bus, it became obvious that the screens were there to prevent anything from being thrown into our midst. Since the U.S. Army rarely planned things like this in advance, the protection had undoubtedly been added following an incident, probably a tossed grenade, I thought.

"Hmm, screened windows. Wait a minute, now, let's see if I've got this straight. We're here to help defend the South Vietnamese against the Communist invaders, right? Why do we need protection from the people we're protecting, who should be our friends?"

"The sarge back at Polk said there were enemy everywhere. He never knew who he could trust, Pete. It's a pisser of a war, but it's the only one we've got," Miller told me.

As we passed through the outskirts and into the heavily populated downtown, I was taken aback by the squalor and abject poverty in which most of the Vietnamese were living. The houses were a few pieces of lumber and cardboard held together with cord and flattened metal beer and soda cans. Many of the locals were cooking on the dirt streets in front of their hovels, squatting near the black pot over a small fire. The smell of their food and its spices and the resulting smoke hung heavily in the humid air. There was also a stronger, rancid odor—perhaps garbage, I thought.

As we moved along I spotted several locals relieving themselves along the streets. They merely dropped their trousers, did their business, then moved on. Therein was the source of much of the odor. We continued along slowly through the bustling heart of the city, moving past thousands of bikes, motorcycles, scooters and a few hundred small cars and trucks. I noticed hundreds of young Vietnamese men walking the streets or riding scooters. Why weren't they in the military? I pointed them out to Mock.

"They couldn't all be on leave, could they?" He shrugged and shook his head slightly. Mock hadn't said much since we left the plane; must still be in shock.

The bus left the city and continued to the compound at Bien Hoa, where we entered through an opening in the barbed wire and watched the gate close behind us—I immediately thought of prison movies where a busload of new convicts pull into the yard. We unloaded, stood in formation until we were called, then went to our assigned barracks and waited to be called again. That night we walked around the encampment to familiarize ourselves with what our life might be like for the next year. Barbed wire enclosed the perimeter, with fighting positions fortified with sandbags and logs every thirty feet. The fighting bunkers were large enough for two or three men to sleep in while one stood guard.

"It would take a helluva force to try to overrun this place. There's a lot of firepower here. The artillery is always on call and I saw some tanks just down the road." Doolittle cupped a cigarette as he spoke. Mock answered, "All I want is a nice typewriter to fire and a desk to drive around and I'll be happy for twelve months."

"Why didn't you go for the enlistment option: an extra year, but a guaranteed job?"

"I took my chances, Pete. I didn't want to do the extra time, so I gambled that I'd get a soft job. We still got a chance when we get assigned to our final unit."

"Yeah, but it's like karma or fate for me. I've always known that I would be in a war someday. As I sat there listening to that Spec 4 in basic tell me I was eligible for almost every school they had, something was telling me, 'It doesn't matter what you do. You're going to 'Nam and fight.'

"So I turned him down. It pissed him off, so he said he was putting me in the infantry. I don't know if he had that much power or what, but here I am."

"So, was it karma, or did you influence the outcome with your preconceived notions?"

"I see your point and I can't really answer your question. I remember a few years back when one of my teachers stated, with damned good foresight, that Vietnam would be the site of the next war. As he spoke I felt a numbness in my heart and something clicked in my brain. I knew, then, that I would be in it. This would be my war. Whether I then consciously set out to make that come true or it had already been predestined is the question. But I know what I believe. I believe it was my karma . . . my destiny."

We had moved back to our barracks in the growing darkness where we alternately regaled and bored each other with tales from our past and plans for our future. Doolittle forwarded a theory that this war couldn't last long and we might be lucky enough to be in on the finish. Miller summed it up:

"Wouldn't it be a blast to take part in a victory parade through Saigon and have all the girls run out and give you flowers and throw themselves at you? You know, like you see in those old newsreels and movies. We'd be heroes."

"Go home a hero. What more could you ask for?"

"Well, Doolittle, I'd be happy just to go home. If we could wrap this little skirmish up by Christmas, I'd be happy enough."

"Amen, Pete, and goodnight, guys."

We moved back into the Army bureaucratic pipeline the next morning, first into formation, then lining up for processing and listening to the NCOs and PFCs throw crap at us.

"Hold on to your papers. Don't lose them."

"Give me your damn papers. What are you doin' with them anyway? Jesus H. on a crutch. Get outta here and take your damn papers."

We filled out forms, answered questions, then trudged back to formation where Miller and I were pulled out for a brush-cutting detail. We hacked throughout the afternoon in the heat and humidity, sweating through our clothes. Miller stopped after whacking down a particularly stubborn bush.

"I don't think I've ever been this hot. The sweat is running down my back and into the crack of my butt like a river."

"First liar never has a chance, man. I'm so hot my hair is sweating."

"I've got pools of sweat up to my ankles in both boots."

"I'm so hot my fingernails are sweating. Your turn."

"It's too hot to complain, Pete. I'm taking a break."

When we returned to the barracks I was so tired I couldn't make it to the mess hall for chow. I drank a ton of water, poured some over my head and slept wordlessly through the night.

At formation the next morning we learned we were headed for Pleiku that afternoon. We were told to clear out of the barracks, they were needed for more new arrivals. I hauled my bag out into the loading area, found some shade and waited for the truck to the airport. As I sat there on my duffel I looked at the other troops milling around or standing in formation—they all looked like they had been hit over the head with a hammer, rendering them unable to function. I was certain that I looked the same to them.

At 1300 hours we headed to the airport, boarded a C-130 cargo plane, strapped ourselves in as ordered and flew to Pleiku. The large door at the rear dropped down for easier loading of cargo and troops. It was left partway open, creating a slight breeze which made the trip comfortable.

The temperature in the Central Highlands was at least fifteen degrees cooler with lower humidity. The almost always cheerful Miller took a quick glance around the area and said, "Hell, this won't be so bad. It's like Oregon weather."

"Yeah, it's like June in Wisconsin, except we don't have all this red dirt. I'll bet that clay gets sticky in the rain," I added, thinking, this really might not be so bad. The drier air and lower temperature had raised my spirits.

As we loaded onto trucks and headed for 3rd Brigade headquarters, I spotted a sergeant leaning on a truck, smoking a cigarette as he gazed at us. He was wearing torn and dirty jungle fatigues and had ugly scratches and pus-filled sores on his arms and deep, dark circles under his eyes. I tried to meet his gaze, but his eyes were two black wells that seemed to stretch into infinity. I was mesmerized by his countenance, but Doolittle broke the spell by yelling at the weary-looking trooper, "Hey Sarge, what's happenin'? You seen any action?"

"Fuckin' new meat. . . ." The sergeant muttered a few more unintelligible phrases, then turned away. Our truck roared off as the bedraggled NCO shook his head.

The base camp was laid out over a slightly rounded, rolling low hill with brigade and battalion headquarters in the center and company compounds around the outside. All of this was surrounded by the barbed wire perimeter and fortified bunkers connected by a series of trenches. It looked formidable enough as we headed into the heart of the compound and were disgorged at the 1st of the 14th Infantry Battalion HQ.

There was more paperwork, then we sat around for several hours waiting for instructions. The sun went down behind the purple-hued mountains visible in the distance as we waited. Finally at 2000 hours a clerk came out with orders. Mock got his wish. He was assigned to battalion HQ as a clerk, Miller went to Headquarters Company, and Doolittle and I went to Charlie Company, an infantry line combat unit. We shook hands, vowed to stay in touch, then went our ways.

Doolittle and I took a short jeep ride over the rounded hill to Charlie Company compound and presented ourselves to the NCO in charge. He found us each a bunk and assigned us to radio watch. At my turn to pull watch, someone woke me up and I dutifully watched the radio for my hour, then woke up the next guy.

The next morning the NCO was being chewed out by the first sergeant because no one called for over two hours. The NCO grumbled that the "new guys fucked up." He then followed the age-old Army tradition of passing the buck by chew-

ing on us, but he hadn't given us any instructions to call in so I
didn't feel bad. After all, I did watch the radio for an hour. The
first sergeant then notified the new guys that we would be attending an indoctrination school for the next week, but today
we would be on work detail filling sandbags. He also informed
us that upon entering the country, we had been promoted one
grade. I was now PFC. I wasn't exactly thrilled beyond words,
but it was a few more bucks.

I spent the day filling and piling the bags along the trenches
and on bunkers and singing along with Doolittle and two other
new guys—Marvin and Hinzman. We sang the chorus of an old
soul song about men working on a chain gang. Even in the hot
sun the temperature was pleasant enough to work in, and we
listened as the Spec 4 in charge of the work detail filled us in on
life in the field. "It's a lot hotter in the jungle and you gotta
carry a helluva load, at least sixty pounds in your pack plus
your rifle and ammo and claymores and flares. It's a lick on ya,
man. And you never know when ol' Charlie is gonna hit you.
You might go a week with nothin' happenin', then hit the shit
every day for a week. You never know." The talking must have
made him tired, as he lay back against the bunker and began
snoring.

That night we pulled perimeter guard in a bunker connected
by trenches with those on each side and big enough for three to
sleep while the other man pulled watch. While waiting for the
sun to go down, the four of us exchanged a little banter. I
started it out. "Well, men, so far this war business is pretty
easy. Fill a few bags, sing a few songs, drink a few brews. Well,
we haven't done that yet but we will. Who said war is hell?"

"Let's just wait until we hit the jungle before we get too
cocky, man," Hinzman said.

"I'd like to spend the whole war right here, fillin' bags or
diggin' ditches. Man, I got no use for the jungle at all," Doolittle chipped in.

"Easy, men, I was just joshing. But, if we have to go out
there, let's get at it. The time goes faster out there, so they say. I
think spending your tour back here would really drag, but, to
each his own. Who wants first watch?"

The next morning I reported to the indoctrination school,

where I learned Vietnamese customs (the U.S. Army version) and Army infantry procedures and tactics. We went on training patrols close to the camp and even spent a night on ambush outside the wire. Nights in the Central Highlands were cool enough to require a poncho liner or field jacket.

Because of our proximity to the perimeter I knew we were relatively safe, and one of the troops explained that the officers and NCOs in charge were "short" (which had nothing to do with their stature, but meant that their tour of duty was near the end) and didn't take any chances. The job of instructor was a reward for good service or a trade for war souvenirs, so the instructors and the school were of little real value to the new soldier. There is an old saying, "An Army travels on its stomach," but I don't think it could even begin to move without favors, bribes and trades within ranks.

At the end of the weeklong school we were summarily dismissed and presumed ready for combat. After another day of filling and hauling sandbags, I was definitely ready for the field. My life was about to change.

2

At 1100 hours on October 16, 1966, Doolittle, Hinzman and I boarded a chopper outside the main gate and flew west by north to the forward supply base. I had been assigned an M-16 and a box of ammo at base camp and upon landing the supply sergeant apportioned the rest of our combat supplies. I began loading myself down with: twelve boxes of ammo and as many magazine clips; four ammo pouches; two fragmentation grenades; one smoke grenade; one hand flare; two trip flares; three canteens; one field dressing; one poncho with liner; an

entrenching tool, and some advice. I hung the grenades and
canteens on my web gear and began loading the ammunition
into the clips, but the worn-out looking sergeant yelled at us:

"Only eighteen rounds in the clip, not twenty or nineteen.
Otherwise the damn thing won't feed 'em right. Keep your
weapon clean or it'll jam up just when you need it."

The resupply chopper landed and we helped load the goods
for C Company, then boarded and rode into the war. We headed
further west across lush tree-covered hills and over a wide valley cut by a winding river, then the noisy bird banked down in a
semicircle and landed awkwardly in a clearing on top of a large
hill.

I jumped off with Doolittle and Hinzman and began unloading the supplies. When we finished, a shirtless black man
looked at us, grinned, yelled, and pointed. "Hey, new meat!
Over there—company CP and Cap'n Simcox." As we headed
toward the CP, a short, skinny Spec 4 stared.

"New guys, well, keep your heads down, your eyes open,
and your mouth shut. You just might make it."

My thoughts were jumbled, but I wanted to ask him a hundred questions like: "What's it really like out here? Were you
afraid in combat? How should I act?" But something in his
eyes made me back off. Like the sergeant at the airport in
Pleiku, there was no focus, no end. His stare went on forever.

Captain Simcox was a short, wiry man with an engaging
grin that seemed too big for his face. He was wearing his shirt
loose and his watch was buckled upside down through his lapel
button and hung down over his heart so he could glance down
and read it.

"Welcome to Chargin' Charlie Company, men. I'm glad to see
you. We haven't had much contact lately, just some snipers. But
we keep beating the bushes looking for trouble and sooner or later
we'll find it. Peterson, Doolittle, and Hinzman—you're all going
to the 2nd Platoon and Lieutenant Canale, a good man. Just do
what you're told and you'll be all right. Dismissed."

The 2nd Platoon was on patrol, so we waited near the CP,
killing time by playing rap poker and checking out the terrain.
At 1700 the platoon filed in along a trail that ran between
bunkers and took positions on the perimeter. As they moved in,

I noticed a feeling, an attitude in the way they carried themselves that said, without overstating: "Don't fuck with me. I've
been there, dammit."

Lieutenant Canale was about six feet tall, brown hair and
eyes, and looked a lot like James Garner probably did when he
was in his early twenties. We introduced ourselves.

"Peterson, Doolittle, and Hinzman reporting for duty, sir."

"Hey, new blood, pardon the expression, and it's about damn
time. We're below strength. You'll like the 2nd. We're called the
Trailblazers because we seem to be on point all the damn time.
Pete—do they call you that? I thought so. You go to the 1st Squad
with Sergeant Watson; Doolittle, 2nd; Hinzman, 3rd." He pointed
to each position in turn, then sent us off.

"Oh, yeah, welcome to Vietnam—toilet bowl of the world.
Have your squad leader send a man for Cs in a few minutes."
He yelled at us as we moved out. I decided I liked him as much
as you could like someone on first impression. Wonder how he
felt about me.

I hitched up my gear and headed to the 1st Squad position
for one more round of introductions. There I met a scroungy-
looking group of GIs relaxing around two fighting positions
while wiping down their weapons and gear. I found what appeared to be their leader and approached him. "PFC Peterson.
Lieutenant Canale sent me over."

"I'm Sergeant Watson. Welcome to the 1st Squad."

Sergeant Watson was a blond-haired Californian who didn't
fit the sterotypical beach bum role. He acted like a farm boy
from the Midwest, like me, and we hit it off from the start.

"Is it Pete? OK, Pete, this is Maddox, fire team leader, you'll
be with him. That's Fears and Vickers. Over in the other hole is
Harrell, McCown, and Curtis. Where you from?"

"Wisconsin. . . . Oh, the lieutenant wants you to send a man
to the CP for C rations."

"Vickers, go pick up our Cs."

Vickers was a skinny (they were all skinny except McCown,
who carried a few extra pounds around the waist), good-
looking young man with a huge shotgun across his lap.

"Fuck a bunch of Cs and the CP. You always send me. Send
the fuckin' new guy."

Sensing conflict, I shifted to get up from where I was sitting to get the rations, but Watson calmly replied, "No, I want to fill him in on some platoon and squad poop that he needs to know. Get the Cs, guy."

Vickers left slowly, cursing as he strode to the CP while Watson gave me a thorough rundown on procedures. He advised me that they hadn't even seen a "dink" in nearly a month and that there was nothing to worry about in this AO. He told me about squad and company policy on patrols, ambushes, LP-OPs (listening posts and observation posts) and night defensive positions.

He said, "If you're not sure about something, ask me or Maddox—got that? Good. Now, did you get a chance to get into Pleiku City, guy?" Watson had a predilection toward using "guy" where most young people of this age would opt for the much used and abused "man," and I saw that it was catching on throughout the squad.

"No, the first sergeant kept us busy when we weren't going to training school. We had line duty and filled sandbags."

"Whenever we get a stand-down, I'll take you to Mama-san's place and introduce you to my girl. She's beautiful. 'Course I don't kiss her, I know where her mouth has been. Remember that, guy, never kiss a whore."

He smiled his wry smile. By this time I was feeling a little over-advised, but the guys seemed to be friendly enough—just ordinary guys in an out-of-the-ordinary place. I hoped that I would fit in, learn fast, and not screw up. Vickers came back with two cases of C rations that he tossed to the ground. Then he reached into his pocket and came out with several letters that belonged to the squad.

"Nothin' for Maddox, one for Fears, one for Curtis, one for me, and nothin' for Sergeant Watson—our fearless leader."

Watson grabbed his M-16 and pointed it at Vickers. "Where's my mail—you took my mail!" He broke out laughing and tried to wrestle with Vickers, who hopped nimbly aside. Watson then took his 16, placed the end of the notched flash suppressor across the wires encasing the C ration box, and gave it a quick twist. The wires snapped and he tore open the box and began passing out meals as he grunted, "Damn 16 is good for something."

He gave everybody three meals to pack away, though most

of the guys took only a few cans. Being at the end of the pecking order, I got ham and lima beans, chopped eggs, and turkey loaf. I had tasted all of them at Fort Polk or base camp and knew these were the worst, but I stowed them in my pack like the other guys did and kept my mouth shut.

"Vick, give Pete your claymore to hump and I'll get him one of the extra batteries for the radio. Might as well break him in good." Watson started to walk away with his meals, then turned back and spoke to Maddox.

"You've got OP tonight. Take your team and the new guy out at dusk. And don't forget to take the radio."

Maddox nodded, then saluted with his left hand as Watson walked to the CP. When he was gone, Maddox spoke, "He's a pretty good ol' boy for one of them California freaks, but he sure gives me a lot of work. I'm always taking point or headin' out to the OP."

"It sure seems that way and it's a lick on us. They use us too damn much," Vickers added.

As the light began to fade, Maddox spoke softly, "OK, guys, grab your poncho and liner and web gear. We'll be heading out to the same OP we had the other night."

We moved out slowly between two bunkers, stepping carefully over their trip-wires, and edged into the dark tropical rain forest. Maddox led us down a well-used trail for about twenty-five meters, then we stepped into the brush to a flattened-out area behind a huge tree. We had good visibility of the trail and some cover. Maddox whispered, "If there were any enemy in the area we wouldn't use the same OP site, but we haven't seen any for a long time. I'll take the first watch, Vickers next, then Fears and Pete."

My first night in the boonies was cold and quiet, giving me time to clear my jumbled mind. I shivered under my poncho liner in the mountain air and watched the stars and the trail and wondered about things: why do men kill other men for a piece of godforsaken jungle? Who benefits? Why is this backward country so important in the world scheme? Why are things the way they are? The stars had no answers.

The OP (observation post) moved back through the perimeter shortly after dawn and headed to the 1st Squad positions. I made a can of C ration cocoa—took the top nearly off a can

with my P-38, bent it back then down into a V for a handle, and
used the can as a cup. As I was sipping the hot liquid, Watson
came walking back from the platoon CP. He had on a ragged,
dirty Army OD (olive drab) baseball cap and looked a lot like a
farmer on his way to the barn—no big hurry, just a man with a
job to do.

"OK, 1st, listen up." I couldn't believe he really said that—
this wasn't a movie. "Second and 3rd platoons will be going on
patrol. We're headin' north up the big valley. We'll be comin'
back tonight, so travel light if you want. Put one can of Cs inside your poncho and wrap it around your belt. We're leaving in
3–0 minutes."

I made a decision to wrap my field jacket, which had kept
me warm at base camp and last night, around my belt and left
my poncho and liner with my pack. Since we were coming
back that night, I wouldn't need my poncho on a sunny day.

The patrol moved out through the undermanned perimeter
of LZ (landing zone) 18M and into the jungle. The sun couldn't
penetrate through the triple canopy of lush tropical vegetation,
making the temperature several degrees cooler as we moved
down the slopes. The squads rotated to keep a fresh man on
point as we had to hack our way through the branches, brush,
and wait-a-minute vines.

When my turn came I strapped my M-16 across my back di-
agonally, barrel down, and began slashing the heavy growth
with the machete. My arms tired quickly and progress was agonizingly slow after we reached the valley floor. There the
growth was so thick that the two platoon leaders made a joint
decision to find a trail. After an hour-long search we found one
that cut along the bottom of the slope and headed northwest.

We made better time on the trail, but by 1700 hours we still
had moved only about half as far as battalion HQ had expected.
We were directed to find an LZ, so we dropped back to the valley floor and tramped out a small field near a stream. The 2nd
Platoon stood guard while the 3rd Herd was extracted and returned to the company LZ. We naturally assumed we would
be next, but word came down from the platoon CP: "C ration
resupply coming in. We're staying here for an Acropolis—
ambush."

"Tell them to bring our packs. We need our packs," Watson yelled.

"Too late. They're on the way."

My heart began to sink a little as I realized I would have to spend the night without a poncho and liner. I decided that it wouldn't be so bad as long as it didn't rain. Surely we'd rejoin the company by tomorrow night.

We finished our C ration supper as Watson filled us in on our ambush position. The platoon would be breaking up into three squad ambushes near the LZ. The 1st Squad and one gun were going to set up along the stream crossing in a line. As the sun dropped down and we prepared to move into position, I unwrapped my field jacket and shrugged into it.

"Look at the fuckin' new guy. Got shit for brains. Just wait," Curtis whispered to Vickers, who shook his head.

I wasn't sure what the hell they meant, but I was warm as we lay along the stream and waited for some activity. The night was extremely dark and cool, but quiet along the trail.

The platoon moved out early the next morning, once again heading north and carrying only one meal. When we broke for noon chow the word came down that there would be no re-supply tonight, so stretch your C rations for another day. I munched on a can of chopped apples, saving my beans and wieners for the evening meal.

We continued heading north throughout the day, then Lieutenant Canale and two squad leaders scouted out an ambush site for the night. Once again I donned my field jacket to the snickers of my squad companions. I asked Vickers, "What's the deal? The jacket's warm and we'll be back with the company tomorrow and I'll get my poncho."

"If it rains on you, guy, that jacket won't hold off much of it and it'll get heavy as hell. Here in the jungle you need a poncho. When it rains, it rains. Second, you never know when we'll get back with the company. They change plans faster than a whore drops her underwear. We might be out here alone for a couple weeks."

I was feeling rather chastened as I slowly finished my beans and wieners and got ready to move into position. I saved one tin of peanut butter for breakfast; resupply chopper had better come in tomorrow. The ambush position was along some rocks just off the trail, was easy to defend, and had good sightlines.

After another uneventful night we finished our meager breakfast rations, then moved along the trail to the nearby river. Our job was to secure a crossing for the combined force consisting of Company C's 1st Platoon and company CP and all of A Company. They were moving out of LZ 4E where they had spent the night. Along with B Company and recon platoon, we were all moving north to make contact with and destroy an enemy force in the mountains east of Plei Djerang.

It began to rain hard and then rain harder as we headed for the designated crossing area, and the water draining off the steep slopes had turned the stream into a raging torrent by the time we reached it. The 3rd Squad was on point and they sent their strongest swimmer across with a nylon rope tied to his waist. He carefully edged into the chest-deep stream, fought the current all the way across, and tied the rope to a tree. The rest of the platoon then crossed slowly.

When it was my turn, I stuck my wallet in my shirt pocket, held my rifle up high in my left hand, and held on to the rope with my right. The water, now neck-deep, was cold and nearly took my breath. I took a few tentative steps, then decided I had to be at least as bold as the other troops so I forced my legs through the rushing dirty water and pulled myself along with my right arm. I looked up after a few minutes and there was an arm reaching out for me and a now-familiar voice ragging at me, "Come on, new guy, grab my arm and get up out of there."

I grabbed McCown's arm and hoisted myself up onto the stream bank. A surge of confidence and a sense of unit pride and responsibility overtook me, so I laid my rifle down and joined McCown in exhorting and helping the rest of the troops as they crossed.

A small rear guard had been left on the other side to greet the combined patrol and guide them across. They arrived at 1300 and immediately crossed the now-receding stream, then Company A moved out to our left heading for the west slopes of Hill 1005. After sharing their C rations with the 2nd Platoon, Charlie Company moved along the side of the hill mass to the east of Hill 1005 while Bravo Company moved onto the hill proper. Recon platoon would then assault to the top of the hill.

We inched along, hacking our way through the jungle while the CO kept in constant contact with the other units. It was a classic combat maneuver being attempted in a jungle terrain with the lowly infantrymen as pawns.

Because of the difficulties we had in battling the elements we barely reached the hill by dark. There, at the bottom, we set up in a defensive perimeter and received a resupply and mail drop. While most of the squad members read their mail or picked off leeches, I hung my soaked field jacket on a limb over a small cooking fire to dry. Curtis was pointing at me, "Look at the new guy now. Wasn't such a good idea humping that jacket, was it? Don't you wish you had a poncho, now?"

"Screw you and the horse you rode in on, Curtis. Don't worry about me—I'll make it."

"Talk about shit for brains. That jacket won't dry tonight."

Maddox had been listening to our discourse and offered, "Drop it, Curtis. I'm tired of listening to you ridin' somebody all the time. Pete, if you put that coat on, your body heat will dry it in a few hours. We'll get you a poncho somehow tomorrow."

I hesitantly put the wet and cold jacket on and began cooking my supper—ham and lima beans with melted cheese, topped with crackers. The steaming repast helped warm my body and raised my flagging spirits. Vickers and I attempted to dig a foxhole, but the going was too tough and rocky so we concentrated on creating a log-and-rock barrier in front of the position.

Watson returned from the platoon CP with the news that B Company and Recon would assault the top of Hill 1005 tomorrow while Alpha and Charlie Companies would close the pincers from the east and west. I surmised that it probably looked good on paper, with neat arrows pointing at the objective. I hoped they remembered to factor in the terrain and weather, but in playing the role of FNG, I didn't raise the questions aloud.

Charlie Company struck camp early in the morning of October 20 in an attempt to make up ground that was to have been covered yesterday. We began climbing to the top of the small mountain range that would lead us to our objective. When we reached the top we intersected a large, well-used trail in the general direction of Hill 1005 and began following it.

The 1st Platoon was leading the way and its point squad

came upon a lone unarmed North Vietnamese Army (NVA)
regular who immediately raised his hands and surrendered. He
was wearing a full uniform and carrying a small pack with rice
and a few personal belongings. Apparently he had deserted and
was looking for a place to surrender—the action had begun.
Sergeant Watson, hearing the news on the radio, grinned.

"Way to go, 1st Platoon. One NVA captured alive. I'm going
to the company CP to check this dude out. I haven't seen a live
dink in two months. Take over, Maddox."

We took the trussed-up enemy soldier with us as we continued to drive toward 1005. We broke for noon chow, but as we
were wolfing down our beans and whatever we heard a torrent of
gunfire, and word came down that Bravo had made heavy contact on top of the hill. Charlie Company saddled up their packs
and moved forward to get in position to block or encircle.

The point squad, still from the 1st Platoon, called back that
they had come upon a small Montagnard village with what appeared to be a family living in it. The company quickly surrounded the village and took the villagers prisoner as suspected
sympathizers. As we continued along the trail the point came
on more stragglers. Some tried to flee and were killed as the
harried troops opened up, while others surrendered and were
added to our collection. I wondered if the casualties were civilian or military, but the 2nd Platoon was the trail element and
information was hard to come by.

Alpha Company had arrived to aid Bravo and assisted them
in clearing the contact area and setting up in a night defensive
perimeter. Bravo had thirteen men wounded by friendly fire; a
jet called in to hit the enemy had instead fired into some rocks
where Bravo troops were waiting. The shrapnel and pieces of
rock scattered among the frightened soldiers, but none were
hurt seriously. The wounded were evacuated, then the two companies settled in for the night.

After the chopper brought water and Cs and extracted our
prisoners, Charlie Company broke up into two ambush sites.
Later as I sat on guard it began to rain, and I realized again why
the others had ridiculed me; it was so cold on that mountain
that my teeth began to chatter. I began to rag myself in the dark.
"Fuckin' new guy. Shit for brains," I whispered while peering
into the utter blackness.

We began a new mission the next morning to reach and take Hill 903. Again, the battalion planned a three-pronged attack on the objective with Bravo hitting it from the west, Alpha from the south, and Charlie Company from the east. As we moved out from our position we got word that Bravo had made early contact, killing one NVA and capturing two AK-47s.

The troops were even more grim-faced than before as we headed along toward the base of Hill 903. We had heard all the reports of battle from Bravo and knew it was just a matter of time until Charlie Company "hit the shit." As that thought was still going through my mind, I heard shouts and a few rifle shots from the 3rd Platoon's point element. We dropped to the ground and waited for orders. The shooting stopped, then Watson was holding the handset to his ear.

"OK, 1st Squad, the platoon is gonna recon by fire through this brush to make sure there's no enemy ambush waitin' for us. Let's go!"

The entire squad rose and every other man began firing as we moved slowly through the brush. I put my weapon on semi-automatic, then blasted away into the bushes as we moved slowly and carefully forward. I made sure I didn't stray ahead of the line where I could get struck and tried to look like I knew what I was doing. The bushes were moving from the rounds tearing into them. Branches and leaves were sliced off and fell toward the ground, seemingly in slow motion. We saw no enemy, and after we had moved about seventy-five feet Watson raised his hand and screamed at us, "Hold it! Hold your fire. Get down and hold your position."

The point had come into contact with two or three NVAs, but they fled, leaving two AK-47s, some 82mm mortar rounds, and some packs with papers. The point squad attempted to follow the enemy troops but they had vanished. We spent much of the day carrying the booty back down the trail to the LZ we had hacked out the night before where a chopper could get in to extract it. Then the company began to climb the hill, but darkness overtook us about halfway up and we were split up into three ambush positions along the trail.

The 1st Squad set up exactly on the trail with claymores and trip flares placed quickly into position. A giant tree with protruding ribs that became roots sheltered us against another frigid jungle mountain rain and cold wind. As we prepared a quick poncho shelter, Maddox and Watson crawled over to where I was huddled against the tree. Watson whispered to me, "Pete, we found you a poncho. One of the dinks left it with his pack when they got out of the area this morning. It stinks, but it's better than getting wet."

I took the stiff piece of dirty, milk-colored plastic and placed it over my shoulders. It did stink, but I felt a lot better knowing I could stay dry through the cold night.

"Thanks, guys, but if that NVA comes back looking for his poncho tonight, I'm gonna be pissed as hell."

As I pulled the midnight watch I huddled against the huge tree and wondered if another NVA might come down the trail, smell the stinking poncho, and think I'm his buddy. I also wondered if the U.S. Army would ever return my pack so I could shave, brush my teeth, and feel somewhat human again. I decided that my pack was lost, as lost as I felt in this cold, wet jungle. I felt like an innocent lamb that had been thrown to the wolves.

3

On the morning of October 22, Charlie Company resumed its climb of Hill 903. Once on the top we joined Alpha Company in their defensive perimeter, shed our gear, and rested for a few minutes. Our portion of the perimeter had several huts which we searched, and we found some packs with clothing and papers in them. While Alpha Company cleared an LZ, we carried the packs out of the huts for extraction.

When we finished loading the booty on the chopper, we settled into a defensive position and took off our shoes. My feet were sore and wrinkled and in need of bathing and rest, but I decided that a little sun would do wonders for them. I told

Maddox: "Nice of Uncle Sam to give us a day off, man. I was really draggin' yesterday."

"The United States Army doesn't give a rat's ass about you or me needin' a day off, Pete. The battalion chopper crashed yesterday and they probably can't find a backup. But, relax and enjoy it. God knows when we'll get another one."

Maddox popped a heat tab out of his pocket and lit it to heat his turkey loaf dinner. I was preparing barbecue beef; I had graduated from getting the leftover C rations to getting a fair grab at all of them. I laughed as Maddox cursed his fate.

"Pete, this damn turkey loaf has to be the worst meal in the whole damn batch. If I shit in the can, it would be a huge improvement, I swear."

"If you got any left over I'll put it on this dead beef."

The squad was beginning to accept me at face value and had begun to include me in their impromptu insult contests, so I tried to hold my own without cutting anyone too badly. I was still feeling my way along through the daily patrols, trying to put things into focus and perspective. I had been told that we were in a safe area and wouldn't see much action, but there was plenty of action for Bravo Company and I had to assume we would see some soon enough. I wanted to be ready to do my part.

At twilight, C Company sent an ambush element from the 1st Platoon while the rest of the troops dug in, fortified their foxholes and put up hooches. I was allowed to share the team's hooch, but I had to leave my stinkin' dink poncho outside. Lying on the cardboard from an empty C ration case felt a lot better than the ground, but after seven days in the boonies I longed for a hard, lumpy Army cot.

Just after dawn, in a heavy ground fog, four or five NVA soldiers walked into the 1st Platoon's ambush position just outside the perimeter. The sudden burst of AK-47 fire followed by the snap of the M-16 brought the entire perimeter to full alert and in motion. Fears and I dove into our fighting position, landing on top of Vickers, and Maddox came sliding in after us.

"Good morning, Vietnam!" Maddox yelled as the noise died down. "Get some, 1st Platoon!"

Fears reached for a cigarette. "I wanna go home. They shooting at us before dawn, man."

"Fuckin' Charlie don't have no respect for a man tryin' to sleep. Wake up and hear that pop-pop-pop of the AK. Damn!"

"As long as you can hear it, you're still alive, guy," I told him.

Fears was trying to calm his trembling hands as he cupped the flame from his Zippo lighter, lit up, and drew hard on the bent Winston. He spoke low, almost whispering to himself, "I hear you, man, I hear you and amen to that. I gotta get outta this place somehow."

The firing was over in a few seconds, then we waited several interminable minutes for some sort of indication as to what the hell happened and what we would be doing. Finally word came down the perimeter from hole to hole: "First Platoon blew the ambush—five Charlies, no kills. One friendly Whiskey-India-Alpha. Charlie *di died.*"

The ambushers were relaxing, waiting to come in to the perimeter for breakfast when the shooting started. The NVA had spotted them first, fired a few rounds, then fled after wounding one GI. Some of the men of the 1st Platoon chased after them, but the NVA disappeared into the fog.

We emerged from our foxhole to finish our breakfast while one man stood guard. After the fog lifted, Alpha Company moved out to the north while we evacuated our wounded man, then slowly headed west by north, the direction that the NVA troops had fled. Bravo was operating even farther west of our area, also headed north. The men of Charlie Company had an uneventful day of patrolling along the high ground west of Hill 903 until 1400 hours, when we stopped on a hilltop and set up a perimeter. In the distance we could hear sporadic gunfire and explosions. The company CP was monitoring the battalion radio frequencies and the word spread rapidly—Alpha Company was in heavy contact. We began to dig in as the jets roared over and dumped their loads, then the artillery took a turn pounding the enemy. As we fortified our holes we waited expectantly for the word to "saddle up" and join the fray. The tension was evident on the faces of the men of the 1st Squad as we heard the firing pick up once more, and an eerie hush fell as we awaited more news. Watson finally hustled back from the CP and began filling us in. "A Company hit an NVA force this morning. They killed two and captured two more. Then they hit a bigger force this afternoon and killed five more. They called in air and artillery and then moved out again. They took some real heavy fire and got two men killed and seven wounded, but they overran the enemy and killed twelve more NVA."

"Way to go, Alpha Army. What happens next? Are we gonna join up with them for the night or are they comin' here?"

"Nothing is set yet, Maddox. Alpha had their dead and badly wounded medevacked and they're gettin' ready to move. The plan is for them to head back to LZ X where we were last night. If they get hit again, I'm sure we'll be called to help."

We set out our trip flares and claymores and rigged a few grenades with trip wires in front of the fighting positions and waited. When Alpha Company started their move to LZ X it was already dark. They humped just over one klick (kilometer), carrying five litter patients that couldn't be evacuated before darkness set in. We listened anxiously for the sound of gunfire and the order to move, but the night was quiet. At 2300 hours the word came down quietly from the platoon CP. "Psst. Alpha made it to the LZ. Pass it on."

We could finally relax a little, but there was undoubtedly a large enemy force in the area and Charlie Company would be joining the fray sooner or later. Our turn was coming, I told myself as I shivered, not all from the cold. I hoped I would produce as well as the men of Alpha Army had, and stay alive doing it.

The next morning Alpha Army sent one platoon out in the same direction they had moved yesterday on patrol and once again they came under fire. The by-now battle-toughened veterans quickly overran the NVA force, killing five of the enemy and capturing more weapons and packs. All this was accomplished without suffering any casualties. The platoon then returned to its LZ and took the rest of the morning off. We heard the news from the battalion "net" as we were saddling up to start our own mission. Watson spoke with genuine admiration for the efforts of our brother unit.

"Ol' Charlie is gonna have to learn not to mess with the Golden Dragons—especially not with Alpha Company. Them ol' boys had VC for breakfast this mornin'. I'm fixin' to put that on my steel pot. 'VC—Breakfast of champions.' "

I looked in the direction of the machine-gun crew and saw

where the thick, deep-Southern accented voice had originated. A large heavyset lad with a big grin and an M-60 machine gun balanced on his shoulder like a toy was rattling on again. "I hope ol' Charlie messes with us today. I'm ready."

He patted the weapon and grinned again. I glanced at his steel pot and saw "Roll Tide Roll" and "Alabama Williams" among some other less savory epithets. "Let me guess. You're from Mississippi, right?"

"Aargh—stabbed in the heart by a dirty Yankee. I'm Donald Williams from Alexander City, Alabama. Everybody here calls me Alabama. Are y'all the fuckin new guy with the stinkin' dink poncho?"

"Yo—how could you smell, I mean tell? PFC Peterson, Stanley R. Everybody calls me Pete or fuckin' new guy, shit for brains."

"Well, I'm almost as new as y'all, so I'll call you Pete. How do ya like it out here. Kinda fun, ain't it?"

"I'm learnin', man. It's something new every day. I hope I've learned enough to get me through a fight. We're due to hit some of that shit that Alpha's been going through the last few days."

"I hope so." He then glanced around and lowered his voice. "Seriously, I don't want that any more than the next guy, but I shot my mouth off a few times and these guys expect me to act like a crazy hillbilly, so I try to humor them ol' boys."

"Your secret's safe with me, guy. Hey, my squad's moving, I gotta go. I expect to hear that 60 playing some sweet music if we hit anything."

"Don't worry. I'll be there. Bringing some pee." I liked the big gunner despite his macho demeanor. I suspected he had been forced to adopt that attitude and create a persona in order to survive in the early stages of Army life. It was not for me to say whether that attitude would serve him well under extreme duress . . . or kill him.

Our mission for the day was to head farther north and meet our brother units in an area designated as the Punch Bowl. Bravo and Alpha companies were moving toward the objective using different routes. Bravo had to chop their way through heavy brush and branches while Alpha and Charlie Company would move along trails most of the way. The 2nd Platoon was given the point and again the reins were handed over to the 1st

Squad. Watson gave the job to Maddox and they plotted an azimuth.

Maddox grunted at us. "OK, fire team, fall in behind me. Be quiet and be alert."

We moved hesitantly at first, along the high ground following the large path, figuring that any moment we could be ambushed by one of the NVA units the battalion had been battling. The pointman, and squad, had the all-important job of preventing any surprise encounter. I was trailing Maddox by four steps and behind me was Vickers, then Watson. If the pointman encountered anything out of the ordinary, he halted the patrol and checked it out or called for help with hand signals.

I was able to pick up the meaning of the signals quickly and even began to anticipate the pointman's needs. Vickers and I would step off the trail and move through the brush as security when he motioned with a flip of his left forefinger in each direction. We would then signal back to him so he could move the patrol forward while we moved along his flanks, ostensibly to flush out ambushers or spot booby traps. As long as the brush wasn't too thick, or the CO wasn't in a hurry, putting out flanks was excellent strategy.

We humped up and down hills and along the sides of steep slopes for the better part of a day, but made no contact. At 1630 hours we came onto the crest of a large hill mass and got the order to hold up. The CO moved up through the ranks and took a small patrol a few meters ahead of the point. I followed along and stood near him as he checked his map, looked through his field glasses, and informed the company and battalion net of his findings.

"Our objective, the Punch Bowl, is down in that valley. We'll hold up here for the night and close there in the morning."

The platoon sergeants and squad leaders met and began laying out the perimeter for the night. I had noticed that whenever we set up in a night defensive position on high ground, the old guys were more relaxed and prone to setting off their insult contests. I thought about it and decided that the enemy wasn't likely to climb the steep slopes and try to attack an entrenched infantry unit, so I relaxed a little also. I was learning. Watson wandered back with the poop. He grinned as he told us the good news that had been handed down from on high.

"Tomorrow we'll be movin' down the hill and set up an LZ. We'll be getting some clean clothes and hot chow. We'll try to get Pete a poncho so we can get rid of that stinkin' one he's been using."

"I'm gettin' used to it, man. I'll tell you, it smells damn good on a wet night." The smell of the piece of plastic, which was probably made in China, had nearly made me nauseous at first, but I had almost become accustomed to it. I had tried to pinpoint the source of the rancid odor; it couldn't be just body odor and sweat, even though he ate different foods (and cleansed himself perhaps less than I did). I remembered the strain and stress my body went through in our short, fierce contacts and decided that it was probably fear that I was smelling. The night passed quietly and we moved down the steep eastern slope of the mass of hills and closed into the objective early the next morning. I hadn't been able to figure out why the area was called what it was, but Watson told me that a battalion-level officer had seen the opening in the mountains and thought it looked like a punch bowl from above. I thought to myself that I was glad it hadn't looked like a toilet bowl. Charlie Company was given the southern part of the perimeter to cover, so we began to set up fighting positions and fields of fire. We spent the rest of the day digging in, filling sandbags, and building bunkers. At 1800, cheers resounded as the word came down, "Hot chow, pop, and beer."

We each received a meal, two cans of beer, and a soda. The Pabst beer was warm, but after more than three weeks without one, it tasted great. During the day choppers had brought a few artillery and mortar pieces to the LZ and they were being set up by their respective units. The Punch Bowl was becoming a battalion firebase, guarded by two infantry companies in the perimeter and Bravo Company on the hill behind us.

The next day, October 26, we received more hot chow, and at 1100 the 2nd Platoon moved to the supply tent near the helipad, where we swapped our filthy fatigues for clean ones. The troops then returned to the platoon area, where we received several large cartons of sundries: candy, gum, cigarettes, writing paper and pens, toothbrushes and paste, and shaving equipment. I felt like I was in heaven, or at least back home, as I scraped off the filth, then the whiskers at the nearby stream. I pulled on the clean fatigues, then glanced at my cohorts.

"Is that really you, McCown? There's a face only a mother could love. And look at Vickers. Hell, man, without the dirt and whiskers, you only weigh forty pounds."

Vickers gave me a small half-smile and his middle finger upraised in the international symbol for *up yours*.

McCown had stuck a cigar in his mouth and was busy removing all the candy and gum in the package and giving it a home in his pack and shirt pockets. He looked up and gave me a smile and his version of an insult.

"Pete, you're not half-bad lookin' without those whiskers and all that dirt. Now, if we can just get rid of that poncho."

It had been a transformation, with the entire company receiving a cleansing of the body and the spirits. I spotted Watson at the CP and walked over.

"Any chance that we might get our packs back?"

"They're over at 3 Gulf—the battalion's forward supply base. They'll try to get them to us, but God knows when, so the 2nd and 3rd platoons will get new ones and you can use the shaving stuff from the sundry packs. I've got you a poncho and liner, so let's go burn that other one."

The 1st Squad gathered in the area between our two bunkers and stood at attention as Maddox and Watson held the smelly "dink" poncho and I sprayed it with mosquito repellent, then Fears stepped forward and lit it. There were no last words or rites, but I thought about a few cold rainy nights in the mountains when that foul-smelling piece of plastic kept me dry. After the ceremonial burning, we toasted it with our beer ration, then went back to our duties. The entire 2nd Platoon spent the rest of the day fortifying our positions and constructing sleeping hooches.

That evening, as I lay back drying my feet and relaxing, Maddox began singing a Righteous Brothers song. Fears joined in and the melody lifted my spirits, sending them soaring over the mountains and the seas before Watson's voice brought me back to reality with a thud.

"All right, 1st Squad. Get five meals packed, we're goin' out in the morning on patrol. Clean your weapons, get some rest."

4

The 2nd and 3rd platoons of Charlie Company, led by a scout dog and his handler, moved out on patrol through an opening in the lines and up the steep hill to the north on a bright October morning in South Vietnam. As we passed through the perimeter established by Bravo Company on top of the hill, one of the grizzled "old guys" in the company recognized Maddox and felt obliged to honor him and the entire company with a salty comment.

"Hey, Maddox, I see you guys got a dog leading you. I thought only blind people needed a guide dog."

Maddox readied a salvo to fire back, but Captain Simcox had overheard and appointed himself defender of the troops.

"That dog has been specially trained to work with humans. And of course, Bravo Company doesn't qualify."

The insults continued, then faded as we headed past their lines to the northwest. Bravo Company then moved down the hill and took over our portion of the perimeter. We were pleased to see Captain Simcox coming along on the patrol, and not just because he had defended our squad's honor. He was extremely well liked among the men for his courage, his willingness to do anything he asked of his troops, and for his abilities to procure supplies and extras when in camp. Maddox said of his coolness, "The Old Man is too short to be running around in the woods. I admire his courage, though. He's not afraid of Ol' Charlie at all. Seems like nothing bothers him."

Watson feigned cupping his groin and answered Maddox: "Yeah, he's got a pretty good set of balls."

The 3rd Platoon was on point, and early in the afternoon their lead element came into contact with an enemy force of indeterminate size. The pointman quickly opened up and reported one NVA down, but the rest of the enemy dropped their packs and some of their weapons and, to use his words, "hauled ass."

The rest of the platoon followed, but the less-burdened NVA had disappeared to the west, always to the west, and sanctuary. A search of the area turned up about a dozen packs, two AK-47s, one RPD machine gun, one SKS carbine, and a B-40 rocket launcher. Artillery was called in and adjusted by the FAC plane, and after the area had been pounded the Old Man called in a chopper to load up the captured armaments. After about an hour Charlie Company moved out again. We were now on full alert and the tension was palpable as we pushed the foliage aside softly and edged along the hilltop, but the enemy was not yet ready to make a stand.

At 1730 we went into a defensive perimeter to break for evening chow. As I nibbled lightly on cold beans and weenies, a firefight broke out about forty feet away. I hit the dirt and scanned the front as the 2nd Squad blasted away. Someone yelled, "Grenade!" and I made myself smaller still as the explosion scattered shrapnel and dirt. There was more yelling that I couldn't understand, then another grenade exploded a little farther away. Despite the fact that I had been sitting in the sun and was still hot from the day's work, chills ran over my body and even my hair was tingling.

I kept my voice as even as I could under the circumstances and yelled softly to Maddox. "Yo, Maddox, what's happenin'? Should we be firing?"

"Hang on, Pete. I think 2nd Squad's got somethin' over there. We'll wait for orders unless they hit our position. Cover your flanks and stay cool."

I remained completely still for another minute or two, then eased onto one side so I could fire if I needed to. After another volley from the 2nd Squad, the firing ceased and the troops edged carefully forward to search the area. They found nothing. The NVA had again escaped into the woods. The word came down as some of the men resumed eating that two NVA had walked up to the 2nd Squad and opened up. The 2nd returned fire and they exchanged grenade tosses before the enemy fled once more.

I didn't feel like eating any more so I stayed behind a tree in the prone position as McCown finished his chicken and noodles and a canteen cup of coffee.

"Hey, guy. How long you gonna stay behind that little tree?"

"Until I find a bigger one, Mac. You assholes told me when I first came to the field that there wasn't any enemy out here. Remember that? Now, you can't take a piss without getting the NVA wet or your dick shot off."

"So we lied. Whaddaya gonna do? Send us to 'Nam?" Vickers replied in a voice shot through with sarcasm.

"I wonder if LBJ knows about all this war shit. Maybe I should go back and tell him personally."

"Yeah, Pete. In about eleven months you can think about that," he shot back. "Think about the Old Man. He's so short he could walk under a snake's belly and salute his asshole. Then he hears this whole shitload of fire and grenades going off. What a way to wind up your tour of duty."

Watson finished his coffee while casting a wary eye to the bushes, dug a little hole for his garbage, and walked to the CP in the center of the perimeter for orders.

We ambushed along the trail that night in two different postures about 500 meters apart, but, despite all the action of the day, the enemy wasn't moving our way on that night. As I thought about all that weaponry we had captured, my respect for, and fear of, the NVA grew measurably. With armaments like those, he wasn't going to keep running and hiding forever. It was now just a matter of time and circumstance until we met head-on. "Watch over me, Lord, make me strong," I whispered silently as I lay along that trail in the Central Highlands.

The 3rd Squad took point as we moved out on patrol once more on the morning of October 28. As we headed toward the northwest the now-familiar but chilling sounds of the AK-47 and the M-16 chattering menacingly at one another sent us diving to the side of the trail. The point element was less than 100 meters from me and I could hear them yelling at one another after the firing died.

"Two dinks! Two of them. One down, one *di died*." Their voices were pitched a little higher than normal in the excitement and terror of the moment. The answer from the platoon leader was in a more normal tone, albeit an affected one. Lieutenant Canale liked to travel just behind the point so he could be on hand for moments like this.

"Hold your position, 3rd Squad. We'll bring the 1st Squad to your right flank and 2nd to your left."

We moved through the brush as quietly as we could in an effort to cut off any escape routes or spot any ambushes along the trail, but the NVA had disappeared. The downed enemy soldier was dead, the bullets having left gaping holes in his clothes and body, and part of the left side of his face was missing. The pointman quickly searched through his now bloody clothes, then shouldered his AK as a trophy. The entire platoon then formed a line and stepped forward on another "recon by fire"—every other man fired as we moved up the gentle slope. We stopped firing, on command, as we reached the crest of the small hill a few minutes later, searched the area, then held up as the Old Man called in the contact. Charlie Company continued the westward patrol, heading down the slope to the valley floor where we met and linked up with Task Force Alpha, which consisted of the 2nd and 3rd Platoons of A Company. The four platoons continued to patrol along the valley floor until 1530 hours, when we stopped next to a stream and set up a night defensive position. The 2nd Platoon quickly tromped and cut enough elephant grass for an LZ and the resupply choppers came in.

One platoon at a time, the troops washed up in the cold waters of the Ya Krong Bolah. On my thirteenth day in the bush I decided to give myself a treat, so I removed all my clothes, dove into the cool waters, lathered up, and had a full bath. As I walked back to our position, buck naked, clothes firmly in hand and my rifle slung, Lieutenant Canale yelled, "Hey, you! Are you in my platoon? Well, get your clothes on. The colonel is coming in. You can't be in a combat zone with no clothes."

Realizing the absurdity of his comments, he grinned and waved me off. I still liked him even though he didn't recognize me. He was an intelligent young man who wasn't afraid to get close to the action and usually had a quick answer, if not always a correct solution, for our problems. He had that air of authority and carried himself with just enough haughtiness to inspire confidence when it was coupled with good judgment. I was glad to be in the 2nd Platoon, if I had to be in 'Nam . . . and I did.

After resupply and a C ration supper, Watson sent Fears, Vickers, McCown and me on OP. We tried to slip quietly through the seven-foot elephant grass to a spot about twenty-five meters outside the lines, where we tromped down enough of the razor-sharp stuff for a position. No trail was near us so we were assured of a fairly quiet night unless we were hit by mortars. If the enemy did come through the grass they would make enough noise to alert the entire side of the perimeter and we could make it back to a fighting position, so we maintained a one up, three down posture all night and rested.

The two understrength companies separated the next morning; TF Alpha crossed the Ya Krong Bolah to work along the south side while the two platoons of Charlie Company moved along the north side, and neither company made contact during the entire day. Late in the afternoon the 3rd Platoon led us into a tiny abandoned village. There was evidence that it had been used recently, so the Old Man decided to set up his command post in it for the night with ambushes on the trails leading in.

We ate our evening meal in the village, then Watson sent me to the CP to ask the lieutenant if he wanted the entire squad sent out on ambush; we had been given the eastbound trail. As I walked past the dog handlers' position I saw Captain Simcox sitting against a tree, rubbing the dog's neck, and singing softly about kicking a dog around.

"Not too worried," I thought to myself. This must be a relatively safe area.

The 1st Squad set up an ambush on a stream crossing by separating into two elements. The back door was covered by Sergeant Watson and one team while Maddox and his team took the kill zone. We couldn't find a comfortable place with cover, so we moved onto a small island in the stream and set up among the rocks. I discovered that if you are very tired, you can block out your thoughts, leave your helmet on, and sleep on a boulder. Nobody crossed the stream or moved along the trail that night.

We pulled back to the village in the morning and then headed down along the stream about 500 meters to an open area. There we cleared an LZ for choppers to extract us—we were headed back to 504C—to the Punch Bowl. My load seemed lighter as we jumped onto the birds and lifted off. Hell, that wasn't so bad. Maybe I can cut this shit after all.

In the three days since we last saw 504C, the LZ had grown into a full-blown firebase complete with artillery and mortar units and their support groups. The bunkers were fortified with logs and sandbags along the now barbed wire perimeter, and brush was cleared for fields of fire. We took positions along the southern quadrant of the base and settled in. The sun was bright and hot, so we quickly constructed a poncho hooch and stowed our gear. Watson procured some C-ration cardboard cartons to cover the ground, then we laid down our poncho liners and began the life of the infantry soldier on break. I took off my boots and stuck my feet into the sunlight to be dried and, hopefully, healed. They were shriveled and rotting and in need of attention. It got cold that night and in the morning a heavy dew lay over everything. I wiped my weapon off with my spare socks and decided to keep it covered, but handy, while we were in the firebase and relatively safe. It wasn't likely that there would be any attack on the base with all of its firepower, but mortar or artillery fire was a possibility.

The paymaster rode into the Punch Bowl in the belly of a Huey helicopter on the last day of October 1966. One at a time the platoons arranged themselves in alphabetical order and shuffled past two portable tables. At the first table I stopped and rattled off: "PFC Peterson, Stanley R., U.S.55880415, reporting for pay." After receiving my pittance I shuffled forward to the next table, where another team of REMFs waited to take my MPC (military payment certificate) and send it wherever I directed. I made out a money order to my parents and one to my brother to repay old debts, pocketed the last ten MPC, and waited for Vickers. He folded a few MPC into his wallet, which he stuck into a plastic bag and rolled up. He shrugged at me, "Easy come, easy go."

"We were in the chips for about a minute, Vick. I kept a few bucks just so I wouldn't feel totally broke."

"Yeah, me, too. Man, Uncle Sam sure don't pay his trained professional killers much, does he? A lousy 165 bucks won't go far even in 'Nam. Let's go over to the supply tent. They brought out a temporary PX."

I purchased a ballpoint pen and a bag of candy, then we returned to the squad area, where Watson greeted me. "Been lookin' for you, Pete. Report to the helipad for loading detail."

I decided this was a great opportunity to get my token gripes in and have a little fun with Watson and Vickers. "Geez, Sarge, thanks a lot. Fuckin' new guy has to do everything. Fuck me and feed me cabbage."

"I wouldn't make you do this shit if I didn't like ya, guy. It'll be a good character builder for ya. Go!" Watson laughed, then turned back to writing a letter.

I unloaded everything that came in that afternoon and sent new supplies and chow out to the troops in the field. It wasn't hard work, but the wind from the rotors drove dust and debris into my eyes and mouth and every pore and crevice of my body. I removed my helmet and shirt and laid them over my rifle and was working hard until a major stepped clumsily out of the battalion commander's chopper and tried to bust my balls.

"Troop, where's your steel pot and weapon?"

"Right over there, sir. I can't unload these birds with them on." I added "asshole" under my breath as I pointed at the pile about twelve feet away.

"Well, put your shirt and steel pot on and keep your rifle closer to you."

"Yes, sir," I replied and added to myself, "get off my ass."

A while later a distinguished-looking middle-aged black major sat down beside me while awaiting a chopper ride. I looked at his insignia and saw he was a chaplain, so I offered him some of my candy but he declined. "At my age, son, you have to watch what you eat and drink or it comes out on your waistline. It's really unfair that when you get older and don't have as much energy to exercise, you still crave all that good food. Take my advice, young man, stay in shape all your life."

I wanted to talk more with him but his chopper came swirling onto the pad. Well, maybe I'd see him again back at Pleiku—if we ever get back there. I returned to the squad at 1730 and watched as the OP moved out through the lines for the night. As the dark closed in, Maddox and Fears conducted a multifarious sing-along on the south side of the perimeter. The radio speaker hissed.

"This is 2–1 Sandbag. How can the OP sleep with all that racket going on? Sandbag-out."

After a quick huddle we broke into a loud chorus of *I keep my eyes wide open all the time.* The laughter that rose up from the ranks and bunkers was good medicine for the entire company and made the time go faster. I was at 335 days and counting.

The next morning, as we were cleaning weapons and gear, the word came down to assemble at the helipad, weapons and pots only. I stuffed a couple of loaded magazines in my pockets and joined the rest of the platoon. We moved to the landing pad and formed up as a company to watch as Captain Simcox turned his command over to Captain Audley M. Federline, a tall young man with an olive drab cast on his wrist. He had broken a bone there four days before in a plane crash. After the ceremony and a round of applause and "Hip, hip, hoorays" for Captain Simcox, the platoons returned to their bunkers, then took turns washing up in the small, leech-infested stream along the south perimeter. I plunged in, lathered up, rinsed off, then headed to the bank to dry off and remove any of the slimy, squirmy, black bloodsuckers that had found me as a potential host.

Maddox laughed at my efforts. "Only two ways to get them little buggers off, Pete. You can burn 'em and burn yourself or give 'em a dose of mosquito repellent." He tossed me a squeeze bottle of the stuff and told me to put a few drops above where the creature was burrowed in and let it run into his mouth. I found one of them about two inches long on my calf and gave him the treatment. It immediately released and fell to the ground squirming. I felt like a dragonslayer as I treated a couple more that had latched onto my ankle. Then, after a tough day of killing leeches, I dried off and changed into clean fatigues.

While we were lying around, Bravo Company was patrolling and again making contact with the enemy. Once more the NVA fled, but Bravo picked off one prisoner and picked up an 82mm mortar pod and a pack. Our night was quiet, but thinking about that mortar kept me extra-alert on my watch. I was ready to dive into the bunker at the first suspicious noise. Mortars—Charlie's got mortars in the area.

In the morning Charlie Company moved out of the LZ, climbed back up the steep slope to the north, and patrolled the

surrounding area. It was a routine patrol but it gave our new
CO a chance to work with and observe his new command and
also gave the men, who had adopted a "show me" attitude, an
opportunity to grade the new captain. We wanted to be led into
whatever fate awaited, but, we wanted a strong leader, not a
pointer who stayed where it was safe and sent troops out on
their own. We wanted another Captain Simcox.

We saw some signs of recent enemy activity—tire tracks
along the trail denoting passage of someone wearing the NVA's
favorite footwear, the Ho Chi Minh sandal. The sandal consisted of a leather insole and two straps attached to a piece of
rubber tire tread.

We returned to the LZ in the early afternoon to see Alpha
Company putting the finishing touches on a huge marker in the
shape of the division patch, a bolt of lightning, on the side of
the steep hill to the north. The sign, about ten feet high and
twenty-five feet wide, was constructed of sandbags dyed with
flour paste. After they finished, Colonel Proctor dedicated the
"Tropic Lightning" logo and named the area Dragon Valley.
Some of the men fired flares and shot off a few rounds as a celebration. The colonel then left on his chopper as we returned to
our positions on the perimeter and began cleaning our
weapons. During the previous night the prisoner had escaped
from Bravo Company, which didn't please their CO. Today, in
what seemed to be an attempt to make amends, they captured
another NVA; this one had an AK-47 and a *Chieu Hoi* safe conduct pass. Just another day, another MPC.

As I wiped the dew from the stock of my M-16 on the morning of November 3, I saw Sergeant Watson heading toward the
company CP for the morning briefing. Vickers was rubbing oil
on his shotgun, checking all the moving parts while Maddox
sat down beside me and removed his boots.

"Whoo! Gas! Where's my mask?" I rolled on the ground,
holding my nose and laughing.

Vickers chipped in, "Talk about chemical warfare, guy. Save
that for the jungle. We're in a friendly firebase here."

"You guys are just jealous. These here feet have walked the
streets of Hotlanta, Gawgia . . ."

"And in the same socks, I'll bet."

Watson came striding back from the CP with a big grin. "All

right, you jungle bunnies, we're going to 3 Golf to pull security for the brigade."

Maddox laughed. "For you new guys, brigade security means palace guard, my kind of duty. A few patrols and OPs, but mostly sitting in a bunker guarding the firebase. Hot A rations, showers, and clean clothes."

"Get your shit together," Watson said. "We're being lifted out at 1000 hours."

I looked back as our chopper lifted off, banked, and headed east. The huge patch with its lightning bolt stuck out as a bold reminder to friend and foe alike that the 25th Infantry Division was a presence in the area to be reckoned with. However, any day of reckoning for Charlie Company, and for me, would have to wait for a few days while we pulled palace guard at Golf. Wonder if Charlie ever gets to pull palace guard?

5

Golf was a large, sprawling, almost circular firebase—the forward headquarters and resupply point for the 3rd Brigade. The 2nd Platoon jumped off the choppers, got their orders, moved into fighting positions on the southwest portion of the perimeter, and immediately began building hooches consisting of ponchos strung over a wire and fastened to pegs. Maddox, Fears and I joined Watson in one position, while Hughes had Vickers, McCown and Marvin in the other. Between us was an armored personnel carrier (APC) and its crew. We felt pretty secure with the extra firepower of the APC and its .50-caliber machine gun beside us and a vast array of concertina wire, claymore mines, trip flares and booby-trapped grenades in front of us. Relaxation became the order of the day and we pulled only single security that night.

Charlie Company lined up for showers and clean clothes after breakfast the next morning. After cleaning my body and face, I returned to the team hooch to discover Maddox and Fears yelling at each other.

"You stole my money, Fears, dammit, and I want it back now! Don't make me come after it, man."

"Fuck you. I didn't take your mothahfuckin' money, mothahfucker."

Maddox grabbed the front of Fears' jungle fatigue.

"Don't call me that. I won't be that guy."

Watson reached in between the two men and spoke softly. "All right, guys. We're here to fight the VC, not each other. Fears, Maddox, settle this without fighting, but settle it."

Fears spoke, softer now: "I didn't take your money, man, but I'll give you five bucks to end it."

Maddox waved his hand in disgust and turned his back. "Forget it. Just stay away from me from now on." Watson took Fears with him to the other squad position and brought Vickers in return.

Things went more smoothly after that and we rested in our hooch throughout the rest of the day until Hughes, who had just returned to the squad as we landed at Golf, came around at 1800.

He was a gentle giant of a man with light brown hair and eyes and when he spoke it was barely above a whisper.

"Pete, you and Vickers and Marvin and me are going on OP. Bring your poncho and liner and web gear."

We moved out through a gap in the wire, which was closed as soon as we went through, then Hughes led the way to a smoothed-out area about fifty meters from the perimeter and we set up.

There was no trail except the one we followed to the spot and we were surrounded by the tall elephant grass, but Hughes decided we would pull 50 percent security. I lay down to rest before my turn on watch, and Hughes suddenly shook me awake.

I whispered, "What? My turn already? I just laid down."

"Naw, man, you were snoring," Hughes whispered back.

"Couldn't be. I never snore. Besides, I wasn't asleep."

"Yeah, Pete, you were snoring," Vickers chipped in quietly. I accepted their judgment and wondered why my habits had changed so much here in the jungle—it must be fatigue.

As I pulled my share of the two-man watch at 2200 hours, I reflected on the men with whom I was sharing a war and a piece of my life. I had grown close to Maddox: I genuinely liked him as a person and admired his soldiering. His piercing blue eyes and enigmatic smile combined with a soft Southern drawl and easy laugh made him a popular favorite among the men and he always had a word or insult for each of them. These engaging features belied an inner resolve that served him well when he was working as a team leader and a flashpoint that became quickly evident when he perceived that he was wronged.

Vickers was a little like me. He had his own shell, a private world that no one could share. He protected himself and made his views known through short, concise statements or wisecracks. Unlike me, he could be genuinely surly and didn't seem to want to get real close to anyone. In the field he humped well, did his job, and, occasionally, moaned about it. He was not Army "lifer" material, but I decided that if the chips were down, I wanted him, and his shotgun, by my side in a battle.

The next morning, November 5, the 1st and 2nd platoons, under Captain Federline, took a short patrol out a few klicks north of the LZ. We secured a village for a civil affairs team, setting up a loose perimeter while they questioned villagers, accepted complaints, and settled claims.

I watched as the villagers stood patiently in line to speak with the team members. They were dressed mostly in the loose, black pajama-like clothing that all rural Vietnamese seemed to wear. The sum of their life seemed to be a few meager belongings, a hut, and a small piece of land on which they grew a few strands of rice for food and market. I pitied them for their seemingly abject poverty, but a part of me envied the simplicity of their existence. We all were seeking the same goals: a roof over our heads, food to eat, some security, and a place in life. Perhaps they had found their place, their purpose, while I was still searching.

When we returned to 3G, the mail had arrived and our side of the perimeter went silent as patrol-weary and news-hungry troops eagerly devoured their letters. The squad had no LP-OP duties this night, so we relaxed and sang songs. Fears and Maddox forgot their differences and did a few duets to answer requests. I guess music and war, like politics, make strange bedfellows.

We continued to operate as brigade security through early November. By day we dispatched short patrols or secured medical or civil affairs teams at Montagnard villages in the AO (area of operations), while at night squads or teams would set up ambushes or OPs. On Sunday the company was rationed two warm beers and a soda per man, and the trading began. Maddox and I were able to get two warm beers for one soda, which we then stockpiled in the hooch while he set out to search for some ice.

He returned after about an hour with a small canister of ice chunks which he had scrounged from the forward mess hall. We managed to get our beers slightly chilled in time for the evening songfest, after which Maddox disappeared. At 2000 hours he reappeared at the team hooch with a case of beer under his arm. Though it was warm, the golden-brown elixir helped us forget most of our cares.

"What's your secret, Maddox? I know you're as broke as I am. How did you get the case of beer?"

"Well, Pete, you have to get to know these guys that work back here in the rear. They realize that they're only a typewriter keystroke away from being in the infantry, so they like to share with us whenever they can."

I filed that information away along with all the other inside stuff I was gleaning from Watson and Maddox. I had this strange feeling that I was going to be in a position to use the information in the not-too-distant future. Because U.S. troops were serving only a twelve-month tour of duty, there would be a large turnover of troops before the first of January, the approximate anniversary of the brigade arriving in-country. If the incoming soldiers were mostly draftees, Vickers, McCown, and I would become the "old guys" of the 1st Squad. The squad would need team leaders and a squad leader and we would be the most likely candidates.

Veteran entertainer and troop-morale booster Martha Raye visited 3G on her USO tour and did a short program of songs and jokes. Vickers, Curtis and I had managed to secure the first row and Maddox arrived late with another case of beer under his arm. He received a larger ovation from the 2nd Platoon than Martha did when she took the small, improvised stage a short while later. She was dressed in OD fatigues and cap. She belted out a few songs and exchanged greetings with some of the troops. Her routines were polished during the last world war and in Korea.

"Where you from, son?" she asked me. "Wisconsin? Know any good cow jokes? I worked in Milwaukee lots of times. Good beer there."

She moved on to the next GI. About halfway through her act, she asked if she could have a drink of my beer. I eagerly handed my half-empty can to her and she drank.

"Aaak. Warm. I hate warm beer."

"That's all we can get, Martha. Ask the brass to give us some ice, would you?"

I decided to sit down and cool it as I felt the stares coming from the mezzanine, a row of boards over barrels where the brass had taken up residence so they could see the show and still look down on us mere mortals. Martha continued her patter and song for about an hour, then closed with the showstopper—"San Francisco." We gave her a standing ovation, then returned slowly to our positions. It seemed strangely incongruous to see such a friendly, familiar American face in such a godforsaken part of the world. In the field, Alpha and Bravo companies were continuing to search and destroy while we lived up the good life. Colonel Proctor visited with chief Quen of the village of Plei Toun and gave him gifts of cigars, cigarettes, candy and soap. In turn, the chief promised to send notice if he received any information about the VC in the area. The war went on.

On November 9, Charlie Company visited the village of Plei Chorr with a medical team to secure the area while they treated forty Montagnards and gave out clothing and gifts. When we returned to the LZ, we were called to the CP for a briefing. As the troops were milling around, Maddox climbed up on a row of filled sandbags and raised his hand and spoke.

"I suppose you're all wondering why I called you here."

The resulting laughter broke any tensions and the real briefing went smoothly. In the morning we would be heading west under the control of the 2nd Battalion of the 8th Infantry. We were given six meals to pack and sent to our positions. The vacation was over.

The choppers banked, then descended swiftly and followed a stream at treetop level for another klick. I saw the purple-hued smoke before I spotted the opening in the elephant grass that had been cut and tromped out by the Special Forces unit in the area. It was barely big enough for a chopper to land in, so the unloading of Charlie Company took some time. The pilots were old hands at this game—ease in, hover, belch the troops out, and haul ass.

The squad moved into the tall, razor-sharp grass and deployed in a defensive semicircle along with other troops while the rest of the company were lifted in. It took about an hour to get everybody on the ground and formed up, then we headed west in a column. The recon platoon of 2nd of the 8th was leading and progress was agonizingly slow, but safer with flanks out for security.

We followed a well-used trail most of the day, crossing the stream on logs and rocks, starting and stopping, and sending small patrols to probe where the map didn't match the terrain. The maps were mostly World War II vintage and many of the landmarks were missing or changed. About twenty minutes after one of our frequent afternoon stops, I saw Watson conferring with Lieutenant Canale. He then raised his hand, turned around, and began cursing in a stage whisper meant for Maddox's ear.

"Dammit all to hell. The 3rd Squad lost a man. They lost Huffman on the last stop. Jesus Christ!"

"How could they do that? Ol' Huffman was slow, but you're supposed to stay in touch with the man in front and behind. Somebody really fucked up back there. How?"

"I don't know, Maddox, but I'm goin' back to find out. We're holdin' up until the Old Man decides what to do. Take over till I get back."

I couldn't figure out how it could happen unless somebody really fell asleep while they were walking—which was possible. As you humped your heavy load along through the humid jungle and nothing happened, you got so tired that you almost became hypnotized by the effort of placing one foot ahead of the other. One more step, one more step, one more step . . . my mind has gone into the sky above all this and back across the sea to my home, beautiful women, cold beer, and loved ones. Yeah, I thought, you could lose track of the man behind you. Watson came back to the squad with a hurt look on his face.

"Well, the 3rd was pulling rear guard and they had Fred as the last dog. That was a bad idea to start with. After the last break was over, the squad took off and the second-to-last guy didn't look back for a few minutes. When he did, Huffman was gone. They sent a patrol back but he must have gone the other way. I fuckin' can't believe it."

"I know you liked Fred, man. Pete, Huffman used to be in this squad. He was strange, but I liked him, too. He was skinny as a rail, but he could hump all day."

"Couldn't we volunteer to go back after him? He has to be still in the area." I didn't think it would hurt to ask.

"The 3rd has volunteered, but the Old Man wants to keep going. The Battalion has made an assault into the LZ we landed in this morning. A Company has moved out into this same AO and he thinks they'll pick him up. The CIDG have made contact and we might be called to help. Shit."

We moved out again, but in his heart every enlisted man in the company wanted to go back for the missing man. As I trudged along I tried to keep my mind focused on the task ahead, but I kept thinking—what if it were me? What would I do? What must be running through his mind? How could the most powerful army on the face of the earth leave one of their soldiers alone in the jungle? God help Fred Huffman as he walks alone through the valley of death.

At about 1630 the column slowed as we neared a small grassy hill. In the distance we could hear the sounds of battle and I saw the RTO run up his long antenna, which had been telescoped together for carrying. I was able to listen as Captain Federline, about ten feet from me, got the battle information from battalion net. He spoke with Lieutenant Canale and informed him that the CIDG had made heavy contact with an NVA unit and were taking casualties.

"I volunteered the company to relieve the pressure on the ARVNs, but they're waiting."

"Sounds like somebody is running from a fight."

Lieutenant Canale answered and shook his head. I couldn't see any good reason to jump into a battle right away, but I wasn't an officer so I kept my mouth shut as we moved into a perimeter and began eating our evening meal of C rations. The CO was still on the horn, and word came down that the battalion was on full alert at the new LZ and Alpha Company had moved west toward us and were on the alert for our missing man.

Captain Federline stayed on the radio as we finished our supper and waited in ominous silence. The sun was dying behind the mountains when Lieutenant Canale came striding toward the platoon from the CP. One look at his face and I knew what he had to say wasn't going to be good.

"All right, men. Listen tight." I had never really heard anybody say that outside of a John Wayne movie, until now. He continued:

"The ARVN are in deep shit and need our help. The rest of the battalion is in the new LZ Lane, but Alpha Company is moving toward the ARVN position on their axis. We are going to head north to a crossing point right about here." He pointed to a mark on his map and went on. "We'll cross that stream, then move up on the high ground to link up with the CIDG and A Company. The Old Man wanted the trail blazer platoon and my best squad on point. That's you, Sergeant Watson. Use your best man. This will be a tough night move, but you men are experienced and I'll be right behind your lead element if you need me. I'll get you an azimuth and we'll get started."

Watson looked at Maddox, who looked away for a long moment before meeting his eyes. Watson then poked his arm gently.

"You're my best man, old dude. Take point."

"She-itt, man. Well, who else? Pete, Vickers, I want you guys behind me. The three of us will take turns on point."

He looked at Watson, then continued talking quickly. "Pete's ready to handle it. Crossin' that river will be a lick in the dark. We'll need the rope, Vick. You're gonna owe me big for this, Watson."

The lieutenant came back to our squad with an azimuth and we buckled our belts and tightened down all our gear. I tried to remember the night training patrols we had taken at Fort Polk, but it wasn't the same. Lieutenant Canale whispered to us:

"This job fits us—too tough for the rest, give me your best. Good hunting and be careful." The ego-stroking had its planned effect; we started out fired-up and ready to do battle if we had to. Maddox led us out of the clearing and into the pitch black that enveloped the triple-canopied rain forest as soon as the sun disappeared. I touched Maddox to get my bearings and reached back for Vickers. God, it was dark.

Maddox led us slowly, as though we were walking on eggs, along a trail on the west side of the stream. I kept my eyes fixed on the back of Maddox's pack. Word came up, "Psst. Hold up. We're losin' contact."

Maddox, Vickers, and I held a brief, whispered huddle to discuss possible remedies for the problem. I suggested holding onto the pack of the man in front, but Maddox interrupted my whispers to reach to the ground, where he picked up some luminous leaves that seemed to be lying everywhere. He stuck a couple in the back of the elastic band around his steel pot and replaced it on his head. They glowed brightly enough to create a dim beacon for me to focus on. I quickly did the same for my pot and we passed the word down the line until the entire patrol was "lit up" to the rear.

We moved stealthily forward once more, sticking to the trail and awaiting word. I was expecting to run into an NVA patrol returning from doing battle with the CIDG and moving in the opposite direction—I kept my finger alongside the trigger guard and my thumb on the selector lever of the M-16. I stayed on one side of the trail while keeping a close eye on the glowing leaves and decided to dive into the brush if we made contact. Vickers moved up behind me and grabbed my pack to get my attention.

"Psst, Pete. Hold up. The lieutenant's comin' up."

I tried to see the lieutenant's face as he slipped past me in the dark. I wanted to sit down with him and discuss this whole war thing and the missing man and this night patrol and crossing that damn river, but I knew I couldn't. It had to have been a tough day for him, also—losing one of your men without a shot being fired. This patrol was probably a chance for him to get back into the good graces of the battalion command. My heart went out briefly to him; I wanted him to be my strong, courageous, inspiring leader. Lead us through the night to victory, make that safety.

Lieutenant Canale, Sergeant Watson and Maddox conferred briefly while Vickers and I stood guard on the trail. After a few minutes Maddox rejoined us and we moved to the edge of the stream a few meters away, where he turned back to us and whispered: "We're gonna cross here. Ready for this shit, Pete?"

He began tying the rope around his waist and readied himself to step in the black water. I decided it was time to say something, so I spoke as gently as I could and tried to keep the fear I felt out of my voice: "I'll be within arm's reach at all times. No sweat, GI."

I wrapped the rope around my waist and saw Vickers do the same. We couldn't tie it since Maddox had one end and the other was secured to a nearby sturdy tree by Watson. If anything happened, we would pull sharply on it and somebody would haul us in; two tugs meant we were across safely. I put my hand on Maddox's free arm and we stepped lightly into the water together, barely disturbing the surface.

In my mind the river assumed the proportions of the mighty Mississippi, which was nearly a mile wide as far north as Crawford County, Wisconsin, my home territory. We couldn't see the other side, in fact, we could barely see a few feet ahead, but we began the crossing with the faith that young men have in their God, their elders and superior officers, their country, and their own personal feelings of immortality. I didn't think that I was meant to die in the middle of a river, in the dark of a November night, in the jungles of Vietnam.

Maddox took the lead, rifle held high in one hand, the other held out for balance. He edged one foot ahead of the other, sliding along the rocky bottom, then brought the back foot up even and hesitated before moving ahead again. The water was cool and the night was unusually quiet as we continued moving. I was one step behind Maddox, and Vickers trailed by about three more steps with the rest of the squad waiting on shore.

Maddox kept sliding along as the water deepened to chest level, making our packs and gear seem twice as heavy. Suddenly I felt a tug on the rope as Maddox slipped, then disappeared with a slight splash. I braced as well as I could on the slippery rocks and pulled hard on the rope. He resurfaced quickly, found some footing, and tried to steady himself. Even in the dark I could see the fear in his eyes and he was shaking like a small child from the cold and the tension. I searched my mind for something reassuring to say.

"Listen, Maddox, I've just said a little prayer. It's all in the hands of the Big Fella now. It'll be all right. Now, I'm gonna take point for a while. You come in behind me." I put my hand on his shoulder as Vickers came up to join us, shotgun held high. He sized up the situation:

"Hey, guy, you picked a hell of a time to go swimming. We've got some work to do here. Want me to take point?"

Maddox found his voice, though it was strained.

"Pete's gonna take it, Vick. I'll be OK in a minute."

"You know, just before I stepped off the bank, I saw the lieutenant move over to the tree where we tied the rope. He had a machete in his hand, so we know he'll cut bait if the shit starts gettin' hot or we keep takin' baths, so we might as well cross this mother," Vickers added.

We started to giggle as quietly as we could. It was the strained, unstoppable laughter of frightened and desperate men who were almost beyond caring.

"We're expendable, Vick. Dead meat. Screw it, I'm taking off for the far shore. We'd look kind of funny out here if anybody could see us. Three guys laughing their ass off in the middle of a river in Vietnam."

"We're right behind ya, Pete. Slow and easy, guy."

I slipped the rope from around my waist then moved ahead of the beleaguered Maddox and began sliding along as I had seen him do. How in the hell do I get into these things, I asked myself. I could've joined the Air Force and spent the war in a comfortable barracks with an enlisted men's club nearby. Screw it. Just plunge ahead as quietly as you can and get to the other side. When I realized I wasn't attached to the rest of the troops by rope, I reached back and grabbed the front of Maddox's web gear, held my rifle in the other hand for balance, and moved out. As I pushed along I felt a strange calmness and confidence, as if the added responsibility gave some necessary meaning and impetus to the job and my life.

The river finally began to get more shallow and I could begin to make out the gray outline of trees and brush on the bank. My heart quickened once more as I imagined the entire NVA waiting in ambush, ready to squash these few puny Americans as they crawled up the bank. I paced myself, one step at a time, until I was just a few feet from the shore when I felt Maddox moving up beside me. He put his finger to his lips, then moved ahead of me to the bank where he searched for a place to climb up.

He spotted an opening in the brush and scrambled up and into the darkness once more. I waited for a few seconds, then he reappeared, looked around, untied the rope from his waist, and secured it to a tree as I crawled up to join him.

"It looks like ol' Charlie didn't hear us despite all the damn noise I made. Vick, give a couple of quick pulls on that rope and let's get the others over here."

It was apparent that the old Maddox was back in charge as he ordered us to set up security a few meters into the woods while he helped the troops climb out of the water. Watson crossed first with the rest of the 1st Squad and quickly set up a defensive half-perimeter. Lieutenant Canale came next with his radiotelephone operator, then stopped to help at the stream bank. It seemed to take an eternity to complete the task and some of the men nodded off while on guard. I whispered to Vickers and Fears as the emotions of the moment came crawling back into my mind.

"That was quite an experience. I was sure the VC were gonna be waiting on this side to pick us apart. We would've been sitting ducks in the water."

"Yeah, but what the fuck. You gotta go sometime, Pete."

"Man, I just wanna get outta here alive," Fears interjected in his singsong manner. "I got a whole lotta woman waitin' for me. Don't be talkin' no shit about dyin'."

"Where do ya think ol' Huffman is tonight, Fears? He's gotta be shittin' bricks about now."

"If he's still able to shit," Vickers added.

"Maybe A Company will find him. If Charlie don't find him first. I'm never gonna be last man on patrol. Man, don't even ask me."

"Huffman, you picked a hell of a time to take a piss. Now

your shit is in the wind, ol' Breeze." There was a note of finality in Maddox's voice which brought the squad to silence.

We finally got the word to move out again. We heard no more sounds of battle from the hilltop, so I took that as an encouraging sign. Maddox, all business now, once more took the point and we pushed into the jungle. To avoid the noises that would announce our presence and position to the enemy, we eschewed cutting our way through the thick foliage. Instead, we pushed the vines and branches aside and went around trees and impenetrable thickets. We could still be heard, but hopefully not pinpointed.

The going was agonizingly slow and we stopped every hundred feet or so to let the CO check his bearings and call in his position to the CIDG and Alpha Company. Milling about in the dark, there was a very real danger of friendly forces shooting at each other. I took a turn on point, straining my eyes to focus on a few feet ahead of me. I would move a few feet, stop, listen, and look, then move again. After about a hundred meters, I relinquished the lead to Vickers and tried to whisper something funny, but fatigue had dulled my brain.

"One good thing about being on point—you don't get as many vines or brambles slapped into your face by the guy in front of you. In the dark, behind somebody, you get all cut to hell."

"All I'm worrying about now is, how close are we to the ARVNs? Do they know where we are? And where is A Company?"

Watson heard Vickers' worries and tried to reassure him. "Just go real slow, guy. If you hear anything at all, drop. The Old Man is coordinating this with battalion, so we'll be all right. Move out, same direction."

After one more stop, Maddox took over the lead again and led us for another hundred meters or so to the top of the hill, then held up. Fatigue from humping and the stress had now almost totally overtaken me, so I leaned numbly against a tree as Lieutenant Canale moved past with his RTO.

"Alpha 6, this is Charlie 2–6. Is that you just ahead?"

There was a little moonlight coming through at this altitude and I saw him put his thumb up and grin to Watson as Captain Federline joined the group.

"We made it, sir. That's Alpha, and the perimeter is just beyond that tree. By God, we made it!"

"Good job, 2–6, men. Now let's meet with Alpha 6 and get this perimeter squared away defensively."

I couldn't believe that we had finally completed our task. We had found the CIDG and linked up with Alpha Company on a hillside in the dark of night with enemy supposedly all around. As the officers moved inside the perimeter to work out the assignments, one of the grunts in Alpha spoke to us.

"Y'all didn't happen to lose somethin' out there today, did ya? We picked up this skinny ol' dude wandering around lookin' like he'd lost his last friend. Says he belongs to you guys, but I think he's a spy and we oughta shoot him."

"I'll be damned. You guys found Huffman? Send him over so I can kick the shit out of him."

"Where have you been, guy?"

Watson was genuinely happy to see the decrepit-looking trooper as he crossed the trail and joined the 2nd Platoon. We had found places to rest along a large trail which led to the top of the hill and the CIDG position. Huffman spoke slowly, and there was relief and a touch of righteous anger in his voice as he told us about his travails.

"I looked up and I was alone. I yelled, but I was scared to yell very loud. Then I ran up the trail but I couldn't see anybody. I thought, I'm fucked now, so I followed the trail to a fork. I couldn't see any tracks or sign, so I guessed left, which I thought was west and went that way. I walked for a while, listened for a while, walked some more. Then I decided that west would eventually lead me to Cambodia, so I reversed myself. A couple hours later I heard noises. God, Americans are loud in the jungle. I stepped out slowly with my hands up and said I was a GI from Charlie Company. They said they had been looking for me. Here I am. Now, why did you guys leave me?"

No one had an answer to his query, but we were all pleased to have a happy ending to the saga as Huffman moved down the line to rejoin his squad. Alpha Company was moving into positions on the north side of the perimeter, so we leaned back on our gear and waited for the call to move. I felt a fiery sensation on my legs, causing me to begin to hop around and swat at them. McCown looked at me and laughed softly in a tired voice.

"Pete, you sat in some fire ants. Take down your pants and brush them off and pour some water on the bites."

"Yeah, sure, you just want to see me with my pants off."

I did as he told me and found only a few of the miserable devils chewing on me, and the water eased the pain slightly. The word came down the line to move out to the south side of the perimeter, so we pushed ourselves a few more meters along the top of the hill. I followed Maddox to a position behind a huge downed tree, where I unbuckled my gear and slumped to the ground, slowly. The tension and the terrain we had traversed had completely robbed me of my strength.

In our arduous trek we had nearly circumvented the CIDG position, going around the west and south portions of their perimeter before coming in on the east. Although it didn't seem so during the patrol, the move had been coordinated well enough that Alpha Company had reached the same point as Charlie Company at the same time. I closed my eyes and felt a nudge on my arm, then another, harder this time.

"You got first watch, Pete. Wake Fears in one hour."

It was 0200 hours when I began my watch. The night movement had taken almost seven hours from inception. I took a position behind the log and fought to stay awake for one more hour.

"Please, Charlie, don't come back tonight. Give us a few hours of peace."

I whispered into the dark. My pleas were answered as the rest of the night was uneventful—the enemy had hit hard, then made a strategic withdrawal to fight another day.

6

Fighting in Vietnam became a series of sporadic firefights and small battles that seemed almost unrelated to one another in the mind of the new guy. For the most part, the grunts followed the old axiom: "Ours is not to reason why. . . ." In reality there almost certainly were plans hatched at an air-conditioned brigade headquarters, passed down to battalion, then laid out for smaller, mostly company-sized elements.

The officers, lifers all, welcomed, even relished these battle plans as an opportunity for personal glory; a chance to advance their careers. Losing men struck a chord in the hearts of most of the line officers—company commanders and platoon leaders—but was viewed as a necessary part of the war effort by all of them.

While the lowly grunt moved along on his twelve-month tour of duty hoping to avoid the enemy and battles, just wanting to get home in one piece, the generals and colonels moved the pawns in such a way as to make battles, and dying, an inevitable outcome in the quest for the almighty body count. The wily North Vietnamese Army regulars and Viet Cong guerrillas preferred to avoid large-scale battles for the most part. Instead, they would hit, run, and wait for the time when the advantages would swing their way. U.S. Army Intelligence would spot an NVA unit movement or encampment, and brigade HQ would order a large-scale combat assault into the area. The enemy, scoffed at as *Charlie* by the brass, but promoted to *Mr.* or *Sir Charles* by the fighting men, would disappear like the morning fog in the warm Vietnamese sun, biding his time, building his strength . . . waiting.

Watson woke the squad at first light to prepare for a possible enemy attack.

"At dawn," he said. "They always attack at dawn."

"Hell, you've seen too many movies. If they couldn't whip these sorry ARVNs, they certainly ain't gonna attack us now with two fortified companies. I'm gonna fix breakfast."

This was the Maddox I knew and respected—the man I wanted to lead me into battle and teach me all he knows. He opened a can of C-ration coffee and started heating a canteen cup of water over a glowing heat tab. I joined him, finding some cocoa and a few crackers in my borrowed pack. I had long since given up ever seeing my original pack with my Gillette razor and personal toothbrush again. Vickers broke out a can of grape jam and a dried C-ration roll.

"You be sure to tell us, Sarge, if an attack starts. I'd sure hate to miss one of those dawn attacks."

Watson grinned sheepishly and pulled out his canteen cup and a heat tab. We were all operating on adrenaline, which we figured could be best reconstituted with caffeine. The CIDG were cooking rice while talking to themselves, probably saying some of the same things we were. Maddox spoke to one, "Hey, ol' dude, lotta VC here? VC here?"

He motioned to the surrounding woods and mimed a soldier firing a rifle. The CIDG trooper, who looked to be at least forty, smiled at the foolish American and humored him. *"Beaucoup VC, beaucoup."*

Maddox grinned back, then turned to us as proud as a new daddy of his language breakthrough.

"Did you hear that? This ol' boy says *beaucoup* VC out there."

"Yeah, we heard, man, we heard. Nice work, interrogating a friendly soldier," Watson retorted, then picked up his hot coffee and headed for the platoon CP. A short while later he returned with orders.

"We need to send three men to clear an LZ to get out the wounded. You think you can handle that with your team, Hughes?"

The men of the 1st Squad seemed to be lighthearted this morning, but I figured that it was just exhaustion resulting in a lack of blood being supplied to the brain or something. There was a genuine threat in the immediate area; the attack on the CIDG had come from an element of the 33rd NVA Regiment. They were positioned here in the western Central Highlands on both sides of the border, and I had learned from Watson that we had been sent here to contact and destroy them. We were lucky to have avoided a showdown on our night trek and now it appeared to be just a matter of time and circumstance.

The line companies seemed to be the bait to force the enemy's hand. This fact rode heavily on our hearts and pervaded our thoughts as we cleared away the brush and loaded the wounded CIDG on the choppers. As long as we were in this area, we were perhaps only minutes away from a battle and a heartbeat away from eternity.

I looked around at the handful of Vietnamese with bandages on various parts of their bodies and noticed that none of them were complaining. I wondered if I could be as composed under similar circumstances. On the other hand, maybe the medics had handed out double rations of morphine and they were sedated.

After the wounded were lifted out, Colonel Proctor flew in with Colonel Shanahan to meet with the company commanders. Then the CIDG and the recon platoon, 2/8th, were lifted out and Alpha Company moved out to the north in the afternoon. Charlie Company remained in the LZ for the rest of the day, allowing the troops to get some needed rest. Just before dark the CO sent the 3rd Platoon out on ambush a few hundred meters away.

Less than an hour later the 3rd Platoon opened up as several NVA regulars walked into their ambush. Our perimeter went into full alert as the automatic weapons fire erupted, shattering the peaceful ennui we had fallen into. I rolled into our foxhole and grabbed the firing mechanism for the claymore mine. If we faced an attack, I would fire it first. Vickers and Maddox joined me in the fighting position as the firing continued. We had questions, but Watson was in a meeting at the CP, so we were left to wonder how the 3rd Herd was doing.

"Come on, 3rd, get some. Get 'em all. If they come this way, we're gonna put 'em in a world of hurt, right, Pete?" Maddox said as the firing stopped.

"We're sure gonna try, but I hope they stay the fuck away. You know, back home, this is Armistice Day. Wonder if Charles has an Armistice Day on his calendar?"

"Mr. Charles probably doesn't know what armistice means. He just humps along with his rice and his AK-47, smokes a little weed and tries to hang my ass out to dry."

"Vickers, you kill me. Your humor is so damn dry. What the hell is that? Jeezus H!"

I wheeled around with my M-16 at the ready as Watson slid into the now-crowded foxhole out of breath.

"Third Herd killed two NVA and wounded another. No friendly casualties at all."

"Way to go, 3rd. Kill 'em all. Sarge, you gotta give us a little more warning when you're gonna come slidin' in. Pete liked to pull down on you, ol' dude."

"Yeah, shit, I thought we were under attack from the company CP, so I was ready to waste them all."

"Next time I'll go to the other hole with Hughes and McCown. You guys'll have to get your news someplace else."

"We'll just find out from Mr. Charles. Hell, Maddox speaks the lingo like a fricking native, anyway. Besides, if you go to the other hole, you'll have to listen to Fears tellin' about how scared he is."

"Yeah, hell, I can get that here, Vick. The 3rd searched the ambush area and couldn't find anymore VC, so they must have *di died*. We'll pull two-thirds security until further notice. I'm going to the other hole and fill them in."

"Be sure to say hi to all the guys for us, Watson. Well, I'm wide awake, so I'll pull the early watch if nobody cares."

"I'll join you, Pete. Vick, y'all gonna be able to sleep?" Maddox asked.

"Yeah, I think the action is about over for the night. Wake me whenever you want, unless I'm dreaming."

Maddox and I continued to whisper for a while, then Watson came crawling back, whistling as he neared the hole.

"Was that loud enough for you guys? I don't want to get my ass shot up by my own squad, if you don't mind."

"I wasn't sure that you were friendly until I heard you doin' that California beach music. Then I knew it had to be you," I told him.

Watson joined Vickers behind the log as Maddox and I pulled the first watch, peering into the darkness, watching as the trees changed shape and seemed to move. No matter how good a picture of the landscape around your position you have painted into your memory, it changes as the light changes and fades, and if you stare long enough, you will see what you fear the most. We had the usual array of trip wires for flares and booby-trapped grenades set out, but our best defense would be the alertness of the man on watch. We were fortunate once more as the enemy was through for the night.

On the morning of November 12, 1966, I rolled out of my poncho liner and sat up behind a tree. Vickers was pulling the last watch and gave me a nod as I shook the twigs and dirt from my fatigues and began taking off my boots. We had to do things backwards in the boonies. At night we left our boots on in case we were attacked or had to make a quick move in the dark. In the morning, if we had time, we removed the offending articles of footwear and aired out our rotting feet. Mine looked particularly bad this morning as I pulled off the filthy socks I had been wearing for four days through the jungle, across streams, and up a few mountains.

"Man, what I wouldn't give for a warm bath and a massage, especially for my feet. Have some lovely, naked, blond Swedish nymphomaniac rub my feet for a while—ummph."

"Let me think, Pete. No, I don't believe the Army provides for that here in a combat zone. But, you can get just about any kind of a massage you want in Pleiku City. I'll show you around when, or if, we ever get back there."

Vickers grinned, then walked over to where Maddox and Watson were lying.

"Come on, troops. Drop your cocks and grab your socks. It's morning in Vietnam. Sarge, you wouldn't want to miss that attack at dawn, would you?"

"Vickers, I'm gonna kill you. I was dreamin' about my girl back in Pleiku doing things to me that are illegal in most of the states back home. Oh, I wish I was there."

"Son, I wish I was in beautiful Hotlanta. There are more pretty girls than you can shake a stick at. 'Course, if my ex-wife would take me back, I wouldn't even look at the others, which is how she became my ex-wife in the first place," Maddox said as he stretched.

"I've heard this one a hundred times before. Pete, you don't want to hear this sad story about a grown man being led around through life by his cock, believe me," Watson added.

I laughed with the others and decided that I would like to hear his tale of woe someday when we got into an LZ with a firebase where I could relax and enjoy it. Watson was stirring some powdered sugar into his coffee when the call came down the line for the squad leaders to report for the morning briefing. We finished our breakfast in relative silence and were cleaning our weapons when he returned.

"Third Herd picked up a few pieces of equipment and two grenades this morning at the ambush site. They're comin' in the back side of the perimeter about now."

The 3rd Platoon rejoined the company as Watson was speaking and the Old Man welcomed them profusely and praised their efforts. We spent another hour or so drying our feet, preparing our gear, and writing letters before Watson came back from yet another CP briefing and yelled: "Saddle up, 1st Squad, we're moving out. First Platoon is on point, we're pulling drag. Stay in contact."

I watched as the 1st Platoon trudged through on point, followed by the 3rd under Lieutenant Shipley, then the company CP. Finally the entire 2nd Platoon moved out slowly before we fell in behind them and took the drag. The 1st led us to Hill 283, where we held up to wait for Alpha Company. When they linked up with us, the word came down to clear an LZ for resupply, then to dig in for the night. One of the choppers received fire as he brought in supplies, but he couldn't pinpoint the source so it was ignored. Hill 283 was a small hill with an open field where some hooches had been standing at one time—perhaps a small Montagnard village or an enemy outpost. We dug in around the open area with Alpha Company occupying the north side of the perimeter along the heavily wooded area. As we were cutting fields of fire and bringing in branches to fortify our fighting positions, some noise went up in the woods near our position. An American Indian from Charlie Company, Charles Beaver, had been working with the machete, cutting brush. One of the troops had spotted a rather large python and wanted to shoot it, but Beaver captured it, then cut off the head and skinned the snake. He then roasted it on a huge fire at his position and invited his side of the perimeter to join the feast and taste the huge reptile. These brave men who faced death every day unflinchingly now hesitated, then a few stepped forward and took a tentative nibble.

"What's it taste like?" McCown asked as he moved to grab a small piece. "I've never eaten snake before, but I'm ready."

"Tastes like snake to me, Mac."

"Tastes like chicken, Pete."

Fears moved hesitantly to the pile of cooked flesh, then cut off a small piece, stuck it in his mouth and grinned. "Tastes like pussy!"

Beaver looked up from his mess kit full of meat. "You mean cat? No. Cat tastes like rabbit."

We all had a long laugh and Beaver joined in, either because he had made a good joke or because he didn't want to be left out despite not understanding—the look in his eyes suggested the former. We returned to our squad positions and settled in for the night. OPs and ambushes were sent out, but the night was quiet.

Alpha Company left the perimeter on the morning of November 13, heading west on a mission once again to search out and destroy the enemy. A Company had been operating in two units while patrolling, Task Force Alpha (1st and 2nd platoons) and Task Force Army (3rd and 4th platoons), moving about five hundred meters apart. Lieutenant Joe Grant, already a legend in the battalion for his heroism in previous actions, led the task force.

Charlie Company as a single unit remained at Hill 283 and prepared for its own patrol. Watson reported the latest news and rumors from the company and platoon CP.

"Bravo moved through the area where the CIDG had their first contact yesterday and found two dead NVA. Only they still call them PAVN so they can call themselves the PAVN hunters. They found a lot of equipment the CIDG threw down as they headed for the high ground and on their way back to the LZ, they picked up a wounded PAVN who said that there were five NVA companies in the area. That's five companies." He put emphasis on the number in his last statement.

"Five! And we're out here at company level patrolling around trying to make contact. What if we run into the whole damn bunch at once with only one company, or even less?"

"Pete, we've got a whole battalion plus help from the 4th Division within a few miles."

I thought about that and wondered what the reaction time for relief would be in this terrain if there was a one-sided battle.

"What are we gonna be doin' today, Sarge?"

"Right now, Mac, we're a reaction force for Bravo and Alpha in case they get in trouble. If they don't, we're going on a short move later today. Get your gear ready and cleaned."

Shortly after 1100 hours the task force hit a large enemy unit while patrolling near a stream. As we were cleaning our weapons on Hill 283, the men of Alpha Company were locked into a heavy firefight about two klicks away. At 1115, Company C was ordered to move to a blocking position on a nearby hill. The word came down the line quickly and we were on the move a few minutes later. It looked like I was about to learn what the reaction time would be.

We moved quickly along the trail to the preselected position, arriving at about 1245 hours. We set up quickly in line across the top of a large hill, bisecting the trail, with only a couple of squads as rear security. Because we had left before eating, some men began breaking out C rations and eating them cold while remaining on full alert. We were eager for news about A Company and, to a man, hoped they would fight their way out successfully. Watson crawled over to the platoon sergeant's RTO to listen to the battalion net for a few long minutes, then crawled back.

"A Company ran into a mess of NVA by a stream. They killed a bunch of them, then pulled back because they were taking mortar fire. They took their wounded to a hill and cut an LZ to get them out. They've called in an air strike, then they'll medevac the injured and join us, and we'll both go back to Hill 283, hopefully."

Captain Federline sent a two-squad patrol from 3rd Platoon out to the rear of our position to check the terrain and make sure the enemy wasn't trying to flank us. As the men slipped out into the rain forest, I relaxed a little. We wouldn't be moving out for a while. Watson kept us informed as to the progress of the medevac and we could hear occasional explosions in the distance.

"They're taking mortars again. The FAC plane is coming up to spot for the artillery. Both units of Alpha are together, so maybe they won't need any help."

I tried to look into the hazy blue eyes of the young, blond noncom as he squatted down to give us the latest update, but they seemed clouded over and I couldn't read his feelings. I wondered if he was as concerned as I was at the very real possibility of combat on a large scale at any moment. It made sense to presume that he was.

At about 1430 the report came that the medevac was completed, all ten wounded out safely, and Alpha Company was moving east. One hour later, as they were crossing the stream, the enemy opened up once more. Apparently they had used the time it took to evacuate the wounded to position themselves for a major battle.

Less than a klick away we lay in our blocking positions and listened in awe and wonder to the terrible roar of automatic weapons firing and mortars and grenades exploding. I glanced at the tight faces of the men around me and knew that we all were experiencing the same feelings of intense fear mixed with the appalling knowledge that our fellow troops were in trouble.

Fears' eyes were wide as he spoke to me: "You ever hear anything like that? I hope they don't make us go over there. I don't wanna go over there. Oooh." He continued to moan in a soft voice as the firing roared once more. We had forgotten about the patrol that was out to our rear, and when they returned we heard the noise they were making and quickly got on line to fire at the enemy that had obviously flanked us. As we readied to fire, word came down from the CP: "Hold your fire, patrol coming back in. Don't shoot!"

We pulled our weapons back as the men from our 3rd Platoon moved back into our lines with frightened glances at us.

"What the hell's going on here? We're friendly, remember?"

I shrugged my shoulders and passed what information we had about the beleaguered Alpha Company and suggested that we had been a little trigger-happy because of those factors. Once more the firing picked up on the other hill and the man from the 3rd nodded in understanding, although there was a disapproving look in his eyes. A few minutes later Watson came half-crawling back once more from Lieutenant Canale's position. I caught his eyes as he began to speak and saw the concern and the fear.

"It's pretty bad. A Company has got a lot of men down and they're about out of ammo. I don't know if they can hold out until we get there, but we're headin' for their position. First Platoon leads off, then 3rd, then 2nd. First Squad has rear guard. We'll be marking our progress by popping smoke every hundred meters. Get saddled up."

Canale turned away from the squad, looked at his old friend, and whispered fervently: "Man, I am way too short for this shit, Maddox."

There were no jokes, no insults, as we men of Charlie Company fastened our web gear and readied our weapons. We knew that we were headed into a buzzsaw and some of us might not come back, a thought so absurd and so real that it was overwhelming. We also knew that the men of Alpha Company were hurting badly and all of them would be dead in a matter of minutes if we didn't make the attempt. They might die anyway, but we would do everything in our power to get there in time. There could be no holding back.

The 1st Platoon led off and the entire company was soon moving toward the battle site. If the enemy had an ambush set up in the area, Charlie Company would have plunged headlong into it, but time was of the essence so we charged ahead through the jungle. In the drag element, Vickers, Curtis and I were counting the meters and popping smoke to mark our position. The fast-movers (jets) were pounding the area around Alpha Company's perimeter, so we were showing them where we were.

The company made it through a thousand meters of thick jungle in less than thirty minutes. When he reached a point about forty meters from A Company's perimeter, Captain Federline tried to make radio contact with the harried Alpha CO to tell him we were coming in. Then he moved the 1st, under the command of Lieutenant LaMotte, and 3rd Platoon, under Lieutenant Shipley, up on line and readied an attempt to break through to relieve Alpha Company.

The 2nd Platoon moved into a rear security position about

thirty meters from the battlesite. The NVA charged once more out of the brush at Alpha Company's positions and I could hear them screaming in English: "GI, you die! GI, you die!"

The tumult and shouting were overwhelming to the remaining men of Alpha, who were down to their last few rounds. Some of the men were saving one round to use on themselves if the worst happened, and it looked like it was going to take place now. They heard the screaming NVA and the roar of their guns and felt a sense of extreme panic, but it was soon replaced by the realization that they were going to die on this day in a miserable, stinking jungle ten thousand miles from home and they wondered why. Then from the command post came a scream: "Don't shoot, Charlie's coming! Don't shoot, it's Charlie!"

Most of the battle-weary men were too harried to understand what was happening as they once more faced the advancing NVA. Those that did hear the confusing command couldn't make sense of it. Hadn't Charlie been coming at them, trying to kill them all day, and now they're told not to shoot? What the hell was going on? Did somebody in the CP snap? Shit, man, I'm gonna die and the CP is telling me to hold my fire.

Less than 150 feet away, Captain Federline, recognizing that he could not be heard in the din, circled his arm, pointed it forward and screamed as hard as he could. "Charge! Charge!"

The men of the 1st and 3rd Platoon surged forward screaming at the top of their lungs and firing toward the unguarded flank of the NVA. The enemy force, totally oblivious to the possible presence of another American unit in the area, had exposed its flank as they drove to eliminate their surrounded and nearly helpless foe. That hunger for the kill would prove to be their downfall on this day. Inside the perimeter, the troops of Alpha were firing their last rounds, praying and quietly readying themselves for the final minutes of their lives as they heard the tumultuous shouting and rapid firing which they believed was another enemy assault. Another scream came from the remains of their CP: "Charlie Company is coming in. Hold your fire!"

Now it started to make sense to those still hanging on. Maybe we're not gonna die. Come on, C Company.

Meanwhile, 2nd Platoon was waiting, still set up in a rear guard and holding in reserve. We took some rounds from snipers hiding in the tops of trees, but we lashed back at them with a few dozen rounds from the M-60 and they fell silent. I listened as the other two platoons screamed and began firing on their way to rescue our battalion brothers as we huddled low to the ground in wonder and fear. I thought it might be better to be in the battle instead of lying in wait, hearing the awful tumult and imagining the worst. The firing from both sides was deafening as the men of Charlie Company tore into the exposed side of the enemy. After the initial cacophony, an eerie silence fell as the voracious GIs changed magazines and got their bearings. In that strange moment, I heard once more an NVA soldier scream at a GI defender. "GI, you die!"

I listened in awe, then heard the voice of a trooper from the 1st Platoon yell back at the surprised enemy attacker. "Not today, VC. Your turn!"

Then I heard a few of the men of the 3rd Platoon give out rebel yells which were quickly picked up by the rest of the American troops and they surged forward once more.

As the screaming men of the 1st and 3rd platoons again hit the NVA, the enemy attackers began to fall from the withering fire. The total surprise, the shouting, and the vehemence of the assault completely rattled and confused the enemy—they literally didn't know what had hit them. As their ranks thinned, the assault on Alpha Company broke quickly and the enemy fled to the west, leaving dozens of dead bodies behind. Some of the GIs chased after them, firing, for a few meters, before returning to the battle site. The troops of Charlie Company, the rescuers, still flushed with excitement and full of adrenaline, then moved in and began to reinforce the perimeter.

The 2nd Platoon held in position throughout the few seemingly interminable minutes of fierce fighting, then held again as a silence fell over the bloodied fields of strife. Lieutenant Canale tried to reach Captain Federline on the radio, but the CO was probably busy setting up a defensive perimeter and surveying the remainder of Alpha Company to determine the command structure. The platoon remained prone, faces drawn, eyes scanning the tree line, guns ready. I glanced at Vickers and asked him, "What do you think, man? Is it over?"

"I sure hope so, Pete. I've never heard anything like that in my seven months. It must be what hell is like."

The lieutenant finally got through to Charlie 6 for instructions, and the word was quickly passed down the line to get ready to move to the battle scene. There was no discussion within the ranks, we merely set ourselves to the task at hand and hoped the battle was over. I thought to myself that if the enemy comes back, I'm about to find out if it is better to be in the battle instead of being a worried bystander. The platoon was placed into defensive positions along the east side of the perimeter that Charlie Company had set up to strengthen and relieve the men of Alpha. The 1st Squad took a spot near a huge tree and settled into a fighting posture. I tried to look through the bushes to the battle scene to set into my morbidly inquisitive mind exactly what had happened and what they were doing now.

Watson was surveying the perimeter, then turned to me. "Pete, go up to the CP and see whether the lieutenant wants us to dig in or what."

My curiosity was about to be sated. I quickly moved through the brush in search of the command post (CP). As I entered the clearing that was the battleground, I saw a sight that gripped my heart and stomach and sent my mind reeling. There, on my left, was a stack of American bodies, some with missing limbs, some decapitated, all saturated with blood. There were at least ten dead men in the pile, with more being added as I stood there, frozen in place. A few feet away, medics and other survivors were working feverishly on the dozens of wounded. Some of the injured men were moaning or swearing at those tending them, but most seemed to be in shock. Scattered around on the ground were used bandages, torn clothing, and abandoned gear and weapons. Along the edges of the clearing at positions where Alpha Company had attempted their defense, I could see more discarded packs and entrenching tools and thousands of spent cartridges. As I walked along in a daze, searching for Lieutenant Canale, I heard a staccato burst from an automatic weapon. I dropped to the ground, but experience had taught me that it was an M-16, so I looked around for the source.

I saw a shirtless GI with a bandage on his left forearm walking along the perimeter, firing into the bodies of the NVA lying on the ground. A few other GIs were trying to talk to him, but he ignored them and continued to fire for a few more seconds. He stopped and handed his weapon to one of the others and put his head in his hands and began shaking and crying. One of the other soldiers put his arm around the shirtless man's shoulders and led him toward the CP, where he sat down and put his head on his arms which were folded across his knees.

The smell of gunpowder hung in the humid air and something else filled my senses, but I couldn't tell what it was, perhaps it was the smell of death, of bodies giving off their death odors. Maybe it was the smell of human flesh, torn asunder, spewing out its essence. I continued along slowly, but everywhere I looked I saw blood and gore. Even the trees seemed to be wounded; there were branches scattered around on the ground and hanging from their trunks, blown away by indiscriminate mortar rounds. I felt like I had descended into hell.

I had seen enough, so I turned around and began heading back toward the squad position. As I passed the pile of bodies something made me take another look. One of the faces appeared to be staring back. He had a startled, surprised look on his face, as if I had caught him in an unnatural act. A few short hours ago these young men were sharing a perimeter with us, joking with and insulting one another, thinking about home and making plans for R & R or for some, the trip back to the World. Now, they lay here on this gentle field, in front of a bamboo thicket, their bodies shattered almost beyond recognition. Something my aunt Ruth had said to my mother when I was home on leave echoed in my mind: "Here it is, 1966, and we still raise our sons up to be cannon fodder."

I hurried away from the pile, as if removing myself from the scene would make it disappear and everything would be like it was before the battle. When I reached the giant tree marking the squad position, I threw off my gear and reached for my entrenching tool. Watson glanced up at me and asked, "What's the story, Pete? What did the lieutenant say? Do we dig in or are we moving?"

"I didn't see the lieutenant, he was busy, but dig in and dig deep. We'll be here awhile."

I had a lump forming in my throat, but something made me speak once more. "And don't anybody ever call me new guy again."

Watson looked at me closely, but let it slide and I tore into the ground with my tool, trying to forget the macabre scenes I had witnessed. How do I carry on after what I had just seen? Nothing would ever be the same again, yet I have to ignore it. But how the hell do I do that? Forget it, bury it, remember the grunt's motto: It don't mean nothin'. But I knew it did. It did to those who died, to their families, and to the survivors who came so close to meeting their fate. And it did to me.

It took nearly ninety minutes to remove all the dead and wounded and police up all the equipment and weapons left ownerless by the battle, and it was nearly dark when we formed into a column to move back to Hill 283. Charlie Company absorbed the stunned survivors of A Company, some of whom were muttering to themselves and staring into space, into the middle of the patrol and we slowly moved out. As the darkness enveloped us, Spooky, a C-130 aircraft equipped with M-60 Gatling guns, circled overhead and dropped flares to light the way. Behind us, an air strike hit the battle site and surrounding area over and over again. It was a fascinating and frightening, almost surrealistic landscape painted by the flares and our fears.

Vickers and I stayed in contact as we trudged slowly towards 283—I felt like I needed to talk with someone to keep the thoughts of the carnage I had witnessed from overwhelming me. I suspected he was feeling many of the same things, but we avoided the subject for the most part. Finally on one of our frequent stops, I whispered to him, "Vick, back there . . . I saw a pile of bodies, Alpha's dead, stacked up, waiting to be hauled away. There had to be a dozen or more . . . and wounded everywhere. It was terrible—the worst thing I've ever seen. Blood everywhere, men moaning. God, I'll never forget this day as long as I live."

"Well, I hope that's a long time, Pete. I could tell it was bad by the number of choppers that came in. You've gotta get past it. Like the armored guys say, 'Fuck it and drive on,' or like I say, 'Fuck me, I'll never smile again.' "

"I believe that, now. I know that I will sure look at things differently from now on. Tomorrow, if we get resupply, I'm getting as many ammo pouches and magazines as I can carry. I don't ever want to get caught short like Alpha did."

The 1st Platoon was on point and they were treading lightly, much as Maddox and I had three nights before. We were following the main east-west trail in the AO and we traveled slowly to avoid plunging into a night ambush. Every shadow, every movement and sound was suspect as we dragged our tired bodies and numbed minds toward Hill 283.

At midnight the artillery battery in LZ Lane fired an illumination round to mark the LZ and we found it and moved into our defensive positions. The 2nd Platoon was sent to the south side of the perimeter where we surprised a couple of local indigenous personnel, probably the neighborhood VC, who were sleeping. They jumped up and disappeared into the woods before the startled 2nd Squad could get a shot off. We didn't pursue or call in the sighting; we were all too tired to care at the moment. Since I didn't have the early watch duty, I collapsed at our team's position, unrolled my poncho, covered up with my liner, and lay there on my back, staring at the stars. I felt like I was seeing them for the first time.

I had been in-country six weeks, and through all that had happened I had felt like I was living in some kind of dreamworld. Nothing was like it was where I had lived in the U.S.A. and I felt like I was sleepwalking through my tour. This day's experience was an awakening at first sight, but then the repetition of shocking events that unfolded to me began to have a numbing effect. I had effectively gone from a dreamworld to a nightmare.

When I took my turn on guard at 0300, I tried to sort out things as they had happened. The events began to play themselves back in my mind, in and out of sequence. Combat now began to take on a different meaning for me. I felt like we were playing Russian roulette and so far the chamber had been empty for the platoon. Next time we went out on patrol, it could be loaded—with screaming NVA. It was a sobering thought, now that I had seen what they could do in battle. I would tread more lightly in the future. Sir Charles had earned my lasting respect on the bloody fields near the Cambodian border.

7

A soft rain fell just before dawn, soaking everything gently, as if God were trying to cleanse the blood from the jungle, to wipe the slate clean. Upon awakening, I unwrapped from my damp poncho liner and began to gather some firewood and cardboard. As the others began to rise and look for C rations, I could sense an enormous sense of despair hanging over us. I lit a heat tab under the cardboard to start a drying and warming fire. I was cold, wet, tired, and heartsick, and although I was in a company of men who had the same feelings, I felt alone.

I could not erase the images that had been engraved in my mind and etched on my soul. I saw again the piles of dead young men, their skin turning ashen, their faces expressing the shock of sudden impact and the realization of imminent death. Their limbs protruded out of the pile like so many grotesque, abandoned mannequins and their eyes, their eyes . . . hollow, blank, but still searching for some kind of meaning. I said a quick, silent prayer while heating a canteen cup of water.

"Guide their souls to eternal peace and give me the strength to endure."

I sipped hot C-ration cocoa and munched on some dry crackers and stared into the fire. A similar scene was playing itself out at most of the positions around the perimeter. After finishing my meager fare, I began to clean my rifle and check my gear. From then on I vowed to check my equipment and weapon every chance I got; I would be ready for the inevitable showdown between the 33rd NVA Regiment and the 3rd Brigade of the 25th. As the morning wore on, word came down that Alpha Company's survivors would be extracted and sent to LZ Lane to regroup. The 2nd Platoon of Charlie Company stretched and covered their portion of the perimeter, preparing to leave. As we moved past some of the troops gathering their gear, one of the grunts spoke.

"Thanks, Charlie Company. Our shit was in the wind, but you guys covered us. Not one of us will forget that—ever."

I felt a sudden surge of pride in my chest. Hey, that's right. We, Charlie Company, saved some lives and kicked some butt while doing it. The unofficial body count was 180 NVA dead.

Maddox, looking much older than his years, answered, "No sweat, GI, you'd do the same for us. Get some beer at the LZ and rest up so you can get back out here for some payback."

Another hollow-eyed grunt interrupted vehemently: "I don't ever want to come out here again. I'm too short for this shit. I just wanna get back home."

"I roger that, trooper, same for me—forty-seven days."

Maddox answered and saluted the handful of survivors. We moved up into the tree line where Alpha had manned defensive positions and ran into a few more grunts huddled around a fire there, one of them burning pages of letters one at a time. I must have been staring strangely at him, for he looked at me with an expression of finality on his face and began a bitter explanation in a resigned tone. "I don't want these to be read by the NVA if I get killed or captured. They could get the names of my wife or parents."

A sergeant with a moustache that drooped down over the corners of his mouth, who was smoking a butt so short that I thought he was inhaling flame, spoke slowly and painfully: "The most powerful Army on the face of the Earth sent a small boy out to do a man's job and we got our butts kicked. We took 50 percent casualties. They better get their shit together, get better intelligence, and a better tactical plan. I'm scared to go back out there now. I'm really scared, Maddox."

His voice shuddered as he spoke from the heart. I thought I saw tears in his eyes, but it could have been from the smoke of the fire or his cigarette. His pain was evident in his voice and body language. He began to lead his men down the path to the LZ as we took the position, but a chopperful of brass had landed and Colonels Shanahan and Proctor jumped out and began shaking his hand. Colonel Proctor spoke, "Good job, Alpha Company. I'm proud of you all. We'll get the bastards."

The sergeant didn't say anything, but I caught his sunken, bloodshot eyes and they spoke volumes. I gave him a tight smile and a nod as he turned and headed for the chopper. The brass continued to make their way around the perimeter and soon stopped at our position.

"You guys must be Charlie Company. That was a hell of a rescue you made yesterday. The whole brigade is proud of us. We're going to make those bastards pay—and soon," the colonel said as he shook all our hands.

I ran the words through my mind and tasted their bitterness. Us? We? Where the hell were you when the shit hit the fan? We? You got a turd in your pocket? I kept those thoughts to myself as they continued along the lines commiserating with the lowly grunts who would have to cash the check he was writing with his mouth and his lifer mentality.

Watson came back from a meeting at the CP a little later and gave us some figures from yesterday's battle. Alpha had suffered thirteen dead and thirty-seven wounded; Charlie Company lost two men in the charge: PFC Mozre Cole and Sp4 Frederick Linder, and had one wounded. Stories of the heroism of Lt. Joe Grant, who rescued two wounded men and destroyed a machine gun before a mortar barrage killed him and nine others while he was trying to save Lt. Terrance O'Brien, swept through the battalion and down to the men of the 2nd Platoon. The enemy body count was thirty-four on the ground, but, based on blood trails and abandoned weapons and gear, an estimated 180 were killed.

The sequence of events was still being pieced together in my mind and I didn't want to forget any part of the whole picture, from our movement into a blocking position through the battle and aftermath. I thought if I could arrange these events neatly into my psyche, I might then be able to move past them to the next challenge. It seemed like a good idea, but I would never forget the death poses of the Americans in that pile or the screams of the NVA as they began their fateful charge. Whatever I did in the rest of my life would be tempered by those events.

Rumors abounded along and within the perimeter of medals to be awarded to Lieutenants Grant and O'Brien and several enlisted men of Alpha Company. Charlie Company was to be recommended for the presidential unit citation for our efforts. As we sat, totally exhausted, leaning on our packs or a tree, weapons ready, we talked about the day within our own circles.

"I think they should give Captain Federline a medal. He did a helluva job getting us there and then leading the charge to break through the NVA 'human wave' attack. That's the kind of leadership that I admire."

"True, Pete, but I think Captain Simcox would have talked battalion into letting him head over there a lot sooner. Somebody screwed up by not knowing the size of the threat in the area. We should have been sent to join up with Alpha right after their first contact. Not that I was crazy about getting into that battle, but they needed us."

Watson sounded a little bitter, and a little scared. Lieutenant Canale joined our group for a short bull session while he waited for orders from the CP and put in his feelings.

"I don't know if that would have helped much, Sarge. Ol' Charlie might have backed off for another day, but sooner or later, we're going to have to fight the entire 33rd NVA Regiment. It's that simple. We're here in their territory and they have to get rid of us so they can continue to demand rice and money from the Montagnards and other villagers and bring supplies out of Cambodia to send on down south. We are here to stop that and the only way we can do that is to break up the 33rd. Sooner or later. . . ."

He paused, then stood up to head for his radio as his RTO beckoned. I broke back in: "So maybe we should bomb Cambodia and see where that gets us. If the NVA are allowed to hit and run back across the border to their sanctuary, we'll have a hard time beating them. If we could interrupt their supply chain. . . ."

"Forget it, Pete," Maddox interrupted. "We can't cross the border and we can't bomb either Cambodia or Laos. Both are neutral. In this part of the world, neutral means pro-Communist."

We were speaking slowly, with resignation in our voices. We were certain an even bigger battle was brewing and we were in harm's way, dangling, like human decoys. I decided I was going to be a well-armed piece of bait, so I asked Watson to order extra pouches and magazines on the next resupply list.

Bravo Company left LZ Lane, where they had moved to the day before in case they were needed to join the battle, and headed west. In the afternoon Charlie Company finally left Hill 283 and headed southeast. The 2nd Platoon led the way with the 2nd Squad on point, followed by the 1st. We moved slowly, stopping every few meters and sending short patrols ahead in an attempt to avoid any ambush. We made a safe crossing of the stream, linked up with Bravo Company at 1600, and together we moved another few hundred meters to a clearing on the top of a rolling hill and held up.

Following a brief meeting we received orders to set up a perimeter and begin digging our foxholes. The 1st Squad had positions along the southeast side of the "wagon wheel," not far from the major east-west trail. We fortified our fighting hole with branches and logs, but at 1730, Watson came to the position as we were clearing fields of fire. He spoke quietly. "We got ambush tonight. I'm going out and taking the whole squad with me. Be ready at dusk. We'll be going back down that trail about a hundred meters and slide off into the bushes. I'll carry a radio and we'll pull at least 50 percent security all night. See you in about an hour."

He wandered off back toward the CP as if in a daze. When he came back it was nearing sunset and we had saddled up to head out. He spoke again of the dangers: "Guys, listen to me. This is no place to fall asleep on guard. The enemy is in the area, we know it and we can't afford mistakes. After we leave the perimeter I want everybody quiet. We'll make sit-reps by breaking squelch twice."

Sit-reps were situation reports that units called in at pre-arranged times to other supporting units. In an ambush or LP setting, an RTO in the perimeter would call to the unit where one of the grunts on guard would be holding the handset to his ear to keep the sound from alerting any enemy in the area. The grunt would then break squelch, or signal, with the push bar on the side of the handset a prearranged number of times to answer. Our code was two breaks for an all-clear. Anything else meant trouble.

We moved out through the lines after dark to avoid observation from the enemy that we all felt was omniscient and ever-present. We had assigned Sir Charles a super soldier label and thought of him, in our minds that had been warped by combat, as a frightening ghost or magic genie who fought when he wanted and then disappeared through his secret door into Cambodia.

After seeing the dead GIs, I thought the likenings were valid. Maddox and I led the way to the trail where we turned right and headed west, and I immediately felt like the old Wild West explorers must have felt when they headed into Indian Country. My paranoia mounted and I could feel eyes burning into me as I moved slowly down the trail. The moon was bright enough to see the shapes of trees and bushes and I thought I would be able to see any moving creature on the trail and they, of course, could see me.

About one hundred meters out we found the broken branch along the trail that had been left by Watson earlier when he and Lieutenant Canale had scouted the area. Maddox and I parted the bushes and waited as the others slipped quietly into a line ambush no more than twelve feet from the trail. We then set up the two claymore mines we had brought along, faced them west, and hid them from the trail with foliage. I followed him and we crawled back to join the ambush and set up the firing devices.

There were eight of us out there and we pulled full alert until 2200 hours, then went to four down, four up until dawn or until company arrived. I had heard the stories of ambushes becoming hectic once they were sprung—a hail of fire, then run like hell to safety. I had also heard the stories of men in ambushes spotting a large force moving through and freezing, letting the entire enemy unit move along without impediment for fear of being overwhelmed. I could imagine either or both of these scenarios happening to the squad as we lay out there, naked to the world.

At 2200, I slid gently and quietly back from the line and tried to nod off for a few minutes. Vickers and Fears had first watch while Maddox and I would take the next one. As I lay there, fighting fatigue and seeing a kaleidoscope of events rush through my mind, I felt a sharp nudge in my ribs. My heart leapt—the enemy must have come into our ambush. Then, Vickers leaned over and whispered that I had been snoring. This was the second time in two weeks, so I knew he wasn't making it up. I was putting the squad in jeopardy with my noisy slumber and it had to cease.

I rolled over and put my head into my steel pot, face first. I didn't have much protection for the rest of my head if we took fire, but I'd leave a pretty corpse and nobody could hear if I snored. It got pretty cool for us dangling out there in the western part of the Central Highlands of South Vietnam, so Maddox and I huddled together for warmth as we pulled our first watch from 000 hour to 0200. Apparently, it was too cold for Charlie also, as the night was quiet.

8

Watson woke the four men who weren't already on guard just as the day's first light appeared in the eastern sky. I supposed he was preparing once more for that ever-present threat, at least in his mind, of an attack at dawn. As the sun began to edge up over the horizon, he broke squelch on the hour to give a final all-clear sit-rep and received orders to rejoin the perimeter in thirty minutes. We continued lying quietly until our surroundings were totally visible, then began gathering the claymore mines we had placed along the trail. Maddox led the way as we moved slowly back to the trail, remembering the adventures of Bravo Company and our own 3rd Platoon, which had run into enemy patrols while coming back from ambushes.

There was no sign of activity on or near the trail, so we carefully eased along it to where it branched away from the perimeter. Watson called the company CP once more to remind them of our presence, then moved up to where Maddox was kneeling beside a rock and yelled:

"Sandbag—ambush comin' in! Sandbag!"

The password was recognized and we walked safely through the men collecting their trip flares and claymore mines and moved to the unused position we had dug yesterday. There, we got the news that we were moving out at 0800, so I swallowed a couple of C-rat cookies and washed them down with a cup of ambition—two packets of powdered coffee, barely diluted with water and piping hot, infantry-style. I was as ready as I could be for another day in enemy territory.

Bravo Company was moving through our lines on their way to a link up with Recon Platoon and the CIDG to check out Hill 271 south of LZ Lane. In the normal stop-and-start motion of a column, a few of the grunts were held up just to the right of the 1st Squad position. One of them sat down against a tree next to our bunker.

"That must have been a hell of a battle you guys in C Company had on the 13th. We were awaiting in reserve back at the LZ, then the radio went quiet for about ten minutes and we thought A Company was gone for sure. Then Captain Federline came on and said you guys broke through and the NVA were running back to the border."

Another grunt, bent over from the weight of a huge pack laden with two claymores, five or six grenades and extra bandoleers, broke in with a terse comment: "Nice work, C Company. We didn't want to come out there."

Maddox, our unofficial spokesman, looked up and answered. "Nobody wanted to be out there, guy. It was a whole lotta hell. Alpha was about five minutes from being totally wiped out. Our 1st and 3rd platoons hit the VC from the side while they were movin' in to finish 'em off. The men up front were screamin' and yellin' and the NVA were screamin' and yellin'. It was a god-awful sound. But ol' Charlie wasn't expectin' us and didn't know what hit him. Our part of the battle lasted only a few minutes, but Alpha was in it all afternoon. Pete got a good look at what was left of their perimeter, but I reckon he ain't ready to talk about it just yet."

He glanced at me, but I shook my head; I didn't think it was the time. He continued, "We came back to Hill 283 after dark. That coulda been another lick on us, but the good Lord must have decided there had been enough dyin' that day, so He guided us in."

He spoke slowly, methodically, weighing each word for emphasis and propriety. The men from Bravo nodded and exchanged knowing looks with us, then the first man spoke:

"Yeah, we've had some tough scrapes out here, too. I hope we can catch Charlie with his pants down before he gets us. This is a dangerous area, man, dangerous."

He paused and took a look at the patrol as it lurched ahead once more, then continued softly, but fervently: "We gotta go. Take care out here, Charlie Company, and keep your head down."

"Same to you, Bravo. Get some out there."

I had noticed the absence of the normal exchange of insults and intercompany banter that usually held forth whenever two infantry units met. It served to underline the seriousness of our situation to me when I remembered that insulting came right after complaining on the GI daily border of social commentary.

The column moved along while we continued to secure our gear and weapons and waited for the word to move out. Maddox looked up with a bemused smile as the word came down that the 1st Platoon was leading off for Charlie Company.

"Must not be a very dangerous mission this mornin'. The 2nd Platoon ain't on point. We can just hang loose, guys."

"Fuck a bunch of point-walkin'. Send me back for rear guard for the next five months, then I'll go home."

"Fears, you're a coward."

"Motherfuckin' got that right, Vickers. I got a lot to go home to. My wife is waitin' with her two legs crossed for me to come back and jump on her."

"You sure 'bout that? I bet she's partying all night with every swingin' dick in town."

"Don't be bad-mouthin' my sweet thang. She knows I'm the only man can put a smile on her black face."

Fears stood up and grabbed his crotch as the squad hooted and I smiled inwardly. Maybe it'll be all right, the insults have returned, at least long enough for the squad to celebrate not being on point. Fears was another of those lean GIs; I had noticed that 90 percent of the troops in the field were skinny. He was about twenty or twenty-one, but looked much older and spoke with the defensive attitude prevalent among young black men from the inner city. An unspoken preface seemed to be a part of every statement that came out of his mouth: "I didn't do it, so fuck you."

He didn't care that everyone knew that he wanted out of the field and would do just about anything to reach that goal. Even knowing that, I could see that he was a decent line trooper who possessed a lot of savvy and lore. For that reason I counted him as a valuable team member and source of information, although I would prefer that he kept his feelings to himself more often.

Watson finally reached down for his pack and told us to saddle up; we were moving out after the 1st Platoon. We followed the trail south and west along the slope of the rolling hill mass until we came to a stream. The 1st Platoon sent a patrol across to check out the area for enemy activity. Farther north on the same stream was where Alpha Company had been ambushed, and the tension was palpable.

We lay down along the trail facing out, peering into the jungle, expecting at any second to hear the familiar and deadly chatter of automatic weapons signaling another firefight and another handful of dirty, frightened young men about to lose their innocence, their health, and, maybe, their lives. There was an unusual silence in the woods, no birds chirping, not a leaf moving. I could hear the men breathing. After a few long moments I heard a rustle, and the orders came down the line whispered from man to man.

"Move out—slow. When you cross the stream, dip one canteen and fill it if you need it."

I quickly undid the top of one of my empty canteens and plunged it into the cool, clear water as I paused and took a quick look around. The vegetation was extremely thick along the stream; you could totally hide an elephant anywhere in the lush, green rain forest. I gave a little involuntary shudder as I thought about the eyes that could be peering at me from a hundred secret places. Move it, kid, move it, I reminded myself as I replaced my canteen and hopped up on the bank—don't give 'em a standing target. We pushed on across the stream and moved southward along the side of another gentle hill. After a few hundred meters we held up again and hit the jungle floor once more.

"Point squad found a camp. Get ready to move up in a hurry." Watson moved up to where Lieutenant Canale was monitoring the radio and lay down beside him for a few minutes, then returned. "The camp is empty. First Platoon is moving through it and they'll pull security on the far side. Third

Herd will secure this side while the 2nd goes in to search it. Get ready to move out and be alert."

The camp was stretched along the side of the hill, tucked in under a double canopy to make it nearly invisible to air traffic, which was light this close to the border in any case. As we began to search into the first few bunkers we spotted it became obvious that this was too much for one platoon to handle, so the 3rd came in to help, leaving their machine-gun crews along the edge for security. There were more than a hundred bunkers, each with several feet of dirt overhead, at least a dozen fighting positions, several mortar holes six feet deep, two ammo pits, three latrines, five kitchens, and two graves with fresh dirt on top. The bunkers were connected with each other and other positions by well-concealed tunnels. Not wanting anything to do with any more dead bodies, I moved quickly past the graves and began searching through an area that contained bloody bandages and resting areas, apparently for wounded men. The lieutenant moved up, took a quick look around, and grabbed the handset to call in the find to Captain Federline.

"Charlie 6, this is Charlie 2–6. We've got what appears to be a huge hospital over on this side. About fifty beds and an operating table, even some bloody bandages. Over."

"Roger that, 2–6. Get me a complete inventory. Out."

We continued to search through the huge complex for the next few hours, counting the bunkers, cataloging the other features, and trying to figure out how we were going to destroy everything, then Watson passed on the word. "Battalion says we'll put a B-52 strike on it later. The official count is 208 bunkers. There are trails leading out of this place in every direction. It looks like we've found the regimental base camp."

"I guess the $64,000 question is—where are they? Why did they leave? The water in one of those kettles over the dead fire back there was still warm. Why would a regiment run from a company?"

Maddox smiled tightly as McCown finished his question. "Mac, I suspect ol' Charlie is not far away at all. The main unit is probably over in Cambodia, resting up and gettin' resupplied and restocked with troops after the other day. We probably just scared up an advance unit. The two graves had bodies in them only a couple days old. Had to be from the battle of the 13th."

We all pondered this somberly for a few seconds, then Watson spoke. "This is probably a forward base camp and staging area for their operations on this side of the border. Their main camp is back in Cambodia."

"Where it's safe from anything we could throw at it. Am I right, Sarge?"

"You're catching on, Pete. Hopefully we can persuade the Cambodian government to close their border to the NVA."

"It would make the playing field more level if that happened. Man, I sure don't feel very comfortable standing around here with the border that close. I can feel those eyes staring at me again."

"You get those feelings, too, Pete? Same-same for me. Let's just *di di* outta here." Watson scanned the bushes around us. The entire conversation had been carried on in low voices, just above a whisper, as if the enemy were unaware of the presence of a loud American force in the area. I couldn't shake off the overpowering feeling that we were being watched, that there was a presence in the camp that I couldn't explain and I wanted to be away from it.

Just before 1400 we moved out of the area and turned back to the northeast. I was happy to be heading in any direction as long as it was away from that encampment and the eerie feelings that prevailed there. Word came down once more, but this time it was good news—we were headed back to LZ Lane, where we had landed five days ago. As we tromped back along the same well-used trail we had taken earlier that day, McCown began musing aloud: "LZ Lane. I hope it's bigger than it was a few days ago. Maybe big enough to have a nice kitchen. Be nice to have a hot meal again."

"Mail from home," Vickers chipped in. "A safe place to sleep. Maybe take my boots off."

I was thinking of my feet and maybe getting a new pair of boots—jungle boots to replace my beat-up regular Army boots. Maddox had been quiet through the conversation, but had obviously been thinking about the possibilities. "A place to wash up is what this ol' boy needs."

Curtis grinned, then spoke one word, "Sex."

"Sex. There's no place to have sex at the LZ unless you're queer, man."

I moved away and put my free hand over my backside while McCown laughed, but Curtis held up his hand. "Sex. I'll be havin' sex with my hand. Old Rosie Redpalm and her five daughters and I won't be the only guy in camp doin' it tonight either."

"Get some, Curtis!" Vickers roared while we all laughed.

Watson glared at us and told us to shut up, but as he turned his head I could see a grin forming on his face. The morale of the platoon had lifted enormously as we crossed the stream, moved past last night's camp and headed for the Lane. There was one more small stream to cross, then we came out of the brush and passed through an opening between two bunkers manned by shirtless GIs relaxing in the sun, but with weapons at the ready. One of the men yelled at us as we trudged toward the center of the perimeter.

"Hey, Charlie Company, you guys are all right. We're what's left of Alpha along this side of the perimeter. Welcome to LZ Lane. If you feel like talking, come on over. I've got a bottle of Jim Beam that I'm saving to drink with you."

"No sweat, GI. I'll be back to see ya," Maddox answered.

It was getting to be a lot of pressure, this being a hero, I thought to myself. It's funny, I don't feel at all like a hero, yet every time I see somebody from Alpha, they treat us like deities—it's a lot of pressure. I hope they can do something to remove the onus from themselves, and from us, in the near future, I thought as we entered the LZ and looked around. It was hard to believe what had taken place in the field of elephant grass since we landed five days ago. The grass, small trees, and brush had been cleared from the stream bank and along the gently rising low hill up to where the forest began. All around the edge of the perimeter were dozens of formidable-looking bunkers fortified with logs and sandbags and ready for action. The battalion support groups had descended en masse with artillery pieces, mortar tubes, crates of ammunition, field kitchens, a forward supply tent and a dispensary. All of these were protected with neck-high walls of sandbags and fortified bunkers that had been dug for all the brass and support personnel in the interior of the perimeter.

I dropped my pack and gear beside one of the 1st Squad bunkers along the stream and slid down the sandbagged wall to the ground. "Man, Mac, I am tired. I'm gonna sleep tonight for the first time since we left 3G. I mean sleep, not doze with one eye open."

"I hear ya, guy. This place looks like it could withstand just about anything Charlie could throw at us. Makes me feel good, Pete. Now, where's that hot chow?"

Watson came strolling back from the CP with a huge grin creasing his war-weary but youthful face. "Pete, Maddox, you're not gonna believe this. They've got the old packs we left up on that mountain a month ago."

"You are shitting me, Sarge. I'd given up on ever seeing that old pack. Let's get the damn things before they disappear into the Army machine again."

Being reunited with my old pack wasn't a major event in my life, but I was trying to muster all the little victories I could, hoping to get my life moving forward again on some axis. The big things had not been going well lately, so every little thing that came out right took on greater significance in my mind. Hot chow and a safe place to sleep were as much as I could ask for, and now I had my pack again.

We lined up for hot A rations one position at a time, then carried them back to the bunkers and consumed the grayish-brown roast beef and mashed potatoes rapidly and mostly in silence. After the meal we gathered around the bunkers, put one man on guard, and, in the highest tradition of the United States Army and fighting men everywhere, began to shoot the bull. We talked hesitantly about the events of the past week and what might happen in the near future, but mostly we spoke of our other lives and our hopes and dreams. I had always considered it difficult to open up my inner self to others, but after what we had been through together in the last few days I let my defenses down a little and joined in the discourse.

I listened intently as Maddox spun tales of his life in Atlanta. "I'm tellin' y'all, there's nothin' more sexy or beautiful than a Southern gal, especially one from Hotlanta. When one of those sweet things opens her mouth and lets that honey drip out, I'd walk through thirty miles of VC territory without a weapon just to listen. Umm. I'm tellin' it like it is."

"I gotta admit, Maddox, a Southern drawl is one of the nicest sounds on earth. Personally, like the Beach Boys, I prefer California girls," Watson said, then he began to sing, off-key.

"Easy, man. If the VC hear that and complain to the Geneva Convention, you're in big trouble. That could easily be considered cruel and unusual punishment."

"Screw you and the horse you rode in on, Pete. You got a girl back home? What kind of girl do you like?"

"No girl, but I like any kind, as long as she's kinda good-looking. I hate carrying a big supply of bags around to throw over their faces. And not too heavy—I like to be able to maneuver them around whenever necessary. But I wanna hear about Maddox and his former wife."

"Well, Pete. It's a long, sad story, but I'll keep it short for ya. She said I wasn't devoted enough to her, so she put my things on the sidewalk and locked the door. Threw me out. But, I'll tell ya, if she snapped her fingers right now and told me to come on back, I'd swim the Pacific in about two hours. I still love her."

"One ol' boy back home used to say, 'I'd drink a mile of her piss, just to see where it comes from.' Now, that's devotion."

"That's perversion. That boy's a *pre-vert,* Mac." I chuckled as I thought about it.

"Well, guys, don't get too loud. I'm going up to the CP hooch to see if I can find out what we'll be doing tomorrow. See you guys later." Watson moved away toward a large bunker and hooch in the interior of the perimeter. The conversation began to wind down as fatigue set in and the men began to unroll their ponchos and liners. I could sense the feelings of security in my fellow squad members and figured that most of them would sleep a little better here at the firebase. I pulled my first watch, then lay down behind the bunker and tried to let myself go. I saw once more the bodies of the American dead and the ground around them red with their blood. I wondered what their last thoughts were and what mine might be in the same circumstance. I wondered also what I could do to honor them. I decided that, instead of forgetting them, I would let the images that were forcing their way into my thoughts be engraved into my heart and soul, to remain therein all the days of my life. I felt this would bestow upon them at least a small degree of immortality. It was the least I could do.

In the morning we rested and waited for orders of the day. I had restored my old field pack and all its goodies (address book, pen, a can of Spam, etc.) to their rightful place on my web belt. I began to write a few notes to people back in the World, while watching McCown eat the equivalent of three C-ration breakfasts without blinking an eye. I really liked Mac and I felt it was mutual, as he spent considerable time showing me little tricks with trip wires and packing gear. I learned from him that you can replace the pin of a grenade with the smaller one from a trip wire—but only if you put it barely into the first opening. I remembered our conversation from a couple of weeks before.

"Otherwise, Pete, it won't set it off. A dink could walk through and just break the wire 'cause it's too tight."

"Mac, that's a dangerous deal settin' up one of those. You could ruin your whole day if you slip."

I watched as he first wired the still-safetied grenade to a small tree, then began the more delicate task of replacing the pin with the slender metal tip of the trip wire.

"Don't slip, Pete. Remember to take your time and keep your hand on the lever till you're sure the tension is right. And, always put the grenade on the side of a tree facing out and work from the back side, then cover it with a branch or something. Then remember where you put it, cause you gotta get it in the morning if it's not tripped. Always remember, the guy who puts it out, brings it back."

"Anybody ever trip one by mistake?"

"Not a grenade. Once in a while somebody trips a flare. After a while you'll be able to do this in the dark."

McCown was the only nonskinny man in the whole squad, packing about 220 pounds on his less-than-six-foot frame. He had disheveled brown hair that was a little longer than most. A smile would leap to his face at the slightest provocation and he had a hearty laugh. Although he was overweight and ate too much, he could hold his own in the jungle marches and often carried extra ammo for the gun crew. He was a good soldier and a friendly man whom I conversed with as often as I could.

He interrupted my reverie by making an announcement to the squad: "Tonight, I'm making Mac's Special Wapatooli Jungle Stew—if we're still here in the LZ."

I didn't know what this entailed, but the squad seemed to think it was a good idea and vowed to help him procure the necessary ingredients. I took off my boots and socks and put my feet into the sun. They were white and wrinkled with huge calluses and some raw skin near the heel and ankle. I still was wearing the boots that had been issued to me in basic training, and although they were well worn they had always hurt my feet. I decided it was time to do my best Maddox impersonation, so I reshod myself and, after informing Watson of my intentions, headed to the forward supply tent.

I had been prepared to throw myself at the mercy of the supply sergeant, but only a young PFC was on duty. I decided in my own best interests to promote him. "Sergeant, I've been wearing these damned regular Army boots since I arrived in-country and they're ruined. Sergeant Watson told me to DX them and get some jungle boots or he'd court-martial me."

"I'm not a sergeant and I'm not supposed to give these out without a slip signed by an officer or the supply sergeant. He's back in 3G and won't be in until tomorrow."

Since flattery wasn't going to get me shod, I tried another tack. "Well, I'm taking these off and leaving them. You can give me a new pair or I'll go back into combat barefoot."

"You in Charlie Company?"

"Yep. 2nd Platoon, 1st Squad—PFC Peterson."

He picked up one of the boots and looked it over. "I can't give you new boots without an order, and they have to be ruined. These aren't ruined."

He picked up a bayonet from the supply bin and cut the boot along the side from the sole to the top. Then he gave me a wide grin. "Now they're ruined. I'll forge somebody's name on the slip. Take a pair of jungle boots and get out of here."

I made sure I had a good fit, then saluted the PFC and headed back to the squad feeling pretty proud of myself. As I approached the bunker, Maddox took a look and grabbed his heart as if shot.

"My God, new boots—jungle boots. Way to go, Pete."

"I owe it all to you, man. You're right, most of these rear guys are OK. You just gotta talk to them right."

"Y'all can take my place as the squad scrounger after I DEROS (date estimate return from overseas), Pete. In the meantime, our orders for today are to strengthen our position, clean weapons and gear, and check with the medic if you got any problems. We're gonna fill some more sandbags and make a wall sticking out each side of the bunker."

"Roger, wilco. Over and out."

We worked along through the warm, sunny day and constructed a chest-high wall, then lay back and dried our feet some more while cleaning weapons. That night, about two hours after finishing our evening repast of hot cream corn and wieners, Mac began gathering his store of supplies. In a huge pot borrowed from the head cook he combined a few cans of C-ration barbecued beef with several others of beef with potatoes and gravy, then added a mixture of tomato sauce and beans that Maddox had bargained for at the forward mess. Someone produced a bottle of Tabasco sauce and Curtis came back from the artillery bunker with a bottle of catsup and an onion.

Mac whooped, not too loudly, in celebration. "Tabasco sauce and onion—I'm in heaven. This'll do the trick. Now, everybody check your Cs. I need more beans."

About an hour later the smell of the concoction was permeating the area and the gun crew was salivating in the next position.

"Umm. Y'all be sure to let me know when it's ready and I'll be over. I've got a small bottle of hot sauce to donate to the cause."

I recognized Alabama's voice and knew the hot sauce would be enough to get him a portion. When it was ready, I was in nearly as much trepidation as I was at the snake-tasting event on Hill 283. I let Mac pour a generous serving into my canteen cup, then took a sip. It was spicy hot but had a rich tomato tang and a strong stock of meat and beans.

"Not bad, Mac, if you like tomatoes." I thought for a second about all the work that he had put in, then added quickly, "And I love tomatoes. It's good, Mac."

"Fuckin' A, it's good," Curtis added.

Maddox and Vickers grunted their approval as they shoveled the spicy liquid into their mouths. Mac grinned and dug into a huge portion of the stew himself as silence overtook us for a few minutes. After we had sated ourselves, Mac finished the last helping in the pot and we all held our bellies, complimented the chef and moaned softly in the cool night air as the stars lit up the sky and the artillery battery began firing a Def-

Con pattern for Bravo Company still out in the jungle. I slapped Mac's back once more, then moved to my sleeping area behind our new wall, where I lay on my poncho covered with my liner. Not a bad day, I thought, not bad at all. New boots, a nice wall, and Mac's stew. Life could be a hell of a lot worse and probably would be soon, so I indulged myself in thoughts of home as I dozed off.

The four men in the position had prearranged a two-hour guard duty roster; I had the 0400 shift. When I felt a nudge on my arm it seemed like I had only slept about ten minutes.

"Wake up, Pete. Come on."

"Oh, shit, Vick. Is it four already?"

"No. The OP says they got movement. We're on alert."

The observation post had moved out across the stream in front of our bunker and slid into the woods just before dark. They had been calling in clear sit-reps until about midnight, when the radio picked up a whispered, frantic call reporting movement in front and to the side of their position. As I pulled myself up to the bunker wall, I could see Watson coming from the CP in a half-crouch, trotting. I knew what he was going to say before he opened his mouth.

"The OP wants to come in. The Old Man says 'Stay there. We're sending help.' We're the help. We're going across the creek to see what the hell is moving."

Watson took the lead as we moved down to the stream and prepared to cross. He took four men with him and moved as quickly and quietly as possible through the water and up on the other side. Maddox, Vickers, Fears and I crossed in the second group and linked up with the rest on a small strip of sand along the far shore. We lay there motionless as Watson made contact with the OP, which had barely ventured into the brush and was less than a stone's throw from the perimeter. I was shivering a little, which I decided to attribute to the cold water I had just waded through, although there was trepidation in my heart. My feet were still in the edge of the stream, so I crawled forward, then waited for orders. A hand touched my arm, then I could hear Maddox whisper. It seemed like he was a hundred miles away.

"We're gonna link up with the OP now, Pete. Be ready." We low-crawled to their position and then went silent to try to hear the noises they were hearing. After a few minutes there was a rustle in front of where we were lying. I tensed and clipped the selection lever of my M-16 from off to fire. I could sense one of the men moving a little to my right, so I waited until he found his position. I heard him move again, then he rolled back toward me and whispered.

"Psst. It's a monkey. Tell Watson it's a fuckin' monkey."

"Sarge, Vickers says it's a fuckin' monkey makin' the noise."

"Is he sure?"

"Are you sure?"

"I saw the monkey. I can smell his shit. Does he want a prisoner?"

"Do you want a monkey prisoner?"

Watson ignored the barb and crawled over to the OP's radio. He worked the handset to break squelch, then whispered his message in the clear, figuring that the OP had already compromised its position with a call for help.

"Charlie 2-6, this is Charlie 2-1 at Oscar Papa. The Oscar Papa has been attacked by monkeys. Over."

"Say again, Oscar Papa."

"I say again, monkeys. That's Mike, Oscar, November. . . ."

"I know how to spell it, Oscar Papa."

It appeared that sarcasm was a wasted art in this man's army, so Watson made his obvious request: "Would like to return to previous night position, over."

"Negative, Charlie 2-1. Remain there to fortify position."

"Roger. Out."

Watson threw the handset down and began cursing under his breath at the mind-set that had decreed his, and our, fortune. I realized that we were doomed to spend a cold night with wet pants here in the brush with the OP, so I tried to get comfortable. Mac moved next to me, then nudged my ribs.

"Tell the Sarge I'm gonna cut some cheese. It's gonna be strong enough to carry back to the perimeter." I rolled over once, whispered to Watson's back, then covered my face. "Fire in the hole, Sarge. Mac's gonna cut one."

The ensuing explosion brought snickers from the squad and the OP, feeling a little sheepish about the monkey attack. The tension that had hung in the air swiftly dissipated and was replaced by a tremendous foul odor and some heavy snickering.

Mac then borrowed a line from the artilleryman's radio jargon as he whispered, "Shot out, Sarge." Watson groaned, then put us on regular alert for the rest of the night.

At first light Watson led us back through the perimeter to our bunker where we started a fire to dry off our pants. I saw Mac looking through his pack. "Are you looking for more beans, Mac?"

"Yeah, I wanna go up to the CP and make some more sweet music."

Vickers laughed and slapped Mac on the shoulder. "I'm surprised nobody got killed when that short round exploded on us out there. That's a better weapon than my shotgun."

We spent the day cutting brush to clear fields of fire and making the roof of our bunker stronger with logs and sandbags. In the afternoon we washed up in the creek, taking turns pulling security. At 1600 word came down to send one man to the helipad to unload the supply choppers. Curtis pointed at me and said: "You're still the new man. New meat gets the shit details. Send the new man."

Something flared inside me and I threw down the sandbag I was lifting and began to speak firmly and earnestly: "No, I'm not the fuckin' new guy anymore. Not after what I've seen and done here in this jungle. I consider us all on even footing now, so don't put any more shit on me as the new guy. I'll unload if Watson sends me, but don't call me that name anymore. Savvy?"

From the gun position I heard Alabama sing out, "Amen, brother. Tell it like it is."

Curtis jumped up from his position and headed toward me, so I turned slightly to present less of a target, but he laughed and stuck out his hand, which I accepted and shook. "You're right. I'll go unload the chopper. No sweat." He spun around and headed for the helipad singing "Summer in the City" at the top of his lungs as he walked along.

We turned back to our work on the bunker, then Watson showed up with a short buck sergeant in tow. There was something in the manner of the diminutive noncom that suggested an infinite desire to be anywhere but where he was. I wondered if the affliction was temporary or if he felt that he didn't belong anywhere.

"You guys remember Sergeant Harrell? He'll be taking the

other fire team. Hughes is going in for a records check. I think Pete and Marvin are the only ones you don't know."

Watson pointed us out, then headed back to the CP as Harrell set his pack down at the other bunker and spoke to Maddox: "Looks like they're building a permanent firebase here."

"Lots of action out here, Harrell. Beaucoup VC."

"Like up in Duc Co in August, Mac? That was a hot area."

"That was a picnic compared to this. We've seen more shit in the last week than the battalion has all year."

The fervor in his voice caused the sawed-off Harrell to stare at him, then go silent. Curtis came back from the chopper pad and began handing out the squad mail he had picked up from Watson. I took my letters and stuck them in my steel pot to read later, then I thought about that sad-eyed trooper from Alpha Company who was burning his mail. He's probably right—gotta remember that. That night Mac, Vickers and I talked about the easy life here in the firebase.

"I'd like to spend the next ten months in a place like this or, better yet, 3 Golf. Sit back, pull line duty, drink some beer, see a show once in a while."

"You'd probably get bored to death back there, Pete."

"Maybe, Mac, but it's for damn sure some of us are gonna get killed out here. When I think of Alpha Company. . . ."

"Don't think about it, Pete. Just be a good boonie soldier and keep your head down when we hit the shit. We'll make it through if we do that."

Vickers' voice trailed off wistfully, as if he were whispering a wish into the wind. Watson sat down with his back against the wall and began giving us the news in a doleful voice: "We're goin' back out tomorrow, guys. Back to the NVA base camp with engineers and demolitions. We're gonna blow those bunkers and destroy everything else."

"I thought they were calling in a B-52 strike on it?"

"Who knows what the Army is thinking? An Arc Light would be safer, but you know the brass is itchin' for a big battle. With that NVA regiment and us in the same area, they'll get what they want. I just hope they've prepared for it."

"Does this mean that you might not re-up, Sarge?"

"Right now, Vick, I'd say no. Head back to California and go to school or work, buy a convertible maybe."

From the next hole Maddox and Fears began to sing a soft duet, so we stopped talking to listen and reflect. I was a little apprehensive, but, like Watson, I knew that since we were in the enemy's territory, we were going to eventually do battle. If it was going to happen tomorrow, so be it.

9

As the sun rose over LZ Lane, I eased out of my poncho liner and took my morning look around. Mac and Maddox were still sleeping behind the wall we had built while Vickers was pulling the last watch. There was a distinct coolness in the air and the morning dew glimmered in the sunlight. I fumbled through my pack to find some cocoa and a heat tab, then lit it and placed a small empty can with holes punched in it for air circulation over it to use as a stove. On top of this, I placed my canteen cup with water to be heated. I asked Vickers if he wanted some coffee or cocoa. He nodded, so I worked my way through his pack and found a packet.

When the water was hot, I poured half in his cup and handed it to him with a packet each of coffee and imitation cream. Leaning against the wall in the morning sun, we were as content as two GIs in a combat zone ten thousand miles from home could be.

"Here you go, guy. Make sure we don't get overrun by one of those early morning attacks. Watson wouldn't approve."

Vickers grinned at my attempt at humor, then added a thought: "He's a good squad leader, Pete. I don't know what we'll do after he's gone. Probably get some green buck sergeant fresh from Germany."

Later we were cleaning our weapons when a chopper arrived

with some brass and a few enlisted men. About twenty minutes after that Watson came striding quickly toward the squad positions with a short, wiry sergeant trailing behind him. I started to think, Didn't I see this yesterday? No, this guy is older and not as short as Harrell.

"OK, 1st Squad. You'll be heading out in about an hour. I won't be going with you; I have to testify at the court-martial in Long Binh for the three guys they charged with desertion in September. Sergeant Belcher here will be your squad leader until I get back in a few days. It could be rough out there, so pick up extra ammo and grenades at the CP."

Belcher introduced himself to the men one at a time. He seemed to be uncertain of himself, not a man used to the vagaries of command. He clearly wished he were somewhere else, like all of us, but he let it show through almost as much as Harrell. He was crowding forty-five, with silver hairs flecking his black mane cropped short in the manner of professional soldiers. He mentioned that he had seen action in WWII and Korea and was about to enter his third war. I hoped he was adaptable; this wasn't Korea and it damned sure wasn't the Big One.

As we lined up to move out, Belcher looked at Maddox. "You'll take point, Maddox."

A quick fire shot into the eyes of the usually placid Georgian, and he practically spat back at the sergeant. "Like hell I will. I've had point the last two times. In this squad we have to take turns and it's not mine."

Belcher filed the outburst away and put Harrell's team out front as we headed out of the perimeter. As we passed between the bunkers at the edge of the clearing, there stood Watson and the platoon sergeant, Leslie, shaking hands with the men of the 2nd as we moved past them. I had never spoken with the platoon sergeant in spite of the fact that we had been in the field together for a couple of weeks and I didn't know him, but I accepted his hand, then moved past him to Watson. He had that shy grin on his face and, although I was envious and wished he could stay with us, I couldn't help but like him. I grinned back as he stretched out his hand.

"Be careful out there, Pete. Charlie could be waiting. Re-

member, I'm going to take you to Pleiku City if we ever get
back to base camp."

"I'll remember, Sarge. Have fun in Long Binh. See ya."

We crossed through a small opening in the morass of trip
wires on the southwest side of the perimeter and headed back
into enemy territory. The fire teams had been rearranged a little
and Maddox now led a group consisting of Marvin, Fears and
me. The other team had Harrell leading McCown, Vickers and
Curtis and they were operating on point. We started out in the
direction of the NVA base camp, then moved farther north to
check out the area of the CIDG contact of the 10th. Battalion
was planning a sweep of the NVA base camp the next day, with
Bravo and Charlie Companies and the CIDG unit with its advisers. As we moved along the main trail toward the hillside we
had struggled so hard to reach eight nights before, I sensed the
anger and resentment in Maddox. He obviously had assumed
he would take command of the squad in the absence of Watson,
but now he had been bumped by another fuckin' new guy, albeit one that outranked him. I caught up with Vickers and
McCown on one of our frequent stops and we hashed the situation over.

"He's steaming right now. I hope he gets over it before we
hit something out here. We need him at his best."

"He'll be all right, Pete. His feelings are hurt, but he'll get
over it fast."

"You guys get extra ammo? I picked up another three boxes
and stuck 'em in my pack. I took a look at the medics getting
ready. They were packing extra bandages and supplies. I sure
hope their information is wrong, but I'm worried."

McCown, who usually sported a grin and a pleasant disposition, showed concern on his rapidly aging face as he spoke. I
tried to lighten his load with a semiserious line. "Easy, big
fella, Vickers and I will take care of you."

We all laughed a little, then the column started up again. I
had also seen the medics loading up while picking up my
ammo and I had a sinking feeling in my heart about this patrol.
Here we were, heading back into that base camp tomorrow
without the 2nd Platoon sergeant and our squad leader. In addition to my field pack loaded with gear, poncho liner and C rations, I felt like I was carrying the weight of the world and my

preordained future. We stopped in the LZ we had cleared for the extraction of the CIDG dead and wounded and began policing up some more abandoned equipment, then took positions and dug in for the night. I believed that the enemy "owned" this area, but Maddox differed.

"I think ol' Charlie will stay away from here 'cause it's already targeted by artillery and air. If anything happens, we just call in the numbers and a strike is on the way. Charlie knows all that shit, too, so he'll cut us some slack tonight."

It was good to hear Maddox talking again and imparting his wisdom to the squad, since I was certain that we needed all the help we could get. Despite all my concerns, we spent a quiet night on that hillside.

Word came down on the morning of November 19, 1966: Charlie Company would be joined by a squad of engineers and would lead the way to the bunker complex, followed by Bravo Company, then the CIDG unit with its advisers and the recon platoon, commanded by Lieutenant Primmer. The 1st Platoon led the way slowly back across the stream and then followed the trail along the side of the rolling hill mass. We reached the edge of the complex at about 1100 hours, then held up and broke for chow to allow the other units to maneuver and move through. As I finished my crackers and peanut butter, a huge brown man made his way down the line, stopped in front of me and stuck out his hand.

"I'm Sergeant Machado. I was platoon sergeant before I got malaria. I'm back now and I wanted to meet the guys who joined the platoon since I left and get their names straight."

"Good to meet you, Sarge. I'm Peterson. They call me Pete."

He moved on to the next position and I began to put my gear back together. I had never put much stock in first impressions, but I wanted to like the big Hawaiian. In Army slang, he was a "pineapple" (Hawaiian) as opposed to a "coconut" (Filipino). The tags were not intended to be racial slurs, although some undoubtedly used them as such. To my way of thinking, Staff Sergeant Machado even looked like a pineapple in his body shape.

Just past noon the other units had moved through, and Bravo was heading south to set up security and a blocking force for a sweep to the south and west by Charlie Company and the

CIDG. Then Charlie Company would turn north and complete a clockwise sweep of the complex, passing within one klick of the Cambodian border. This was the plan, if all went well. As the units began to move into their positions, all was still going well.

The engineers had decided to construct the LZ around a huge bomb crater on the edge of the complex; there they would receive the explosives and supplies they would need for demolition of the bunkers. We were still awaiting the orders to start our company sweep when firing broke out in the direction of Bravo Company's movement. I hit the ground and quickly scanned the area to my front as the firing continued sporadically, then eased for a few minutes. I took a glance at Sergeant Belcher a few feet away and could see the fear plainly on his face. I turned back to Maddox on my left and saw more of the same, so I spoke as calmly as I could. "What do you think, Maddox? Snipers, maybe?"

"We'll find out damn soon. Bravo has probably held up to figure out how to react. In a few minutes they'll move out again and we'll be able to tell by the noise how bad it is."

It happened just as he said; a few minutes later Bravo took extremely heavy fire as they moved out. The severity of the attack caused the feelings of uncertainty and anxiety to turn into unbridled fear as we listened to the terrible sounds of the battle and prayed Bravo Company would break the siege. The prayers were answered a few minutes later, but not as we had hoped.

"All right, Charlie Company, saddle up. We're moving out." Colonel Proctor had decided to move us up on the exposed right flank of the recon platoon to try to break the enemy attack at that spot. As we moved down the trail I was last man in the squad behind Fears, Maddox, and Marvin and just ahead of the CO, Captain Federline, and his radiotelephone operator. We branched off the large main trail and began pushing through the brush to the right. We were just below the crest of the tree and brush-covered slope and could hear firing, explosions, and people screaming not far away. My heart was pounding in my throat as I realized that any second I would be in the mouth of the beast. My feet did not want to move, but something, discipline, blind obedience, faith, kept me and the other men of Charlie Company moving forward into the conflagration.

I glanced back at the CO, then moved my eyes quickly back to our exposed flank as my peripheral vision noticed that the bushes were moving toward me. I stared harder; they were moving toward me. My heart leapt into my mouth and froze. Things began to happen in slow motion as I started to turn my head slowly to warn Captain Federline of the danger while my body started to lower itself in self-preservation.

"We've got movement—enemy—on the right!" I yelled the warning as I dived to the ground, but halfway through my words the advancing, camouflaged NVA soldiers began firing. As I hit the floor of the rain forest, I quickly fired back a large burst. I then flipped out the empty magazine and the thought zipped through my mind that I needed to fire on semi to preserve ammo. I fired several more bursts at the moving trees and saw a few of them fall and lay still. A surge of adrenaline, raw energy, or bloodlust shot through me. I had killed. Better yet, I had killed and was still alive. So this is what it's like to take another human's life. Well, if I hadn't, they would surely have taken mine.

These thoughts raced through my harried mind in a millisecond as I changed magazines. Around me the others were firing into their own particular "kill zones" as the enemy appeared to be everywhere. My mind was racing along at breakneck speed, but something reminded me that while I was hitting the ground, I had also seen the captain going down. I turned my head in his direction and saw him lying still about four feet away. Near his left shoulder there was a widening red stain.

I checked back to the front and saw that the enemy had stopped advancing for the moment and was instead firing at us from concealed positions. I reached for my bandage attached to my web gear and began to slide toward him. A burst of fire tore into the brush and ground around me, so I slid back again and rolled behind a skinny tree about three feet to his left and slightly down the hill, where I yelled: "Medic! The Old Man is hit. Medic!"

I began firing into the trees and brush on the top of the rolling hill, then once more tried to reach out for the wounded man. Once more the AK-47 burped and the rounds whistled and buzzed through the air around me like angry hornets, so close it made my hair stand on end. I couldn't understand why I hadn't been hit by one of the bursts that whizzed past my face and head. Why the captain and not me? I also realized that trying to reach him was tantamount to suicide, so I rolled back to my tree and fired another short burst with my left hand into the largest tree in front of me. Apparently my enemy had no view of the left side of my tree, so I exposed that side of my body while firing.

In my state of near-panic I tried to keep contact with the rest of the squad in hopes that someone would appear and begin barking orders that would turn the tide of the battle. I looked to my left and saw Marvin and Fears huddled close together and hugging the ground. Next to them was a CIDG adviser in a green beret and camouflage fatigues. He had a bandage on his left arm and was directing fire for Marvin. He apparently had been separated from the rest of the CIDG and probably had been damned glad to see us coming to help. He caught my eye and I sensed that he was concerned that, since I was slightly behind him I might accidentally send a round or two his way. I signaled that I was firing in the direction of the big tree directly to my front. He nodded, then grunted, "Just be careful that you don't shoot your own men and conserve your ammo. Be sure you have a target."

I saw Maddox a little farther down the line, behind a good-sized tree, working on his rifle feverishly. He had it broken down and was trying to extract a jammed round from the breech. He had a look of panic on his face and spoke in a high-pitched, almost strangled voice. "Pete, can you help me? My damn rifle won't fire. Can you get me the pistol from the captain? I need a weapon."

I shook my head slowly and tried to find my voice. "Can't do it. Every time I try to move to help him, the bastards fire a burst right through here. Look."

I put an empty magazine on the end of my rifle barrel and held it out just to the right of the tree I was cowering behind my tree of life. The enemy weapon opened up once more, ripping the air with its staccato message of death. I looked back at Maddox and gave him a sympathetic look, then returned the fire at the invisible foe. Every fiber in my body wanted to get up and go to the downed officer, roll him over, and tend to his wounds, but my brain reminded me of the sound of the bullets coming at me. I tried to see his face, but his eyes captured mine as he screwed up his mouth and tried to speak. I could see and hear the pain and terror. "Please . . . help me . . . help me. . . ."

I wanted to say, I'm sorry, I can't. I'm sorry, but I didn't think he could hear or comprehend. I was extremely frustrated and began firing once more at the tree line. Come on, dammit. Show your face once. As if to answer me, another burst of automatic weapons fire came tearing into my little tree and a few of the leaves were shredded and fell to the ground around me. I squeezed myself into a smaller profile and began shaking from fear and frustration. I fully believed that I would die any second and wondered once more why it hadn't happened already.

Finally I saw a medic approach from a little below and to the right of the captain. I pointed to the front. "They're firing right through here. You can't get to him until we get these NVA out of there. Don't try it."

The medic ignored me and crawled to the side of Captain Federline, then began to gently roll him over. The enemy weapon burst into action once more and at least three rounds tore into the medic's arm and chest. He fell back with a surprised look on his face, then began screaming. "Medic! I'm hit! Oh, God! Medic, help me, help me!"

I fired another burst at the suspected source of the enemy's murderous fire, then waited a few seconds and tried to roll to the aid of the two wounded men. Again, a heavy burst drove me back to my tree, shaking and cursing, on the verge of tears. I wanted to scream at the injustice of it all—God, why won't you let me help them? My mind again checked through all the possibilities. Should I act like the brave but foolish medic and die bravely? The practical side of my brain answered no, I could do no more than bandage them if I did get through unscathed.

My first job must be to destroy the enemy position so someone else can help the wounded and we can get them to an LZ. To that end I squeezed off a few more rounds in the direction of the cursed tree line.

After another thirty minutes of holding in position and avoiding the ubiquitous sniper fire, another medic appeared from the brush below us and began crawling toward the wounded, moaning men. I yelled, "No! Don't try to help them.

They're firing right through here. This is their kill zone. If you try, you'll get killed. Don't do it, man."

The medic hesitated only a second, then reached for the other medic to roll him back off the captain's legs. As if on cue, the deadly NVA weapon spoke again and the medic took rounds in the face, chest, and arm and was thrown backwards to the ground where he moaned once, then died. I swore as loud as I could, then rolled to the left side of my tree and saturated the enemy's tree with a full magazine.

The Green Beret looked at me. "Take it easy, man. We gotta figure out a way to get your captain out of there."

I had figured out by this time that we had suffered severe casualties and the command structure was collapsing. I thought about the enemy and what he might do next and the logical thought came back: if he knows how thin we are, he'll try to overrun us. I counted my magazines—still five more left. I'll have to be more selective in my firing from here on; can't afford to run out. I checked to see how the captain was doing and saw that he was still breathing, but quiet now. I glanced at the motionless medic and saw that one of the enemy's bullets had torn off most of the left side of his face. Somehow I had begun to harden myself to the horror around me, so the dead man's disfigured face didn't bother me as much as it would have an hour before.

Turning back the other way I saw Maddox was lying quietly behind his tree, holding his useless weapon to his chest like a doll. Farther down the line I could hear sporadic firing, an occasional explosion and more yelling. I saw Fears next to Maddox, on his left.

"What's happening down that way, Fears, can you tell?"

"I ain't goin' down there to find out, man. I know that Lieutenant Canale is hit, Mac is hit and Belcher is dead, and all our asses are in big trouble."

He lay back down behind the tree and buried his head. Maddox was moaning or swearing softly, incoherently. Overhead, the jets were making a run at the enemy positions between us and the border, pounding the jungle with their small bombs and rocket fire and an occasional burst of napalm. I felt a small surge of confidence; someone was still able to call in air and artillery that could keep us alive. Behind us in the crater, the engineers were still blowing down trees and sawing them to clear an LZ. The buzz of the chainsaws in the background, mixed with the chatter of automatic weapons and grenade and bomb blasts made a macabre symphony.

I was starting to wonder how this would come out—it certainly wasn't like any damned Hollywood war movie in which the men die bravely and quickly and the good guys, always Americans, prevail and all is well. There had been a very real danger of the enemy charging out of those trees and overwhelming our thin green line before help could arrive, but that danger appeared to be passing as the air and artillery bombardments had apparently broken the enemy's resolve. They were now content to pin us down and thin our ranks with deadly accurate sniper fire and grenades; perhaps they were waiting for reinforcements, too. I forced myself to turn back to the wounded men and I could see that the first medic had apparently stopped breathing. Captain Federline was now groaning softly and only I knew what he was trying to say: "Please . . . help me . . . help me. . . ."

The 3rd Platoon had been held in reserve at the LZ to help provide security for the engineers. Finally they were ordered to move in behind us to relieve the pressure and enable us to get our wounded back to the LZ. The 3rd Platoon leader, Lieutenant Shipley, appeared in the brush to my right rear, looking puzzled, so I pointed out the now obvious kill zone and told them to stay clear. I glanced at the eyes of the grunts who crawled up behind me and saw the abject fear that I had felt when we entered the fray. They had been holding in position, listening to the terrible battle, imagining the worst and praying they wouldn't be summoned to join it.

I nodded and motioned some of them to move to their left where it was safer as Shipley asked questions about the status of the captain. "Is he still breathing? Can you get to him?"

"He's still breathing but I can't move toward him. This is where the fire comes through."

"Do you know the status of your platoon? Lieutenant Canale?"

"The lieutenant is down. Sergeant Belcher is down. There's a lot more dead or wounded, but no word is comin' down the line."

"Well, we've got resupply coming in to the LZ, so don't worry about ammo. We're gonna pour some fire into the tree line, then try to get the wounded out. Pass that word down."

We got the word down as far as we could, then opened up on Lieutenant Shipley's signal. It felt good to make an offensive move, even if it did resemble all the defensive firing we had been doing the past couple of hours. There was silence following the volley, then a couple of shots rang out from the big tree in a defiant answer. A tall and extremely skinny GI with a pencil-thin moustache on his hawk-like face was kneeling next to the lieutenant and peering into the trees ahead of us. He pointed and yelled, "I see one and I can get him."

He fired one round, then another one. I heard a small crash as the leaf-covered NVA soldier fell from the tree. "I got the son of a bitch. I got him!" he yelled, sounding surprised.

I wasn't sure, but I hoped that he had shot the man who had made my life miserable and had ended several others. We had been pinned down for over two hours and it was time to retrieve our dead and wounded and move them to a safer place where they could get proper medical care. In the first minutes of the battle, feelings of panic and urgent self-preservation had nearly overwhelmed me. Then as the battle continued, they had been replaced by feelings of doom, fueled by frustration at our inabilities and by the terrible events unfolding around me. As time passed it became obvious that the enemy was not going to overrun us, but was satisfied to stay hidden and pick us off. I was now feeling tremendous fatigue from the stress of combat and shock from the carnage, but an awareness had crept back into my heart and mind: I will live through this. Now that we had an officer to take charge once more, I reached down to find some inner strength to carry me as events continued to unfold.

The Green Beret must have had some of the same thoughts as he turned toward us and said, "All right, let's get your CO outta there. Are those medics still alive or wasted?"

"Both look to be dead. Captain's still breathing."

As he began organizing us to make the attempt to move the captain, I decided it was time to take another chance at rolling across the kill zone. This time I made it with no firing; either the sniper had been alone and was dead or the others were biding their time. I pulled one of the dead medics off the captain's legs, then we grabbed his legs and shoulders and moved him as gently as we could to the bushes behind us. The Green Beret pulled out a large knife and started to make a stretcher out of branches and ponchos. I looked down the trail and saw two men half-carrying and dragging Curtis, who was wounded in the leg. Somebody yelled out, "Help that man. Get him to the LZ."

Maddox and I grabbed his legs and two guys I didn't know took his shoulders and we moved him back to the brush and tried to find a couple of branches. After a lot of cursing and grunting, we finally got a stretcher constructed and lifted Curtis onto it. He was moaning and telling us how much it hurt as we lifted the dead weight and started off through the thick brush. After we had gone about ten feet a sniper opened up in our general direction. You could hear the rounds tear into the trees around us, some of them ricocheting, so we lowered the wounded man roughly and hit the dirt. He cried out as he bounced on the ground, then quickly became still so he wouldn't draw fire.

The 3rd Platoon had moved into our abandoned positions and now they quickly answered the sniper's rounds with a few volleys of their own. Curtis groaned at us from the ground. "Don't worry about me. Save yourselves. Leave me, it's OK."

"Shut up, Curtis. You've seen too many movies. We'll get you to the LZ in a few minutes."

I didn't feel as flippant as my answer, but it seemed to jump out of my mouth on its own and it fit the occasion. I was learning things about myself that I had been unaware of previously. Now, I would learn if I had enough courage and strength to get back up and start carrying the wounded man out under fire. I started up along with the other three men, each grabbing a corner and lifting the dead weight and headed once more toward the main trail, somewhere ahead of us. We struggled and staggered as we toted the burly Curtis and had to set him down every few feet to take a new grip. Finally we set him down, moved him off the makeshift stretcher, and restructured the poncho on the poles. With the poncho pulled tighter, the load didn't sag as much and we moved a little easier. Another sniper opened up, but one of the men shook his head and said we should pretend that it wasn't coming at us, so we continued through one last clump of bushes and onto the main trail. We stopped once more and rested as Curtis began babbling and laughing. "Morphine must have kicked in. I'm feelin' good, now."

Once more we hefted him and set out up the slight incline toward the LZ. Although it was easier going on the trail, the combination of fatigue and dead weight made the load occasionally bump along the ground and Curtis would moan and then apologize for doing it. Another Green Beret met us on the trail. He had his right arm in a black sling and was limping slightly as he hobbled along, bush rifle in hand. His face was gray from fatigue and loss of blood. "Goddammit, pick that man up. The four of you should be able to carry him easily. Move along. Get him up to the LZ."

We were a little shocked and annoyed at his outburst, which I figured must have been caused by pain from his wounded arm, but Curtis, in his near-delirium, shot back. "What the fuck are you gonna do, send us to 'Nam? Leave these guys alone, they're gonna carry me to LZ Lane."

The Green Beret, in his tiger-striped jungle fatigues, hobbled off toward the battle scene, looking for someone else to help or curse at, I assumed. After about an hour of lifting and carrying, stopping and lowering, we made it to the LZ. Doc Cabral was caring for the wounded men lined up along the south and west side of the bomb crater. I saw the engineers still sawing and leveling logs on the far side and there were a few scattered stragglers of the 2nd Platoon spread around in the bushes. I found a spot along the main trail, just a few feet from where Cabral and another medic were working feverishly, and sat down against a tree, facing south in case any enemy came through behind Bravo's lines. In the absence of orders from any higher authority I decided to stay there and watch for my squad members.

The wounded continued to pile up along the trail as the medics waited for the LZ to be finished. I watched the harried Cabral as he assigned them priority numbers. He shouted out to no one in particular, as if answering a question. "I'm assigning numbers based on the severity of wounds, not rank. Captain Federline goes first. He's the one with the worst injury."

No one dared question the authority of a medic on a day like this. Some of the wounded men were moaning and bitching, some were pleading for help, and some were silent; silent because their wounds were so severe they were rendered nearly comatose, or so slight as not to cause them much pain or discomfort. I saw another stretcher bearing Lieutenant Canale arrive at the scene; the men carrying him collapsed much as we had after bringing Curtis this far. The lieutenant was trying to speak as Doc Cabral inspected his wounds. Part of the back of his head had been shot away and you could see his brains through a hole the size of a silver dollar. He was babbling at no one.

"Charlie sure can shoot . . . sure can shoot."

He was obviously under the influence of morphine and Doc tried to placate him by telling him the chopper was coming.

"Chopper comin'? Tell him to hurry . . . hurry."

His voice trailed off, then I saw Doc Cabral's eyes glaze over and remembered how close they had been. Another group of stragglers came up the trail carrying more wounded and a few hobbled in on their own. Would it ever end? I saw Hinzman, who had arrived in the field with me a month ago, being carried by men of the 1st Squad. His eyes were closed and there was a terrible purplish color on his face, streaked with blood. He must have taken a round that set off his smoke grenade in addition to his wounds—it was an eerie sight. Vickers was standing in line with a bandage on his arm. I asked if he was all right.

"Just some shrapnel. I'll be OK, but they'll have to take it out, it's still in there."

"Where's Mac?"

"Dead." He spat the word at me in an accusatory way as if I had caused the death, but I realized that he was in a state of shock and wasn't upset at me.

Then it hit me—Mac is dead. I felt useless as I remembered how we had told him we would take care of him just two days ago. I bowed my head slightly, then asked again. "Any word on anybody else? I saw the Old Man and two medics get it right beside me and I couldn't do a thing."

"Belcher's dead. Sergeant Machado's dead. A bunch more wounded."

"Yeah. I helped carry Curtis. Lieutenant Canale's up there in real bad shape. Hell of a day."

The first chopper came in slowly and unloaded some ammo and a few clean-uniformed officers and noncoms from the rear. Apparently the battalion was moving quickly to replace some of the downed command structure that was plaguing us. I spotted Maddox and Harrell milling around and waved at them. They moved over toward me, then Maddox veered off toward Doc Cabral and began talking to him. Doc was shaking his head and Maddox walked away and sat down with the wounded men. I saw Fears in the line holding his leg and moaning aloud. "Doc, I hurt my leg real bad. Please send me in."

Doc Cabral was directing the loading of the medevac chopper that came in behind the one with the ammo resupply and, as it lifted off, I could see another one circling above. I felt some small sense of relief that the wounded men were heading for the MASH units and hospitals, but what about the rest of us? What about the sick at heart, the dispirited men who had passed within an eyelash of death's door and were filled with anguish, remorse, and pain so deep that it couldn't be reached by normal means? Must we continue to go through the same motions out here and face it all again tomorrow or another day? I kept all these thoughts to myself as Marvin staggered in and joined Harrell and me along the trail. I had consciously placed a layer of hardness over my heart and my outer feelings after the battle and aftermath of November 13. I now had to add another layer to a growing callousness of spirit, which seemed to be the only way to survive the tremendous emotional stress. It was becoming impossible to think straight, to acknowledge right from wrong, to know when to care. I wondered if I was losing my mind.

I snapped out of my trance as Maddox stumbled into our position and sat down. I tried to ask him if he was all right, but he was lost in his own world and wore a blank expression. After a few minutes he got up and walked toward the edge of the crater and sat down again. I wanted to help him, but I had to take care of myself first and I thought we should stay in a guard position. I looked at Marvin and Harrell and saw the same frozen countenance, a result of shock and fatigue from the battle. I wanted very much to know what they, and all the others, were thinking. Were they affected in the same way as me?

Harrell began to speak softly: "Pete, I'm next in line to lead the squad. I don't want it. I don't want anything more to do with it. Maddox can't do it now, either. You take it, Pete, if they come around and ask for a squad leader."

"Let's just wait until they get squared away here, Harrell. Maybe they'll bring out some replacements for us."

Due to the excessive numbers and the size of the LZ, the evacuation of the wounded and dead could not be completed before dark. The survivors in Bravo Company, the CIDG unit and the recon platoon joined the remainder of Charlie Company in a large perimeter around the crater band of the LZ for the night. We moved a few feet ahead and dug a huge foxhole with dirt stacked high in front. I found a big tree to rest behind when I wasn't on guard and sat down and opened a can of beans and wieners. The smell and sight of it nauseated me so I threw it away, then sucked the juice out of a can of peaches.

As darkness fell, Maddox rejoined our position but remained silent and morose. As I pulled guard I was certain that, any minute, thousands of NVA would come firing out of the trees and kill us all. I spoke to Marvin in the dark as we pulled first watch together. "Did you do any praying out there, Marvin? I don't mind admitting I called on the Big Guy a couple of times."

"He's a wonderful man, God is. Wonderful."

Marvin wasn't much for conversation, but I needed to talk to someone, to say something, so I continued: "Word is, they had to leave McCown, Belcher and Machado out there. Sniper fire was too heavy to get their bodies today. They know they're dead, but still, man, we should have gone back to bring them out. Americans don't leave their dead."

"Yeah, you're right, man."

The conversation ended there and I withdrew into myself as the beleaguered battalion prepared for nightfall. A full squad had gone out down the trail as an OP for this side of the perimeter. At about 1900 the artillery forward observer began to call in defensive concentrations, an essential and exacting task considering the logistics. One of the DefCon rounds came in short, due either to a mistaken coordinate or a faulty round, wounding a few men and killing one. A rescue party of medics and troops was hurriedly sent to the site and brought the OP back to the LZ. The men came staggering in to the center of the perimeter, glancing around wild-eyed and frantic, like captured wild animals. I didn't think my heart had any more room, but the sight of these beleaguered souls caught up in a frenzy not at all of their choosing, put another load on it. It was a tragic climax to a horrible day for the entire battalion.

As I lay behind the tree, unable to sleep and certain of attack, I pondered the events of the day. We had been forced to pull back, although not routed, and some of us would live to fight another day. I wondered how the enemy felt in his camp this night. Were they celebrating a great victory, planning another attack tomorrow, or were they reacting much like us, grieving their losses and wondering who won? I knew we had slain a great many of the enemy with air, artillery, and ground fire and I had seen a few of them fall before the first barrage from my own rifle.

Tomorrow will tell, when we add up the friendly casualties and count the enemy bodies. Tomorrow will tell, when we return to the battle scene and retrieve our three remaining bodies and challenge once more for that miserable piece of ground. Tomorrow will tell, when we examine our souls to determine our personal casualty list and to find if we have anything left to give for ourselves and for our fellow man. Tomorrow will tell.

10

Incredibly, the sun rose again on the morning of November 20. It peered over the edge of Dragon Crater and splashed across my back as I was pulling the last watch. It felt good as it warmed my bones—if there was just some way to get it to shine on my heart. I looked through my pack to see if I had any fruit, but could find only a round tin of C-ration cookies. I opened them and munched one down, then sat motionless, waiting for the inevitable order to move out once more to the battlefield. I tried not to think about what had transpired on that bloody ground only a hundred yards or so away yesterday or what might be out there today, but my heart was filled with melancholy.

There was a flurry of early activity around the LZ as a chopper brought in more ammo and a few new men, then took out some more of the wounded. The helipad was located about sixty feet to my rear at the northern edge of the crater on a bed of logs put together by the engineers. The extended perimeter of the wounded and war-weary battalion stretched back to the north and east and covered most of the hill mass south of the stream that delineated "Indian Country" in my mind.

Captain Beal took over as acting company commander of Charlie Company and a grizzled, skinny staff sergeant, Sergeant Nuckols, became the new 2nd Platoon sergeant. The word came down from battalion that Captain Federline had died from his wounds in the early morning hours. To keep from thinking about it too much, I wiped my M-16 down thoroughly, checked my ammo and magazines, and picked up a couple of extra grenades. I didn't know what would be waiting for us in that cursed base camp, but I made sure I had all the armaments I could carry.

The morning reports had put friendly casualties at eighteen dead and almost fifty wounded in the battalion. The unofficial body count of NVA dead was set at 360 from accounts of ground troops and spotter planes. The battle was being touted as a great victory for the battalion, but those of us who had been on the line, fighting for our lives, knew the truth. We had barely held our own, and for a long while it could have gone either way. On the ground, in this fight, I did not believe there was a victor.

The 3rd Herd led Charlie Company toward the battle scene as the other units held in reserve at the LZ, now named Dragon Crater. Since Fears had somehow convinced a medic that he was injured, the squad was down to just four men, one of whom, Maddox, was only partly there.

Harrell was a new man today, taking command of the under-manned group and keeping us in operating order. When the company went on line for a sweep of the area, he crawled into bunkers to check for enemy soldiers before blowing them with grenades. We had some leadership and were working as a unit once again. In spite of the heavy pall that hung over us all, it felt good to have a mission, to keep moving, and to be able to focus on the task at hand. We were shaking off our lethargy, aided mightily by the absence of our enemy.

We found the bodies of McCown, Belcher, and Machado and, to the relief of us all, they were not booby-trapped or vio-lated in any manner. We had heard the horror stories about the enemy's desecration of bodies, so I had been prepared for the worst. However, the NVA had obviously not returned to the battle scene after their withdrawal at sunset and were not on hand to contest our actions today. We searched, but not too ea-gerly, for tunnels where some of the enemy were undoubtedly hiding, but found none. We retrieved the bodies and a large amount of abandoned gear and equipment, then began a body count of the enemy dead in the western quadrant of the battle area.

As I reached the area where I had been pinned down for nearly three hours, my heart sped up a little and a lump formed in my throat and chest. I saw dark stains on the ground where the captain and the medics had fallen and once again I ques-tioned myself and the fates. Why? Why was I alive and three others dead from wounds suffered within a few feet of me? Should I have tried to do something more—perhaps attacked the enemy position or flanked it? Did I do the proper thing or was I just afraid, too afraid to move? Or was it all preordained, bound to happen the way it did? I had no answers to these ques-tions and I felt a strange guilt for being alive, as if I should apologize to those who no longer were.

Having completed our assigned tasks, we moved back to the crater and took a noon break.

Captain Beal reported 166 NVA bodies still on the ground just in our sector—if the count was even close to correct, even I might have to concede that it was a victory for the battalion. How could the 33rd NVA continue to function as a regiment after losses like these? Perhaps this was the decisive battle we had all been preparing for and fearing over the last ten days. I did not let my hopes rise enough to believe it, but the thought lingered in the periphery of my mind and made my heart a little lighter.

During our sweep the rest of the dead and wounded had been extracted, and the battalion was preparing to move out back to LZ Lane, since a B-52 strike had been set for 1500 hours and all of the units had to be in the firebase before that time. We moved out just behind Bravo Company and just ahead of the CIDG and the recon platoon. As we crossed the edge of the crater I saw the Green Beret who had fought beside us, with the bandage still on his arm, sitting on a short stump. He nodded at me and spoke a few words of encouragement to Marvin, then we moved on into the jungle.

Because of the size of our force, we moved quite quickly along the trail, not concerned with ambushes or snipers. Bravo Company of the 2nd/35th, a sister battalion, had been lifted into the area as a reaction force the day before and linked up for the short move to the LZ. We arrived at 1430 and took up residence once more near the stream. At 1500 word came down to get into the bunkers.

"B-52s in the air. Over the target in five minutes."

We heard a terrible shriek as the bombs tore through the air, then a tremendous muffled series of explosions when they hit the ground. Although we were a couple of miles away, the ground shook and dirt fell from the roofs of our bunkers onto our backs. I looked at Marvin and Harrell and let my thoughts run on.

"By God, that should slow them down a little."

Marvin allowed himself a slight grimace and answered, "Mr. Charles best be diggin' in."

"We'll find out how good those NVA tunnels are. If he's not real deep, his shit will be weak, man. Them ol' boys are bringin' some real pee." I tried some Army jargon.

Sergeant Harrell had been sitting quietly as the bombs fell and the earth shook. He nodded his head and looked up.

"There's only one thing more powerful than an Arc Light and that's an atomic bomb."

"Or one of Mac's farts, God rest his soul," I added.

After the strike, the platoon sergeant's RTO walked along the bunkers and passed the word that anybody that had medical problems should head to the dispensary. I took a look at the slight shrapnel wound in my hand and decided to get it flushed out and bandaged. As I stepped inside the heavily fortified bunker, I met a young medic in clean fatigues and shiny boots. He asked me how I got the wound and I told him about the battle and the deaths of the medics. He lowered his voice, then asked for more details in a reverent voice.

"Did they die doing their job, their duty?"

"They did that. They were both very brave, but foolish under the circumstances."

"A medic is taught to help the wounded and disregard his personal safety. They did what I would have done, I think."

I didn't argue with him; he was evidently new in the country and had seen no action. His baptism would come soon enough, since he would probably be replacing one of the two dead men in the field. I flexed my hand, which he had washed with peroxide and applied a large strip bandage to, then nodded at him as if I approved his work.

I told him to keep his head down, then headed back to the bunker where I cleaned my weapon once more and then ate my first meal of the day: roast something in a gray gravy. After dark I sat behind the bunker and let my mind wander back over the past thirty hours. I replayed the entire firefight, flinching inwardly at the chatter of the AK-47s and the thump of the grenades. I saw the captain fall to the ground, more clearly than I had yesterday, and doubts began to gnaw at me.

I could have reacted quicker, or dove at him and took the rounds meant for him, but what would that prove, except to change the identity of the dead man?

I should have recognized the threat earlier when I saw the strange up-and-down movement of the brush-covered NVA soldiers as they closed in on us. I felt again the anguish, the tremendous frustration and sense of failure as I lay behind my tree unable to reach the dying men. One thing kept burning in my mind: I should have shot the moving bushes at first sight instead of hesitating the split-second that it took to formulate into words my warning. That slight hesitation, that half-second, was the difference between life and death for one man and led to the demise of two brave medics. I should have shot first and asked questions later.

I was unable to reconcile in my heart and mind whether I had acted properly in my behavior toward the wounded men. Was I correct in my prudence or were the medics right with their bravery and their death? The only thing certain was that I was alive and had to go on. Although I would never be able to put these thoughts out of mind, I had to somehow control them, or they would surely control me.

Maddox was struggling within his own mind, trying to get his emotions under control. He had also seen the death of fellow soldiers close-up and he had faced the enemy with no weapon, save his grenades, for the duration of the battle. The strain had been tremendous and he was cracking under it. I tried to talk to him, joke with him, and though he showed some interest, there was no light in his eyes. I didn't know what to do for him and it deepened my despair.

As the sun began to surrender to the horizon, Sergeant Nuckols led half of the 2nd Platoon to a large ambush position about seventy meters south of the perimeter along the stream bank. As we dug in along the east side of the creek, I could see spider-holes along the other bank. I wondered how and when the enemy had crawled that close to the firebase, then I remembered that the CIDG had been posted on an OP out here a few nights before and they dug the same one-man foxholes that the NVA used. The night passed quietly and we managed a few needed hours of sleep.

On the morning of November 21 we got our gear ready for another move back to the contact area. I watched Harrell as he headed to the platoon CP and waited for his return so we could find out our place in the patrol. After a while Sergeant Nuckols stopped and told the three of us to join the 2nd Squad since Harrell would be heading for Pleiku for health reasons. I shook my head and wondered how this Army could operate without any noncommissioned officers, but kept my tongue silent and headed to the 2nd Squad.

This time a rested and partially restocked Alpha Company returned to action and led off, with Bravo Company, 2nd/35th, following a few minutes later. After another thirty minutes the men of Charlie Company headed out on a more southern route.

The other units would head for Dragon Crater, then wait until we got into position to act as a blocking force and a reserve unit. They would then kick off a sweep of the battle area.

We stopped to break for noon chow in an area where we had spent the night a week earlier. We took defensive positions and checked out the demolished fighting holes we had occupied. Finding no sign of enemy activity, we relaxed a little and munched on Cs. I looked at Maddox, who was lying between the trail and a huge tree, curled into a ball. I thought he was sleeping, so I nudged him and said teasingly: "Hey, guy, you're supposed to sleep when we're back at the firebase. There's a couple of Playboy bunnies from the club in Atlanta here to see you."

I saw that he was shaking like the proverbial leaf in a storm, so I put my hand on his forehead to see if he was hot. His face was covered with sweat and he stammered as he tried to speak to me, but nothing came out. I asked him, "What's wrong, ol' dude? You look a little peaked."

"Pete . . . Pete. I feel terrible. I'm hot and cold. Get me some help, will ya?"

"Medic, got a man with a fever."

The medic took his temperature, then looked at Maddox, shook his head, and chuckled quietly as he spoke.

"You got 104. How'd you manage to raise it that high? All these guys want out of the field and you figured out how to do it. All right, here's your tag. I'll see if we can get a chopper in here."

Maddox managed a feeble grin but was too weak to speak. I picked up his pack and started to ransack it.

"I'm taking your fuckin' peaches, man. You'll be eating fresh fruit in Pleiku while I'm out here winning this damned war. Don't you feel guilty?"

He tried to manage a wink but the effort was too much. It took about twenty minutes to get the medevac chopper in, and after I helped load him on and send it off I felt more alone than I had since I arrived in-country. Mac and Belcher dead, Vickers and Curtis wounded, Watson in Long Binh, Fears gone somewhere, and now Maddox headed for the hospital. It had been a long three days and it wasn't over yet.

Word came down to saddle up and hit the trail once more to

get into position. When we set up we were about 400 meters north of the crater, in position to intercept any forces heading either in or out of the base camp. I could hear small-arms fire once again in the distance—the all too familiar pop-pop of the AK and the heavier bang of the M-16, firing in a series of small bursts. Occasionally I could hear the loud blast of a grenade or the muffled whump of one detonated inside a bunker. One of the radiotelephone operators (RTOs) passed down the word that A Company had taken fire from five or six NVA. They returned the fire and killed two of them. I felt a little surge of empathy for them—get some, Alpha, but my heart was heavy and my mood was somber as I realized that we were only moments away from the battle scene and would be called quickly if things got hot. I repeated fervently—get some, Alpha.

We held in place as the two companies moved out once more to sweep the area. This time B Company, 2/35th, took fire and held up to allow air and artillery to soften the enemy's position. The RTO continued to supply us with information on the progress, or lack of it, as he received it.

I wondered how much softening those damned NVA needed—if an Arc Light couldn't soften them up, what the hell could we do. I knew what the answer to that was and I didn't like it: we had to go in and dig them out by hand, if necessary.

After the artillery strike the men of Bravo moved out once more and again came under heavy fire. They overwhelmed one bunker and found a dead NVA regular with a little dirt thrown over him and a machine gun with its barrel still hot and smoking. They decided, with the Colonel's blessing, to pull back again and call in another air and artillery strike to pound them some more. Alpha Company took no more fire and held their position to the east of Bravo while the engineers tried to destroy the bunkers in their area. Both companies pulled back to the crater for the night while Charlie Company remained in a reserve position not far away.

We set up in a tight company perimeter around the knob of a small, brush-covered hill just south of the stream. Rangel joined Marvin, Alexus and me in our position and I dug in and set up my claymore mine and trip wires just like Watson, Maddox and Mac had shown me. Late that night I heard a thrashing coming down the line. I couldn't tell if it was one of our guys, but I figured it had to be because of the noise and location, so instead of firing I challenged him.

"Halt. Who the fuck goes there?"

"Sergeant Nuckols. I'm doin' a perimeter check."

"Advance and be recognized. You got the password?"

"Tonto."

I knew it seemed ridiculous to have a perimeter check in a combat zone, but I figured he was trying to impress his new command, so I played along and gave him the answer.

"Lone Ranger. Advance and state your business."

"Just checkin' to see if anybody's on guard."

"Not a bad way to get killed. You might want to pull your circuit in a ways to stay out of the wires."

"Yeah, I guess. Where's the next position?"

"Just over there—machine-gun crew. Go back this way."

He staggered off through the bushes and I could hear him challenge the gun crew and the incredulous answer: "What the hell are you doin' out there?"

The rest of the night passed quickly and I managed to get a couple hours of rest before the morning started to break with a pink haze over the tree-lined eastern hills. "Red sky at morning. Sailor take warning," I remembered. It's a good thing I'm not a sailor, I thought, then thought again. Hell, if I was a sailor, I wouldn't be going through all this shit. I'd be pulling watch over some empty ocean, knowing full well that North Vietnam didn't have a Navy. I'd be counting the days until I could get to a liberty port for some women and lots of booze. The only combat I would see would be when somebody bad-mouthed my ship or stole something from me.

My thoughts returned to the jungle, where I chewed on my cold beans and wondered if I'd ever even get to see Pleiku City, where Watson said the women and the booze were plentiful, easy, and cheap. Seemed like a lifetime away.

The game plan was much the same for the morning of November 22; the two companies started on another sweep of the base camp. The right flank of Bravo Company this time made heavy contact with an estimated two dozen NVA. Once more I listened to the distant firing and awaited orders to join the battle. B Company pulled back again and called in air and artillery to pound the enemy. The companies remained linked together, but were unable to maneuver freely and perhaps put the enemy into the jaws of a trap because they were prohibited from crossing the border. Because the battle was being waged on a rather large scale, brass and reporters from Saigon were checking out all the action, so no surreptitious border crossings were attempted.

The 3rd Brigade troops had been under the control of the 4th Infantry since coming into this AO. As we sat in our position we received word that the commander of the 2nd Brigade of the 4th Division, Colonel Miller, decided to call us all back to LZ Lane and hit the area once more with B-52s. It was the best news I had heard in several days and the only logical move left at his disposal. I was sure that the colonel and the other members of the command staff would have liked to pour troops into the area until the enemy was overwhelmed and slaughtered, but the rules of engagement didn't allow us to infringe on the sovereignty of a neutral country—Cambodia. We all knew that they weren't neutral at all, but that's the way the political game was played. I shrugged into my web gear and readied to move.

The other units moved past our position, then Charlie Company followed them back to the firebase. We closed into the LZ in midafternoon, then cleaned our weapons and rested. Sergeant Nuckols was trying to get to know the platoon and let us know him by bullshooting with the troops, so he made the rounds of the platoon positions. He was also looking for a candidate for noncom preparatory school back at Pleiku, and after talking to the remaining squad leaders and some of the troops, he picked Alexus to go. Alexus, a man of damn few words, nodded, grinned, picked up his rifle and pack, and headed for the helipad. He would be out of the field for a minimum of two weeks. I had arrived in the field a few days before Alexus, but though I envied him, I did not resent his good fortune.

Just before dark two shots rang out from the east side of the perimeter. I moved to the bunker and stood watching and listening for further action, but nothing happened. After about fifteen minutes, word came down that an NVA had tried to surrender by holding out a *Chieu hoi* leaflet which promised safe conduct, but a jumpy Alpha Company trooper shot him dead. I hoped that I could restrain myself a little better than that if the situation presented itself to me, but I couldn't condemn the shooter after what he had been through. Charlie had just picked the wrong place to surrender, I decided. I thought about Vickers and was certain he would have spoken these memorable lines that he had said to me a few days and a different world ago: "Fuck me. I'll never smile again."

I wondered if I ever really would smile again as I headed for the piss tube located slightly downwind from our bunker. As I stood there urinating on Vietnam, a warning was shouted down the line from bunker to bunker.

"Arc Light. Bombers on the way. Over target in approximately five minutes. Into the bunkers."

I shuffled over to the bunker and passed the gun crew hunkering down into their hole. Something about the way they were crowded together, like hobos warming themselves over a fire in a trash can, struck me as humorous. I yelled over, "Hey, you guys, spread out. One grenade will get you all."

One of them yelled something back, but I waved and headed for my bunker. I decided to sit on the edge of the hole rather than crawl down into it. If a bomb did come too close, I could quickly hit the bottom. A few seconds later I heard once more the high-pitched "shriek of death" and wondered what Charlie was thinking out there in his bunker as the bombs descended. I also heard again the muffled explosions and felt the earth shudder in protest as the projectiles tore into it.

I shuddered a little in unison as I thought of the possible death and destruction they would wreak on the humans in harm's way and on the innocent animals of the tropical rain forest.

After the strike I moved over behind the wall and rolled out my poncho liner. I saw Alabama readying his sleeping position at the next bunker and called to him: "Hey, man, what do you think? That oughta put a lick on old Charlie. Maybe we can finish that sweep in peace."

"I shore hope so. This whole dang place gives me the creeps, Pete. You reckon those were thousand pounders they dropped?"

"No doubt. Those Air Force dudes know how to fight a war. Load up with big stuff, fly over the target and drop them, then fly back home for a steak and a beer."

"Them ol' boys don't know what real war is. Give me a couple of them on my gun crew during a firefight and I'll show 'em how we do it on the ground."

"I sure wish I could have had your gun beside me the other day. Maybe I could have saved the Old Man and the medics who died. Maybe not, either, but I would have been able to cut through the brush a lot easier."

"I hear ya. In front of me, some of those damn VC tried to hide in the bushes, but I just cut it down with the gun, then shot them as they tried to run. That felt good."

I looked at him, but all I could see in the dark was a big grin. I made no judgments, for I could recall all the feelings that coursed through my mind during and after the battle. I remembered especially the feeling of tremendous power I had experienced when I saw the NVA soldiers fall as I fired my weapon. Yes, it did feel good, but it was tempered by the regret that it had to be this way. Why is it, whenever old men have disagreements, that young men must die?

Surely there must be a better way, but not until they learn how to get along without fighting. Like other young men throughout the annals of history, I'll just follow orders and march in step into the fray.

Once more, on the morning of November 23, 1966, we headed into enemy territory. By now the "Battle of Dragon Crater" had taken on international status. Reporters were on hand from CBS, AP, UPI, *Life* magazine, *Stars and Stripes,* and various other organizations, lolling around the CP and the helipad. Most of them were trying to hitch a ride to the scene of the action and a few were willing to hump along with us to get the story. The battle was being played up as a huge victory for the 3rd Brigade and the brass weren't going to miss any opportunity to grab some publicity.

Remembering what Mac had said four days ago, I glanced at the dispensary and saw the medics loading up extra bandages and morphine again, so I piled as many magazines and grenades as I could manage into my pack or on my web belt. This time I would be even more ready. As we lined up to head out, I looked around at my fellow troopers and they were also laden with extra weaponry and ammo. There was an air of determined boldness about the men; their faces were set and only the eyes gave a hint of the apprehension that we all felt in our hearts. It was as if we all had decided that, even though we don't want to go out there again, we're going out there to kick some butt and take some names.

Charlie Company led the way out of the firebase and back on to the main trail. I was in a team with Marvin, Rangel and Jack Betta under Sergeant Bennett. As we headed down the slight hill to the stream where it all had begun many days before, I felt the old familiar fears begin building again. Each time we crossed that stream, my heart sank and my brain went on double alert. I told myself, today. Today, I'm ready. There won't be any more of this pinned down by a sniper shit. Today is our day.

When we reached my line of demarcation, the stream, I could see that it was a dirty gray with traces of gunpowder in it, and it was no longer a flowing creek; it was dammed by trees and earth that had been blown into it. The bombs must have hit near here and, I figured, I can't drink this shit anymore.

As we stopped around the crater we took defensive positions and broke for noon chow. I could see tree limbs broken off and piles of dirt where the bombs had fallen to the south and west. After the engineers cleared out the LZ, choppers began arriving with a mortar platoon, and the recon platoon was dropped in to pull security for the CP. Lieutenant-Colonel Proctor flew in with his aide to direct the operation from the crater. Two things crossed my mind as I watched him jump out of the chopper: it must be safe and it must be big. This was probably his chance for glory and he was determined to see it firsthand . . . from the crater.

We pushed out of our loose perimeter at 1300 and got on line for the sweep. As we moved out, the mortar crew was firing rounds over our heads to pin down any enemy troops in a classic Army fire and movement. The devastation of the base camp was awesome: the ground was torn and tossed about and trees were downed or stripped bare of leaves and branches, leaving the trunks standing like naked sentinels. There were huge craters everywhere in the area of the camp, which looked a little like pictures I had seen of the moon's surface. I saw a pair of tan fatigue pants hanging about twenty feet up in a denuded tree, and at the bottom of the tree was a dead, naked NVA with his hand raised to his forehead as if in salute or as a shield.

We found a few bodies and some useless gear in the impact area and moved through to the edges of the camp, where we had fought bitterly four days ago. The brush and trees were still standing there, so I was pushing through them cautiously when I saw a movement. I flipped my selector lever to automatic, but something made me hold my fire. As I stood there, weapon at the ready, the bushes parted and a photographer and another man with *Life* stenciled on their jungle fatigues stepped out. The photographer took a picture as I exploded.

"What the hell are you doing out here? Do you know how close you came to getting yourself killed?"

"I do now, troop. Hey, we're just doing our job, keeping the folks at home informed about our men in combat. You guys are big news right now."

"Not here, not in front of me. Stay behind the fuckin' line of men on the sweep. Jesus H. Christ, *Life* magazine in the jungle."

I was shaken by the experience, but I realized that I couldn't do my job that way, so I tried to inject some humor into the situation to Betta.

"I believe that we are fighting this damn war with the wrong weapons, man. If we get a camera and a tape recorder, we can go anywhere safely. Am I crazy, or are they?"

"They're *dinky-dau,* Pete. But, if you hadn't pulled down on them, they probably would have splashed our faces all over *Life* magazine and we would have been famous war heroes."

"Screw a bunch of heroes. Heroes usually wind up dead and I've seen enough dead. I guess they knew their shit was a little weak when I locked and loaded, huh?"

I laughed and unwound a little, but it was good to realize I had some emotions left. We pushed on through the bushes, then started back to the south where we linked up with Bravo Company to begin a sweep through the complex underneath the artillery and mortar barrage intended to keep the enemy away from the bunkers or pinned down in them. The engineers would then come in behind us and blow up the remaining bunkers. As we began to move through the heart of the camp, I was walking around a huge crater when I heard a loud whistle and a mortar round landed and exploded about twenty feet to my right. I hit the ground, then rolled over and down into the crater.

As I crawled back out I looked at the men to my right and

saw about ten men lying on the ground. As I got closer I saw that two men were quite obviously dead, with one of them nearly decapitated, and several of the others were seriously wounded. Sergeant Bennett stood up with an anguished look on his face and held his hands over his ears in pain. A photographer snapped a picture and a medic grabbed him and pulled him back to the ground. The rounds stopped going overhead and a calm settled in as the medics bent to their work. After determining that the rounds came from our own mortar crew, we carried the wounded and dead to the LZ and continued on our way. It was the third time in the last six days that injuries and death had resulted from friendly fire—I felt like we were getting it from all sides. I was surprised how easily we all accepted this latest carnage. I surmised that the horrendous experience had become all too commonplace for us; in order to continue to operate, we had to make it a routine.

Just past 1700 we held up our sweep and began to set up in a perimeter when it became obvious that we weren't going to get through the camp on this day. We dug in on the east side of the "wagon wheel" and once more I went through the motions of setting up my trip wires until I remembered Mac's advice and concentrated on my task. After I finished we broke out some Cs. Betta feasted on a can of ham and lima beans while I munched crackers.

"How can you eat that shit, man? That looks and tastes like I imagined gruel would taste."

"Nothin' to it. Just open a can of your finest U.S. Army cheese spread and put it in with the beans as you heat them. Ham and lima beans with melted cheese, now that's good."

"I'm from Wisconsin and I know cheese. That's not cheese."

"Close enough for me. I heard 3rd Squad say that they went on a water run and shot a dink down by the creek."

"They sure as hell weren't going to drink the water we saw back there, were they? That stuff was poison."

We were relaxing a little as it looked like the NVA had either disappeared over the border or been vaporized. We did not let our guard down since every man knew that we were less than a klick from the Cambodian border, but the tension was lessened slightly due to the size of our unit and the lack of contact during the sweep. Our squad pulled 50 percent security until midnight, then went to one up, three down until dawn.

In the morning, as we sat around the hole sipping coffee, we heard a clamor to our left rear. After a few minutes one of the company RTOs walked by to relieve himself in front of our position and gave a report.

"When we started to dig in last night, the guy from CBS and the other reporters found this hole already dug and used it. This morning they started to complain about the terrible stink around them, so they called one of the platoon leaders from Alpha over and he looked in and found a few bodies. It's a frickin' tunnel and they think there may be forty or fifty bodies inside. It really stinks."

"That must have been that fifty that I killed the other day, Betta—and I did it with one clip."

"I musta killed that many just in hand-to-hand combat, Pete."

I hadn't known Rangel very long except to see that he was quiet, very proud of his work, and thought he was being passed over and prejudiced against by the Army. He probably was. He was of Mexican-American descent and spoke with a heavy Latin accent. He had taken over the fire team and decided it was time to finish our bragging contest.

"There wouldn't be many left if you guys did what you said you did. It's time to move out."

The rest of the mopping-up operation began with the three companies again on line. We moved through the camp, then held in position less than 500 meters from the border as the engineers blew the rest of the bunkers. As we sat or lay in a line on the ground listening to the muffled, mostly underground explosions, I glanced around at the undermanned platoon and wondered when we'd get replacements. As if to answer my question, the grizzled Sergeant Nuckols came stumbling through the brush toward us.

"Hey, you guys got any extra pound cake? I'm starved."

"Pound cake and peaches are like gold out here, Sarge. The best I can do is ham and lima beans—Betta's personal favorite."

"I'd rather eat dink rice than that shit. Did you ever see anything like the way those bombs chewed up that camp? We're gonna be moving out of here and back to Lane as soon as the engineers finish their work. Went a lot easier than I thought it would. Sure you ain't got some fruit?"

"No fruit. Any word on when we'll get some replacements? We're short on men, especially experienced men."

"Maybe we'll find out something when we get back to Lane."

At 1130 hours we began pulling back to Dragon Crater, where the mortar platoon was loading the last of its men and equipment on a chopper for extraction. After they left, the engineer company with its remaining demolitions and gear took the next bird. Within minutes of their liftoff, the oversized patrol headed out of the LZ and took the now-familiar trail back to the battalion firebase, LZ Lane.

After finding positions in the crowded perimeter, we lined up for Thanksgiving dinner which had been prepared at 3 Golf and flown in. We feasted on turkey, gravy, potatoes, and some kind of pumpkin dessert. There was a rumor of ice cream, but our side of the perimeter didn't see it—the brass probably scarfed it up. I ate with Betta and Mize and we made short work of the hearty repast, then watched in amazement and gratitude as the platoon RTOs passed out our beer ration—two cans of warm brew. Mize and I decided to put ours in the creek to cool slightly while we stood watch and shot the bull.

Alabama Williams joined us on the creek bank as the day grew murky and edged inexorably toward night.

"Hey, Pete. Y'all heard anything on the loo-tenant?"

"Not a thing more. He had a severe head wound, man. He may survive and never be the same."

"None of us will, Pete. None of us will."

"You got that right, Bama. What do you think of Sergeant Nuckols? He's been around for a while."

"Yeah, I guess. I hope he realizes that this ain't Korea."

"If he doesn't, you'll straighten him out."

"Yup. I will. I hear that Robert Stack is visiting the troops here. I wonder if that ol' boy will come down to the lines and talk to me. I've never talked to a movie star."

"To paraphrase Vickers, fuck a bunch of Robert Stacks. I'd like to take that dude out to the Crater and spend the night on OP. We'd see what kind of war hero he is, pronto."

"Get some, Pete. I take it you don't care for heroic movies about war."

"I used to. I loved war movies, especially when the hero killed 500 Japs or Germans and came back to a big parade and all the girls kissed him. I couldn't wait to do that myself. Well, here I am and it's nothing like any movie I've ever seen. Welcome to the real world. Welcome to Vietnam, asshole."

"These guys don't know how to die right, do they, Pete?"

"Sure don't, Mize. Sure don't. Let's drink that beer."

Later that night the B-52s with their cargo of death laid down another blanket of devastation near the area of the Alpha Company battle of November 13. It didn't take a genius to deduce that the infantry would be checking out the area in the morning. I lay on the ground, covered with my poncho liner, thinking about my new friends, Betta and Mize, and my old companions, Maddox, Vickers, Watson, and, of course, the dead, always the dead. Captain Federline's eyes came piercing into my thoughts, my dreams, and my heart, always searching.

On the morning of November 25, Charlie and Bravo companies of the 1st/14th once more moved to the south and west to search for enemy activity. The battalion thought that the NVA's 33rd Regiment had been virtually eliminated as an effective fighting force, with casualty estimates running as high as 550 and many more suspected dead in bombed-out tunnels. It was our job to sweep the area bombed last night and search the surrounding jungles for any remainder of the regiment.

We moved out through the lush vegetation, avoiding the trail and hacking out a path to the site. The entire 2nd Squad alternated on point, wielding the machete in a losing battle against the jungle growth. It was extremely difficult labor—the pointman would shed his gear and weapon and pass it back to the squad to split up and carry and begin whacking away at the vines and brush. The second man would stay close and keep an eye on the surrounding terrain for enemy activity. After a few minutes of arm-numbing work, the pointman would gladly relinquish his duties and the machete to the next trooper.

After about two hours of this, we came across another smaller trail heading in the general direction that we were heading. We followed it more slowly and carefully, mindful of the proximity to the ambush site of the 13th. Once more we came to the stream, which by now was a stopped-up, gray, stagnant pool. My mind kicked into a higher state of alert despite my fatigued arms and back as we neared the battle site. Before we reached it, word came down to double back a few hundred meters to an LZ we had used previously and to hold up so Alpha Company, 2/35th, could join us.

Alpha was replacing its sister unit, Bravo, in the field and being lifted from Lane to the LZ we were guarding. They were being ferried in by only one chopper, so the lift took the rest of the day. We dug in and fortified our positions, I put out my claymore and trip wires, then I retreated to a spot behind the branches we had lain along the front of the hole, and rested. The night went slowly, except when it was my turn to sleep, and it was peaceful.

The next day the other two companies moved out early to make the sweep of the bombed area. Charlie Company remained to police up the food containers and empty ammo cans left by the combined units, and then moved on a different trail in the same direction as the others. We stayed a little east of the two companies doing the sweep and discovered another small complex with about two dozen bunkers, a few huts, foxholes and latrines. The complex was only a few days old and we immediately began blowing up and grenading the bunkers while keeping a wary eye out for the residents of the camp.

We completed our task, then headed a little farther south to an open area and held up just past noon. The other units completed the uneventful sweep and joined us about an hour later. We took our noon break and I finished my last can of Cs—a can of chopped eggs and ham. I held my nose and forced a couple of spoonfuls down, but the taste was horrendous and I threw most of it into the brush. I wondered if we would get a resupply soon, but the word came down, "We're going back to Lane. C Company will get lifted, the others will walk back. Charlie Company—to the LZ."

The choppers whisked us from the makeshift LZ to the firebase in a matter of minutes. Finding our place in the perimeter was becoming a routine now, so we tossed our gear down behind the bunker and awaited further orders. The rumor mill was working overtime with the hottest item being a stand-down back in Pleiku. I took it all with the proverbial grain of salt, but I noticed the medics at the dispensary were packing some of their equipment away, so perhaps there was hope.

After our highly forgettable evening meal, Sergeant Nuckols came loping along down the line checking the platoon bunkers and stopping to talk with the inhabitants. He was smiling as he gave out the official news. "We're heading to Pleiku tomorrow. The whole battalion and artillery, mortar, dispensary, everything. It's an official stand-down for restructuring and replacements, and you guys deserve it."

Our spirits were lifted immensely by the news and by a beer ration that was passed out a few minutes later. I took my two cans and joined Mize and Alabama on the edge of the stream where we reminisced and pondered the future. I felt a deepening sadness when I contemplated the events of the past fortnight. I thought about the men we had lost and the momentous changes on those of us who survived. No matter where I traveled or what I encountered, I knew that all the days of my life would be tempered by my personal involvement in those incidents of death and destruction along the Vietnam-Cambodian border in the "Battle of Dragon Crater" during the month of November in the year of the Lord, 1966.

11

The morning of November 27 dawned hesitantly, with no bright sunshine or blue skies to greet the troops of the Golden Dragon Battalion, just gray low-hanging clouds and a very real threat of rain. Morale had been raised immensely by the news that today was "bug out" day and we would be heading to brigade base camp—the rear, if there was a rear in this terribly unconventional war. I finished a C-ration breakfast of pecan roll and hot cocoa, then took a short stroll along the perimeter. The men of the artillery and mortar platoons were already dismantling their weaponry and stacking crates of ammo on the helipad, and the medical unit was boxing its gear for transport. The battalion was moving, en masse, and there was excitement in the air.

The movement promised a new beginning, perhaps in an area of operations closer to the base camp in Pleiku or pulling security around some airport. I let my mind wander over these various items on my fantasy menu, then selected an appointment as instructor in orientation camp located near Saigon. I thought my combat experience would qualify me for the position of teaching the FNGs how to survive, and I would be willing to bet that I could hold my own with the other instructors in the bars at night. In my state of near-somnambulation, I stumbled over a piss tube, then caught myself and straightened up quickly, saluted it, snapped my mind back to reality, and continued my tour.

I saw a few soldiers working on their steel pots, replacing the tattered cover with another of camouflaged cloth or, more likely, a sandbag. These covers became a canvas for those with an artistic bent and, more important, a bare wall for grunt graffiti. Soldiers gave vent to their feelings by drawing popular cartoon characters, naked girls, or weapons and writing epithets or slogans. Artistic talent being in short supply, most grunts merely used a pen or magic marker to denote their feelings at the time whether humorous, sacred, altruistic, or profane.

The things I saw ran the gamut from the simple: *Bong the Cong; Cong Killer; PAVN Killer; War is Hell (Heck);* to the religious: *God Bless America;* a drawn cross with *Jesus Died For My Sins* around it; to the geographical: states and/or cities; to favorite sports teams; to the slightly more profound and irreverent: *Yea, though I walk through the valley of death, I will fear no evil, for I am the meanest SOB (MF, Bastard) in the valley; John Wayne Sucks, Ho Chi Sucks, LBJ Sucks;* and *God Isn't Dead, He's Hiding In Canada.*

On my own pot I had attempted a Tropic Lightning patch (a lightning bolt on a palm leaf) and had written: *2nd Platoon Trailblazers.* On the narrow elastic band which circled the pot and held the cover in place I scrawled the date 11/19, then an *M,* for McCown, and an *F,* for Captain Federline, in memoriam. On the back I added a graffito I had seen on a wall on State Street in Madison, Wisconsin: *Lady Bird loves Dean Rusk.*

Once more I brought my wandering mind around to the battles and the men who fought. We had landed here on the edge of this creek seventeen days ago, but it seemed much longer. Certainly, to some it was a lifetime. I thought about those men and wondered if they had known what they were fighting for and did they think it was enough to die for? I wasn't sure that I did. We had come here to seek out and destroy the enemy in his stronghold, and we had done that, but now we were leaving the territory for him to reclaim, it seemed. Mine is not to reason why, but I do reason, and I wonder. I will still follow orders, but not without question. I know that the Army is only able to succeed in battle through rigid discipline and unswerving loyalty to chain of command through almost blind obedience of orders, yet I will demand some validity before I charge after the enemy. I must know why, why, and why.

It took the better part of the day to remove all the heavy weapons. They were lifted by sling and carried away dangling below the choppers. Around the perimeter, troops were tearing down bunkers, lancing the sandbags and dumping the sand into the holes, burning the logs and empty bags and anything else that couldn't be carried out. The choppers began ferrying men to 3 Alpha, where they lined up and boarded another flight of choppers to Pleiku. As my bird landed at Lane, I hopped on and hung my legs over the edge as I had seen other old guys do. As we soared high and away, I looked back at the section of jungle that we had fought so hard to control. I decided that spitting on it would be symbolic of my feelings, but after I let fly the rotor wash was so strong it blew back in my face. Rangel was sitting next to me and a smile creased his dark countenance for the first time I had seen.

"Pete, Vietnam is spitting on you, man."

It was even more symbolic than anything I could have done. I wiped my hand across my cheek, arched my brow, and tried to give him a wry smile.

"Ain't it the truth, Rangel. Story of my life."

I wondered if the North Vietnamese would filter out of the jungle and go through our garbage as the stories said they would. We had stabbed holes in the cans and thrown them in holes or fires, but if they got to them soon enough, they could still salvage most of the contents. I also wondered how many of the enemy were still alive in the hills along the border and who would fight them if they did replenish their ranks and become a threat to the Central Highlands again. Probably the damn Golden Dragons again, but, until then, I'll rest easy in Pleiku for a while.

It had begun to rain as we left Lane and was still coming down when we landed outside the west gate at Camp Enari. As we formed into companies to march into the base, the 4th Infantry band played a few patriotic songs and the Red Cross Doughnut Dollies passed out coffee and treats from the back of a truck. We marched smartly into the camp and down the muddy red clay road to the battalion area, then took a left into what I recognized as Charlie Company compound.

My heart swelled a little and my chest puffed out as the band played *Stars and Stripes Forever* and my step got lighter and much brisker. We were bloodied but unbowed; we had been staggered, but were victorious. Now we were "home" and I turned my thoughts to sleeping on a cot and hot chow, showers and cold beer and sodas, but mostly to the fact that I would be safe. I could walk around the compound without fear of ambush or booby trap or sudden death, and it felt good.

We stood in company formation and listened as the first sergeant praised our actions on the border, informed us that we would maintain proper decorum while in his company area, and would make all company formations. He told us that clean fatigues, underwear, and socks would be available tomorrow morning and that there was plenty of water for shaving and showers.

Then he pointed at an old pop cooler off to the side of the CP filled with beer and turned us over to our respective platoon sergeants. Sergeant Nuckols quickly called his squad leaders together, then ordered them to disperse us to our platoon tents. The squad leaders merely pointed to the tents and dismissed us. As I neared the nearest 2nd Platoon tent, I heard a commotion and a familiar voice yelled out, "All right, you miserable jungle bunny, get your ass in this tent, now!"

Recognizing the voice of one Thomas Maddox, I laughed for the first time in years, it seemed, pushed aside the flap, and stepped inside the dirty tent. I threw my gear and weapon on the first empty bunk and started pumping Maddox's hand with my right while accepting a cool beer with my left. I then slapped Vickers on the back, as his right arm was bandaged and his left hand was occupied with a can of Carling. I was home and it was time to drink beer and trade insults.

"OK you rear-echelon shammers, show some respect for the real combat veterans. The line doggies are back."

We clapped each other on the back till we ached, all the while exchanging insults around the room. Watson was there, along with Fears and Harrell and several new faces. Though I had known these men barely six weeks, I felt a closeness to and a kinship with them that I had not felt before; we had become brothers of the blood and comrades in arms. Part of each of us would live in the others for the rest of our lives, I thought, as I stood in the center of the tent and proposed a toast.

"To those brave men who didn't come back from Dragon Crater, and to those who did, God bless us all."

"Amen, brother. Roll, Tide."

Watson sat down on the bunker next to my gear and asked, "What happened out there, Pete? Did we kick their butt, or did they just retreat and wait for another day?"

"I don't know, Sarge. I do know we had a high body count after the big battle, then Alpha hit some shit when we swept the area a couple days later. But after the second B-52 strike there was nothing but stragglers and dead bodies. If Charlie didn't make it across the border, he's dead. I'd like to think that we hurt that 33rd Regiment badly, thanks to the air and artillery."

"Pete, word is that you did a hell of a job out there."

"Shee-it. In all honesty I laid there behind my little tree and watched the Old Man get it and two medics die trying to reach him. All I could do was fire my weapon and curse the fates."

"I couldn't even fire my fuckin' weapon," Maddox broke in. We all laughed ironically.

"A few other 16s jammed out there, according to the complaints I've heard," Watson said.

"I still wake up sweatin' and screaming. Damn that Mattel toy," Maddox added.

"You know, for a long time out there it was a real cluster-fuck. We could have broken if the NVA had come at us in a wave once more. That Green Beret helped us stay together until

Lieutenant Shipley and his platoon arrived, but he didn't really take over, just made suggestions. In my opinion, that battle could have gone either way. We supposedly won, but all we did was hold them off by continuing to fire until the air and artillery could drive them back to the border. A lot of men, good men, died in the effort. Mac, the Old Man, Machado, Belcher. How's Lieutenant Canale doing?"

"I think he's in Japan, Pete, or maybe the States by now. Head wound like that, not much they can do."

The tent went silent for a long moment, then I spoke softly: "I saw this in a movie once and it fits." I stood up, saluted, and grabbed a cold beer from the tank. "With your permission, Sergeant Watson, I'm going to get very drunk."

The group of us in the tent did, indeed, get very drunk that night in base camp.

The next morning I staggered to company formation with a thick tongue and a pounding head and tried to be attentive as the first sergeant made a few announcements to the troops. "Each platoon send me two men for KP and three for work detail. Try to send me new guys and men who've been in the rear. No passes today, get cleaned up and rested."

I passed on breakfast and staggered back to the tent where I ran into Watson, who put his arm on my shoulder. "Pete, you deserved that drunk last night, but take it easy, man, before you kill yourself."

"Sarge, you're my squad leader, not my mother." He looked a little crestfallen at my rebuff, so I added, "I'll be all right, Sarge, thanks."

"OK, Pete. But, if you ever wanna talk. . . ."

I spent the rest of the day hiding in the tent, cleaning my weapon and gear and writing a few letters. In the afternoon I headed for the water tank, where I washed my entire body for the first time in a month, then shaved and headed to the supply tent for new fatigues. When Maddox came back from work detail we sat on the steps to the tent and spoke quietly about the times we experienced in the jungle.

"I really missed you out there, guy. How's the malaria?"

"No malaria, just a fever. I'll never forget that day—the 19th, Pete. I was so damn frustrated, and scared."

"Same for me. At first I thought we would be overrun and

killed, then it got better, but I couldn't help the Old Man or stop those medics from committing suicide in the name of doing their job. They were extremely brave, braver than I, but also extremely foolish. Yet, I wonder. . . ."

"Don't think about it too much, Pete. It'll eat you up."

"It's already chewing on me pretty good. Let's get some beers, guy."

"Only if you promise not to get totally stoned. Watson is takin' us to Pleiku City tomorrow."

At morning formation Top Sergeant Ellis informed us that we had to be clean enough to pass his inspection before receiving passes for town. I headed for the water tank, where I lined up in front of one of the rough, makeshift benches and shelves and took care of my daily lavatory needs.

I hunted up a pair of clean fatigues from my locker and stood in line at the clerk's office along with Maddox and Vickers. After receiving the valuable piece of paper, we loaded into the back of a deuce-and-a-half (2.5-ton) truck and headed into town.

I surveyed the terrain and the people (LIPs, local indigenous personnel) and wondered how they could carve an existence out of the hard red clay that turned into sticky mud during the monsoon season. The land rolled between mountainous stretches into an undulating plain covered by bushes and small trees and an occasional group of huts. The people grew rice (where they had access to water), root crops (yams or potatoes), corn and fruits. They took their meager wares to market in Pleiku City, picked up a few piastres, bought what they could afford, then trudged back to their hovels. They didn't appear to be in any danger, at least not here in the Central Highlands, yet we had come ten thousand miles to fight for their freedom from communist oppression, had we not?

Pleiku was a disappointment at first glance, and at second glance it wasn't much better. There were a few multistory buildings and Watson said there were some beautiful French colonial mansions on the edge of town, but most of the shops and places of business were small, run-down one- or two-story structures. Where there was curbing, it was broken and in need of repair, but mostly the streets were dirt from side to side. The locals wore a mixture of black pajamas and western wear and there were a few Montagnards walking by themselves dressed in loincloths with a blanket wrapped around. As we passed along, more than once I saw a local drop his trousers and relieve himself along the street, then move along as if nothing were untoward.

Vickers saw me staring at them and reminded me, "Screw it, Pete. It don't mean nothin'. You just learn to ignore it and drive on."

"Yeah, man. I guess we aren't going to advance them into the twentieth century just by being here. They've got to police their own ranks and learn about hygiene. But you'd think they could at least cover it up."

"Hey, flies gotta eat, too, guy."

As the truck pulled to a halt near a tree and in front of some ramshackle shops, I took a closer look at the boxlike structures thrown together by enterprising refugees and displacees from the countryside. It seemed to me that Vietnam was slowly losing its identity as the natives flocked from small villages and farms into cities and campside villages to find a way to separate the rich Yankees from their dollars, or MPC. Our presence had changed their economy, sense of values and way of life. With our dollars we were making their lives easier, but in the process we were destroying their culture.

Unfortunately, in the case of females, the fastest way to make good money was to sell your body. Entire families would encourage and abet the daughter, or sadly, in some cases the mother, into the oldest profession in order to assuage the oldest need—sexual gratification. Here in Pleiku City the girls usually worked in a bar, persuading the lonely GIs to buy them Saigon or Pleiku tea (colored water which was 100 percent profit for the owner), and, of course, they also offered other services.

"OK, GI. You numbah one. I give you numbah one boom-boom, you give me 500 p. for short time. 1,000 p., long time."

If you were interested in something of a different carnal nature, a simple query would bring this reply, "You give me two dollah, I give you chop-chop."

We sauntered down the dirty street like sailors on leave in an old WWII movie and were led into a place that Watson called Mama-san's. I had a measly two dollars in my pocket, and this lack of legal tender in combination with a slight hangover left me strangely uninterested in sexual endeavors, so I sat, suppressing yawns, until Maddox woke me with a whistle.

"Would you look at that! Sergeant Watson, I apologize for even thinking she would be just another bar girl. She's fine."

He drew out the last word with a leer. She was almost as dark as the others, but her eyes were slightly rounder and her lips were less full, but still pouty. Her hair was long and dark, but more brown than black and she stood taller than the others. She obviously was of mixed French-Vietnamese descent and appeared to be the best of both worlds. She had the slender Oriental figure although there was a hint of European fullness in her bosom and hips.

"Pete, Maddox, this is Han Lee. She's part French, part Vietnamese and all woman."

"Indeed, Sarge, indeed. She'll do just fine," I said.

Maddox excused himself to find Vickers in the next room.

"I'm past my PCOD, so I better get the hell outta here before I jump on her. See y'all later."

Watson led us to a table in the back of the room where I saw another Eurasian delight even more beautiful than Han Lee. She had smoldering charcoal-gray eyes and a totally dispassionate manner which ignored my long glances. Watson tried to link us, but it wasn't to be.

"I don't know her real name, but I call her Sue. Sit down, Pete, talk to her."

I sat, but while parts of my body were glowing, my tongue was knotted. She continued to act as if I didn't exist and I felt like maybe I didn't. I heard Han Lee asking a question.

"You Fust-Fohteen like Raht-san?"

"First-Fourteenth, uh, I guess. How'd she know that?"

"You've got the division patch on your sleeve and only three battalions are here in the brigade. Not hard to figure."

"Fust-Fohteen go to field Decembah Seven. You wait-see."

My jaw dropped and I glanced quickly at Watson, whose eyebrows shot up along with his shoulders in a shrug.

"I don't know what the hell she's talking about, man. It's news to me—I couldn't tell her. I didn't know."

"All Fust-Fohteen go back to field Decembah Seven. I know."

"Oh, man, Watson, I can't do this. I can't hang around civilians—bar girls who know more about what we're doing than we do. I'm gonna split, man. Later."

I jumped up and strode back to the bar to find Maddox and Vickers to tell them the strange story of unrequited love and intrigue in the back room. I now needed a stiff drink, but Mamasan's was not the place to get it, so I ordered a 33 and slugged it down. One of the bar girls sat down beside me and ordered a Saigon tea, which she consumed rapidly. I laughed at her and told her I had no money, but she ordered another and brought me another 33. I shrugged and allowed to myself that I was, indeed, still thirsty, so I poured it down my parched throat. She replaced the empty bottle with a full one and continued to consume the colored water. Vickers saw what was going on and warned me, "Pete, she's running a tab on ya. Before you leave, she'll make you pay for the beers and her tea."

"She can't make me pay. I'm broke."

"I warned ya, guy."

Vickers shrugged and walked to another table to talk with Mize while Maddox and I continued to b.s. and suck on 33s. After an hour or so of talk, it was time to look for the truck. As I got up to leave, the girl came up to me with a tab and wanted 500 piastres for my "bill."

"Five hundred p. You pay 500 p."

"No, no. I drank two 33s. You drank the tea, you pay for it, I didn't order it."

"You numbah ten, you sonbitch. You pay 500 p."

I protested loudly, then opened my wallet to show the girl and the bartender I was flat. They shouted and cursed at me in Vietnamese and English while I continued to protest my innocence.

Finally I turned away from their angry, scowling faces and headed outside, shaking my head and fist at them.

"Vick, you were right, man. They tried to convince me that I owed them for the drinks, all right. That really steams me—I've never run away from a bill that I felt that I was responsible for, but that girl ordered those drinks on her own. I might owe for two 33s, but that's all."

"Don't worry about it, Pete. This isn't the first time they've pulled that crap and it won't be the last. If old Mama-san is there the next time we come to town, I'll talk to her and straighten it out. Let's get the truck."

As we rolled along the blacktop road back to Camp Enari, Maddox lay on the truckbed floor and talked.

"I'm so short I could walk under a small dog and scratch his balls, so I'm not exposing myself to any snipers. I'll ride here."

"If we hit a mine, you'll be the first to know about it," Watson pointed out to him, but Maddox smiled and nodded off.

I was pondering the events of the day in my head and was having some trouble reconciling statements of Han Lee.

"Sarge, do you suppose Han Lee has been listening to some REMF clerk shoot his mouth off, trying to be important?"

"I reckon so, Pete. The next time I see her . . . if I see her again, I'll tell her not to pay any attention to those guys. 'Course, she won't listen to me, anyway, I'm just one of her many boyfriends, I guess. I really thought we had something going between us, but. . . ."

"Hell, Sarge. You're goin' home, guy. You'll find some nice California girl back there that's just as good."

"But not as beautiful. She's the best-looking girl I've ever seen in my life."

"Sarge, if you do see her again, try to find out the name of the asshole she heard it from. I'd like to get a piece of that guy, whatever he is, officer, noncom, draftee. I'd like to point out that he could be hanged for shooting his mouth off."

"Remember, Pete, some of these guys back here have a lot of power and know how to fuck you over. They can lose your pay records, your mail, or fuck up your promotion chances. Be careful with them."

"Sure don't seem right to leave it like that, but. . . ."

"Just say fuck it and drive on, guy."

"Fuckin' A, man. Well, fuck it and drive on, then."

We pulled into the company area, reported back to the company clerk, and then headed to the tent. After downing a nondescript Army supper, we moseyed to the entertainment area, an outside movie screen with a few rows of rough wooden benches, and watched a John Wayne movie about war on some island in the Pacific and groaned in unison at the phony heroism and the cheap theatrics. At the end of the movie there was an addendum noting that the movie was made with the cooperation of the Defense Department.

"Whoa, you could knock me over with a feather, Pete. Ol' Duke needs to get a real job, maybe here in 'Nam." Maddox's voice dripped with sarcasm as he spoke.

"It just goes to show ya, man: in war, movies are hell," I replied.

There was no beer available in the company area and no one had any money to send to another area, so we hung around the tent and wrote letters to kill the night.

After the First Shirt took morning roll call and gave us the orders for the day, he produced a slender young man with blond hair and blue eyes and a single bar on his collar and helmet. He introduced the modest youth as Captain Childers, our new commanding officer. Captain Childers, Stephen A., from Alton, Illinois, told us he had graduated from West Point, had been in-country for a few weeks, and was glad to have a chance to command such a well-known company. He said we would be spending about eight to ten days in camp on stand-down while we added replacements and healed wounds. He appeared to be sincere but very green, and I shook a little inside as I thought about our last CO. I didn't want to look at him or get to know him at all, which was probably an irrational feeling, but it was so pervasive I couldn't ignore it.

After the captain finished his remarks, Top Sergeant Ellis reminded us that today was the last working day of the month of November, making it payday, and that we would be lining up by platoon at 1000. After dismissal we walked back to the tent and began cleaning our gear and waiting for mail call and the payroll line. Harrell was cleaning his locker at the end of the tent in anticipation of leaving soon for the World, as we now called the United States. He walked over to my bunk and handed me a metal crest to wear on the front of my baseball cap while in base camp. It was the insignia of the 1st/14th Infantry: a golden dragon on a red background with a blue ribbon furled almost all the way around it. On the blue ribbon, in gold, were the words: *The Right of the Line*—the battalion slogan. I thanked him for the gift and asked him about the slogan's origin.

"The story I heard was General Grant attended a victory parade and ceremony after the Civil War and was asked where the 1st of the 14th should stand. He answered, 'To the right of the line.' This has always been the place of honor in military ceremonies. So wear it with pride, Pete."

I didn't quite understand why I had been singled out for this gift which he had purchased back at division HQ in Hawaii. Harrell was a loner and not at all liked by the men of the platoon, apparently because of his ability to "sham" out of field duty. Perhaps because I had not taken part in the hazings and had not mentioned his weak moments at Dragon Crater, he felt he owed me something. Whatever his reason, I thanked him again and immediately placed it on my cap, put my cap on my head and began a search for a mirror. When I joined the payroll line, the crest drew glances and comments from the men regarding its authenticity as compared to cheap Vietnamese copies.

We managed to procure some American beer and real whiskey for a GI payday party that night and Vickers, Maddox and I drank another night away. Sometime during the early evening a handful of replacements arrived and found bunks on the other end, away from our revelry. The next morning Watson stepped inside the tent to talk with us and yelled: "Jesus Christ, look at all the new meat! Do you guys even shave yet? The first time ol' Charlie pops a cap, these guys are gonna fill their trousers. But I won't be there 'cause my days in the field are over. Done."

He reared back his head and gave a long, loud yell: "Shooooorrrrttt!"

"What about me, Watson?"

"Maddox, you're done, too. We're REMFs for a few weeks, then on to that Freedom Bird."

"Back to the World. Look at the fuckin' new guys. They can't believe it. Hell, guys, in about 350 days you'll be short, too—or dead!"

I had been watching Maddox closely as Watson gave him the news, and it was like a huge weight was lifted from his head and shoulders. He had a smile that creased his angular face from ear to ear and lit up his side of the tent. Even though the celebration reminded me that I still had 306 days to go, I was happy for both of them, but mostly I hoped the tormented Maddox could find peace for his heart and mind. Although I had never broached the subject with him or anyone else, I was certain that he had suffered an emotional breakdown that had caused the fever and gotten him out of the field. He had come under extreme mental duress during the battle of the crater when his weapon jammed, and he had not yet recovered. He'll be all right as soon as he gets home . . . he'll be all right. We'll all be all right, when we get home . . . home.

We took the Pleiku Express back into the city that afternoon and headed for Mama-san's Bar. When I stepped inside I saw again the face of the bar girl who tried to hustle me before. I tried to pay her for the beers I had drank, but the hatred that showed in her face and came through her voice made me change my mind, so I wheeled around and headed for another bar. I found Mize outside and we wandered along the streets like tourists, sidestepping the street urchins who were trying to sell their sisters with their singsong pitches, "Hey, GI, you numbah one, you boom-boom my sister? 500 p. She nice virgin, OK?"

Most of the urchins wore discarded American or Vietnamese military shirts and cutoff trousers, but this particular lad had on an old plaid shirt buttoned to the neck and a baseball cap.

As he made his pitch I saw him eyeing my Timex watch, and his hands were exploring my back pockets for a bulge that might be a wallet. I tried a new line with him.

"No, no boom-boom. Me cherry boy."

"Ah, cherry boy. You want chop-chop? 300 p."

"No chop-chop. No boom-boom. And don't touch me."

I made a motion like I would break his arm, which he understood and told the others, who backed off. Mize and I stepped together into the American Bar, a long, narrow room with an extremely high ceiling from which a very old fan hung suspended. We drank a few 33s then wandered the streets of the city, looking over the various shops and talking about home.

Mize was even more skinny than your average skinny soldier, yet in the field he humped the PRC-25 radio for the platoon leader without any problem. His gawky face and shy grin fronted for a quick mind and pointed wit. He was from Indiana, married, and quick to complain about the slowness of the mail service. He hadn't heard from his wife for almost two weeks and feared the worst. I told him there was probably a pile of letters waiting for him somewhere, but he was not to be consoled. To shut him up I took him back to the American Bar, where I bought him another round of 33s and we sang along to the antique jukebox until it was time to head back.

Watson and Maddox provided the necessary liquid refreshment at the 2nd platoon tent and we serenaded the night away by singing every song we knew and a few we didn't. We made the acquaintance of the FNGs, including Kevin Patterson, Arnold Martinez, Larry Vansworth, Thomas Underhill, Ray LaBarge and Rushinski. We talked a little about their homes and ours, and I began to ache for the sight of the hills of southwestern Wisconsin and my family, an ache that could be soothed only by an overindulgence of alcoholic beverage. It also eased the recurring nightmares of the faces of Captain Federline and the medics with the torn bodies that tortured me day and night, whenever I had time to think. Only the liquor could drown the twisted thoughts. I really didn't know what else to do.

It's a strange war in a miserable and destitute country, I thought, as I ambled awkwardly to the piss tube. We're fighting for these people who are trying to separate us from our money and seem to hate us. The news from home tells of students protesting the war by marching down the streets, chanting, "Hell no, we won't go." Here in Vietnam students are also rioting against their government and, indirectly, against the U.S. and the war. Buddhist priests are immolating themselves to protest their government and the war. Even the fighting men would like to cease hostilities and leave the country.

Now, if that many people are against this war, why are we still here? Hmmm, because we follow orders from our government, where we are represented by legally elected officials in whom we put our faith, and we can't be pushed around by anarchistic protesters. I would rather fight than be aligned with rabble-rousers who protest by day and attend pot parties all night, I think. So, here I am. I believe that my mind is getting more twisted every day. It's getting harder to tell right from wrong and good guys from bad guys from where I stand, which is pretty strange because where I stand is in front of a piss tube.

The next morning Maddox stayed with us and Watson moved into the NCO REMF tent, a sort of halfway house for noncoms on their way into or out of the country located near the clerk's office. After morning formation and breakfast Sergeant Nuckols gathered the platoon together to check the makeup of his squads. Since Fears was on KP, Marvin and Vickers were on sick call, and Maddox was a REMF, I was the only member of what had been the 1st Squad, before our recent battles and DEROS had destroyed the structure, to report.

"Who the hell are you and where's the rest of the squad?"

"PFC Peterson. The rest are dead, wounded, sick or shamming."

"Well, get back there with the 2nd Squad. As soon as we get the replacements lined up and the sick guys back, I'll set up permanent squad rosters. Now, I want you to meet your new platoon leader, Lieutenant Lesko."

Lieutenant Lesko was a short, skinny (what else), bespectacled man who looked like he should be teaching English literature at a small university in Massachusetts. To become a good platoon leader, a green lieutenant had to inspire respect and a little fear. I found it difficult to believe he could inspire any fear, but respect would come from deeds, not stature or carriage. He told us he was glad to be leading us and he was sorry to have missed the battles of the border. I glanced around the compound as he spoke, whispering to no one, but wanting all to hear.

"Don't bullshit us, lieutenant. Just do your job."

He finished his speech and turned us over to Sergeant Nuckols, who dismissed us. The new guys went to the indoctrination school, a few men headed for work detail and Maddox and I returned to the tent once more to kill some time.

"What's the first thing you'll do when you hit Atlanta?" I asked him.

"After saying howdy to my family, I'm going to this café I know. I'm gonna order the biggest steak in the house, well done, with fried onions and hash browns on the side. Ooowee, I can't stand it, Pete, let's go to town."

"Second Platoon gets no passes today. We're out of luck."

"Stick with me and I'll have you in downtown Pleiku before noon today."

We headed for the NCO tent first, where we rousted a sleeping Watson, then Maddox began his spiel. "Remember that night when you put me on point to cross that river when we thought the NVA regiment was waiting?"

"Yeah, yeah. Piece of cake."

I laughed at his characterization of the situation and said, "Piece of shit, guy, was more like it."

"Well, ol' dude, you still owe me big for that and I'm here to collect. Second Platoon is supposed to be in camp today, but we want to go to Pleiku for a steak. Cover for us," Maddox said.

"Shit, guy, what can I do? I can't give passes, only the clerk's office can do that and it has to have the Old Man's signature."

"Cover for us. If anybody asks, we've gone to the laundry. We'll hop on the truck and get off at the laundry outside the gate, then grab a ride into town. Back in two hours, nobody will know."

"OK. But if the MPs grab you, I can't help. You know, I've seen guys risk court-martials for some leg before, but this is the first time I've seen it for a steak. Get some, guys."

We filled a laundry bag with fatigues and rode the Pleiku Express to the laundry, jumped off and waved at the guys going to town. We turned in the clothes, then moved unobtrusively back to the road and jumped on a small, rickety, old Lambretta truck for the ride to Pleiku. After a harrowing ride, we paid the grinning, maniacal driver 100 p., then strode down a street with a raised dirt sidewalk along the sides. Maddox led me to a small shop with a sign on the front that read TAN THANH and smelled of burnt meat and Vietnamese spices. We passed through the small barroom into an even smaller room with a lean-to kitchen attached to the rear. We sat down at a table and relaxed as an elderly Vietnamese man approached.

"Maddox, numbah one fliend. You want food—chop-chop?"

"Yeeh, Minh. Two steaks with fries, and don't say flies, it's fries. There are too damn many flies here, anyway. And two Tiger beers, none of that damn 33."

Among the American troops, 33 had become the favorite Vietnamese beer of most. It had a robust flavor, if you could get past the formaldehyde used as a preservative, which caused an odor and a slightly offensive aftertaste. Maddox preferred Tiger brand, which had a lighter taste and not as much preservative used in its preparation. We sipped the beers slowly as Minh leaned over his grill and cooked the meal. He brought it on a plastic military platter and set it down in front of us, cut it in two pieces and slapped a piece on each of our plates. The steak was huge and the potatoes plentiful. I had to saw for a few minutes to get a piece of the meat, which should have been a tip-off, but I bit into it and tried to chew. It was delicious, but tough as leather and had a strange, exotic, gamy flavor. Maddox grinned at the look of puzzlement that crossed my face.

"Now, you can tell the folks back home that you've eaten water buffalo. And it's damn good, right?"

"It is good, but man, it's tough."

After we finished our pleasant repast, we took our tired jaws to the street to search for a ride back to the camp. We jumped back on another Lambretta, driven by another grinning local, and joined a couple other GIs for the wild ride back. We hopped off at the laundry, grabbed our clothes, still undisturbed in the bag, and headed up to the gate. The MPs looked at the laundry bag and waved us through, but after we had moved about ten feet up the road, one of them spoke to us.

"You know, if you guys weren't from the 1st of the 14th, we'd bust your ass for being AWOL. Don't come down here again without a pass. Got that?"

A couple of smart remarks shot into my mind, such as, How about when we go back to the field through this gate? Do we need a pass then? And, what are you gonna do—send me to 'Nam? But I let them stay there while Maddox answered:

"Roger that, man. We owe you one."

It didn't matter how they knew about our transgression. Because of the reputation of the Golden Dragons, we had been given a break and we were grateful and a little proud. We walked back into the company compound with our heads held high. Top Sergeant Ellis, who was as short as Maddox, stared at us but said nothing and we moseyed to our tent.

We spent the next few days on construction projects and short patrols and an occasional morning inspection while we added more replacements to our depleted ranks. The new men were slowly assimilated into the company, but while we were eager to flesh out the platoons, we were reluctant to head to the field with so many FNGs. As the days started to drag a little because of this drudgery and harassment of our rear-echelon life, I began to believe that the field wasn't so bad after all. I tried to stay busy during the days, and nights were filled with guard duty or drinking.

When I wasn't busy, when I let my guard down, I thought about the battle, the captain and his eyes, and the medics. I could still see the medic with the look of surprise on his face as he was shot and the bone protruding through his forearm as he slumped across the captain's legs . . . I guess I always will.

Sunday, December 4, the company was called to our second formation of the morning in the commons area between the mess hall and the clerk's office at 1100 hours. We were called to attention by the new CO, then given parade rest. There was a line of boots along the edge of the yard with steel pots resting in front of them. A hand-lettered placard rested against each helmet, bearing the name of one of the members of Charlie Company killed in action in the border battles. My eyes passed along the line, reading the names, one by one, until they came to McCown.

I fixed on his name for several seconds, then passed on down to the end where I knew I would find Captain Federline. I again fixed on his name and held it there, trying to communicate with him, or his memory. I gave him a mental salute and hoped he could see this, somehow. The CO introduced Colonel Shanahan, who gave a few perfunctory remarks, then turned it over to the chaplain, who asked God to bless the memory of these brave men. We were called to attention and the bugler blew a stirring rendition of taps. A lump formed in my throat and threatened to burst out of my mouth in a sob and my eyes burned as I listened to the heartrending tones. I felt like this wasn't enough, that a man's life should be worth more than this menial ceremony, but I consoled myself with the knowledge that these men had surely been given decent funerals at home by their loved ones. I returned to the tent and contemplated the vagaries of war and its effect on Man.

On the morning of December 6, 1966, Captain Childers announced that we would be leaving for the field the next morning, just as the harlot, Han Lee, had predicted a week ago. We spent the day readying our gear, cleaning our weapons and replacing ammo and equipment. I had received a small Insta-matic camera from home and I wrapped it in plastic and packed it away in the NVA ammo pouch I had policed up from the battlefield at Dragon Crater. Then I put the pouch on my web belt between my canteens and grenades so I could get a few shots in the field when the action was slow.

Platoon Sergeant Nuckols called a meeting after our evening meal at the mess hall. He managed to mix a little humor with the announcements of squad assignments. The "new meat" had been picked over by the squad leaders and the rest was dispersed according to needs.

"Pete, what squad are you in?"

"First squad."

"Wrong. You're in the weapons squad with Sergeant Wilson. Martinez will be the gunner until Williams comes back and you and Vansworth are assistant gunners. Sawlski will carry the other gun with Scheffel and Chase as assistants."

He went on to name the other squad affiliations while I pondered this particular turn of events. One of the things I had decided to particularly avoid during my tour of duty was the machine-gun crew, but somehow here I was, an assistant gunner. My duties would include humping several hundred rounds of M-60 ammunition and feeding it correctly into the gun when it was being used. The machine gun was a valuable weapon in times of firefights because of its ability to bring accurate and deadly repetitive fire onto the target quickly. As such, it was also a prime target for enemy snipers and sappers, causing life expectancy to hover just above that of an officer in combat situations.

I retreated to the tent and tried to figure out how I could get back into a light weapons squad without humiliating myself or extending my tour, but nothing came to mind. Maddox was still hanging around the tent, so I asked him about it.

"Well, Pete, you'll just have to bide your time and wait for the right opening, then pounce. Let the Sarge know how you feel and do a good job where you are. Be a good soldier and they'll remember it when you ask for something."

"If I live that long."

"Can't look at it that way, ol' dude. The M-60 is a tremendous offensive weapon that can make the difference in many a battle. Remember that, and work hard at making your gun crew the best. You'll be all right. I've got confidence in you."

"I wish I felt that way, guy. I've got no desire to be on the gun crew at all."

I thought about his advice as I tried to sleep later that night. I wondered what we were heading into, where we were going, what was the situation and why didn't they tell us these things. I finally fell asleep and dreamed once more of a terrible battle with enemy bullets whizzing by my head, pursuing me as I cowered behind a tree. I saw the captain fall once more and look into my eyes, pleading for help while I remained unable to reach him. I woke up sweating, moaning and felt tremendously exhausted. I felt like I was losing this battle and I didn't know what to do about it. I was extremely frustrated, my mind was getting frayed in the process and I didn't know how long this could go on without losing my sanity. I lay awake on my bunk and waited for the new day with trepidation.

12

I reported to Sergeant Wilson, who directed me to the tent where Chase and Alabama had been staying. Once there, I was laden with 300 rounds of 7.62mm ammunition in belts of 100, which I placed around my neck and under one arm or the other. I was advised to get rid of some of my 5.56mm ammo since I would be feeding the gun during any action, but I had only to think a few seconds to realize that I should carry all that I could manage—remember Alpha Company and learn from it. I piled all my gear outside and ate a short breakfast, then picked up five C-rat meals from a table outside the supply tent and found room for a few cans in my pack. I put a few more cans in a sock and hung it from my web harness, from where it dangled down over the pack. I was ready for the field, but it was the heaviest load I had ever humped.

I said my good-byes to Maddox and Watson, who said they would both be here at Christmas when we were due to come back in, then we marched loosely from the compound to the chopper pads just outside the west gate. As the chopper lifted off, I took a long glance back at the camp and realized that the time had gone too slowly there and that the field was, indeed, the place to be for the next 300 days and nights. Stay busy and the time will go by much faster. The quicker the time goes, the sooner I can go home, where everything will be all right.

It was a leisurely trip to our LZ, the Punch Bowl, where we had spent a few days back in October, an eternity ago. We off-loaded and set up in a loose perimeter until the entire company was on the ground. The former artillery firebase was deserted now, with only a few scattered sandbags where there had been fortified bunkers and gun placements. We kicked out to the north by east, up the steep hill mass past the fading Tropic Lightning logo and along the high ground.

As we stepped into the bushes, my jungle sense returned immediately. I lowered my voice, checked my gear to make sure all my weaponry was accessible and quiet, then placed my finger along, but not around, the trigger of my M-16 with my thumb on the selector lever, ready to flip it to semi or auto (rock and roll). Yeah, Charlie, I'm back.

There was no shortness of confidence among the veterans of the border wars as we returned to the jungle with our new men and old memories. While I would miss Watson and Maddox and others who were dead or wounded, I knew that my pride and the sureness of my abilities would overcome my personal fears and depression. While I did not desire combat duty, it seemed to be my karma.

Martinez, a short, wiry Hispanic-American from Orange, California, lifted the heavy machine gun to his shoulder and we fell into our spot in the column. He stumbled several times as we climbed the hill, then the going got easier on top and we humped several klicks on the hill mass before breaking for noon chow. As I heated my ham and lima beans, Martinez produced a bottle of hot sauce and offered me some.

"Here, Pete, try a shot of this on that crap."

"You're humping hot sauce. Not bad for a new guy."

"You know, I could get my mom to send me some tortillas and we could use some of these Cs to make tacos. Sound good?"

"Sounds damn good, guy. What else do we need?"

"Well, we can't get fresh vegetables, so we could save up our cans of barbecued beef, beans and tins of cheese and I'll get the shells. We'll go from there."

"Think it will make that gun any lighter?"

"Jeez, I hope so. That sucker weighs a ton."

We headed down into a valley after chow, then climbed up another mountain on the other side. About halfway up the steep slope, Martinez slipped and fell hard on his side. "Oh, shit, man. Can you take the gun for a while, Pete? My shoulder is killing me."

"I was wondering how long it would take you to ask for help. You take this belt of ammo so I've got a free shoulder to hold it. Remember, if we hit anything, I'll put the gun down and get away 'cause you're the gunner."

I humped the gun up the hill mass and a few hundred meters along the rolling high ground before Martinez said he could take it back. The damn thing did weigh a ton and I could still feel it in my shoulder a long time after returning it to Martinez. At 1730 we closed on a rounded hilltop for the night and set up in a perimeter. As he put the gun down, Martinez let out an audible sigh that was almost a groan. After a few minutes' rest, we dug a huge foxhole and put up a poncho hooch.

I showed the two new guys how to set out trip flares and a claymore while my mind flashed back to McCown and his instructions. It still hurt a lot to think about him, so I borrowed a machete and began cutting brush to extend our fields of fire while Martinez and Vansworth cleaned the M-60. Through all this, our squad leader spent his time talking with Sergeant Nuckols. They had served together on a previous tour of the country as door gunners on choppers and Wilson was apparently trying to make the best of this connection. It was only one day, but already I didn't like him. It was only one day, but already I liked Martinez and Vansworth and knew we'd get along. As rain began to fall, we sat in our hooch and cooked our supper in relative silence caused by our extreme fatigue from climbing up and down steep mountains while laden with the heavy gun and extra ammo. When guard duty was over, sleep came easily in the cold, damp mountain air.

After shaking off the stiffness, the next day we continued along the mountain range for two hours, then descended the slippery slopes in a snakelike fashion. Martinez fell several times, but emerged from each unhurt and cursing like a veteran trooper. Upon reaching the valley floor, we broke for noon chow as the sun came through the clouds. I threw off my gear and removed my shirt, soaked with perspiration, and laid it across a bush to dry in the sun. Martinez and Vansworth followed my example, then I opened a can of crackers and a tin of peanut butter and nibbled away. Martinez began wiping down the gun while Vansworth leaned against a tree and asked, "What do you think about our squad leader, Pete?"

"He sure doesn't waste any time with the squad. I see him over there suckin' up to Nuckols again. I think he's looking for a rear-echelon job and I hope he gets it. Chase would make a good squad leader."

"What was it like on the border? They told us at the school that you guys did a hell of a job out there."

I hesitated for a long minute before answering, then tried to make my mind a blank and just let the words roll. "It was a bitch. I truly believed that the battle could have gone either way early on. We held because we had fire discipline and air and artillery power to wear down their ranks. We lost most of our command structure in the field and had a lot of jammed 16s, but we held and they broke." I paused for a few seconds and stared at the sky, then said, "HQ says we won a tremendous victory, but I say we held on."

"Were you scared during the fight? I mean, what was it really like?"

"Was I scared? Who, me? Fuckin' A, I was scared. I can't really tell you what it was like, you'll have to learn for yourselves. Trust your instincts and be alert. Keep your head down, your eyes open and your mouth shut and you might just make it. That's the advice I got. Now you got it."

We stayed on the valley floor most of the afternoon, following a wide trail in the warm sunshine. We had seen no sign of the enemy during our first two days, so morale was high and the men were exchanging insults and jokes as we moved along. We returned to the high ground and set up for the night at 1700. After picking off the leeches and digging a foxhole, we set up our watch rotation and I slept heavily, without dreaming, through the cold, peaceful night.

Charlie Company continued its mountain odyssey the next few days—up, down and, all too often, along the sides of the steep slopes. Alabama Williams rejoined the gun crew and he and Martinez alternated carrying the M-60 with Vansworth joining the other crew. I felt this would help me in my escape from the weapons squad; they already had enough men and I wouldn't be missed. I filed my arguments away and continued to follow Maddox's advice to be a good soldier and wait for my chance. Each night we were exhausted and eager to stop, but each morning we awoke a little less fatigued as our bodies quickly became accustomed to the grind. We took our resupply drops on the tops of the mountain, usually early in the morning, then headed out again. After seven days we had seen no enemy and were following cold trails.

On December 15 we had orders to meet the resupply chopper at 1700 at an LZ nearly twenty klicks from where we began the day. We humped along the hill mass, down into valleys, across streams and back to the top of another low mountain range with only a short stop at noon. When we finally staggered into the prearranged clearing at 1650, word came down from the CP and passed through the ranks, "Good job, Charlie Company. Hot chow is on the way."

It had occurred to me during these daily movements that this was a training exercise for all the new guys, a "shakedown cruise" with no enemy, but lots of rugged terrain to get us into shape and restore confidence in ourselves and one another. If a small pocket of resistance was met, even better. I couldn't figure out how they arranged to have the enemy cooperate, but I liked the idea. After the hot supper, I talked with Fred Scheffel from the other gun crew as we waited to go on ambush-OP for the night.

"Scheffel, aren't you DEROSing soon? What the hell are you doing out here in the field?"

"My idea, Pete. I hate it back there in the rear. When I get back to the World, I'm going to ask for duty in Germany. I was born there and I want to see what their life is like now. Maybe I'll live there someday."

He had a throaty voice, like a man who had smoked too many cigarettes, which he had, and a hearty, raspy laugh. Once we got out on OP, we tried to whisper to one another, but the fatigue and the light air made us slightly giddy and we began giggling and couldn't stop. The radio hissed, "Oscar Papa, we hear laughter out there. What the hell's goin' on, over?"

"Is it VC laughter or friendly laughter, over."

"Charlie Oscar Papa, shut down the noise. Stop it, over."

Scheffel put on his stern face and answered, "Roger. We'll stop it if it comes this way. Out."

We then dissolved in gales of suppressed laughter, until Scheffel started coughing and rolled on the ground. Chase told us to stop it, but it was out of control for a few minutes, until I moved to the other end of the line ambush. We were acting like schoolchildren, but were helpless to do anything about it. After our watch was over, I tried to rest, but the adrenaline was still flowing, so I looked at the stars and made my mind a blank.

We continued along the high ground all the next day, following a wide, well-used trail in the thin air. In the afternoon, we stopped along a crest to watch an air strike on a mountain range across the valley. The sleek jets swooped down like graceful diving birds delivering their cargo of death and destruction. We were running short of water, so I borrowed a machete from Mize, who humped everything, and whacked into a good-sized bamboo tree. The liquid came coursing out, cool and not totally unpleasant to the taste. The word came down to continue the move, so I shrugged into my gear and we started our descent to the valley below.

We stayed in the valley that night, not far from a stream where we washed ourselves and filled all our canteens. I made sure we dug our hole deeper and extended our fields of fire even farther because we had given up the high ground. Alabama and I cut a couple of large branches to form a parapet while Martinez and Wilson put up a hooch, which was the first work the squad leader had done on a gun position since we began the mission. It was about fifteen degrees warmer on the valley floor, so we were able to spend the night in comparative comfort.

We continued to move along the valley floor the next day, looking for the elusive enemy, feeling secure in the knowledge that he probably wasn't in this area. During one of our many stops, I took a quick look at Sergeant Nuckols' map and noted the red dots marked in our AO (area of operations). I tried to figure out where we were, then extrapolate where we were going and where we had been. To my eye, it looked like a giant circle, but I didn't really care. The morale of the company had raised immensely and we were working together as a unit.

After our noon chow, we moved another two klicks and came upon a monastery with a well-tended garden and lawn with paths. Because Buddhists hated the Catholic-dominated Saigon government, some of them had aided the Viet Cong by hiding weapons and supplies for them in their monasteries. Charlie Company pulled into a loose perimeter while the CO and the platoon leaders searched the premises guided by the monks.

The gun crew covered the trail as usual and shot the bull.

"I heard these monks hide weapons for the VC, Pete."

"The Thieus are Catholic and there's no love lost between the Catholics and the Buddhists, Alabama, so maybe some of them are VC sympathizers, but these ol' dudes seem peaceful."

"Didn't some of these here Buddhists set themselves on fire down in Saigon? Seems like a tough way to prove a point."

"The Buddhists that immolated themselves thought it was the only way to present their argument—to protest the mistreatment of Buddhists by the Saigon government. I guess more wars are fought over religious differences than over any other cause."

"Where the hell do we fit in all this, Pete?"

"Which story do you want, man? The domino theory states that if Vietnam falls, the rest of Southeast Asia will follow, then the Philippines, then California. Martinez would wake up some morning and find the Communists running Disneyland."

Chase had been listening in and decided to interject, over a laugh. "Fuck me, Pete. I'll never smile again."

"There's also the belief that the U.S. is the policeman of the world, the protector of peace-loving people, like these in South Vietnam. The military establishment, of course, loves that one. Isn't that amazing?"

"Well, we should be able to stop Communism anywhere, I believe. Anyplace in the world," Alabama stated fervently.

"Why can't the South Vietnamese fight their own battles, protect their own homes?" Chase had jumped totally into the conversation now and had posed the question of the day, and year. I struggled to find an answer; my mind was troubled by the assumed moral rightness of my country's positions that had been ingrained in me since childhood and the obvious lack of national pride in the soldiers and civilians we had encountered.

"Well, we've seen them fight, and if we weren't here, this country would fall. The ARVNs and the CIDG don't fight very well. But I wonder myself, now that I'm here, if the South Vietnamese really care."

"Somebody must think Vietnam is a valuable country, Pete. The U.S. is spending a lot of money and spilling a lot of blood to keep it going. I wonder if there's some oil or minerals in the ground that we have our eyes on."

"Could be, I haven't got all the kinks worked out in my personal theory yet, but I believe that our leaders are concerned about all that we've talked about and they've made the decision to protect South Vietnam. I've always believed that our leaders are doing the right thing for our country and I still do. I'll do my duty, but. . . ."

"But, this war is different, right, man?"

"Chase, this war is strange, not like we saw in the movies. Nobody dies right, and the bad guys don't stand and fight and always lose."

A yell came down the trail from our squad leader: "Saddle up, gun crew, we're moving out!"

The search had turned up nothing, so the company moved away from the monastery and to the top of a small mountain where we set up our perimeter. That night as I sat on watch with a poncho liner over my shoulders, I thought about our conversation. Why was our war so different? I grew up with movies that glamorized war and the good warriors. Our side always won and the heroes seldom died or were injured seriously. Everything was so neat, so black-and-white (even when it was in Technicolor), the big guy was the hero and the guy with the moustache or the Oriental with big teeth was the villain. He had to be defeated to preserve the future of the free world. No sacrifice was too great and we would be victorious because we were morally right and better looking.

We had been raised on the presumption of American rightness and the belief that using might to preserve that rightness was both necessary and correct. So, to prevent the advance of Communism throughout Southeast Asia and God knows where else, and to preserve the American moral rightness, was it not our manifest destiny to provide less fortunate countries with financial aid, arms and young men, because it was the right thing to do?

But this war was *not* like the movies, TV or history books. Our war had no front lines, we did not know who among the local citizenry was a farmer, who was a guerrilla. Except for the Yankee dollar, the Vietnamese showed latent hostility to or, at best, grudging acceptance of the American presence, and we didn't know why.

Individual and collective responses to the first taste of combat have been well chronicled in the past by some of the finest authors—Hemingway, Crane, et al., but there is no adequate preparation for the actual carnage and destruction that one is exposed to and becomes a part of. In this respect, our war was like so many others, but where was the moral certainty that provided the fighting men of other wars their desire, their strength, their righteous vigor? The GIs of WWII seemed to be possessed with an assurance, a conviction that kept their morale high, their minds alert and their bodies moving. Part of this perception could be attributed to movie portrayals, but conversations with veterans of the "Big War" also revealed these characteristics.

This appeared to be the difference between wars and those who fought them. The only episode of morale boosting at our level came back at camp when the band played to welcome us home and later when the first sergeant praised our actions in combat. I took a look at my watch in the moonlight and realized it was time to wake up Martinez. Maddox was right—I was thinking too much; my head hurt from all these contemplations.

We stayed on the high ground all the next day, following the trail and relaxing in the cool air. In the afternoon, we came to a fork in the trail where the company split up; 2nd Platoon stayed on the high ground while the rest of the 1st and 3rd went with the CO down the trail to the valley. It was presumed that the trail we followed would bring us back to the valley, but we came to a halt at a sheer cliff at about 1800. Rather than back-track to the fork, the 2nd Platoon was ordered to stop on the hill with our backs to the cliff.

Because this was the highest mountain in the area, the air was considerably colder and the wind whistled through the trees, brush and our hooches. We had attached the poncho halves to trees to keep them anchored, then huddled together inside for warmth while one man kept watch. Again, the night was peaceful and the cold, light air made my sleep dreamless.

We came down off the mountain and joined the company in the valley for resupply and morning briefings. We were ready for another day of moving and climbing, and the battalion HQ didn't disappoint us. Word came down the line that Bravo Company had lost a man to sniper fire yesterday in the valley. Since we hadn't seen any trace of the enemy, I decided to ignore the news until it was official, but I checked my rifle and ammo just in case. We humped along the sides of mountains most of the day, then climbed a particularly steep mountain at 1600. On the way up, Sergeant Leslie passed out and had to be carried to the top, where a medevac chopper dropped a line and hoisted him out. The company continued along the ridge, then climbed another crest and settled into a high plateau for the night.

As we were finding our positions and shucking our gear, from somewhere on the perimeter a voice sang out "Climb Every Mountain." The words of the popular song brought a laugh from the totally exhausted troops. It seemed to us that, indeed, we had climbed every mountain in the Annam Range, but there would certainly be more tomorrow. After the chop-pers brought in roast beef sandwiches and cold juice, we settled in for another quiet night in the mountains.

We stayed in the natural LZ most of the next day, moving only a short distance along the high ground to another plateau, then dug in again. Alabama and I quickly put up a hooch, then we relaxed and told stories until dark. I took the early watch, moved to the side of the hole and leaned against a large tree. I was trying to make my mind blank, to remain alert while float-ing along, when I heard a distinct "Fuck you!" from the woods directly in front of my hole.

I snapped my head to attention and wondered if the enemy was taunting me or if some GI had sneaked to the front of my position. I listened breathlessly and heard, once more, "Fuck you!"

By now I was getting a little exasperated, then I heard someone come up behind me and I recognized Scheffel's laugh. "What the hell is coming off, Fred?"

"Pete, you just got the official welcome to Vietnam. That was the famous fuck you lizard. Some guys say it's a cuckoo bird, some say it's a monkey, but it's a gecko lizard, and he just gave you the word."

"Story of my life. 'Fuck me' is right. The folks of my hometown would never believe what I've been through over here."

"There's no way the people back home can understand what's happening over here, Pete. They see a little on TV or in the newspapers, but that's just the highlights, not the real stuff."

"How're you holding up under all this humpin'?"

"I don't care if we hump a hundred klicks as long we don't see any action. I'm down to twenty days and a wake-up. See you in the morning."

We finally descended into the valley the next day and walked along barren rice paddies and cornfields, meeting no resistance—just a walk in the sun. After noon break, we continued in an eastward direction with the 2nd Platoon leading the way. The point squad came upon a small secluded village with neat gardens and a beautiful, clear spring. It was like an oasis. Since we were in need of fresh water, we decided to stop, search the area and fill all canteens. After the gun crew had taken a secure position, I took all the empty canteens, looped them over a stick and headed for the water. As I dipped them in the cool, clear water, I glanced around at the ville and spoke with Vickers.

"This is like Shangri-la compared to other villes."

"Yeah, look at their irrigated garden—fresh vegetables."

Chase came over and pointed out a villager working. "Look at that ol' dude. He's got a real complexion problem. Are you thinking what I'm thinking, Pete?"

"Looks like leprosy. Never seen it before, but that's what it should look like."

As the word got around, some of the troops began to empty their canteens and spit out the water in their mouth as they retreated. From my limited knowledge, I surmised that it was not the communicable type of the disease or they would have been more isolated. The medic agreed as we took a long drink and tried to point this out to the troops.

"No sweat, guys. If the disease was infectious, the colony would be on an island somewhere. Drink up."

I scooped my canteen into the cool water and drank once more, but the average GI would rather believe an unsubstantiated rumor over the apparent truth, so most of them refused to fill up. Those of us who weren't so restricted by popular beliefs strolled through the colony with the captain on an inspection tour. The residents, all males, were happy to have visitors and gave us a quick tour of their gardens, which were flourishing and weedless. The lepers possessed a self-reliance and pride in their accomplishments that was not evident in other villages. After a brief rest, we bade them farewell and moved forward.

We made a night defensive position on a small knoll in the valley and dug in. As we put up our hooch, we talked. "Pete, what're you gonna do when you get home?"

"That's a long time from now, Alabama. I guess I'd drink some good Wisconsin beer and eat some of my mother's cooking. Her Sunday meals—chicken and noodles with peach pie for dessert are the best food I've ever tasted. I can almost smell them now."

"Naw, that's Martinez' feet. He's got his boots off."

"You're just jealous, man. Hey, how did Vickers get the wound in his arm?" Martinez was lying beside the hooch with his feet up on a limb.

"Shotgun!"

"Yo, Pete! Whaddya need?"

"New guy wants a war story. Tell him about your wound."

Vickers walked over to our position and sat down. "Not much to tell, guy. We moved out of Dragon Crater to help out Bravo and Recon and tried to flank Charlie, but he was waiting. He hit us on our right and shot us all to hell. We hit the dirt and were pinned down by automatic fire and grenades. I took some shrapnel in the wrist, but it didn't hurt much. Lieutenant Canale tried to lead a charge, but he took one step and was shot in the head. Belcher, Machado and Mac—all dead. Hell of a day, right, Pete?"

Vickers had spit the words out almost mechanically, not unlike gunfire. While it had obviously been painful for him to talk, he looked more peaceful after finishing. The light was dying and I was feeling tired and listless in the night air, but I felt he needed an answer.

"Hell of a day. I'll never forget those days on the border. I know you new guys are anxious for some action to prove yourselves, but trust me, you don't want that kind of shit, for lack of a better word. Now, I'm goin' on first watch."

After my watch I fell into a deep slumber and dreamed the enemy was coming at me, shouting and shooting. I fired and fired; even though I could see the bullets hitting them, they kept on coming, but they were shooting at the man next to me. He fell, and looked at me and his eyes burned into me.

"Pete, wake up. You're moaning and talking." Alabama was speaking as he shook my shoulder.

"What did I say?"

"Nothin' much. Just mumblin'. Go back to sleep and dream about boom-boom or home."

I tried, but I wondered what I was trying to say—I'm trying to help? I lay awake until my next watch, then slept fitfully, but dreamlessly till dawn. Dawn was becoming my salvation, my reprieve from further nightmares and punishment. It was not only easier to see the enemy in daylight, it was easier to banish ghosts. My life had come to this.

The next day we climbed up a small range after receiving resupply, then eased along the ridge in the afternoon. There was an electricity in the air as we anticipated the news that we would be going in for Christmas. Tomorrow would be the 23rd, surely we would go in tomorrow. The lack of a visible enemy and the nearness of the holiday had brought out the little boy in us on top of that peaceful mountain in South Vietnam.

As we finished our breakfast the next morning, word came down that we would be humping down off the mountain and about six klicks across the valley to a road. There, trucks would pick us up for the trip back to base camp for the three-day Christmas truce. We immediately began to lighten our loads by poking holes in unwanted C rations and burying them. We would hump to the trucks with a light load and a light heart.

Base camp was undergoing a few changes, I noticed, as we pulled into the company compound. The rear-echelon sham-mers had been constructing some wooden barracks and the perimeter was being adjusted a little to allow for new trenching and bunkers. The present trenches were populated by rats who were beginning to overrun the troops at night, so the troops were attempting to kill and bury them. Alabama allowed, "Maybe they oughta leave the rats alone and bury some of these rear-echelon assholes."

We jumped off the trucks and fell into a company formation, got a quick welcome and were dismissed for the day. I headed for the 2nd Platoon tent where Maddox was waiting with a half-barrel filled with cold water and cans of beer. I wrung his hand and then poked a hole in a cold can of Strohs and ex-changed a few verbal jabs with him. We had received our let-ters somewhat regularly in the field, but all packages and magazines were held by the clerk until we came back.

Now, the mail call consisted of a huge bag of Christmas packages and goodies. We opened the well-packed containers and sampled the home goodies, eschewing the usual Army sup-per. The cookies, cakes and canned goods were passed around for everyone to taste and wash down with 3.2 beer. In the safety and luxury of base camp, it was time to unwind, relax and en-joy a few of the comforts of life in the rear. But, at least for me, it was not a time to forget. That night, I drank until I could feel fatigue and darkness closing in, then succumbed to it.

13

First Sergeant Scott Wolfe, a replacement for our present top kick, Sergeant Ellis, who was preparing to DEROS, walked out of the company HQ, called the company to order and began to speak in a voice that you could plainly hear if you were in-country and suffered no great afflictions of the ear.

"I understand you men did another fine job in the field. I commend you for that. Now that you're back in the company, I expect to see the same cooperation you gave your officers and noncoms out there. Back here, I'm God. I expect you to follow all my orders to the letter. If you cross me, I'll come after you. I may not be able to whip every swingin' dick in the company, but I'll damn sure get my sandwich in. Now, this morning, there will be cleaning solvent and kerosene available at the supply tent. Clean *all* of your weapons and replace all damaged gear. This afternoon, there'll be organized sports and a special supper in the evening. Platoon sergeants, take charge of your men."

I hadn't really planned on risking my paycheck or my health by getting into trouble with any of the cadre, but I guess a new First Shirt feels he has to make his presence known and be ready for anything. I suppose that's how the old Army did things, but, hey Sarge, we're McNamara's whiz kids. We don't need to fight each other anymore. It's almost 1967 and this is our generation's war, such as it is.

We had stored the M-60s in a large waterproof box with a hinged lid just outside the gun squad's tent. We got them out and gave them a thorough cleaning, wiped off all the belts of ammo, then turned to our M-16s. After another forgettable noon meal, we lined up for platoon competition in volleyball, basketball and football, with the 2nd Platoon taking first place in total points to win two cases of beer. We retired, with prizes in hand, to the platoon tent and relaxed with a few brews until word came down through the person of Chase, who burst into the tent and began filling us in.

"Here's the poop. New Top Sergeant Wolfe is preparing a pizza supper for the entire company. Afterwards, in the mess hall, there'll be a party. Each platoon will put on a skit of some kind, so let's figure out what we'll do, guys."

We spent the next two hours trying to line up volunteers for a skit, but all we could muster was Mize, Alabama, Chase, Vickers and me. As we continued to drink beer and work on it, the whole idea began to sound ridiculous. We finally decided that if we were still close to sober at the time, we would ad lib something about a TV newscaster interviewing troops as they got ready for an OP. We lined up for supper and watched 1st Sergeant Wolfe cooking and cutting some genuine pizza. We were each doled out two slices and took it with our beer to a table. It was damn good, which set us to wondering how he could do that well, considering the limitations on supplies in a combat zone. Of course, ours is not to wonder why, or how, but then we had little else with which to occupy our minds.

At the party, all the troops were in a festive mood, so we threw caution and stage fright to the winds and stepped in front of the company with our skit. Chase acted as the newscaster with a broom handle for a mike. He asked Mize, a typical trooper playing a typical trooper: "Trooper, are you ready for OP?"

Mize, who had been hesitant about performing in front of a crowd, was now quite drunk and not shy at all. He bellowed out an answer that could be heard down in the trenches: "Am I ready, or am I ready?"

To lampoon a new regulation requiring all troops to carry a mosquito net at all times, we had covered ourselves with nets and wrapped them around our weapons. I had armed myself with several containers of mosquito repellent and no rifle, so Chase asked me, "Troop, where's your weapon?"

"Sir, there's a fine if you're caught without mosquito spray, but no fine for not carrying a weapon. So when it's time for OP duty, I say—let us spray."

Chase then turned to Alabama. "What do you do on OP, son?"

Alabama, who was also feeling no pain, was carrying a decrepit old guitar. To answer the question, he strummed it a little and tried to sing: "I keep my eyes wide open all the time."

The crowd of entertainment-hungry troops laughed and cheered, spurring Alabama on to greater heights. He stopped singing, stared at the guitar as if it offended him, then began smashing it on the floor. He jumped on it several times to complete the demolition as the crowd roared their approval. I couldn't be sure if he was caught up in the frenzy of the moment and having fun, or if something had snapped, unleashing pent-up frustrations in a near-maniacal fashion with the company joining in vicariously. Whatever it was, we all felt better after his performance.

After the skits, the Old Man said a few words, then led us in some hymns and Christmas carols. He tried to wind up with "Silent Night," but someone started to sing the refrain from a popular country song and we all joined to give a particularly heartfelt rendition of "I Wanna Go Home."

I had heard it sung better, but never more emphatically than the version of the troops of Charlie Company on Christmas Eve in the Central Highland, South Vietnam, at least 10,000 miles from home.

After the party, a handful of us began touring the compound singing carols. We received a few laughs, no compliments and several requests—mostly to shut up. Captain Childers ordered us back to our tent, then walked with us and sat down for a few songs and beers. He preferred Army marching songs ("I've Got Sixpence"; "Caissons Go Rolling Along") and tried to teach us the words, but we were beyond learning. I wanted to like him; he was friendly and sincere with the professional edge of a career-oriented officer. I looked at his face, then caught myself staring into his eyes and dark memories came welling up.

I moved away and found myself another beer as he bade us goodnight and advised us to keep the noise down and get some sleep. We then tried to close out the festivities with the national anthem, but we began to receive legitimate death threats from the surrounding tents, so Vickers led us in a closing song, the unofficial Army hymn.

"Hymn, hymn. Fuck hymn."

We then slapped high fives all around, clapped each other on the back for a job well done and staggered into our bunks. It was, indeed, a Christmas Eve well spent and certainly one to remember.

The sun rose and shone brightly on Christmas morn, 1966, in the Central Highlands, warming the air and the heart. I awoke slowly, groping about with one hand until I found a can of Coke, which I downed in two gulps. I then worked my way to the water tank and put my head under the spigot and let the refreshing water pour over my pounding head for a long minute. The cool water helped, so I brushed my teeth and scraped a few whiskers off the face of the morose stranger that appeared without invitation in the rusted steel mirror.

After a short breakfast, I retreated to my bunk and reread some old letters while trying to hold my throbbing head still. Since there was no morning formation, I took a much-needed nap until Vickers woke me at noon and informed me that there was a turkey dinner at the mess hall. I managed to choke down a healthy portion, then the first sergeant hosted a party for some orphans from a nearby mission, complete with Santa, a concept of which they had no grasp, and presents, one of which they did.

That night, Martinez was wiping down the .45 pistol that he and Alabama took turns wearing when the other carried the machine gun. He twirled the pistol on his finger, cowboy style, then aimed it at the floor and pulled the trigger. A terrific explosion resulted sending me and the other old guys to the floor while the new guys looked around, dazed. Martinez quickly checked the chamber to make sure no more rounds remained, then holstered the weapon and handed it back to Alabama with a flourish.

"There you go, Alabama. Works real good. Now, did you want me to test-fire the M-60 while I'm at it?"

"Fuckin' new guy. You fucked up and coulda killed somebody." Alabama was trying to be stern, but a grin was working the corners of his mouth.

"You got something against floors, Martinez? The management here at Holiday Inn West will be highly pissed," I added.

"Sorry guys, I fucked up. That's a lick on me."

"Reminds me of a time back home in Alexander City. . . ." Alabama started, then I cut in: "Here's a dime, big guy. Call somebody who gives a damn."

"If you know how to write, get some paper and a pen, Alabama. Write somebody who gives a shit," Vickers quickly put in.

"You guys are all same-same *dinky-dau*. I'm gettin' some shuteye. Gotta hump that damn gun tomorrow." Williams crawled into his bunk as Fortunato from the clerk's office came in.

"What the hell's going on here, men? Top wants to know who fired at what."

"Nothing serious, man. There's a tunnel under our tent where VC come out every night and kill three or four dozen of us. Martinez saw them open up the lid and shot twelve of them with one round."

Fortunato started laughing at Martinez' and my story, then said, "I'll tell Top it was just another new guy fucking up. Got any beer?"

"Negative. We sucked it all up yesterday. Oh well, as Scarlet said, 'Tomorrow is another day.' "

"Say hi to the First Shirt for us." I waved at him as he headed out the doorless doorway still talking to nobody in particular.

"Don't let the new guy come near me. I'm at nine days— shoorrtt!" His famous cry of the short-timer's bird echoed throughout the compound, then silence fell.

"See you guys tomorrow, if Martinez doesn't kill me tonight," Vickers cracked.

"Amen, brother. Buenas nockers. See y'all mañana."

"Much grass, redneck. See you in church, guys."

I was really beginning to like these guys and hoped that Martinez wouldn't kill me until we got to know each other some more. I filed away into my little notebook of life that Christmas ended, not with a whimper, but with a single bang at base camp in Pleiku.

It was more of a lighthearted company that headed off to war on December 26. We knew from the beginning that we were only going to be out for five days, until the New Year two-day truce starting on the 31st, so we joked and insulted as we loaded on the choppers for the short ride to the LZ. After jumping out into a dry rice paddy, we formed up and moved out to the east and crossed a huge empty valley, then climbed to the top of a low mountain range. My legs felt good this time out and fatigue didn't hit until we stopped moving for the day. We dug in and did our usual night duties, then I warmed up some beans and waited for my turn at watch.

I thought about Maddox and how he had felt out of the circle this time back at base camp. Well, hell, he was going home—couldn't feel too sorry for him. I hope he's still there on the 31st. We'll have a proper farewell. I slept well in the mountain air once more, dreaming only of girls and cows, for some damn reason. Must be a correlation there, somewhere.

We headed along the crest of the hill range throughout the next morning, then started down a grassy slope. The elephant grass was so high the men kept losing track of each other, so we held up every few minutes to allow any stragglers to catch up. The valley floor was brushy and extremely thick until we came to a huge clearing where everything was brown and dead. There were dead mice and other small creatures lying in the dried-up leaves and weeds, the brush was dying and the trees looked like they might be. I took a look around and spoke to Sergeant Bennett, now leader of the 1st Squad and an acknowledged flake.

"This must be that spray they talked about back at Fort Polk. That's some bad stuff, dude. They say it kills everything."

"They oughta spray this stuff all over, then ol' Charlie wouldn't have any place to hide."

"If this shit kills monkeys, it'll probably kill me and you, too. I don't want anything to do with it, Sarge."

"Easy, man. The Army wouldn't use it if it was dangerous to troops, I know that."

We came to a stream on the edge of the "dead zone" and the word came down the line to fill canteens as needed. I shook my head.

"Not me, guys. Not until we get farther away from that poison. A man once told me, 'Don't shit where you eat.' This comes under that heading. I'll wait."

"The Army says it won't harm humans in small amounts. That's good enough for me. We've got the greatest country in the world backing the troops and they wouldn't do anything that would be dangerous to your health. It's as safe as mosquito spray."

"Yeah, Bennett. That's why they put the skull and cross-bones on the containers. We put shit like this on weeds back home and the warning on the cans says it will kill you. I'll just wash this shit off my boots and get the hell out of here."

I did wash my boots off in the stream, which was undoubt-edly already polluted from the stuff, and we headed farther up the valley until we came to a natural clearing where we set up in a perimeter. We still hadn't seen any enemy in the entire month, but I didn't mind. The warmer valley air felt good, but I didn't sleep well, thinking about all those dead creatures and wondering how safe that spray really was.

We continued along the valley floor until late the next after-noon when we climbed to the top of a low hill and received a resupply of C rations and mail. We set up in our night defensive position (NDP) there and the perimeter went quiet while the troops sorted through the mail. The gun crew set up along a large east-west trail that ran along the crest of the ridge. The M-60s were almost always placed where the main force of the enemy was expected and where there were good fields of fire, whether natural or man-made.

The Army's prevailing attitude regarding the enemy had them charging out of the jungle in human waves to be chewed up by machine guns blazing their deadly rounds across well-defined fields of fire to preserve the sanctity of freedom-loving peoples everywhere. Who are we to cast aspersions toward Army procedure? I guess you need a plan, no matter how ill-advised it may be, something to give order and discipline to our actions, and meaning to our lives.

As we began to set up our watch schedule, an OP from the 3rd Platoon moved out past our position and we exchanged some good-natured bantering, in the manner of fighting men.

"Third Herd on OP? We'll have to be real quiet, men, so we don't wake those guys out there," Scheffel cracked, then roared his smoky laugh.

One of the troops recognized him and answered, "I've got your position marked as a DefCon, Scheffel. If we get hit, I'm calling in the four-deuce on you."

Jack Betta joined in the insults from the next position. "Why are you taking all those ponchos and liners out there? You're supposed to be on alert all night, not sleeping."

"They're just to fool the VC. He'll think we're going to be asleep and sneak up, then we'll capture him alive."

"Whatever you do out there, 3rd, don't laugh. War is not funny, war is hell," I said, loud enough for the platoon CP to hear. We were feeling pretty confident that Charlie wouldn't climb up here and attack us, so there was some major b.s. and classic insults flying and our morale seemed to be as high as the elephant grass we had been through yesterday. It was another quiet night in the Highlands and, even though I knew better, I hoped that we could spend the next nine months working this area.

As Charlie Company came alive at dawn, the OP came straggling back up the trail. The young trooper humping the PRC-25 radio paused to wipe his brow. "Man, we must have been eight or ten klicks out. Did you hear the terrible firefight we had last night? We must have buried thirty or forty VC this morning."

"Obviously new meat. You're overdoing it, son. Make your lies a little smaller," I told him.

"Hey did somebody saw a tree down out there? I swear I heard a chain saw. You guys have any engineers with you out on OP?" Scheffel asked.

"Fuck you and feed you cabbage," the radio-laden grunt replied.

"Nice comeback. You sound like a lizard I met last week," I put in.

"Come on through, guys. I'm feelin' friendly today, 'cause I'm shooorrrttt!" Scheffel yelled for the whole perimeter to hear. "Twelve days and a wake-up."

"Thanks for reminding me. I'm at 278 and a hiccup," I answered.

Scheffel was part of the Charlie Company that came over with the 3rd Brigade in January. It consisted of career officers and noncoms and a force of mostly enlisted men mixed with a few draftees. A few of the troops reached their discharge date and had been replaced by draftees, like Vickers, but the company as a whole had retained that old Army flavor. There was a camaraderie and pride that existed when whole units landed in-country and began their mission. The morale was higher, in large part due to the continuance of command structure and smaller unit (squad, platoon) makeup. This naturally resulted in good performance in the field.

I could see the breakup of the "old Army" as the men neared the end of their twelve-month tour of duty and I wondered what effect the replacement of these enlistees and lifers with green draftees would have on future performance. I was one of these draftees, but I had been afforded the privilege of serving with the old line troops under severe duress and I knew it would be difficult to carry on the tradition with these new young men. As I continued meditating, I was rudely interrupted by the prosaic cry of the squad leader.

"Saddle up, gun squad, let's go!"

We eased back down the other side of the hill and set off once more across the rolling plains. A spotter plane circling lazily overhead suggested we check out a Montagnard village just a few klicks from where we patrolled, so we obligingly shifted directions and reached it just before noon. We set up security, then the CO and some of his platoon leaders began to look through the seemingly friendly hamlet.

The Montagnards were darker in skin color and lived separately and autonomously from the Vietnamese, with whom they were almost at war.

Having been treated as undesirables by the South because of their color, habits and language, some of the tribes had been cooperating with the North Vietnamese. U.S. Special Forces had been trying to persuade them to fight against the VC and NVA in return for money and special favors. The tribesmen that were convinced to do so operated on their own and owed no allegiance to the Saigon government, which they hated.

These villagers lived in thatched-roof huts, some on stilts to avoid rainwater that washed through the dry streambed next to the hamlet during the rainy season. They raised rice, corn, root crops and fruits, some livestock and lived simply, much as their ancestors had. When we entered one of their villages, it was almost like stepping back in time.

After an hour or so, the word came down to move out and

we passed through the ville on our way south. As we moved carefully along the thorned hedge fences, I got a chance to observe some of the people. Some of the women were breast-feeding babies, which brought stares and lewd comments from some of the men. I heard some comments from the 1st Platoon: "Hey, Chester, did you see that? She was givin' that kid some titty."

"Yeah, man. I'd like to get some of that and I've got somethin' for her." Chester grabbed his crotch and yelled at the woman, "Hey, Mama-san! You want some of this."

Their squad leader laughed and told them to move out past the woman, who kept her eyes averted. I wondered what she was thinking.

There was a coarseness that ran through these men which was embarrassing at times, frightening at others. The reason appeared to be that they had been snatched from homes and loved ones and plopped down in the middle of a jungle and told to kill those people who are trying to kill you. To many of these young lads, being in the Army and being here absolved them of any moral obligations, effectively turning them into lowlifes and criminals—if there can be any such thing in a combat zone. I pondered whether being in a place that was morally deprived, that is, a combat zone, did indeed give one the latitude to commit acts that would be deemed felonious in a civilized world. If one was raised with traditional values, I decided, he must hold on to those cherished beliefs, regardless of the circumstances. This could be the focus point that holds one together when the world turns into chaos, as it did for me and the men of the battalion during the weeks on the border.

A few of the troops had purchased, or stolen, copper bracelets from the tribesmen and wore them proudly as we headed back in a southeast direction, to the mountains. These bracelets had become an identification badge of the infantryman, and woe to any rear shammer who had the audacity to put one on.

Charlie Company continued to move east and south, over mountain and across valley and stream, still encountering no enemy activity. On December 31, as promised, we humped to a road where we met, and loaded onto, trucks from base camp. After unloading and shucking our gear and weapons at the platoon tent, we lined up alphabetically for pay. As I stood there in line behind Kevin Patterson, I looked around at the activity in the bulging compound. There were even more new guys in as replacements and the old guys hadn't started leaving yet. I recognized those who had spent the five days with us, but the others were new and it would take a few days before the names connected to the faces. Ahead of me in line, I spotted House and Malarik and behind me were Rushinski, Underhill and Vansworth.

I saw two new sergeants sitting in front of the mess hall—an E-6 named Brittain and an E-5 buck sergeant, Kushinski. I expected that the sergeants would be squad leaders to replace guys like Watson, who was DEROSing soon, and Leslie, who had collapsed on Hill 1400 and was given a rear echelon position.

We procured some beer and hard liquor, then toasted the New Year and old memories in the platoon tent. Conversation, while it was still lucid, reflected on personal experiences in-country and our lives back home. Promises were made, lies were told, songs were sung and personal relationships were bonded further on nights like this. I felt a closeness to these men that I had never felt before; the strains and stresses of combat, the common bonds of abject fear and joy of survival had made us kinsmen forever.

At midnight, we took our party outside and began singing "Auld Lang Syne" as the perimeter lit up. Flares were shot into the air, turning the night into an eerie near-day, while rifles and machine guns sprayed the night sky, the tracers pointing like crimson fingers to the stars. 1966 was now history and our performance could be judged by the gods and arbitrated by mere mortals, but could not be undone. As I sat on an overturned water can watching the pageantry and hoping no innocents were in the line of fire when the thousands of rounds came back to earth, I said a silent prayer for health, strength and for peace on earth in 1967. God be with the fighting man in South Vietnam.

14

The morning of the first day of 1967 dawned hard and cool in Charlie Company compound. At our formation, called to make sure no one had gone into town on New Year's Eve, Underhill, an FNG, stood shakily in the last row. I watched out of the corner of my eye as he did a very unmilitary right-face, then began throwing up. When his name was called, he was unable to answer, but several of us vouched for his presence.

"Yo, he's the guy with his head down. He's partly here."

After roll call, the Top Sergeant walked briskly back to where Underhill was now standing shakily and looked him over.

"Trooper, are you sick?"

Underhill swallowed, shook his head and whispered almost imperceptibly, "No."

"Maybe I should put you on shit-burning detail today. That sound good?"

The shaky trooper fought down another wave of nausea as Top continued his harangue. "All right, dress that line and give that vomit a military burial after dismissal. Put Underhill on KP and platoon sergeants send me two more men each. Company, dismissed!"

The company was called back into formation at 0900 hours for a ceremony to award medals to those who had been nominated for their actions during Operation Paul Revere IV. After a brief speech lauding their efforts, the battalion commander read the citations, then passed out a Silver Star to Lieutenant Shipley of the 3rd Platoon and several Bronze Stars to some of the other men, including the lieutenant's RTO.

No one in the 2nd Platoon was awarded anything, possibly

because the people who do the nominating, officers and non-coms, were killed or wounded early in the battle of Dragon Crater.

Nevertheless, if Lieutenant Shipley, who came late to the battle to conduct the withdrawal of forces, deserved a Silver Star, everyone who fought near me deserved one, especially the medics. No one was braver than those men. A rumor floated around that Belcher was nominated for the Medal of Honor for jumping on a grenade, but it couldn't be substantiated.

After the ceremony, the CO informed us that we would spend one more day in base camp before leaving on January 3. We would move out to the firing range to test fire all weapons tomorrow, then clean and ready all gear for movement the following morning. He added, "For those of you not on work detail, there will be passes and a truck to Pleiku at 1100."

Vickers and I lined up for the precious piece of paper, still stamped with Captain Simcox's signature, then boarded the Pleiku Express along with Mize and several new guys. When we hit the city, we jumped off the truck and headed for Mamasan's Bar where Vickers did some fast talking and I offered her 200 piastres for the incident last month when I drank free. Mama-san studied me for a minute, then smiled and said, "You nice boy. I take 200 p. You give me 200 more p. and take girl. Numbah wan boom-boom." She laughed and pushed me toward the girls.

Vickers asked her, "Why so cheap, Mama-san? First of the month, usually the price is higher."

"Twenty-five leave. Fourth come in. Cheap bastards. You go to Qui Nhon—two days. Take girl now—200 p., short time."

The price was reasonable, but one look at the yawning, bored-looking girls sitting around the table was enough to turn off my sex drive. I turned to Mama-san. "Where are Han Lee and Soo? They would be worth a lot more."

"Gone. Maybe Da Nang, maybe Saigon. Numbah ten girls." She growled out the words with disgust, so I decided it was not my fate to make connections with the most beautiful girl in the country, or maybe the Orient. Vickers, Mize and I sipped a few drinks while listening to a cheap jukebox, then rode the truck back to Camp Enari at 1600.

Upon our return, we wandered back to the tent and tuned in

Armed Forces Network on Vickers' radio. Our new favorite deejay, Chris Noel, came on at 2105 and she had a voice that could melt down the barrel of an M-60. As I listened, I conjured up visions of her playing the songs only for me, whispering to me in her dulcet tones. She had a voice that put me in mind of silk sheets, for some reason. I supposed that every GI in 'Nam had his own fantasies of her, but that was their problem.

Down at the other end of the tent, several of the new guys were gathered around Malarik's bunk and it looked like he was holding hands with them, one at a time. I yelled at them, "Hey, new meat. No holding hands on the first date. What the hell's coming off, guys?"

One of the new guys looked up and replied in a hushed voice, "Malarik's telling our fortune by reading our palms."

Danny Malarik was a dark-skinned young man of Hungarian descent from New Jersey who had a great sense of humor and worked hard at fitting in wherever he went, it seemed. I thought about this latest twist of his character that he was now showing and then yelled down at him, "Malarik, bring your sorry ass over here and read my dirty-assed palm."

I don't know why I was using such foul language, maybe because I was uncertain and somewhat bemused about this particular practice of predestination. He came down next to my bunk and asked, "Are you sure you want some damn gypsy predicting your future, Pete? I could be wrong, or worse, I could be right."

"I'll be the judge of that. Read on, MacDuff."

He took my hand and traced along the different lines of the palm with his finger while showing a concentrated look on his swarthy face. Then he dropped my hand. "I'd rather not, Pete. No hard feelings, man?"

"Hey, read it. Tell me what you see."

"OK. I'm not bothered by anything on your love line or your life line, although both have slight breaks in them. But, judging by your age, I see a large break in your health line not long after your next birthday. When is that—May, June?"

"May 30th. What does that break mean to you, and more importantly, to me?"

"To me it signifies a major health problem, probably not a disease. More likely, a severe injury, almost fatal." He hesitated, then added, "It's not fatal, though, Pete."

"A severe injury and it just so happens that I'm serving a tour in Vietnam. I'll be going home four months after my birthday, or will I?"

"It'll be close. Could happen here or maybe an automobile accident back home."

I didn't know quite what to think, but I wasn't going to let anybody think that it was going to bother me. I searched for the proper comeback. "You know, Malarik, it's a good thing I don't believe in this shit or I'd be worried."

"I could be wrong, Pete, but the lines never are, and that's the way I see it. I'll get you a beer, man."

He brought me a Schlitz from the barrel at the end of the tent and I quaffed it quickly. Neither of us said anything else about the reading as we sang old songs with Chris and sucked down beer. I thought about it later, while lying on my bunk, but I decided I couldn't waste time worrying about something I had no control over, so I filed it away under ominous portents and went to sleep.

After our usual morning routines, we humped out through the main gate, took a loose right turn, then proceeded along the perimeter to the firing range. The entire battalion, so it seemed, had converged on the huge range to test their weaponry; HQ had heard the many reports of jammed M-16s and had officers roaming the firing line to determine the cause. I burned a couple of magazines through my rifle on semi, then flipped the selector another notch to auto, or rock and roll as it was known in-country. The weapon burped out most of the rounds, then jammed. I called one of the officers over, but he wanted to blame me, not the weapon.

"You must have misfired, troop."

"Screw it, I didn't misfire. The weapon is jammed."

"You probably didn't clean it properly."

I looked closely at him, but he wore the uninterested air of a career man who wasn't about to rock the boat, so I decided to try a different tack, à la Vickers. "Well sir, you can fuck me, I'll never smile again."

He gave me a long glance, then shook his head and moved on down the line to the next jammed 16 and pronounced it dirty. I borrowed the shotgun from Vickers and fired it once. It kicked like a Missouri mule in heat, causing Vickers to laugh as he saw me wince and flex my shoulder.

Martinez fired the M-60, then put a magazine through his M-16. Alabama then unholstered the .45 sidearm and handed it to him, then yelled: "OK, Martinez, time to fire the pistol. Everybody watch your feet. Lock and load."

I fired the M-60 for a few rounds, then borrowed an M-79 bloop gun from Fred Huffman, the lonesome end. I blooped a few rounds out into the trees behind the range and felt an immediate surge of adrenaline. To be able to cause remote explosions was the ultimate sense of power to an infantryman. I waxed enthusiastically to those around me: "I gotta have one of these. When I get back to a rifle squad, I'm gonna hump one of these."

"What about close-in combat, Pete?" Vickers asked.

"Then I'll hide behind you and your shotgun, Vick. But I love the way you can bring pee down on their ass from a long way off with this baby."

Miller, whom I had last seen three months ago, was in line to test a shotgun he was humping. We exchanged greetings and compared our tours thus far. He belonged to the security platoon, which was about to undergo a change in name and mission. Their job now was providing security for the HQ and occasionally patrolling the area around base camp. Renamed the attack platoon, they would be in the field in the new AO, operating along with other line units. Miller was looking forward to it.

"I'm glad. Time goes too slowly when you only take an occasional patrol. I got tired of guard duty in the rear."

"I'm here to tell you, Miller, that life in the boonies is far from desirable. They shoot at your butt out there. Oh, well, you'll learn soon enough. Do you ever see Mock?"

"Once or twice since we've been here. He hangs out with the other clerks up at brigade."

We vowed once more to stay in touch, then said our goodbyes and I joined Charlie Company as we formed up to head back. Once in the company compound, we tore down our weapons and washed them in cleaning solvent or kerosene, then wiped them down and worked on our gear. I replaced my spent ammo and picked up an extra grenade and flare, then declared I was ready. We packed all our excess gear and clothing away in our lockers and hauled them to supply for storage. It sure seemed like we were moving.

Sergeant Nuckols called a platoon meeting at the mess hall for the early evening. He went over new assignments, then told us we would be assigned to the 1st Cavalry during the mission. After the hoots and derisive comments died down, he told us we would travel across the Central Highlands east to the coastal plains not far from the South China Sea. We had no idea of what to expect in our new AO or when we might see Pleiku again. Rumor had reared its ugly head and declared that we would be relocating to the east coast with the 4th Division taking over here.

Maybe it would be easy duty, like the past few weeks here—lots of humping with no enemy. Nuckols wound up by mentioning that the battalion was recruiting a long-range reconnaisance patrol (LRRP, pronounced "lurp") team and asked if anyone wanted to volunteer for training and duty. I ran it through my mind, hesitated for a minute or so as I thought that this might be the way to fight the war, then dismissed it; I wanted to work my way up in a line unit. A few of the troopers expressed mild interest, so he told them to report to the clerk if they were serious. As the meeting broke up, Nuckols remembered that he had nobody to carry his radio and asked if anybody wanted to volunteer. Since Mize was carrying the lieutenant's radio, and he and I had become fairly close in the last month, I made the plunge.

"I'll carry your damn radio. When do I start?"

I was becoming a different person. I never would have volunteered for anything before and I'm still not sure why I chose to do so. But I did.

"Pick it up tonight. Mize will show you what you need to know and I'll see you in the morning. I sent La Barge to the clerk's office to replace Fortunato. He recommended him to the first sergeant and he said that was good enough for him, so we lost one more man."

The platoon was dismissed, then Mize and I hung around as

Nuckols wondered aloud, "Who in this platoon should I recommend for promotion? I haven't been here long enough to know all these men and I ain't gonna recommend any new guys."

Even though he wasn't asking us, I decided it was as good a time as any to speak up. "There are quite a few guys who have been in-country seven or eight months with no promotions. They've seen a lot of action and deserve some rank and extra pay. Vickers, Mize, Bennett, Fears. They all deserve a promotion, and if you've got any left over, I'd sure take one."

He laughed, then wrote down some of the names before leaving for the clerk's office. Mize grinned as he began to show me the workings of the PRC-25 radio.

"I doubt if that will do any good, Pete, but thanks for trying. I got a wife at home who would love to see a few extra bucks come home every month."

"Hell, man, you guys have been through a lot here in the last few months and you do deserve a promotion. And, dammit, I do, too, after that shit we went through in November. Now, show me that damn radio procedure."

We spent the next couple of hours going over proper procedures and Mize showed me how to carry the monster and how to pack the extra batteries. I threw off my extra grenades and flares and shifted things around on my web gear until it felt right, then we hit our bunks. Before we could get to sleep, Williams and Martinez came in with a case of Pabst that I decided I should partake of, since it was a Wisconsin beer. At slightly before 0200, I finally found my bunk again and immediately fell asleep.

It seemed like my head had barely hit the canvas of the bunk when the runners came around from the clerk's office to wake us up at 0430. We fell into loose formation, then filed in for a last breakfast of powdered eggs and bacon. After pouring down a few cups of hot coffee, we moved back to the tent and rounded up our gear. At our second morning formation, we were assigned to trucks and began to move toward them at 0700. As I shuffled along with the radio, I saw Maddox coming out of the mess hall, heading toward me, canteen cup filled with coffee in hand.

"Hey, old dude, where've you been the last few days?"

"I didn't feel right being with you guys, so I moved in with

Watson and the other short-timers. I had to come to say good-bye to you, Pete. As you probably know, I'm heading back to the World in a couple of days."

A lump began to form in my chest and worked its way into my throat as I realized I might never see him again—the man who had taught me the most about war and survival.

"Well, my main man, you've almost made it. I'm really happy for you, Maddox."

He offered his hand and I grabbed it and then clasped him lightly on the shoulder. "I'll write, Pete, I swear it. Keep your head down out there. I really liked working with you. Anything I can do for you when I get back to the States?"

"Yeah, man. Call my parents when you get time. Tell them I'm doing fine."

A silence fell over us as we struggled with our emotions and fought to keep them from showing; we were soldiers and no one must see our inner feelings. I gave him the number to call, then tossed my radio and gear aboard the truck. I looked at him, then jumped up to the floor of the truck bed.

"Good luck wherever you wind up, Maddox. I'll never forget these times, especially the night we crossed that river. Take care, old dude."

The truck's engine was started now and we began edging along the road toward the gate. I stood up in the back and whipped a smart salute at him, which he answered even more crisply.

"Golden Dragon, Maddox!" I yelled over the roar of the truck and the pain in my heart.

"Right of the line, Pete. Give 'em hell, 2nd Platoon! So long!"

I sat down and leaned back against the side of the truck as we left Camp Enari, heading east, looking for new battles, new stories to tell. I had been sincere; I would not forget Maddox and the times we had, the battles we had fought, the ground we had covered, just being together. Now, however, I was moving into another phase in my life as a warrior and I had to turn my thoughts to the immediate future. I took the radio handset, depressed the squelch button and called Mize.

"Charlie 2–6 Romeo, this is Charlie 2–5 Romeo. Radio check, over."

"Roger, 2–5 Romeo. Read you Lima Charlie. How you, over."

"Two–6 Romeo, Read you same-same. 2–5 Romeo, out."

One of the new guys spoke wistfully as we rolled out of the main gate and began to follow along the highway. "Anybody know where the hell we're going?"

"We're going east, man. Wherever the action is, Charlie Company, especially the 2nd Platoon, will be there."

PART TWO

COASTAL PLAIN

15

The trucks carrying Charlie Company, 1st/14th, motored along Highway 19, over the rolling plains of the Central Highlands, past the rickety villages of Le Trung and Suai Dai, heading for the mountains on the first leg of our journey. As the truck bounced along the bumpy road, thoughts bounced in and out of my head. Did the rest of the battalion ride on trucks or were they choppered? Don't know and it doesn't matter. What was the enemy going to be like? VC or NVA regulars? In our last AO, we knew where we stood. The enemy consisted mainly of NVA regulars, feared and respected by us, who were trying to kill us. Sergeant Nuckols said he thought we would be dealing with both NVA and a large contingent of local VC in this area. It could be a different kind of war, just when I was getting used to the old one, in a manner of speaking.

Occasionally the trucks would dip into a valley with hills rising on both sides of the road. Even though there were choppers flying by sporadically, a handful of VC could pop up, fire a rocket, toss some grenades or satchel charges, then *di di* as we tended our wounded. I monitored the company frequency to find out if any of the front trucks had trouble, but the ride was peaceful in the morning. At 1000 the trucks halted and the word came down the line, "Take a break, stretch your legs, smoke if you got 'em, take a piss, let it all hang out. Ten minutes."

I gave Mize another radio check, then stood and walked around for a while.

"Pete, how's it hangin'? How the hell could you volunteer to carry a radio? You must be *dinky-dau*—that PRC-25 is numbah ten, GI."

"I probably am a little nuts, but the radio is better than the M-60, Chase. If the gunner went down, I'd be carrying that damn thing. I can learn from being close to the command center, but I still want to get back to a rifle squad."

"Do you suppose there are any of our troops patrolling these hills as we pass through? Mang Yang Pass up ahead would be a great place for an ambush."

"I think somebody said that the ARVN were in these hills."

"Oh, that's great. I feel a lot better already."

Finishing our break, we hauled our refreshed asses to the trucks and hit the road again. When we reached the pass, somebody yelled, "Mang Yang Pass, lock and load. Steel pots on, full alert."

As we crept along the bottom of the huge ravine, with mountains rising on both sides of us, Vickers grunted. "If Charlie doesn't hit us here, he's missing a helluva good chance. We're dead meat here."

"Dead meat is right, GI. Even with choppers overhead, it would be over before they could drop down. But, hell, Vick, nobody lives forever."

"I don't want to live forever, Pete, just a hundred years or so, then get killed by a jealous young man 'cause I stole his girlfriend."

The trucks pulled out of the pass unscathed and you could almost hear a collective sigh of relief. We were in 1st Cav country and as we passed their base camp at An Khe, you couldn't miss the giant replica of their patch on the side of a hill. The patch featured a horse's head, then a diagonal black slash on a field of yellow. The sign pointed out that we were in 1st Cav–Airmobile country and denoted the various units sequestered in An Khe.

Chase shouted to no one in particular but for the edification of all, "You know what that patch stands for? The horse they never rode, the road they never crossed and the yellow was the reason why. Fuckin' First Cav–Airmobile Assholes."

We all joined in the derisive laughter, but I remembered that we would be attached to them in our next AO. Since it probably wasn't a good time to remind the troops, I kept my silence. I also kept my silence as we rode through another shantytown where the children came screaming after us, begging for food. Alabama stood up in the truck and threw cans at them as hard as he could. I shook my head at the incongruity of the scene; he was feeding them, while possibly trying to kill them with a full can to the head.

I looked away and we motored on. The Highlands flattened out and became the fertile valleys of the coastal plains as we cruised slowly through Binh Khe, then An Nhon. The conversation turned to comparisons of various duty tours in-country. Betta started it off with his observation, "Door gunner is numbah one job—bring pee from above and unload troops, then get the hell out when it gets hot. Maybe I'll put in for a transfer to air support."

"Choppers make a hell of a nice target. Maybe armor would be the place to be. Pour out the heavy shit, then *di di* after their ass when they run," Vickers put in.

"They make an easy target for mines. You could get fried inside pretty easily, Vick," I added.

He nodded, then Chase spoke up again. "Artillery would be OK if you didn't mind turning deaf in a few years."

"The short rounds and friendly casualties would finish me. Man, I couldn't do that at all."

"So, what the hell do you think would be better than the infantry if you had to stay in the field, Pete?"

"Maybe be an adviser with an ARVN unit. Wouldn't even have to carry a weapon, just pick one up when the ARVN hit the shit because they always seem to drop theirs and run. But the best job would be a pilot—fly the fast-movers or B-52s. Get in, drop your shit, get out of Dodge, go back to Thailand and have a beer with a numbah one pretty young thing rubbing your back. You wouldn't even have to see the death and destruction you caused. Yeah, that's the job."

"How do we get to be a pilot?" one of the new guys asked.

"You need a college degree, plus flight school. Basically, you can't get there from here."

"I think I'll stay in the infantry and wait for a rear job. When Sergeant Leslie leaves, there'll be an opening in supply," Vansworth said.

"Good luck, guy. When that job opens up, there'll be dozens of grunts suckin' up to their platoon sergeant."

It started to rain lightly as we eased through the streets of Qui Nhon, the largest city I had seen since Saigon. I saw a trooper walking out of a bar with a pretty girl on his arm. He yelled, "Hey, are you the First or the Second of the Fourteenth?"

"First, and the whole battalion had that girl last week."

He laughed at Chase's insult and continued along as did we. It was getting late in the day and we were getting hot and hungry under our ponchos, but the trucks continued another ten miles before pulling off the road onto a huge open grassy field.

The trucks made a huge circle and we unloaded onto the wet grass. Sergeant Nuckols told us to get as comfortable as we could, so we immediately began constructing hooches around the truck. We wanted to build a fire for warmth, but there was no wood to burn, so we lit heat tabs and cooked hot coffee and cocoa. Nuckols jumped into the truck cab over the protests of the driver, who wanted to lie down.

"Nobody in the truck cab but me—orders from my CO."

"Well, call your CO if you think it'll help, but I'm in and I'm not getting out," the crusty Ranger sergeant answered.

I opened the door and tried to wheedle my way in to the warm and dry cab as the rain shower became a deluge.

"Sarge, you need your RTO in case the CP tries to raise you." He shut the door, then reopened it a bit and my hopes rose, but he grabbed the radio and closed the door and locked it. I crawled under the truck and wrapped my poncho around and under me, then prayed the truck didn't move without warning and that Charlie didn't zero in on it for a mortar attack. My first night in the new AO was wet and cold, but I took some comfort in knowing I wasn't alone in my misery and that we were safe.

The sun broke through the early morning haze, quickly drying our fatigues and raising our spirits. I gobbled down a can of crackers and cheese, swallowed a cup of cocoa, then got my radio and ran a check with Mize. Nuckols emerged from the truck, told me to make him some coffee and ran his own radio check. I handed him a heat tab and a pack of coffee out of his pack and told him it was his coffee. He grinned and lit the tab to heat his water while I put all my gear together.

Nuckols took his canteen cup of coffee to the morning briefing, then returned a few minutes later with the morning word. "We'll be getting on the choppers at 0930. Heading out to a small LZ called Santa to replace a 1st Cav unit. Get the word out to the squad leaders and tell them to meet in the center of the field for extraction."

The choppers lifted off right on time and headed east, then south. I noticed the terrain was more level than the mountains, with wider rivers and lots of rice paddies. There were a few hills and some mountains in the distance, but it was closer to sea level and the humping looked like it might be easier here. We landed in a LZ struck between a wooded tree line and a creek. It reminded me somewhat of the way Lane had been laid out, but it was smaller. We jumped out and waited for the rest of the company to arrive. I noticed a group of 1st Cav troops standing around a position, waiting for orders to head to the LZ.

"You guys hit any bad shit around here? We came from the Cambodian border area where we had some terrible battles with the NVA. Human wave assaults, shit like that. Hundreds of dead NVA regulars. It was hell."

"Well, last week the 2nd VC Regiment overran a firebase, but we came to the rescue and fought them off barehanded. Killed about 500 and only lost a half dozen or so."

"My dad always told me that the first liar doesn't have a chance. Seriously, what should we look for here?"

"Lots of VC action. Snipers, booby traps, hit-and-run. You can't tell the friendlies from the enemy. The Papa-san you see in the rice paddy working every day could be counting your numbers and looking for a good place to put a mine or booby trap. Gets to ya."

"I guess that was one good thing about our last operation, our enemies wore khaki uniforms. The bad part was that there was so damn many of them."

"Well, there is said to be a division, the 3rd NVA, in this province, but we've never hit anything bigger than a company here in the Bong Son area. Well, there's our chopper, good luck to the 25th and keep your head down."

"Take care, 1st Cav. Keep it down."

The north side of the LZ was bordered by higher ground with small trees and brush, so the CO sent orders to get OPs up there immediately. We found a centrally located bunker for the platoon CP and Mize and I began improving the site with sandbags and branches. We piled the bags up three feet, then topped it with a poncho roof: two ponchos snapped together over a branch and tied down on the sides. Then Mize took a stick, inserted it into the hoods of the ponchos and across the horizontal tent pole, thus raising the roof slightly and improving the water runoff. We placed several pieces of cardboard along the ground and put one more poncho across the front for a doorway. It wasn't pretty, but it was shelter.

It rained hard all night, but we stayed dry until 0300, when the drainage ditches Mize and I had dug could no longer hold the runoff that streamed down the slight slope. The water began to seep in under the sandbags and through the cardboard we were lying on and, in a matter of minutes, we were getting wet and cold. Mize and I earned the honor of stepping out in the deluge to enlarge the ditch while Sergeant Nuckols and Lieutenant Lesko gave directions from inside. We finally managed to turn the tide and returned to salvage a few hours of sleep.

The 2nd Platoon received their marching orders the next morning—a two-day patrol to the west, then south. I loaded four meals into my pack, then strapped the radio to the upper part of my harness so the weight would be carried on my shoulders. It was heavy as hell, about twenty-five pounds with the extra battery, but I shrugged my shoulders a few times, got it situated in place, leaned over at the waist a little and fell in behind the platoon sergeant.

The patrol followed the stream which was now swollen from the all-night rain. It had stopped now, but the skies were gray and overcast and ready to open up again at any minute. I knew that sooner or later we were going to cross the damn stream (climb every mountain, ford every stream) and after slogging through and along rice paddies all morning, we did ford it and checked out some abandoned hooches. We found no enemy sign, but I did see a lot of fruit (bananas, pineapples) and rice. This appears to be a fertile area, but where are the people?

At dusk, we set up on a low hill covered with brush and trees. As we were shedding our gear and getting ready to dig in, two choppers flew over, circled around and opened fire on our position. I hit the ground, found the nearest tree and hugged it as they poured out M-60 fire. The seemingly endless fire from the sky tore into the trees and hit the ground with soft thumps, like a deadly hailstorm. Lieutenant Lesko screamed at the CO on Mize's radio, "This is 2–6, choppers firing on us—call them off!"

"Oh shit, here they come again! Mother humpin' assholes," Mize yelled.

Mize was trying to find the gunship frequency while Sergeant Nuckols and I popped smoke grenades and tossed them. The choppers continued to circle, but held their fire as we held our positions, afraid to move. The radio hissed, "2–6, this is 6 Actual. We've got them stopped. Pop colored smoke only to mark your position. White smoke marks enemy activity in this AO, over."

"Six, this is 2–6. I hope we get our shit together before somebody gets killed. Thanks for the help. 2–6 out."

It had been a frightening experience, although it lasted only a few seconds. As the door gunners opened up with M-60s, I felt my sphincter tighten and my heart was pounding louder than the guns. Some of these chopper pilots and their crews were trigger-happy, more so than could be justified, and we had just had the distinct displeasure of meeting one. The eyes of the new guys were a lot wider after the incident. Kevin Patterson, entrenching tool in hand, walked over to the CP and asked, "Do you get shit like this often?"

"Everybody craps on the infantry until they need some dirty job done. Then they love us, man. I was drafted," I said.

"We should have turned Alabama and Martinez loose on them." He laughed as he headed back to his position and resumed digging in.

As the shock and terror wore off, we returned to the menial tasks of excavation of holes and construction of hooches. I quickly learned that one of the many tasks of the RTO was digging a hole for the CP since officers and noncoms didn't even bother to carry an entrenching tool. I asked Sergeant Nuckols about this and he explained it to me this way: "It could set a bad precedent. If I carried it, I might be tempted to use it and we couldn't have that. Being an NCO has to mean something more than just extra pay and stripes. If I'm a platoon sergeant, I ain't diggin' no damn hole."

Mize and I set up the hole, the hooch and the command center, complete with long antennae for better reception on the radios. When we were finished, Mize waxed philosophically. "You know, Pete, it doesn't really matter who shoots you, the VC or our side, either way you're dead."

"It would seem like such a waste to die by friendly fire. You'd not only be giving your life for your country, but to and by your country. It's not right. Command structure and discipline regarding firing procedure needs to be tightened."

"You oughta run for public office someday, Pete."

"Well, maybe I will. Here's my speech: 'Folks, I've never stolen an honest dollar in my life and all I ask is a chance.' "

"All right, you guys, knock that shit off and get me a radio check with the OP."

Anything coming through the brush would have been heard for a half-mile, so we relaxed and spent the night on light security. The next morning we continued to patrol down through the fertile valley, crossing the river twice before heading due south toward a low mountain. We broke for chow, then slowly moved up a trail that had been well-used, although not lately. At the crest we paused to check out some old fighting positions destroyed by bombs or artillery, then rested awhile as Lieutenant Lesko made connections with the firebase command.

"Charlie 6, this is Blazer 2–6, over."

"Go ahead, 2–6, this is Charlie 6 Romeo. Actual is with Golden 6." Golden 6 was Colonel Miller, who was now battalion commander.

"Roger, 6 Romeo, 2–6 reports 1800 ETA. Request hot Alphas."

"Roger, 2–6, wait one." He came back on a few minutes later.

"Blazer 2–6, request granted. Later, Charlie 6 out."

We trudged on down the north slope of the mountain, then crossed the stream once more and across a few rice paddies to the LZ. We were tired, wet and hungry for those hot A rations we were promised. I dropped my gear at the 2nd Platoon command tent, then set my radio inside and got in the chow line, a couple of troops seated on C-ration boxes doling out the food from OD insulated containers. As the first few men started down, Colonel Miller arrived with Captain Childers to talk to the men. He took a glance at the food.

"What the hell is this? I've got men coming from a long patrol and they get cold fuckin' weenies and creamed corn. Get me a radio."

He grabbed the handset proffered by the company RTO, then demanded and got the battalion frequency.

"This is Golden 6 Actual. I want some hot, I mean, *hot* chow out here ASAP. Enough for a platoon. Cold drinks, too. You got that? Golden 6, out."

He shouted loud enough for most of the perimeter to hear, then tossed the handset back to the RTO. Needless to say, the men of the 2nd Platoon were visibly impressed, casting glances of admiration at the colonel. But, favorable impressions and admiration do not a full stomach make, so I asked myself: what would Maddox do? I grabbed Mize and we followed our noses to the artillery field kitchen, where I explained our plight to the cook.

"Hang on, I've got just what you need," he said. He disappeared into his pantry, then emerged with the ever-present OD insulated container filled with about 100 hamburger patties. Large, round, mouthwatering hamburger patties, still warm and ready to eat. He grabbed a can of catsup and placed it on top.

"I hope this will help. I was going to make hamburger gravy tomorrow, but this is more important. Sorry, no bread, we bake tomorrow, but eat hearty, leg."

"Thanks, artillery, we owe you one. Remember the Trailblazer Platoon the next time your firebase perimeter gets overrun."

We placed the canister on the ground at the chow line and turned the men loose after grabbing a few for ourselves and the CP. There was stale bread in the line, so we were able to make sandwiches complete with catsup. Colonel Miller returned after the chopper landed, off-loaded the hot As and jumped into the serving line to help pass it out. He couldn't understand why the troops weren't too hungry.

"Here, son, have some more of that roast beef and potatoes. You troops sure don't eat much for infantry."

When Lieutenant Lesko explained the situation to him, the colonel had a good laugh, then roared once more. "That's what I like, expediency under pressure in a combat zone. I want that to be a Golden Dragon tradition."

I had a feeling that he would be a hands-on type of officer

and we would be seeing a lot of him at LZs around our AO. After we settled in, the night went quietly as Mize and I took turns on radio watch.

The sun made a brief appearance the next day, then the clouds moved in and we waited for the rain. Sergeant Nuckols became quite ill and needed rest, so the 2nd Platoon was held in reserve for two days. To kill some time, I took a walk around the perimeter and checked out the other hooches to see if I could improve ours. I saw a sign outside the hooch occupied by the 1st Platoon CP designating it as the Phu Cat Hilton and decided we needed one on our hooch. I rounded up Vickers, the only man in the platoon with any artistic talent, and we came up with the following: 2nd Platoon Seldom Inn.

Because it was Saturday, the Army gave us our weekly liquid ration (a misnomer since we received it whenever the Army felt like passing it out)—two beers, a soda, all warm. The trading and mixing and matching began once more.

"One Coke for two beers. Who likes Coke?"

"I'll take that action. I can't stand warm beer."

"The Army has three kinds of beer, Pete: warm, warmer, and skunky."

"I especially get a kick out of their weekly beer ration, Mize. I've been here over three months and this is my third ration. Somebody in the rear is sopping up my beer."

"Fuck the rear. Fuck the Army. Fuck LBJ and Ladybird, too," Fears put in.

"That's a lot of screwing, Fears."

"Fuck you, too, Alabama, you cracker."

"You better not. You'd *never* go back to your mama."

Fears had failed in his attempts to land a permanent rear job, although he had spent several days there during our December OPs. He continued to gripe about everything that happened and looked for his opening. What he was doing was similar to what I was doing, except I had better motivation toward the job and my place.

The next day, I took my radio and gear and joined Sergeant Bennett's squad on daytime OP. We set up on a small hill 100 meters in front of the perimeter, then removed our boots and put our bare feet up to the sun to dry while hoping the enemy didn't come along. As the time dragged on, we became aware that boredom was rapidly becoming a major concern. To a young man filled with the piss and vinegar of his years, having nothing to do was almost as bad as having something dangerous to do. We made it through our fourth day in the AO without any enemy activity and time was standing still.

On Monday, January 9, the 2nd Platoon was given a mission: clean up the area and replace the piss tubes, which wasn't exactly what we had in mind. However, we did a thorough policing, then dug up the tubes and replaced them with empty artillery shell containers set into the ground at a 45-degree angle. The soldier in his quest for relief could present arms and open fire. After we finished one of the tubes, Chase moved to baptize it and saluted. "Permission to relieve myself, Romeo Tango Oscar Peterson?"

"Permission granted, weapons squad leader Chase, fire at will, or whoever you see."

He did a smart right face, went to parade rest, then started to sing as he did his chore.

"When Sunny gets blue, her eyes get sort of cloudy. . . ."

As he finished, I stepped up and performed similarly but sang a different song. "I've got the whole world in my hands. . . ."

After the chores were done, we headed for a platoon bath run in a small rice paddy just south of the helipad. There was about a foot of water in the paddy, so we plunged in and lathered up, then did a wash and rinse before stepping out to remove the leeches and commiserate.

Alabama was faced with the sight of a huge leech on his member. "That ol' boy must be real hungry. He's bit off a lot more than he can chew. Give me a lit cigarette, no make that a lit cigar." He took the cigarette from Martinez, then hesitated for a few seconds before burning it off.

"This is the first time anything ever sucked on my whang before. Kind of a shame to kill it."

"Somebody has got to take that country boy to town. I'm kinda glad I got out of the gun squad when I did."

"Hell, Pete, I guess if you suck up, you can get a better job anytime."

That one stung, but I vowed to myself to keep it light.

"You mean if I suck and blow, I can get Colonel Miller's

job? Who do I start with? Look, man, I wanted out and Nuckols needed an RTO. I took it and I'd do it again. Besides, it's not who you know and who you blow, it's who you meet and who you eat, Alabama."

The bantering continued, but no one really seemed to care one way or the other about who carried what or how they got the job, as long as they could do the work. I put on my clean fatigues and headed back to the CP, where I cleaned my gear and got a new battery. We were going on patrol in the morning and I wanted everything to work perfectly.

We climbed the small hill to the northeast and entered a small valley that was a mirror image of the one we had patrolled earlier in the week. Again, there was no evidence of enemy activity and the platoon returned to the firebase empty-handed. I slogged to the CP, dropped my gear and radio and set it inside the hooch as the rain began to fall. It continued to rain intermittently for the next thirty-six hours. Inside the CP hooch, we lapsed into a quiet, brooding mood, letting our thoughts slip across the bonds of time and space to home and loved ones.

The four of us showed each other pictures and exchanged perfunctory comments and compliments as the rain pelted the poncho roof. By the second night the spell was getting heavier, so I strolled down to the perimeter to exchange pleasantries and insults with the line doggies. I felt like I was losing my standing as one of them after eight days with the radio. I stopped in the gun crew's hooch and listened as Alabama gave us his views of the world.

"Pete, did you meet Underhill yet? You know, I hate blacks, but he's a helluva nice guy. I cain't figure that out."

"How can you hate an entire race of people? You will not even meet one-tenth of 1 percent of the black race in your rednecked life, yet you despise them. How does that wash?"

"My daddy and grand-daddy hated 'em and I hate 'em. I hate their attitude, their walk, their ugly faces. . . ."

"Whoa, man. You know, we've been through a lot and I respect you as a man and a soldier, but you are racist and I can't condone or respect that."

"Well, that's not gonna change me. You know they always hang out together. . . ."

"And whites don't?" I interrupted.

"You know what I mean. Niggers act like they got some kind of secret, inside information when they meet and start bopping and dapping. Whites don't do that shit."

"You've got to open your mind and see the real world, man. You're stuck in a Southern time warp."

"Don't bad-mouth the South, Pete. I won't stand for that. You haven't lived down there so you can't know how we feel or why. Don't be so quick to look down on my people."

"Well, Alabama, I consider you a comrade and I'll fight by your side, but I disagree with what you say and stand for."

Mize stuck his head in the door of the hooch and interrupted us. "Pete, come on back to the CP. We've got a decision to make tonight."

I climbed out of the gun crew hooch into the rain, then turned back to get in another thought to Alabama. "You better get a camouflage scarf for that red neck of yours, guy. The VC will spot it a mile away. Later."

"And you need some bandages for that bleeding heart problem of yours, Pete. That'll kill you someday."

I lifted the flap of the CP hooch and crawled inside with Mize. Nuckols flashed his flashlight on me briefly. "Pete, the battalion needs two men from Charlie Company to attend NCO school back at base camp in Pleiku. It's our turn to send one of them. Lieutenant Lesko and I decided on you. What do you think about that?"

He obviously thought he was giving me a hell of a deal, but I wasn't entirely sure. Life at base camp drags, but I'd be out of the field, away from the leeches and rain and the enemy.

"I'm willing to go, but what about Mize, Vickers, Rangel and the others with more time in-country? They should get first crack at this."

"We need men who are going to be with the platoon for a long time. Those men will be DEROSing in a few months. It's between you, Sawlski and Williams. We picked you."

"Well, I'll go, but I hate to leave all this rain and mud."

They laughed, then Lieutenant Lesko spoke. "It's two weeks of leadership training at the NCO Academy. If you graduate in the top five, you get E-5 stripes. I'm expecting that of you, mister."

I lay in the dark, listening to the rain, pondering the twists of fate that had placed me in this spot and now were moving me toward another adventure. Well, I would try to be a good garrison soldier, but I always had difficulty with inspections and the pettiness. I would give it my best and let the chips fall where they may. I slept fitfully and dreamed of Alabama shooting at me and laughing as I ran.

The next morning, the company was getting ready for a long patrol. Chase stopped at the CP to pick up Cs for his troops as did Vickers for the 1st Squad. I figured they deserved to hear the news from me.

"Guys, they're sending me into NCO school. I know you've both got more time in-country, but Lesko and Nuckols want somebody with a lot of time left so they won't have to replace squad leaders as often. I've got eight and a half months, so I'm their man. I don't like the way you guys have been treated, and I'll understand if you're pissed at me."

Vickers replied laconically, then picked up his meals. "Hell, Pete, you're only doing what any other GI would do under the circumstances. Nobody is going to do anything for you, so you've got to cover your own ass first."

Chase slapped my hand. "You're buying a case of beer the next time we go in for a stand-down, you lucky asshole."

"I will buy that case of beer. You guys keep your heads down out there."

Patterson stopped at the CP with my radio on his back. "What the fuck did I do to deserve this thing? Pete, you lucky son of a bitch, what the hell is my call sign?"

"It should be Asshole 1, but you're Blazer 5–0. Nuckols is Blazer 5 or Charlie 2–5, depending on who's calling. Really, it's not so bad, Pat. Just imagine you're carrying a case of beer and take care of it."

"Get real. This mother's heavy. It'll be waiting for you when you get back."

"No, no, no. I'm rid of that albatross for good. It's back to a line squad for this dude. Take care, Pat."

I watched as the company disappeared into the trees, then carried my gear and weapon to the helipad where I found a resting place and soaked up a few warm rays. Just as I was feeling sleepy, I heard the *whup-whup* of the rotor blades cutting through the morning air. After it landed, I helped unload the supplies, then jumped on the Huey helicopter and flew to the battalion LZ, where I checked in with HQ and was directed to a truck which took me to the airstrip. I showed them my flight orders and they put me on the manifest for the next flight to Holloway.

The C-130 lifted off with a dozen or so troops and some cargo at 1100. I sat near the back and watched the countryside slide past through the half-opened cargo ramp. This country is so damn green and lush, yet the villages are such dumps. Why had a country with so much potential been unable to take advantage of their resources? Had the French siphoned all the profits and abused the working people, creating hatred and the eventual backlash that led to their defeat, much as all colonial powers had done through history? There was widespread poverty throughout the countryside, yet this is a land that could feed itself and still be able to export food to the world under the right circumstances.

Another incongruity of this war-ravaged country was the sight of a mansion surrounded by rows of trees stuck in the middle of nowhere near the mountains that marked the edge of the Highlands. The stories that we heard told of French payoffs to the VC and the Saigon government to allow them to operate these coffee or rubber plantations and be insulated from the war efforts of both sides. These were people who had a good life here and were willing to pay to keep it. Not all plantation owners were of that cut, however, and there had been great battles in the rubber plantations farther south.

A change in the pitch of the engine noise precluded the descent into Holloway Air Base. I deplaned and walked through the large terminal and looked for a ride. Outside I spotted a small Army truck with 3rd Brigade, 25th Infantry markings and walked over to it. A Spec 4 emerged from the terminal with a youthful looking second lieutenant in tow and greeted me.

"Hey, dude, what's happenin'? You just in from Qui Nhon?"

"Yeah, can you drop me at Charlie, 1st of the 14th?"

"Can do. You guys should have been here the last few nights. We've been getting a few mortar rounds at Camp Enari and here at Holloway they're getting more."

"Good deal. You boys in the rear deserve a piece of the war, too. Makes you appreciate your job more."

He snorted, then started the truck and roared off to camp, arriving at Charlie Company compound about fifteen minutes later. I thanked him profusely for trying to scare the hell out of me with his driving and saluted the still-silent, green lieutenant. I could empathize with his shock at the first sight of his new duty stop, but after he got used to it, well, it just would get worse. I walked through the wire gate and turned into the clerk's office.

"PFC Peterson reporting, Clerk LaBarge. I'm back for NCO prep school."

LaBarge told me the first sergeant was up at battalion HQ and sent me to grab a bunk and get squared away with my gear. I found my footlocker in the supply shed, then headed for the old 2nd Platoon tent. The place was deserted and the bunks were missing, so I moved to a different tent near the clerk's office and found an empty bunk on the far end away from three shammers.

I decided to check out my locker and discovered that some rear asshole had broken the lock and stolen my Golden Dragon crest pin from my baseball cap. It was the only thing missing, which raised my suspicions, but I decided it wasn't worth worrying about.

I put my gear and weapon away and hit the hard bunk for some rest. When I opened my eyes again, it was dark outside and there was dim light over the bunks on the other end where a REMF was reading a skin magazine. I staggered up to the clerk's office and encountered LaBarge again.

"Yo, my main man, LaBarge. Got any Cs? I slept right through supper. Best sleep I've had in a long time, though."

"I figured that's what happened, so I had one of the guys on KP fix up some sandwiches. Come on over to my tent for chow and beer."

LaBarge had a small, circular, blue tent with sandbags piled up about four feet on the outside. Inside there was room for two men to live, or one to live comfortably—LaBarge lived alone. He had all the comforts of rear life: cot with air mattress; cooler, well stocked; radio, record and tape player, and some softcover books.

"Not bad. Apparently you couldn't find a maid to clean the place and make your bed."

"I'm working on that, Pete. I got most of this stuff from Fortunato and some from the PX. Have a beer. It's imported all the way from the U.S.A. and contains 3.2 percent alcohol."

I felt like I was in a different world from the LZ I had left this morning. It was still the dry season here while the troops were slogging in the mud back there.

"How is life in the rear? Does time go slow here?"

"Sometimes it really drags and I'm ready to transfer out, but there are lots of interesting things to do here in my job, so I guess I'll hold on to it."

"Do that, troop. Your job here is important. We need somebody we can rely on. No matter how boring it might get, don't give in to the temptation to head back to the boonies. Do your job and go home satisfied."

I finished one more beer and stepped out into the cool Central Highlands night air. The sky was clear and beautiful and the moon was so bright you could read a book. I needed no light to find my way back to my bunk.

I spent the next three days getting my clothes and boots ready for the morning inspections at the school. I met Koger, the 1st Platoon's nominee who would be my schoolmate, and we took our fatigues to the cleaners located at the PX. The Vietnamese workers cleaned and pressed them and we picked them up the following day. We asked around and found out a few things about the school, mostly that it would be Mickey Mouse stuff. On Saturday, Koger and I were put on work detail with the other shammers and we spent the morning constructing new barracks. After our noon chow, we disappeared from the scene and no one came looking for us, so we napped in one of the abandoned tents.

Sunday night, I thought I was prepared for the Academy, so I went to the mess hall to watch a Jonathan Winters movie, *The Russians Are Coming,* but it didn't seem funny and I was almost happy when the camp was put on alert and the lights were put out. I went to the tent and lay on my bunk, thinking about prejudices. What causes hatred to hang on and sometimes even grow stronger through generations of families? After mulling it over, I reckoned that if your parents treated you well, showed you love while protecting you and providing for you, you would be hard-pressed not to hate what they hate. But, when you begin to mature, shouldn't you start to break the molds and get out from under the pressures that forged your behaviors, your likes and dislikes? I guess in some people, even reaching an age of reason cannot rescue them from the fears and inhibitions imposed upon them in their tender years. "Fear, that's what causes it. Fear of the unknown."

I fell asleep after midnight and dreamed once more of the eyes of the captain on that fateful day, then woke up thrashing and sweating. I staggered to the end of the tent and woke up the FNG there to ask if he had any booze. He waved me off, so I went outside and passed the clerk's office.

One of the shammers was on duty, so I tried to talk with him, but he was nearly asleep and resented my intrusion. I went back to the bunk and lay there, thinking that it had become quite self-evident lately that my mental state left a lot to be desired, but I still didn't know what to do about it. Finally, I dozed for an hour or so until Koger woke me for breakfast. We then shaved, dressed in our best fatigues and headed for our new adventure.

16

January 16 produced a bright but cold morning, so Koger and I wore our field jackets to the Academy, then stopped and hung them at the front of the one-room building. The NCO in charge lined us up alphabetically, brought us to attention and gave us a quick inspection. I glanced at the other troops in line and figured I was in trouble; most of them were REMFs with spit-shined boots and tailored fatigues with a crease so sharp you could shave with it. Of the thirty candidates, I estimated that eight were grunts, another six to eight were artillery and the rest were members of the Remington Brigade (desk jockeys).

I earned three demerits (belt, boots, hair—hair?) and no merits and then we were marched single-file inside, seated alphabetically, then given the rules of the Academy: inspection every morning; candidates would be addressed by number on seating chart; class ratings would be determined by academic standing, inspection points (I *was* in trouble), field work and peer rating.

The staff would pick an acting platoon leader and squad leaders each day and the bottom five in rankings at the end would automatically fail the course. The Army had decided that fear of failure was as powerful an incentive as the rewards of success, or the NCOs and officers in charge wanted the power to punish a subordinate arbitrarily. Either way, the policy sucked.

After the introductory phase, we received a two-hour lecture on command structure with intermittent questioning of the class. It became quickly evident that I had two major challenges at the Academy: to try to break even at inspections while scoring in the other categories, and staying awake in the classroom. I glanced around and saw I was not alone; shoulders slumped and eyes were blinking as the sun warmed the air and baked the tin-roofed building. The instructor, Lieutenant Primmer (former recon platoon leader in the 1st/14th), was an interesting speaker, but I was losing the battle. When he called my number (19), I managed a noncommittal answer to his query, then lapsed into a semiconscious stupor, confident the law of averages would protect me from further intrusions. On this day it did.

After more dreary lectures in the afternoon, we were finally dismissed and headed for the company compound. I knew that I was doomed from the start with the inspection, since I did not possess the hand or the eye to make me look good in a uniform, nor did I believe that looking good was any measure of a man and his abilities as a leader. However, I would try and, to that end, I took my spare fatigues to the cleaners for pressing, then returned to my bunk and went to work on my boots and belt buckle. I spent the night bringing my scuffed jungle boots to a dull luster and taking the tarnish off the buckle. My eyes and arms ached and I slept soundly all night.

Day two of school was a little better. At the inspection I

made no merits, but I received no demerits, an outcome which I considered a victory. During the inspection and subsequent classroom lectures, I discerned that a pecking order was being established. A couple of clean-cut, spit-and-polish troops in the first row had scored well on inspections and were trying to answer every question and dominate discussions. The staff we had seen thus far was delighted with the efforts of these two and they looked to be top five material. A tall, husky black man named Warren, a line trooper from our sister battalion, 1st/35th, had come to the classroom with an unshaven face, unpressed fatigues and a starched antiestablishment attitude. He had, of course, taken the most demerits in the inspections and then dared to question the instructors during class.

The instructors would become incensed when challenged, then would question the integrity and motive of the provocateur rather than address the issue raised or modify their beliefs. It was typical Army—pound the square peg into the round hole, pound it and pound it into submission.

I thought about these things as the day progressed. I agreed with some of the things Warren was saying, but some of the time he just seemed to be striking out at an authority figure. In the classroom, he had a platform to espouse his views, so he was availing himself. I wondered if he understood that his behavior, which would be admirable in a college lecture hall, was costing him in the more restrictive Army classroom.

The next morning we arrived early and I saw a chance to talk with Warren and Brown (one of the first-row favorites). I was prepared to dislike Brown because of his smooth mannerisms and sometimes patronizing attitude, but I soon learned he was an infantryman and a veteran of these battles in the rear and could be a valuable friend. What I had perceived to be phoniness was really an honest attempt at showing he was the best; there had been some problems in his past, and he wanted to get his rank back. This appeared to be his way back up the ladder.

I started out, "I've been in the classroom for two days and managed the answer to one question. I understand most of the stuff they're throwing at us, but it doesn't interest me. How the hell do you guys stay focused?"

"Well, I've been in the Army five years and believe me, it's all a game," Brown said to the growing audience. "If you play by their rules on their time and turf, you'll do fine. I've been an E-5 before and I know how to play, so next week when they announce the top five, I expect to be there. I'm not sucking up to anybody and I don't give a damn if anybody thinks I am. It's part of the 11th Commandment, men."

Warren spoke bitterly. "I don't like their games and I don't intend to play any more than I absolutely have to. Those assholes are just skating along 'til their DEROS comes up, so I'm gonna raise hell and give my opinions every chance I get."

Brown answered in a calm voice, "These guys will eat you alive and not give a damn, Warren. I can see you don't care about the promotion, but man, don't think they won't stick your ass in the bottom five without batting an eye. If you give them shit, you'll get it back doubled."

I stuck my nose back into the conversation. "I'm somewhere in between you two in my beliefs. I don't like this Mickey Mouse shit either, but I will play along while I'm here and continue to bend the rules to my satisfaction when I'm back in the field. I would like to have the promotion, mostly for the money, but I agree with Brown, they'll screw you over and leave you for dead, Warren."

"I'll take my chances. I've only got three months left on my tour and in the Army, so I've got nothing to lose. Besides, a man ain't much if he don't stand for somethin'. Besides, what are they gonna do—send me to 'Nam?"

We all joined in the chorus for the last four words. Koger had been listening and nodding, but spoke up now. "I'm kind of in-between, too, but more like Brown. I might stay in the Army, so I'd really like to get the rank before I go back to the World. Rank comes hard back there."

"You know, Lieutenant Primmer's not a bad instructor," Brown said. "I like his lectures, thorough and professional."

"He was recon platoon leader for the 1st/14th over on the border," I added. "They got caught by the NVA a couple of times, so he's battle tested."

Warren's eyebrows shot up. "I didn't know that. Still, he could be a little more receptive to criticism during the questioning. And those two lifer sergeants, Moore and that red-headed prick, O'Malley, they're doofless." He was reviving an old basic training term to describe their ineptness.

Koger interjected, "That's what we can call Moore—Sergeant Doofless."

"And O'Malley is red on the head. . . ."

I interrupted Brown, "Like the dick on a dog."

We all collapsed in laughter, then tried to pull ourselves together as the whistle sounded.

We had our first written test and I began to show my strength as I scored 100 percent. My plan was now solidified: score the highest on academics, break even on inspections, do my best on fieldwork and let my peers think what they would. I now knew I could make the top five, if the staff was open-minded and the candidates got to know me. As the week dragged on I tried to appear alert and receptive as the staff continued to fawn over Brown and Carter, a pudgy but spotless clerk. At times I wanted to stand up and yell, "What the hell has this got to do with leading a squad into battle along the Cambodian border?" But I kept my silence in order to stay on the good side of the staff.

On Thursday, January 19, we finished classes and returned to a somber camp. LaBarge waved us over and said, "Captain Childers was killed in action today near Phu Cat. Lieutenant Bordner, Sergeant Kushinski and PFC Franks were wounded while checking out a tunnel complex. That's all we know right now."

My mind was clicking, trying to make sense of this latest blow. I tried to bring his face before me and I couldn't remember what he looked like. Then I felt guilty about the fact that I was back here skating, shamming while men were dying in my company. After regaining my composure, I realized that sort of thinking was counterproductive since there was little one man could do to prevent the death and destruction that happened in war. I had already learned that lesson all too well.

LaBarge and I joined Koger in his tent for some beer and sad country music after chow. We toasted and mourned our fallen leader, though we hardly knew him. I found out his full name from LaBarge, then proposed a toast.

"To Captain Stephen A. Childers, Charlie Company commander, who has shuffled off this mortal coil. May his soul be in Heaven an hour before the Devil knows he is dead." It was a sad night in Charlie Company compound.

I actually looked forward to the start of classes the next morning; I needed something to occupy my mind and break the spell cast over me by the bad news. I broke even again at inspection, then fastened my eyes and focused all my attention on Lieutenant Primmer's lecture on military intelligence. In the afternoon we were tested again, this time on land navigation. Again, I scored 100 percent—two out of two. Before dismissal, I learned that I would be the fourth squad leader tomorrow—not a singular honor, since everyone got to lead a squad during the two weeks of school. However, it was a chance to show the staff and the other candidates something about me and my abilities.

As a squad leader, I took part in the Saturday morning inspection, as an inspector. I praised the grunts and found fault with the REMFs in their pressed fatigues and spotless boots. Carter had been praised by the platoon leader as he passed by in review, but I got real close to his face.

"Did you shave this morning, son? Well, next time get a little closer to the blade. One demerit." It felt great.

We filed into the classroom and listened as Lieutenant Primmer gave a two-hour lecture on the Battle of Dragon Crater, complete with chalkboard illustrations. I sat spellbound as he told of how the ARVNs performed abominably while his recon platoon held the enemy off. He told of how the lines of Charlie Company were breached, but the enemy was eventually repelled by fire superiority, discipline and timely resupply. He said the official body count was 232, but he thought it was much higher, like other Army officers, I thought. As he wound up the lecture, he turned from the chalkboard, smiled ever so slightly and said to the candidates, "And that was the day the 1st of the 14th lost its cherry."

His words touched some chord, some juvenile strain that still surged through the hearts and souls of a good share of these boys—these men, especially those members of the rear echelon. Some of them laughed nervously, one or two guffawed, while the grunts nodded, smiled and added a silent "Yeah." But I didn't smile; regarding the events of November 19, 1966, I knew I'd never smile again.

I also thought that Primmer had played loose with the facts. He overstated the performance of his recon platoon, which was understandable, and oversimplified the overall significance of the loss of command structure on the field. His statement that the 1st of 14th lost its cherry on November 19 ignored the baptism of blood we had suffered six days before when Alpha Company was nearly annihilated, and the battles that Bravo Company had fought. In all, it was a self-serving lecture. I knew, however, that I couldn't talk about the battle without choking up, so I remained silent and his "facts" stood.

After the last class, Koger and I invited a few of the candidates to his tent for a few beers. Warren was the only one to show up, and he could only stay for a short while. "I've got line duty at 2000 hours, but I'll have a couple."

"We don't have to pull perimeter guard or work details while school is in session here in company."

"Yeah, but you're white, your first sergeant's white and your company clerk is white. Go down to the line right now. Most of the guys there are black."

"I can't argue the facts, but let's look at it further," I said. "Most of the shammers, at least in Charlie Company, are black, so it follows that they would serve on most details."

"I'm not ready to concede that most shammers are black, but if they are, it's because they are looking for an example, someone to follow. In a lot of cases, that's a shammer, a guy who has time to read about what's happening in the world and how to react as a black man."

"A militant black man?"

"You could say that. It's a fact when a brother gets a job in the rear, he tries to help other blacks do the same. Also, and don't minimize the importance of this fact, a lot of the brothers don't think it's our war, man."

"Is it just a white man's war, then, Warren?"

"I'm not sure about that. You know, I love my country, too, but there are a lot of things that need changing. One of the militant brothers said it like this: the black man shouldn't be fighting the yellow man for the white man."

"I'm from the Midwest, Warren. Back there we still believe, at least they did when I left, that America is in this war as a country, one people. Does that make us naive or simplistic, or are we just really patriotic?"

"I think you're content with the way things are and would like to see it continue. The black power advocates would like to tear it all down and start over with a different power structure."

"That leaves a tremendous gap between the two," I said. "We've got to find a way to bridge it or compromise in some way—tearing down the power structure is anarchy."

"I personally believe that we have to work within the system to improve our lot in life," Warren added.

Koger then broke into what had been just a two-way conversation. "Shouldn't that include the lot of all underprivileged and downtrodden, no matter what their color might be?"

"Sure, but they need to get involved, too. Well, I gotta get ready for line duty. I hear your CO got wasted, Pete." Warren sat down his empty beer can and stood up to leave.

"Yeah, wasted. Joined the choir invisible. Paid his debt to nature. Another white guy dying for his country." I put some sarcasm into the remark.

"If he believed he was dying for his country, he should be honored. But more and more blacks believe that they are dying for a white man's causes and country. Do you know how it makes me feel to see the Confederate flag flying over some hillbilly's bunker? I'm still fighting for America, but not for that peckerwood. If some redneck buys it, it's not a great loss to me."

He started to leave, then stopped at the door. "Pete, I know you're listening to what I say, and to me you're a righteous dude, so hear this: big changes are coming, I just hope they're peaceful ones."

"Warren, you're an articulate spokesman and I believe the situation today needs men like you. Stay involved and keep your head down."

He gave me a raised fist, then the peace sign; I responded with a thumbs-up and hand-salute. His words stuck in my mind long after he left. It was obvious that I had naively believed that I cared about civil rights for blacks because I had favored integration and voter registration. In actuality, I had shown very little grasp of the problems and had no solutions. But, I did care, in my own bleeding-heart way, I was just isolated up to now. From this point on, I vowed to search for signs of intolerance at all levels and fight it where I could.

The Sunday schedule called for only two hours of class on methods of instruction. As we were leaving the compound, the first sergeant flagged us down and challenged us. "Hold it right there, troops. Where the hell do you think you're going? It's Sunday."

"We've got class today, too, first sergeant."

"Yeah, we're going to Sunday School."

He didn't know whether to believe us or not, but he smiled slightly and let us pass. After the two-hour lecture on giving lectures, we were sent home with orders to prepare a ten-minute speech for the next day. Once back in the tent, I began to work on a lecture concerning the makeup and duties of a rifle squad. I had no problem writing it, but cutting it to exactly ten minutes was harder than I thought it would be.

Koger and I rehearsed together, one speaking while the other listened and checked the time. When we reached the nine minute mark, the other would signal to wind it up in one minute. Around midnight, we were satisfied enough to knock off for the night and sip a beer while listening to Johnny Rivers on his record player. Then I retreated to my bunk and listened to the rats racing along the floorboards. My trusty mosquito net kept them at bay while I slept.

Another cool, crisp Highlands morning greeted us as we walked up over the crest of the rolling hill that the camp was built on. Coblentz, a short wiry troop from artillery, was the platoon leader for the day and he called us crisply to order and led the inspection. I took one demerit for my boots, but I didn't really care about the chickenshit stuff anymore. If I didn't make it on my academics and field performance, I didn't want it. I could feel the tension in my stomach as I entered the class-room, but I told myself it couldn't be as bad as being pinned down by automatic weapons at Dragon Crater.

The morning dragged on, but after chow break the class split into groups and began the lectures. Brown, Warren and Koger went early, but I was second to last. As I listened to the early speeches, I ran over some of the things that had happened to me over the last four months. I surmised that I had been challenged a few times and, within the limitations imposed on me by my Midwestern rural upbringing, had answered them fairly well. This was merely another small challenge, yet when my name and number was called, my heart leaped into my throat and for a second I *was* more frightened than I had been in battle.

As I began to speak I glanced at Warren, who was giving me the OK sign, and Brown, who was holding small signs marked from ten to one. He checked his watch and flipped one over each minute to aid the speaker in timing the length of the speech. Because of my rehearsals, I finished within ten seconds of the limit and Brown whispered as I walked by, "Good timing—the best so far."

The instructor, Sergeant Moore, critiqued the lecture and noted that I had used a few too many hand gestures, but otherwise it was fine and would score well. I felt relieved, but was getting a little tired of the school and life in the rear. Too much harassment, too many damn regulations and silly rules, too many meaningless tasks and duties and way too much time on your hands. That night Koger and I listened to Chris Noel on Armed Forces Radio and shot the breeze.

"I'm ready to go back to the line, man, to the boonies. Life back here is a real drag. You gotta get stoned to feel good and the body can only take so much of that. Set me free."

"I could stay here for another two and a half months and not miss a thing, Pete. I'm not looking forward to seeing the platoon again. I hate that grind."

"Have you learned anything in this Mickey Mouse Academy? Hell, we gave speeches today, but did anybody listen to anybody else? It's almost all cut and dried as to the top five. Brown, Carter, Ogg and you are in if you don't screw up, but Warren doesn't have a chance to make it and he's the only one here I'd want to serve under in combat. And I might lose out because of my frickin' demerits. There's something fundamentally wrong here, Koger. The Army needs men like Warren in a leadership position."

"We can rate him at the top on Friday, Pete."

"Yeah, but he's gone. Chop-chop. The staff and the rear assholes will rate him low. This staff sucks and so do the spit-shining desk jockeys. Send me to Bong Son."

"You'll be there soon enough, Pete. I hope it's what you are looking for, man."

After inspection and a short briefing, the staff marched us to an open area on the west side of the camp where they opened up the formation and put us through a rigorous physical training session. We started with a few warm-up exercises, then several of the candidates took turns leading us through ninety minutes of push-ups, sit-ups, jumping jacks and squat thrusts. The two weeks of soft living and rear beer began to take its toll as the sun climbed into the cloudless sky and the temperature rose. About the time I thought I was going to drop, the session was ended and we took a ten-minute break to cool down.

Following the break, we began a period of close-order drill. Candidates who had not led the class in PT instruction were given the chance to put the platoon, as we had been designated for the exercise, through a set of maneuvers designed to move us down a road, then around the field and back to the starting point. A few panicked immediately, giving the wrong directions and sending us marching into the sides of bunkers and buildings where we gleefully did exaggerated pratfalls and moaned. It was the first real fun the group had together since the school began. One of the REMFs, Hayes, started like this: "Right, turn and forward, Ho! I mean, stop! Wait! Halt! Left face. Again. Shit—no, don't! Halt!"

A few of the troops were sharp and prepared and had little problem moving the platoon correctly. Carter, the staff favorite, started us out, "Platoon, right face! Forward—march. Left . . . left . . . left, right, left."

We moved smoothly down the road, which ended just ahead, as he pranced alongside. As we neared the fence, he panicked and forgot the command to reverse our movement (to the rear, one march). He sputtered for a minute before yelling, "Reverse, ho!"

We crashed into the fence, did phony flops over the top strand and rolled on the ground laughing. It was the funniest thing I had been a part of in Vietnam.

"A reverse, ho? What the hell is that, man?" somebody yelled.

O'Malley came running to the scene, his face even more red

than its usual scarlet hue, and began screaming, "Get up, god-dammit, get up! Show some respect to your drill leader. Pla-toon, ten-shun. Take over, Carter."

I whispered loud enough for most of the platoon to hear, "Watch out, Brown. Carter's goin' for numbah one with the staff. Look at old Red on the Head suck up to him."

Despite all the repetition, a few more of the candidates pan-icked, sending us into moments of happy disarray. One of the troops had a thick Southern twang which, combined with the singsong cadence, made him totally undecipherable. His com-mands came out like this: "Toon, tain-shat! Layuft haaccce! Far-wort hahch."

"Speak English, man," Warren yelled. "I've only got three more months to get through this class."

The unexpected levity combined with the physical activity raised the spirits of the class and, as we marched smartly back to the classroom with Brown leading, I remembered the words of the prison commandant in a famous war movie: Be happy in your work. On that morning, in that place, we were happy.

I checked the scores for our MOI lectures on the board at the classroom and I received 23.5 out of 24, again the highest. There was little doubt that I was leading in academics and had no trouble with my drill program. I felt that I must be at least close to the top five, so I would "keep on keepin on,' " in the words of the song.

The class loaded into trucks and headed to the firing range for a demonstration instruction and participatory exercise with explosives that afternoon. After the lecture and two blasts, each of us was given a small piece of C-4 (plastic explosive), a blast-ing cap and some "det" cord to make our own charge. Because of the potential for danger and fun, the class was more inter-ested and excited than usual and the afternoon flew by. We each got to blow our charge, accompanied by whoops and cries of joy as the juvenile in all of us emerged for a while.

That night Koger and I laughed as we recalled the drill lead-ers marching us into fences and bunkers.

"Carter, I loved it. He fell apart and couldn't remember his name, let alone the commands. My sides still hurt."

"And that ol' boy from Mississippi. When Warren yelled out, I fell down. It sure felt good to laugh for once, Pete."

We listened to Chris Noel again until one of those over-whelming silent moments hit and neither of us could speak, or wanted to. I went to my tent and told the shammers to turn off their music and light, wrapped my hopefully ratproof mosquito netting around the wire frame over my bunk and let the fatigue overwhelm me.

The class returned to the range the next day for some basic infantry maneuvers—fire and maneuver, fire and movement. Again each candidate got a chance to lead a squad through one of these by yelling commands as the troops lay down a base of fire for their comrades who were maneuvering or moving. We were using live ammo to add realism, so the grunts were quiet and attentive, while the desk jockeys were acting like they usu-ally did. I tried to put on my "jungle face" for maximum safety and effectiveness, then made a quick decision: when a REMF was behind or beside me, I would lag back. It could cost me points and possibly a top five spot, but I did not want to be shot by a desk jockey in starched fatigues on some puny exer-cise.

After a lot of cursing, sweating and some bleeding, I made it through the designed course as a leader, then moved back into line to serve as a squad member. When Carter took the squad, he tripped and fired a half-dozen rounds into the rocks just over our heads.

"What the hell is the matter with you!" I screamed. Some-body else yelled, "Put the fucking safety on or I'll shove that ri-fle up your ass."

I had hit the ground immediately, then glanced around. The grunts were all down, the REMFs were still up and the artillery and armor were undecided. I looked at Koger, and then we laughed and walked through the rest of the exercise. We lis-tened to the critiques, then loaded up and rode to the gate.

As we marched back to the classroom, Carter took some heat from the line doggies, but I laid off. He was trying to maintain his composure in the face of severe hostility and there was something brave about that. Hell, he probably didn't ask to be sent to 'Nam as a clerk . . . whoa! Now I'm feeling sorry for some rear asshole whose biggest problem was trying to decide which pair of spit-shined boots to wear that day—and he almost killed me. I really do have a bleeding heart problem; this place is costing me my sanity.

That evening at the clerk's office, LaBarge and I reviewed the latest round of rumors: One, the brigade would be spending the next five months in the Phu Cat–Bong Son area; two, the brigade would join the division in Cu Chi; three, the battalion would pull palace guard for brigade HQ or at some air base until we were at full strength.

LaBarge insisted there was no factual basis for any of these stories that were making the rounds and said he had heard very little about future plans. "Who's running the company now?"

"Lieutenant Guidry from battalion HQ. We'll get a new CO to relieve him next month."

"Guidry? He got a Silver Star for action with the Cacti, didn't he? Good man."

"That's the one. He's just on loan. The tunnel complex was filled with supplies: food, clothing, weapons and ammo. There was a hospital in there with an operating room and beaucoup maps and documents. It's a regiment HQ. We're the big news in the brigade right now."

"Charlie Company strikes again. Wonder who was on point that day. Probably Kushinski of the mighty 2nd Platoon."

On Thursday, two Academy staff members led the candidates on a dual-purpose patrol. They wanted to check us out in patrol situations and, at the same time, battalion HQ wanted to see if there was any VC activity in the small ville a few klicks to the west. The sun was hot, the village was sleepy and showed no signs of enemy activity, and the patrol was uneventful. On the way back, we stopped at the range and went through forward observer procedures and called in a few smoke rounds. It felt good to stretch my sore, tired muscles, but again I was getting tired of the grind and the harassment. That night we reviewed the material we had covered and quizzed each other in preparation for the final exam the next day. The competitor in me wanted to do well, but the pragmatist wanted to get it over and get on with my tour of duty.

The staff and acting squad leaders moved quickly through the Friday morning inspection, lending further credence to my belief that they had already picked their favorites and were merely going through the motions. If this were true, I was again in trouble in my efforts to attain top five status. All I could do was write a good final test and let my marks stand for me. It was too late to change my methods.

Lieutenant Primmer announced the remaining schedule: review of all courses this morning followed by the final exam after chow. After the exam we would rate our fellow students on their deportment and leadership qualities. He then led us into a review of military justice as we tried to discern which points were likely to appear on the exam. At 1100 we were dismissed for a two-hour chow and study break.

There were fifty questions in the test requiring written answers of several lines each and some mathematical work. As I worked through the pages, I discovered that one of them was duplicated, so I ignored it and completed the test in about ninety minutes. I waited outside with Ogg for the rest to finish, then returned to fill out my rating sheet. I studied each of the names and numbers and tried to honestly rate each candidate. When I came to Warren, I happily lost my objectivity and placed him in third place, despite his refusal to accede to the rules of the staff.

Koger and I walked back to the compound together and found some beer at the EM club on the hill. At his tent, we listened to some sad country songs and drank beer. I asked how he did today. "I think I did all right—maybe three or four wrong. We both should be top five, Pete. That would make the first sergeant happy."

"I really don't know, man. My academics are fine, MOI tops, fieldwork good. But I didn't volunteer in the classroom or join the discussions very often. It could cost me. But, hell, I really don't care. I know my qualifications and I'll get my rewards from Charlie Company."

While eating pancakes and greasy, hard sausages at the mess hall the next morning, LaBarge broke the news. "Word came down last night, Pete. Koger made the top five, you fell short. You missed one page of questions on the exam."

I explained what happened, then hurried through breakfast and headed for the Academy staff hooch. As I waited at the door for Lieutenant Primmer, I wondered if I should whip a battalion greeting on him (Golden Dragon, Sir), but decided that I should not suck up—let the case ride on its merits.

"Sir, PFC and Candidate Peterson, someone made an error and there was a duplicate sheet of questions of my exam. I did the page once, then skipped the duplicate."

Sergeant O'Malley, standing at Primmer's shoulder, puffed up and turned crimson. "There were *no* errors made in correcting the papers, I did each of them myself," he yelled at the top of his voice.

I insisted that the lieutenant check my test scores and then decide if I was likely to miss one whole page of questions. He checked my perfect scores, nodded, then told O'Malley, "Dig out the test paper. There's obviously been an error."

The redheaded sergeant found the paper, handed it to the officer and said, "I made no errors. He had one page wrong."

Lieutenant Primmer rifled quickly through the test and found the blank page, which he showed me. I pressed my point. "Sir, check the previous page, it's the same questions. I saw no need to answer them twice."

"Yes, I see. It is a duplicate. That brings you up to only four wrong—92 percent. Totaling your scores now moves you up from eleventh to sixth place—still not top five."

I sneaked a quick glance at the standings and saw I had dropped to second in academics, but my peer rating was only tenth. I couldn't see my staff rating, but they obviously hadn't rated me in the top five, either. My mind raced over the series of events; if my peers had rated me tenth, it was because I had not answered enough in class. I could understand that, but I could not understand the staff not putting me up high enough to make up for that. I believed that the error had, by virtue of causing the staff to think I had not taken the test seriously, lowered my academic standing enough that when the staff made their final ratings, they ignored me in figuring the winners. Now, when the error was pointed out, they didn't feel they could bump another person out of his spot, so they crucified me.

It hurt, but I didn't see any way out of it, so I wheeled around and headed to the classroom. I had a bitter taste in my mouth as Ogg inspected me. I was still angry as we filed into the room and sat down. My first impulse was to head for Charlie Company compound and request an immediate return to Bong Son to rejoin the real troops, but I cooled down and tried to swallow the bitter pill. I was angry at my fellow candidates for not being a little more discerning, and at the staff for screwing me over, but I would get my puny diploma, then file my complaint through the first sergeant.

Ogg nudged me as we sat waiting for Lieutenant Primmer. "I saw you had a total of three demerits on the board, so I made you even with three merits."

"Thanks, man. That's all I ever asked for—an even shake."

Old Red on the Head read the announcements for the day, "Graduation at 1300 today. Wear clean fatigues and shined boots, baseball cap. Now, I'm going to pass out a sheet of paper for each of you. We want you to rate the Academy and give us your suggestions and complaints. Be sure to put your number on the bottom. Don't worry, no one will know what's on the sheets but the staff."

He left and I went at the blank sheet with a fury. I complained that the staff was partial to starched fatigues and shined boots and didn't see the soldier inside them. I stated that they had picked their favorites the first few days and showed partiality to these candidates throughout the two weeks. I said the field work should count more on the score of each man and instructors should pay more attention to the way candidates conducted themselves under pressure of leading while out there. I added my number, then handed in my sheet and felt better for a while. O'Malley took the papers and disappeared while Lieutenant Primmer gave us a small speech praising our efforts.

O'Malley came back later. "Now, we've got some sore losers who say that the staff showed favoritism and picked the top five last week. *I do not* have favorites. This course is well balanced and puts the best candidates in the top spots."

Warren raised his hand, then stood up to speak, "If you believed everything was all right, why did you ask for suggestions, which, incidentally, were supposed to be confidential?"

O'Malley turned so red I thought he would explode. He yelled loud enough to be heard by Lieutenant Primmer outside, "We thought somebody might have something constructive to say, but I guess not. Class dismissed until 1300."

I felt betrayed and abused, so I decided to skip the ceremony, but Koger told me the First Shirt was going to attend, so I swallowed what little pride I had left and found some clean fatigues. I dug my camera out of my locker and took it along to get some photos of myself and the classroom. Maybe someday I'll want to remember this place.

There was enough brass in the classroom to start an ammunition factory: the commanding general of the 3rd Brigade, two colonels, two majors, two captains and Lieutenant Primmer. Also in attendance were Sergeant O'Malley with his red face, Sergeant Moore, the top five with smiles on their faces, Warren with his chip on his shoulder and I with my wounded pride. The ceremony didn't last long, so we rounded up a few of our favorite former rivals and invited them to Charlie Company compound for a few beers after evening chow.

Koger and I moved a cleaned-up trash barrel into his tent to use as a cooler and filled it with Strohs and Millers. The physical activity gave me some time to think and I decided that if my reluctance to change my attitudes about speaking up and passing inspections had caused the class and staff to ignore me, then my falling short could, in part, be placed on my shoulders. I was fully aware of the Army's ways and by not adapting to them, I managed to salvage some personal pride while losing a prized promotion. Also, I should have taken the duplicated page to the instructor during the exam; maybe my high academic rating would have swayed the staff. But this was all after the fact; if I must be an also-ran, I'll be a good one.

Brown, Warren, Coblentz and Ogg joined us as the sun fell in the western sky over Pleiku. Brown brought a bottle of Ten High, Coblentz toted a small bottle of rum, Warren carried beer in every pocket. We congratulated the three top five finishers, then Warren and I proposed a toast. "For those brave souls and assholes who weren't in the top five, but graduated with their pride intact."

Brown added, "Hear, hear. Well, you gotta admit we had fun and nobody was shooting at us."

"Nobody but Carter . . . and O'Malley."

"That peckerwood. I'd like to get him in Alpha Company compound tonight. I'd turn that racist inside out."

"Ogg, do you agree with that—O'Malley a racist?"

"Definitely. If I were braver and more eloquent, I would have accused him of it in class. I'm sorry, man."

"Don't waste your time being sorry," Warren responded. "Stopping bigotry and racism is the duty of all free men."

"The only thing necessary for evil to triumph is for good men to do nothing," I quoted. "Right on, brother."

LaBarge and 1st Sergeant Wolfe joined the gathering and made the rounds, shaking hands and patting backs. Wolfe spoke, "Congrats, Koger, good job. Pete, I'll be making a personal inquiry on Monday about that foul-up. If it helps any, your name is on the next promotion list. You'll be a Spec 4 as of next Wednesday."

"Thanks, first sergeant. That does help. Can I offer you a cold one?"

"Just one. I've still got to work on next week's duty roster. You two have tower guard tomorrow, so don't get too soused. Monday, you'll be heading back to Phu Cat."

"Good. I'm ready to be a line doggie again."

After Top left, we continued to drink and commiserate until after midnight, when I fell asleep on the floor next to the beer barrel.

LaBarge shook me awake at dawn with a harsh growl, "Wake up, Pete. Come on, man, you've got tower guard at 0700. Get some breakfast and report to my office."

My head was pounding, my tongue and mouth were dry and my stomach was churning. Still, I dutifully raised myself and went to the water tank, where I let the water cascade down over my head for a few minutes. I forced down some coffee and toast at the mess hall, then reported to LaBarge.

"PFC Peterson barely reporting for duty. Any chance I could get a one-day pass to recuperate?"

"Negatron, troop. If you're gonna run with the big dogs, you gotta learn how to piss in the tall grass. Tower number five will be your home for the day. You'll be relieved for noon chow. Carry on."

"Roger, wilco. Over and out. To the tower."

I managed to make it to the perimeter and found my tower, then I leaned on a post for a long time. Finally, I slowly made the climb up the wooden ladder and stepped onto the platform. I sat down in the catbird seat and put my feet up on the sandbags. There was a little breeze at the twenty-foot elevation, so I felt a little better. The morning dragged by and the breeze died down as the sun climbed, taking the temperature with it, making me hot, dusty and in a foul mood until the relief man appeared at noon.

After making my way through Army chicken-fried steak and washing it down with lots of juice, the afternoon went much better. After my duty was over I passed through the mess hall where I groveled for a loaf of bread and took it to my hooch and I retrieved a small canned ham my parents had sent me from my locker. I opened it and sliced it, then grilled the slices on a makeshift C-ration can-stove and some heat tabs. A can of C-ration processed cheese and a dab of mess hall mustard added the final touch. I washed it all down with a can of warm soda—ah, bliss.

I had my gear ready to go early the next morning, but LaBarge found me in the mess hall, choking down Army powdered eggs.

"No flight today. Tomorrow we take pay to the company. There'll be a shower run at 1400, but you've got the day off, then line duty tonight."

I went back to my bunk, reread and answered my old mail, then rested until 1100. Then I got permission to leave the company area and headed up to battalion HQ, where I stopped at a desk in Finance and straightened out my pay allotments. At 1400 a few of us climbed on a truck and motored to the other side of camp where we discovered a nice shower area in an artillery compound. I scrubbed off the red clay dust and lingered for a few minutes, then donned my clean fatigues and felt like a million bucks. That night I pulled line guard with three shammers—I sat and slept on top of the bunker as if to segregate myself from their inane prattling and watched an uneventful night roll by.

LaBarge held my pay out of the company field payroll, so I collected it before we headed for the airport. I left most of it with him, told him about the allotments that would take effect next month, and where to send it this time. At Holloway, I boarded the C-130 and contemplated my present position. I really didn't want to go into combat, but life in the rear is so full of boring details and people impressed with their sense of power that it is even less inviting. My goal was simple: to get through the next eight months in good health. To that end, I would continue to be a good soldier, because a good soldier was more likely to survive.

I leaned back and closed my eyes for a few minutes, then I heard the roar of the engines as they wound up. I relaxed as the plane moved into position for takeoff, then felt the surge as the big bird finally roared down the runway and lifted off. My adventures with the rear echelon at the Academy were over. It was time to put the unpleasantness of it behind me and head back to reality.

17

The hulking C-130 kissed the tarmac and rolled to a stop at the airstrip near Phu Cat. I followed the finance officer and clerk as they procured a truck and we rode to the company area inside a large firebase named Trains. This entire area was called Bronco Beach by the 1st Cav, who had been operating here for the past year. As the truck slowed, I saw Mize and Vickers lining up for pay call and I felt like I was home. I jumped down, clapped them on the back and we exchanged handshakes.

"Greetings, men. I'm your new reenlistment officer. Like to get you to re-up for six years and add another year to your tour here in beautiful Vietnam. What do you think?"

"I've got your re-up right here, guy." Vickers grabbed his groin and we shared a low laugh.

"Good to see some real troops. Everybody OK in the 2nd?"

"Well, Pete, you shammin' mother, life's tough out here, but we've got no platoon KIAs (killed in action), so we're cool. How'd you do?"

"Bombed out, Vick. Shot down by the rear echelon. Just missed the top five, but unofficially, you, me and Fears are Spec 4s as of tomorrow—the first."

"It's about damn time. Nine months as a PFC is long enough. If we can find some brew, we'll celebrate."

The guys continued to fill me in on company action over the past two weeks, then I searched out the platoon CP and reported in. Nuckols grunted a greeting, but Lesko spoke.

"Welcome back, troop. I heard about your misfortune and if you'd like, I can make an official complaint with battalion HQ. We can't let them jerk the infantry around."

"If it's all the same with you, I'd like to forget the whole damn thing and get back to work here. I'd like to join a line squad and use my training."

Nuckols and Lesko exchanged glances and shrugged.

"Bennett asked if he could have you when you got back, so I guess you belong to him. He's goin' on R&R pretty soon, so maybe you can get some jerk as a squad leader. Did you hear about the tunnels?"

"I sure did. You guys are celebrities. Look at this."

I pulled out a clipping I had torn from the *Stars and Stripes* daily newspaper and read it to them.

BRIGADE FINDS BRAS, PANTIES

AN KHE, Vietnam (IO) Two sets of items essential to the support of North Vietnamese female cadre were captured by the 3rd Brigade of the 25th Inf. Division which is participating in the 1st Cav. Div.'s Operation Thayer II.

Two pairs of bras and panties were wrested from Communist control in a cave complex by elements of the 1st Bn., 14th Inf., some 290 miles north of Saigon.

The brigade of the Tropic Lightning Division discovered the feminine garb while searching and destroying what is believed to be the underground headquarters and field hospital of the 18th North Vietnamese Army Regt.

"You think ol' Walter Cronkite talked about Charlie Company on the news?"

"Could be, Sarge. You guys did more than the 1st Cav was

able to do in a year. You took away their support. 'And that's the way it was, January 31, 1967.' "

Lesko ignored my pun and asked me, "Pete, what did you think of the school? Should we send anyone else when our turn comes or is it a waste of time?"

"They do a lot of good things—land navigation, defensive tactics—and they do a lot of Mickey Mouse stuff, sir. I think when the present staff DEROSes, it'll be better."

I swallowed the rest of my complaints along with a healthy dose of pride and joined the 1st Squad at one of their bunkers just inside the wire next to the west gate. The company was pulling "palace guard" for the forward brigade HQ, which consisted mostly of line duty and short patrols and a lot of sitting around the perimeter.

As the sun went down, Bennett, Vickers and I lay back against the wall of the huge bunker and told stories. I noticed that the temperature was warmer here in the coastal plains and the night would be pleasant. I heard a distant *pop-pop-pop,* then suddenly the 1st Cav boys on the north side opened up with everything they had. After a few minutes, they went quiet again and we had not moved.

A half hour later, another sniper opened up and the rounds hit our bunker just above our heads with a noise like a boxer hitting a heavy bag. We scrambled around to the other side and continued our conversation as the artillery fired flares and the 1st Cav opened up again.

"Way to go, arty, now they can see their targets."

"Welcome back, Pete. Charlie missed you."

"Looks like it. Man, that 1st Cav is a trigger-happy outfit."

The others took their poncho liners inside the bunker to get some sleep and I took first watch up on top behind a low wall of sandbags. Now that I was back in my element, I was intent on proving myself to my squad, platoon and company and most important, to myself.

I took a self-guided tour of the perimeter the next morning and found that it wasn't nearly as big as Camp Enari, more like 3 Golf. There were a few units of the 1st Cav, an artillery company, and room for one company of our battalion. On the northeast side was a large field where the Assault Helicopter Battalion kept their choppers and personnel and next to that was a storage area. I saw the hooches where forward HQ was located and noted that they were quite temporary, so I guessed we probably wouldn't be staying here very long.

The 2nd Platoon stayed in the perimeter for the day as the 1st went on patrol into a nearby village. That night the firing started again about 2100 while Huffman was on watch and the rest of us were talking on the back side. The 1st Cav opened up once more, firing blindly, then stopped while the choppers went up and began dropping flares. Martinez had wandered down from the gun position and when one of the flares began descending almost directly onto our position, he grabbed my arm and we stepped out from behind the bunker's wall and began singing in the descending illumination, "Mammy, how I love ya, how I love ya!"

The sniper opened up as Vickers, Huffman and Bennett joined us and we dashed around to the safe side again and collapsed in laughter as a few rounds pounded into the bunker.

"If you don't like the fuckin' music just say so, don't try to kill the singer," Bennett yelled into the night.

"Everybody's a damn critic," I added.

"I better get back to my bunker before Chase has a bird."

Martinez began to walk away, then began to limp and did his Walter Brennan–Real McCoy imitation. "Dagnabit, Little Luke, I told you not to sing."

We were a loose group, a platoon that hadn't seen any real action for a while, and the revelry helped pass the time.

After breakfast the next morning we grabbed a C-ration meal and saddled up for a daylong patrol. We headed down a wide dirt road into a heavily populated ville with decent housing and well-dressed citizenry. It looked like the locals were able to make a good living here in this flat, fertile area, which led me to believe that the VC would have a little more trouble selling their programs. I stopped and searched a well-constructed French colonial house now inhabited by a middle-aged Vietnamese merchant. He was selling soda pop and a few other sundries from the veranda and his daughter was mixing the soda in the kitchen.

We moved on through the village and then back onto the heavily traveled road. Security was lax with all the Vietnamese moving along through our ranks, so I relaxed somewhat and enjoyed the balmy weather. One of our orders was to stop all

ARVN troops to check their identification papers. If their papers were not proper, we took them in for questioning. It was an attempt to stop infiltration into ARVN ranks, but it was a distasteful chore for me. Even though I questioned their courage and fighting ability, I didn't think it was righteous to harass and detain them, thus causing them shame in front of their families and friends.

After our fruitless search, we headed back to camp, passing dozens of villagers returning to their homes after a day of work. Some of them were cleaning ladies, barbers or laundry workers with access to the base; they certainly would know the locations of targets for snipers. As we trudged along, I wondered if anybody ever questioned the local workers on the base. The patrol returned to camp with no further incidents in time for hot chow. As I finished my gray beef and potatoes, Nuckols stopped in.

"We need some poker players. CP at 2000. Keep it quiet."

Fancying myself an intelligent gambler, I moseyed up to the tent, found a comfortable spot on the sand and joined Lieutenant Lesko and Sergeants Nuckols, Brittain, Kushinski and PFC Schmitt in what I thought was going to be a friendly game. Five hands and $75 later, I stood up and excused myself.

"I'm checkin' out, guys. Not my night."

"Stick around, Pete. Get back in later."

"Negative. I think I'll just go on down to the wire, put a flare in each hand and wait for the snipers. It'd be less painful."

Bennett greeted me at the back of the bunker, "Well, that didn't last long. What happened?"

I asked him for a match, then took my last dollar out of my pocket, lit the match and burned the piece of MPC.

"That's a better way to get rid of money. Here's another rule to live by: never play poker in a combat zone. You can't bluff a guy who could die tomorrow."

We had a good laugh, then went outside to wait for our sniper, who checked in at 2215.

"This guy's no dummy, Bennett. He always fires high—up on the bunker or over our heads. He knows that if he hits one of us, we'll have to come out after him with night patrols and ambushes and that would ruin the game for all of us."

"Kinda comforting havin' a friend out there, ain't it? Maybe he works here and doesn't want to lose his job. When the VC come around, he says, 'Yeah, I know where to fire and I'll do it every night. Just give me a rifle.' Then he makes sure he doesn't hit anybody and the 1st Cav never gets suspicious. Well, all this talk makes me tired."

He wrapped his liner around him and tried to sleep while I took the 2300 watch and wondered why I had ever thought I was a poker player.

On the morning of February 3, I became a squad leader. Sergeant Bennett came back from the CP and screamed, "I'm goin' on R&R, assholes! Yeehah! Pete, you are now in charge of the 1st Squad. I'll see you pricks in about a week, or maybe two if I can sneak around base camp. Adios, mothahs."

I knew that this might not sit too well with some of the guys who had been in-country longer than I, so I spoke to them:

"This is how it is. I am the squad leader. I expect your 100 percent support, but I'll do the job whether I get it or not. Let's work together and be a good squad. Anybody got anything they need to say or do?"

Vickers spoke up, "You're the man, Pete. What you say, goes."

Rangel said nothing, but his dark eyes were smoldering and spoke volumes. I would have to be a damn good leader or he would be all over me like flies on a piss tube. The platoon was ordered to patrol to another large village in the same area we had forayed into yesterday. As we waited near the west gate, I checked the men's gear and weapons and reminded them to clean it all when we returned. A short, stocky man approached and began looking us over. His nametag read Weinberg and the insignia on his collar said major. He finished looking over the troops, then spoke a few words to us.

"As you were, troops. Getting ready for patrol, I see. Another day, another chance to excel, men. Good hunting."

"Doesn't that just make you wanna puke?" Martinez whispered.

"The guy needs to get a real job somewhere," I added.

We headed back down the same road and then veered south. The ville was quite similar to the last one, with good housing and bicycles everywhere. We spent a few hours searching and found no suspicious activities or supplies, then returned to the camp early in the afternoon, settled in to our positions and watched the steady stream of locals passing by. As we relaxed, orders came down: send out a squad, stop everybody that comes along for ID check, bring in those without proper papers.

"I don't like this kind of harassment shit, Vick, but orders is orders, as they say. OK, 1st Squad, saddle up light. Web gear and weapons. Let's go."

We moved out through the gate, set up across the road and began stopping people, using a few Vietnamese phrases to communicate to them what we wanted.

"Dung lai." (Halt.) *"Dura tay len."* (Put up your hands.)

"Toi kham ong." (I will search you.)

"Dura tay len dau." (Keep your hands on your head.)

A few of them failed to show proper ID, so we had to detain and escort them to the company CP, which required more botched pronunciations on our part.

"Lai dang kia." (Walk there.) *"Dung noi chuyen."* (Do not talk.)

One of the troops made a swipe at the breasts of a beautiful young girl on a bicycle, which immediately drew my ire. I decided that I had to make a stand and a statement, not just a warning.

"Troop, do not treat a female that way, ever. Not in this platoon, and especially not in this squad."

"Hey, she could be VC, man. She could be the one firing into the perimeter at night."

"If you have evidence of that, we'll take her in for questioning. Do not use that VC shit as an excuse to harass or assault the locals, especially a female. We're Americans, not Nazis."

"Shit, man, she's just another dink."

"And you're just a soldier, and I'm just your superior. Leave her alone."

He glared at me, but moved along and the young lady pedaled away quickly. If she had not been VC, the abuse from an American soldier, supposedly her protector and ally, might just turn her into one. After a couple of hours, we had sent about fifty villagers into the camp and the word came back—enough.

We had performed our task a little too zealously, perhaps, but I was happy to give the order to move back inside the wire. Once there, I gave the men a few minutes of rest, then ordered them, in a nice way, to clean weapons and gear. I took out my cleaning rod and some solvent and began going over my own M-16. Vickers and Huffman sat down beside me.

"I think I'd rather be back in the mountains fighting the NVA. There I was more sure of things. I hated the enemy because he was trying to kill me. I don't hate these people, but I have to treat them like they were my enemy. How can we say we're over here fighting for them when we do this shit?"

"I don't know, Pete. Don't seem right to me either, but some of these people are VC sympathizers and suppliers. I'm sure the boys in Intelligence will find the guilty ones and let the others go."

Whenever I saw Huffman, I wondered how he had ever made it this far. He was as thin as the proverbial rail and you never knew where his head was; he always appeared to be looking off into the distance somewhere and thinking deep thoughts, but rarely expounded on them. Then I would think about his getting lost in the jungle near the border and being found by Alpha Company and I realized that he was one of those guys that was going to make it through with only a scratch or two—he was walking in sunshine.

As the day drew to a close, local villagers began gathering at the gate in front of our position to find out what had happened to their family members that we had detained. I wished that I could go to them and reassure them that all would be well, but I didn't know if it would. I tossed them a few cans of Cs over the wire and then we settled down for our hot chow—which also didn't seem right. As the sun began to set behind the mountains, they began to wander off down the road, still lamenting the fates in their singsong language. I was glad that they were gone, but I figured they would be back in the morning and I hoped the "highers" would let some of the detainees go. As we finished our meal, Mize came sauntering down from the platoon CP with a grin on his face.

"Hey, 1st Squad leader, send a couple of men to the mess hall, they've got a shipment of ice cream and nowhere to store it. Come on."

For some reason, there was a huge load of ice cream that the cook had no room for in his freezer, so my squad received three gallons of various flavors and we dug in. It was the first ice cream I had tasted in months, so I gorged myself along with the rest of the squad. If Charlie had attacked that night, he would have found bunkers full of overstuffed GIs burping in their sleep.

The relatives of the detainees did return at first light and some stayed most of the day. While I couldn't understand their language, I knew what they were saying and the mood they were in. We geared up for another patrol and stepped lightly around and between them as I led the platoon out of the gate. I vowed that if I was ordered to conduct another ID check, I would find that most of them had enough identification and would detain only the most suspicious.

We made another fruitless search through another large village made up of prosperous-looking merchants and, a few houses away, filthy hovels. There were definitely more poverty-stricken people here than in the previous villes. We returned slowly back up the road, hoping the throng had disappeared. When we got to the gate, the crowd was much smaller and we got the word that some of the detainees had been released and the rest sent to a camp nearby. My old bleeding heart was aching that night as I lay wondering how we could capture the hearts and minds of these people while we were harassing, threatening and jailing so many of them. Then I heard the reassuring *pop-pop* of our regular sniper. I could understand what he was doing and why he had to do it and it was almost music to my ears. I better be careful—I'm starting to lose the handle again.

The word came down bright and early via Mize: "Squad leaders up to the CP for briefing. Now."

I listened as Lieutenant Lesko filled us in on the day's mission, a Chinook lift out to a valley about ten klicks away. There were several villages in the valley and the citizens were suspected VC or suppliers. I took the word back to the men and told them to grab one C-ration meal as we were expected to return in the evening. As I lined them up on the field near the helipad, I realized that this was the test, the challenge that I had been preparing for in my mind. I knew that while I could and probably would perform well personally under conditions of extreme duress, now I was about to find out if I could lead men in the basic struggle for our existence. I was ready and I think the men were, too.

We loaded onto the cigar-shaped, double-rotored, ugly Chinook helicopter and lifted off for the west. We choppered over the low mountains, then descended into a lush valley where we jumped off and lined up for a sweep. After the entire company was deployed, we moved out toward the first ville and began searching. A young man suddenly began running from one of the huts in front of the 1st Platoon's sector.

In an attempt to make him stop, one of the grunts yelled, *"Lai dai! Lai dai!* Goddammit, *lai dai!"*

When he kept running, a few of the men opened up and brought him down. A search of the body revealed no weapons, but also no papers, thus making him a declared VC kill.

It didn't seem right to kill an unarmed man, then declare him an enemy, but he was running and refused to stop. He was probably a VC, but I wish he would have stopped and surrendered. Surely he didn't believe he could outrun a bullet from an M-16, did he? I pushed it to the back of my mind and kept a close eye on my men and the huts we were searching as we moved through the ville. The questioning and detaining of villagers who did not have proper papers took all day and when it was finally ended we had evacuated over 300 suspects. We had no more incidents and when the evacuation was completed, the Chinooks picked up the company and deposited us back at the base camp.

As I lay back against the bunker, I noticed that my knee was extremely sore, so I limped over to the medic, a big Texan, who swabbed it, then peered at it.

"Looks like a cactus needle to me."

"Probably better send me on to Tokyo to recuperate for a month or so, huh, Doc?"

I laughed as I spoke. I remembered then that I had first met this medic back in November at Lane when he had bandaged my hand and listened while I told him of the two medics who tried to help Captain Federline and died. I put the thoughts quickly out of my mind.

"No more sham time for you, Pete. I'll just put this bandage on it and you keep it clean."

I spent some time thinking about our role lately as the beat cop of the area; stopping people and checking their papers, sometimes arresting them and taking them in. I didn't like it, even though it was relatively safe. Tomorrow we were going on a patrol over the mountain to the east coast, where Captain Childers was killed. Maybe that will be a real mission.

I choked down some ham and eggs, chopped, in the morning, then carried my canteen cup of coffee to the CP.

"Any good rumors, Mize?"

"We're heading back to Pleiku to join up with the 4th."

"No, no, a thousand times no. I guess I could handle it, but I think the men would prefer Bronco Beach. What else you got?"

"The 2nd Platoon is nominated for a Bronze Star for their service over the past months."

"I didn't know there was such a thing, but we damn straight deserve it. I'm proud to belong to the 2nd, but then I haven't got anything to compare it to. What about the company? Weren't we nominated for the Presidential Unit Citation or something like that?"

"Haven't heard a word about that, Pete. We deserve it after savin' A Company, though."

We humped around to the east side of the perimeter, then headed toward the mountains a few klicks away. The going was easy until we reached the base, but we wound around the brush-covered gentle slope until we reached the area where the tunnel complex had been discovered.

We broke for chow, then searched along the rest of the area for another three hours. The engineers had packed explosives into the tunnels and then blown them by remote control. According to Patterson, the entire mountain had apparently settled about three feet after the explosion. We found no evidence of recent activity, so we formed a loose perimeter and called in the Chinooks. Doc Bowman walked over to where I was waiting.

"How's the knee, Pete? Any problems?"

"Loose as hell, Doc. Feels good now."

With no flat ground for an LZ, the Chinook settled in butt-first against the slope and hovered, so I directed the men to watch the rotors and come in at an angle to the rear ramp. The deadly blades were whirling just a few feet off the incline, but the troops avoided them and loaded on for the supposed trip to Trains. When we landed at a smaller firebase a few klicks farther west, I got the men squared away and headed to the lieutenant's position.

"What the hell is this? Where are we?"

"It's called LZ Illini. We're going to spend the night here and then we'll get a new mission tomorrow. We'll cover this part of the perimeter. There's a stream over there if the men want to wash up. We'll have a briefing in the morning."

I took a case of Cs down to my men and listened to them.

"What the hell are we doin'? No base camp, no hot chow. Did they tell you anything?"

"Not much. We're here for the night, then somewhere else in the morning. Get used to it. If you eat their damned ice cream, you gotta go where they send you."

"All the way. I'll never smile again," Vickers said.

The squad leaders gathered at the platoon CP early in the morning of February 7 and listened to Lieutenant Lesko.

"The 1st and 2nd platoons will lift out to this small LZ, then patrol the area and set up observation-type ambushes during the Tet ceasefire. The CO will be patrolling here near Illini with the 3rd, and the 4-Deuce platoon will set up here. We'll link up later in the week. Take four meals per man, resupply tomorrow afternoon."

We all looked at the map, then Sergeant Brittain spoke, "They don't know what to do with us, do they? They bounce us around from here to there, messin' with our minds. Christ, just give us a mission and turn us loose, for God's sake."

"Most of us are combat tested and the new guys are eager. We'd acquit ourselves well under any circumstances," I added as Chase nodded.

Nuckols cocked an eyebrow and fired back, "Wait a damn minute, Pete. One of my rules is no fancy phrases from squad leaders. Keep it simple, dammit."

"All right, sergeants, get your squads on the pads for liftoff at 0900. Move 'em out." Lesko folded his map and dismissed us.

We lifted off once more and headed west. As we soared over the first escarpment and began to wind our way down, I felt the old involuntary tightening of nerves and muscles. Although it had been a long time since our last combat assault into a possible hot LZ (the two most dreaded words in the Airmobile Infantry lexicon), the reactions were the same as if it were yesterday. I jumped off the skid while the chopper was hovering at three feet, rolled over once and started looking for my men while listening for fire. I moved the squad inside the tree line where we waited as the rest of the two platoons landed.

"Rangel, take your team over to those rocks and set up. Be alert. LT says beaucoup dinks here."

I spotted Lieutenant Lesko and Sergeant Nuckols at the edge of the clearing and headed in that direction for orders.

"Pete, put your squad on point. Follow an azimuth of 260 degrees along the high ground. We're in the vicinity of the Oregon Trail, which is a main supply branch off the Ho Chi Minh Trail. We could run into enemy anywhere, so be alert. Put your best man on point."

"Sir, I'll be on point with Vickers alternating."

"I don't want my squad leaders on point. Don't you have anybody else who could do the job?"

"I haven't had a chance to train anybody else. I'll start today if it looks safe. But I'll take the lead to get us started."

"OK. I'll be in the 2nd Squad with Sergeant Brittain."

I didn't tell the lieutenant that I was chomping at the bit and wanted to get out on point where I could feel at home. We moved out along the ridgeline following a small trail that soon veered north. I notified the CP, they ordered me to stay on course, so we got out the machetes and started hacking our way along. The brush was not real thick on the high ground, but we followed our azimuth into a steep canyon where it got thicker and the going was much tougher.

Vickers, Rushinski and I changed shifts every twenty minutes as we slashed our way across the valley floor. We quickly sweated through our jungle fatigues and began cursing the elements and circumstances that surrounded us. As we neared a stream, the radio that Sergeant Nuckols had assigned to me crackled.

"Charlie 2–1. This is Blazer 6, over."

It took me a few seconds, then it hit me that I was being paged, so I grabbed the handset and depressed the talk bar. "This is Charlie 2–1. Go ahead, Blazer 6."

"2–5 will proceed with you, 2–1. 2–2 and 2–3 will proceed with Blazer 6 down the spider to Point Alpha on your map. Rendezvous at approximately 1700. Over."

"Roger. Rendezvous at Point Alpha at 1700."

We crossed the stream slowly, then cut our way back to the ridgeline where we encountered another trail heading west. It looked like it had been used recently, so I took over on point and we eased along on full alert. After an uneventful hour I held up my hand to halt the column, then installed Rushinski as the new pointman with as many instructions as I could think of in a few seconds.

"Go easy. Move your head back and forth slightly, scanning everything. Watch for wires, loose dirt, broken twigs and dead leaves or weeds. Keep your finger alongside your trigger guard and pointed straight ahead and your thumb on your selector. If something happens, drop, flip your 16 on rock and roll and let her go. If anything looks, feels or smells wrong, let me know. I'm right here."

I probably overadvised him, but I was a little concerned with the fact that none of these new guys had any combat experience and we were in enemy territory, to my way of thinking. We continued along the ridgeline for another hour, letting our shirts dry on our backs in the cooler air and easier going. At 1600, Blazer 6 advised 2–5 that he had reached Point Alpha and we should make a turn to the north and join him there. I sent a small scouting party into the bushes off to our right and they came back to report.

"There's a steep dropoff, almost a cliff, with no trail, and it extends all along this ridge. We could go back to the stream, but it would take a couple of hours at least."

"The loo-tenant wants us to close with him in one hour. Let's go down the cliff and see if we can make it on time," Nuckols decided.

I loosened the sling on my M-16, slung the weapon over my back and tightened it, then began to climb down. It wasn't a sheer cliff and I was able to find handholds of rocks and brush, so I began to ease down the steep slope while the others waited. Just when I was feeling confident, a small tree that I was holding on to pulled loose from the rocks and soil and I slipped and slid the last fifteen feet, landing hard on grass and brush. I stood slowly, checked myself, found no fractures or major contusions, then motioned to the others to come down.

It took about twenty minutes to bring the rest of the troops down, then we struck out immediately for the lieutenant's position. We hacked our way along through the thick brush on the shoulder, then down into a gentle swale and back up the other side where we staggered into the perimeter set up by the rest of the 2nd and all of the 3rd platoons. Mize sent us to our part of the perimeter and we flopped down to rest for a few minutes before digging in and cutting fields of fire. It had been a long, hard day of up-and-down searching for the elusive enemy and we were totally fatigued. But it was a good feeling, at least for me. The day had gone rapidly and I knew my tired and sore body would put my mind to rest easily enough tonight. I took off my shirt and let the sweat dry slowly—it felt good to be back.

18

I knew it was morning when I heard Mize sing out: "OK, squad leaders to the CP! Now!"

I groaned a little as I stood up, then shook off the stiffness and headed awkwardly toward the CP hooch near the center of the wagon wheel. My left leg and arm were sore from the fall I took, but it was nothing serious. Sergeants Brittain and Braggs and Spec 4 Chase were already seated around a map spread out on a poncho and I plopped down beside them. Lieutenant Lesko sipped hot coffee out of his canteen cup, then greeted us.

"Good morning, men. First things first. 2–3 has a sick man, so they'll cut a small LZ for a medevac. Now, in case you didn't know it, this is the Chinese New Year, Tet. A truce has been declared and we hope the VC will keep it, but we'll be prepared if they don't. We're going to proceed down this spider to here, then head due north to Point Bravo, here. There, we'll set up an observation and get a resupply. 2–2 will lead off. If we come to a cliff, send for 2–1. Any questions? 2–3, get started on that LZ."

"Sir, I think all the men of the Fighting 1st should get a Ranger patch for their work yesterday," I joked lamely. Lieutenant Lesko rightfully ignored the jibe.

"Stay in touch, men. Carry on."

It took about thirty minutes for the 3rd Squad to cut down enough trees and brush for the chopper to land, but finally I heard the *whap-whap* of its rotors as it neared our position. By this time, the poncho liner–wrapped troop was shaking and his teeth were chattering while the sweat ran down along his face. Malaria was the obvious culprit, according to the medic. All of the troops were given, and were expected to take, a daily pill, Dapsone, and a larger weekly tablet, Chloroquine Primaquine, that would choke a horse. From my spot on the south side of the perimeter, just off the trail, I listened as Mize called in the medevac chopper.

"Dustoff 32, this is Blazer 6, waiting for pickup, over."

"Ahh, roger, Blazer, should be over your position in less than one mike. Pop smoke, over."

"Roger, Dustoff, smoke popped, over."

The wily veteran Mize never said the color of the smoke in the clear in case some enterprising VC, waiting with a radio and smoke canisters, might pop the same hue to lure the pilot into a deadly trap. After a few seconds the pilot came on again.

"I see yellow smoke, Blazer. Can you affirm, over?"

"Roger, yellow smoke popped, bring her in. Blazer out."

The chopper danced over the crest and into view, then dropped into the narrow LZ, hurling dirt, leaves and small branches into the air. As part of the never-ending initiation ritual, old vets would remain silent when new guys laid their poncho or shirt across a bush, then roar with delight when the rotor wash sent it sailing. I held on to my steel pot and watched as a bare-chested grunt guided the bird into the landing zone, then two others helped the wobbly sick man get on. They laid him gently on the floor, tossed on his weapon and gear, then the bare-chested troop gave the pilot a thumbs-up and waved him away. The bird sashayed around as it lifted out of the narrow slit in the forest, like it was performing some sort of mating ritual, then banked and headed east for the nearest mobile hospital.

Shortly after, we broke camp, filled in all the foxholes, buried our garbage and geared up for the patrol. Our packs

were two meals lighter, so the going was a little easier as we
headed back to the stream. We followed it to the southwest,
moving slowly and as quietly as possible. I put Rushinski, then
House at the head of our squad and told them to pretend that
they were on point, hoping they would at least get the feeling. It
was an easygoing walk through the jungle during a truce.

In the afternoon we pulled away from the stream and headed
north once more. I could hear the machetes whacking away at
the head of the column and could imagine what they were
thinking and saying as they toiled. At 1600 we began climbing
another ridge and a few minutes later we reached what Lieutenant Lesko decided was Point Bravo. We relaxed, threw off
our gear and dug in as we awaited the resupply chopper and,
hopefully, a mailbag. At 1700 the bird arrived with the hoped-
for treasure, C rations and PFC Marvin, back from sick call. As
usual, the perimeter went quiet as the news-hungry grunts read
and reflected.

We lay around the perimeter the next morning until 0900,
then Sergeant Nuckols sent my squad and one of the gun crews
on a mission. We cut back to the stream and found a trail where
we set up in an ambush-and-observe posture. We had just settled into a lazy C ambush when the radio came alive with a
message from the platoon CP.

"2–1, this is 2–5, over." He didn't wait for acknowledgment.
"Get your butt back here. We're gonna flip-flop to a new Lima
Zulu (LZ). Do you hear?"

"Roger, 2–5. On the way. 2–1 out."

We pulled in our trip wires and claymores and *di died* back
to the small LZ where the men of the 1st Platoon were already
lined up waiting for the first lift. After they were lifted out, we
grabbed a water break, then loaded on the second lift and
headed west by south. The choppers lifted us over the nearest
range of small mountains, then swept quickly down into a narrow valley with a large trail visible to us as we descended.
There were a few open fields on the lower slopes of the smaller
hills. On one of these was an occupied LZ, our target.

We landed smoothly on a flat area in the heart of LZ Alpha-
Alpha, then jumped off and were immediately replaced on
board by the men of Alpha Company, who had been working
out of the camp. The 2nd Platoon was sent to cover the south

half of the perimeter, while the 1st took the rest. I received orders to take my men to the southeast part of the perimeter where I noticed two things: a nasty odor hanging over the area and a large trail cut off by the perimeter wire. Apparently it had led right through our position and down the slight slope to the creek below, where it joined the Oregon Trail. This could be interesting, I thought.

I took a quick check around our sector and decided that this was not a good place for an LZ. It was surrounded on three sides by higher ground with trees and ground cover to hide an approaching enemy force. The fields of fire were severely limited on the south and east sectors and the grass was high and thick on the west. I went with my men to cut as much brush as we could, but our vision was still obstructed by large trees. Rushinski walked back to the bunker and groaned, "Sheesh, Pete, couldn't we find a place that smelled better than this? Either somebody's dead or Alpha left an open garbage dump around here."

"We'll check that out in the morning. Right now, Chase and I are going to find an ambush site for tonight." Vickers and Mize joined us as we followed the trail out past the wire and along the spine of the small hill. We found a spot where the trail made a sharp bend in front of a large tree surrounded by brush. Chase and I decided to set up in a line ambush just past the bend in a patch of heavy brush.

"Pete, let's set a booby trap right by the tree. I'll get some C-4 and wire it to a claymore firing device and we can put a couple of Willy Peter (white phosphorous) grenades up in the branches with a trip wire."

"Hell, Chase, let's make it real bad. How about a can of gasoline or kerosene? We could blow a huge ball of fire out there. What we didn't kill would be scared to death." I had been kidding, but Chase jumped on the idea.

"Fuckin' A, man. Gasoline with C-4 wired to the back of the can and Willy Peter grenades inside. A bomb. I've always wanted to build a bomb."

"There's some gasoline down by the CP bunker. Alpha Company had some engineers in here with their chain saws and they left it," Mize put in.

Almost every boy loved to play with fireworks, but we had

the unique opportunity to take it to a much higher level. We were going to build our own bomb. I decided to back the troops in the ambush down the trail a little and make our kill zone about thirty feet from the bomb site. If the bomb was detonated, there wouldn't be anybody left in that area to kill, anyway. Later, I gathered the men of Vickers' team and Alabama's gun crew and briefed them on our plans.

"Here's how we want it to work, guys. The gun will face south, the rest of us will face southeast. If Charlie comes along, the gun crew lets them go past. If it's just a small force, Vickers' team will open up on them and the gun crew can take what they miss. If it's a large force or if some of them escape the fire, Chase will blow the bomb and we'll head for our back door, which is the opening in the wire."

Chase grinned and poked my shoulder. "For the first time in ten months I'm looking forward to a night ambush. Let's get it on."

Chase was almost giddy as we put on our web gear and checked to make sure nothing was going to make noise. I don't know where he got the energy, but as we went through the wire, he was grinning and lugging a five-gallon olive-drab canister with a small stick of C-4 already wired to the outside. He gently placed the can in some brush just in front of the tree, then connected the wire to a blasting cap. Vickers and I set up two trip wires, then I crawled quietly to our ambush CP that doubled as rear guard. I was behind a decaying log where I could see the tree, the gun crew and Vickers' team while keeping an ear open to anyone coming through the brush behind us. Chase was on the other end of the log, peering at the tree and his bomb. It would be his call as to when to blow it, which seemed to be fitting.

I had put the men on 50 percent security until midnight, then one man on until dawn, but there was enough anticipation to keep most of us awake for several hours. It was a thrill to be involved in something out of the ordinary, something that would get the attention of the entire perimeter and be the center of conversation for a few days, thus raising morale. It was a great idea and I hoped we would get to use it; all we needed was a little cooperation from Charlie. But, just when we needed him, the enemy failed us again and the night was totally quiet.

In the morning we carefully pulled the bomb apart and carried it and our dreams back to the perimeter. Chase was particularly distraught at the turn of events that deprived him of an explosion and carnage.

"Damn, Pete, this bomb was a hell of an idea. I know it would have worked great. Where the hell was Charlie?"

"The same old story, Chase. You can never find an enemy when you need one. Maybe they saw us put it together and said, 'This must be that crazy 2nd Platoon we've heard about. We better stay away from those assholes.' Maybe we can use the idea again."

The ambushers rested in their positions in the morning hours, giving me time to contemplate my first overnight ambush as a squad leader. I gave myself a passing grade for the setup, but an incomplete for performance. The heavy stench still hung over this side of the perimeter, so I figured it was time to take a small patrol to search for the source of it. A few meters to the left of the trail and just outside the perimeter, we found a disgusting mess.

The men of A Company had been going just outside the perimeter to relieve themselves, which was proper procedure. The problem was they didn't follow sanitary procedures or exhibit common decency in disposing of their waste. The Army procedure would be: dig hole, defecate, and cover with loose dirt from hole. Some men preferred to use the entrenching tool as a pick, with the blade at a right angle. They would then stand the shovel on its handle and sit on the blade, resting chin on hand and elbow on knee with hips and buttocks hanging over— sort of a poor infantryman's Rodin on a makeshift stool.

Incomprehensibly, the troops of Alpha dug no holes and simply walked away from their wretched refuse when they finished relieving themselves. There were dozens of smelly, fly-covered deposits in the small area about thirty feet in front of the 1st Squad bunkers. We returned to our positions and retrieved several entrenching tools and then went back to the ugly scene with T-shirts or towels wrapped around our lower face. The flies buzzed around our heads and landed on our arms.

"Man, I thought I was through with this crap, pardon my pun, when I came back to the field. Join the Army, see the world. Bury shit." Vickers had a way of icing almost every word with a coat of heavy acrimony.

"The next time I see somebody from Alpha, I'm going to raise some hell, Vick. There's no excuse for this." I was adamant in my feelings, also; Alpha had done wrong.

Alabama strolled out from his gun position down the line. "So that's what that smell was. I thought so. You know, most of the 1st Platoon in Alpha is black. They were on this side of the perimeter. They did this."

"Well, if you can point out the difference between white and black defecation, I might buy your statement. But it all smells the same to me."

When we returned to the perimeter, the 2nd Platoon was making cleanup trips, a squad at a time, to the stream on the north side of the perimeter. I took my squad down, dipped my whole body into the cold, clear water, then lathered and scrubbed myself thoroughly in an attempt to rid myself of the awful odor and sight. This was followed by the ritualistic removing of the leeches and the redonning of our dirty and smelly fatigues. I washed my shirt and towel and wrung them out, then carried them back to the LZ. It felt good to be cleaner, even with dirty pants and socks.

That night I began to suffer intestinal burning and cramping along with a fierce need to purge myself. I was barely able to get away from the bunker before having to drop my trousers and let fly. I noticed that several other men were experiencing similar problems. Dysentery had struck, undoubtedly carried by flies that had come in contact with the refuse, then toted the germs to us. I wrapped my poncho and liner around me and lay there, groaning and holding my lower belly and cursing the slovenly troops of Alpha Company.

The 2nd Squad leader, Sergeant Braggs, took an OP a few meters up the Oregon Trail as the light drew dim. As they neared the site they had picked out before dark, they met several VC on the trail. Both groups, shocked and surprised, hesitated for a heartbeat then opened fire. Braggs and his men put several hundred rounds in the direction of the enemy force, then moved quickly back to the perimeter. The entire perimeter went on full alert and I crawled grudgingly out of my cocoon and into our bunker.

After a few minutes, I duckwalked quickly back to the CP, where the lieutenant was talking with Braggs. Braggs was visibly agitated and shaking as he cupped a cigarette.

"There were a lot of them, sir. I saw four or five firing and I'm sure there were more behind them. They had packs and weapons. Jeez, that was close."

Lieutenant Lesko talked with the FO, then called Charlie 6 to ask for a fire mission. Charlie 6 asked if it was really necessary, since he had to go through brigade and they had to go through Saigon to clear any fire mission during the Tet holiday. Saigon then probably had to go through Washington for final clearance. It was a hell of a way to run a war, but then I already knew that. I returned to my bunker while he started the negotiations and pondered our lack of visibility and fields of fire to our front. I took Rushinski and crawled to the wire, where we put up two more trip flares, then we hustled back to await the possible enemy attack. There was a feeling of anxiety and concern—how big was the unit? Were they just passing through on the Oregon Trail or would they probe the perimeter and attack? I felt another burning urge and stumbled to a spot just to the left of the bunker and dropped my pants.

At 2230, Mize crawled close to our position and hissed, "Get in your holes, we're gonna put HE all around the perimeter and Willy Peter on the trail." Artillery began to crash into the trees and on the hills around us a few minutes later, occasionally sending deadly pieces of shrapnel whizzing near our bunker. It was dangerous, but I felt more comfortable and confident as the fire mission roared on. The firing continued for almost thirty minutes, then sporadically off and on through the night as the missions were repeated as DefCons. During the lulls, I could hear noises and sensed movement just outside the perimeter. Luckily, I didn't need to relieve myself anymore. I don't know what frightened me more—the possibility of an attack from the front or from my rear.

Morning finally arrived for the beleaguered men of the 1st Squad. Vickers, Rushinski and I went to the wire to disarm and remove our flares and mines, then we continued into the tree line to check for activity and to relieve ourselves. When we returned, I had the men police the area to make sure we had covered everything that we had deposited. Dysentery was running rampant through the squad and during the night a few of the men had been searching for a safe place to "assume the position" only to have nature make its sudden call before they could drop their trousers. I sent an armed patrol to the stream so they could wash out the clothing, *after* filling the canteens.

I realized we were probably perpetuating the life cycle of the organism that had attacked us by using the stream as a laundry, but I saw no other way to get their clothes clean and restore a little of their dignity. It began to rain as we joined the 2nd Squad to make a sweep patrol through the previous night's battle site. We moved slowly through the brush along both sides of the trail until we reached the spot. Braggs motioned from behind a tree to some bloody packs still lying on the trail. Vickers, Huffman and I moved across the trail to set up security while the others searched. Huffman spotted a body, which he pointed at without speaking. I glanced at it and saw it was a uniformed VC with no weapon, his face torn and violated by two M-16 rounds.

I pointed out the spot to the others, then moved gladly into a semiperimeter about forty feet away. I had seen enough dead bodies to last me through my tour and if I wanted to see more, I needed only to close my eyes to see them again and again. The 2nd Squad searched the body, then Lieutenant Lesko ordered us to leave it and the packs on the trail to attract the enemy into returning for them. The 1st Squad was ordered to set up an ambush on the trail during the day, with the 2nd returning at night.

I scouted down the trail and found a good offensive position about 300 meters from the LZ where the trail made a sharp bend. I put five men into a position between some rocks and heavy brush just off the trail and sent Rangel and two others about fifty meters back toward the LZ. They would act as rear security and guides in case the ambush area got hot and we needed a quick retreat. The five of us caucused, then set up our kill zone along a stretch just past the bend. I decided to let no more than four men enter the zone, then Vickers would open up on the last one when he was in range. The rest of us would try to pick off the others while I fired the claymore, then we'd retreat to the rear guard or the LZ if we thought it was a large force.

We played everything straight on this mission. Perhaps it

was the rain or the dead VC and bloody packs that reminded us that we were only a finger twitch away from being a weekly statistic. I believed that the enemy would come down the trail any minute and the tension was thick enough to cause my sphincter to snap shut for a few hours. With the rain killing the sound, I crawled to where Vickers was lying.

"I think they're waiting for night to come back. If it's just a small group, they wouldn't want to get into any action in the daylight. Air and artillery would kill 'em."

I had no idea if what I said had any semblance of truth, but I felt like I had to say something. I felt a great need for companionship out there on that trail, in the rain, waiting for Charlie.

"I hope you're right, Pete," Vickers whispered back. "This isn't the right place or time to fight."

"What is the right place or time?"

"When I'm back in the World and you guys are in an LZ with the battalion and have all the firepower you need. Then they can attack."

I had been holding the radio handset up to my ear and I heard a hiss and a low voice break the silence. "Charlie 2–1, this is Blazer 6. Give me a sit-rep. Break squelch once if all clear, twice if trouble, over."

I pressed the bar once and he acknowledged and said he'd call again in thirty minutes. I placed the handset inside my shirt to keep it dry and fixed my eyes back on the trail. At 1600, with no activity in the area, we were called back to the LZ. We slowly worked our way down the trail to Rangel's position, where they were huddled together under two ponchos draped across low branches. I waved them in behind us and we headed for Double Alpha, which looked a lot like home in spite of the odors and poor defensive positions.

Vickers and Rushinski gathered some empty C-ration boxes and a few dead limbs and we threw in some heat tabs and started a fire that we huddled around to dry our clothes and poncho liners until darkness began to fall. Then we put out the fires, crawled into our bunkers and put up ponchos over them to stay dry from the now-cold rain. At about 2100 sniper fire tore into the northwest side of the perimeter and we went on full alert. The 2nd Squad OP-ambush returned to the perimeter despite seeing nothing—they were a little skittish.

As the night wore on and the rain subsided, I heard movement and what sounded like snatches of conversation from the woods just outside the wire. I reported the possible activity to Lieutenant Lesko and requested artillery. He quickly agreed and started the procedures while I kept the squad on full alert as the noises continued. I couldn't be sure if it was VC, rats or monkeys, but I saw no reason to take chances.

When the barrage of shells finally tore into the woods, I breathed a sigh of relief and lowered our security status to 50 percent. I low-walked over to Rangel's bunker to inform him of the change, but he had already placed those men on regular night security. I decided this was not the time or place for our confrontation, but I put a mark next to his name in my head. There were noises and movement throughout the night, so we continued firing occasional barrages to keep Charlie guessing. The stress of the situation and the dysentery combined to keep me awake most of the night, so I was tremendously fatigued in the morning.

I staggered to the CP with my weapon in one hand and my entrenching tool in the other, ready for the meeting, the enemy and my bowels to call. Lieutenant Lesko laughed and shook his head at my predicament, then lent an ear as I complained.

"Sir, could we get water on resupply? The rain washes our excrement down the hill into the stream and we drink the water. We can't avoid the bacteria that way. And are we ever going to get clean clothes?"

"I'll request the water. No clean clothes yet. They treat us like the orphans we are in this AO. Big news—Colonel Miller is coming to the LZ for a visit, so be sharp."

"Maybe we can arrange some sniper fire or an ambush."

"Just be good soldiers while he's here."

When I got back to the squad positions, the men had a huge fire going and were standing around drying off once more. As I watched, Fred Huffman, whom I called the Wanderer, turned to look at me and one corner of his liner dipped into the fire. The synthetic material burst into flames sending Huffman diving for cover while Rushinski stomped it out. I took the liner to Mize at the CP.

"Can you get me a DX on this? As you can see, it was hit by fire. Give it to the colonel when he comes in."

"Will do. You know, Nancy Sinatra made a visit to the battalion LZ and I was hoping we'd get her out here, but higher says the area's a little too hot now."

"Probably a good thing. If she had come out here and got a look at me, she would've wanted to stay and where could I put her? We do all that humpin' all day and I couldn't handle more humpin' at night."

"She did say those boots were made for walkin'."

"I'll show her what those boots were made for. Too bad, Nancy. When is the 'Wild Man' coming back?"

"I'm sure he's sittin' somewhere with his feet up, havin' a cold one. Get some, Bennett. Oh, the lieutenant wants to see you."

Lesko was kneeling on the ground in his hooch, looking over his map. As I appeared at the front, he began to speak. "Change of plans, Pete. Take your squad out to this point," he pointed at a trail junction, "for a daylight observation and ambush. Pick up 2–5's radio."

"Sir, could I have a gun crew? They could make the difference if we hit anything."

"All right, take one of Chase's crews, but no bombs out there today. Golden 6 might not like it. Be outside the wire in two zero minutes."

"Roger, sir. Once more into the breech."

"You know *Henry V?*"

"Not personally." Lesko never laughed at my jokes, so I continued, "I did see the movie with Olivier—some great oration. Outside the wire in twenty mikes, sir."

Chase sent Alabama to me and we set out along the trail to the south. We moved slowly in the drizzle, past our ambush and bomb site, then down across a ravine and up another hill. I found an outcropping of rocks overlooking the trail and we set up in a line ambush with a small rear guard. Since we had no real "rear door," I decided that we would fire on the front of any group that appeared and use the trail as our escape.

I heard and saw the colonel's chopper as he came into the LZ and although I could neither hear nor see what was going on from 500 meters away, I knew what was happening. Lieutenant Lesko was bowing and scraping and Nuckols was wishing he was with us. After about twenty minutes the bird lifted off once more and headed east.

We spent an uneventful day huddled under our ponchos behind the rocks and my mind reflected over the events of the past few days. We had been in constant danger, but despite the contact, sniper fire and the probes, no one had as much as a scratch. Morale was OK, but would be higher if we could shake off the dysentery and the rain. We were still understrength, but the influx of new men had eased the problem somewhat.

We were especially short on NCOs, the backbone of the Army. The brigade had arrived in-country in January 1966 at full strength, but as the men completed their twelve-month tours and DEROSed, they were replaced by draftees with five months in the Army and no rank. This should make promotions easier to obtain for GIs like myself; the Army needed sergeants and I could do the job. I snapped out of my ennui as the radio crackled and we got the word to come into the LZ.

We slogged back in time to dry out and warm up some Cs. I swallowed some crackers and cheese and hoped it would stick around long enough for me to get a few nutrients. When the CP asked for an OP, I sent Rangel and pointedly ignored his glare. See, I told myself, I was already acting like a sergeant. At the evening meeting at the CP, Lesko reported on the visit from Colonel Miller and his entourage.

"Golden 6 was happy that we're seeing some action here. He doesn't like ceasefires. 'Stack 'em up like cordwood,' he says. They want kills."

"Just like all the rest. Come out to the boonies and stack 'em yourself, John Wayne."

"The CO, 3rd Herd and the Weapons Platoon will join us tomorrow here. Stay in touch with your OPs and the CP."

I took the news and Huffman's new liner back to the bunker and settled in for the night. Huffman thanked me. "FTA, Pete. I'll guard this with my life." He saluted, then turned away, stumbled and fell into the bunker. After finding out he wasn't hurt, I laughed and wrapped my own liner around me and waited for my colon to send another message. The enemy appeared to be frightened away by our artillery as we had a peaceful night.

I watched the next morning as the first chopper landed and a tall, ruddy-faced man in his mid-thirties jumped off—Captain Eklund had arrived in Alpha-Alpha. He returned Lieutenant Lesko's salute, then quickly took charge of the perimeter and the unloading men. He set the 3rd Platoon on the east side and extended the defense a little farther in that direction. The Weapons Platoon set up their mortars in the center of the perimeter near the landing pad and began digging holes for their shelter. The CO then suggested that since Lieutenant Lesko had such a fine hooch, he might consider donating it to the company CP. Lesko and Nuckols grudgingly moved southward to get closer to the 2nd Platoon. I felt a sense of comfort and power now that we would be operating at a company level—we had more strength and quicker access up the command structure.

The rain slacked to a light mist, then stopped in the afternoon and we began drying and cleaning weapons, gear and clothing. Our fatigues were caked with mud and smelled of sweat and excrement; our boots were wet and our feet were shriveled and most of the squad had diarrhea. The medic had nothing that would help us, so we ate crackers and cheese and suffered openly. Around 1500 the sun broke through and I sent half the men to the open part of the perimeter to expose and dry their feet in the welcome rays. The rest of us hung our fatigues on bushes and kept watch, then switched places after an hour.

A lone resupply chopper found its way into the LZ just before 1700, bringing hot A rations, mail, supplies and a couple of returning troopers, including one short, redhaired Texan with an obvious hangover and clean fatigues.

"All right, you mother-humpin' assholes, get your shit together, I'm back."

Bennett had returned. He spent the next hour regaling us with tales of his R&R and how he and his wife didn't get out of their hotel room the first two days. I told him about the enemy activity and our dysentery and told him the squad was his. Since it was our turn to send out an OP, I volunteered to take it out, but he declined my offer.

"You keep the squad tonight and I'll go on OP with Vickers and his men. I'll square it with Nuckols."

With no rain, I hoped we might get a good night's rest, but Vickers reported in at 2115 with noise and movement. The CO monitored the call, then called artillery to bring in flares and we watched as the flickering golden light filtered through the trees and bushes while the OP laid low. Nothing happened for a while, but about ninety minutes later Vickers was on the radio again, whispering, "2–5, this is 2–1 Oscar Papa. Beaucoup movement and noise. We can hear the VC talking and laughing."

The platoon CP was just behind my position now, so I crawled back and joined Nuckols as he monitored the radio and asked if I could answer Vickers. He handed me the handset and lay down on his poncho.

"This is 2–1. Hold tight as long as they don't come after you. They must not know you're there. We're only a few feet away and we're ready. 2–1, out."

Sit-reps were negative until 0230, when Bennett came on the horn, his voice strained. "OP coming in. OP coming in *now!*"

"Roger, Oscar Papa. Get in here."

I scrambled back to my bunker and passed the word quickly along our side of the perimeter. "OP coming in. Sandbag, sandbag! Hold your fire!" Vickers, Bennett, Huffman and House came stumbling through the wire with poncho liners rolled under their arms. I had crawled down to the wire to greet them and make sure they weren't followed, then set a trip wire across the opening and aimed a claymore in that direction.

I whispered to Bennett as he crawled to the bunker, "You just had to start trouble your first fuckin' night back in the war, right?"

"The bastards were really close. They were laughin' and raisin' hell."

Vickers leaned over and added in a whisper, "I think they're drunk, I heard one guy belch."

"Well, let's add some fire to their party."

I called the company CP and reported the OP return and requested firing of previously recorded DefCons. As the shells began screaming through the night sky toward the woods, I slid into the bunker and confronted Vickers.

"What the hell does a VC belch sound like, anyway?"

We repeated the DefCons a couple of times, pouring a heavy barrage onto the woods, then the night went silent.

The next morning we patrolled all through the area and found no trace of the enemy, who had become nocturnal in their activities since we had arrived. During the day they stayed out of sight, then moved personnel and supplies down familiar trails after dark, while we could only guess at which point they might pass near our LZ, ambush it and hope for contact. It was our mission to stop the enemy's use of the Oregon Trail to re-supply VC units in the coastal plains and kill them. So far, we had only mixed results.

Bennett eased slowly back into the saddle as squad leader, spending the day asking me questions about the terrain and enemy sightings. We went over the maps together, plotting out ambush sites as the patrol checked out the trails. We returned to the perimeter in the afternoon and relaxed in the sun. At 1800 clouds began to move in and the rain followed shortly after. I still was battling the bug, so I spent most of the night outside the bunker wrapped in my poncho, feeling cold, wet and lonely.

While Bennett and Vickers tried to start a fire in the cold, driving morning rain, I moved to the wire to check the wires and claymore. I was astounded to see that one of the wires was clipped and the flare was missing. Further examination revealed that one of the claymores was turned around to face inward. I called Bennett to the scene, then we decided we would set a grenade under the claymore with the pin pulled when we put the mine back out at dusk. Perhaps we could give Charlie a taste of his own medicine. I marveled at the ability, patience and courage of the VC who could creep into our wire, evading our trip flares, and turn our weapon against us while avoiding detection. This was going to be a tough enemy to defeat.

Sergeant Brittain led a patrol out to the southwest, away from our position, and around the hill. Their point element discovered a tunnel and the entire patrol set up a security around it. A thorough search found another tunnel leading to a complex. Several volunteers were willing to forgo the cold rain for the interior of the tunnels, despite the inherent dangers involved. The 1st Squad was pulling rear guard, but I would not have volunteered anyway because of a slight case of claustrophobia.

Lieutenant Lesko radioed a report on the find to the Old Man, who ordered a full investigation, which he wisely would wait for at his hooch. Brittain's squad searched through the tunnels and found a large cache of rice, a few weapons and ammunition and some papers. Further into the complex, they found an underground hospital with a surgical unit.

By late afternoon the search was completed and we returned to the perimeter. We restarted our fire and tried once more to dry off and warm up. I was excused from OP duty in deference to my frequent bowel movements, so Vickers took three men out about fifty meters while Bennett and I set up our booby-trapped claymore. I curled up just behind the bunker and munched on crackers as the cold rain fell. The night was quiet and I retrieved the grenade and mine before the OP came in at daybreak.

On Thursday, February 16, we finally left LZ Alpha-Alpha. The Trailblazers moved slowly out through the wire and headed southwest, past the tunnel complex that would be blown by engineers later in the day and toward the mountains. We were leaving the rest of the company and Sergeant Nuckols, who was ill with the dysentery that had hit much of the company, behind as we worked our way along through the lush tropical growth. After three hours we had moved only about a klick through the jungle when we came to a large ravine. The steep-sided gulch was slippery with mud and as the platoon began to cross it, the rains started again. We slid down the hillside, grabbing at branches to slow our descent.

"Fuck it. I hate this shit," Chase exploded in front of me. I slid by him and, as calmly as I could muster, recited, "U.S.55880415. U.S.55880415. U.S. . . ."

I was using my Army serial as a mantra, reminding myself I was only a draftee, had no say over my fate and would be out of the service in about a year. Chase began taking up the chant, but he was using his enlistment number, which began with an RA, signifying regular Army enlistee. I laughed as I fell down again.

"You missed my point, but it's all right if it helps you get through this shit."

The chant moved up the line for a while, then came back from the CP in a different form. "Shut the fuck up. Do you want the enemy to hear us?"

"I forgot. He can't hear the damned machetes whacking away and all the other noise we make coming through the brush."

Chase looked at me and began singing, under his breath: "We gotta get outta this place, if it's the last thing we ever do."

After we struggled up the other side of the ravine, we continued cutting through the jungle for another 100 meters or so, then came onto a trail heading up and around the nearby range of small mountains. Lesko conferred with the CO, then called Bennett to the trail.

"Take your squad and scout this trail. When you reach a position you can defend well, call me and we'll leapfrog."

We headed west, then south along the well-defined trail. I had point for the first time in a week and I immediately felt the change; the scouting patrol became a mission to discover if the trail was safe and a personal quest for some higher meaning. I was home on point. We climbed slowly along the trail which worked its way along the side of the low mountain. If Charlie decided to ambush us, it would be difficult to escape, so we moved carefully.

Finding no fresh tracks or signs of recent activity, I led the squad to a swale near the top of the range and between two crests. Bennett reported our position to Blazer 6, who ordered us to go to the highest point while he started toward our position. We continued to ease along the ridgeline to the west, which was now a gentle slope, and quickly reached the high ground. Once more Bennett radioed the LT and told them to come on up while the troops pulled security along the trail both ways. It had been a long, hard day and the rain was still falling in the cold mountain air, but it felt good to be on high ground.

As the rest of the platoon made its way to our position, I studied the map, retracing our steps and checking out the area. We were about three klicks from Double Alpha, but it was a trip that would take several hours under the best conditions. If we had any major problems tonight, we would face them alone. Sitting on top of a mountain in Vietnam during the rainy season was not on my list of favorite things to do. We were very wet, very cold and very tired and in no mood for any enemy probe or sniper fire. If any VC had messed with us, we might have chased them all the way to Hanoi.

19

On February 13, the 1st Battalion of the 14th Infantry Regiment began its participation in Operation Pershing in the Phu My District. The battalion was given an area of operation in the southern part of the district where it conducted search and destroy, cordon and search, and village search operations as well as extensive ambushes. Village search and cordon operations were conducted in conjunction with the National Police. During this span, the enemy suffered 89 KIA, 21 captured and 28 weapons seized. The battalion losses were three KIA and 25 WIA.

The sun didn't break through, but the rain finally stopped before dawn. The platoon broke camp and filled their holes, then headed down the westward slope of the small brush-covered hill. In the valley below, we forded a small stream, crossing it slowly to allow each trooper to fill his canteens. Rangel and House, on point, came across a small trail and we followed it around a ridge jutting out of the low mountain range, then entered another valley, smaller and narrow enough to almost be called a draw.

The trail got wider, but still looked like it hadn't been used in weeks. Lieutenant Lesko stopped for a communications check to see if we were still in radio range of Charlie 6, so Vickers and I moved into the brush to relieve ourselves. The dysentery had finally begun to clear up and I was feeling better until I saw several huge bunkers dug halfway underground facing the trail. I felt a tremendous surge of déjà vu coupled with an urgent sense of danger, so I quickly jumped behind a large tree. After assessing the situation, I judged it to be a deserted enemy camp of indeterminate size.

We hustled back to the lieutenant with the information, then followed an excited Lesko as he took an inspection tour of the camp. He radioed Charlie 6 with his report and the platoon was ordered to search all the bunkers for rice or documents that might have been hidden for later use. The lieutenant put the gun crews and a few other men on security, then put the rest of us to work. We used our flashlights to shine into the dark interiors, but found nothing but bugs and mice. The search was completed in early afternoon and the platoon received orders to follow the trail and search for a suitable LZ.

Rangel found a spot clear of trees and we began stomping down the elephant grass and cutting brush. The labor paid off when the bird landed and we unloaded hot A rations. Lieutenant Lesko helped serve the chow and seemed to be pleased with the way things were going. Morale was high, buoyed by the discovery of the bunkers and the hot chow, but I thought about how tenuous our situation would be if the bunkers had been occupied. I didn't like the feel of the area and I decided to raise the issue with Bennett as we finished our meal.

"We're really pushing our luck here, dude. Ol' Charlie saw the chopper land, so he knows where we are. Just a handful of them could raise some hell with us. We should have moved before dark."

"Yeah, Pete, I feel same-same, but the Loo-tenant's been lucky so far and now he thinks he can do anything, so just fuck it and dig in, man."

We did dig in and I made sure the hole was extra wide and deep, but Charlie wasn't ready to tangle with us even at platoon size and the lieutenant stayed lucky.

I took the point next day, leading the platoon away from the small LZ, up the draw and toward the mountains again. We found a trail heading up the slope, so I halted the column while Vickers and I scouted ahead for a fresh sign, but there was none. The patrol continued up the gentle slope, reaching the crest by noon, then took a chow break at the junction of the trail we had followed and a larger one that ran along the ridgeline. I pulled out a can of beans, then moved over to the gun position where I sat down next to Martinez, who was checking his feet for leeches or blisters.

"Martinez, also known as Gus Peppergut, my main man,

how about loaning me some of that hot sauce for my ham and
lima beans? Now that I've recovered from the trots, I could use
something spicy to wake up my taste buds."

Martinez, hearing the knock of opportunity, replied, "Trade
time. What kind of cigarettes did you get?"

Each meal contained a four-pack of cigarettes, a small pack
of toilet paper, gum, a spoon and a can opener (P-38). I had
stuck the cigarettes from mine into the band around my steel
pot, so I pointed to it.

"Salems. If you can't smoke 'em, Salem. Want them?"

"Negatron on the Salems. Lookin' for Marlboros."

"Here's my best deal. Whenever I get Marlboros or Win-
stons, you get them. In return, you give me an occasional dose
of that wonderful hot sauce."

"Sounds good, Pete. Here you go." Martinez handed me the
bottle, then spoke again in a mock-serious voice. "Do you suppose I could get a blow job with that deal."

"Not from me, but if Alabama was any kind of gunner, the
next time he's in Pleiku, he could get two of them, then come
back and give you one."

"Better yet, he could get one, then come back and give me
two." Martinez was giggling now.

Alabama turned to us with a look of disgust on his face,
which I swear looked like the map of his home state, complete
with mountains and rivers. "You boys are queer. I don't do that
shit. That's numbah ten."

"Don't knock it until you try it, man. A good blow job is
definitely numbah one," Martinez said.

I took the proffered sauce and liberally doused my beans,
then crushed a few crackers in with it and dug in. One hour
later the platoon moved out to the south on the large trail which
was bordered by brush on both sides. As we reached a slight
bend in the trail, I noticed some more bunkers ahead, plainly
visible alongside the trail. I slipped behind a tree and motioned
to the others to be alert.

"More bunkers along the trail. Pass it to the lieutenant," I
whispered to Vickers.

Not long after, Lesko came walking lightly up the line and
whispered to me, "Any enemy sign or movement at all?"

"Nothing yet. Probably abandoned, or we'd be dead by now. I guess we better crawl up and check them out." I sighed.

Bennett pointed to Rushinski and Vickers to go along with me. We slipped from tree to tree, then crawled up to the first low mound. I pulled the pin on a fragmentation grenade and looked for a place to drop it, then gave a loud warning: "Fire in the hole!"

The explosion was muffled by the packed dirt and logs, making a *whump*. Rushinski stuck his head into the hole and declared it empty, so we moved on and repeated the procedure, then realized we would quickly run out of grenades. We soon discovered there were rows and rows of the mounded fighting positions, all deserted, leading up to the apex of the mountain where we detected larger and deeper ones—obviously command bunkers. This was apparently a large base camp, perhaps regimental size, but it looked to have been abandoned some weeks, perhaps even months, ago.

There were sleeping areas, latrines, bunkers for heavy weapons and connecting paths. Since the VC, or NVA, had not destroyed or mined the place, they obviously intended to return sometime, which didn't make me feel entirely secure. It was like November again; I could feel eyes staring at me, but I tried to shake it off.

After hearing the reports from Blazer 6, Charlie 6 ordered the platoon to begin mapping the area and diagramming the bunkers and find a spot for an LZ. We moved into the abandoned command center and constructed hooches around the bunkers. It was cold on that hill and I wondered as I lay under my liner behind a huge tree, where are they and are they coming back?

During the night the sky cleared off and the sun made a rare monsoon-season appearance in the morning. I dug into my pack, pulled out my OD T-shirt and hung my smelly fatigue jacket on a bush to dry out. We were in our fifteenth day with the same clothes, so the air was getting pretty rank, but the platoon was learning to operate and behave as a cohesive unit—in part because of the harsh conditions.

Word came down from the CP: 1st and 2nd squads search for more bunkers and an LZ site; 3rd Squad and a gun crew would make a water run back to the stream we had crossed two days ago. I gave a little involuntary shudder as I thought what might happen if that VC regiment met the water party. We checked out the entire area for an LZ, but it looked like the choppers were going to be landing in the valley and we would be carrying all supplies up the mountain. The lieutenant rejected this notion, to my relief, because we did not have enough men to secure an LZ and the bunker complex and it would be too easy to be ambushed while carrying the supplies.

The final solution was to cut and blow down enough trees out of the side of the hill just below the crest to allow a chopper to put one skid on a log and be unloaded. The engineers sent out two chain saws, which were lowered from a hovering bird, and we began to cut. Sergeant Brittain, a giant of a man, and a member of his squad manned the saws first and the trees fell against each other for a while, but by 1700 there was enough room to get the chopper in. The gutsy pilot slowly edged down into the narrow opening, clipping small branches with his rotors as he sashayed back and forth and stuck one skid against the makeshift log platform we had devised. We unloaded C rations, lots of C-4, tetrytol, mail, hot As and a grinning Sergeant Nuckols.

The chopper returned a little later carrying a squad of engineers with more saws and the rest of their tools. We carried the explosives about 100 feet to the CP on top of the mountain, then settled in for hot chow and mail. I dug into the ham and potatoes, then relaxed as the sun slowly faded in the west. It was a beautiful sight from the mountaintop, but the air began to cool immediately and we got inside the hooch. The engineers volunteered to pull watch with us, but I declined; they had a big job to do tomorrow, so we would pull watch and they could rest easy.

When my turn came, I thought about what would happen if an artillery round would land on the bunker with all the explosives. Then I mentally shrugged and decided it was doing no good to worry. The top would be blown off the mountain and we would be scattered along the slopes. We would never know what hit us and there wouldn't be enough remains left to bury, so why worry? In the cold, thin night air, I wrapped my poncho liner security blanket around me and slept like the proverbial log.

The engineers fueled themselves with coffee and a heavy C-ration breakfast, then went to work early in the morning, forming charges to use on the hundreds of bunkers spread over the massif. Two of them, augmented by members of the 2nd Squad, continued sawing trees and building a better platform at the LZ. We started blowing the bunkers in the morning, then held up as Colonel Miller and Captain Eklund flew in and stepped gingerly onto the logs.

The 2nd Platoon was the big news in the brigade because of the find and Golden 6 was basking in the reflected glory as he walked among the bunkers followed by his entourage. I had the distinct feeling that he would have been happier if they had been occupied when we found them; bodies would have been stacked up like cordwood, his favorite expression, in that event.

The men were laughing, shouting and generally cavorting like kids as they got a chance to play with powerful fireworks and destroy an enemy lair at the same time. Because there were over 200 bunkers and only a few men making charges and blowing them, it took over two days to finish the chore. The bunkers were stretched along the ridgeline in both directions for more than 100 yards, then like water spilling over the sides of an overfilled barrel, extended down the slopes of the mountain. At the end of the second day, February 21, the only bunkers left were at the mountaintop command center, which was our campsite. These would be blown in the morning as we took our leave.

Despite a light rain I decided it was time to celebrate, so I put out the word—a can of something spicy, preferably from home, hot sauce or any condiment would entitle you to a C-ration can of jungle stew, à la McCown. One of the engineers came up with some Tabasco sauce, another had some tomato juice and, incredibly, an onion. I had some dry soup mixes sent from home and Martinez had his hot sauce.

Using a mess kit over a small fire, we browned some C-ration ground beef in its own grease, added the onion, juice and hot sauce and let it simmer. I then filled my steel pot with C-ration beans and wieners, added my tomato soup mix and water and heated it over another larger fire.

Chase was helping me prepare the feast and mentioned an old adage: "Necessity is the mother of invention." I replied with a new one that came to me: "Jungle stew is the ugly stepchild of war and monotony."

As the smell wafted over the perimeter, we began to get requests for portions, so I added some C-ration pork and ham to the meat and more water to the steel pot. After one last liberal dash of Tabasco sauce, I combined the meat and broth and let it simmer for a few more minutes. Finally, after bluffing my way through the entire preparation, it was time for the taste test. I took a good-sized spoonful, slugged it down, then reached for my canteen. After swallowing enough water to cool my mouth, I managed to gasp to the waiting troops, "It's perfect! Line up and dig in. This is Mac's recipe, I think, and we made it in his memory."

The compliments were profuse as the GIs dug into the hearty stew, but what else could they say? It was late, they were tired and very hungry, which makes for an appreciative crowd. If the enemy had stormed up the hills in the night, he would have met a cloud of noxious gas as the beans and hot sauce began to work on us. I believe that the American soldiers sitting on top of that mountain in Binh Khe Province bonded a little over a pot of Mac's jungle stew.

Bennett returned from the CP and passed on the orders of the day for February 22 to the members of the 1st Squad. He began to take down his hooch as he spoke. "The whole damn platoon will move out today. Our squad will work as rear guard for the engineers as they get ready to blow the rest of these bunkers. The rest of the platoon will pull guard around the LZ until 1100 when the lift starts. We'll go out on the last two choppers with the last of the engineers."

"Where to next, master?" Vickers asked.

"LZ Illini."

"Illini? Hey, hot chow, showers, clean clothes, right?"

"Wrong, Vickers. The whole fuckin' company is goin' on a combat assault to another area back in the lowlands."

"Have gun, will travel. Brittain was right. They don't know what to do with us, do they?"

"Sure seems that way, Pete."

After the rest of the platoon left, the squad set up on the trail and I ambled over to the storage bunker set on the south side of the hilltop and was surprised to see a substantial amount of explosives still there. I thought for a minute, then asked the corporal working there, "Don't tell me we have to carry that back to the LZ and load it on the chopper. I think any one of us can come up with a better idea than that."

"No sweat, GI. We're gonna blow the last few bunkers, then we'll set a timed charge to blow the command center while we're in the air."

The engineer in charge sent his men to the LZ just before 1100, then waited for the last chopper to land with Bennett, Vickers and me. When it did, he set the timer and we all loped to the LZ and jumped on the bird. He explained the situation to the gunner by yelling in his ear and giving him hand signals. The gunner grinned and gave him a thumbs-up, then let the pilot in on the story. He graciously climbed, then circled gently while pitched to one side so we could have a good view. The engineer counted down the last ten seconds on his fingers; I knew he was a good demolitions man because he still had five on each hand. As he closed his fist, the hilltop exploded in a ground-hugging cloud of dirt, rocks, branches and blasting powder. We exchanged thumbs-up all around, slapped fives and grinned and made "whooo!" sounds as the pilot turned and headed for LZ Illini.

The adventure of the bunkers on the mountain had been a good diversion from the real war. The men of the 2nd had enjoyed the activity and the isolation from the danger of the lowlands and the harassment of rear echelon types. We had worked together to complete the mission, and now we must use that cohesiveness to make it through our tour of duty.

We barely had time to grab a few Cs at LZ Illini before the company headed out again on a combat assault. The very words sent an anticipatory shudder down my back and there was a somber mood hanging over the men as we readied our gear. The new LZ was prepped with artillery and gunshot fire before the Hueys ferrying the troops of Charlie Company came swooping in two abreast. We leaped out onto a grassy field, then scattered along a low dike that bordered a rice paddy. It was fifteen to twenty degrees warmer in the lowlands and more humid, so the sweat popped onto my brow quickly as we hustled into a column and moved out. We stayed away from trails, cutting our way through the brush and elephant grass and headed for an unknown, to me, objective.

After traveling slowly for a couple of hours, we reached our night defensive position and went into a wagon wheel. Bennett came straggling back from the CP with the bad news. "We're goin' on ambush again tonight. Pete and Vickers, take one other asshole and find us a good site."

We took Rushinski along and directed him to find a suitable spot; as a new guy, he needed more experience, but I liked his attitude and willingness to learn. He picked a bend on the trail we had crossed earlier. Vickers and I then asked a few pertinent questions.

"Why is this a good spot for an ambush?"

"We'll have good fields of fire and good cover behind those bushes and trees."

"What about surprise? Is there any chance we could be discovered by the enemy first?"

"If we set up in kind of an L, we could see him as he comes in either direction and unless he hears us, he'll never know we're here."

"Where's your back door?"

"The back door would have to be the path back to the company."

"Not bad, Rushinski. What if the enemy somehow spots us, cuts us off from the company and attacks us?"

He hesitated for a minute, then answered: "We could head back to the LZ where we landed today and call in artillery."

"We might hit our troops—the company," Vickers broke in, then continued, "I think we should head for the LZ, but call Charlie 6 and have him call in artillery since he knows the location of both spots."

"That's damn good, Vic. I agree with you—let the Old Man handle the artillery. We could hold out for quite a while if we could find the place in the dark. All right, let's get back."

We slipped back to the LZ, grabbed some chow and some rest and waited for dusk. Huffman had left for R&R, but we still had eight men—eight good men. Vickers, Rangel, Bennett, Marvin and I were considered old guys, while Rushinski, House and Malarik were the new guys. We meshed well and I liked working with this squad. We moved to the site and set up in a lazy L-shaped ambush near the bend, but there were no guests at our party again—where were they?

The platoon split from the company and moved south the next day, following the trail we had ambushed the night before. We moved slowly in the morning sun, stopping to send out scout patrols every few hundred meters and looking for anything suspicious. At noon we stopped along a clear stream and broke for chow. I walked over to the edge and discovered a beautiful sandbar about fifty feet away, stretching along the stream bank for at least 100 feet. I told Vickers, "Back home we call this a creek or crick, rhymes with prick. On the map it's a river; the Army calls it a stream and Charlie Company calls it a spider. I call it beautiful."

"I hope old Blazer 6 calls it a swimming hole. I could use a bath."

Charlie 6 was sympathetic to the 2nd Platoon's personal hygiene problems and gave us permission to spend the afternoon in a perimeter by the stream. Sergeant Nuckols sent a gun crew to the other side for security, then each squad got an hour to bathe and swim. I wore my filthy fatigues into the refreshingly cool water, then pulled them off and washed them with hand soap. After rinsing, I hung them on the nearest bush to dry, then lay down on the warm sand. We were all loose and relaxed as we spent a lazy afternoon in the shade or on the beach.

Since you have to pay the piper if you're going to dance, the 1st Squad was sent on ambush on the trail to the south once more. Bennett and Rangel had scouted an open area just past a small grove of trees. We set up in the tree line and ambushed the clearing. Again there was no activity and I settled in next to Vickers and Malarik and thought about home.

We rejoined the CP just past dawn, finished a leisurely C-ration breakfast and received orders to patrol to the north. We moved out away from the stream and up a large gully, then back around a small hill. On the south side of the hill, we picked up a large trail that looked as if something had been dragged along it. A few meters farther along we found the fresh track of a very large cart, which we presumed was a tiger since they were indigenous to the area, although not a common sight. I took the point from Malarik and brought Vickers and his shotgun up with me, then I told Bennett and the squad:

"We don't know how hungry this animal might be, but we should be alert in case it's an enemy tiger and is pissed off at GIs. I want the shotgun right beside me. That should stop him if he attacks. I'm taking my weapon off safety, but I want the rest of you to keep yours on. I don't want to be shot in the back by a trigger-happy trooper."

"OK, Pete. I'll be right behind Vickers with the radio. Try to take the tiger alive, in case the Old Man wants him for questioning." Bennett was wearing his usual wild grin as he answered.

"Fuck a bunch of questioning," Vickers cracked, "my shotgun will ask all the necessary questions and give the answer."

He stroked the barrel of the big gun as if it were a pet, then we moved out more carefully than at any time since November on the border, peering carefully at every bush and tree. We lost the tracks quickly, but continued along the trail and around the hill until we came to a clearing. I heard one of the men yell, "There he is—over there!"

He pointed off to the right into some low brush. I glanced quickly, but saw only a flash of color, then nothing as whatever it was slipped into the trees more than 100 meters away. Some of the men wanted to pursue it, but Sergeant Nuckols brought them up short.

"Let him go. We've still got a mission here."

"Yeah. And why would you want to kill such a beautiful animal, anyway?" I asked.

"So he doesn't kill us," House put in.

Our mission was to continue to scout this side of the valley, so we moved back into the tree line and resumed our patrol. A few monkeys scolded us as we violated their territory, but we found no enemy, although the trail had been recently used. There were tracks and relatively fresh elephant dung on the wide path; I suspected that the beasts were being used to haul supplies for the VC. The trail went up over the ridgeline into a different AO, so to avoid any chance of a mishap with a friendly unit, we returned to the stream perimeter in time for a resupply chopper with a mailbag. We relaxed in the wagon wheel and dug in for the night and I dreamed about tigers and elephants storming the perimeter.

The platoon continued to patrol the area around the LZ the next day, this time heading south, then east to climb the nearby hill, then back to the perimeter in the afternoon. We bathed and swam once more in the cool water, then took the rest of the day off. At 1700, Sergeant Nuckols came walking toward the 1st Squad position with that familiar troubled look on his face.

"Bennett, Pete, come on. We're gonna scout out that stream crossing just south of here for an ambush tonight. The lootenant is gonna take some men and cross over here to the village and ambush just outside it, so we'll have Alabama's gun crew and your squad and my radio."

We looked over the crossing, then moved about thirty feet farther south where a larger trail came in from the west and formed a Y with the north-south path. The trails followed irrigation ditches used to transport water to the rice paddies, so they were lower than the surrounding terrain, especially near the stream. In the daylight, the confidence that is prevalent among young men with rifles working together led us to believe that we could ambush the site despite the drawbacks of poor visibility and no real fields of fire. We worked out a plan to set up along both branches of the Y and back along its trunk to a nearby rice paddy, which would be our rear door. When we came back after dark, it looked different—more ominous.

"I don't know, Bennett. Can we do this without gettin' somebody killed?" Nuckols whispered as we stopped at the rice paddy just to the west of the site. Then he made the decision.

"Hell, we're here, let's do it. We have to be able to retreat quickly so they can't throw grenades on us while we're in those ditches or we'll be dogmeat. Who you puttin' on rear guard?"

The moon was shining up over the hill to the east and I could see a glint in Bennett's eyes as he glanced at me and spoke softly.

"Rangel and his team—Marvin and Malarik. Pete and me will take a fork of the Y and Vickers, Rushinski and House will take the other. We'll put the gun crew up in the paddy to hit anything that comes from the west. Whaddya think, Pete?"

"I think we should let the rear guard handle anything that comes from the west. Let's put the gun crew across the trail from the Y and let them cover the south. Sergeant Brittain is ambushing the north trail farther up, the stream is on the east and the lieutenant is ambushing farther west, so anything we see will probably be coming from the south."

"We'll have to make sure we only fire in a north or south direction to keep from killin' each other."

"No sweat. We'll be laying in the ditches, so the crew will be a couple of feet above us. I think it'll work—we've got a lot of firepower on the trail."

Chase looked at me, then at Nuckols and gave a barely discernible nod in the moonlight. "It'll work. I'll take the men over and set our fields of fire to the south with one man covering north. I wish we had a bomb, Pete. This would be the place to use it."

"I hear ya, guy. Be alert over there, Chase."

He led the gun crew down the trail and placed them behind a low scrub bush on the white sand along the stream while the 1st Squad deployed along the Y. Because the area was surrounded by water on the north and east and bordered by the ditch-trails on the other sides, they were actually on a little island—with very little cover. Mize joined Bennett and me on the south branch while Nuckols stayed with the radio at the junction of the branches a few feet behind us.

Vickers took Rushinski and House to the north branch, about twenty feet from us, and set up a claymore. As the full moon eased up into the night sky, I realized that the men in the gun crew were sitting ducks on the white sand. They're probably scared to death—well, no, it looks like they're sitting up talking. Jesus H., they're sitting there playing cards in the bright moonlight. I stifled a laugh, then rolled back a foot or so and whispered to Bennett.

"Listen, if we see or hear anything, we gotta open up right away, then get those assholes out of the open. They're in deep shit and don't have a clue—look at 'em, they're playing cards."

Bennett raised his head a few inches, took a quick look, then lowered it and I could feel his body shaking as he smothered a laugh. He hissed to me, "They're fuckin' playin' cards. I can see Alabama's teeth in the moonlight, grinning. I don't fuckin' believe it."

Unwittingly, we had made the gun crew the bait for our ambush. I had not taken into account the light of the moon when we picked the site and made our plans so I felt personally responsible for their fate. This was not Trailblazer strategy; we didn't hang anybody out to dry. After about an hour they were still playing as if they were back in base camp and nothing had happened, so I relaxed a little and Bennett took a nap.

As I sat there, wondering who was winning in the card game, I saw movement coming from the right. Figuring it was a trick of the night and tired eyes, I strained, looked again and saw a figure in the shadows then at least two more sneaking north on the main trail. They appeared to be trying to creep closer to surround the highly visible gun crew and were oblivious to our presence. I flipped my 16 to semi, then poked Bennett and Mize. Mize was already bringing his weapon to the firing position and I saw Bennett's face tense up in the moonlight, but he brought his rifle up and nodded. I pointed to where I was going to be firing, then we opened up to the south and southeast at the shadowy figures—as much to warn the gun crew of the danger as to hit any of them.

In less than a heartbeat, it seemed, I heard the trusty hammering of the M-60 as Alabama began pounding away. Then I heard the familiar popping of an AK-47 as the enemy weapons found their voice. I stopped firing for a second to get my bearings and check my grenades and heard Bennett's strained voice: "They're shooting back. They're firing at us."

Since we were all still alive and pretty much in charge of the situation, I figured it was time to inject a little levity into the harried circumstances. "Yup, that's the way it works. We shoot at them, they shoot back. The one who shoots best, wins the battle."

"I'm too short for this shit, man," Bennett snapped back.

Mize, who was even shorter, looked at me and grinned, then changed magazines and fired another burst to the south in case any reinforcements were moving up. I fired a few more rounds, then my weapon jammed. I started to panic, then remembered what happened to Maddox at the Crater, so I took a deep breath and picked up a grenade. I slid down in the trail and motioned to Bennett and Mize about my weapon and watched the action.

I could hear the VC yelling at one another and I felt my heart beating like a jackhammer somewhere up high in my throat. I was a little frightened and frustrated, but somehow excited as the adrenaline rush took over. Bennett fired another burst at the trail to the right, then his rifle jammed, too. Then I heard a cry from the island. "I got him. I pinned him right to the tree."

There was no doubt about the origin of the voice; the big

redneck had hit something, hopefully an enemy soldier.
Vicker's shotgun barked twice, then silence fell over the area
until I heard a stage whisper emanating from his position.

"I'm gonna blow the claymore. Get ready."

There was a tremendous roar and I felt the back-blast rush
just over my head, tearing into the brush. Had we been a few
inches higher at our position, we could have been injured seriously by it. In the background I could hear moaning and low
shouting in Vietnamese. I crawled back to Sergeant Nuckols
with Bennett and we held a brief strategy meeting. We all
agreed with the cagey platoon sergeant that it was time to with-
draw while our luck was holding.

"I'll take the rear guard and head for the paddy. I can set up
a position there. Get the gun crew and follow as soon as you
can."

"Give me your weapon, Sarge. Vickers and House can stay
with me and I'll bring the crew as soon as you're set up."

We moved over to the north branch and waited until everybody had disappeared up the west trail, then I hissed over to the
guys lying low on the sand.

"Psst, Chase. You guys ready to *di di?*" then realized the VC
would immediately know what we had planned. I had to get my
head on straight.

"Yeah, Pete. I thought you'd forgotten us. It's time to get the
hell out of here."

"Get down. We're going to toss a couple of grenades, then
bring you over."

Vickers and I hunkered down and tossed a grenade each
way, then I crawled back to the edge of the main trail.

"Come on over, one at a time, gun first. Give me your name
first, then I'll put out my hand and you come across. Go."

"Alabama here, Pete."

"Bring it over, Alabama."

He stepped tentatively onto the trail, then grabbed my arm
and stepped across to safety. Martinez and Rich then followed
before the squad leader, Chase, pulling rear security, came.
"Chase here. I wanna go home, Pete."

"OK, Chase. Don't forget your cards."

Chase snickered a little but gripped my arm hard and
squeezed it as he came across our line of demarcation. House

led the way to the rice paddy while Vickers and I took the rear security. We backed all the way to the paddy, Vickers holding his shotgun steady in the trail position until we passed Rangel's position and the two-foot dike running along the edge of the field.

I lay down behind the dike and relaxed for thirty seconds until Sergeant Nuckols gave me back my jammed rifle and took his. I quickly broke mine open and screwed together my cleaning rod, then poked the spent shell from the chamber. I closed it again and jacked another round into the mechanism and hoped it would fire. Word came down from Nuckols, via Mize.

"Everybody down. Artillery on the way."

We were no more than seventy-five feet from the ambush site, so when the shells came screaming in they sent shrapnel and debris whizzing past us as we hunkered down behind the dike. Sergeant Nuckols waited until the initial barrage had ended, then asked for a number for the fire mission. Intermittently through the night, the man on radio watch called in the mission as the ambush team hunkered down behind the dike.

"Firefly, this is Charlie 2–5 Alpha. Fire mission, over."

"Go ahead, Charlie 2–5."

"Firefly, give me number 1–0, over."

"Roger, 2–5, wait. 2–5, Firefly. On the way, over."

"Roger, on the way—out."

After calling in the mission on his watch, Bennett came over to me and showed where a piece of metal had torn into his poncho liner and it was still smoldering. Bennett was becoming a basket case, but maybe we all were. I remained tense and wide-awake, fearing a counterattack throughout the night, but the men caught some sleep behind the dike. As the adrenaline rush wore off, a deep fatigue had set in on them, but I was still soaring.

Somewhere across the wide-terraced paddies to our rear, the lieutenant and the 3rd Squad were ambushing a trail to a village. If they had to fire, we might have to leap over the dike and into the brush to escape injury, only to expose ourselves to any enemy that might still be lurking in the area. During my watch, I repeated to myself over and over again: "Don't open up. Don't open up. Just leave us alone the rest of the night."

Even after my watch I was still keyed up, so I remained

awake and replayed the harrowing incidents in my mind in slow motion. I could see again the shadowy figures sneaking, almost dancing, past me to surround the gun crew. I wondered—what if we had waited another few seconds? Would we have been able to lure more VC into the kill zone, or would those who already were in it have opened up and wasted a few of the gun crew? I decided we had acted correctly and in the nick of time.

It had been a dangerous but thrilling night of action and high drama and no one was hurt, although I could still hear the buzzing of the enemy's rounds as they tore over my head and the back-blast of the claymore. It reminded me of something that George Washington had said after a battle in the French and Indian Wars. "I have heard the whistle of the bullets, boys, and there's something romantic in the sound." As long as you don't get hit, George, I thought, you might be right.

The rest of the night went calmly and the 2nd Squad joined us in the morning. We all huddled behind the dike as one more fire mission was called in, then we crept quietly down the trail to inspect the site. As we moved through the Y on the trail, it became evident that a pitched battle had been fought. Lying on and along the trail were spent casings, empty magazines and the detonator for the claymore that had been fired.

I could see one body leaning against a small tree in front of where the gun crew had made its stand. We found no more, but there were several blood trails leading into the water, none of which emerged on the other side. The wounded VC must have followed the stream until they found a safe area to patch themselves up in, or perhaps to die. I went back to the dead man and noticed how it was impossible to look very good after a sudden demise; stripped of all dignity and poise, the body freezes into a contorted caricature, the face an exaggerated mask. I turned away. I didn't need another face to lodge itself into my memory.

Sergeant Brittain made a loop in a nylon rope and tossed it over the head and shoulders of the body. After making sure that everybody was clear, he gave it a jerk and pulled it a few feet to see if there was a booby trap. It was clean, so one of the men searched the pockets of his black pajama uniform, but they were empty. The radio came alive and Sergeant Nuckols informed us that the "loo-tenant" wanted us to join him and the

3rd Squad at the village for a sweep, so we policed up our gear and left the body in the trail.

We moved across the rice paddy in small groups of three or four men abreast, staggered to prevent one weapon from bringing us all down. As we entered the hamlet, a familiar sight occurred. A black-clad young man emerged from one of the huts and headed down a trail west. Two members of the 2nd Squad opened up, but he disappeared into the brush. A search of the spot where he had last been seen showed a spot of blood, but there was no further trace. They searched for a tunnel or spider-hole, but amid mounting frustration, they found nothing. Sergeant Nuckols yelled, "Sergeant Brittain, did you find him?"

"Negative. One blood spot, then nothing at all."

"Did you check for tunnels? He must be close by. They can't just disappear, like ghosts."

I gave a low grunt, then nudged Bennett. "Sometimes I think they do just that. Disappear like ghosts."

"Well, there's one that didn't disappear. Alabama took care of that."

"I still can't believe that we didn't bring down two or three when we first opened up. They were right there in front of us. Ghosts, I tell ya."

We finished our sweep with no further incidents and returned to the small LZ where we dropped our packs and prepared to rest. My nightlong high was descending rapidly, being replaced by a frustrating numbness and aftershock. I was frustrated by the escape of so many VC, although some of those would probably succumb later to their wounds. I was very frustrated by the failure of so many weapons; five in all had jammed over two days. I was numbed by the potentially dangerous situation into which we had been placed.

The ambush had been a qualified success, but it had been perilously close to being a catastrophic failure. A heavy feeling of fear mixed with futility began to weigh me down and depress me. I felt like I had been lucky so far, but my turn was coming. Just as I closed my eyes, Mize came to our position and gave us the news.

"Golden 6 is pissed because so many got away, so the LT is pissed. Now we gotta clean our weapons and test-fire them."

"Fuck the colonel and the lieutenant! The damn things jammed. They weren't dirty. I think they're defective."

I had exploded without reason at Mize, who wasn't the enemy, although I was beginning to wonder who was. The colonel wanted a big body count, the lieutenant was worried about his future and we were the pawns. Bennett confirmed the news as he picked up his rifle.

"Clean 'em, then pick up fresh ammo and we test-fire later. The fuckin' colonel wants ambushes again tonight, so we're goin' farther south down that trail."

"Why doesn't the colonel come out here and go on an ambush with us? The bastard's a chicken," House complained.

"Right. We could put him with the gun crew and let him play cards. Hey, Chase! Whose deal is it anyway?" I yelled down to the next position.

He grinned at me, then put his finger to his lips and moved his hand to his shoulder and simulated ripping his chevron off. I nodded, yeah, you could get busted if the lieutenant hears about it. No sweat, GI, my lips are sealed.

After cleaning, the weapons test-fired the new ammo well, with only a couple of incidents of jamming. I decided to keep my cleaning rod in my jungle fatigue shirt pocket where I could reach it in a hurry. Usually it was a spent shell that didn't eject that caused the malfunction and the rod would solve that problem with one swift plunge down the barrel, that is, if Charlie didn't mind waiting while I did it.

At dusk it began to rain, further deepening my depression, but we saddled up and moved down the trail, then cut across the rice paddy before doubling back to a point about 300 meters south of the previous ambush. We hunkered down behind the paddy dike and ambushed the trail where it bent away from the stream. I fervently hoped that no VC would happen along this miserable, wet night and my prayers were answered.

20

The 1st Squad—the wet, disconsolate and totally fatigued 1st Squad—made its way back to the LZ after another night ambush. The men threw off their gear and looked for a dry place to crash.

Mize gave us the news that we would be picked up in the afternoon and dropped into a new LZ about fifteen klicks away. I cleaned my weapon again, then got an empty plastic battery cover from Mize and wrapped it around the end of the barrel—if anything happened, I could fire through it easily enough. After that, I crawled into his hooch, wrapped my liner around my wet body and slept for the first time in three days.

At 1500 we loaded onto a Chinook and took a leisurely flight north where we plopped down in a grassy area near another stream and joined the rest of the company. Bennett and Rangel scouted an ambush site in a wide gully to the east and the squad returned there at dusk and set up in an L-shaped posture along a small trail. The light rain continued all night and the only thing that moved was when Bennett had to crawl back into the bushes to relieve himself. Bravo Company reported contact, so we knew there was VC activity in the AO, but we were in no hurry to find it.

On the last day of February, we moved back to the point of insertion, grabbed a quick C-ration breakfast, then the entire company moved out. We crossed a narrow valley, then started climbing the low mountains to the west, winding our way from slope to slope, always moving up.

At dusk, when we finally reached the highest crest, we were extremely weary and miserable, but our spirits leaped a little when the lieutenant gave us the word.

"Hack out a small LZ. Hot As coming in."

We quickly hacked and tromped out a one-ship LZ and brought in the bird with the food. It wasn't very good and it wasn't very hot, but we were tired and hungry, so it was a feast. After dining, we dug in, put up our hooches and rested safely on the mountain.

The Trailblazers received a day off as the entire company relaxed and waited for their pay on the first day of March, one day late. It was a needed reprieve from the constant stress and strain of always being alert, a break from uncertainty and fear. Here, on this giant hill in Vietnam, we were safe from all but an attack with rockets or mortars. There was, however, another enemy that stalked us relentlessly at times like these: boredom. As we relaxed, we tried to fill the empty hours with conversations.

"Pete, I want you to come with me to the meetings at the CP from now on. I'm getting shorter every day and I want you in on the decisions and sharing the responsibility."

"Yeah, OK, if Rangel will let me. He really thought he should have been squad leader when you went on R&R."

"Screw him. He's leaving before I do, so he knows we have to break in a new man. You want me to talk to him?"

"No, I'll do it if he causes any trouble. I'll probably have to show him where the bear went through the buckwheat."

"Whatever the hell that means. But don't let it affect you out here."

Bennett smelled his fatigue shirt and winced.

"Man, I hope those assholes bring some clean clothes out with the pay. How long has it been since we've had a change, Pete?"

"Let's see—twenty-four days by my trusty diary. You know, POWs get clean clothes more often than the 3rd Brigade does. The bastard brigade—that's us."

"There you go again. Pete for Senator."

"I'd rather be king. Then I could make things happen."

We were interrupted from further drivel by a shout from the CP. "Squad leaders, get up here!"

"Come on, Pete. Let's see what we can do." We strolled about fifty feet across the top of the mountain to the platoon CP and sat down to hear the latest. Lieutenant Nelson, who had replaced Lieutenant Lesko without fanfare late yesterday, made his first presentation to the cadre. He introduced himself, then told us what he expected, which wasn't much different from our other platoon leaders. He then said a chopper was on the way with our pay, hot chow and mail, and that we should line the men up alphabetically.

"Tonight the 1st Squad will ambush the main trail on the south slope. I'll be with the 2nd Squad on the north slope and Sergeant Nuckols will stay with the CP. Scout your sites this afternoon and move out at dusk. Good hunting."

It was too soon to make any lasting impressions, but I was pleased with the news that he was going on ambush with the troops. I heard the *whap-whapping* as the resupply chopper came into view and descended on the LZ, where it had its contents removed swiftly. It reminded me of vultures tearing at the belly of a dead beast. I saw two men get off, one carrying a large bag, probably money and vouchers. The red mailbag was tossed to the company CP first, then the mail was sent down to the platoons after sorting.

The clerks set up two card tables and the men filed past the first to receive their pay, then to the second where a Spec 4 in a clean, pressed uniform offered to help the men set up their finances. He took their MPCs, which hadn't even had time to get dirty in their hands, to send home in money orders and made recommendations about deductions that could be made automatically each month. Since I had taken care of my particulars while back at Camp Enari, I was waved through, so I took my remaining $29, picked up my letters and went back to my hooch. A little while later, Underhill came strolling toward the position with the *Stars and Stripes* in his big hand.

"Stanley, my man." He always called me that and I called him Underbrush or Underdog or just Hill. "Did you get your *Sporting News* today?"

"Negative, old dude. When it comes, you're next in line after me."

Underhill had played minor league ball with the Detroit organization and liked to read about the game at all levels. He continued, "Spring training should be started by now. Maybe I can read about some of my old teammates moving up the ladder."

"What league did you play in, Dog—Rookie?"

"I played in the Rookie League, then some A ball. I hit .300 in both leagues and I believe I can hit .300 in any league."

"That's where it has to start—in your mind and in your heart. But here in the Jungle League, .300 won't get it. You better hit closer to 1.000 if you want to get back."

"You played some ball, didn't you, man? I can tell."

"I played some country ball, but nothing organized. I could hit a little. My dream would be to be an announcer. 'Here's the two-and-two pitch to Underhill. He swings and hits a drive to deep left field! It's going, going, gone! Detroit wins the pennant!' I could do that."

Underhill was grinning broadly and slapped my shoulder as he said, "I promise you, I'll be there in Detroit and you can interview me after I hit it."

"It's a deal, Hill. Are you done with that paper?"

He tossed me the paper as he climbed to his feet and ambled off with the athletic black man's strut. We had made the promises with the typical infantryman-in-combat fervor, but like most vows made in stressful situations, they would probably be forgotten.

I glanced at the headlines denoting various American victories across the Vietnamese countryside and wondered why the NVA and VC didn't surrender since we were kicking their butts so regularly. Maybe Charlie doesn't read *Stars and Stripes*.

We ambushed the main trail that night, but since the company was behind us and the enemy would have to make a steep climb to attack, we pulled light security and got some rest in the cold night air.

The choppers arrived to extract us at 0900 and we flip-flopped to another landing zone—LZ Wire, where we formed up and moved out as a platoon toward the hills to the west. We climbed for a while, then found a trail that led to the ridgeline. We followed it along the crest for a half hour until Sergeant Kushinski, leading the 3rd Squad, halted the column and sent for the new lieutenant. He had found more bunkers.

The 3rd Squad moved into the complex while the rest of us pulled security. After an hour of searching, the word came down that we would set up here for the night. Nuckols, Brittain and Bennett set up the defensive positions and we cut away the brush and dug in. I opened a can of peaches to celebrate begin-

Chapman with Vietnamese children in front of a typical village hooch.

Pete scribbles a letter home. Bennett is at rear.

In battle gear. Standing, left to right: Vansworth, Chase and Martinez. Kneeling: Sawlski, Rich and Alabama.

Jack Betta and Kevin
Patterson at Chu Lai base
camp, May 1967.

Fears, McCown and Harrell.

Pete and his C rations.

Alabama with his
"Zippo lighter."

Alabama (kneeling) is ready for action, while Mize, Rushinski, Huffman, Pete and Vansworth relax.

Rich, Pete and "crazy" Sergeant Bennett.

Maddox and Vickers in lounging gear, November 1966.

Martinez and Pete at Chu Lai, July 1967. (Courtesy of Donald E. Williams)

Mize, Lieutenant Lesko and Fears question a villager.

ARVN regulars "winning the hearts and minds of the people" through intimidation.

Vickers and Lieutenant Nelson with a Vietnamese girl.

Champion football and volleyball team at Pleiku base camp, Christmas 1966. Sitting, left to right: Vansworth, LaBarge, Alabama, Rushinski and House. Standing: Pete, Patterson, Vickers, Fortunato and Huffman.

Ringo. (Courtesy of Fred Vickers)

Fred Vickers rides shotgun. (Courtesy of Fred Vickers)

Vansworth, Underhill, Pete and Sawlski at Chu Lai, June 1967.

On patrol near Chu Lai. From left: Lee, Nuckols, Cain and Lieutenant Nelson.

Party time for Mize, Maddox, Pete and Vickers.

Martinez, Sawlski, Vansworth and Alabama at Pleiku, December 1966. (Courtesy of Kevin Patterson)

Chase, Mize and Pete pause for refreshment.

Robert and Joni Peterson on their wedding day, June 19, 1971.

Sergeant Nuckols, Alabama, Patterson and Vickers gather for a reunion in the late 1980s.

Soldiers Grove veterans Bill Becker, Pete and Tom Moran.

Pete at the Moving Wall in Chicago, June 12, 1986.

A 21-gun salute following the scattering of Robert Peterson's ashes at the Highground in Neillsville, Wisconsin, on May 29, 1994.

ning my fifth month in-country; it was always the best of the Army Cs and I felt content as I sipped the syrup and squished the peaches between my teeth. I wrapped myself in my poncho liner against the cool wind and the platoon spent another peaceful night.

As we finished breakfast the next morning, Sergeant Nuckols came over to the 1st Squad position and gave us our mission: we were moving due west about three klicks, back to LZ Alpha-Alpha. The choppers in the area had spotted enemy activity in the now-abandoned LZ and we were going in quietly to try to catch some of them. I looked at Nuckols and Bennett.

"I thought this terrain looked familiar. I don't have any fond memories of that place—I had dysentery all the time we were there. Stinkin' cesspool, beaucoup enemy activity. I guess it's just a 2nd Platoon kind of place."

"Glad you feel that way, Pete. 1st Squad is on point." Nuckols laughed.

"Who else would be on point?"

"Remember, we're going as quietly as possible," the old sergeant said.

"The U.S. Army doesn't do anything quietly," Bennett reminded us all.

Bennett put my team on point, so I put Rushinski in the lead and fell in behind with Vickers and Malarik. We moved out slowly following the trail that would bring us into the LZ where the squad had positioned two weeks before. As we neared one of the ambush sites we had used then, I detected a strong, musky smell in the air. I motioned to Bennett and Nuckols to hold up, then lowered my voice and spoke to them:

"Charlie's close by. I can smell him. He's either right near us or he just left. Vickers and I will take point and we'll be movin' slow."

"All right, Pete. I'll call the loo-tenant and he can let the Old Man know what we're doin'."

Nuckols didn't have to add "be careful"; it was in his tone of voice. I moved with Vickers into the lead and we edged out with extreme caution since I was always convinced that a good portion of the NVA Army was waiting for us wherever we went. I held up as we reached the gully that ran from where we stood about 100 meters down to and alongside the east edge of the old camp, but since there was no other way to safely reach the goal, I began to cross it. I followed the trail into the gulch, watching closely for trip wires or anything suspicious. Finding nothing, I edged up the slope to the other side with the strong odor still in the air.

I began to scout around as Vickers joined me on the other side and then I heard a rustling noise. Vickers and I hit the dirt together and seconds later a grenade exploded, but not close enough to hurt anyone. I waited and peered into the brush, expecting an attack or, at least, some gunfire, but nothing happened. Vickers and I crawled off to the side of the trail and found some trees and again we searched the area visually. I could see no movement, nothing untoward, so I motioned the rest of the squad to cross the gully. As they joined us, I took my fire team farther down the trail, scouring the bushes and trees as we moved. My heart had slowed somewhat and I tried to figure out what had happened; I knew we had not tripped a wire.

To the right of the trail was an open area where you could see along the side of the LZ and across to the hill on the other side of the stream. I heard Vickers yell, "VC! There! Across the creek—on the hill."

Some of the troops began firing, but the range was too far for the M-16 or the shotgun. Alabama then brought his M-60 into play, walking a line of fire up to the fleeing black-clad guerrillas. One of the figures hit the ground, but the other reached down, almost without breaking stride, and grabbed and dragged his companion the last ten yards or so into the brush. Alabama fired another burst or two into the vegetation, but they were gone and we were too far away to even pursue.

"Damn, they're fast! If they ever have an Olympic event called buddy-dragging, they're a cinch for the gold medal," I said.

Bennett quickly rounded up Rangel and his team to go across the stream and up the hillside to check the area while we pulled security. They found nothing and returned to meet us at the LZ where we found signs of digging in places where GIs had buried their trash. The VC had apparently been looking for discarded food and supplies when their lookout spotted us and detonated a grenade to warn them and slow us down. As I stood on the spot used as a helipad, I looked to the west at a low ridge that stuck out of the hills a couple hundred meters away and saw three or four more VC looking back at us. A few of the trigger-happy troops opened up again, but their targets were well out of effective range and the VC merely walked away into the trees.

Lieutenant Nelson called in gunships to strafe the area, then sent Sergeant Brittain and his squad over to check it out. Kushinski took his squad to check out the tunnel and hospital complex while the 1st Squad remained as security for the CP. After an hour, Brittain radioed back.

"2–6, we found lots of fresh sign, but no VC. We're gonna break for chow. When do you want us back at the Lima Zulu?"

"2–2, stay put until 1400."

At 1420, after the 2nd Squad had left their position and were on their way back to the LZ, several VC came out of the woods again and began looking around to see what they had left.

"Look at that. Either they've got the biggest balls in the world or they're really hungry," I yelled as I pointed them out. Lieutenant Nelson already had the coordinates ready, so he called in artillery without a marking smoke round, but they disappeared while the rounds were in the air. I laughed and spoke to Chase and Bennett:

"Ghosts, I tell ya. Here one minute, gone the next. They must have heard the whistle of the rounds in the air."

"Well, Pete, if they want to dig up C rats, let's give them a little surprise," Chase interjected, "Just before we leave, we'll booby-trap our garbage."

He showed how we could pull the pin on a grenade and cover it with an overturned can, then cover the can with dirt. The VC would dig into the pile, discover the can and lift it. The grenade would fall out and arm itself. If the VC were not alert, it would be good-bye, Charlie, as Chase strikes again. As we sat there congratulating him for thinking of such an evil trick, a small green snake emerged from a clump of bamboo next to where Vickers was sitting. He whirled and rolled out of the way as Bennett and House whacked it with their rifles. The bamboo viper, as it was known, is just one of the many deadly snakes in Vietnam, so Vickers was slightly upset as he remained standing and filed his complaints.

"Fuckin' snakes. We gotta fight the VC, the weather, the jungle and the damned snakes. I'll never smile again."

The choppers whirled in a few minutes later and we headed for LZ Wire to join the company. The mighty 2nd Platoon had spent another busy day in the jungle, spotted and fired on about a dozen enemy—some armed—dodged a grenade, called in artillery and survived a snake attack.

Colonel Miller would not be happy with our body count, but we had suffered no friendly casualties. We pulled perimeter guard at Wire that night and rested.

Bennett remained at the LZ to catch a chopper to brigade HQ for some medical work, so I took the squad once more as we headed out on company patrol. We headed north, up a large valley, then onto a low hill range to a saddleback between two bigger hills, where we broke for chow.

Nuckols came stumbling toward me with a pound cake in his hand. "Pete, I still can't believe it. You actually smelled the VC. What'd they smell like?"

"Strong musty, almost sour smell, like sweat, but stronger. I suppose I smell their discharges—sweat, urine, feces. They eat differently, bathe differently and they crap differently. And this nose can pick that odor out, no problem."

"I should put you on point every day, man."

"No way, José. You'd have a mutiny on your hands. I'll do my share and more, but not permanent point. That's a ride home in a body bag, with a nice tag on my toe."

I could see down into the valley below, so I oriented myself with Bennett's map, mentally checking off landmarks as I finished my boned chicken. After chow, the company moved down into the valley on the other side of the hill and the going became easier as the vegetation was cut down for paddies and fields. The 1st Platoon, on point, held up near a large stream and the company was moved into a perimeter next to it. We spent the rest of the day bathing and swimming and then received clean fatigues for the first time in twenty-eight days. The men were almost giddy as we threw our filthy, torn, smelly jungle uniforms into a pile and pulled on the clean ones. I tucked in my trousers, rolled up my sleeves, then got into chow line and feasted on some unfathomable Army stew while wondering about the lack of mail.

"You know, Vick, I was really beginning to get attached to those old fatigues. I smell funny now. Can't figure that out."

"That's clean you're smelling now, Pete. Something you haven't smelled for a while."

Alabama joined us to talk about the past few days. "I'm tellin' ya, I'm gettin' tired of doin' all the work around here. I got that one in the ambush and another yesterday. What're y'all doin' out here, anyhow?"

"I guess we should all carry extra ammo for guys on the guns. Hell, we could just get you a mule or an elephant, then we could stay back in base camp."

"Well, maybe we could keep you around to put on OP or somethin' like that. I don't mind admitting that I was little worried on that ambush the other night. When I think back on it now, y'all put us out there as bait, didn't you?"

"Not purposely, 'Bama. But none of us took into account the full moon and the bright sand. But, you assholes were playing cards. You were shuckin' and jivin' instead of pulling full security like you should have been. Right?"

"You got that part right, buddy. As long as nobody got hurt, it's somethin' to laugh about, Pete. Well, we live and learn."

"I guarantee you, I learned—I learned a lot."

Nothing bothered the resting company that night, so we patrolled on up the valley in the morning, cutting our way, sweating and cursing. The valley floor was covered with dense brush and thick, tall, razor-sharp elephant grass, so despite moving all day, we covered little territory.

We searched on for the ethereal Victor Charlie, crossing the river whenever the going got too tough. We spent the late afternoon searching for a spot big enough for a Chinook to land in, finally coming to a broad expanse where we tromped and cut down the thinner brush and grass and brought in the big birds. The company was flip-flopped in two flights to LZ Coral on top of the highest mountain in the surrounding area, commanding a wonderful view—an excellent spot for a firebase.

We moved through the already-manned defensive perimeter and set up our own positions nearby on the same ridge. It was actually cold there and at our platoon meeting later, Sergeant Nuckols mentioned to Lieutenant Nelson that we could use some wool sweaters to keep warm up here. Nelson said he would requisition some; he had seen some on the artillery crews. He then doled out extra pairs of OD wool socks for the entire platoon. Kushinski—Ski to us—by now, advised us to put the clean ones on and wrap the wet ones around our waist to dry them out with our body heat. Nelson then advised us that there would be no ambushes tonight.

"Rest up. There have been sightings of heavy VC activity in the valley below and we're going down there tomorrow. Intelligence and the 1st Cav know that Charlie is in the area, but can't find him. Maybe Charlie Company can."

It was raining as we moved out the next morning along the ridgeline, then edged our way down the slippery slopes of the mountain. The rain and mud soured our disposition and we cursed as we slid along to the valley below. We stopped for an extended noon break while the CP decided on our next move, so I walked through the squad with my 16 strapped across my back and a bottle of mosquito repellent in each hand.

"Leech patrol. Leech patrol. Drop those drawers and off with your boots. They're everywhere!"

I made the men search themselves for the parasitic devils, then we sprayed them with a little of the repellent. They obediently and greedily sucked it in and fell off, writhing in agony. The repellent didn't do much for mosquitoes, but it was deadly to leeches and helped start a fire when your heat tabs were wet. After chow, we continued to patrol the valley floor, then retraced our steps and began the onerous task of climbing up the muddy slopes to return to Coral.

We wound our way up, climbing at an angle to the right, then back to the left, slipping and sliding and swearing at the fate that put us here. We finally reached the firebase late in the afternoon, then moved to the positions we had held the night before to begin the drying-out process in our hooches. The trek up the muddy slopes had tired us all, but I managed to respond when Mize called the squad leaders to the platoon CP. Nelson was waiting with a grin, wearing an ugly but warm-looking olive drab wool sweater.

"How do I look, men? There's one for every swingin' dick in the company. No ambushes tonight. Tomorrow we go down the south slope where we pick up a trail and follow it into the valley. We'll search and destroy down there for two days, then get further orders. Questions?"

"Any mail today, sir?"

"You got mail yesterday. Hell, this is the Army, not Boy Scout camp. Dismissed."

He was slurring his words a little and speaking too loud. I wondered where he got the booze out here—did he hump it? As long as he did his job and didn't put the men in jeopardy, I didn't care if he drank tiger piss, but I would keep an eye on him. Leading men into combat required steel nerves and a quick mind and alcohol was not conducive to either. In my hooch, I listened to the rain fall and wondered when we would get a real mission in an area of operations where we could work for a long time. We were being bounced around like an ugly orphan from one AO to another, always on short operations. The bastard brigade, that's us, all right.

In the morning Bennett showed up on the first chopper into the LZ. He rejoined the squad and immediately began complaining about the rain as we saddled up and got ready to move out with the company. We cut back through the perimeter of the firebase, then headed down the steep hillside to the south, picking up the trail after a few minutes. We eased down into the valley once we got on the path and began our patrol. The sweaters and meals weighed our packs down, but the going was fairly easy along the trail. We found no sign of recent activity in the mud and despite making our presence known, there was no sniper fire.

At about 1600, after an uneventful day in the light rain, we came across a larger trail, almost a road, which led us to an abandoned church in an open area. There were a few other old hooches in the vale, but the church was the most prominent feature. We stopped and set up a perimeter around it and some of us walked through the shell of the bombed-out structure. It was hard to tell how long it had been in this condition, but I saw slogans written on the shattered walls in French and others boasting of the prowess of the 1st Cav and other units. Some of the men began adding their own names and unit designation to the graffiti, but I still felt like it was a place of worship. I felt a calmness as I sat on a piece of timber and reflected on the last time I had been in a church, but I couldn't remember when or where it was. I decided to retreat to my squad position and think about something else.

We set up an LZ in a flat area and the Army sent out a hot

meal. I wolfed down the ham and gray-green beans before the rain could ruin them, then walked over to the gun crew position and sat down in Alabama's hooch with Martinez. He greeted me, "Hey, Pete. What's happenin', guy? That chow could use some hot sauce and chiles, huh?"

"You'd put hot sauce on ice cream, I s'pose?"

"I might, if it was Army issue ice cream." Martinez then added, "Pete, I want to be in your squad. I saw you guys work point that day in Double Alpha and I think I'd be a good point-man."

"Are you tired of the gun?"

"A little. Mostly, I wanna be in a line squad, go on point, maybe make squad leader before I go home. I don't think I can do that here in the gun squad."

"One thing at a time, Gus. I'll talk with Chase and see what he says—then Nuckols will have the final say. We can always use a man who wants to walk point."

"Make sure that Chase understands that it's nothing personal, I just want a change."

I did some thinking as I moved toward the other gun crew hooch. With Bennett, Rangel, Huffman and Vickers all leaving at the end of next month, I would need replacements and I didn't want them all to be new men. Chase had no objections if he got a strong body in return, so I talked with Bennett, who also thought it was a good idea and agreed to bring it up with Nuckols in the morning. It continued to rain softly through the night, but I felt more at peace next to a church; it kept me warm and safe through the night.

Bennett, Chase and I approached Nuckols with our request in the morning as he sipped his C-ration coffee. He listened to the request, then turned to Chase. "You havin' any trouble with him, Chase? I know those damn California freaks don't make very good soldiers."

"Negative on that. He's a good man who wants to get out of the gun squad."

"And into the 1st with Bennett and me. He wants to be a pointman."

I added this knowing the value of a good pointman to any unit. Nuckols grinned and shrugged his shoulders. It looked like he approved of the deal.

"Hell, yeah. Let's give it a try. Just like the major leagues, huh, Pete? Tradin' players."

"Right. Martinez for a player to be named later."

"I call Louisville my hometown, just down the river from Cincinnati, so I follow those damned Reds. You got a favorite team, Pete?" Nuckols threw away the rest of his coffee and hauled his bony frame up. He couldn't weigh 140 pounds, but it was all grit.

"Used to be a Braves fan, but they moved to Atlanta, so I figured, screw 'em. I'm a Packer fan all year long."

Chase had been listening, but he spoke up. "Go, Cubs. Go, White Sox."

"And take the Bears with you," I added.

We took the news back to Martinez at the gun crew's hooch. "As soon as Chase gets a replacement, you're in. Don't fuck it up, old dude."

"All right! You won't regret this, Pete."

Alabama cast a bemused glance at me, then asked, "Pete, how'd y'all get so much pull with Nuckols? You change jobs, go to school, get rank, make squad leader. I've been here about the same time as you and I'm still humpin' this damn gun. Man, this Army sucks."

It was a legitimate complaint and it deserved an honest answer, so I gave it a shot. "Alabama, I'm not sure; maybe it's because I'm a few years older than you dudes. Maybe it's because I listen to what he says and take his advice. Maybe Bennett tells him good things about me. I don't know. I do know that I work as hard as anybody here, so I don't feel bad about my rewards."

Chase interjected with his soft voice, "Willie, I'll be gone in less than two months. I plan to recommend you as gun squad leader at that time. You deserve that."

"Well, now I feel better. Thanks, buddy. Sorry if I shot my mouth off out of turn, Pete."

"No sweat, GI. You were only saying what your heart felt. Just don't shoot off your pleasure maker, guy."

I hustled back to the squad position as they were tearing down the hooches and packing their gear. I quickly changed my socks, then took point to lead the company across to the other side of the valley. Due to the absence of rain and the fact that we would be heading back to Coral later in the day, morale was high. I shot a straight azimuth, then followed dikes along the paddies to stay out of the mud. With no enemy to detain us, we reached the foot of the mountain just before noon, then broke for chow.

Later I found the trail and led us up the steep gradient and back to the LZ and those beautiful, earsplitting 155-millimeter cannons. After we had settled into position, I headed to the CP with Vickers to pick up any mail. Mize informed us there was a barber available in the perimeter, so we dropped off the mail and went back to get a haircut and afterwards, I shaved for the first time in four days.

As we were finishing evening chow, one of the men spotted some Vietnamese in the valley. In a futile gesture, several men opened up and the Vietnamese returned the fire. Word got up to the Old Man, who directed his forward observer to bring the artillery to bear. We watched as a very professional-looking barrage covered the area of the sighting, then returned to our holes.

"Well, Vickers, Charlie finally makes an appearance, so we'll undoubtedly be chasing his shadow tomorrow."

"Have shotgun, will travel. Hell of a life, huh, Pete?"

The night was calm but cold, so I donned my sweater and stayed in our hooch until it was my watch, then wrapped my liner around me and moved behind the sandbags. Nothing moved all night and just before dawn it began to rain again.

Because of the overcast sky the choppers couldn't fly, so we built a huge fire, cooked our C rations and huddled around it to stay warm in the morning. Mize sang out, "Squad leaders, to the CP."

Lieutenant Nelson greeted us, "Sergeants, we'll get stale if we lay around this hill, so in thirty minutes we're heading back down the trail to this point." He held up his map and pointed to a red dot. "Point Alpha. We'll wagon wheel there tonight in an ambush posture. Take three meals and full gear. Get your men ready. 1st Platoon will be on point, then we'll fall in with the Old Man. Questions?"

"Sir, it looks like they're just getting C Company out of the way again. When do we get a real mission?"

"I haven't been here long enough to know what's going on with higher, Sergeant Brittain. I just follow my orders and treat each one as a mission. I'll discuss it with the other platoon leaders and see what we can do, but until then, I expect you to carry out your orders."

We tore down our hooches and wrapped our ponchos around our web belts, then fell in behind the 1st Platoon and Sergeant Able. They led the company along the ridgeline to the east, then we descended partway to the valley before stopping on a flat, low hill about three klicks from the LZ. Scouting parties were sent out for ambush sites, then the company set up in a perimeter for the night. As if someone flipped a switch, the rain stopped and the skies brightened. Mize yelled, "Send up some men to help unload hot As. They're on the way."

I volunteered to help unload the unexpected repast that Charlie 6 had requested as soon as the overcast sky broke. We slopped down our beef stew, then headed out to our ambush sites.

Vickers, House, Rushinski and I ambushed the trail from behind a huge tree as the rain began to fall again; it was a quiet night.

Morning, March 10—back into the valley to check out a ville. We moved carefully along the trail as we neared the group of huts surrounded by a brambled hedge. The ville appeared to be abandoned, but there were plenty of signs of recent activity. Vickers and I eased into the first hooch, poking our way along with weapons at the ready. We found cookware and pots clean and used; someone had been living here. Over in one corner Vickers spotted a large round screen made from reeds or grainstalks and used for sifting impurities from rice and various other chores. He kicked it away and found a spiderhole underneath.

We each took a frag grenade and pulled the pin, then tossed them in and dove out the door. "Fire in the hole! Grenade!"

The grenades blew as one with a muffled *whump,* then we stepped back inside and saw that the hole was a little larger. Vickers handed me his shotgun, then stuck his head and shoulders into the opening and glanced around.

"Nothing in here. There's a solid dirt floor under the dirt that was blown loose, so there's no tunnel down there."

We left the scene and rejoined the platoon. Nuckols and the lieutenant were standing under an overhang to get protection from the steady downpour as the other troops searched the remaining hooches. Nelson was talking to Captain Eklund, then turned to Nuckols.

"Back to Coral, Sergeant. We've got point, so form the men up and move out ASAP."

We could see the firebase sitting on top of the big hill, but to get there we had to slog through rice paddies, then brush, then climb the steep trail in the driving rain. By the time we breached it we were dead on our feet and ready to sack out. We headed to our former positions and reconstructed our hooches, then crawled inside. I pulled my dry wool sweater out of my pack, threw off my wet fatigue jacket and put on the smelly pullover. I glanced at Bennett, who had just arrived from a short meeting at the CP.

"No ambush tonight, just regular security. Now, I'll trade a barbecue beef for just about anything. Any deals?"

I tossed him a boned chicken, then heated the beef just outside the hooch door. I had learned the hard way about the noxious fumes heat tabs make in a closed area. I added some cheese to the meat and spooned it on some crackers. It wasn't good, but it was hot and smelled good enough to make Bennett want to trade back again. With four of us in the position, we each pulled only two hours guard and managed to stay dry enough to get some sleep.

The rain let up in the night and the sky brightened somewhat in the morning. Bennett went to the CP meeting alone while I relieved myself. I told him we both would have the same result when it was over: a big pile of shit. He came back and spread the news.

"All right, you miserable SOBs, get your asses in gear! You're gonna get clean clothes and you're gonna clean yourselves up. The big brass is comin' from brigade HQ. And, you lucky assholes will get your booster shots today."

"Who's coming, Colonel Miller?" I asked.

"No, it's the big boss man, Colonel Shanahan, comin' in to inspect the gun placements and the line troops."

"I wish that potlicker would have been with us yesterday. He could have checked out those hooches. I can see him now, a full-bird colonel down on all fours, with his head stuck in an enemy bunker. . . ."

Vickers was interrupted by Bennett. "Instead of up his ass!"

The little sergeant roared his deranged laugh. Sometimes I was certain that he had gone round the bend.

After washing up and shaving in our steel pots, we lined up for booster shots; this time it was immunization against cholera. Spec 4 Bowman, the intrepid medic, was busily inserting needles into arms and egos.

"Did that hurt, trooper? No? Well, let me try the other arm. It's supposed to hurt."

Martinez was just behind me in line, so we conspired to feign passing out when we reached the inoculation desk (card table). When the desk jockey asked for my shot records (immunization certificate, carried by all military personnel), I handed it to him, then keeled over onto the sandbags with Martinez falling across my legs. Bowman didn't miss a beat.

"Pull down their pants and I'll throw the syringe at their butts from here. I think I can hit something."

We quickly leaped to our feet and bared our arms. "Doc, you gotta work on that sense of humor. With your help, we could have scared some of the new guys."

"Man, I just want to get this over with. I don't like this duty any more than you do. I'm considering reenlisting in order to change my MOS (military occupational specialty). I'm just not cut out to be a medic. Get it? And you said I didn't have a sense of humor."

We headed back to our bunker, flexing and working our inoculated shoulders and carrying our clean fatigues, which we would change into when the colonel was on his way. A resupply chopper brought in hot chow at noon, then we took our mail back and began to police up the area around our bunker. At 1430 the word came down that the colonel's chopper was in the air—change fatigues, clean weapons and look sharp.

The Huey set down on the landing pad and the brass began to pile out—Flamethrower 6 (Colonel Shanahan), a major, two captains and a lieutenant. They began to check out the artillery positions while Vickers, Huffman and I stood by our bunker; we were afraid to sit down and soil our fatigues. Bennett was talking to the medic about the headaches he had been having since the mortar round exploded next to him. I knew it had been bothering him and I supported his trying to get assigned to rear duty for the last six weeks of his tour. The phrase "too short for this shit" was working its way into too many of his utterances.

As the colonel and his entourage worked their way through our section of the perimeter, he shook a few hands and would occasionally say a few words to one of the troops. Suddenly I got one of those portentous feelings: I knew he was going to stop and talk to me, unless a sniper dropped him in the next few minutes. I whispered to Vickers and Huffman: "He's going to stop here and talk—get ready."

Like clockwork, the colonel eased past the previous few bunkers with a mere nod and a perfunctory salute, then stopped at ours.

"How long have you been in-country, son?" he asked me.

"Sir, I've been here almost six months. Vickers and Huffman are going on eleven months each."

"Veterans, ah? Did you see action on the border?"

"Yes sir, all three of us." I stifled a sudden impulse to tell him about Huffman getting lost, then found, over there.

"Did you kill any NVA over there?"

I pointed past the grinning Huffman to Vickers and he spoke up. "We got our share and then some, sir." He patted his shotgun.

"There were some tremendous battles there, but we made the NVA pay dearly, then chased the rest of them back to Cambodia. I'll bet that shotgun came in handy."

"Right, sir. It could bring some pee," Vickers added while Huffman grinned.

"How do you like those jungle boots? Are they working out for you?"

"Sir, this is a fine boot," I said. "It lets your foot dry out and then breathe after getting wet; it's comfortable and has a steel shank in the arch for protection. I like it a lot."

I felt like a shoe salesman and realized that I was blathering on too much, so I stopped. "Did you know that President Kennedy authorized and helped design jungle boots?" he asked.

I didn't know, but it hardly mattered now. He was long gone although I was here in large part because of his life, his leadership and his death. The colonel shook our hands, saluted smartly and told us to carry on, then headed on around the perimeter. One of the captains in his menagerie looked at me with raised eyebrows as if to say, "What are you sucking up to him for? That's my job."

Flamethrower 6 and his minions left shortly thereafter and life at the LZ returned to normal. I sat down in our hooch and opened one of my letters from Ens. George Fetty, one of the handful of homeboys from our tiny town serving in-country. I also had a first cousin, Lt. Doug Peterson, USN, who piloted a jet from the decks of the USS *Intrepid,* and three friends, Donald Moran of the 1st Cav, recently wounded, Wayne Dull, USMC, and Harlan Longmire, USAF, all doing their bit for the hometown and the USA. I read about the ensign's exploits in the South China Sea, then wrote back a quick note about how we were winning the war here.

Later, in a pensive moment, I borrowed a felt-tip pen from Vickers and printed a new logo on my steel pot cover—"The Searcher." He studied it for a minute, then asked, "What's the meaning of that, Pete?"

"I saw a movie by that name with John Wayne. He and Jeffrey Hunter searched for years for a girl, Natalie Wood, that was kidnapped by the Indians. Sort of like what we're doing—searching and finding nothing."

"I wouldn't mind searching for Natalie Wood my damn self."

I tossed him the marker and continued talking. "The colonel seemed to be all right. I know he's preoccupied with the damn body count, like Miller, but I kinda like him. Maybe one of these days they'll figure out that getting a high enemy body count is the kind of attitude that will send a lot of GIs home in body bags."

"Man, I hope so. Didn't MacArthur say we should never fight a ground war in Asia?"

"You got that right, Vick. We're fighting a war of attrition in jungle terrain against an enemy that is fighting for their lives, and in some cases, their homes and families. We've got to use all our firepower to win. We're just spinnin' our wheels if we continue to fight like this—go in, fight for a while, then leave and let the VC have the territory back. It doesn't make sense."

As I glanced at him, he shrugged his shoulders and I knew what was coming.

"Fuck me, I'll never smile again."

21

Two things happened the next day that ran contrary to recent events; it didn't rain and we got another full day off. We hung around the perimeter all day, cleaning our weapons and gear, answering mail and insulting one another. The chaplain from battalion HQ flew out to the LZ and held a Protestant service with communion. Afterwards, he made the rounds of the bunkers, speaking with those who wanted to talk. I told him about the bombed-out church we had seen in the valley and how peaceful I had felt there.

"Yes, well, you were in the presence of God there."

"How do we figure the presence of God in a combat zone? To me it doesn't add up."

"God is in your heart and soul always."

"Not during a firefight when I'm firing my weapon into the body of another human being. God can't be with me then."

"Perhaps God is helping you strike down your enemy—the enemy of your country."

"Perhaps, sir. You know, we have to search the bodies and empty the pockets of the dead enemy. Most of them have pictures of their loved ones and letters from them. I think my enemy believes his God has sent him to strike me down, so where does He draw his distinctions?"

A silence fell over us and was interrupted by the familiar *whup-whupping* of the rotor blades on an incoming Huey. The chaplain stood up and put his hand on my shoulder. "That's my ride. I understand your frustration and I hope I can come back and talk with you again. Until then, may God bless you and keep you . . . and give you peace."

I sat there feeling frustrated and alone after he left until a voice rose out of the CP hooch twenty feet away. "This is *my* platoon and don't you forget it!"

Lieutenant Nelson was yelling angrily at Sergeant Nuckols, who came out of the hooch with a red face and tight lips. I suspected the lieutenant had been drinking again, but I still didn't feel like I could do much about it, unless he tried to go into a combat situation while under the influence. There, I would take my stand. However, if the lieutenant believes that he can operate a platoon without the complete cooperation and participation of the wily Nuckols, he's wrong and because of that we all could be dead wrong.

At 1730 another chopper arrived with hot chow and a beer ration—one warm can for each man. My first beer in more than a month was too warm to drink. I figured it would cool some during the night, so I set it down in the shade and laid down on the sandbags covering the bunker.

Bennett leaned on the side wall and wanted to talk. "Pete, we're goin' on a combat assault, just like the fuckin' 1st Cav tomorrow. We'll jump off on Hill 450, then sweep down to the valley here. I'll be going back to Bronco Beach either tomorrow or the next day for tests on my head, so you'll take the squad again."

I kept my eyes closed, but I knew he was standing there with that hangdog look on his Irish face, waiting for me to say something at least mildly amusing so he could let go a crazy laugh. It had come to this: my wisecracks and Vickers' dry, understated humor were the highlight of the squad's social life. I felt like I couldn't let my public down.

"I can see the medical report now. X rays of Bennett's head show nothing . . . or maybe an image of a woman's crotch."

He started to snicker in the low, base manner that men use when discussing women and sexual possibilities. "I think they'll show a little red-faced guy holding onto his package with one hand. . . ."

I interrupted, "And his other hand is making the peace sign?"

"Just half of it, Pete. This half here!"

He roared as he flipped me the bird, then I rolled over to nap, knowing he was happy for a while at least.

The next morning we did leave Firebase Coral, lifting out at

0900 and heading north. We soared along for thirty minutes or more, then the choppers descended, banked left and hovered over an open field on a hill. I leaped out at about five feet, landed hard and rolled over in the grass. I shook my head and looked around to get my bearings, then headed for the tree line. It was another day, another mission, another chance to excel.

The 3rd Herd led the company down a huge gully into the valley, where we came onto a small stream which we followed to where it met a river, then followed the river to the northwest.

Eventually we came onto an old deserted bunker complex and stopped to check them out. After looking over a few of them, the CO decided they weren't worth investigating further or blowing up; they were in such bad condition that they would need major reconstruction to be useful to the enemy.

We patrolled farther north until late in the afternoon when we came to a large open field with good fields of fire. The Old Man picked this as our NDP, so we dug in and set up our armaments and trip wires. As we finished our foxholes, a lone black-clad figure appeared near the tree line about 200 meters away. Our side of the perimeter opened up, but he disappeared and, strangely, we received no orders to pursue.

"Like a ghost. Here, there, everywhere, nowhere," I said.

"I don't believe in ghosts, Pete. They're just fast and smart—too smart to stick around and fight," Bennett replied, then added, "You know, I hate those damned VC 'cause they're the reason I have to be over here, but I admire their balls."

He was, of course, using balls as a synonym for courage, but it left me an opening to give him a needle and question his manhood. After all, this was the U.S. Army, an outfit that traveled on its insults, wasn't it?

"You check their balls a lot, do you, Bennett? You wouldn't be one of those light-footed ol' dudes, would you?"

He grimaced at me, then answered. "No, dammit. I mean their nerve, the way they draw fire that could kill them—on purpose. I'm a married man, asshole."

There was no further activity at the perimeter and Charlie Company rested easy.

Following the same procedure as yesterday, Charlie Company jumped on choppers in the morning, flew a dozen miles or so to the southwest, then watched as the gunships poured rockets and machine gun fire into an LZ. When they had finished their prep, we swooped down, jumped out and charged into the tree line once more.

Bennett returned to Bronco Beach for medical tests, so once more the squad was mine to lead. It was difficult to impress any sense of stability on the troops due to the changing of the leaders so often, so I tried to keep the differences in our styles to a minimum in order to maintain their morale and efficiency levels at a workable level. I had pledged to myself that I would do everything in my power to keep the men safe and send them home whole. My ulterior motive would be while doing that, I would be making my own tour of duty safer and healthier, also. I also had promised myself that I would not ask my men to do something I would not do.

We formed up and moved out along the shoulder of a big rounded hill, then picked up a large trail and followed it into the valley. As we eased down the gradual slope, I could feel the warmer air. We were only a few miles farther inland, but it looked like the monsoon season hadn't arrived here yet. It was dry and hot and I told Vickers, "We're back in Vietnam, Vick. Won't need those sweaters down here, guy."

"Yeah, man. Looks like we'll be using that mosquito spray for something besides starting fires. The leeches and mosquitoes will be thick in this swamp."

We moved slowly along a trail that was the only dry land visible in the marshy valley. There were a few old hooches, long since abandoned, but no other sign of life anywhere. We broke for noon chow and remained in a long column along the trail to eat our C rats and pick off the slimy leeches that had made their way into our trousers and boots. It was hot and quite humid in the narrow, wet valley and we began to sweat profusely as we continued along the trail, which followed a small stream. In the late afternoon, we found a large patch of ground that was slightly raised above the marsh and the CO decided this would be our NDP.

After setting up the positions, we attacked the leeches again. I took off my right boot and found a blood-soaked sock and a particularly large and busy one sucking away near my ankle. I removed him using the repellent method, but the blood continued to flow due to the anticoagulant he had injected into my bloodstream. I finally got it to stop by lying down, propping my foot on my pack and tying a sock around my leg as a tourniquet.

About an hour later a resupply chopper came in with C rations and mail. I saw Sergeant Brittain heading for the chopper and wondered where he was going, so I yelled at Mize: "Where's Brittain going? He hasn't been here long enough to have R&R."

"He's been reassigned to Recon Platoon."

I jumped up and hobbled over in my bare feet and saluted him as he waited to get on the bird. "Good luck, Sarge. Keep your head down."

He gave me a blank look, then we shook hands. "Yeah. Well, see ya, Pete."

We hadn't spoken ten words to each other in the time he had been with the platoon and I knew he resented my leading a squad, but I had no ill feelings toward him and hated to see the platoon lose a good man. With Recon he would have his own platoon, so he could decide who the squad leaders would be, to the extent that availability and enemy bullets would allow. I hoped that he would cut some slack if circumstances dictated that a Spec 4 was the right man in the right place; rank in this war didn't necessarily translate into leadership abilities. I did know one thing about the Sarge, though, he never showed fear.

As I returned to my position, I saw Sergeant Kushinski huddled with the platoon leader and the CO with Nuckols nearby. Mize informed me that Ski had lost his map somewhere during the afternoon patrol. Nuckols was in favor of sending him back to find it and the Old Man agreed.

With less than two hours of daylight left, he took the 3rd Squad on a search mission. When he returned at dusk, he was still minus the map and the brain trust then had to assume it had fallen into enemy hands. He had marked our AO on the map and had written all the call signs, frequencies and code words on the margin. Now all of these would have to be changed. As I glanced at the usually ebullient Kushinski, he had the look of a contrite dog, complete with sad eyes, and I could almost see his tail tucked between his legs.

When we attempted to dig a hole, the seepage made it a losing proposition, so we put up our hooches and sprayed repellent over our skin and pant legs. Because of the swamp, I felt that the only way the enemy could hit us was coming down the trail or with mortars. The first was unlikely and highly defensible, so the company played the odds of the other possibility and won, as the night proceeded peacefully. Our real enemy here in this wet domain was the slimy, almighty bloodsucker.

We had been scheduled to proceed west along the stream, but the plans were changed due to the swampy conditions and to allow the battalion HQ to switch all codes and frequencies. Our new mission was to make short patrols in the area and be ready for pickup at 1500. I led an eighteen-man patrol along the stream, staying on the trail, confident that no enemy would be lying in wait in the quagmire. I kept my map stuck in the buttoned cargo pocket of my fatigue pants—each pant leg had a patch pocket halfway down with a strap of OD nylon on the inside to wrap around your leg, which ostensibly would keep leeches out. I wrapped the strap around the pocket with the map and fastened it. I wasn't about to lose that precious paper.

As we rounded a slight bend in the trail, I could see in the distance a few elephants grazing along the base of the hills. Even at 500 feet, their majesty and massiveness filled me with awe. I pointed them out to the men and we spent about fifteen minutes resting and observing the huge mammals as they up-rooted small trees and foraged. It seemed to remove me from the combat zone if only for a few minutes and my mind felt refreshed as we headed back.

At the LZ we pulled off our boots, socks and damp clothes and let them dry along with our feet as we lay in the sun. At 1500, we loaded onto the birds once more and were lifted out of the swampy area. We soared around on an eagle flight for an hour or more, then finally landed on a ridgeline a few miles west of our previous location. The entire company was placed on the elongated ridge one platoon at a time, each separated by a couple of klicks. The platoons then were further broken up into three ambush patrols and by nightfall there were nine ambushes along eight klicks of the ridgeline. We were trying to catch the enemy moving along the high ground at night.

I led my squad and one gun crew to a site on an east-west trail and set them up in an inverted C formation with the gun facing west and Vickers' team facing east. The rest of us covered the middle and would face the kill zone if anything came along. While there was brush on the site for cover, either side of the ambush could rush to reinforce the other if needed. Nothing moved along the high ground that warm night; Charlie seemed to be still biding his time.

We remained in our ambush positions the next day until the sun began to bear down and the temperature climbed at mid-morning. I then took the men up into the shaded tree line, where we set up in a loose perimeter and took turns cleaning weapons and catching up on sleep. Vickers rubbed down his shotgun as I sat down beside him, and he turned to me. "Is there a plan to this, Pete, or are we just jerking off here? Not that I'm complaining about laying in the shade, but what's the point?"

"I guess they still don't have a real mission for us, Vick. We're just pawns for the 1st Cav to do with as they please. But, I'd like to lay in the shade on a hill like this for the next six months. They could just leave us all here and put it in their reports: C Company secures Hill 308. The enemy could come in once a month, we'd shoot it out with nobody getting hurt, he goes away and we all relax."

"Never happen, GI. I'd settle for it, though. I'd settle for anything safe for my last six weeks. I'm so short I could hide behind one sandbag."

"Maybe we can talk with Nuckols and find you and Bennett something in the rear in a couple of weeks or so."

"Don't worry about it, guy. I'd just get in trouble back there. Some asshole would try to order me to clean latrines or something and I'd have to explain how this shotgun might go off and accidentally blow somebody to hell. Screw it. I'll stay here in the field where I know what's happenin', at least part of the time."

"Ol' Rangel leaves at the end of this month. He never mentioned anything about the rear either. You guys are damn good soldiers. I hope some of that rubs off on the new guys."

"Yeah, well, 'rots of ruck' with them. Rangel is still pissed at you, Nuckols, Bennett and the Army for not letting him be squad leader. It grinds my butt a little, too, but I understand the reasons behind your getting the job and he doesn't."

"Or he doesn't want to. Anyway, as Confucius said, if he can't take a joke, fuck him."

"Time for a him. Him, him—fuck him."

At 1700 we received orders to proceed down the steep hill to join the others in an LZ for hot chow and supplies. We followed the trail partway, then I shot an azimuth to the coordinates and we headed straight down the slope and arrived at the LZ as the Huey was unloading and we heard a disconsolate cry in a highly recognizable voice.

"Hello, you scabby assholes. You're the most screwed-up squad I've ever seen and I'm here to save ya."

"Welcome back, Doolittle. I mean Bennett," I answered.

He winced at the comparison to Doolittle, a trooper who had entered the country when I did and had made a career out of getting out of line duty. Strangely, he had been a good recruit at Fort Polk, but the actual combat had raised a specter in him that he had been unable to confront. As we lined up for chow, we received orders to retrace our steps and resume our ambush posture after eating, so I ate lightly. Martinez walked over with a canteen cup in his hand.

"You like this orange drink, Pete?"

"It's all right. You got a deal for me?"

"Roger. I know that you don't like iced tea. So, when we get orange drink, you get mine. When we get tea, bring me yours."

I carefully poured the still-chilled drink into my canteen to drink when we reached our ambush site. It took us more than an hour to climb back to the spot as we had to stop four times for cramp breaks to relieve those who had eaten too much. It was dark when we finally got to the top, so I held up the patrol and Vickers and I crawled ahead to make sure the ambushers didn't get ambushed.

My heart was racing a little as we crept along into the brush in anticipation of bumping into or facing the fire of my imagined enemy. We found nothing, but my hand shook a little as we gave the prearranged all clear signal by clicking our gun barrels three times. Bennett clicked back and brought the rest of the squad back to the site and we spent another peaceful night. I toasted the squad with my orange drink when I took my watch at midnight.

The squad joined the rest of the 2nd Platoon in the morning for another retrieval followed by another insertion, this time into a wide valley split by a meandering stream. The vale was unpopulated, but showed evidence of recent activity by either local farmers or VC, which, I had learned by now, were often the same person. We swept down along the stream on a wide trail that bordered the empty rice paddies and coconut groves. I took point along with Vickers and Rushinski following behind. I had been extremely tired in the mountains and the heat of the valley was pulling the last bit of energy out of me now. I surmised that it was the combination of the weeklong bout with dysentery and general lack of sleep that was bringing me down.

We found a small idle paddy surrounded by a dike and Lieutenant Nelson decided it would be a good NDP. It hadn't been used for several seasons and the brush had sprung up along the dike providing good cover. As we set up the fighting positions that evening, we spotted some red smoke lifting above the brush 200 meters to the south. A fire team from the 2nd Squad was dispatched to the scene, but they returned forty minutes later empty-handed, saying they had found nothing in the fading light. I caught Bennett's eye.

"Looks like it was one of those 'short' patrols—go out far enough so the perimeter can't see or hear you, then sit down for a while. Come back later with a negative report."

"Yeah, well, we've all done it, Pete, when we thought the orders were dangerous or stupid, but on one like this, you should check it out. It could come back to haunt us all tonight."

"I guess it comes down to who makes the final judgment call. . . ."

Bennett interrupted me quickly to state forcefully, "Which has to be the man on the scene—a field decision."

"So self-preservation becomes the strongest motivation, ahead of unit pride, patriotism, or job performance. I guess that's just part of the old Eleventh Commandment: cover your own ass first," I surmised.

"You can't argue with it, Pete. Not in this war. You, me, Vickers, Huffman—we've seen too many dead and wounded men to follow some of these stupid fuckin' orders that we hear. One of these days you're gonna get an order to patrol out someplace and you won't understand it. You'll have to decide whether it's worth it to expose you and your men to the enemy or just set down in the brush and fake it. Like I said, I've seen too many men die."

The mood was getting somber, so I did what I do best—tried to lighten it up. "And I've seen too many mountains, too many wet, cold nights without sleep, too many days without a hot shower, a warm cot and a cold beer. Can I have an amen for that?"

"Amen, brother. I'd like to have some of that self-preservation from these damn mosquitoes. Look at 'em. They're as big as helicopters."

We covered our visible skin with repellent, which was supposed to be odorless to prevent the enemy from detecting you, but if a VC couldn't smell this repellent there was something wrong with his nose. It had a pungent odor of musk and kerosene and it made your skin sticky so the dirt would stick to it. The mosquitoes descended on us with a fury throughout the night and you could hear light slaps around the perimeter as troopers forgot where they were and tried to kill the offenders by hitting themselves. It seemed to me that the only thing the sticky liquid repelled was the olfactory sense of the wearer.

By morning we all looked like street urchins from a Dickens novel, so we moved quickly to the stream that was present in every valley in Vietnam, one squad at a time, to wash up. I pulled my razor out of my pack, rubbed some hand soap lather into my whiskers and began to shave using the water as a mirror. By the time I was done I had two or three nicks that were bleeding, but I felt cleaner and fresher.

Bennett led a seven-man patrol down into the wide valley to the southeast, following the trail and stream. Sometimes it seemed like we'd been doing that forever. Vickers, Huffman and I joined Chase and a gun crew behind him as we checked out the area. We moved along easily until the stream began to wind closer to the hills on the west, so we looked for a place to cross. After a few minutes we came to a fording place, with rocks laid close enough together to form a walk.

Vickers and I crossed first, since we were old hands at leading units across water. When we climbed up the opposing bank we were hit by a tremendously offensive odor of rotting meat. We did a quick check and found a dead, uniformed NVA soldier in the bushes nearby; he had to have been there close to a week. I waved to Bennett, and after the rest of the patrol crossed he called in the find to the CP. I saw his face tighten, then screw up in disgust as he listened to the reply on his handset.

"Jesus Christ! They want us to search the body, then leave it. I don't believe this shit."

"Who were you talking to?"

"Nuckols. Here, you talk to him. See what you can do."

I proceeded to give a report and some gentle persuasion. "2–5, this is 2–1 Fire Team Leader. The body has been searched by whoever wasted him. His pockets are inside out. His flesh is deteriorating badly, and the maggots and flies are having a ball. He's been dead at least five days, so we're going to cover him with dirt to prevent the spread of disease. Can you roger that and square it with higher?"

"Roger. Wait one, 2–1 FTL."

Bennett grinned and gave me a thumbs-up and I winked back as the radio crackled again.

"2–1, affirm on your request. Cover it and move. Out."

We threw a few helmets full of loose sand on the body and topped it off with rocks. "I don't know why we're doin' this, guys, but I saw it in all those fuckin' western movies, so pile up the rocks," Bennett remarked.

"Why didn't the ones who killed him have the decency to bury him?" Rushinski asked.

"Left him as a reminder—a notice to other VC. If you mess with us, you get this. Most of the units do it, but I'm not sure it has any effect. Some of the units leave a playing card. The ace of spades is supposed to be some kind of death symbol," Bennett replied as he poured the water out of his canteen. "I just filled this SOB in the river, but with a dead body this close, I'd rather go thirsty."

"VC! There! Three, no four," Alabama yelled and began to open fire on the figures fleeing into the brush about 150 meters away. We grabbed our gear and weapons, fired a few rounds and went in pursuit. We found one blood splotch, then lost their trail in the thick foliage. The troops fanned out over the area and combed it, but they had disappeared. After thirty minutes Bennett took another radio message and told us, "Search for a few more minutes, then we go back to the NDP. I'm sure they're a mile away by now, anyhow."

"Or in a tunnel right under us. They're ghosts, man," I said.

"Well, Pete, that one ghost bleeds. He's hurt bad."

The further search was fruitless, so we trudged slowly back to the river, crossed it and continued on to the perimeter. Lieutenant Nelson was waiting for us as we came in.

"Good work, men. I gave you one KIA. Get some chow and join me at the CP at 1900."

As we walked back to our position on the perimeter, I wondered aloud, "So we get credit for a KIA, but for which one? The one we wounded or the one we buried? If the unit that killed that dude gets a KIA and we get a KIA for the same one, the enemy body count is all fucked up, man."

"Don't knock it, Pete. Higher wants a body count, the lootenant gives 'em one. It's a game, but lifers have to play it or get left behind," Bennett answered.

"Following their convoluted processes, we could go sit on China Beach at Da Nang and send in a body count every day. At the end of our tour, we'd have won the war and you and I would be full-bird colonels."

"That might be the only way we can win this fuckin' war, Pete. I've been here damn near eleven months and we ain't makin' any progress. I thought when I got here this would be over by Christmas, man, but. . . ." His voice trailed off, a voice filled with enormous frustration and deep bitterness. I stared at him for a long minute, then once more reached for a way to lift him up.

"They told us the same thing when we came over, Bennett. But they didn't say which Christmas, guy."

"I guess you're right, Pete. Fuck me and feed me beans, they could at least fight the damn war like they wanted to win."

With that, he opened a can of peaches and walked around the perimeter sucking the juice. He looked like a lost child, but he also looked like one of us, like he belonged here.

At dusk the lieutenant led us to a preselected site in a coconut grove where we set up in a perimeter ambush. The moon was brighter than I had ever seen it; I pulled out a letter that I had received yesterday and began to reread it in the light. I saw Rangel on guard and I sat down beside him and we whispered for a while.

"You're getting awful short, Rangel. You'll probably go back to base camp next week."

"Yes. It's time and I'm ready to go home. Want to take a look around?"

He handed me the starlight scope and I hefted the instrument and tried to check the watch area and the perimeter. The device was bulky and heavy and a distinct burden on the troop who humped it. The squads took turns carrying and using the lone scope in the platoon and squad members carried it only part of a day. At night the man on watch used it to see in the dark, supposedly. I had never been able to see anything with it, so I couldn't vouch for it.

"Maybe the moon's too bright, man. I still can't see shit out there."

He took the unwieldy instrument from me and moved his head slowly around the perimeter, then giggled softly and poked me. "Straight over there at three o'clock. Somebody in the 3rd Squad is beating himself."

He handed me the scope quickly. Once more I tried to find something and managed to get a hazy, indistinct scene of rapid movement. I gave the scope back and peered with my 20–15 vision at what certainly looked like Smith masturbating near a tree at his position. I thought about creeping up to ride him, but remembered that men had been killed for less, so I lay down on the grass and thought about the Army and the warm night and men and their strange behavior. Then I laughed softly along with Rangel.

We sat around the grove all morning of the next day, cleaning weapons and writing letters. I told Bennett about the experience with Smith and he yelled, "Smitty, were you on watch at 2200 last night?"

"If that's ten o'clock, yeah. Why?"

"Well, it seems that our position had the starlight scope on you and it looked like you were tryin' to put out a fire or somethin' in your pants. That right?"

He turned red and stammered a little, then Lieutenant Nelson heard the uproar and came over to the position with a puzzled look on his face. "Hey, you guys are making too much noise. What's happening?"

"Let me tell you, sir, about Smith's little peccadillo," I began, but Smith interrupted.

"Hey, my peccadillo is as big as anybody's here."

I laughed so hard the tears formed in my eyes and my stomach ached from shaking. Rangel related the story to the lieutenant, who chuckled and walked away, shaking his head.

At 1400, Sergeant Ski led the platoon back to the southeast and through an abandoned village. As we climbed a dike to cross another idle rice paddy, the deadly *pop* of an enemy rifle brought us all back to reality. RTO Patterson spotted the VC heading toward the woods and the platoon got on line and opened fire, then the 2nd Squad pursued the two fleeing soldiers. After they returned, the platoon swept the area and found a body where the enemy had first been spotted. Nelson was nearly beside himself as he called the CO with the news.

"Charlie 6, this is 2–6, over."

"This is 6. Go ahead."

"I've got my foot on one Victor Charlie Kool-Aid (killed in action). 2nd Platoon strikes again. Over."

"Good work, 2–6. Continue the mission. Out."

I sat down next to Patterson to grab some rest and water. "You know, Pat, this is all your fault. You could have ducked down behind the dike and ignored the sniper and he would have gone away eventually."

"Hey, I'm just a killing machine, wasting my time carrying this radio—I should be in a line squad. I fired once from the hip; I probably should get the kill."

"You can have it. Is the man still drinking out here?"

"Sometimes. I haven't seen him drunk out here in the boonies, but he still packs a bottle. Sometimes he makes me carry it for him."

The platoon started to move, so we found our places and headed toward our position in the coconut grove to spend another night. Despite the heat and the mosquitoes, morale was high and combat stories prevailed as the Trailblazers settled in for the night. I thought about Bennett and hoped he could hold himself together for another month, then wondered how much longer I could hold myself together.

22

Lieutenant Nelson split the platoon the next morning, sending Sergeant Nuckols and his RTO, the medic and Alabama's gun crew with the 1st Squad. He took the remaining two squads and the other gun crew and worked an ambush-observation on the north side of the stream, while we moved out to work the south.

Vickers took point and Bennett and I fell in behind him as he led us back across the river and toward the abandoned ville. We held up just to the northwest of it, then Bennett and I scouted for a place to set up an ambush. There was a large sinkhole where the ground had dropped about three feet over an oval area about twenty by thirty feet. We placed the entire patrol into this depression where we could cover the trail and the fields around the village.

It was hot and dry, but there were shade trees along the edge of the hole to block out most of the sun, so we kicked back and went on light security. The medic, Doc Bowman, went on a tangent about the language and the difficulties of understanding it. He sat beside me and asked, "Pete, do you understand any of it?"

"Not much. Sometimes it sounds melodious and other times it's guttural and choppy. In our job the trick is to make sure they understand us, so we use a few key words and phrases mixed with GI slang, some French and pantomime."

"I wonder what *no bich* means. They use it like when they don't understand us, but what does it translate to, literally?"

"You sure it's 'no bich'? Maybe they're saying *no Viet,* meaning we're not speaking Vietnamese so they don't understand us."

I wasn't even half-serious, but it was boring just sitting there, so I was trying to get a rise out of him. He exploded. "Christ! I should have known better than to ask an infantryman a tough question. I gotta get my MOS changed to get into something where I'm challenged."

"You've been saying that for a month now. Do it or shut up about it. I don't see any anchors on your ass."

He glared at me, then rolled over and faced the other direction. I then fell back into my old ways and tried to lighten things up by saying to no one at all, "You know what MOS stands for? My occupation sucks."

We whiled away the steamy day until the late afternoon (evenin' to Southerners), when the sun began its inevitable slide and the skies turned hazy. Fred Huffman had shinnied up a coconut palm that stood just alongside the sinkhole. We continued to lounge around while he clung to the tree about eight feet up, when suddenly he began whispering to us in an urgent voice.

"VC, VC there!"

We grabbed our weapons and followed his pointing finger with our eyes. There, in the day's late gleaming, were six or seven black-clad figures scurrying along the trail from the abandoned village toward the stream. Apparently unaware of our presence, they were not running, but walking quickly, prancing in the Oriental manner, almost in cadence. They were carrying what appeared to be weapons on their shoulders or in their hands.

There was a low hedge between our positions and the branch of the trail they were using, so the patrol crept out of the sinkhole, sneaked up behind it and slowly raised their heads. I felt strange as I took a long look at the figures in the gathering dusk and sensed something was wrong. Then it came to me that they were carrying hoes and farming utensils, not weapons. I started to yell, but the entire patrol opened up almost as one. I screamed as loudly as I could, "Hold your fire, they've got hoes, not rifles!"

The continuing volley drowned me out, so I poked Vickers, motioned to him to stop, then yelled again at the others. "Stop shooting! They're civilians."

I sank to one knee in frustration and saw Vickers looking at me and nodding his head. I looked at the faces of the men who were still firing and saw that they were in an almost frenzied state, a zone of their own. For the first time in weeks, maybe months, they had an easy target within range and unable to escape and it was payback time. Payback for all the sniper fire; for all the disappearing acts the enemy pulled; for the cold, rainy, sleepless nights; for the leeches; for the men lost on the border; for all the frustration and all the loneliness and for not letting us go home. The men of the 2nd Platoon were going to win this one. The firing finally stopped when all the Vietnamese were lying on the grassy field at the edge of the trees.

"Sergeant Nuck, they were civilians. They had hoes, not weapons. They were farmers." I had spoken in a monotone, trying to place no blame or shame.

"He's right, I'm pretty sure, Sarge. We should have held up."

I could hear Vickers speak in a low voice. Nuckols looked at me blankly, his eyes and face showing that he wasn't yet comprehending what we were saying. Finally he spoke in a terse voice that was hard, but lacked his normal confident edge. "Let's check it out."

The now-silent men moved slowly toward the fallen Vietnamese. I was in a fog, my mind numb, trying to piece together what had just happened. Martinez and I peeled away from the rest to check on the first two casualties—two young women about thirty feet from the others. They were lying on their backs with their bodies slightly twisted. Each had been hit by at least six rounds and was bleeding profusely from various places, yet somehow they were still breathing. Pieces of bone were visible in large gaping wounds; viscous tissue had been violently torn from their bodies and was seeping into their black clothing along with their blood. One of the women had a head wound so deep you could see her brain.

I knelt down and saw that their faces were contorted by the pain and in their eyes was a questioning, pleading look that pierced to my soul. I knew there was nothing we could do to help them, but I tried to clear the blood and tissue from the face of the first woman. She was young, maybe twenty-five, with a hard face, but one that hinted at comeliness. She had at least one foot in the hereafter and my heart filled with remorse and anguish as I saw the light fading in her eyes. I wondered what kind of life she had lived until now and how the circumstances of her existence had put her in this spot at this time. What about her family? Certainly she had children who were at this very moment waiting for her in that village on the hill.

From somewhere I heard a voice yell at us, "We can't get a chopper in. Battalion says they're on another mission and they can't spare one to pick up wounded VC. Do what you can 'til morning."

Nobody gives a damn about the Vietnamese, I thought to myself. These women aren't going to live until morning. Hell, they're dying in front of me and nobody cares. Well, dammit, I care, but I can't do anything about it, they're still going to die.

I saw the medic stand up from where he was working on some of the others and look toward us, but I found myself waving him back. These women were only a matter of minutes from death caused by the severity and multiplicity of their wounds and no one on this earth could help them.

I stood up to curse at somebody or something then looked at the imploring eyes of the first woman and sank quickly back to my knees and began wiping her face again. If she was going to die, she deserved to be touched or held or something. I glanced at my companion, Martinez, and saw he was holding the head of the other woman. Just then, he looked up. "She's gone, Pete. Dead."

His voice was strangled and he sounded like he was talking to me from inside a barrel. I was falling into a semistupor as I looked at the face of the woman lying in front of me. Her breathing was even more shallow and as I gently wiped her forehead with my towel, she stopped and her human spirit left this realm.

I tried to empty myself of emotion, but the anger and frustration and sorrow began to overwhelm me. I stopped for a second to pray that whatever higher plane these young women and the others had aspired to would be granted them. I thought about asking for forgiveness for all of us, but I didn't think we deserved it. I walked over to where the rest of the troops were setting up a loose perimeter around the rest of the casualties.

There were two more dead, a man and a woman, two slightly wounded and a small boy who had survived unharmed somehow.

"It's a miracle that boy made it through without a scratch. He sure is lucky," Alabama said.

"How the hell do you figure he's lucky? We just made him an orphan today. That's luck?" I snapped back bitterly at the big Southerner because he had spoken to me and thus became my target. I was going to add that we had also made the boy a VC, but I was concerned that someone might decide he was another threat that needed to be eliminated.

Alabama struggled to remain collected as he answered me. "Pete, dammit, they looked like armed VC in a hostile fire zone. We did what we had to do."

"We should have ordered them to halt—yelled *lai dai* at them. If they did, we had prisoners. If not, we fire a warning shot. If they point their weapons . . ." I picked up one of the hoes and pointed it at him in the near-dark. ". . . then we could always shoot them."

"That's easy to say now, Pete. . . ."

"No, it's not," I interrupted. "It hurts like to hell to say it, but we have to take responsibility. We were wrong. Wrong."

I walked back with Martinez to where the bodies of the two women were lying. Tears of frustration and anger welled into my eyes, but I choked them back—no one here would see me cry. I stood up as Lieutenant Nelson arrived on the scene with the rest of the platoon and began his report to the CO.

"We've got four VC KIA, two WIA and one detainee. They were carrying packs and rice. 2–6, out." He turned to me for some reason. "Now the Old Man says he can get a chopper in. Get ready to load on the wounded and the prisoner. It'll be here in five minutes."

I strolled back, still in a state of shock, to where the wounded Vietnamese farmers were lying and saw Bennett kneeling beside an injured elderly man, holding a bandage to his wound and wiping his face with the other hand. The sight of the crusty, profane Irish sergeant trying to make the wounded more comfortable brought the lump back into my throat. He looked up at me, "We shoulda killed them all. They shouldn't have been out here, especially near dark."

"Yeah, it's not like it's their country or anything." I tried to see his face, but it was too dark. I thought to myself, you're not fooling me, Bennett. I know you care. I can see it.

I told him a chopper was on the way and we were to load up the wounded and the little boy and he nodded. Then I thought about what had happened and my role in it. Good God, why didn't I get the medic to help those women? Maybe they could have lasted until they were medevacked. Maybe I was wrong and they weren't wounded so badly. No, I had seen enough wounded and dying people by now to know that these women were on the verge of death and in extreme pain and I had been told that no chopper was coming. I would live with the conclusion that I had made, whatever its aftermath.

After the chopper picked up the survivors, the platoon moved to a nearby field in the moonlight and set up in a wagon wheel for the night. Some of the men broke out their C rations, but I wasn't hungry. I thought again about the people of the large village over the hill, where these farmers were undoubtedly heading, waiting for their loved ones. How could this have happened? What kind of army allows its troops to be placed in a position where this can take place? What kind of war is this? How can the mightiest country in the world have so much trouble fighting a war against a Third World nation? Why weren't the South Vietnamese doing the fighting? God almighty, could the protesters be right? Was this war wrong?

These questions coursed through my mind during the night as I lay under the stars. When I closed my eyes, I saw the figures fall once more and the faces of the anguished women came before me, their eyes pleading and searching. It has been said that the first casualty of war is truth; if so, then the second must be innocence. My innocence, which had suffered severe injuries in November, was now mortally wounded, lying on the bloodied ground with the shattered bodies of the Vietnamese peasant farmers. I finally napped for a few minutes just before dawn; I didn't care if the enemy attacked then, as Watson had always feared. Maybe we deserved it.

The questions continued to plague my mind and my heart was heavy as we returned to the ambush site the next morning. Captain Eklund flew in to inspect the bodies, then we buried them in some nearby bunkers. Some of the men were laughing and joking, but Martinez, Vickers and I were struggling with our emotions while trying to keep poker faces and Bennett stayed off to one side.

I couldn't make myself look at the bodies or walk on the bloody ground, but I knew I had to come to grips with this incident, this massacre, this bloody tragedy and make peace with my ghosts and demons if I wanted to remain mentally stable and fully functional. But I also knew that I would never forget this place and time and what had happened here.

I resolved to try to live with my judgment while always remembering the results. Now I had to get on with my tour of duty and try to be a good soldier. I knew that this event would influence the way I reacted and performed, but I would try to focus on the task at hand: the mission, always the mission. I added yet another layer of callousness to my soul while my inner spirit wept. It was my destiny, I guess, but was it the destiny of the peasants to die on that field on that day, or did they just stumble into the wrong place?

After the captain left, we moved back to the stream and set up in a daylight observation position near the crossing. The sun was unmercifully hot, as if we were being punished for our sins, so we found shade and rested. In the evening we moved to an ambush site farther east and south of the river. As we set up, I spotted movement outside a hooch on the other side of the river. I borrowed the lieutenant's binoculars and zeroed in on an NVA soldier in full khaki uniform talking to a black-pajamaed VC. I motioned to the men to get down behind the paddy dike and get ready to fire.

The two soldiers were barely in range, so I brought Huffman with his bloop gun up beside me and ordered them all to open fire. I fired a half dozen rounds into the area myself and watched as the targets fled, first into the small structure, then out again and into the brush. We stopped firing and the 1st Squad moved across the stream as quickly as we could. The area was deserted when we reached it, but the NVA had left some ammunition and two ChiCom (Chinese Communist) grenades that he probably had been delivering to the VC.

We checked out the nearby bushes and Rangel grenaded a bunker behind the hooch, but the blast threw shrapnel back through the opening striking Rushinski in the arm. He had been lying down in the bushes, but somehow a piece of metal found him. He complained of some pain, so I called the CP and told them we were coming back with a wounded man who probably needed evacuation. I fully expected to be fired on by the two soldiers as we recrossed the stream, so I sent the men by twos. I felt like there was a target on my back as I hustled into the water, but nothing happened. As Vickers and I reached the halfway point in the stream, the FO brought in artillery on the target area and we moved on into the perimeter.

It had felt good to fight a real enemy, even though we made no captures or kills. This was more like what we were supposed to be doing—firing our weapons at the enemy, pursuing him and seizing some of his weaponry. The combat hadn't erased the previous night's action or forgiven us our trespasses, but it did ease the pain by showing us we could still function as a fighting force. As men, we didn't panic, crumble or fail; we carried out the mission at hand. I slept a little better that night, mostly because I was exhausted.

We humped to the east early the next morning, moving about three klicks to join the rest of the company. At noon we jumped on Hueys and choppered out to another valley where we swept through and searched until 1500. Then we received orders to wagon wheel for another extraction in one hour. At exactly 1600 we loaded back into the choppers and went on a combat assault to a ridgeline a few klicks farther north. We jumped out at about four feet, formed up and moved on line into the woods. Our mission was to serve as a blocking force in a trap being set for a VC regiment that intelligence had placed in the immediate area. The slight, cool breeze of the hills was immensely refreshing and I thought it would be nice to spend some time here.

"Hell of a war, huh, Pete?" Bennett asked.

I looked up as the short Texan plopped down beside me. "Yeah, but it's the only one we've got. Man, they're sure jerking us around—here, there, everywhere. If somebody farts crosswise in the DMZ, they'll send us."

"Fuckin' A, they will. Pete, what did you think about that ambush the other day?"

"I'm not ready to talk about it, man. I don't know if I ever will be."

"It was a helluva deal, man, but they put us there to ambush the trails. Those people had been moved out of there weeks ago, but they came back and they got killed. . . ."

"That'll show 'em," I remarked as sarcastically as I could.

"That shit don't get it with me, Pete. I fired at them because I thought they were the enemy and would try to kill me sooner or later—nothing else. I feel bad, but it happened and we can't change that, so let's move on."

"Fuck it and drive on, as the boys in armor say. Well, I don't mean to cast blame on anybody else, 'cause I'm as guilty as anybody. I'm just trying to figure it all out, Bennett."

"Yeah, but they never should have been there."

"Maybe we shouldn't be here," I whispered softly.

Vickers had been listening in and now ventured an opinion. "Could be those people had been delivering rice to the VC to pass on to that NVA soldier who showed up yesterday. Maybe there were VC. At least they were probably sympathizers or suppliers. I truly believe that."

"I'm too tired to argue anymore, men. Wake me when you DEROS."

They were right when they said they shouldn't have been there, but I didn't want to think about it during the rest of the day since it would be filling my nights for some time to come—of that much, and no more, I was dead certain.

The enemy regiment failed to show up that night or the next day, so we moved out along the ridgeline and down into the nearest valley where we set up another blocking position. Word came down that Flamethrower 6 was pissed because the VC didn't cooperate and fall into our trap. The term "body count" kept popping up whenever officers talked to each other. It seemed that securing or pacifying an area was secondary to "getting some kills" in strategic planning. This truly was becoming a war of attrition, which concerned me deeply since I had read that Uncle Ho and General Giap had an army of more than a million men and would tap their population for as many as they needed—men, women or children. Since we had less than 100,000 fighting men, airpower and artillery would have to kill a lot of enemy soldiers for us to be victorious.

Doubts were nagging at me as the platoon moved into a

large rice paddy to wagon wheel for the night. I opened a can of fruit cocktail and slowly sipped the juice as I lay behind a dike and let my thoughts roam. If Charlie continued to pick and choose his sports, using sniper and booby traps to thin our ranks, what would happen to our morale? Could we win this type of battle?

Chase interrupted my contemplation by lying down next to me. He started a pitch, "Pete, my main man, I've gotta take my R&R or lose it, 'cause I'm going home in thirty-three days. They've got two openings for Tokyo. Do you wanna go with me? We'll rent motorcycles and climb Mount Fuji and just kick back. Sound good?"

"It certainly does. I wasn't planning to go until May or June, but some of the things that have happened lately have got me down. I could really use some days away from here. When do we go?"

"Fifteen April. Six days and five nights. Are you in for sure?"

"I'm in. I'll write home for money ASAP."

I had grasped at this straw like it was a giant life preserver and I was drowning in the South China Sea—well, I was drowning in a sea of frustration and heartbreak. Chase headed back to the CP to reserve the spots and I dashed off a letter home. Just thinking about reentering civilization for a few days and nights had my spirits soaring. Life wasn't so bad, after all—until I dozed off and flashed back to the deadly ambush and the burning eyes of the dying women. I awoke with a start and a feeling of remorse in my heart. I lay awake under the stars for several hours before taking a nap before dawn.

The 2nd Platoon humped two klicks to join the CO and the rest of the company in the morning. After a meeting of the platoon leaders at the CP, the entire unit then moved out to sweep the valley. Late in the afternoon we came to a large creek where we halted to refill our canteens. One of the squads of the 1st Platoon discovered a deserted bunker complex while setting up security. We grenaded a few of them without incident before deciding they were empty, then the word came down that we would hold up here until twilight.

Three choppers came into our site with mail, hot chow and

some officers from brigade HQ. The pilots shut down the engines so the officers could hold a meeting without shouting, then fired them back up as the conference ended. The choppers with the officers aboard belched smoke, then died and would not start again. The gallant officers moved to another bird and flew out of the LZ. The crew of the afflicted Huey worked feverishly on the engine as unsolicited and unappreciated suggestions poured in.

"If you guys haven't made this month's payment, let 'em repossess it."

"Did you check the muffler bearings?"

They withstood the taunts good-naturedly, but finally surrendered to the gods of flight and called in a salvage bird. This helicopter version of a tow truck came swirling in a few minutes later; it had a slightly different rotor sound, more of a *whip-whip*. It was slightly larger than the Huey and had four giant legs that protruded out a few feet, then down, like a praying mantis. This enabled the tow bird to straddle the wounded Huey, which by now had its rotors removed, and have it attached for extraction.

While the chopper settled over the Huey for the attachment, it looked like two giant awkward birds trying to mate. Bennett yelled, "All right, choppers, get it on."

I laughed a little and added, "Now there's something you don't see every day."

The men applauded and waved as the rescue vehicle lifted the Huey off the ground and slowly headed east for repairs. We then saddled up and headed downstream to our ambush position, feeling happier for the distraction. We had stayed fairly busy since the *incident,* so it hadn't hampered the unit's effectiveness as I had thought it might.

When I did think of it, usually at night, my heart ached and the melancholy left me dejected and emotionally spent. I realized that I had to keep forcing it to the back of my mind and to the dark corners of my soul. I would have to deal with it later, but now I had to survive and help others survive, so I covered it over and pushed it back.

After another quiet night we continued to patrol down the valley and then along a range of hills on the west side. We humped up over a finger of the hills, hacking our way through the brush. It was extremely hot, so we moved slowly and replaced the men with the machetes every few minutes to prevent heat prostration. Mize was close to DEROS and had shed his radio to spend his last few days in the field as a member of the 1st Squad. His presence on my team had raised my morale a few more notches; he always seemed to be relaxed and in control of his faculties.

Sergeant Ski and the point squad came on a small hooch, half-hidden in the brush. The squad surrounded it and Kushinski carefully checked the interior. He then moved back to Sergeant Nuckols and reported that the hooch contained explosives. Nuckols took a quick look and said, "Get the loo-tenant up here."

Nelson inspected the find and made a report to the CO. I took a look inside the door and saw about twenty grenades, a few rockets and some plastic explosives. It was hardly a large cache but, nevertheless, an important find. Higher ordered us to blow it in place, so the rest of the platoon set up in a perimeter while Nuckols and Ski prepared the hooch for demolition and I fetched their supplies.

Nuckols asked me for a wire and firing mechanism from a claymore and we got some C-4 from Huffman so they wouldn't have to shape the charge using the enemy plastics. He molded the C-4 around the blasting cap and placed it with the enemy munitions. We piled the rockets and grenades around the charge, then backed off into the bushes, got clearance from all the squads and watched from the prone position as Nuckols detonated it. It made a resounding explosion, hurling shrapnel and debris 100 feet or more into the jungle. We grinned at each other like kids who had just blown up the neighbor's mailbox on the 4th of July, then slowly packed up and continued the patrol.

We moved back to the valley floor, then rejoined the company and followed the stream southward until we found a good ambush site. We settled on an open field with dikes for protection and good fields of fire. The moonless night was deathly quiet; I slept some and didn't dream. I supposed this was a result of my suppressing all thoughts and I wondered how long I could postpone facing reality and how the others were doing with their emotions. I'm no doctor, but I figured we all needed to get drunk and sort it out, while it was still fresh.

A cheer went up from the men of the company in the morning when the choppers came in sight over the range of low hills and then eased down into our LZ. The word had come down earlier that the company would take time to bathe in the stream and get a change of clothes. I dug into my pack and found a bar of soap wrapped in plastic, then took my razor and toothbrush and headed for the water.

The stream was just cool enough to be refreshing in the morning sun and the water was clear and seemed to be clean. I dove in, lathered up and dove again. It felt so good that I almost forgot where I was. After a few repetitions, I felt like I had removed not only several weeks of dirt and grime, but I had also shaken loose an oppressive layer of guilt and depression. I climbed up on the sandy bank where I shaved off three days of whiskers and a month-old moustache—it was time for a new beginning. Clad only in olive-drab shorts and a boonie hat, I paused on the bank to give a Tarzan yell. I felt better than I had in weeks. Should it be this easy?

That afternoon we loaded onto choppers again and headed on a combat assault farther east on Hill 701. The gunships peppered the slopes lightly, but the bare mountain stuck up above the surrounding hills and was obviously deserted. As we jumped off the choppers on the ridgeline we were hit by a refreshing breeze. The company was set up as a blocking force along the ridge for a battalion sweep in the valley below—a sweep that was meeting stiff resistance. The 2nd Platoon was ensconced on the highest point of the mountain—the rounded peak. Because of the elevation and the open terrain, we were safe from everything except a mortar attack.

As darkness began to gather, it became cool on the mountain but, because it was dry and secure, no one complained. In the valley beneath us, sporadic fighting and firing began to break out as the units settled into their night perimeters and began claiming their territory. Before we could hear the sound we saw the red tracers streaking their way along the landscape, warning of death and destruction. Occasionally a tracer would hit something solid, then ricochet at a different angle, creating surrealistic patterns in the night. Every few minutes a flare was fired by the nearby firebase and the night took on a different look; the fighting men would pause for a few seconds to recheck their targets, then resume their deadly assault.

Being a mile or more from the battle sites, we could only surmise at the intensity of the fighting, but if the amount of ammunition being poured out of the perimeters was any indication, the troops down there were fighting for their lives. The battalion network kept a steady chatter of updates and requests for more information. The new RTO switched on his speaker and we listened as if it were a baseball game.

Charlie Company was on standby to be flown in if needed, but it appeared from reports that none of the ground forces was in danger of being overrun. The reports noted that two choppers were shot down, but we had seen no crashes from our vantage point. They had probably been hit, then landed safely or headed back to the firebase for repairs. The VC were apparently firing a .50-caliber machine gun and mortars as well as small arms. As I sat there watching the kaleidoscopic specter, someone sat down beside me and I heard a familiar voice.

"Pete, how ya doin'?"

"Koger, my man, it's been a while. Aren't you about ready to get on that Freedom Bird?"

"Three weeks, man. Glad to see you're still in one piece. I wanted to give you my home address in case you ever get down to Louisiana again."

We talked for a few minutes more, then said our good-byes, since we didn't think we'd ever see each other again. I put his address in my wallet, then rolled out my poncho and liner and lay down after the firing eased back to bursts and potshots. I knew that we were headed down into the valley in the morning to an uncertain fate, but I thought it would be a good chance for the 2nd Platoon to redeem itself. In my mind, I felt there should be a penance or an act of contrition—some kind of settlement for our recent actions. Although we could not revisit the past or raise anyone from the grave, perhaps a test by fire would be our reparation. Perhaps I was thinking too much.

I turned my thoughts to the men below as I lay there listening to the muffled thumps of the howitzers firing and the screech of the shells as they rent the night air. Out of empathy and concern for the line doggies hugging the ground on those fields below, afraid to sleep, I lay awake on Hill 701.

I quickly swallowed the last bite of crackers and washed it down with straight coffee as I heard the choppers heading toward the mountain. It was morning, March 27, 1967, and we were about to head toward the site of last night's frenzied action. The 2nd Platoon moved down off the peak and joined the rest of the company waiting at the LZ as the choppers swirled in. The Hueys dropped us off a few minutes later west of a large village and we went on line to sweep through to the east.

There was tension on the faces of the officers who expected a pitched battle for the ville, but I felt like it was just another mission, another opportunity to excel and, even more important, another chance to redeem ourselves. The forward observer began calling in artillery, which screamed over our heads and crashed into the village as we moved out. Since we were directly in line with the fire, the fear of a short round was nearly as real as the fear of the enemy.

The village turned out to be deserted and after a short pause we continued toward our objective, the nearby low hills. By the time we reached the foot of the hill, the artillery had been pounding the slopes for twenty-five minutes. It was extremely hot in the valley and my water supply had dwindled to nothing, so I stopped at a tiny stream to refill. The water was dirty and gray from the shells that had exploded in the area, but I scooped one canteen full in case we couldn't find anything else.

Sweat was pouring down our faces as we struggled up along the brush-covered slope, praying that Charlie wasn't dug in on top, knowing that if he was, those slopes would soon be covered with GI blood. Luckily the enemy had chosen not to fight this day, as the hills were deserted. After reaching the top we settled into a blocking position for Alpha Company, which was sweeping the valley on the other side of the hills.

Our new orders were to remain on the ridge overnight, so I notified the CP that we were extremely short on water. We reclined under sunshades made by fastening our ponchos to bushes until the late afternoon when the resupply chopper came in and blew away the loosely fettered shelters. We unloaded the water containers and the precious mailbag, retrieved our ponchos and settled in for the night. I read my letter and watched the western sky turn red, then once again turned my mind off. It was getting a little easier to detach myself from my surroundings, to think of nothing, to harden myself, but I felt I had lost touch with reality. Or was survival out here the only reality?

Once more we jumped on choppers in the morning and moved to a valley farther north, landing in an LZ secured by ARVN troops. We immediately moved south and set up in a blocking formation, then waited as the ARVN forces swept toward us. Their sweep netted nothing, so after a long chow break, Charlie Company swept to the west, moving through several tiny villes and capturing four suspected VC with grenades and field packs full of rice. With prisoners in tow, we turned north and entered a larger village in the late afternoon.

The 1st Squad surrounded a large, well-built dwelling on the edge of the village. Bennett, Mize and I entered it to check for enemy activity and saw a family of four preparing its evening meal. I decided to check the thatched roof for hidden weaponry, so I poked it with my rifle. It seemed to be moving. I stared at it, then yelled to Mize.

"Hey, this friggin' roof is alive. Holy underwear! It's full of snakes."

Mize laughed and put his arm around me. "Come on, Pete. I'll protect you. 2nd Platoon is settin' up right out here for the night."

He led me to a spot along a hedge less than twenty-five feet from the hooch. Although the sun was slipping below the horizon, there was enough light to see more snakes crawling around the hedge and my skin began to crawl with them. I had no great fear of the slimy critters, but all snakes in Vietnam were supposed to be poisonous and I wasn't pleased with the notion of sleeping in their midst. Mize threw his poncho liner down on the ground next to the hedge, lay back and grinned at my discomfort. He laughed as he told me:

"Hell, Pete, they won't hurt you. And if they did bite, it wouldn't hurt for very long."

"Right, Mize, about thirty seconds or twenty-two steps. Whichever came first."

We had all heard the legend of the deadly 22-step snake that was supposed to be the scourge of the Vietnamese jungles, so named because twenty-two steps were all you made before dying if one of them bit you. I volunteered to go on a one-man ambush, but Nuckols and Nelson laughed at me and sent me back to the squad, so I found a pile of wood the family had been using for their cooking fire. I moved it piece by piece into the open field about fifteen feet from the hedge and laid my poncho and liner on top of the pile and tried it out as a bed. It was as rough as anything I had ever slept on, rougher than the boulder in the stream over on the border, but I was convinced it was snakeproof.

Mize duckwalked out to me and whispered, "Pete, you're on OP out here. A sniper could pick you off with one shot, man."

"I'd rather be shot than bitten by a snake. I figure the VC will think I'm *dinky-dau* and won't waste a bullet on me."

I lay on my hard, lumpy pile, certain that I looked like an offering on a sacrificial altar in the open field, and marveled at Mize's ability to spit in the face of danger. He wasn't one of those celluloid-inspired heroes that would run into a hail of bullets to rout the enemy, but he just plain wasn't afraid. Nothing bothered him. That night, fortunately, nothing bothered any of us.

Charlie Company continued to sweep the valley the next morning in the hot sun. It was bone-dry and we trudged along in the dust until Bennett came strolling up from the middle of the column where he had been talking with Nuckols. He yelled at us: "Listen up, crowbait! You assholes are going to be choppered to LZ Litts this afternoon and tomorrow on to Pleiku. So don't get killed this morning."

The load got lighter and no one paid much attention to the heat as we humped another klick to a large field near a small stream. We broke for noon chow and rested in the shade until 1600, when the choppers picked us up and lifted us to Litts, where we took positions on the perimeter of the large firebase, took off our boots and relaxed. After a meal of hot A rations, Bennett, Nuckols and I rounded up two cases of beer for the platoon to split up. I drank my cans while lying on the roof of our bunker and watching another hazy, orange sunset. The guys were feeling pretty chipper, so we sang some old rock songs and ballads and talked until the beer was gone.

The landing strip at Litts didn't look long enough for the

C-130 to land on and stop, but the pilot touched down on the runway, reversed the engines with a loud roar and braked to a stop just in front of the fence. Then he swung the cumbersome aircraft around and brought it down to the end where we were waiting and shut it down. After the plane was refueled, we loaded on and the pilot fired up once more.

As we roared down the short runway, Bennett looked at me with a fixed grin on his freckled face. "No sweat, GI. He's probably done this before."

The big craft lifted off with the wheels clearing the wire fence by about a yard and we headed to Pleiku. The trip took about forty minutes and most of the guys nodded off to the drone of the engines. After an easy landing on the huge tarmac runways of Holloway Airport, we loaded onto trucks and motored to base camp. After settling in and shedding our gear and weapons, we marched up to brigade HQ where the company went through a records check.

That night there was beer in the mess hall and a steak fry at 1800. The beer was cool, the steaks were tough but delicious, and the ice cream for dessert almost fooled us into thinking we were civilized. It was the first trip to base camp since the battalion left in early January, so the men took advantage of the beer and a night off. However, due to the early flight and the big feed, we all quickly tired and headed for our bunks. I took a few cans back to one of the platoon tents and laid down on a bunk.

Rangel was cleaning out his locker, getting ready for his trip home. I offered him a beer, which he refused, and a toast. "Rangel, I hope you find what you're looking for in life."

He looked up briefly, nodded, then bitterly answered, "I should have been squad leader when Bennett was gone, not you. I was in line, so it was wrong for you to get it."

"Rangel, I just follow orders. I was told that it was my job, so I did it. And, I did a good job. If you want to get pissed, get pissed. I'm sure that Nuckols and Nelson gave me the job so they would have a man in place when Bennett DEROSed—and you're leaving before him. Hell, go ask them why they gave it to me."

"I think maybe you sucked up to get it."

He actually snorted with derision as he spoke. I stared at

him for a minute, then decided that it wasn't worth fighting
over or talking about any longer.

"Fuck it, Rangel. If your head clears, I'll talk about it with
you. Otherwise, adios."

I went for a walk around the compound; it felt good to be in
the night air unencumbered by a weapon. Mize and I sat on the
ground outside the mess hall and talked for a while, then I
yawned, went to my cot and was asleep when I hit the canvas.

I shrugged off the slight hangover the next morning and
started cleaning out my locker. I found some mildewed items
and took them outside to a burn barrel where a fire was already
consuming some of the waste of the area. I saw Bennett coming down the sandbag-lined path, so I leaned over the fire and
began rubbing my hands together.

"Fire feels good on a cold day, man. Come on over and
warm up, Bennett."

The temperature was already in the 70s under a cloudless
sky. He shook his head. "You're gone, Pete. *Dinky-dau.* Nuts.
Careful you don't roast your weenie there."

After taking care of personal business and lining up for pay,
I saw that the beer coolers were open once again in the afternoon. The word had already come down that we were heading
back to Litts tomorrow, so we imbibed heavily as 1st Sergeant
Wolfe and the cook roasted a pig. It was a tradition that dated
from the days when the 25th Division was stationed in Hawaii:
company stand-down means pig roast. Those who preferred
steak got it, but the pork was sweet and tasty.

Nelson emerged from his tent wearing a new insignia: the
silver bar of a first lieutenant. Feeling a little cocksure and
more than a little drunk, I shook his hand, congratulated him,
then poured half of my beer on his head. As it cascaded down
his face and onto his shirt, a flash of anger and retribution
showed in his eyes. In that brief second I saw my life in the
Army up to then flash before my eyes; I was certain that he was
going to bust me to private or belt me. The instant started to
drag a little, but then he stifled his feelings, grinned and
slapped my back.

"Thanks, Pete, but don't ever do that again."

I handed him my neck-towel to wipe himself, then poured
what was left of my beer over my head in sympathy. Mize was

standing nearby, so he poured his beer over his head and several other troopers did the same, thus defusing the situation totally. As we wiped the beer from our faces, I saw Sergeant Nuckols raising his hand and asking for our attention. "Listen up, men! Staff Sergeant Brittain was killed today. Recon platoon got in a firefight with a large VC unit and he was shot along with two others."

The group went silent until Sergeant Able of the 1st Platoon raised his beer can in a salute. "To Sergeant Brittain—for his country, in the line of duty and all that shit. So long, Sarge."

We tipped a few more, but the edge had been removed from the festivities, so we broke off into smaller groups for conversation and serious drinking. I was celebrating one year in the Army and six months in-country, but the loss of Brittain made it a somber party. The compound went silent about midnight, but Mize, Vickers and I continued to drink and talk until 0200, then unsteadily made our way to our cots.

Bennett's voice tore into my aching head at 0700. "All right, you miserable drunken assholes, get up. We're goin' back to war."

I moaned in concert with Mize and Vickers, then stood like I was testing sea legs and began throwing my gear together. We had said our good-byes last night, but Mize rose unsteadily from his cot and began shaking hands again.

"Pete, I'll miss you and your wisecracks. Vick, you only live a few hours from me. Come visit me in Indiana. You guys keep your heads down. I won't be there to take care of you."

We said our last farewells and swore we'd write. I don't believe that God or man holds a grudge if you don't keep a promise made in a combat zone, which is why there are no atheists in foxholes or on OP. I was leaving another good friend, but I was happy for him and I hoped he would find peace at heart.

As the C-130 lifted off the tarmac and headed east, I let my thoughts roam over the previous weeks. I hadn't dreamed of the November battle and Captain Federline for some time, so I spent a few moments recalling those incidents. The images no longer filled me with horror; I now felt frustration and a deep sadness as I reflected. And, I felt guilty, but I don't know why.

When my mind clicked forward to the moonlight ambush on the stream in February, I smiled as I pictured the events in my mind and heard Bennett saying, "They're shootin' back."

Then I shifted my mind ahead again to the March 20 disaster and I saw broken bodies lying on the ground and my heart hurt. I ached for those poor dead farmers and their departed souls. I wondered if there was some way God could let us all rest in peace, but I doubted it.

I opened my eyes to stop the emotion from overwhelming me. Most of the troops were dozing, so I began to wipe imaginary dust from my rifle. The engines changed pitch as we began our descent into LZ Litts and I forced myself to think about the short runway and the fence to clear my mind. We hit the dusty strip and the pilot (who had the balls of a cat burglar) stood on the brakes to bring the ugly hulk to a stop with the nose just short of the fence. I imagined I could see the cocky flyboy sitting in the cockpit laughing maniacally as he pulled off yet another one.

We climbed out and headed to the south side of the perimeter where Vietnamese civilians were selling sodas. I bought a warm Coke, shook it and sprayed it into my mouth to remove the cottony feeling. After a couple of hours of withering in the hot sun, two Chinooks landed just outside the wire and we loaded on board and flew to LZ Ship, where we found positions in the perimeter and slept off our two-day respite from the conflagration.

23

Early the next morning, while it was still just warm, we moved out and down the slopes of the hill and into a long, narrow valley. We humped for about three hours, seeing nothing, then moved up to the top of a small hill and entered the perimeter of LZ Wire. We were given a short chow break, so I walked around looking for a water bag or tank. I passed a group of men unloading pallets of mortar rounds and then did a double take at a familiar-looking face.

"Rogers? Rogers? It is you. How the hell is it hanging, home?" We did a clumsy white man's half-assed soul shake.

"Pete. It's been a while, man. Let's see. You went to candy-stripe school at Fort Polk, so you must have come in-country in October."

"Yeah, 3 October. I'm with the 1st of the 14th. Goin' on another combat assault in about thirty minutes. You gettin' any— rank, I mean?"

"Up for Spec 4. Not as fast as infantry, but I'm not complaining. Well, I gotta get back to work, Pete."

"And I gotta go jump off a perfectly good chopper. Take care of your damn self, guy. See you back in Wisconsin someday."

"Keep it down, home."

It had felt like reunion week for a few minutes, meeting somebody from near my home with whom I had gone through Basic, but now it was time to load up and ride off to war. The choppers took the company out to another huge valley with another wide stream cutting through the middle of it. We moved out as a platoon and swept through a nearby village, moving slowly and checking every hooch. This was a fertile valley and the village was made up of hooches that were well-constructed and clean. For a nice change, the people wore multicolored clothing, which seemed to be a sign of stature, if not affluence. We picked up two likely suspects, young males without proper identification, and fired at several others who escaped into the thicket and totally disappeared.

Reports had had the VC maintaining a presence in the valley, collecting taxes, taking a share of the crops and drafting the young males for their army. We were sent in to find and detain or kill these VC. The villagers had been putting up with their presence for years; whether out of sympathy for their cause or just as a matter of survival was open to conjecture.

After we finished the sweep, the three platoons met outside the village, where we wagon wheeled for evening chow and got orders, then each of the platoons broke off in different directions for night ambushes. The 2nd Platoon CP, with the 2nd and 3rd squads and a gun crew, moved to a low hill overlooking a huge valley. Martinez had joined the squad to replace Rangel, so he and I scouted out an ambush spot along the wide trail that followed the river. We set up there in a line ambush where the trail dipped into an irrigation ditch, with a rice paddy dike as our escape route.

During the night there were sporadic outbreaks of firing on the other side of the river, so we had to change our position to find protection from stray rounds. Bennett learned on the radio that the firing was coming from ROK (Republic of Korea) troops who were well known for shooting first and often, then asking questions. If we had to operate in this AO for long, we would need a lot of cooperation and coordination between the friendly forces. As I lay along the trail, I thought about the men I had served with who had gone home, some of them in body bags, some alive but wounded and some with wounds of the heart and deep scars on their psyche.

I wondered how they were really doing; did they have nightmares, dreams about their experiences? Were they able to put any of the bad times behind them, or did they wake up sweating and moaning, like I did? I wondered, but I had to come back to the present and confine my worries to my tour of duty and how to survive it. I must create the possibility of a future by taking the present one day at a time, one careful step at a time.

The 2nd Platoon hooked up again with the company for a sweep southward down the valley in the morning. When we reached another village, the 2nd was put in a blocking position on the south side while the CO led the other two platoons in a search. They took two more prisoners while we tried to find shelter from the relentless sun.

I took a position across a paddy from the ville with my fire team and was joined by Chapman, the forward observer and his RTO. Chapman and the radioman found a coconut tree and decided to retrieve some of its fruit. First Chapman tried to climb it, but it was too straight, so he gave up and sat in the tree's shade while the RTO then shinnied up slowly and reached for the coconut. He grasped it and broke it free, then lost control of it and let it slip. He yelled, but Chapman had time only to turn slightly before the earth-bound coconut struck him in the lower back.

He cried out and went prone, then continued moaning, as we

gathered around him, wondering how to report this freak injury. He groaned even louder, then implored us to call the medic and a dustoff chopper. Bennett called the platoon CP, the medic hurried over and decided he should indeed be sent back to the nearest MASH for treatment. After the dustoff extracted the fallen soldier, his RTO left to find the company CP, so we cut open the offending coconut and feasted on our ill-gotten gains.

"He almost gave his life for a friggin' coconut. How do you figure that, Pete?"

"Can't figure that, Gus. I sat here watching it unfold and I can't make any sense of it. 'Course, my brain's fried in this sun."

We spent most of the day waiting for the Old Man to finish his sweep, then moved out to join him on the north side of the ville. We moved into a perimeter, then relaxed as the CO called in for resupply and hot chow. Nuckols rode the chopper back to base camp, then flew to Pleiku to process for his R&R to Hawaii. As the sun sank, we moved out into platoon ambush positions once more. The 1st Platoon reported movement near the large village all night and flares lit up the area, but nothing moved at our site near the river.

Just before dawn we grabbed our gear and headed out across the dormant rice paddies as quietly as we could. We humped about three klicks in the dawn's early light in an attempt to surprise the Viet Cong who might be spending the night in one of the large villages. The huge valley was dotted with sprawling collections of hamlets that sometimes were connected and often shared the same name with a number added. As we passed some of these villes in the dark I could see the glow of dozens of little cooking fires as the matrons of the houses prepared the morning meal. I had a little pang of homesickness, but it was quickly deflected by the shields of heavy callus that had formed over my soul.

Once we reached our objective, the 2nd Platoon took a blocking position just outside the hamlet and the CO once more led the sweep with the other two platoons. We set up behind a paddy dike and broke out our rations. I edged over to the CP and finished my cocoa while talking to the lieutenant.

"Sir, how long do you think we'll be in this valley? This is pretty good duty—a river nearby for swimming, coconuts, not many VC."

"Word is, we get a real mission at the end of the month. We go north to Quang Tin Province to join the 196th, replacing the Marines to pacify the area."

"Explain pacifying."

He smiled at me, then snorted a little. "Make the area calm and peaceful so the people can live there safely."

"To continue to search and destroy, then mollify?"

Patterson and acting platoon sergeant Kushinski were listening while finishing their chow. "There it is, man. We're now attached to Task Force Oregon and operating in their AO, but we're still a bastard brigade," Kevin said.

"If the ROKs would settle down, I'd like to spend the rest of my tour here, except for my R&R, which is why I'm here. Are Chase and I set?"

"You're on for the 15th, Pete. Tokyo." Nelson said, then quickly added, "Got any peaches to loan me?"

"Negative on the peaches, as always. When you get a can of those, you gotta eat them right away before you get wounded or killed and lose the chance to enjoy that nectar. Well, better head back to the fighting first."

After the Old Man and the rest of the company finished their search, they evacuated three detainees, then the company moved back to the river where we set up in a perimeter and whiled away the heat of the day by swimming and bathing, one platoon at a time. The water was refreshing after another hot day in the dusty rice paddies, so I swam and cavorted like a teenager back in the World. Chase popped out of the water next to me and reminded me of our pending rendezvous with real life in Japan.

"Six days and five nights in lovely Tokyo, man. We'll have a ball: sightseeing, motorcycling. . . ."

"Drinking, girls. I hope you haven't forgotten those."

"That, too. Drinks will be cheap at the Army post bars, but girls are something else. The price is steep in Tokyo."

"Maybe we can meet some nice girls and party a little."

"Yeah, I'm past my time anyway. Meet some nice girls and spend some time talking. I like that."

"You take this stuff seriously—no sex within forty-five days of DEROS? Seems to me that's an overreaction."

"Maybe, but I'm taking no chances. I've got a girl back in the World and she's numbah one with me."

"Xin loi, Chase. *Xin loi."*

The company continued the same routine over the next two days—an early morning move into position, then the CO and the 1st Platoon search and sweep while the other two platoons hold blocking positions. After sending in the detainees, we moved back to the river area for rest and chow. At dusk, we broke up into platoon elements for the night, then split the platoons for ambushes spread across the valley floor.

Although activity continued around the heavily populated villages at night, the trails and stream crossings remained free of movement. We began to feel loose and relaxed in the absence of the enemy, feeling our only danger was getting in the way of a ROK bullet. Morale was high as it had been at base camp and we were able to break in several new platoon members, including McQueen in the 1st Squad.

On April 6th, Chase cut his foot badly while swimming. He was medevacked to the nearest field hospital where they took fourteen stitches to close it. I wondered what this would do to our plans for Tokyo, but I decided I couldn't do much about it. As the engineers say, I'll blow up that bridge when I come to it.

The entire company finally received orders to search the largest village of the chain, which had a population of at least 2,000. It sprawled across a good portion of the valley floor close to a low hill mass and was known to Alabama as New York City. The RF-PFs (Regular Forces, Popular Forces) sent an interrogation unit in by chopper to question any suspects among the villagers and to separate the VC probables for evacuation. The Ruff-Puffs, as we called them, were eager to impress the American units with their expertise and ability to extract information.

As we gathered suspects and herded them into one of the village squares, I witnessed the man who appeared to be the head interrogator whacking people over the head with his stick if he didn't like their answers. I volunteered my team for bunker searches to escape the frightened and imploring expressions on the faces of the villagers. As we moved through our portion of the hamlet, crawling into bunkers and spider-holes, I heard a shot. Not long after, Patterson came down the trail, his radio on his back and a grim look on his face. His lips were tight as he spat out the news.

"The son of a bitch shot her. Just fucking shot her."

"Who shot who, Pat?" I thought I knew, but I was trying to figure out a way to calm him. He sat on a bunker and shook his head.

"The Ruff-Puff with the stick. He hit this woman, she said something to him and he shot her. Pulled out his .45 and shot her in the head. What the hell, man?"

"Christ in a wheelbarrow. I wonder sometimes, Pat, what the hell kind of a war did we get into here. I guess we just have to remember the grunts' slogan, 'It don't mean nothin'. Don't mean shit.' "

"Tell Vickers I'll never smile again," he answered.

He headed back to the CP and we continued our search, but a burst of AK-47 fire sent us scurrying behind the nearest bunker. The AK makes a lighter sound than the M-16, more like popcorn popping, magnified a few hundred times. After determining that the fire wasn't aimed at us and hearing no orders to search for the source, we ignored the sporadic potshots and continued the mission. At noon we took a chow break around a tree near several bunkers.

"Vick, trade you a ham and lima for just about anything."

"Negative, Pete. Here, take this beef, but I don't want your damn lima beans. Man, I'm ready to go home—twenty-seven days and no more of this shit."

"Yeah, I hear ya. I'm ready for R&R, too. How do you react to this shit, Vick? You've seen more than I have, so how do you get through it?"

"I'm numb, Pete. You can't let it get to you or you'll go *dinky-dau*. You have to say it doesn't mean shit and then feel that way in order to keep going."

"But it's hard to do that when you see this shit and know that most of it is contrary to everything we were taught while growing up. It's getting to me, guy."

Captain Eklund called in a Chinook to carry off the dozens of detainees and the Ruff-Puff unit. The Ruff-Puffs were going back to their quarters for a hot meal while the civilians were headed for a detention camp (stockade) where they would be grilled extensively, then reeducated and indoctrinated. Some would be pressed into duty in the South Vietnamese Army; some would remain in prison if their answers were wrong; some would be released to return to their families.

That was how it was supposed to work. However, I suspected that anyone who suffered the beatings, indignities and other physical and emotional torture inflicted on them by the South Vietnamese government sycophants would be of little use as a soldier or citizen. In effect, they were creating a constant crop of potential VC. In truth, most civilians wanted little to do with either side and resented the intrusion of fair-skinned foreigners, but the abuses at the hands of their countrymen made them easier targets for the VC recruiters.

We continued to search the villages of the valley without major incidents. The 2nd Platoon had become the unofficial blocking force for the company, except at "New York City." The other platoons would take turns sweeping a ville and picking up a handful of suspects that were dispatched to the rear by Huey or Chinook, if there were enough. The weather stayed very hot, with daytime highs of 100 degrees or more, but there was ample shade and we used the nearby river to bathe and cool off in every other day. We would tune in the Armed Forces Radio Network, lounge in the shade and let our minds go free, sailing them across time and space, to the World . . . home.

During the morning of April 9, Charlie Company moved down off Hill 109 and began moving past the first large village in an attempt to sneak up on the second one. Battalion had sent out a scent dog and his handler to check out the bunkers and tunnels and he was walking with us. As we passed an old man watering a large bull water buffalo, the bull lifted his head and sniffed at us. The dog, sensing danger or something different, barked and growled and the bull immediately lowered his head and charged. The dog handler didn't hesitate—he raised his M-16 and fired three rounds into the huge bull in an attempt to protect his dog. The bull sank to his knees, then rolled onto his side and died. Within minutes, rigor mortis or shock set in and his legs stiffened and pointed straight out.

The old man began yelling in Vietnamese and people came

streaming out of the closest ville. We moved into a loose perimeter as the CO radioed higher for instructions. The ugly Americans had struck again, killing the village's only bull, a prized possession. About an hour later, when all our nerves were on edge in the blinding hot sun, a chopper landed. Two officers stepped off, approached the old man and started counting out bills. The old man was still surly but finally he walked off, muttering, and we continued our mission.

When we broke for chow, Vickers began to chide one of the guys.

"What are you gonna do tonight? I saw you lovin' up that mutt last night."

"He was jerkin' him off. I saw that," another added.

"Hey, the dog's gotta have some fun, too," the soldier protested as the squad roared. Laughter was becoming our way of coping with the absurdities of war.

After noon chow I asked Martinez if he wanted to take Chase's R&R since Chase would still be in the hospital with his serious laceration. He pondered it for only a few seconds.

"Yeah! That's the best idea I've heard since I got here, man. I need to get away for a while. I can borrow some money from Vansworth. Thanks, Pete."

I felt good knowing I would be with someone I knew while in Tokyo, and I had grown to like Martinez in the time he had been with the platoon and my squad. That night the platoon set up near the river again and watched the sun go down in a violet haze. At about 2200 the ROKs opened up again, sending us scurrying for cover as the rounds buzzed angrily over our heads. We hugged the ground or nearby trees as the lieutenant grabbed the handset and screamed: "Stop those goddam ROKs before they kill us!"

The order must have been passed along, because the shooting stopped and we gradually resumed our positions. I dug a body trench about eighteen inches deep and stayed there most of the rest of the night, but the ROKs were quiet.

Another morning, another ville, another blocking position for the 2nd Platoon. As we positioned ourselves along a hedge just east of the targeted hamlet, Bennett spotted an old man working in a field near us. He decided we should question him, so we encircled the old dude and Bennett spoke, "Hey, Papa-san! Any VC here? VC?"

He swept his hand toward the bushes and hedges surrounding the village, but the old man grinned and said nothing. Bennett reached into his pack and pulled out some cigarettes and a can of very warm beer.

"I've been carrying this for a week. Papa-san, you like beer? Like 33?" He pantomimed sucking the beer, then opened it and gave it to the old man. The peasant sipped a little, then grinned and took a big drink. Then he motioned us to follow him to a nearby hooch. I put my weapon at ready and lagged back with Martinez as Bennett, Vickers and the old dude entered the hooch and came out with an old bottle. Bennett laughed, "Hey, guys, it's party time. Papa-san chipped in with some rice wine here. Let's give it a try."

He poured a little into his canteen cup and the four of us sampled the mysterious elixir. It was thick, dark and heavy with sediment, but it was definitely alcoholic and strong enough to take your breath away. Bennett then hit on another idea: "Let's pretend like we're drinking with him and getting drunk. Maybe we'll get him loose and he'll show us some weapons or something."

"You've seen too many movies, man. Won't work, but since I've got nothin' else to do today, I'll go along with it," I said.

We raised the cup to our lips and pretended to drink, then emptied it into the grass behind the old man's back. Papa-san finished the warm beer and some of the wine, then fanned his face and grinned. We laughed, staggered around a bit and fanned our faces. Inexplicably, what I had thought was an extremely bad idea began to work. The old man motioned us to follow him as he staggered toward an irrigation ditch with a tunnel tucked in under some bushes along one side.

He pointed at the tunnel, then backed off. I put my weapon on semiautomatic, then looked at Bennett, who whispered, "VC there, Papa-san? VC?"

The old dude just pointed, then staggered off to his hooch. Bennett strode up to the edge of the ditch, then turned.

"I don't know the words for 'get the hell outta that hole and surrender, assholes.' "

I stifled my laugh and dug out my little U.S. Army phrase card and began murdering the Vienamese language once more.

"This'll have to do. *Buong sung xuong. Dura tay len!*"

Martinez and Vickers stood at the ready as I yelled again. *"Buong sung xuong! Dura tay len!"*

Two young male Vietnamese came out of the hole with their hands raised. I motioned for them to come out of the ditch. *"Toi kham ong."*

I told them we were going to search them, but they had nothing on their bodies. Martinez took a long look in the hole, which was only a few feet deep and empty.

"We got all there was, Bennett. Nothin' more here."

"Drop a frag in there just to be sure."

Martinez pulled the pin on a pineapple grenade, held it for a second, then tossed it into the hole. Nothing moved or made a sound after the explosion, so Bennett was satisfied that the hole was truly empty. We took the prisoners to Lieutenant Nelson and told him the story, embellished by some heavy bragging.

Although he was elated with the prisoners and the job we had performed, the only reward we received was no mail and an ambush site on the side of Hill 109 that was covered with rocks and briars. The degree of discomfort was such that we slept fitfully if at all when we weren't on watch. Anything coming down the trail that we overlooked would have had to deal with our displeasure firsthand, but no one came.

On April 11 the platoon moved to a blocking position on the south side of one of the interlocking villes, then began searching the bunkers and holes along the hedgerow that surrounded it. One of the new guys stopped to relieve himself and, while watering the Vietnamese landscape, he focused on a patch of dead brush near him. After finishing, he kicked the brush aside and discovered a hole.

"Sergeant," he yelled, "I found a tunnel."

Every sergeant in earshot came running. Kushinski wanted to go into it, but Lieutenant Nelson stopped him with the reminder, "No, you got shot once already in one of these. Get me a tunnel rat."

Dynas (we called him Jake, because Chase thought he looked like a Jake should) finally volunteered to crawl into the hole, so we outfitted him with Alabama's .45, put a grenade in each shirt pocket and gave him a flashlight. Just before he entered, Kushinski tied a nylon rope around his waist and whispered in his ear loud enough for all of us: "This is so we can drag your body out." Then he laughed.

Since Ski was too big to take a poke at, I muttered to Patterson. "Geez, send that asshole back down without a rope. We don't want him back."

Dynas crawled into the entryway of the tunnel, then stopped after a few feet. His boots were still visible and we could hear him thrashing around. He yelled back, "That didn't take long. I'm at the end of the hole, but I found some uniforms."

He passed back some pale green uniforms back out of the hole, then scrambled out into the daylight and stood up.

"Just a spider-hole, I reckon."

The rest of the squad had turned their attention to the NVA army issue, so I gave Dynas a thumbs-up and told him, "Good job, man. I can't do that shit. The hole closes in on me. Claustrophobia."

"Don't mean shit, Pete."

He had jumped into our jargon quickly for a new guy, but regardless of his blow-off line, I could see a little fear around his eyes and mouth. Bennett picked up one of the uniforms and told the troops, "This puts me in mind of the battle over on the border. If you new meatheads see a bunch of these coming at you, you better have your shit together or Charlie will hang your ass out to dry."

I tried to clarify and overemphasize what he had said: "Charlie is out here wearing black pajamas. That was Mr. Charles from Cambodia and North Vietnam we fought back there." Of course, the old battles were always the worst and grew more vicious with each telling.

Sergeant Kushinski and his RTO carried the uniforms back to the platoon CP and the 1st Squad continued to search the hedgerow. The sun was well up in the cloudless sky and the temperature was in the 90s, slowing down our life juices and our reactions. Then sniper fire crackled over our heads and we hit the hard, dry ground and hugged it. As we lay there, Bennett saw another old man digging along the edge of the rice paddy. He yelled at him, *"Lai dai! Lai dai,* goddammit, Papa-san!"

Bennett started to stand up, but the sniper opened up again

and we could hear the rounds whistle over us. We all ducked and when we looked up again, the old man was trotting away at a decent clip.

"Lai dai! Lai dai!" Bennett screamed.

The old man moved a little faster toward the hedge. Bennett raised and opened fire. The old man dropped to the ground in a loose heap and lay still. I jumped up beside Bennett. "Jesus, Bennett, he was an old man."

Then I looked into his eyes. He was gone. His pupils were dilated, there was no light, no expression. They were vacant. He held his rifle pointed forward in a grip so tight his knuckles were white.

He was in another world, so I spoke again, more softly. "It's all right, man. Relax, it's Pete. It's cool."

After a few minutes his eyes began to light up as he slowly returned from whatever zone his tortured mind had thrust him into. He turned to me and spoke in a strangulated whisper: "I shot him. I shot him, right?"

"Looks like it, man. You all right?"

He grunted, then something inside sent him into his sergeant routine. He started walking toward the body, barking orders.

"Secure the area. Search the body. Check him out."

Huffman checked the body, but he was clean. He was also very dead with three gaping body wounds. It was getting easier to look at dead bodies and I realized I was becoming desensitized and incapable of much outward feeling. It wasn't a pleasant thought, but I felt my mind must be creating some sort of survival mechanism. It was just another body and I would carry on.

Bennett moved over to the hedge, got down on his hands and knees and began digging around in it, and I warily eased in beside him. I wasn't sure what he was doing, but he found a spider-hole about three feet deep and reached down and fished around with his arm and hand inside it. After a few seconds he came up with a .30-caliber carbine and held it up for the platoon to see. He muttered to me as he shook the weapon defiantly.

"I knew he was running after a rifle. I knew it. I knew it."

The body was left for the next of kin, who were gathering as we headed back to our position on orders from Lieutenant Nelson. Bennett appeared to be all right, but his lips were drawn in a tight half-smile as he gave his report.

"The old man started running as I walked toward him. I yelled at him to stop. The sniper fired, he kept on running, I shot him. We found his weapon a few feet away."

Lieutenant Nelson reported a VC KIA to the CO, who accepted the report without question and the life of the old man was ended without ceremony on our part. I sat under a shade tree and ran my thoughts quickly past the events, then let the whole thing slide out of my mind like water off my poncho.

Patterson plopped himself down beside me as we took our noon break. "Good news, Pete. When the resupply chopper comes in, you and Martinez are headed back to Uplift, then to Pleiku for processing and R&R."

I let out a long sigh, then grinned. "I really need it, man, but hell, I'm broke. I didn't get any money from home, so all I'm carrying is twenty-three bucks. You got any spare scratch?"

"No, but Schmidtt always wins at poker. I've heard he carries a wad. Check him out."

I found Schmidtt finishing his beans and procured a loan of a hundred bucks, then began to unwind. It was really going to happen. Martinez and I flew back to Uplift where we met Alabama, who was back there for medical reasons. We drank a few beers, also for medical reasons, and spent the night safely behind an extremely large bunker.

We flew to Pleiku on a Caribou, arriving at noon at a nearly deserted air base. An airman told us to find our own ride to the base camp, so we headed down the highway with our packs on our backs and weapons on our shoulders. About a half mile down the road we spotted a watering hole, just another ramshackle building with some gaudy pink and blue paint splashed on it. We entered, had a few drinks to clear the dust of the coastal plains out of our throats, totally ignored the bored-looking bar girls and tried to figure out how we could afford to live like kings in Tokyo on our meager finances.

After spending a couple of hours there, we finally spotted a truck with the proper markings on it and waited for the driver, who hauled us to the company compound, where we reported in.

The first sergeant gave us copies of our orders to Tokyo, via

Cam Ranh Bay, then followed up with verbal orders to hit the
mess hall for steak supper and then to the perimeter bunkers for
line duty. The steak was halfway decent, by Army standards,
and the line duty was quiet.

The next day we updated our records with a medical clerk.
Searching hard for something to bug a couple of line doggies
about, he decided we needed another plague booster shot before we could leave the country, but then left it to the clerk in
Cam Ranh to catch and sent us over to Finance. After squaring
away all our paperwork and clothing, we lay around waiting for
the top kick to send us to the station in Cam Ranh Bay for out-
processing. That night we sat in the clerk's office talking when
the screen door was almost torn from its hinges by a huge
blond GI who staggered into the room, hatless and highly ine-
briated and looking for somebody to cross swords with. He
muttered and cursed at us for a while about his tough year.

"You fuckin' cocksuckers—shammin' back here while I
risked my life. You can all kiss my ass. *Right now!*"

I took umbrage at his tone, his manner and his mistake in
lumping me with a shammer, but, since he was a giant of a
man, about 6–4 and 240 (he grew as we retold the tale later), I
took it quietly. As he continued haranguing the five of us (Martinez, Vansworth, LaBarge and an FNG), I finally decided to try
my skills at defusing a situation with some reasonable man-to-
man conversation. It was a terrible idea and I should have
known better.

"Well, guy, I know it's rough out there, but you're not alone.
I've been in the boonies for seven months now and. . . ."

"Fuck you! You—you're all assholes and I oughta kick the
shit outta you!"

He pointed a huge, wavering finger at me and I knew my
shit was shaky, so I tried to figure out a way to get past him in
order to retrieve my equalizer—the M-16. He was standing in
front of the screen door and that was the only way out, so I began to scan the room for another weapon of any kind. The rifles
of the clerks were hanging on the wall behind the giant, so I
grabbed the only item I could find—a stapler. He might kill me,
I thought to myself, but I'll staple his ears to his head. He continued to stare at me for several long minutes, which dragged
into hours in my mind, as I tried to figure out where I was going

to land and in how many pieces. I wasn't afraid during the face-down, probably due to the various trying circumstances I had been faced with before or maybe my brain had passed the point of no return. However, I did believe that my facial features were about to be rearranged. Maybe he sensed that, for finally, he growled, "Ahh, shit. You assholes. . . ."

He wheeled and crashed out through the door into the night and the room went silent. I waited until I was certain that he was well out of earshot, then spoke. "And stay out, jerk, if you know what's good for you."

The men laughed and I sighed. Martinez then asked, "Who was that prick? He's not from the 2nd Platoon."

"I'm not sure he's in our company. Maybe Weapons Platoon. Pete, you stood up to him. You weren't afraid of him. . . ." Vansworth started to say, but I interrupted.

"Sheeeitt, man. I'm gonna need new fatigue pants. He coulda kicked my butt all the way around the compound and not even got tired and I thought he was going to. I felt like a one-legged man in a butt-kicking contest at a definite disadvantage. I'm gonna head back to the tent and get my weapon. If he shows up there, he'll be looking at the business end of an M-16."

Whoever the giant was, he disappeared for the night and wasn't seen at roll call the next day. After a breakfast of SOS (shit on a shingle, aka chipped beef and gravy on toast), Martinez and I hopped a ride to the airport and caught a flight to Cam Ranh Bay. We were on our way.

24

Cam Ranh Bay was rightfully called the safest American base in Vietnam, being located on a peninsula that jutted eastward into the South China Sea and was guarded on the west by Marines and Army infantrymen. On the base was a huge Air Force compound and support bases for the Army and Navy, as well as one of the busiest airports in the world. Any U.S. serviceman assigned to Cam Ranh Bay had all the luxuries of home at his disposal, and more: electricity, air-conditioning, refrigerators and freezers, movie theaters, EM, NCO and officers' clubs on every street, cheap maid service, comfortable housing and good food. As Martinez and I walked by yet another air-conditioned officers' club, he said, "This must be what they call a hardship tour, Pete. Helluva way to fight a war."

"War? What war? I can't believe we're still in 'Nam."

We checked in and were assigned to a roomy wooden barracks with screened windows and a real ceiling and floor, which was being cleaned by a Vietnamese woman. I lay back on my cot, looked out the window at a group of troops returning from their six days of paradise and definitely recognized one of them, whom I hailed.

"Sergeant Nuckols! You rednecked peckerwood. Welcome back!"

He was returning from Hawaii and looked like he'd been hit by a typhoon—clothes wrinkled, shoes scuffed, face unshaven and missing his garrison cap, but still able to walk.

"Pete, Martinez, how are ya? I had a great time with my wife. Saw Don Ho at a nightclub. Right now, I need a beer and then some sleep. Come on."

We found the EM club, where he stayed for two beers before

staggering back to his bunk. Martinez and I drank a few more of the fifteen-cent brews, then retreated slowly to our cots and faded away.

We went through out-processing the next day, receiving lectures about desertion and its penalties, then received our plague booster shots. Finally we took a truck to the airstrip where our flight was called at 1800. As I boarded the Pan Am 707 liner, I saw several round-eyed American girls smiling at me—and everybody else that was boarding. I consider Asian women to be among the most beautiful in the world, but there's something vibrant, wholesome and outgoing about the girls of the USA that you cannot find elsewhere. I reached across the aisle and poked Martinez in the shoulder.

"It's happened. I've died and gone to heaven. If I'm sleeping, don't wake me."

We arrived in Tokyo at 0100 at the U.S. base where we checked in and tried to find out where we could go at that hour. A Japanese tour operator was circulating through the crowd of GIs, promoting his hotel in Atami, which was a small city about two hours away. A four-night package, consisting of a room and coupons for discounted food and drink cost about 1,600 yen, or fifty U.S. dollars. It seemed like a good deal to me at the time, so we snapped up the opportunity, then moved into the next room where we rented some cleaned and pressed civilian clothes. After the operator had garnered a dozen troops, we boarded a bus and headed for Atami.

The bus passed through parts of Tokyo, which was still bustling in some places at that hour, but I couldn't get the full flavor of the city through the windows—I hoped I would have enough money left to be able to spend the last night somewhere in the huge metropolis. We arrived at the hotel about an hour later and were given blankets to lie down on in a banquet hall. The package didn't begin until the following night, so we lay around and drank the complimentary quart bottles of Nippon beer until the floor felt softer, then napped.

We spent the next five days in Atami, a seaside resort town of about 50,000, south of Tokyo. We resided in a new multi-story hotel, the New Fujiya, which rivaled any of its American counterparts in cleanliness and service. There was a tiny swimming pool on the second floor, a fine dining room, gift shop and a bowling alley in the basement. Each morning and again in the afternoon, we headed to the pool, which was only ten-by-twenty feet, and soaked ourselves while enjoying a libation served by a short and dumpy but friendly waitress who was trying to learn to play the guitar and sing Dylan songs.

The group was squired part of the time by a lovely tour guide, Kazuko, who showed us parts of the town, took us to a sukiyaki party where we wore kimonos and drank too much sake, and kept us informed. Martinez and I found a wonderful neighborhood bar where we drank beer with shop owners and soaked up the local flavor. The people were friendly and courteous, except for the students protesting against American nuclear submarines docking in Japanese ports, and even they seemed to understand that we were on vacation.

Ten other servicemen were using the package, and on the second day we all received a message to report to Suite One on the top floor of the hotel. Once there, Colonel Salvatore, a Clark Gable look-alike in mufti, advised us that there was a Russian trade delegation visiting the city and staying at the hotel. He warned us, "Stay clear of them. Do not give them any opportunity to create an incident. If you meet them in the street, step aside. If they come into a restaurant or bar where you are, leave quietly. Do *not* speak to them. Got that? Any questions, men? Good. Carry on."

And carry on we did, especially at the sukiyaki party where real geishas attended us, but would not speak; I deduced that they spoke only Japanese. The Russians did arrive at the hotel the next day complete with heavy fur coats and hats. They would not even look at us or acknowledge our presence; one could imagine the briefings they had received about us. I tried to write a letter home in the lobby while the Russians waited for their rooms and Colonel Salvatore lurked in the background, but the paranoia was too stifling. Later that night as we wandered from one bar to another, we met a large group of them, and since they showed no signs of sharing the sidewalk, we stepped out into the narrow street to avoid any trouble, then gave them the international signal for "you're an asshole"—the upraised middle finger.

The days flew by and it was time to leave with the group on the bullet train for Tokyo. At the last minute Martinez and I scrapped our plans to spend the last night in Tokyo and instead rented another room at the New Fujiya and moved our bags down one floor. We had been staying in tourist rooms, but now we had a large place with bedrolls on the floor, a refrigerator and a table. Once more we made our way to the pool and began to soak in heated bliss, a well-appreciated morning ritual.

"I wonder if I'll ever really feel clean again, Gus. My feet haven't cleared up yet and I've still got this damn jungle rot on my arms and legs. I've had a heat rash since December. Man, I swear I'm going to shower three times a day back in the World."

"I hear ya, guy. I'm gonna live on the beach at Malibu and swim all day."

He paused for a minute, then continued, "People back home have no fucking idea what's going on in 'Nam. I can tell from the letters they don't have a clue."

"No way we can tell them, either. If we put the truth in a letter, they wouldn't believe it or it would bother them so much they wouldn't write back. I can do without a lot, but I gotta have some mail."

Martinez stared at his hands for another long moment. "Pete, what about that day we shot those women? How can things like that happen? We didn't mean to kill any civilians, but they're dead. It bothers me a lot."

I leaned back against the side of the pool. We were on the shallow end, sipping a morning beer and when I looked at Martinez, I could see the pain in his face and the anger and hurt in his eyes. He was in mental agony and I didn't know if there was any way I could help.

"It bothers me when I think about it, too, Gus. I believe that when you do wrong, you have to pay for it, whether it's on a criminal level or some sort of religious judgment day. But this whole war bothers me so much I think my heart is going to burst, sometimes. This war is nothing like we were raised to believe it would be. In the movies there's a good guy and a bad guy. The good guy always wins and everybody cheers, the band plays and the girl, who's always pretty, runs into his arms. When somebody died, they would sprawl on the ground, then say something brave and uplifting while the violins played softer. I'm not naive enough to believe that life is like the movies, but I did believe that life rewarded the people who did right and I was led to believe by my government that what we're doing in 'Nam was right. I don't know what the hell is right anymore. I've seen a lot of people die already, some right next to me, and none of them died like he was in a movie. Do you know what one of them said?"

I stopped, Martinez waited, then motioned for me to go on. "He said 'Help me, mama. Please take me home, mama.' Why don't they put that in a fuckin' B movie? I tell you, man, it's gettin' to me. I sometimes believe I'm cracking up. The only time I feel good anymore is when I'm drunk."

"They never kill civilians in a movie, either, Pete. They all come out when the Americans take the town and give them flowers and kiss them. Never kill civilians. . . ."

His voice trailed off, so I jumped in again. "Man, we've got to stop this. I've thought about that day a lot and I now believe that, given the circumstances and our standing orders, the patrol reacted with correct procedure. It was wrong, but it was right, if you know what I mean. We all have to learn to deal with it on a personal level, somehow."

"Pete, you don't have to say *we*—you didn't fire a shot at all. You saw who they were and tried to stop us."

"I was there and I was a team leader, so I share the guilt." And the shame, I added to myself. I could see Martinez was struggling with his feelings, so I tried to change things. "OK, men. Here's the plan of action. Down to the wharf for some food, then to the polka bar for drinks. Saddle up!"

We tried to fight off the depression caused by the memories we had conjured up and the knowledge that we were going back to Vietnam tomorrow. We started with a huge meal at a tiny upstairs restaurant that had a great view of the sea, then finished the day and night at the polka bar where we drank, sang and danced with the bar girls. Our finances were nearly depleted, but our troubles were forgotten as Martinez and I made our way slowly and carefully to our room, laughing and singing like children.

The next afternoon, after a long hot bath, we bade good-bye to the giggling maids and waitresses, managed to keep our balance while bowing to the staff at the front desk, then boarded a bus to the airport. We waited until 0200 for our flight, which arrived in Cam Ranh Bay at 0630. Six hours later we flew to Pleiku and hopped a ride to base camp. It was raining hard when we reached the company compound and I slid along on the red clay into a tent and fell on a bunk. As I sat there trying to make sense of the whole thing and break through the culture shock, I heard Martinez snoring. I was comforted by the sound; it told me that he had a little peace, for now, but I knew that both of us had a long road to travel.

25

In February 1967, U.S. Command put together three orphan Army brigades into a (containing) force for Southern I Corps to relieve the Marines of secondary problems in that portion of their zone. The 1st Brigade of the 101st Airborne Division was used as the dominant unit and was joined by the 196th Infantry Brigade in early April. The task force was code-named Oregon and on April 20 was given to the III Marine Amphibious Force. The 3rd Brigade of the 25th Infantry Division, under the control of the 1st Cavalry Division, was ordered to Chu Lai by the end of April.

On April 28–30, the 1st/14th Battalion TAC CP moved by air from Phu My to Chu Lai and the rest of the battalion closed by convoy. The battalion assumed the mission of security for the Chu Lai Defense Command and conducted search and destroy operations, night ambushes, search and clear, cordon missions and relocation of civilians.

Welcome back to the real world. The rain had stopped, but the red clay mud was slippery and sticky as we plodded to the morning formation. I looked at Martinez and softly shook my head.

"From the Land of the Rising Sun to the land of the rising scum, pardner."

He bowed slightly, Japanese-style, and answered, "Mushi-mushi."

Top Sergeant Wolfe gave a brief rundown of the company's activities in the field. I was happy that no one had been killed or wounded recently and was actually looking forward to seeing some of the troops. As Wolfe finished up, it began to rain again, so we tromped back to our tent and started to get our gear ready for the trip back to the field tomorrow. Then we flopped onto our bunks and commiserated as we listened to the rain.

"Oh man, thirty-six hours ago we were in a spotless hotel in a clean city and country where they handed you a warm wash-cloth after you went to the latrine. Now we're back in the toilet bowl of the world."

"Xin loi, Pete. I wanna go home, but if we can't, let's at least find some beers."

"Later. I'm gonna catch up on my letter-writing first."

The rain eased later, so we found some beer to wash down the leathery steak supper and watched an old Bogart movie in the mess hall before retiring. As I left the hall, I spotted Fears, formerly of the 1st Squad, who had somehow spent the last couple of months working in the rear. He told me he was going home in a few days, so I shook his hand and wished him well. He had made it, and made it his way—who was I to say what was right and what was wrong? If Fears was nothing else, he was a survivor.

We planed from Camp Holloway, Pleiku, to the Chu Lai airstrip the next day, then took a truck to Bronco Beach and grabbed the afternoon resupply chopper, which took us out to rejoin the company just in time for evening chow. I exchanged greetings and insults with most of the 2nd Platoon, then joined the 1st Squad as they dug in and built rain hooches near an old, abandoned shrine. I walked over to the shrine, knelt and said a loud prayer.

"God, take me home or back to Japan. Get me out of this place and away from Bennett. Oh, and God, please have a sense of humor."

It got a couple of chuckles, then we crawled into the hooch

to escape a sudden downpour. My first night back was quiet as I reacquainted my body with the feel of Vietnam soil. The rain eased the next morning, so I wiped down my rifle and ammo with the towel I had managed to liberate while back at base camp. I looked up as Bennett came back from the platoon CP with a huge grin creasing his ruddy face.

"Listen up, assholes! I've got good news and more good news, if your name is Bennett or Vickers. This afternoon, we meet the choppers at 1600, then head into a new base camp up north. We're gonna pull perimeter guard there for a few days while we get some new men and join Task Force Oregon. For us two, this is our last day in the field. We're goin' home."

"Good deal all the way around, but especially for you guys. Why don't you two just ease back with the platoon CP and let Gus and me take the point. You deserve the break, even if you are a little nuts."

"No, Pete, I'm stayin' where I always am—in the front. If it's my time, it doesn't matter where I am. You and I will be on point."

"And I'll be right with you two pricks," Vickers added.

"Remember, if it wasn't for us pricks, you cocksuckers would starve," Bennett shot back.

We set out to sweep through a village and began to take sporadic sniper fire as Bennett laughed and yelled. "Been like that for three days. Snipers and leeches."

The large part of the company moved slowly through the ville, finding nothing and pushing nobody out to the blocking platoon. We broke for noon chow, then the CO with the 1st and 3rd platoons swept through a second village while the 2nd blocked and searched through some hedges and ditches a hundred meters to the east. As we moved across a small cultivated paddy to get into position, Bennett spotted a VC jumping into a ditch no more than twenty feet ahead of him. He took off in hot pursuit with the squad trailing and wondering what was happening. As I neared the ditch I heard a shot and a yell, so I hit the dirt and crawled quickly toward Bennett, who was lying immobile at the edge of the irrigation ditch. He raised his head slowly and I could see that his face was ashen as he tried to speak.

"He shot me."

A surge of emotions rushed through my mind and I was certain that Bennett had been mortally wounded because I had not forced him to stay back with Lieutenant Nelson. He raised his head once more and said in a much steadier voice. "He shot me right through my shirt collar. Look!" He poked his finger through a hole and laughed in his deranged manner again.

"My last fuckin' day and I almost get killed, Pete."

By this time I had regained all of my jungle senses and had pulled the pin on a grenade. He took it from my hand and tossed it where he thought the VC might be hidden. Just to be safe, we tossed two more into the ditch, then crawled over to the edge and peered in. An opening to a tunnel was barely visible under the lip of the bank. Under Bennett's direction, Martinez and Vickers tossed grenades into the hole and we all hit the dirt. The resulting blasts were followed by a sudden exodus from several exit holes nearby, as a half-dozen VC took off running toward the village. We fired a quick low barrage at the scattered flight of frenzy, then had to cease because of the presence of the company in the ville. A few more VC ran in the other direction as the platoon blasted away, downing two of them while the others fled into the brush, pursued by the 2nd Squad.

Bennett paused at my side. "Geez, Pete. Almost bought it on my last day."

"Well, you depraved asshole, I told you to drag ass with the lieutenant. He never gets shot at back there."

We moved back to the paddy near the ditch, where Bennett sat down with his back resting against a dike. "I'm not movin' till the choppers come. Where's Vickers? You OK, man?"

"Nothing to it, guy. They're afraid to shoot at me."

Vickers was using the same sardonic tone he had used the first day I joined the company in the field a hundred years ago. It seemed that nothing ever ruffled the guy. The two of them remained down behind the dike until we moved again to a large paddy where we were extracted.

We headed north and were unloaded about a klick away from our new base camp in the Chu Lai area. We walked across bright white sand into the perimeter and up a small hill around which the camp was sprawled. There the platoon sergeants assigned us to bunkers and we moved into the huge structures formerly manned by Marines.

The entire 1st Squad was assigned to one huge bunker, about twenty-by-twenty feet, with fortified sandbagged walls and fighting positions on the inside and on top. The bunkers were connected by slit trenches running between them. The Marines had constructed a fine defensive facility—an enclave along the main north-south artery of Vietnam, Highway 1. Bennett, Vickers and I tossed down our ponchos and liners behind the main edifice of our bunker and began to discuss the war.

"I know I'm repeating myself, but when I got here the men were all sure it would be over by Christmas. Now, it's almost May, I'm goin' home and we haven't won nothin'. It feels bad—empty." Bennett spoke in a resigned voice laced with bitterness and sorrow.

Vickers nodded in agreement and added his thoughts. "I remember the same thing—guys saying we'd wrap this up quick-like and get back to the World." He grunted in disgust, then continued, "It hurts, yeah, but I'm going home and buy a motorcycle and ride off into the sunset."

"Man, I wish I was going with you guys, but I've got five more months of this hell. I don't believe we've made any progress in the war in my seven months. Even the victories on the border didn't count for much, because we left and Charlie probably took over again. In order for us to win quickly, we need ol' Charles to stand toe-to-toe with us because then we'll destroy him, but he's too smart for that. We could bomb North Vietnam back into the Stone Age, but the politicians are afraid the Chinese might enter the war. Maybe we'll change tactics, but then it would take a long time to win, so my war effort now focuses on one thing—to get my ass home safely."

"There it is, guy. Cover your own ass first."

Martinez came hustling out of the bunker. "Holy shit! Rats! VC rats attacked me. You guys are smarter than you look, staying out here. Got room for me?"

"The old pros outfoxed the rats again. If you look closely, you'll see we're also protected from sniper fire by the bunker and if we hear mortars, we roll over into the trench and pray," Bennett explained.

"Ah, Bennett-san. You numbah one short-timer, but still *dinky-dau*," Martinez said.

We took a shower run the next day, then the platoon shifted positions to cover the west side of the perimeter as the 1st Platoon went on a short patrol. In the afternoon we were issued clean fatigues and welcomed several new guys to the platoon. I knew at least two of them were mine, to replace Huffman, who left last week while I was gone, and also Vickers and Bennett. We moved once more that night into bunkers along the northwest. There the two short-timers and I held a long talking session while lying on top of the bunker under the stars.

On the morning of April 27, Vickers got the call from the temporary CP to get his gear together. He moved down to a couple of the other bunkers and made his farewells, then returned and shook hands all around. I held onto his hand and looked into his dark, unfathomable eyes for a long minute, then he shouldered his gear and shotgun.

"I'll be seeing ya. I'll send my address, so we can get together when you get back, Pete. You keep your head down and your asshole tight 'cause I won't be here to bail you guys out with my shotgun. I'm gone."

"I'll never smile again, Vick."

He managed a small grin, then nodded and headed to the clerk's tent and a truck ride to the airstrip a few miles away in Chu Lai. I climbed to the top of the bunker and sat for a long time alone, reflecting. I hoped Vickers could put it all behind him and get on with his life, but could it be that easy? He's actually going home. Home—my thoughts of home were hazy and indistinct by now. I blew out an audible sigh, then climbed back down to earth, to reality. My wish for Vickers was that he could find peace and reasons to really smile again.

We changed positions again that night, moving down off the hill to a bunker near the camp road that led to Highway 1. The new position jutted out almost into a graveyard on flat ground and wasn't nearly as defensible as the hillside bunkers, but the fields of fire were good and no one could sneak up on us. We received a beer and soda ration and Bennett quickly downed his, then talked each of our new guys (Allen, Fryer) into giving the battle-scarred veteran one of their cans of beer and sucked them down also.

We spent the entire next day inside or in the shade of the bunker as the temperature moved back up over 100 degrees.

Martinez came over to the bunker from the next position and complained about how Danny Malarik and his continuous line of bullshit was driving the guys crazy in that position. We lay around and filled the new guys with as much lore and our own line of b.s. as they could soak up. After the sun finally went down, we moved back to the top of the bunker where Bennett went into his famous act.

"Shooort! I'm so short I can't make a shadow. Six days."

He danced around for a few seconds before we heard the incessant sound of an AK-47 popping off a few rounds. One of them thudded into the sandbags near us, forcing Bennett to dive behind the barricade while I laughed.

"See, man. They heard you. The VC want you. Keep your ass down."

"Ah, they're just sayin' *xin loi* to ol' Bennett."

The rest of the night was quiet, but I noticed that the little Texan crawled down off the top and slept inside.

The next afternoon I sent Martinez to lead a patrol with part of the 1st Squad and a gun crew. I had tacitly taken over the squad and needed at least one fire team leader with experience. This was an opportunity for Gus to learn the ropes and accept responsibility while in a leadership position. I climbed to the top of the bunker and watched as they headed out through the wire, across the open paddy and disappeared into the jungle. I felt a little like a mother hen whose chicks were leaving the nest for the first time. Bennett climbed up beside me and went into his routine.

"Pete, I know where we can get some beer and whiskey. It's Saturday and I'm *shoorrtt,* so let's get drunk."

He took up a collection from the remaining squad members, then set out for the collection of quonset huts that made up the CP. An hour later he returned carrying a case of Strohs.

"I need one man to carry another case down. Send somebody down to the main gate to buy some ice from the Vietnamese; they bring some in on bikes every day." He paused, then wiped the sweat from his face. "Texas is gonna seem cool compared to this. It must be 110 easily."

I took another new guy, Galaviz, to the gate where a couple of young Vietnamese lads had cakes of ice wrapped in several layers of burlap and plastic. I haggled with them for a few minutes, then we settled on a price, which I told the new guy to pay. He paid without batting an eye and we toted it back and packed it with the beer in a huge burn barrel. A couple hours later, when Martinez brought the patrol back, we rewarded them with a cold brew, then joined them.

As we leaned back to suck them down, the radio crackled. "Charlie 2–1, this is 2–5, over."

"Go ahead, 2–5, this is 2–1."

"Send me one man for NCO school, ASAP."

I looked around my position and realized we had mostly new guys plus Martinez, Malarik and House.

"Martinez, you're the obvious choice, but I can't spare you right now with all the old guys leaving. You'll get the next slot. That leaves Malarik or House."

"Malarik sucks—send him," Martinez said quickly. "You know he's the type that'll finish at the top of his class. He will, you can bank on it."

When he got the news, Malarik quickly grabbed his gear, thanked me profusely and headed for the CP. I shrugged, "If he finishes in the top five and gets his stripes, and he will, I'll have Nuckols send him to another squad or platoon. This one's not big enough for the two of us."

By nightfall, we were feeling very little pain. The air turned a little cooler and the first flight of giant mosquitoes from hell moved in. Bennett had been missing from the bunker for some time, but I wasn't concerned until I heard a commotion from near the 2nd Squad position. I advised the rest of the squad to stay put, then shouldered my rifle and ambled over to check things out.

I saw Lieutenant Lesko, now with the 1st Platoon, and Sergeant Nuckols watching as three men tried to pry a drunken Sergeant Kushinski out of the perimeter wire. Nuckols sent me to help, so I threw off my fatigue shirt and eagerly dove in. I heard a wild, familiar laugh that I recognized as Bennett's; when I spotted him, he had one arm around Ski's neck, trying to cut off his air. Ski shrugged, grabbed him with one arm and tossed him aside like a rag doll. I helped him up and looked at him—his grin was as wide as I had ever seen it and his eyes looked like something you would find on a giant bug.

"You OK, man?"

"Let me go! This is the most fun I've had all year."

Kushinski was about 5-11, 195, but it was all muscle, even the part between his ears, so it was said. He had been drinking all day, then began creating an uproar after dark; somehow he had wandered out in front of his bunker and into the wire. The MPs at the gate heard him and alerted the CP—Nuckols and Lesko got the message and headed down to investigate. Nuckols had tried to talk Ski into calming down and sleeping it off to no avail, then Lieutenant Lesko gave him a direct order to get out of the perimeter fence and report to the company CP. There was no reply and Nuckols then tried to placate Lesko.

"He's too drunk to understand, sir."

Lesko was steamed at what he felt was a major offense. "Let's just call the MPs, have him arrested, then we can court-martial him whenever he sobers up."

Nuckols spoke quietly, but forcefully for the defense. "Go easy, sir. He's been in combat, seen men die and got wounded himself. Let's let him sleep it off, then you can discipline him later."

In the meantime, several of us decided to high-low the raging bull. I barreled into his knees with an attempted cross-body block while the others grabbed his arms. He staggered, went to his knees, then jumped back up and began kicking and thrashing even more forcefully. I felt a tremendous pain in my rib cage, then lost all my air.

As I lay on the ground, gasping and moaning, Bennett screamed at the enraged Kushinski, "You crazy Polack, we're just trying to get you into the bunker so you don't get killed, you stupid son of a bitch."

Lesko threw up his hands and spoke for all of us. "All right, let's leave him there for tonight. Put a couple of men here to guard him. If he attacks them, tell 'em to shoot him. As far as I'm concerned, he's gonna lose some rank."

Bennett and a couple of guys from the 2nd Squad continued to brawl with him for a few more minutes, while I held my ribs and laughed, but Ski was immovable. We finally gave up and left, laughing and bragging, and the Polack spent the night in the wire. In the morning I could see him lying there from my bunker, body and face bloodied and battered, clothes tattered. Finally he staggered back to his bunker, grabbed a canteen and poured its contents over his head and face. That done, he picked up his weapon and gear and headed meekly for the CP and his personal judgment day. Nuckols related to me later that he had been fined and would be skipped on the next promotion list. He reappeared a couple of days later, a meeker and contrite fellow, and stayed with his squad.

I spent the day recovering from too much liquor and an extremely sore rib cage. We made a shower run to the nearby Army base and I soaked as long as I could to help ease the pain and cobwebs. As bad as I felt, I knew Ski and Bennett felt much worse. We took sniper fire again that night, but I slept like a rock after my watch. It's strange, I mused silently, how combat soldiers come in from the field for a break from the fighting and almost always start fighting with one another.

The entire company loaded onto amtracs (armored personnel carriers) and headed down the road to the main gate. There, leaning against a sandbagged bunker, stood Bennett with his gear, weapon and a sheaf of papers rolled up in his hand and I knew immediately this was his farewell. He yelled over the engine noise, "So long, you mother-humpers. I'm goin' home, back to the World! *Adios,* suckers."

Then he laughed that diabolical laugh and pointed his finger at me as I went past on the lead APC. I gave him the thumbs-up, then yelled back at him, "Thank God, I couldn't take any more of you, man. *Vaya con dios,* you neurotic bastard."

The fresh-faced second lieutenant in charge of the APC looked at Bennett, then at me and shook his head. He obviously thought we were both a little crazy and he was at least half-right. The amtracs unloaded us a few klicks to the west and we swept back through paddies and fields to Highway 1, where we loaded back onto trucks and came back to camp. The patrol had been totally without event, but the hot sun took its toll, forcing at least several days' worth of beer out through my pores.

When we got back to camp, we were issued a can of beer and soda as our weekly ration. I climbed to the top of my bunker in the fading light of day, leaned back and toasted my father on his birthday. Then I toasted Bennett and Vickers, who were homeward bound. I was alone now—I had to call the shots and shoulder the responsibility. There were no other crafty veterans in my squad to turn to for advice or wisdom.

Martinez was a good man and the others would come along, but they all needed guidance. I wanted to stay close to the men, but to be a good leader, one must distance himself somewhat in order to remain objective and dispassionate while sending them to perform tasks that could lead them to death or dismemberment. I vowed again, however, that I would ask no man to do what I would not do.

As I neared the platoon CP the next morning, Kevin Patterson waylaid me and made a pitch. "I want to get in your squad, but Nuckols won't let me. I think he needs me to take care of him. Can you help?"

"I'll work on him, Pat. I need some good experienced men. He listens to me . . . sometimes."

An hour later the blades of the Huey slapped their way through the already steamy morning air as the pilots began their descent into a large rice paddy. We leapt out and moved to the dike on the north side near some palm trees. The company formed up by platoon, then began a sweep patrol, moving east, back toward the base camp. The patrol was designed as a training mission for the new men, so we bypassed a village and followed trails along the wet rice paddies as the sun beat on us relentlessly.

An AK opened up from somewhere and broke the spell that the sun had put us all under. We jumped off the trail into the muck and waited as the company FO, Strohman, called in artillery on a nearby hillside. I looked at the new men and saw that although their eyes were wide, they appeared to be more confused than scared. The artillery rounds tore into the brush-covered knoll and, after twenty minutes or so, we resumed our patrol. Later in the afternoon we received sniper fire again, once more without casualty. We repeated our reaction, then moved out again, putting one foot ahead of the other, pushing ahead . . . pushing.

By the time we reached base camp our fatigues were drenched with sweat, which left more layers of caked salt residue on the green surface as they dried. We headed slowly for our bunkers, dropped our gear and collapsed. We were exhausted, but we were young and most of us were in great shape, so the physical labor was a challenge and it felt good. I poured a canteen over my head and let it drip onto my shoulders as I watched the sun close out another day in Vietnam, another X on my mental calendar.

The next day we took a short platoon patrol out through the wire a few klicks to the north, then doubled back to the base camp, passing through a small village which we searched, but not too thoroughly—just another training mission. Back at the camp we took a shower run to clean off the grime and cool down. The tepid water felt as cool as a mountain stream in comparison to the midday heat of a summer day in the southern part of I Corps, Vietnam. On the truck ride back I sat next to Nuckols and pumped him.

"I need another experienced man to work with in my squad. I've had Rangel, Huffman, Vickers, Bennett reach DEROS, Malarik at school and House tells me he wants to join the LRRPs (long-range reconnaissance patrols). I need somebody like Patterson and he's ready to go."

"Pete, I hate to give you my RTO. He's the best in the company. I'll give you somebody else. Who do you want?"

"Give me Alexus or Betta. Either one would be good."

"You've got Alexus. Now you owe me a pound cake when we get back out to the field."

"You drive a hard bargain, Sarge, but I need Alexus. When you get ready to turn Patterson loose, I want him, too."

"You're trying to corner all the good men, Pete. I'll have to give you more of the tough jobs if I give them to you."

"That's fair enough. Give me the men, I'll do the job."

I didn't mean to sound like I was bragging, but I was sincere in offering to do the tough chores if I was provided with hand-picked, reliable men. That night we lay on top of our bunker, drinking some Vietnamese beer we had procured through the wire and listening to radio reports of a village being burned down by the Viet Cong. For a while I thought we might have to move out on armored personnel carriers to join the fracas, but higher decided on a heavy artillery barrage instead.

On the morning of May 4 we loaded on choppers and headed west by north. The Hueys soared peacefully along in formation and I became slightly mesmerized staring at the relentless greens and browns. As we neared the predesignated LZ, the door gunner on my side pointed and said something into his mouthpiece, then began pumping lead into the tree line. "Oh shit—hot LZ," I thought to myself as I jacked a round into the chamber of my semi-trusty 16. The bird hovered about three feet over a soggy rice paddy and we jumped into uncertainty once more.

After the insertion, the company sloshed to a dike with a wide trail running along the top of it and formed up. The 1st Platoon then led us along the trail west with the 2nd and 3rd following in order. I was in the middle of the 2nd with my seven-man squad, four of whom were virgins—FNGs with no more than a month in-country. The trail was junctioned to the north by a well-used path which cut up and over a small brushy knoll. The 2nd Platoon took the lead on this branch of the trail and moved forward, led by the 3rd Squad, then Sergeant Nuckols and Patterson, then my squad. The 3rd Platoon and the company CP followed us as the 1st continued on the main trail to the west.

As we neared the apex of the small rounded hill, there was a flash and a loud explosion in front of me. I felt the shock wave and a small shower of rocks and shrapnel hit my uniform and face. I hit the dirt and directed my men to flatten themselves facing outward and be ready to fire.

As the dust cleared, I heard shouts and moans and a voice cried out, "Medic! Medic! Get up here on the double—men down!"

I told Martinez to stay alert and watch the men, then headed forward to see if I could help. There were four men lying on the ground, most of them moaning softly or swearing. Two of them were only slightly wounded, but one, a new guy on his first operation, was lying on his side, crying and swearing at the same time.

"My leg! Where's my goddam leg?"

I looked down at his legs—the right one had been severed just above the ankle. His boot, with foot and ankle still in place, was lying about ten feet away, sitting in the middle of the trail like an abandoned toy, still laced up and ready for action. No one wanted to go near it as if they thought it was contagious.

"Help me! Give me my leg. Oh, God!"

The new guy continued to beg for his leg, so the medic picked up the boot, laid it down by his good leg, then told him in a soothing voice, "It's all right, man. I got it back for you.

Take it easy and let the morphine work. We'll get you out of here and back to a hospital."

Doc Johnson had replaced our previous surly medic and the platoon took an immediate liking to the short, soft-spoken black man. He continued to minister to the severely wounded man while the company medic hustled up the line and worked on the other two.

I saw Patterson standing nearby with his shirt off, working his arms and shoulders and realized he was the fourth wounded man. I walked over to him and he spoke excitedly, "Pete, I guess I tripped the wire. It blew me into the air, but the shrapnel went into my pack and canteen. I got my shirt and pants wet from the water in the canteen, but I'm OK, I think."

I patted him on the shoulder, told him to sit down and headed back to my squad as Nuckols called in the medevac chopper. I filled my men in on the action and sent two of them to help carry the wounded back down the trail to the paddy for extraction.

Martinez noticed some blood on my face and tossed me his metal mirror. I examined my sweaty countenance and discovered a pockmark near the corner of my mouth where a piece of shrapnel or rock had struck me. It stung a little from sweat, but the damage was minimal. I told Martinez, "Well, it's your squad now, Gus. I'm going in for two weeks' rest and pick up my Purple Heart."

"I've got your Purple Heart—right here."

He grabbed his crotch as he answered. Captain Eklund came walking by, then stopped as he spotted me. "Peterson, I thought you got wounded—or was it Patterson? You look all right to me."

I decided not to mention my wounded visage as the men came staggering by, carrying the wounded new guy on a makeshift poncho stretcher. They had lain the severed, booted foot exactly where it should have been and were being as gentle as they could. The other two wounded were hobbling along behind with the help of some men from the 3rd Squad.

"I didn't even get to know his name, but maybe it's better that way, Gus. I don't really know anymore."

"I wanna go home—or back to Tokyo, Pete."

A feeling of gloom pervaded the atmosphere as we continued down the trail and finally emerged into a marshy area with another fork heading southwest. The 3rd Platoon then followed the trail to the north, while the Trailblazers settled into a small area behind a dike. There was an empty hooch which was utilized as the platoon CP and we took positions around it for the night. I didn't sleep much as another image joined my parade of ghouls—a severed foot in a boot and a man screaming for his leg. It was getting harder to feel anything through the layers, harder to care. I wondered if I still had a soul.

We spent the next two days feeling out the area, exploring the trails and small hills, taking sniper fire as we moved. The fire usually came when we were on a trail near a village or across a paddy from a hill. Charlie was accomplishing several things when he raised out of his bunker or tunnel, took aim—or not—then sent his staccato message of death toward our ranks.

The firing alerted others that we were near; it could lead us to chase him and wind up in an ambush or booby trap; it would delay and somewhat disorganize the advancing troops. If the fire or booby trap happened to wound or kill a GI, Charlie was an even bigger hero.

We tried to vary our responses to the random attacks in order to not fall into a routine. Sometimes we would send men after the sniper, sometimes we called in artillery and, a few times, we just ignored it and continued the mission. As we searched the area on May 5 we discovered numerous bunkers and spiderholes where snipers could hide after completing their nefarious tasks. We grenaded each hole and I marked their location as closely as I could on my map so I would be alert the next time we were in the area—hopefully, I could pinpoint them for artillery if we were fired on again.

The platoon set up in a perimeter near an abandoned village and I was eating my beans and wieners when the next burst of AK-47 fire tore into the ranks. There was plenty of daylight left, so I led half the platoon across a field into the brush in a fit of angry energy and frustration. The fierce dash helped assuage our frayed nerves although we found only some spent cartridges near a bunker we had grenaded earlier. Alexus tossed another frag into the opening, then checked it out, but it was empty.

We retreated slowly to our perimeter, feeling certain that the sniper would open up again as we crossed the field and he performed on cue. The burst of fire sent us scrambling into the dirt as curses and cries of frustration and anger rang out. Since it was getting dark we called in artillery and moved back into our NDP. Once there, I instructed the men to dig our hole deeper and larger, then I dug a body trench to sleep in. I felt a gathering sense of despair and loneliness as I lay staring at the night sky, waiting.

In the morning I took my squad down the southbound trail on a short observation patrol. We moved along on cat feet, constantly checking for wires and any disturbance. Finding nothing, at 1000 we linked up with the 1st Platoon and they returned to our perimeter with us. The entire company then moved two klicks north along the main trail. As we neared the large collection of hooches that marked our destination, sniper fire from two sources pinned us to the ground. We responded by calling in another barrage of artillery fire, then swept into the ville with weapons at the ready. There was no more resistance, but we rounded up fifty-two villagers and sent them in to be relocated, interrogated and reeducated. I was beginning to feel like a truant officer in a real tough neighborhood and I didn't care for it.

Again, late in the afternoon, moving to a defensive position, we received fire. We again called in artillery and closed into a perimeter for the night. Once again we dug deep, and my entire squad scraped out body trenches for resting or sleeping when they weren't on guard in the foxhole. Also, once again, I maintained full alert until the early hours. Paranoia and uncertainty were stalking me in the night shadows, pushing me toward the edge. I needed one of the old guys to talk with, but I was now the old guy in my squad and it threw an added and unwanted burden on me at this particular moment. I had to pull myself together and be a leader and I had to do it alone. People, American soldiers, were counting on me.

26

Charlie Company was extracted early the next morning from the large paddy to be deposited into a valley farther west. As we swept down toward a small field near a huge village, I saw the chopper to our right firing into the brush, then our right door gunner opened up. When we hit the dry paddy, I led my squad off the Huey and through the haze of colored smoke used to mark the LZ to a dike on the west side of the small field. The noise and swirling dust further distorted the chaotic scene, which I viewed detachedly, as though in another world, having a strange, abstract dream. Finally, I brought myself back to earth and told Alexus to take over while I duckwalked over to the CP for instructions.

Captain Eklund had found a dike to set up behind and from there he gave the officers and noncoms a quick rundown of the AO as he knelt over his map. "There's been a lot of VC activity in this valley lately. As we came in, four choppers took fire, so we know Charlie is in the village. Our mission is to round up the villagers and detain for evacuation. 1st Platoon, block here. 2nd and 3rd will sweep through. Let's move in 0–5."

We were moving toward the village on line when the sniper fire began again. Instead of hitting the dirt, I motioned the men into single file and we hustled as fast as our load would let us into the village unscathed. More and more I had let my instincts take over in stressful situations. With my heart and part of my mind disengaged from the fray, I felt no fear, no anger, no remorse—nothing. Although it helped me get through these harrowing times, I felt as if I were losing some control when I allowed this mind-set to take place.

The company sweep proceeded westward from a wide trail

through a portion of the village and stopped at a river, then turned south and slowly moved into the large part of the ville. We struggled through bramble thickets and around piles of firewood, searching all of the hooches and bunkers. Almost every hooch had a large mounded bunker with a dirt roof at least three feet thick. The structures were large enough for a family or a contingent of VC, so we took time at least perfunctorily to search each one and brought the denizens out into the daylight. The heat and humidity were, as always it seemed, unforgiving.

Since the village was considered pro-VC, we rounded up all the residents and moved them to a nearby paddy for extraction. While we were herding them along the trail, we came under fire from a hillside on the south side of the village. The 3rd Platoon, under Lieutenant Lesko, moved toward the source, then held up as the snipers opened up on full automatic. Lesko quickly called for artillery and the rounds came screaming through the air directly over our heads just moments later.

The lieutenant ended the fire mission, then the 3rd Herd moved forward through the village once more. I had been pulling rear guard with my squad but, in the absence of orders to the contrary, I decided to join the 3rd in their hunt. An unsearched portion of the ville lay between the paddy trail and the sniper's hillside, so the grunts moved through this area, looking through the hooches as they moved along. One of the troops stepped into a well-constructed house of brick, wood and mud with a thatched roof. As he entered, the unmistakable shrill scream of an artillery round sent most of the troops diving to the ground as it crashed through the thatched roof and exploded on contact with the interior.

Shock and chaos reigned over the next few minutes as men were staggering around in disbelief and confusion. At least five men were lying on the ground, wounded, while others sat holding their heads, trying to connect their minds back to reality, hoping that they could just close their eyes and wake up back home. Lieutenant Lesko had been in the area of the explosion and was walking around with a trickle of blood running down his face, mumbling incoherently.

I spotted Sergeant Able, who had hustled up with his platoon to help, and pointed out Lesko's condition to him. He began organizing the troops into an operating unit and I followed suit by moving my squad into a security force so no VC would take advantage of our situation. The platoon medic was tending the wounded; someone called the company CP and they were moving quickly to the location and had already called medevac choppers. It occurred to me suddenly that no one had checked out the status of the soldier who had entered the hooch just prior to the explosion. I assumed he was dead and possibly dismembered, but he deserved an accounting.

Sergeant Able had been thinking the same thing as he took a poncho from the pack of a wounded man and motioned to me. "Come on, Pete. Let's see what's left of him."

Upon entering the hooch I was struck by the lack of structural damage—six men had gone down from the explosion, but the building stood. There was a gouge on the floor where the shell had probably struck and exploded, some shrapnel in the walls, but little else. I forced myself to look for the body and saw a boot with a foot still inside. Something was screaming inside my head, but I forced it back.

"Not again. No, Jesus," I mumbled.

I tried to find that "iron man" mind-set, but I was already too involved to detach myself. I began to chant to myself over and over, as I leaned over the severed extremity, "Don't mean shit, don't mean nothin'."

I put the boot and foot on the poncho Able had lain on the floor. As my eyes became adjusted to the dark, I saw other parts and pieces of flesh and bone strewn around the room. I spotted a portion of the torso thrown up against the wall, still partially covered by a shredded piece of olive-drab jungle fatigue. Very gently, we lifted it onto the poncho, then looked around the room.

"Jesus, where's the rest of him. There should be more pieces somewhere in here." Able was whispering as he got down on his knees to search further. He picked up a couple of fist-sized pieces of tissue and set them beside the torso. "It's not fair. It's not right. There should be a body when a man dies."

"Maybe the rest was obliterated, Sarge. The helmet's missing, too. The round might have hit him on the head and exploded. How the hell can this happen?"

My mind was reeling, but I tried to wear a mask, a frozen poker face; maybe that way I could keep myself under control.

We threw a couple more small pieces of the poor dead infantry-man on the poncho, then carried it outside where we tied it up like a laundry bundle and tagged it. Able looked around in confusion for somebody who knew him.

"What was his name? Anybody know his name? Pete, you know?"

"No—I don't want to know, man. Not now, anyway. I just want to go over to that river, jump in and come out on the other side and I'd be home."

The company medic took charge of the bundle and I stayed until he loaded it gently on the medevac chopper. Then I rejoined my squad and sat down on the dike. I took a canteen and poured the water over my hands one at a time and tried to wash the blood, the smell, the tissue and all my memories away. I wondered how I ever could smile again.

After the wounded were extracted, the remains of the company moved back on the main trail, which ran along the edge of the village, picking up a few more detainees along the way. Most of the men had a twisted, haunted look on their face; in their frustration, a few of them wanted to punish the prisoners. Martinez swung his rifle at the head of an old man who tried to get away. I tried to soothe him.

"Whoa, man. I know how you feel, but we can't do that. It wasn't his artillery round that caused the damage. We've got to stay cool."

It was good advice, but I was falling apart myself on the inside. How could this happen? Why should young men, in the prime of their lives, be subjected to such horrors?

After overseeing the evacuation of the 100 or so detainees, Company C set up in a perimeter between the village and the river. We were all still on edge, but we received only a few short bursts of sniper fire, which we answered with another barrage of HE and WP. Since we were no longer on the target line, there was no real danger of a misfire or short round. The explanation that filtered down was that the guns were reloaded while they were still hot from the mission and they cooked off—fired themselves. As to why they were reloaded, I wasn't familiar with artillery procedure so I couldn't be certain if someone would have to answer for the fatal error.

I wondered who would answer for the unknown casualty?

Who would explain it to his family? The harassing and mentally debilitating sniper fire continued the next day as we swept through the large village again, then continued along the brush line to another smaller ville about a klick away. This one was deserted, with only a couple of bunkers to blow, so we continued down the trail to the next one.

We were searching a few hooches scattered along the way when a different, heavier-sounding automatic weapon opened fire. We flattened ourselves as the rounds whistled overhead and I heard someone yell, "M-60! Christ, Charlie's got a fuckin' machine gun!"

Since it was close to noon, I crawled over to a hooch and sat up against it away from the line of fire and opened a can of diced apples. I began to dig into them and yelled at my men. "Might as well have some chow, guys. We'll be firing artillery for a while to keep ol' Charlie's ass down."

I wasn't really hungry, but I thought the men needed an act of bravado—something to slap back at the ghostly snipers and say, "See, we're not afraid. We're gonna chow down instead of running and hiding." It helped ease the tension and the men began to show life again. After the barrage of artillery fire ended, we continued into the village, which was strung along the edge of a rice paddy and back over a slight brushy rise to the south. We searched every deserted hooch and bunker, working, sweating and swearing in the heat until near dark. Then we set up in a perimeter along the south side of the same ville. The 2nd Platoon manned the side of the wagon wheel along the main trail and a branch that cut off to the east.

We tried to dig a foxhole but the ground was so hard and rocky that we had to instead find some branches for a barricade. Just before dark, sniper fire tore into the perimeter again, hastening our preparations and tightening our sphincters. I moved my pack and gear to a tree about six feet behind our position which I would use for protection while resting. I had a feeling that we wouldn't get much sleep that night.

The night was quiet, but as dawn began to break, I heard several pops in the distance and a soft whistling noise in the air. Glancing up, I saw what looked like Roman candles slicing through the air toward us. I yelled, *"Incoming!* Rounds coming in!" Then I got down behind our flimsy barrier.

The rounds exploded as they landed along the west side of the perimeter. I heard someone yelling, "Mortar! Mortar!"

I watched and waited as several of the shells exploded in front of my puny barricade and was certain that we were in for trouble, but there was very little shrapnel and the explosions were small. I muttered to the men with me, "Must be rifle grenades—not much shrapnel, just some noise. Just like concussion grenades."

The attack ceased after a few seconds and we waited for the assault that might now come, but everything went quiet. I spoke quietly to the closest positions to check them out. "Alexus—any injuries over there?"

"Negative, but I gotta check my pants."

"Alabama—you guys OK over there on the gun?"

"We're OK. They'll have to do better than that, Pete."

I smirked a little at the confidence of the big Southerner, but it made me feel better knowing he was just a few yards away with his deadly M-60. It seemed miraculous that over twenty rounds had fallen on our part of the perimeter within thirty seconds and no one had a scratch. I continued to check the brush line in front of us, but Charlie and his friends had obviously fired their ordnance at our lines, then *di died*. I trotted up to the CP to report in person to Sergeant Nuckols.

"Was it mortar, Pete?" The old Ranger sergeant appeared a little anxious as he awaited my answer so I affected a calm air.

"Nah. Explosions were too small. More like rifle grenades. But, I'll tell ya, ol' Charlie's got his shit together in this valley. My asshole is twisted so tight, you could cut washers off it for a week. Mercy!" Maddox would have been proud of my embellishment.

"How are the men holding up, Pete? Any problems?"

"The new guys are getting a real baptism, but they're doing their job. We need something good to happen out here."

We swept back along the other side of the large paddy, which stretched through the valley. There were more groups of hooches, almost connected into villages, and we diligently searched every one. Some of them had been lived in recently, but we found no supplies. We continued to take occasional fire and began to answer it with bursts of our own that got no results, but made us feel good for a while. At dusk we set up in a perimeter around a small village. Nuckols set the 1st Squad position on a square corner that jutted out into the paddy, right on the main trail. The ground was soft, so we dug a huge foxhole and I cut my sleeping trench right next to it.

Then, despite no real appetite, I broke out my ham and lima beans and nibbled on the cold, greasy mess. Dragon 6 wanted to visit us, but sniper fire at his chopper drove him away, which seemed like poetic justice to me—he should get a taste of what we're facing down here.

More fire laced into the perimeter as darkness fell, but the 1st Squad was dug in well and in my trench I looked at the stars and wondered what the dawn would bring.

I lay there awake and alert until my first watch at midnight. With three men in my bunker, each of us pulled two ninety-minute watches during the night when we were on single security. I had just finished my watch at 0130 and was getting ready to crawl out of the foxhole to wake up the next man when a bloodcurdling scream followed by an explosion shattered the night stillness.

For some reason I knew instantly what had happened; a grenade had landed next to a troop in his foxhole and in that instant, realizing he had no escape, he gave out a death scream that ended with the blast.

I could hear all the bewilderment and frustration, the terrible fear and, finally, acceptance in the horrifying few seconds that the scream lasted. It began like a baby crying for his mother, then became a youngster wailing in protest. The scream suspended itself in the air and my mind for what seemed like minutes, but was really only a flash. Later, I could still hear the pitch change near the end as the primal beast inside the man roared in bewilderment at life's ultimate mystery and then I heard resignation as the scream and his spirit departed. I said a quick prayer for his agonized body and soul.

The entire perimeter went on full alert and the 3rd Platoon opened up, but the phantomlike VC had crawled under, or stepped over, the carefully set trip wires, tossed his package of death and was gone. The man who screamed was, indeed, dead and two others were wounded by the attack—all members of the 3rd Platoon, which had been given the toughest sector to defend. They were strung along the edge of, and partway up, a low rise with brush in front of them—since we had waited until dusk to move in, they had no time to expand their fields of fire or remove the cover. The other two men weren't badly wounded and the medevac didn't want to come in at night unless it was critical, so the evacuation was set for morning.

I thought about spending the rest of the night in the hole, but I decided my sleeping trench afforded me a better chance of escaping a grenade. In our minds the enemy began to grow in stature once again and seemed capable of anything, while we were the helpless giant, flogging and flailing around blindly. At 0300, after no further probes, I put the men back on regular alert, but I still couldn't sleep. What next, or who's next? Once again I didn't want to learn the dead man's name; I barely spoke with the troops from other platoons. Don't get to know too many people, don't make friends, it's too hard on you when they get wasted. Just add another layer of hardness to the heart and move along.

With the morning sun came more sniper fire from the east—across the paddy from my position. Another sniper joined in from the west and we huddled in our holes as the artillery pounded the suspected areas. When the medevac chopper tried to dart down the valley for a quick extraction of the dead and wounded, the snipers opened up again from three directions. The pilot brought the ship in and held it at a high idle as the casualties were loaded. I noticed the men glancing at the walking wounded with envy.

"They're gettin' outta this shit, man. I'd love to trade places with them."

I heard Allen mumble to Fryer as the chopper lifted off and headed east, toward the MASH unit and safety. As soon as he cleared the ground, we opened up with everything we had across the paddies and into the hillsides. We had no targets, but it felt good to release some tension. I decided it was time to show some bravado, so I stood up and walked casually to the CP where Nuckols yelled at me.

"Get down, Pete. You'll get your ass shot."

"Screw it. We can't let a few snipers dictate how we're gonna operate in this AO. Let's get on with it. Where are we going today?"

Before he could answer, I heard the radio crackle. "Charlie 6, this is Dustoff 2. Does that complete your medevac, over?"

"Roger, Dustoff, thanks much."

"OK, Charlie, just wanted to let you know that I took a round in the leg during the extraction. Nothing serious. Dustoff 2, out."

Nuckols grinned wryly and praised the flier. "Welcome to the war, pilot. He's got balls so big he can't sit down to come in here under fire the way he did."

"Well, that's his job—to pick up the wounded. Our job is to get wounded, or killed, I guess," I replied as succinctly as I could.

We swept on down into the village where we had taken the rifle grenades, then moved farther along to the southwest and crossed the paddy. We found yet another ville and swept through it, flushing two young males out into the paddy where they were grabbed by the 3rd Herd, waiting in a blocking position. They fit our description of VC and could have been part of the local cadre which had been setting up the booby traps and sniping at us. It was a minor accomplishment, but it raised our spirits measurably.

We dug in early for the night on the south side of that same village. I continued to question the placements of our NDPs, but in a constructive manner, hoping that our platoon leaders would take it up with the CO. Lieutenant Nelson was gone on R&R, but I thought Nuckols knew more about strategy and tactics, anyway. I was certain that the men would prefer walking a klick or two to find a more defensible position on higher ground rather that setting up in or near a ville. The Army continued to operate in the manner of the 500-pound gorilla—we'll put up a perimeter anywhere we want. The problem was, troops were getting maimed and killed and it was time for a change in strategy.

About midnight a grenade exploded somewhere near a 1st Platoon position. They responded with a hail of fire and the perimeter went on high alert again. Although there were no physical casualties, nerves were frazzled and the fear and adrenaline set our hearts pounding once more.

At 0200 a burst of automatic weapons fire tore into the NDP, again sending the company into a small frenzy. Ol' Charlie knew what he was doing and we were dancing to his tune.

No one could be sure of the source of the fire, so we didn't fire back, but the FO called in a few rounds into our preselected targets—a shot in the dark, but it was something. The area in front of my position lit up like an eerie campfire scene as someone or something popped our trip flare at 0315. We hosed down the area with our 16s, then waited with eyes peeled and hearts in our mouths, but nothing further occurred. They were playing a deadly game with us and we were unable to thwart them. I remained awake all through the night, certain that an attack, or at least a probe, was imminent.

When dawn finally broke mercifully, the beleaguered troops of Charlie Company were all hunkered down in their foxholes. I checked the area in front of our position, but found nothing but an expired flare. I directed the men to stay alert, then headed for the CP to report. Along the way I noticed that all the officers were still in foxholes—they were getting smarter. Fear has a way of doing that to a man.

"*Goooood morrrning,* Vietnam!" I said. "At the 1st Squad position, trip flare popped, we fired, but no sightings. Charlie's jerkin' our chain, messin' with our minds. I haven't slept since we came into this damn Death Valley."

I sat down next to Nuckols and blew out a sigh as he answered. "That's a good name for it, Pete. None of us are gettin' much sleep out here. I'm gonna make some suggestions to the Old Man when we meet this mornin'. You got anything to bring up?" I grasped at the straw like a drunk reaching for that first drink.

"Yes! How about sending a squad or two to find a good NDP in the afternoon, somewhere on high ground? Let's have a mad minute a couple of times at night. Just open up to keep Charlie off guard instead of the other way around. Let's take the initiative, not sit back and let him pick away at us and drive us crazy."

Nuckols let a small grin cross his haggard face. "I'm gettin' to know you pretty well. You said about what I thought you'd say. I like your mad minute idea. Maybe we can keep Charlie away from the perimeter."

I went back to my hole and tried to fix some coffee, but fatigue and stress made my hands shake so badly that I could barely hold the canteen cup. The company saddled up and moved out at 0900 and began to sweep south. About an hour later, the sniper fire began from another small ville. The CO called in Batman 26, commanding officer of an APC unit that was operating in an area just east of us. He sent two of the amtracs to a hill overlooking the village and from there they pounded it with their .50-caliber machine guns while we watched and cheered. The huts shuddered, gave off a puff of dust and some of them collapsed when the rounds tore into them and a few palm trees were broken in half. It was a new tactic and an impressive sight.

"Get some, Batman!" Alexus yelled.

I yelled back, "If anything can scare ol' Charles, it's a fifty up close."

After they finished their prep, we swept through the hamlet with no further sniping. As we neared the south edge of the ville, three armed VC raced out toward the tree line to the west. The entire 2nd Platoon opened up, but the VC made the woods, where one of them stopped and fired a burst at us before disappearing. Fryer put a couple of M-79 bloop rounds into the area, but they escaped our fire. An ensuing search of the tree line was fruitless, so we headed back and resumed our mission. We had been having a pretty good day, but it was now tempered by the discovery that a troop in the 1st Platoon had taken a flesh wound from the last burst of fire from the VC.

The medevac chopper came under fire once again as it swooped in to pick up the wounded man, but no further casualties resulted. At 1500 we moved east to an NDP near a stream where we cut an LZ and called in a resupply chopper. I watched as the men unloaded several cartons of fragmentation and M-79 grenades. Later, each defensive position was given several frags and bloop rounds to throw and fire at predesignated times during the night. With grenades blasting in different spots around the perimeter every few minutes, Charlie would find it more difficult to approach us. We had taken the initiative and it sent my spirits upward slightly.

As I moved to the CP to check for mail, I saw Lieutenant Nelson step off the last chopper and look around. I walked over to him, threw a crisp salute and reported, "Damn glad to see you, *sir!* How was R&R?"

"It was great, Pete, but I leave you guys alone for a few days and all hell breaks loose. Where's Nuck and the CP?"

I led him to the platoon CP where Nuckols broke into a big grin and slapped him on the back. "Welcome back, Loo-tenant. We've got a bitch of a war here—snipers and grenades and booby traps. Sit down, have some coffee and I'll tell you about it."

Lieutenant Nelson probably wasn't the greatest officer in the free world, but he had a definite streak of cockiness—an aloofness that set him off from the men and demanded our support. I was genuinely glad to see him back; we needed every edge we could muster as it had become a war of nerves, and we weren't winning.

That night we had our most restful night since we had come back to the field eight days before. The intermittent grenade tossing and M-79 firing had made Charlie's forays into our perimeter a little too dangerous. The extra level of security provided some needed sleep and gave our morale a boost.

As we crossed another stream to look at another small ville in the morning, we took more fire. The lead elements hustled across the stream to safety, then held up as Captain Eklund called in Batman again to pound the suspected fire origin area with their heavy weapons. After the fire mission was complete, the 1st Platoon moved into the village and began searching while the 2nd and 3rd blocked. They flushed out two young men who tried to make it to the brush, but were cut off and detained by the 3rd Herd. The 2nd Platoon then acted as a holding force for prisoners and detainees from the ville.

The 1st rounded up over fifty civilians and VC suspects from the sprawling village, who were extracted at 1700, then the company went into a wagon wheel for the night. We called in the resupply choppers and stocked up on mail, C rations and armaments. We continued our practice of throwing and blooping grenades for the second straight night, and again we were secure.

The 2nd Platoon took a short patrol the next morning, heading east on a trail through heavy brush and then along a narrow paddy. We had been sent to explore a smaller glen that branched eastward from Death Valley between two low wooded hills. I was leading the patrol, trying to break in the new men by pointing out things and sharing accumulated lore, when once more an AK-47 opened up. This time it was punctuated by the rustling of the brush next to my face and an angry whistling of rounds just over my head.

I threw myself downward and to the left, landing on my shoulder and side, then flattened myself on my chest. After a few seconds a growing rage replaced fear and caution and I jumped up, flipped my safety on automatic and angrily sprayed the hillside. I yelled a few choice epithets at my unseen assailant, then led the patrol into the brush to continue our mission. My ragged nerves were even more shaky as I tried to focus on the task at hand and I felt like I had taken another step toward the brink.

After finding some abandoned hooches and no more activity, we returned to the company perimeter located next to the stream, where we lay around all afternoon and even took some refuge from the sun by splashing in the stream, using its high banks to cover us from snipers.

As night closed in we fortified our streamside foxhole with a couple of large branches and more dirt, then set up our watch. For some reason we stopped throwing grenades, but continued firing Fryer's M-79, and the night defenses went untested.

In my sleeping trench just behind the hole, I could hear and smell the creek as I lay staring at the enormous panorama of ultimate beauty spread across the night sky. I pondered my destiny again. What twist of fate had caused the Viet Cong sniper to fire a few inches too high? Was my story not quite over? Was Death Valley my final journey, or just another valley in Vietnam? I knew I was thinking way too much, but I couldn't shut off my mind, just most of my feelings.

On May 14, Sawlski and Underhill took point for the 3rd Squad and led the 2nd Platoon away from the perimeter to the southwest and into another vale. We searched yet another village strung along the east side of an elongated, narrow rice paddy that stretched the length of the valley and ran from hill to brush-covered hill. We herded the remaining residents out to a trail along the edge of the ville, then waited for the Chinook chopper to pick them up.

The 2nd Squad found a large cache of rice in one of the hooches—far too much for the population of this village alone.

Because of our recent combative situations, we decided that the rice was not being stored for later sale, but was indeed a cache for the VC. After reporting the find to the CO, we waited for orders. At 1200 we received word that a Chinook was on the way to pick up the detainees and we were to burn the rice.

The troops, with Lieutenant Nelson helping, poured mosquito repellent and lighter fluid on the grain, then threw heat tabs into the pile and set fire to it. I had to turn away. I was born and raised on a farm and I knew about the sweat, strain and devotion required to bring a crop to harvest, and I could appreciate how difficult it must have been to do so without machinery. It hurt me to see the food crop destroyed and I could see the anguish and loathing in the eyes of the villagers—was this the way to win their hearts and minds?

After the extraction of the detainees, we rested while the 3rd Squad scouted out ambush sites. That night we ambushed the junction of two trails, but although the dark night was filled with suspicious sounds, there was no probe or activity.

Bravo Company made a combat assault on a valley a few klicks away the next morning. Two of the Hueys ferrying troops were shot down by the VC, resulting in the wounding of several men, some seriously. The ominous cloud of despair I had been laboring under since we moved into the AO got a little darker with the news.

The platoon patrolled farther up the small valley, then turned to head back for a resupply rendezvous with the company CP. As we humped through the brush, we could hear two choppers headed for the same LZ. Suddenly, they opened up on our narrow valley, the door gunners peppering away out of every window, it seemed. We dove behind trees and Lieutenant Nelson began screaming into his radio handset from behind a huge tree that he had been walking past.

"Get those fuckin' choppers off our backs! They're gonna kill us!"

I popped a smoke grenade, then yelled at others, "Pop smoke! Pop smoke! Get some smoke out."

Several puffs of smoke began to make their way ever so slowly up through the thick foliage as the machine-gun rounds continued to slash away at the jungle, some of them ricocheting angrily from tree to tree. I huddled close to my own large tree, safe behind its ample girth, and flashed back for a second to a similar attack in January. The rounds ceased after a few more seconds and the choppers swept on down the valley while a few of the men screamed their frustrations while questioning the heritage and sexual orientation of the pilots and door gunners of the Hueys.

This was the third time I had been fired at by an American chopper and I had seen several short rounds and accidental firings of artillery land on our forces. It seemed that just when you think you've got ol' Victor Charlie's weaponry figured out, the U.S. Army screws up and hits you with some of your own. It didn't happen this way to John Wayne or Errol Flynn in the movies, so what the hell was going on? We picked up our re-supply at the LZ and pitched our bitch at the CO, who replied that the ships' crews were trigger-happy after the shootdowns with the Bravo Company assault in the morning. The entire platoon was jumpy and irritable as we returned to the valley and set up in an ambush for the night.

The next day, we rejoined the company at the LZ near the stream, then immediately headed east to check out another area. As the temperatures climbed past 100 degrees, the men began staggering and falling out. The squad leaders passed the word up the ladder and Lieutenant Nelson finally gave us a long break in the shade. It was so hot even the VC snipers took the afternoon off. At 1700 we climbed a small hill and began digging in for the night. The resupply chopper came in with hot chow, but there was no mail, so we dug in, fortified ourselves and lay back to wait for whatever this night would bring. I was called to the platoon CP where Nuckols filled me in.

"Before it gets too hot in the morning, we're moving out. We'll hump about five klicks east to meet up with the APCs for transport to Hill 54, our newest base camp. We're getting a few days off, Pete."

"God knows we need it, Sergeant Nuck. My batteries need charging and the men need some rest and beer."

I staggered back to my squad and gave them the news. Like me, they were relieved but not overjoyed. We had seen too much lately to get excited about a few days in the rear.

Since we moved into this vale of death, I had picked up the pieces of an American blown up by his own artillery, heard a death scream from a fellow grunt trapped in his foxhole with a grenade, withstood a rocket attack at dawn (Watson would have nodded sagely), been sniped at daily including having the bushes around my face snipped off by one, burned rice in front of the villagers who had grown it, and watched some of my fellow platoon members shoot an unarmed man. I was physically exhausted and mentally distraught, and I was becoming more and more certain that the sword of Damocles was hanging over me and the thread that secured it was slowly unraveling. In my mind, there seemed to be no chance in hell that I would get out of this war—this maelstrom—alive.

27

A weary, tattered Charlie Company headed due east on the morning of May 17, sticking to the large trail, which soon became a road. This trail was the one most used by the residents of these valleys as they traveled to the coastal villages like Quang Ngai. Because of this frequent use, the trail was not mined by either side, so we could set our own pace and relax a little. As we headed over the crest of the last small hill range, I saw the South China Sea beckoning once more in the distance. We continued on down onto the coastal plain and waited in an abandoned group of hooches stretched across a broad expanse of white sand. With the war a few klicks behind us, the men began to loosen up and unwind.

The APCs picked us up at 1000 and deposited us at the main gate of our new home—Hill 54. It was another old Marine base, but smaller than our last camp just a few miles down the road. We tromped up along the road to the CP with as much pride as we could muster. We had been bloodied again and we had bent, but we did not break. The First Shirt pointed out the quarters for the troops, the mess hall, supply tent and dispensary. They were all tents or wooden frame buildings that looked like they wouldn't stand up to any stiff breeze. There was a transient look to the whole damn place, which was fitting for an orphan outfit such as ours. We headed for one of the tents just around the hill from the CP, unloaded our gear and began to make the necessary arrangements that would bring us back to a semblance of normal life.

I led my squad to the supply tent, where we picked up some clean fatigues, then we took turns pouring tepid water into the shower barrel for each other and trying to scrub off some of the grime. Later we received a beer ration, then I led a short patrol to the EM club—the Dragon's Lair—where we pooled our finances and augmented the meager ration several times over. It was an afternoon of drink, reading and answering mail and rear chow, followed by a night free of grenades and enemy probes. One squad from each platoon spent the night on ambush outside the base camp perimeter while the rest of us slept on the board floor of the tents, but we slept well.

The next day we rode a truck to the beach, where we spent a few hours swimming and drinking beer at a small EM club. We returned at 1700 and I found out it was my squad's turn on night ambush. I soaked my head in water for a while, wrapped my wet towel around my neck, then took the men through the wire on the south side at twilight. We moved out about 150 meters, scouted out several likely sites, then waited until it was completely dark to move into a line ambush near a trail fork. No one came along and I let a melancholy mood sweep over me as I gazed at the stars and pondered my place in the universe.

For the next three days we lay around base camp on air mattresses or poncho liners atop the hard boards, resting and making only an occasional foray into town. Town, which we called Chu Lai, was the collection of makeshift hooches that sprang up near every military base camp in the country and the world, complete with prostitutes and merchants who would sell anything. It drew us with its promise of liquid refreshments and, just possibly, a good-looking girl or two.

But, alas, the good-looking girls had been shipped out to Da Nang and the other larger cities where GI money flowed down the dirty streets. Martinez and I strolled along Highway 1, which served as the main street of this gathering of hovels, and looked around.

"Gus, my main man, take a look at those bar girls in there. I'd have to say they were somewhat lacking in facial fairness."

"Pete, they'd make a statue weep, but let's go in anyway."

We sucked down a couple of Tiger beers, then sauntered back through the main gate and returned to the sedentary life of a REMF. I missed Vickers and the maniac, Bennett, and wondered how they were doing back in the World. I strolled over to the CP and harassed LaBarge for a few minutes, but he was busy. It was a relief not to be in mortal danger, but the heat was stifling and we were bored stiff. So, we drank and talked and lay around thinking . . . thinking too much.

There was a feeling that ran deep into my essence, touching the edges of my every thought—a feeling of despair. I felt as if I was being forewarned—I remembered Malarik telling me on Christmas Eve that my health line was broken and I tossed it off with a joke. Now, five months later, the prophecy was alive in my mind because of the terror we were confronting on a daily basis in this new AO. I couldn't laugh it away anymore, so I drank myself into a state of nirvana.

At 1500 the platoon loaded onto APCs, headed out a few klicks, unloaded and humped to a preselected area for an overnight ambush. The APCs would carefully retrace their path, checking closely for mines that might have been quickly set after they had passed the first time. They were usually safe enough in daylight, but once darkness fell, Charlie could hide mines easily and blow the APC as it rolled over. On the 20th, after unloading and getting into ambush position, we heard a *whump* in the distance, then Lee switched his radio to Batman's frequency, held the handset to his ear and listened to the report. One killed and three wounded—no wonder they got so nervous when the sun went down.

The ambushes close to the base camp didn't turn up any results. We remained on regular alert and were able to sleep when the mosquitoes allowed it. I continued to sleep only fitfully, spending much of the time looking at the stars, searching for answers and fighting the sense of foreboding that was weighing me down. This country's war had taken away my innocence and my youth and now I felt I was in danger of losing my ability to function.

On the morning of May 22 we loaded onto the APCs and rode them most of the day, patrolling the area, then blocking for the other platoons while they searched a large village. Activity was minimal, but the sun was merciless and the heat oppressive, so much so that the men became lethargic even in the shade. Rivulets of sweat worked their way through the layer of dust on my face as I sat propped against a tree. One of the radios was tuned to AFRVN to lift our spirits somewhat. At 1400 they reported that the official temperature in the Chu Lai area was 116 degrees Fahrenheit. Shortly after hearing that, the CO led us slowly back to Hill 54 and the tepid shower water and we were given the rest of the day and the night to recuperate. I took off my fatigues and let my feet and crotch dry in an attempt to stop the rashes that had invaded those parts of my body.

We spent the next day cleaning our gear and weapons after learning that we were heading back to the field on the 24th. Most of the time was spent in reflective silence or writing letters, but we did get some beer for the evening. The heat was overpowering again, but we got a short rain shower in the afternoon, which I basked in with my clothes removed. That night we moved out to a trail crossing for an ambush and fought a bloody battle with the Quang Ngai Province mosquitoes.

As the rotor blades slapped their way once more through the morning air, I climbed aboard a chopper and sat on the edge of the floor in the open doorway and let the cool air rush past my face. It reminded me of a summer evening back home, riding along with the car window open. I snapped back to reality when the chopper dropped down to treetop level and the door gunners opened up. These guys had lost some friends and machines and were pretty jumpy. I watched as my squad jumped off, then felt a hand pushing me hard. I half-fell and jumped into the paddy, then whirled in a flash of anger with my M-16 raised and pointed at the offending door gunner, who stood behind his M-60. We stared into each other's eyes and faced one another down for a few seconds, then the bird lifted off. I made a quick note of the chopper number, then flashed him the larger half of the peace sign.

"Them assholes think they own that ship, Pete."

Sergeant Nuckols laughed, then motioned me to join a platoon meeting. I trotted over to the paddy dike, still steaming.

"I'm sure I'll meet him again if I live long enough, Nuck."

While Lieutenant Nelson coordinated the morning's activity with the rest of the company on the radio, Nuckols let me in on the plans.

"We're going to sweep through Thon Hai 2 while the rest of the company blocks. You lead us in and watch yourself."

I took the point with Allen and we moved quickly across the paddy to the ville. As we neared the first hooch, sniper fire rang out through the already stifling morning air. I led Allen around the corner of the mud-walled hooch, then signaled the others to find cover, but Alexus had already taken care of it. In a few seconds, before we could locate the source, the firing stopped and the troops of the 2nd moved on into the ville and began searching the hooches.

The 3rd Squad was moving through some hooches near a ditch when two young men began running from one of them toward the nearby hills. Sawlski chased them, firing as he ran, but they escaped into the tree line. Sally loped on back to the platoon, sweating and panting, but grinning.

"I almost got the bastards. I saw the dirt kick up between their feet, but they're too fast for me. This damn pack and all this fucking gear slowed me down."

We continued to search slowly and thoroughly through the large village, pausing often for water breaks, then took our noon chow in the middle of the hamlet. I was finding that I had no appetite because of the heat and the stress, but I munched on C-ration crackers and sipped water to keep me going.

After several more sniper attacks, we found ourselves still in the village at the end of the day, so the company joined us and set up a perimeter. At 2230 hours a burst of automatic weapons fire tore into that perimeter, slightly wounding one man in the 3rd Platoon.

We answered with a long salvo of artillery fire, but no one had any illusions about silencing the snipers that way. We had to catch them on the ground, in the open, which seemed to be an impossible task. The company, and I assumed the battalion, were enormously frustrated by the VC tactics.

The next day as I finished sipping my morning cocoa,

Sergeant Nuckols called me to his position and made an announcement. "Pete, we're gonna make you a buck sergeant. Whaddaya think of that?"

"It's about damn time, man. I've been doing the job of an E-6 for three months now."

I grinned so he would know I was at least half-joking. I had been a squad leader at least part of the time from February through April, and with Bennett gone now had the job full-time. In the Army's grand scheme of things (TO&E—table of organization and equipment), it is a position to be filled by a staff sergeant.

"Loo-tenant Nelson and me had to sign three waivers while we were in base camp. One of them stated that you were in the top 2 percent of the company—whatever the hell that means. You'll probably get your raise next payday. Remember, new E-5s buy the beer."

"That's one custom I'll gladly go along with. That extra money will be nice, but I appreciate mostly your confidence. Thanks, Ranger."

I had to quickly forget the promise of a promotion as we tromped through the rice paddies. We followed a trail into a shaded area where cool, fresh water bubbled up from several springs and made a small pond that drained into the nearby rice paddies. We searched the small hill overlooking the glade and discovered the VC liked the area also. There were several bunkers that had been used recently along the side and top of the hill. We could hear gunfire in the distance and went on alert. The radio crackled with the news and I could hear Sergeant Nuckols ask Patterson softly, "Who got wasted?"

The 1st Platoon had taken casualties—five wounded, including Sergeant Able with a scratch in his eye. After Lieutenant Nelson listened to the reports, he then informed the CO of our find and we received orders to stay at the area overnight and ambush the trail that ran through the area.

We climbed the small rise overlooking the trail and the springs next to it and dug in. Alabama claimed an enemy bunker for his M-60 crew, while I moved a few feet farther up to the hilltop to set up the 1st Squad positions and listened to him laugh because he didn't have to dig.

It was pitch black that night as I lay next to Martinez and

Galaviz with the radio handset propped next to my left ear.
Somewhere between 2300 and midnight I heard a soft metallic
click from the gun position and my mind came to full alert—
somebody's flipping their safety onto fire. As I slid into the foxhole, I flipped mine also, then poked Martinez and pointed to
the gun crew, barely visible in the pale moonlight. Just then a
burst of fire from that position sent the perimeter into a frenzy,
then it was silent once again. I waited a long, heart-pounding
second, then whispered to the crew.

"You guys all right? What's happening? Talk to me."

"A dink walked right up to us and Snow shot him dead. He
never knew we were here."

I made a mental note that Alabama seemed to drawl more
when he whispered, then reported the events to the CP and received orders, which I relayed.

"Snow, my man. They want you to search the body."

Snow's voice was shaky as he answered me. "I ain't crawlin'
outta this hole till daylight. You want him searched, you search
him."

"Snow, Captain Eklund wants the body searched for
weapons or documents. You shot him, you gotta search him."

I heard Alabama whispering to him in a persuasive manner.
"I'll be right here to cover you. Just jump out there, check him
out, jump right back in."

I decided to boost his confidence even more and if that
didn't work, I would crawl down and search the body myself,
even though I hated the chore.

"Snow, Alabama, get down. We'll blow our claymore to
make sure the area is clear. Then you can go out."

We blew the mine, then Snow crawled out to the dead man
and checked him over. He was back after a few seconds with a
pack that he handed to me. I got back on the horn and described the contents to the lieutenant and Charlie 6.

"One VC military style pack, no weapons, some rice, some
greens, some paper."

"Any writing on the paper?"

"Too damn dark to tell and I'm not putting on a light."

"Roger, 2–1. Tell the gun, good job. Out."

I decided to fulfill the orders to the letter.

"Psst, Snow. Charlie 6 says good job. Way to go, gun crew."

We tried to settle back to our normal night routine, but our nerves were still jangled. About an hour later I heard one of the RTOs at the company CP call the platoons and announce in an extremely somber voice, "Be advised that a friendly artillery round from a Navy H and I mission has landed near our position. Charlie 6 and one other are Whiskey India Alpha. Out."

The news hit me like a ton of manure. I wanted to stand up and scream at the skies, give vent to my pain. What the hell are we doing wrong? Why don't we all just go home? We can never defeat an enemy as cunning as this one when we keep making deadly mistakes that kill and maim our own men. Can't somebody do something? Instead, I burned inside and lay awake the rest of the night.

Martinez noticed my silence the next morning and tried to make a few jokes, but I was having none of it. I respected, admired and genuinely liked Captain Eklund and was angered and deeply hurt by his loss. We had heard this morning that he might lose his leg, but would pull through, and the other man, McGinnis, was in stable condition. I put my personal feelings aside and tried to get into the proper frame of mind as we headed down off the back side of the rise, but every day it seemed to get harder.

The platoon headed toward the northwest, across a large paddy where Charlie made us dance behind the dikes twice before we made it across. No one was hit, but we were tremendously agitated by our inability to strike back. We stopped in a brushy area for a water break, then continued due west along a trail toward the ville next to a river. As we crossed the last narrow stretch of paddy, another sniper opened up and sent us scurrying. I hustled with my squad on into the ville and searched in vain for him.

Under a spreading tree, a lot like a maple back home, I found more than a dozen empty .30-caliber shell casings. The sniper had climbed the tree, spotted the platoon moving across the open paddy and fired a clip, then hurried down and away. I wondered how he had missed all of us from here; it should have been easy pickings. I marked the spot on my map and etched it in my mind, next to the other hot spots I had been filing away over the last few weeks. The next time we came near this ville, I would have Fryer put a bloop round into the center of that tree.

We held up on the edge of the village, now abandoned except for the resident snipers, and waited as the other platoons joined us. We commiserated with several troops from other platoons, only to have Charlie send us scattering with another quick burst from his AK-47. We hurriedly moved the troops into a defensive perimeter and began digging in. For a change, there was no wordplay, no bitching—the men were openly worried. Allen spoke quietly, asking, "Pete, is Charlie kicking our ass or what? We can't do anything out here without gettin' shot at or grenaded."

"I know, man. It's frustrating as hell, but we've got too much firepower for Charlie to take us on head-to-head, so he snipes and booby-traps, hits and runs. And, he's damn good at it. But, if we keep after him, we'll rout him out."

"I think," I added to myself, then I tried to lighten it up.

"Remember, guys, if you get killed, I'll personally visit your girlfriends and tell her how you wanted me to take care of her. That's the kind of squad leader I am."

"Nobody can take care of my girl but me," Allen shot back. "Nobody else would measure up, if you know what I mean."

The sniper fire continued sporadically throughout the night, and around midnight the 3rd Platoon OP was hit by grenades and rifle fire. They pulled back to the perimeter with one man slightly wounded. Shortly after, the OP that I had sent out came under fire and beat a quick retreat to friendly positions. Charlie had us ducking, hiding and playing his game—it was frighteningly embarrassing. A powerful Army infantry company was reduced almost to groveling before a few guerrillas. But, they were damn good guerrillas.

We were kept so off-balance and busy, I hadn't had time to work with another new man in my squad—Garland Walker, from Alabama. I told him to listen to me, Martinez and Alexus and he would be all right, then threw him to the wolves. The platoon had also received a new staff sergeant, Marshall Cain, a lifer who had been in the Army for eight years. Sergeant Nuckols hadn't decided what to do with him yet. He had the rank to take my squad, but that wasn't going to set with me and the Ranger knew it.

The snipers continued firing almost at will the next morning as we hunkered behind trees and in foxholes to finish our C rations. We answered with artillery and machine-gun fire, but they were on a large brush-covered hill and spotting them was impossible. I volunteered to take my squad up the hill, but we had orders to move in the other direction, so Charlie had his way with us until we left. Since the incoming fire was heavy enough to bother the chopper pilots, we burned our trash and DX items and took the slightly wounded man with us as we headed back across the paddy.

"We're running, Pete, and it really burns my ass, man."

Martinez spat the words out and kicked at the ground. I felt the same way, but I wanted the squad to focus on the enemy.

"We're retreating, yes, but we don't have a CO, and we need to regroup. We'll come back to kick some ass, GI. Just think of it as advancing in the opposite direction."

We cut through the brush as much as we could to evade the eyes of the snipers, then headed due east for about three klicks. As we crossed the last hill range, once again I spotted the South China Sea in the distance and knew we were relatively safe. Charlie didn't follow us and nip at our flanks and heels, partly because of the better visibility, but mostly because of the APCs and their powerful .50s, which were only a few minutes away. With the sniper fire gone, the company set up near a stream for the night and dug in leisurely.

We took a resupply chopper with hot chow and cold drinks and relaxed as the night went quiet. Nuckols directed me to take an OP out, so I took Martinez and his team and McQueen on the radio to a large tree to the west of the perimeter. I slept a little for the first time in four nights and felt secure until battalion reported a large force was moving near us. Despite that report, the night remained quiet and a grateful Charlie Company replenished their bodies and spirits with sleep.

As I sat down beside the Ranger sarge for morning chow, word came over the horn that Malarik, who had finished at the top of the class in battalion NCO Academy, had just finished in the top five at 4th Division Academy and had received his second promotion in two weeks. Nuckols grinned as he gave me the news.

"Well, Pete, now I've got another E-6. What the hell am I gonna do with them?"

"Well, they're not gonna get the 1st Squad. Send Malarik to

another platoon. Both of them need sergeants. Give the 2nd
Squad to Cain as soon as he's ready. Boyer's gone half the time,
anyway, and doesn't want the job."

"Yeah, that's kinda what I was thinking. But, if Boyer stays
and Cain wants a squad, I gotta give him yours."

"Well, I'm not going to work under somebody else now, so
if that happens, you can get me a transfer out." I didn't want to
leave, but I did want him to know that I was serious about keeping my squad.

Before he could answer, the morning resupply arrived and
Malarik stepped off and rejoined the platoon, with Boyer heading
back for R&R. Nuckols temporarily assigned Malarik to the 2nd
Squad with Cain as squad leader, which left me assuaged for the
moment. After the meetings broke up, the 2nd patrolled down the
main trail, actually a road leading to the coastal villages, looking
for daylight observation and ambush sites.

As we reached the crest of a small hill, Lieutenant Nelson
decided this was a good place to set up the CP. He sent the 2nd
Squad and a gun crew with Malarik and Cain down the trail
120 meters where it made a curve and branched to the south.
They set up in an L-shaped ambush—now called a "peach" by
higher. I took my squad into the thick brush along the crest of
the hill to find another observation post. There was a line of old
bunkers dug into the side of the hill which we checked for
booby traps, then moved into. The bunkers had been there for a
year or more, probably dug by troops from the 3rd Marines.

Fryer and Martinez put up their ponchos as a sun shield and
we relaxed, secure in our bunkers, safe from snipers and hoping
for a free afternoon. An hour or so later as I scanned the trail
back to the coast, which was visible in the distance, I spotted a
column of Vietnamese heading west toward the 2nd Squad ambush site. I motioned to my squad to get down and keep alert,
then grabbed the radio handset.

"2–6 and 2–2, this is 2–1. Troops or civilians headed toward
the 2–2 peach, over."

"Describe them, 2–1."

I took another look, then quickly got back on the net.

"Be alert, 2–2, the leader has a weapon. Can't see any more,
but there is at least one weapon."

"2–1, 2–1, this is 2–2. Let me know when they're in my peach. I want them all."

I lowered my voice so the sound wouldn't carry on his end and hoped he would take his cue from me. "Hang on 2–2, let me call it from here. They're rounding the bend. Wait . . . wait."

I realized I was holding my breath, so I released the push-bar, grabbed some air, then resumed my traffic control while my stomach tightened. The Vietnamese suspected nothing and followed their pajama-clad leader along the trail.

"Wait, 2–2, they're almost there. On my signal. . . ."

A burst of fire rang out, followed by a salvo from every member of the ambush team. The leader of the column fell to the ground as the others fled in several directions.

"Son of a bitch! They're gettin' away, Pete!"

Martinez yelled, then stood up and began firing at the flee-ing figures. I put my hand on his barrel, then told the squad that firing might endanger the 2nd Squad if they chased after the enemy. We watched in frustration as the ambush team searched the body and showed no interest in chasing the others. Mar-tinez was seething.

"Fuckin' Malarik did it. I know he did. Malarik opened up too soon, the glory-hungry bastard."

Cain was on the radio giving a report to Lieutenant Nelson.

"2–6, 2–2. We've got a dead VC with a burp gun, Chicom grenades and mines, some piastres and a watch. He has some paperwork, must be a honcho."

I broke in agitatedly, "The peach was popped too soon, man. There are at least seven VC in the bush. They should be chasing them."

I was furious, but tried to get myself under control.

"This is 2–6. Cool it, 2–1. 2–2, continue report."

"This is 2–2. I didn't see where the others went, but we defi-nitely got the leader and his weapons."

Screw the leader, I thought, go after the others. It seemed to me that Nelson was content to tally the important kill and not worry about the others. The radio hissed again.

"2–2, this is 2–6. Bring back everything but the body and his clothes. Be here in 1–5 mikes. We're calling in air."

I waited for my chance to call in, but he came back with,

"2–1, 2–6. Dial up 48–80 for air support. They're waiting for your call. Call sign is Quick-Strike 1–6. Do you copy?"

I rogered his call, then dialed the Navy pilot.

"Quick-Strike 1–6, this is Golden Charlie 2–1. Come in."

"Roger, Charlie 2–1, whaddaya got?"

I gave him the coordinates of the trail junction and asked him to blanket the area north and south of it with napalm or whatever he had. By this time the ambush team had retreated to the platoon CP, so I had my men hunker down in the bunker and watch the show. The fast-movers screamed into action a minute or so later and laid down a blanket of exploding steel and fire into the bushes north of the junction. I heard the *whump* as they dropped the napalm, then watched as the orange fireball formed—fire from the sky had to strike fear into anyone in its path.

"Charlie 2–1, how'd that look? Over."

"That's real pretty, Quick-Strike. You got anything left for another run 200 mikes on the sierra side of the tango?"

"Negative on that. You want another strike called in?"

"Negative. We'll check it out on foot. Thanks for your help, Quick-Strike. 2–1, out."

I called 2–6 to give some more of my opinions, but he was too giddy to listen, so I took my squad over to the south trail and looked around, but it was far too late. We then returned to the CP and watched in chagrin as Malarik and Cain basked in their glory. I liked Cain, but when he was first placed in the platoon, Nuckols sent him to the 1st Squad. He couldn't work under me because of the rank differential and I couldn't work under him because of my experience and attitude. He hadn't said anything, but I know he resented losing out to an almost-E-5. I approached him and asked, "Who fired early?"

He pointed at the pile of booty. "Doesn't matter. The guy we got was loaded, Pete. Burp gun, grenades, money, papers. Must be a big wheel, maybe VC cadre."

Martinez was still steaming and let some of it out. "Screw it. All but one got away. That fuckin' squad."

I put my hand on Martinez' arm and led him away. We headed past the loot and found Nuckols counting the money. I tried to interest him in the story as I saw it.

"We know Malarik fired early and blew the whole deal. They could have gotten them all if they waited. The lieutenant thinks they did great, but they blew it, Sarge."

He looked at me, then motioned me to calm down and returned to the pile of piastres. The money was sent in to HQ on the evening chopper, with the proviso that the platoon would get free beer on the hill next time in. Nuckols took the watch and Lieutenant Nelson put a tag on the weapon with his name on it; if no one stole it, a likely scenario, he could sell it or try to ship it home. War souvenirs were going like the proverbial hotcakes back in the rear, with the desk jockeys and wannabes exchanging them for air-conditioning or other plush favors. With little else to do in their spare time, they figured out ways to send them home complete with combat stories. It made me want to vomit when I heard about it.

We moved off to rejoin the squad, then shortly after, the platoon saddled up to meet the company in a wagon wheel. As I lay in my position that night, I thought about the ambush again from our view: it was a simple operation. You wait for the center of the column to reach the center of your kill zone, then open up. Malarik was a fine garrison soldier, but I wondered if he would make it out here in the field. I knew I didn't want to be around the next time he made a mistake in judgment—somebody might get killed, maybe me.

I thought about the Vietnamese; the leader must have been a local VC cadre officer who was in town collecting taxes, supplies and "volunteers." Some of these dudes had no weapons, so they were probably being taken to join the VC for training and indoctrination. At the very least we bought them a little more freedom with the slaying of the official. I remembered that one of the induction officials wore a pistol as he led us around back when I was in Milwaukee for my preinduction physical. I realized I was thinking too much, yet again. I saw Martinez on guard, so I rolled over and whispered, "Fuckin' Malarik—what a doofus."

I saw his teeth gleam in the moonlight as I lay back down on my poncho liner.

For our sins, the next day we were given a murderous patrol through the brush. We spent almost the entire day cutting and hacking our way through the heavy stuff as the sweat poured down our faces and saturated our soiled fatigues again. At 1500, it began to rain. The cooling effect was wonderful, but our gear and clothes were drenched as we headed into an NDP at 1800. Then the rain suddenly stopped, so we laid our shirts across the bushes to dry as the sun reappeared. We built rain hooches on the top of a small hill and Charlie left us alone for the third night in a row, respecting our high ground and the proximity to the APCs and tanks.

I lay in my hooch wondering why we were cutting through the damn brush. Why not go back to Sniper Valley or even Death Valley and keep on truckin'? Must be because we don't have a CO and battalion wants us busy out here while some other company rests on the hill. That's gotta be it. Well, no use losing sleep over that—this is a pretty safe area, so enjoy it. I better quit talking to myself and get my head together. Who knows what tomorrow will bring? I couldn't shake that ominous feeling of dread and apprehension.

28

I took the point with Martinez to lead the 2nd Platoon back into the brush the next morning. We cut our way along the ridgeline of the hill where we had spent the night, then picked up the main trail east. We followed it slowly and carefully to the river, where Lieutenant Nelson gave the word to hold up while he asked the Old Man, Lieutenant Guidry, on his second pinch-hitting tour with Charlie Company, if we could wash up. He gave us permission to take a two-hour break and the men took turns washing and standing guard. After scouring off part of a week's grime, Martinez and I found a shady area under a tree beside the river and relaxed until he suddenly had a notion.

"Yo, Pete, isn't today Memorial Day?"

"I don't know anymore. It's all one big, bad dream. Seems like I've been here since Christ was a corporal. Hell, if it's Memorial Day, it's my birthday."

"Your birthday's on Memorial Day? You sure?"

"I think so. Every year, they have a parade on Memorial Day back home. I always told my younger brothers and sisters that the parade was for my birthday and they bought it. They probably still think so today. Messed up their minds good."

"Well, happy fucking birthday, Pete. And many more."

"Yeah, well, if ol' Charlie don't cut us some slack pretty soon. . . ."

I didn't finish what I was thinking, no use getting anybody else caught up in my morbidity. I closed my eyes and a kaleidoscope of thoughts about my tour of duty and all that I had seen and done flashed into my head. My mind passed over so many things, then stopped for a moment to reflect on the commanding officers of Company C I had known. When I arrived in the company, our CO was Captain Simcox, who left the company on November 1 of last year; then Captain Federline, KIA eighteen days later; Captain Childers, KIA January 19; Lieutenant Guidry, temporary in January; Captain Eklund, WIA; Lieutenant Guidry again. Maybe it was me—I was the jinx. I went over to see Sergeant Nuckols and expressed that view and made an offer to take a job in Saigon tending bar at an EM club, but he failed to see the humor.

In the afternoon we saddled up and moved northeast, away from the stream, rejoined the company at 1600, set up in a perimeter and dug in for the night. The resupply chopper came in to our LZ with hot chow and mail, so I caught up on my letter reading and writing while following the shade of a thick bush alongside my position. Around 1830 the CO and a forward observer began setting up DefCons for the night by firing the obligatory smoke round first to make adjustments.

I heard the first round fire in the distance, then shriek through the air and something made me look up to follow it. As the smoke bomb burst with a pop, the canister came hurtling free and, although it was still only a growing dot, my untrained eagle eye could see it was heading for my position. I spoke calmly to the CO, about thirty feet away.

"I think you better add five-zero meters to that shot, sir."

"What's the problem, troop?"

I took another quick glance at the canister, waited for a two count, then rolled quickly to the side as it crashed to the ground exactly where I had been sitting.

"That's the problem, sir," I said, inclining my head as casually as I could toward the canister, half-buried in the sand. The CO and FO were both startled but then began laughing at the comic aspect of the scene and my actions. The FO, a tall blond Californian, then spoke.

"We like to keep our DefCons as close as possible to our lines. Is that close enough?"

"Close enough. You know, ol' dude, it's my birthday and I'm glad somebody remembered, but, please—add five-zero meters."

It was my birthday, and although the boonies weren't my first choice as a place to celebrate, we had taken no fire and had no contact today—practically a walk in the park. For one more day at least, I had been given the gift of life. I lay on my back and stared at the skies and wondered how things were going back in the World. Did anybody still remember me . . . us? Their sons and loved ones? There were now a half million of us over here and we felt like we were alone and forgotten.

The next day the entire company moved out through the brush and slashed our way along the crest of the low hill range. At noon Lieutenant Guidry got a radio message to get on a chopper that was leaving Hill 54 to pick him up. We quickly slashed and tromped out an LZ for his extraction, then set up a perimeter and waited for his return. Two hours later, he landed and gave out the news—Charlie Company was going back to base camp tomorrow. A slight ripple of relief moved through the company as the news was spread.

The 3rd Platoon then led the revitalized company out of the brush and into a tree line alongside a paddy where we received a chopper with hot chow. We moved back to the high ground after chow and we dug in and dreamed of cold beer and showers, clean clothes and all the rest that Hill 54 meant. In the background I could hear the jets pounding Death Valley for the third day in a row. I supposed that another company, perhaps Bravo, was heading out tomorrow to make room for us at base camp, and to make another run at Charlie. I wished them godspeed.

On the morning of June 1, I led my squad, the 2nd Platoon and Charlie Company two klicks to a trail junction for a rendezvous with the APCs. A chopper had stopped earlier at the junction and dropped off donuts and milk cartons in a thermal insulator for a morning treat. Since no security had been left to guard them, I checked all around the containers for booby traps, then tentatively opened one and grabbed a milk carton. My taste buds were honed and saliva was almost dripping as I tipped the container to my mouth. The smell hit my nose just before the liquid hit my mouth and I spat it out as soon as it touched my tongue. I yelled in disgust, "Sour! Don't drink this shit. It's spoiled. Those rear assholes struck again. Why didn't they pack it in ice?"

The donuts were all right, but with only warm canteen water to wash them down, it just wasn't the same. I had really wanted some cold milk. I could hear the APCs roaring down the trail, so I rinsed my mouth once more, spat it out and consoled myself with thoughts of rear chow and beer. I climbed on the lead APC, as was my custom. I had the idea that if Charlie was going to blow one up, he would let the first one or two go by. I knew, deep in my mind, that it was just as likely that he had left a mine set to go off on contact with the first one, but my routine was set. After all, I had now survived eight months of hell and it was no time to start changing my methods, so I climbed up on the lead APC.

We arrived at Hill 54 at 1300, then showered and shaved, put on clean clothes and lined up for pay. The first sergeant had some beer chilling, so we celebrated my promotion and pay hike by quaffing a few. When the beer ran out, I left the company CP, rounded up a few squad members and headed for the EM club—the Dragon's Lair. We whiled away the afternoon by reminiscing and passing around a generous measure of solace over our cold brews. For a few hours our troubles were forgotten.

At 1800 an alert was sounded. Someone had reported a force moving a few klicks away and Lieutenant Nelson, ever in search of glory, volunteered the 2nd Platoon. Grumbling and moaning, we staggered back to the platoon tent, picked up our weapons and web gear, then formed up outside. I put on my helmet and decided, since I was not feeling any pain, to have some fun with the situation.

"Platoon, A-ten-shun! Now, listen and listen tight. We're gonna meet those APCs at the gate in five minutes. We're gonna double-time down there, singing and yelling like Trailblazers—the best damn platoon in the whole U.S. Army. Are you ready?"

"Yes, sergeant!" They roared out the answer as the other platoons looked at us wide-eyed. Knippel, of the 3rd Herd, yelled over, "You guys ain't so fuckin' hot, Pete. You act like you're the only real troops over here, but we're as good as you."

"Who's going out now, asshole? When the going gets tough, the 2nd Platoon gets going."

I faced the platoon and did my best DI imitation. "Pla-toon, ten-shun! Right *faace!* Forward—*maarch! Lay-eft, raht, lay-eft.* Double time—*ho!*"

I began singing one of the refrains that all recruits learn no matter where they took their basic training. "Here we go, Blazers, here we go!"

Then I switched to "Gotta run! Love to run! Gotta kill! Love to kill!" as we moved down the road to the gate. As we loped past the officer's mess, I saw Colonel Miller with Lieutenant Guidry and few other officers looking at us and shaking their heads. Since we were still in the Army, where nothing ever goes completely right, the APCs were late at the gate and the alcohol-inspired, almost magical spell was broken. Sergeant Nuckols came strolling down to us, shaking his head and grinning.

"You guys are nuts. You know what Colonel Miller said? He said, 'Them's not soldiers. Them's savages.' "

I laughed and wiped the sweat off my face. It had been fun, in a perverse way, and it had cleared away the bitching and moaning. When they arrived, we jumped on the tracks and headed around the perimeter, then southwest toward the site where the enemy had been spotted. The APCs halted while we scanned the area, which appeared to be deserted until I saw movement near a bush about a hundred meters away. I nudged Allen, who had spent five days at a sniper school in April learning how to kill from a distance and now lugged a heavy M-14 so he could prove it.

"Allen, you got a tracer round for that 14?"

He reached into his pocket and handed over a tracer and then I asked for the weapon. I released his magazine, jacked the round into the chamber and took aim. Then I held up and spoke to Allen again. "You know, you remind me of Barney Fife, who couldn't carry a loaded gun. Whenever trouble started, he'd reach in his pocket for his bullet. Anyway, I am about to put a round into the top of a bush where a VC is hiding, gentlemen."

They laughed as I settled into a firing position, then popped the round where I had last seen the movement. The tracer laid down its blazing orange path in the growing dusk and a Vietnamese man stepped out with his hands up after the round whistled into his hiding place. Several troops opened up and the poor guy hit the ground. When the firing stopped, he stood up and waved his hands, trying to surrender. I tried to stop laughing and yelled, "All right, you dead-eyes, take him prisoner. We'll be here all night if you keep trying to hit him. Bring him in."

I leaned back against the .50-caliber gun on the top of the track to speak to the officer in charge of the APCs. "Sir, do you have some rope so we can tie ol' Uncle Ho's arms. We'll take him back to the colonel for supper."

The lieutenant looked at me and shook his head slowly. "You guys are fucked up. Let's get the hell out of here."

"Sounds good. There's beer to be drunk and lies to be told. OK, Savages, let's go home!"

Even though I suspected the Vietnamese had a weapon stashed nearby, we couldn't have found it in the dark, so I made sure everybody was loaded on and we turned for home. We made it back without further incident, turned in our prisoner and headed back to the EM club to top off our night. We were feeling pretty good about ourselves and proceeded to let everybody within earshot know about it. We could see the looks on the faces of the REMFs, and it wasn't envy—but we didn't care. We were the Blazers, no—we were the Savages.

Martinez and I headed down the dusty road to the main gate the next morning, then turned left and walked along Highway 1, the dirty main street of the place we called Chu Lai. We scouted out all the hovels and finally found a somewhat decent place to sit ourselves down and have a drink. We spent the morning consuming a goodly amount of 33 beer and totally ignored our 1200 curfew. A rather large Marine was also in the place, drinking and letting everybody know how the Marines had cleaned up the countryside. I let it pass for a while, but as much as the beer had loosened his tongue, it had fried my brain. I started getting angry the longer he bragged, so I finally had to ask him, "If you jarheads have really cleaned the VC out of this area, who the hell has been killing and wounding the men of Charlie Company for the past month?"

"Ah, there's nothin' out there. You guys are just the fucked-up Army—the Marines have killed everything."

Martinez poked me in the arm and growled at me. "Pete, I'm usually the guy who gets hot. What the hell are you doing with this jarhead? Let's go."

"No, man. He owes us an apology for badmouthing us and lying. Marine, you're wrong and you should face up to it."

"Why don't you Army pussies just run along to your camp."

He was standing now, spurred on by liquor and ready to do battle, as was I, but before anything happened, the MPs came into the hooch and told us to head back to camp, since curfew was two hours ago. I reluctantly put on my cap and stepped out into the punishing afternoon sun, then moseyed toward the gate. Something inside me had apparently wanted my face to get beaten on, but my senses were slowly coming back as we returned to our platoon tent.

The place was like a nursing home during naptime—no movement at all in the heat. The guys were scattered all around the floor, so I picked up the platoon radio and headed for the shade of a nearby bamboo thicket where I threw down my poncho liner and tried to nap. As I dozed gently in the late afternoon, the radio came alive with a message.

"2–1, this is 2–5—are you there? 2–1, come in."

"Go ahead, 2–5. This better be good."

"I need a man for NCO prep school—who ya got?"

I hesitated. I had promised Martinez would be the next to go, but I didn't want to lose a good man now. I decided to make one of my famous bargains with the Ranger.

"2–5, Martinez is the man, but I need a replacement and Patterson wants to join my squad. Could you spare him?"

"2–1, you're always trying to get my RTOs. I'll give you Patterson, you give me a good man to carry the radio. Send Martinez in the morning and check with me. 2–5, out."

Radio procedure had become more relaxed to fit in with the

atmosphere of base camp. This was a place to ease away from the harsh realities and burdens of the war, a place to rest your body and your mind, although I needed alcohol to ease the pain in my heart.

All the beer I had been consuming had dulled my senses and eased my nightmares. I wasn't forgetting anything that had happened, but it wasn't pervading my every thought at this time; I considered that an improvement and to the extent that it helped me forget, I thanked the beer. In the boonies, I had slept only an hour or so most nights so I didn't have time for dreams, and my nerves were constantly on edge. Hill 54 was helping rejuvenate my body—my mind would have to take care of itself.

When I gave Martinez the news, he fought to conceal his elation, but it bubbled through. He led a patrol to the EM club for more beer, then to the mess hall where we scrounged a few pieces of ice. Back at the tent, we set up our waste barrel cooler and began drinking in earnest. One of the company LRRPs, Stach, found a guitar and began singing Simon and Garfunkel songs. We all joined the mournful chorus of "Homeward Bound" and let the melancholy roll over us. It was just another night on Hill 54.

In the morning the 2nd Platoon slowly and reluctantly readied their gear for patrol duty. At 1000 hours we marched in quick step to the front gate where we boarded APCs. I mounted the first one and set up on the front edge, according to my death wish. As we headed out of the main gate, I saw Martinez standing at attention. I whipped a salute at him and got a beauty in return, so I yelled:

"Do good, dammit—you're representing the Savages!"

He grinned and waved and the APCs moved down Highway 1 to the south, passing by small stands where Vietnamese would sell anything to the rich Americans, even their families. We turned off the road and plunged into the garden of an elderly couple who stared daggers at us, then began cursing in Vietnamese. I don't know why the officer in charge of the tracks picked that spot to head west, but I suspected it was the general attitude of most ugly Americans—we're here to help these people, so let's destroy their crops and villages, use their women, then give them money and expect them to be grateful. In an area where we were supposedly pacifying the countryside and winning hearts and minds, we were doing neither.

The patrol headed west for two more klicks, then dismounted and scoured the countryside, which appeared to be deserted. In the late afternoon we found a site for an NDP, then waited until dark to move in. We set the platoon up in a perimeter, then I took an OP out about seventy-five meters and set up behind a huge bush. The moon was bright, so Ralph McQueen, whom we had made RTO, and I struck up a conversation about the world. We carried on in low tones for about twenty minutes before the CP called with a succinct message, "Shut the fuck up out there!"

It wasn't the time for one of my wisecrack answers, so I let the harsh message stand unchallenged. As we lay there, resting and listening to the sounds of the Vietnamese coastal plains, I heard another transmission on the handset, which was now pressed to my ear as I pulled the early watch. The brigade LRRPs were under fire somewhere in the low mountains to our west. The 2nd Platoon was put on standby to attempt a rescue or reinforcement of the five-man patrol, but apparently the siege was lifted and nothing further happened that night.

We moved two klicks south the next day, to a stream where we held up for a few hours and were able to wash the dust and sweat off. That evening, near dusk, we set up in an ambush nearby, then heard another of those mysterious intelligence reports that crop up every few days. This one had over 100 VC or NVA reported in our area. We immediately moved to the nearest high ground, a low hill overlooking a smaller trail, but they didn't come our way.

Given the success they were having with the type of war they were waging, there was no reason to believe that Charlie would come out in force. Still, the grand plan of the U.S. Army seemed to consist of our being able to thwart the sniping, the booby traps and mines, the line probing and the sapper attacks until they did strike en masse. Then, we would destroy them and call it a great victory. Considering the climate, the terrain and the godawful uncertainty of events, our task was immense.

The APCs, as faithful as a Greyhound bus, met us the next afternoon for pickup and conveyance back to Hill 54. I headed immediately for the shower brigade where Underhill and I took turns pouring water into the overhead barrel for one another.

After a shave, we walked down to the wire and purchased some 33 from a lad no more than ten, then found a deserted bunker to relax in. I held my breath when I took a drink to avoid the smell of the preservatives, but the cool beer hit the spot and we drank in silence.

The 2nd Platoon had the night off but the 3rd Marines from down the road had a Custer (in June, an ambush was a Custer) that was taking fire, so they pulled back and we went on alert for a while. No one really wanted to go out and get his butt shot at while rescuing a damned Marine, but we would follow orders. Luckily, none came. I wondered if my jarhead friend was ducking fire from those VC that he had cleaned out of the area; the thought made me chuckle to myself. Careful, next you'll be talking to yourself and answering. I grabbed another 33 and chugged it.

There was a common malady among the grunts in the field in Vietnam: as you moved through the jungle and along paddies, you couldn't avoid getting scratched by the ever-present thorns and briers. Without proper care, which was impractical if not impossible in our circumstance, they would invariably become infected. Pus-filled sores would form, then fester and become like boils. These sores would itch and burn all day, then ache when the temperature dropped at night. In the boonies, when it was safe we tried to wash them, then let the sun dry them so they would scab over.

Here at base camp I headed to the dispensary to see what they could do for me as both arms were nearly covered with the ugly festering sores that we called jungle rot. I sat on a bench and waited to be called in, but the medic who came to the door saw my problem and handed me some Phisohex medicated soap to wash them with and a needle with which to lance the cores. I took the offerings and asked, "Is this modern medicine's answer to jungle rot? I should just get some leeches, huh, Doc?"

"They would probably work as well as anything we have," he answered, then shrugged and added, "Dig 'em out and clean 'em. That's all the more we can do."

When he said "all the more," he stamped himself a Southerner to me, probably a Georgian. I was finally getting accustomed to the inflections, drawls and colloquialisms that made up the regional accents of the U.S.—just another benefit of modern Army life. Here in a combat zone, we rolled the accents together with radio jargon and came up with our own language, sort of a jungle-speak.

I poked at a few of the sores to get some blood and pus flowing but the pain was excruciating, even to a combat-toughened grunt, so I decided to soak them to soften the afflicted areas. The medic then coated the sores with an antiseptic salve and wrapped my arms from elbow to wrist with gauze and tape. I walked self-consciously to the 2nd Platoon tent and became the target of quite a few ribs from the squad.

"Did you get an *owee* in the field, little fella? Did the nice doctor kiss it and make it all good?"

"I'll show you what the doctor kissed and you can do the same."

It was all in good fun and I took it that way. That night, after getting orders to take out an OP, I tore off the white bandages, which would shine like a beacon in the moonlight. The sores still ached, but I saw no way to continue treatment without an extended furlough from field duty, which wasn't going to happen.

On June 7, I took my squad to the main gate where we loaded onto the backs of tanks and went on patrol. We moved up Highway 1 several klicks, then turned left and headed up a road along the side of a steep hill. The ride was bumpy and rough, so I tried to shift my position to get more comfortable. Just then, the tank hit a large rock and I was thrown over the side. I managed to grab on to a metal rung with one hand and keep my legs free of the track, but I was in a precarious position. I glanced down and saw I was dangling over the edge of the road where the hill dropped off for a couple hundred feet. It wasn't a sheer drop, but the incline was steep enough to make me roll most of the way down the hill. It didn't take much imagination to realize that I was about one more slip away from big trouble.

A strange calmness came over me and I looked at Ralph MacQueen, who was manning my radio. I maintained my grip with my left hand and reached out my right, with my rifle, to him, saying in the calmest voice I could muster under the circumstances, "Ralph, would you take my weapon, please?"

He grabbed it; I grabbed onto another rung and, with a loud grunt, swung myself back on board. Ralph laughed so hard I thought he would pass out or fall off.

"Pete, you were so cool. I would have panicked and fell, but you stayed as cool as an ice cube, man. 'Ralph, would you take my weapon, please?' You kill me."

I shrugged and we continued on our way like it hadn't happened. Hell, the jungle was full of VC trying to kill my ass and now I tried to fall off a tank and over a cliff. I couldn't let that happen; nobody would believe it.

The tanks let us off on the top of a bare hill where the sun seared into our bodies and brains, again robbing us of our spirit. By the time they picked us up, we were tired, fried and mad at the world. When we got to Hill 54, I headed for the EM club and purchased two cases of beer for the squad. We tried to replenish all the lost fluids while celebrating my receiving official orders for promotion to E-5, effective May 30, 1967. I was now an E-5, a buck sergeant.

Kevin Patterson, my new squad member who was certifiably loony, and I talked well into the night. The feelings of despair and impending doom continued to weigh on me, but the beer was a wonderful buffer. I wrote in my tiny journal, "Ralph helped save me, but I'm not very confident. When will I get it?" Then I lay down on my poncho liner spread across the board floor and slept.

The 1st Squad got the next day off, in return for night duty—an OP. While it was still only moderately hot in the morning hours, I took a walk around most of the perimeter. The road from the main gate made a Y at the base of the hill—to the right was the mess hall and kitchens, the EM club, chopper pads for resupply, large barrack tents (forty feet by fifteen feet) and water tanks for the troops on this side of the hill. I stopped and cut back along a footpath past the crappers and piss tubes, stayed above the dispensary and stopped into the company CP to see what was happening. Malarik was sleeping on a cot there, an NCO perk that I disdained. No one else was stirring, so I moved on.

The path led me back to the road on the south side of the hill, where I glanced in on the supply hooches and then headed back down toward the gate. On my right now was the chapel and quar-

ters for the rear echelon personnel. I spotted a small boy at the
gate with some bottles of Coke and beer, so I purchased three bottles of soda and stopped into the barbershop manned by two Vietnamese barbers. It was located just inside the wire and jokes were
made about it being a spy nest for the VC.

I sat down in one of the U.S. Army barber chairs and gave a
soda to each of the smiling barbers, just as I did back home. I
let one of them cut my hair short, then paid him a few MPC and
headed back toward my tent. I looked at the ubiquitous bunkers
at the perimeter, which were designed to repel the Communist
hordes that we weren't likely to see, as I passed by. They were
all the same—square, dirty and uninviting, except in an attack.
The platoon hooches were located about halfway up the gentle
sloping hill and there were more bunkers scattered around inside the perimeter in case of mortar attack.

I passed by a tent where a few of the NCOs slept and
thought about Sergeant Kushinski, now banished to the Recon
Platoon, where maybe he's found his niche. He was a good
enough soldier, just hated officers and drank a little too
much—well, he's not alone there. I climbed the steps at the
back of the 2nd Platoon tent and looked inside. Since line
troops and REMFs avoided each other like the plague, most of
the men were just lying around on the board floor, trying to get
comfortable. Activities on the day off included sleeping, reading and writing letters, listening to Armed Forces Radio, talking or just staring.

When a grunt had been in-country for any extended period
and had seen any real action, he developed the look—some
called it the thousand-yard stare. It was an almost blank look
that said nothing, but conveyed everything and became the
fighting man's all-encompassing tool, shield and means of escape. Some crossed over, propelled by awful realities into a
nether world that probably exists inside all of us, returning only
to communicate with nods and grunts. There was no fire in the
eye, just blackness, emptiness. You could see forever . . . and
ever.

I sent the squad out without me to the OP that night, then
got a few beers and joined the crew at the CP, so I could moni-
tor the radio. Sergeant Nuckols chided me, "Don't baby-sit 'em,
Pete. Let 'em alone. They're grown men and they'll be OK."

I nodded at him, then grinned, winked and answered, "But think about how long it took me to shape this squad up. I had to trade around and send guys away to school just to get rid of them. Now, I've got the best squad in 'Nam."

I knew Malarik was in the next room, and would rise to the bait. "Does that mean you wanted to get rid of me, Pete? Me, Danny Malarik, the Great Hungarian?"

"Danny, I told Sergeant Nuck that the 1st Squad wasn't big enough for the two of us."

"That's right, Pete, you did. Now, I've got to send him to the 1st Platoon to get rid of him."

Staff Sergeant Able of the 1st was leaning back against a footlocker, looking at us with his one good eye—the other had been scratched badly by a bramble, probably an enemy thorn, and was a deep red and nearly closed. He smiled and joined in on the roasting.

"Thanks, guys. What the hell am I gonna do with this trigger-happy gypsy? I need guys who'll follow orders."

The story of the premature ambush had made the rounds on the hill, but Danny was bearing up under the abuse by refusing to admit his error and showing absolutely no remorse. He truly believed he had done no wrong.

"Well, Sergeant Able, we could trade him to the Marines. They always need more cannon fodder," I added.

"Nah, I wouldn't do that to anybody, even Malarik."

We continued drinking and haranguing the Hungarian until the omnisicient company clerk came in and announced, "Lights out, men," and meant it.

While the others bedded down on cots at the CP, I stumbled along the path to our tent. I noticed that it seemed hotter and smellier here on the lee side of the hill. I took my poncho and liner back up the hill, where I lay gazing at the heavens. The mellifluous odor emanating from the crappers and piss tubes hung in the moist night air, permeating my olfactory senses with every breath. Ah, the essence of man. Take away my burdens, dear Lord, I prayed.

There was no beer to be found the next day, so Sergeant Nuck and I commandeered a jeep and went on a search patrol. We drove south on Highway 1, then turned into a Navy pier, where Nuckols tried to talk an ensign out of a few cases, but he said the Marines had cleaned him out. We finally wound up in a club for ROK troops where the Ranger told stories of his days on the peninsula during that war. His use of a few Korean phrases and the names of cities and provinces in the country convinced them he was for real so they sold us a few cases and we headed for home, expecting to be shot or court-martialed and not giving a damn. However, no one seemed to notice we were missing, which was almost the worst punishment of all.

Another day of lying around in the dirt of Hill 54 left me ready to go back to Death Valley—almost. We put our beer on ice to let it cool, then sucked it up at night. There was no activity in our sector for the third night in a row. Maybe the papers we found on the dead VC officer were right. Maybe they would try to take Chu Lai in July. Well, if that must be, let's get at it.

The discovery of a bamboo viper in the thicket I had been sleeping near chased me back inside the tent to sleep. I stepped gingerly around Betta's legs, which were sticking out into the aisle we had left down the middle of the tent. He was suffering from an infection in his right leg, which caused him great pain. He was medicating with antibiotics and painkillers and spent most of his time sleeping in a near-delirium and working his way along the floor into the aisle again.

Then someone would bump his sore leg and cause him to start moaning. He belonged in a hospital, but an infantryman couldn't get sent there unless he was seriously wounded or running a temperature of 104. I wondered what the requirements were for REMFs. I listened to the others snore and fart for a long while, then dozed fitfully.

In the morning the squad moved out once again with the APCs and spent the day guarding 105mm howitzers while they registered. We sat on top of another hill and watched them blast away; it seemed to me that HQ was just trying to find something to do to keep us busy. That night, as we again replenished our lost fluids with beer, the 3rd Squad was sent out to chase another VC rumor that was baseless.

I had been baked almost brown in the sun and the beer made me light-headed and almost drunk in a short while. I walked away from the group, found a deserted interior bunker and lay down on top. After a few minutes I passed out or went asleep and woke up at 0230. I got my bearings, then returned to the tent and thought about tomorrow. We were heading back to the field, back to the business at hand and I had better be ready. The beer, which had laid to rest many of my nightmares, had also dulled my senses and taken away the edge that I needed. It was time to pull myself together.

29

The 2nd platoon climbed onto the APCs that lurked at the main gate like a row of armed turtles, then rode down the highway again. Once more we turned west across some farmer's field and I imagined this happening to my father's farm and the anguish it would cause. We patrolled along the coastal plain, still east of the first hill range, throughout the day, but saw nothing. On the way back to camp the lead truck got hung up while crossing a steep ditch, then mired down quickly in the loose sand.

The next APC behind it turned around and backed up, then hooked on with a chain and tried to pull the first one. It, too, became mired, as the crew cursed their fate and the approaching dark; they were genuinely frightened at the possibility of being out in the field after dark. The infantrymen merely lay around on the ground and ate a few C rations and made bad jokes.

Finally a third truck with a longer chain was able to stay on solid ground and pull the others out. Once they were all out, the APCs headed for home again, stopping only to drop my squad and a gun crew at a stream crossing where we set up in night ambush. It was cooler there than at base camp and the night was calm.

I let the men wash up in pairs at the stream in the morning, then we headed onto a small knoll to watch the trail. We had been advised that eight VC armed with submachine guns were moving through the area, but they didn't come our way. The 2nd Squad had spent the night a few hundred meters away from us and today they were ambushing the same trail as we were, on the other side of the low hill range. Just before noon, five VC, one armed, walked into their sights. They killed one and captured four others and, once more, became the darling of the platoon and company as the praise for them came over the radio. Patterson snorted as he listened, "That fuckin' squad is looking for medals and they don't give a damn who dies to get 'em."

"Yeah, but, when Nelson's got a tough job, we'll get the call." I had added that out of bravado and a little envy, but at the same time I was relieved that the VC hadn't come our way. I knew, however, that we were ready for anything. I was proud of my squad and certain that they would acquit themselves well under most circumstances. I had impressed on them countless times my feelings about responsibilities: "Do your job; do it well and your tour will be easier and safer, for you and for your fellow soldier—me."

The sun was, as always, unyielding, so we stayed in the shade the rest of the day. We remained as alert as we could, but the heat was creating a state of torpidity among the squad members. I waited until the welcome night enveloped us, then led the ambush team down to an overhang where we could cover the trail as it entered a pass between the hills. We lost radio contact with the others because of our particular position, but I was cognizant of their exact location and we needed merely to climb the hill to regain our voice.

After another quiet night, we began humping toward Hill 54 early in the morning to escape most of the heat. By taking only a short break, we covered the five klicks in less than two hours, then threw off our gear and rested. After showering and changing clothes, we took the rest of the day off and were able to catch up on our correspondence.

I spoke with the Staff Sergeant Cain and others in the 2nd Squad about their recent success. They were buoyant and a little cocky, but I didn't mind. I actually hoped they would get called on a little more when things were tight, but I knew that my squad would be there. I expected and wanted to be the squad chosen to lead the platoon or company through; it was a matter of pride, and logic. If my squad was leading, more soldiers would get through the crisis safely. I firmly believed that, and while it was a source of pride, it was also a tremendous burden on my shoulders.

I was down to my last three months, plus two weeks or so, and I wondered if I could stand up to the stress of survival and of leadership for that long. I also worried about what would happen to my squad when I was gone—who would take over? Alexus would DEROS about the same time I would; Martinez would be the logical choice if he made sergeant at the NCO school, otherwise, maybe Patterson. He had shown a real knack for infantry tactics as used in Vietnam and was considering Ranger School after his tour ended.

As we lay around for two more days, resting, I thought more about these things and became convinced that I needed another leave; I needed to get my mind straight again. If I could get a seven-day leave next month, I could come back refurbished and ready to complete the last two months of my tour with renewed vigor. It would also be, perhaps, my last chance to see more of the Orient.

I decided to aim for Bangkok or Taipei, since GIs who had been there had informed me that they were the cheapest places to visit. The leave would also give Nuckols and the lieutenant a chance to break in a new squad leader. By the end of the second day I was convinced that this was a necessary course of action, so I headed to the company CP, armed with all my arguments and reasons.

"Sir, I'm a mess inside. I need a leave to get straight. Can you help me get a week off next month?"

Lieutenant Nelson thought about it for a minute, which I took to be a good sign. He seemed to be weighing the options. "Sergeant Pete, I'm going to be leaving the field late next month to become the executive officer for the company. I want you to stay with me until then, and as XO (executive officer), I'll get you that leave in August or September."

Sergeant Nuckols quickly raised up off his cot, put his finger on my chest and spoke forcefully. "Pete, you ain't gettin' outta the field for no damn leave. We need you, so get your men ready. We're headin' out in the mornin'."

I trudged back to the platoon tent and told the squad to clean their gear and weapons and replenish their ammo. While they were doing their chores, I dug into my emergency fund for a few bucks, then rounded up two cases of beer and some ice and we spent the evening sipping beer and listening to Bravo Company on the radio as they sprang a successful ambush and killed several VC. I felt like we were at a football game and our team had scored a touchdown. We sacked in early; tomorrow we would see Sniper Valley again and it could be tumultuous, even deadly.

The feeling of despondency began closing in on me as I stared at the night sky. Something is going to happen, but what, and when?

The refrain from a popular song, "Here we come again," kept going through my mind as we neared our drop-off LZ. The door gunners of our Hueys prepped the area with machine-gun fire, then disgorged us in a small paddy. We took no sniper fire, but little time was wasted as we formed into platoons and moved out. I put Patterson on point and he led us along the trail away from the small valley where we had landed.

As the sun began to take its toll, the platoon moved gingerly through a brush-lined pass between two small hills and into a small village. The place was abandoned, but we checked all the hooches and bunkers still standing for recent activity and found no fresh signs. Late in the afternoon we moved to a night ambush position in a grove of trees adjacent to the trail we had followed into the ville. The 3rd Platoon, two klicks away, reported two WIA—one from a booby trap, one from a sniper.

At the CP, Sergeant Nuckols informed me that we would be trying a few different tactics, trying to catch Charlie off guard and presenting less stationary targets. "We're gonna scout out night ambush sites in the afternoon, then move off a klick or so to pick up resupply. When it starts to get dark, we'll move back into the Custer site. During the day, we'll set up small ambushes along trail junctions or on high ground. We're gonna try to wait for him to move, then get him."

"Aren't these the tactics we talked about last month in Death Valley? Did you finally get through to somebody?"

"I hope so, Pete. I talked to the loo-tenant about it and he talked to the Old Man. I feel better knowing we'll be workin' this way. We were sittin' ducks before."

"If we could just pick off a couple of snipers, the morale would sure jump. The men are scared as hell out here—and they should be."

"Are you scared, Pete?" Nuckols had that sorry-I-asked-but-I-have-to-know look in his eyes.

I hesitated only a second. "Me? Scared?"

I paused for dramatic effect, then continued in a lower voice that I tried to lace with conviction—heartfelt conviction. "Every fuckin' second of every fuckin' day. I don't eat, can't sleep, can't think right out here. If I survive, I know I'll never be the same as I was before—never!"

Nuckols avoided my eyes and stared hard at the ground. "Same-same. You described me perfectly, man."

The VC avoided our ambush site, so we held tight through morning chow, then I led my squad on patrol into another abandoned village. We set up an observation post in some heavy brush and watched as some women and children moved back into the rubble, picking through the debris, possibly trying to put their lives back in order. They had been unceremoniously rousted and forced to move out with only what belongings they could carry. I thought about how painful it must have been for them to leave the only home most of them had ever known—forced out by the Saigon government as personified by the Ruff-Puffs and their sponsors, the Americans. As much as I tried to empathize with them, I had to refrain from concerning myself with that facet of our war-making effort while I was on a mission. I had men to guide and worry about. History would have to pass judgment on our efforts.

In the afternoon we returned to the platoon CP, then doubled back to the paddy to meet the chopper. At dusk we moved into the brush near our observation post for an overnight ambush. There was plenty of movement in the village—I suspected some of the Vietnamese were trying to reestablish their families in the ruins of what once had been their home. Their plight continued to weigh on a part of my mind, but I kept my eyes and senses focused on my task. Nobody came near our position and there was no movement in the ville at dawn, so the platoon headed west.

The acting CO, Lieutenant Guidry, had been with the 2nd Platoon for two days, but was ready to join the 1st, so we met them at their observation position, dropped him off, then headed southeast. We humped slowly and cautiously for a little over two klicks, then set up on a trail junction for the day. Late in the afternoon, I took a recon patrol to scout for a night location. I picked a highly defensible position on a knoll with good fields of fire and a high bank overhanging the main trail.

I took the patrol back to the platoon CP and we ate our evening C rations (I nibbled some crackers washed down with warm water) and waited for dark. As the heavy evening shadows dissolved into the growing dusk, we moved into the night defensive position and set up a perimeter. Lieutenant Nelson and his FO began calling in DefCons, then for good measure put some high explosives on the hill mass to the west. Immediately there was a secondary explosion which I heard and spotted from my position and reported to the CP. Lieutenant Nelson looked bemused as I told him what had happened.

"Good job, Pete. At dawn, take your squad up there and check it out."

I thought to myself, "Thanks a lot, sir. See if I ever report another secondary." I got a couple of hours sleep on the hillside, but something kept intruding into my dreams. We had had three days with no casualties, but it was just a matter of time until Charlie caught onto our new tactics and adjusted his own. When that happened, I hoped we had enough sense to make another shift—with that in mind, I began to mull over what else we could try out here. When I finally fell back asleep just before dawn, I dreamed that a giant pair of eyes were pursuing me everywhere I went, even behind a tree. I thrashed myself awake and found some coffee. "Not gonna let me rest, are you, guys?" I whispered to the demons as I lit the heat tab and waited for the water to get hot.

The platoon moved out early in the morning and crossed the wide paddy to the west. The bulk of the men waited in the brush while I took my squad up the hill to check out the secondary explosion I had noted last night. We were operating on the very western edge of our AO, close to 101st Airborne Division territory. I hoped that our higher had coordinated our movements with theirs—I didn't want to get ambushed by another American unit, especially not by an airborne outfit.

We investigated an old campsite with some fresh signs that caused us to move along the ridgeline cautiously. This was where Charlie was hanging out when he wasn't harassing the troops of Charlie Company, but he wasn't around to fight today. We continued to search, but could find no sign of recent explosions, so we headed back down the hill.

Lieutenant Nelson decided to call in for a resupply chopper while we were still near the big paddy, but when the pilot brought it in, he was greeted by automatic weapons fire. The crew quickly tossed out the supplies and got the bird airborne in a few seconds—they had the routine well practiced by now. As they pulled up, one more burst tore through the humid air, adding an insolent exclamation point to the attack. The FO called in Boomer to pound the offending hillside while we picked up the supplies and headed into the tree line on the other side of the paddy.

Sergeant Nuckols sent my squad ahead to scout an NDP north of the large paddy. I spotted a bomb crater about twenty meters inside the tree line and we set up around that for the night. We put an OP-type ambush with a gun crew back at the edge of the woods where the trail came across the paddy and lay in wait. I wasn't able to sleep and couldn't see the stars because of the foliage, so I broke squelch on my radio to let the OP know I was coming out to join them. I left Alexus in charge of the squad, but I was certain that we were safely ensconced around the crater.

The crater was away from the trail and the VC couldn't creep up on it without announcing themselves with noise, so the only vulnerable spot was the ambush. It was hidden back in the brush, but since GIs have trouble remaining quiet for long, a VC moving along the trail could be alerted enough to throw a grenade and *di di mau.*

I paid my nightly homage to the stars, then spent some time trying to spot something through the starlight scope, which again proved itself to be a useless tool in my hands. After an hour or so I needlessly told the men to be extra alert, then crept back to the silent perimeter, using our prearranged number signal to pass safely. The password of the day was "fourteen." When challenged with a number less than that, I must answer with one that would add up to the password number. It was simpler than memorizing a password and its challenge, although occasionally we had a trooper who had to hesitate as he counted up his fingers and toes.

As the morning broke and light filtered through the jungle canopy, Lieutenant Nelson was moving to the edge of the bomb crater to relieve himself. He stopped, leaned over to inspect the hole a little closer, then yelled "Jesus H. Himself! There's a live bomb in here. Nice goin', Pete, you wagon-wheeled us around a 500 pounder. Sidney, get me the Old Man."

Sidney Lee, now solidly entrenched as the RTO for the lieutenant, called Charlie 6 as Lieutenant Nelson shook himself down then grabbed the handset. Charlie 6 responded to the problem, "I'll get back to you."

A half hour later as we sat there alternately making jokes and praying the VC wouldn't drop a mortar round squarely in the crater, the message came down from the CO. "Leave a security squad to guide the engineers; demolition team on the way. Move the others at least 500 meters away."

I took my squad and the FO's RTO due west across the narrow part of the paddy and partway up the steep hill marking the end of our AO. We set up in a day ambush along a trail near an abandoned VC campsite. Sally, now leading the 3rd Squad, and McQueen, Nuckol's new RTO, moved about 200 meters north of my position where they set up near a small village. The 2nd Squad, under Sergeant Cain, waited near the paddy for the engineers. After they arrived, they worked about two hours carefully setting a detonation charge on the bomb before the message came over the horn.

"Fire in the hole! Big fire in the hole!"

Then a tremendous explosion shook the ground and sent shrapnel flying through the surrounding brush. Patterson and I shared a glance as we listened to the dirt and metal rain on the paddy below us, then he grinned and said, "Can you imagine what would have been left of us if Charlie had booby-trapped that mother? Nothin' but puckered-up assholes—wow!"

"Yeah, I can imagine. Able and I picked up what was left of that guy from the 3rd Herd. You remember, he was in that hooch when the artillery round cooked off a few weeks ago."

I shuddered involuntarily as I thought of it. Patterson continued to reflect, then spoke again. "If that happens to me, I hope that at least my middle finger and my rectum are intact. Then I can still give the finger to the world and let 'em kiss my ass."

He laughed so hard at his own remark that he had to sit down and collect himself. I chuckled and watched as the chopper flew in to pick up the engineers, then heard the radio come alive once more.

"2–1 and 2–3, wagon wheel with 2–2 and the CP. Out."

I gave the squad a saddle-up signal and stood up to buckle my web belt. From somewhere near, several bursts of automatic weapons fire resounded almost at once. I hit the ground, grabbed my rifle and listened to the relentless, angry flat chatter of the M-16s interspersed with the more hollow urgent popping of an AK-47 and some other unknown weapon. I realized quickly that Sally's squad had opened up and was also taking fire. I held the radio handset to my ear, waiting for a break in the firing. There was a brief lull, then three more M-16 shots, then silence. I held the mouthpiece close and spoke slowly, belying my feelings.

"2–3, 2–3, this is 2–1. Do you need help? What's happenin'?"

McQueen answered with a loud, breathless voice. "Three dinks with grease guns came out of the village and saw us. They opened up and Underhill and Sally shot all three."

"Are they all dead?" I could hear my own voice and it was almost as excited as McQueen's.

"Deader'n fuck! And no friendly casualties."

"Good job, 2–3. We'll be holding here about 200 mikes south if you need us."

I passed the word to the men and told them to be alert for any stragglers coming down the trail. Tension was replacing the excitement in my head as I knew there could be more enemy coming down off the hill to check on the firing. I heard McQueen report to Lieutenant Nelson and get the unnecessary orders to search the bodies. They removed the weapons and grenades from the corpses, then pulled back to join the 2nd Squad and the CP. After they were in position, I brought my squad across the paddy and made the platoon whole again. The 2nd Squad took point and we moved to a small brushy knoll about two klicks away where we set up our perimeter, then dug in for the night. Word came down for the squad leaders to meet at the CP. As we sat down, the radio crackled again.

"Charlie 6, this is Golden 6 Romeo. Do you have recommendations for citations?"

Before Charlie 6 could answer, Lieutenant Nelson got on the net. "This is Charlie 2–6. Underhill is recommended for the Silver Star."

The CO and Golden 6 acknowledged his interruption as Nelson basked in reflected glory, but I felt a wrong was being committed, so I interjected mildly, but with a definite undertone so no one could doubt my purpose. "What about Sally? He was there, too, and he's the squad leader."

I looked at Sally, who had a blank look on his face, as if he were still in shock. Underhill was also strangely quiet and morose, but he nodded as I spoke. The lieutenant added Sawlski's name to the list, then informed us that we had to return to the ambush site to take photos for battalion.

We looked at each other and I spoke, "Nobody wants to do that, sir. It's bad strategy and bad luck to go back there this soon and I think it's a repulsive idea to take pictures of dead bodies. I'm against it."

"We're going back at first light, Pete. You lead us, then you can take security around the village while we take the photos. You're dismissed. Good job, 2–3."

Duly chastened but hardly repentant, I gave Sally and Underhill a thumbs-up, then returned to my position to reflect on the day. The look on the faces of the two men told it all: they had taken automatic weapons fire close-in; had looked death in the eye and escaped. I knew what was going through their minds, over and over: "Why? Why am I alive and the VC dead? Where is the line drawn?"

It was almost too much for the mind to comprehend, so you try to accept it at face value. I closed my eyes and mumbled a silent and fervent invocation to whatever God was listening: "Peace be with you, Sawlski and Underhill—and with us all."

Late that night word came over the battalion net that the VC had used a .50-caliber machine gun to shoot down the chopper containing Batman 6, the commanding officer of the APC company that operated in our area—no word of casualties. The game was getting nastier.

As I cautiously led the platoon back to the battle site in the morning, I pondered this new piece of information: Charlie had Soviet and Czech rifles and grease guns and .50-caliber machine guns. It seemed like he was building up to something in the area—maybe *Chu Lai in July* was his objective. It would only be a matter of time, it seemed, before the VC put the men and the weapons together in the right place at the right time (albeit their time) and we would have the battle we were waiting for. Despite the fact that Charlie was doing well with his sniping and hit-and-run tactics, he could not win a war this way. If he wanted to win, he had to try to defeat a sizeable American force on the field. That was what the battalion was waiting for, but I hoped he wouldn't try it today.

We reached the area of the firefight just before noon and the bodies were still there. Lieutenant Nelson and Sergeant Nuckols took pictures while the 1st Squad pulled security. I noticed that Sawlski and Underhill avoided the scene and continued to remain silent. After the mission was completed, we retraced our steps and headed east. We broke for noon chow at our night position, then packed up and moved two more klicks to join the company CP. The sweat restained our fatigue shirts, adding another day's worth of salt to the stiff and stinky fabric.

When we finally reached the company perimeter and removed them, the shirts dried quickly and turned a chalky greenish-white from six days' perspiration—you could see each day's sweat line, like the cross-section of a tree. We took our position and I picked up mail and resupply items for the squad, then we washed up in the stream that made up the east side of our perimeter and rested in whatever shade we could find. One of the men was doodling with a felt-tip pen, so I borrowed it and printed "Savages" on one side of my steel pot cover and "Solitary Man" on the other.

The platoon stayed with the company in a night perimeter near the stream. I let my fatigue shirt hang on a small branch and dug a black T-shirt out of my pack to wear in the dark. The temperature dropped from three digits to the mid-80s at night and it was comfortable after the sun disappeared. It was also "Charlie time," but not near us that night.

It continued to be almost unbearably hot the next day. We stayed with Charlie 6 and moved to a new perimeter site back in the brush, then lay around in the afternoon to beat the heat. The foliage was extremely thick so there was plenty of shade and it would be difficult for the VC to sneak up on us. The 1st and 3rd had split off on their own, so we were the sole escort of the CO as he learned the ropes and the territory.

The 1st Platoon reported they had found an M-1 rifle and wanted credit for one kill, which the Old Man was delighted to give. If this travesty was being repeated throughout 'Nam, the enemy body count was being grossly overstated. The lies began at the bottom, as troops tried to please their platoon leaders and field officers tried to please their seniors with high counts, and almost certainly continued up the ladder to Westmoreland. If these inflated reports bred overconfidence or complacency, it could ultimately result in increased dangers for the line troop. The mind-set of an infantry officer who believes he can whip any enemy force with only a small unit because he believes the Americans are killing VC at a ten-to-one ratio could be the worst enemy for a GI in the bush.

Resupply had also been a problem since I had been in Vietnam. We had great difficulty in getting some supply items, such as a .45 pistol for the M-60 machine-gun carrier to wear as a side weapon, or K-bar knives, yet when we passed through battalion or brigade HQ, there were plenty of REMFs walking around with shiny .45s on their hips and a K-bar on their web belts. When we met one of these "toy soldiers," we would whip out a smart salute, then laugh and shake our heads.

As I lay there in the brush somewhere near Thon Hai 2 in Quang Ngai Province, I wondered if the supply division was exhibiting yet another symptom of Army overconfidence. The feeling could be, "Let's sell this stuff to the guys back here. Hell, the guys in the field are killing all the enemy, just look at the kill ratio. They don't need anything else." Maybe I was thinking too much, but lying there thinking was better than sleeping and dreaming those dreams.

In the morning the CO and Lieutenant Nelson sent Sergeant Nuckols and my squad on patrol along the stream. I led the patrol for a ways, then put Patterson on point to give him experience. As he replaced me, I told him, "Just sweep all the mines and booby traps out for me."

The thick growth and heat began to wear us down quickly,

so I proposed that we walk down the streambed for a while. Nuckols concurred and Pat and I stepped into the calf-high water. It felt cool and refreshing, so I dipped my filthy sweat towel into it and wrapped it around my neck, still dripping. I had been carrying the nearly-rotten towel for two months and it stank, but I rinsed it when I could and it felt good when we reached water and I could dip it. It was another item that the Army couldn't or wouldn't supply, so we purloined one when we could at base camp.

We moved downstream for about 200 meters until the water pooled up and got too deep. We fought our way back onto the bank through the heavy brush and finally found a small trail. There were signs of VC movement in the area: pressed-down grass, some torn paper and that smell—the smell of VC and of danger. I motioned to Nuckols, pointing to my nose and then touching my finger to my lips for silence. We found an empty bunker that I marked on my map, then I got word to report back to the CP for a short meeting.

When I got back, the word going around was that Alpha Company had captured forty-six VC. Later, after we settled into a night defensive position, I discussed this with Patterson.

"Alpha must have stumbled over some old Vietnamese civilians as they tried to surrender. No way in hell they could capture forty-six of anything. The old Alpha Army before November could have, but they were never the same after those battles over there."

"Hey, maybe they caught forty-six cases of the clap—VD, not VC, Pete." I ignored his gibe and continued to ramble on about my feelings.

"You know, this war is getting more and more fucked up, Pat. The way I see it all now is, I intend to be the best soldier I can as it pertains directly to me. No volunteering, no heroics except to save my own ass, for the next ninety days."

"You talk it, Pete, but when the shit hits, you'll be there in the front just like always."

I thought about that for a minute, then answered softly. "I hope not. I want to lay in the back and direct traffic. Let somebody else be a hero."

"I hear ya, guy. But if Charlie hits us tomorrow and pins us down, what'll you do?"

I couldn't tell if Pat was asking a question or making a rhetorical statement, so I answered. "Probably jump dead in his shit and put a real lick on him, hang him out to dry, put his shit in the wind, kick ass and take names."

He picked up on my lingo and jumped in, "Stack 'em up like cordwood, bring some pee. Did we forget any?"

I could hear him chuckling in a low growl as I crawled over to check on Alexus' position. It was my goal, my vow, to never let anyone fall asleep while on guard, so I checked whenever I was awake, which seemed to be all the time. Alexus was on guard and he gave me the finger and we both grinned in the pale moonlight. I whispered in a conspiratorial tone, "Listen, guy, battalion says there are 10,000 NVA coming right at your position tonight. Maybe you better give me your cans of peaches or fruit cocktail for safekeeping. I'll give them back to you in the morning, JP—or is it PJ?"

"It's Mr. Alexus to you and you can put my chopped eggs up your ass, but don't touch my fruit. Now, leave me alone so I can sleep."

I really liked Alexus, he seemed to view everything as though he had seen it all before and wasn't about to be bothered by it. Underneath that cool demeanor however, I suspected that he was smoldering like I was. I moved back to my position and lay down behind a small tree to wait for Charlie, my watch, dawn or sleep, whichever came first.

We picked up yet another trail early in the morning, moving slowly from one valley to another through a brushy pass. Alexus put his team on point and I came in just behind him. The heavy brush made the entire trail a potential ambush site, so we edged along and were still a klick away from our destination at noon. We broke for chow and I put my squad on the south side of the trail on a gentle grass-covered slope, then opened a can of crackers and a tin of cheese.

The 2nd Squad was on the other side of the trail, just at the edge of the brush. As I munched I heard a grunt yell, "Grenade!"

I took a quick glance on my way to the ground and saw someone picking up something and throwing it into the brush, then I heard an explosion. The platoon went on immediate full alert, facing out with rifles ready. Silence fell for about five long seconds, then somebody yelled, "Everybody OK? Let's check the area."

I rose to one knee and saw the 2nd Squad crouching low and moving into the elephant grass and brush. A few minutes later they returned empty-handed, then began praising their fellow squad member Dynas, better known as Jake. Jake apparently saw a grenade hit the ground at the feet of his squad, picked it up and threw it back. One of the men said fervently, "You saved our asses. When I saw that grenade, man, I thought it was over, but Jake just picked it up and threw it back. Sheeitt, man."

I strolled over and put out my hand to the reticent Dynas. "Helluva job, Jake. I don't know if I could have done that."

He remained silent, but allowed a tight grin to work on the corners of his mouth—at least, I think it was a grin. His hands were still shaking as he accepted the congratulations and adulation of his grateful squadmates. Lieutenant Nelson got on the horn and notified Charlie 6 of the deed and when we finished our patrol and set up for resupply, Golden 6, his own damn self, flew in to pick up Dynas and make him a bona fide hero. The word was, he showed him around HQ and recommended a Distinguished Service Cross. For the rest of us, his chopper carried hot As—some kind of ground meat with mashed potatoes and corn. I ate a few forkfuls of the stuff, then sipped on my canteen cup of fruit drink and spoke with Patterson and Allen.

"When you think about heroes, you have to think about Dynas. Look at what he did. Without him, we wouldn't have had a hot meal and cold juice. Here's to Jake!"

I yelled the last part and those that heard me joined in the toast. Underhill walked over, sat down and managed a few words. "He must have been a ballplayer with those quick hands and good arm, Pete."

"Just like a southpaw first sacker fielding a grounder and throwing a runner out at home. Like Norm Cash."

"Right on, Pete."

He flashed his big white-toothed smile for the first time since he had helped waste the three heavily armed VC, then quickly stood up and moved back to his position. I knew what he was going through on the inside and I felt for him, but that was all I could do.

The mail arrived as we finished our meal and dug in for the night. I thumbed through a newspaper and read a story. "Hey, Pat, it says here that Westmoreland reported to Congress that we're winning the war, but he needs more men and Congress said OK. They're drafting 29,000 in August—a new high for the war. How does that grab you?"

"Let's think about that, Pete. If we're winning the war, why the hell does he need more men? Westmoreland sucks. They should put me in charge—I'd take the 2nd Platoon into Hanoi, grab Ho and get out of town fast. Whaddaya think?"

"You could put Dynas on point and have him throw everything back that comes at you."

"That was a hell of a thing he did, Pete. I wonder what I would do."

Pat arched his brow and pondered the situation while the conversation stopped for a minute.

Then I added, "It had to be all reaction. You can't really plan something like that—I mean, you tell yourself that if this happens, I'll do that, but when it comes down to it, would you follow through or just react? Or, in your case, would you grab your crotch, your butt or your head?"

Dynas had done a tremendous deed, but how do you place that in the order of things? I thought about it as the jungle creatures began their nocturnal symphony and came to a conclusion: it had all happened within three or four seconds and three or four soldiers were alive and unscathed because of what he did. I decided that was all we needed to know.

The next day we moved back down the valley, crossed the stream and followed a narrow trail through the brush to a large open valley where we sat up in a daylight observation post. As we neared a collection of huts, sniper fire came tearing into the line of men, but somehow missed all of them. I hit the dirt, then rolled over into the brush and looked around at my men to see if anyone had been hit. I saw Alexus, lying on the ground about fifteen feet ahead, looking back at me. A question was on his face, making its way through his lips. "Pete, why can't I just get a flesh wound? How about I stick up my hand and get one?"

I smiled and giggled a little, then the sniper opened up again. "OK, Alexus, on three! One-two-three!"

We both brazenly and stupidly stuck up our nonfiring hands,

exposing them to the sniper, but when he stopped firing, we were both unscathed, as we had supposed we would be. The FO called in artillery and saturated the area, then we moved on. Late in the afternoon Alexus had another problem: he began complaining of chills, fever and aching all over. By the time the medic reached his side he was shaking so badly he couldn't hold the thermometer in his mouth.

The medic wrote out a tag and tied it on his collar. "Looks like malaria, Alexus. Did you take your pills?"

Alexus couldn't speak, but he nodded in the affirmative. I squatted down beside him and looked in his eyes, but they weren't focusing. He was burning up and freezing, so I reached for his pack and removed a can of peaches.

"You won't need these, man. You'll have nurses feeding you and rubbing you all over. Damn."

He tried to smile, but groaned instead. I put my hand on his shoulder and tried to comfort him a little.

"The chopper will be here ASAP. You couldn't get hit in the hand, so you figured out a way to get malaria. What a man! I'll be in to join you with my flesh wound in a day or so."

The medevac arrived a few minutes later and we loaded him aboard; I was down to one team leader with two weeks' experience. I asked Sidney Lee, Nelson's new RTO, to check on the status of Martinez, who should have returned from the school. He reported back to me a little later that Gus had made the 4th Infantry Division school roster and would be back when it was over. I shrugged and told Nuckols that I wasn't going to send any more men to school because they were all finishing too high and I couldn't get them back. I continued, "It must be that excellent on-the-job training they get from their squad leader."

"I'm sure that's true, Pete. That's why I can't let you go on leave."

The 2nd Platoon stayed in a peaceful grove of trees for re-supply and night perimeter. I set up my positions on the west side of the wagon wheel with an OP fifty meters out in the bushes. As we sat under one of the large trees, Pat sat and told me of his plans.

"I talked with Sergeant Nuckols and told him I wanted to be a Ranger. He said I could cut it, so I'm going to give it a try. If I get the transfer and it works out, I might re-up."

"Whoa, man. Medic, I've got another man out of his head. Are you nuts or just tired of living like a human?"

"Well, I'm still just thinking about it, Pete. Maybe I'll just get the transfer without reenlisting."

"Now you're talking, guy. Here, finish off these peaches I got from Alexus. I gotta check the perimeter."

I crawled toward my position, thinking that I was starting to act like a mother hen again, but with Alexus and Martinez gone, I wanted to be sure everything was in order. I had to get Martinez back or trust Rushinski to be a team leader. He had been in-country five months, but had been sick or injured a lot and hadn't had a chance to show leadership qualities. I caught a glimpse of a red glow at the next position, so I found a pebble that probably had been there for a thousand years and threw it at them and hissed, "Sheeez. Cover your butt."

Cover your butt—wasn't that what we all try to do? He did, I relaxed a little and found my stars—it was a beautiful and peaceful night.

The platoon remained in the same peaceful valley for another day and night. I took my squad on a short patrol south of the perimeter, then returned to sit around and let our feet and jungle rot dry. We had plenty of shade in the grove and we used the trees for cover, so no snipers bothered our Sunday afternoon break. The medics flew out from Hill 54 and broke out the soap with hexachlorophene so we could wash out our sores and feet. After my feet had dried in the sun for a while, I found my cleanest pair of dirty socks and put them on. It was day eleven of our current operation and all our clothing was sweat-soaked and filthy.

That night I sent Allen out on OP directly in front of my position, then leaned back against one of the trees and joined Fryer on watch. At 2215 a burst of automatic weapons fire reverberated through the narrow valley. Directions and distances are deceptive at night, but I estimated the shots were fired to our northwest about 250 to 300 meters away. I heard a hiss from behind me and Nuckols edged up to my tree.

"Bring in the OP, Pete."

I weighed it quickly in my mind, then dismissed the order as premature and leaned over to whisper to him my reasons.

"Negative. I don't think they were firing at us. Could be a trick, just like in the western movies. Let's hold on for a few minutes."

"All right, we'll wait. But, if anything happens, get 'em back in a hurry."

We waited, but nothing happened the rest of the night. At dawn, I pulled in the OP and gave my opinion to the squad. "An old Indian trick—make some noise, get the enemy to check it out, then zap him. I hope the Old Man doesn't fall for it."

I sipped my cocoa slowly, then heard once more the clarion call of destiny and I already knew what was coming. It was my karma, or it was at least the standard operating procedure of our battalion.

"Squad leaders, to the CP!"

30

Lieutenant Nelson was sitting on a partially inflated air mattress and leaning against a tree while drinking his morning C-ration coffee. The ends of the air mattress were forced by the 150 or so pounds on his six-foot frame to protrude upward at about a seventy-degree angle and looked like a pair of ugly water wings. The lieutenant, like me, rarely ate and kept his hair cropped close to his head, so with his shirt off he resembled one of the survivors of a death camp after World War II. He tossed away the rest of his brew, picked up his map and began to speak to the assemblage of squad leaders, RTOs, the medic and the FO.

"Sergeant Pete, you'll lead the 1st and 2nd Squads on patrol up along the paddies following the valley to the west. Find out what you can about last night's racket. Maybe it was an accident. Charlie shot Charlie."

Sergeant Nuckols, in his twelfth year of weaning himself from cigarettes, lit up his fifth of the morning and surmised, "Coulda been an execution. The VC sometimes will off a village chief to scare the people into helping them." He thought about that for a minute, then corrected himself, " 'course, there aren't supposed to be any inhabited villes around here."

I tried to keep my voice even as I spoke, but a little sarcasm made its way through. "Maybe it's a trap for those eager Americans who check out every damn noise and movement that they hear. I know ol' Charlie is just laying out there. Waiting. For us."

"We'll be just a few minutes away if you need help. You already have the frequencies for Boomer and Dustoff or you can call me and I'll bring them in. Do it!"

Nelson waved us away, like some potentate dismissing the peons, so Sergeant Cain and I rounded up the squads and checked their gear and ammo. Cain naturally resented being under the command of someone with seven fewer years of military experience and one less stripe, but in the finest tradition of the U.S. Army, he kept his mouth shut and got on with the job. I was a little uncomfortable with the arrangement myself, but I had no doubts that I was the most qualified man for the job because of my time in-country. Cain was fast becoming a proficient squad leader, however, and I figured he would be the platoon sergeant after Nuckols had DEROSed. We pored over the map together and plotted out a circuitous path, avoiding the open paddies as much as possible, then started out to the north to follow it.

As we left the shady glen and stepped into the broiling sun, I continued to wrestle inwardly with a dilemma imposed on me. Should I follow orders, accept responsibility and keep the work ethic that had been instilled in me years ago on that farm in Middle America, or should I avoid the snipers and ambush that I knew could be waiting? This was one of those patrols that Bennett had talked about months ago. I could stop in the brush 200 meters out, give the men orders to be quiet, then rest for two hours and return with a false report like I had seen others do. This would be a safe choice and I would be following my recent personal dictum—no more heroics, cover my own ass first and keep the men healthy.

At 200 meters I halted the patrol, grabbed the handset and

called in. "Golden Charlie 2–6, this is Golden Charlie 2–1. Over."

"Go ahead, 2–1, this is 2–6."

"Radio check. How do you hear me?"

"Lima Charlie, 2–1. How you?"

"Same-same. 2–1, out."

I looked at Patterson and Allen and some of the others and wondered if they could sense my inner conflict. No one spoke for a couple of minutes, then I took my dirty sweat towel and wiped my face, pulled out my map and pointed to marks on it as I spoke with Cain and Patterson.

"We're going to check out these three areas: this old ville here, then back through the brush to the trail junction down here, then we cross the paddy to check out this area where we stayed last week. We could get sniper fire in the ville or on the paddy and we could get ambushed anywhere, so be extra alert. Pat, take your team on point, I'll be next in line, then Sergeant Cain and the 2nd Squad. We'll reverse the order when we come back. Any questions? No? Must have been a helluva presentation then. Head 'em up, Pat."

I stuck the map into my pocket and we headed to the abandoned village we had searched last week. The men gave the half-burned hooches and blown-out bunkers a thorough check, but there was no evidence of any kind of recent activity, so we headed back to the trail junction and took a ten-minute break. It was ridiculously hot again so I checked the men for dehydration and was pleased to find them in good shape. After the break we headed west to the edge of the paddy where I called up Cain to meet with Kevin and me in the brush. I looked at the paddy that seemed to stretch forever, but was in actuality less than fifty meters across.

"Pat, take your team across and secure the other side, then I'll bring the rest of the squad. When I'm across, Cain, send your squad in two shifts. Be careful, we're surrounded here on three sides by brush and high ground, so don't waste any time out there. Go."

Patterson led Walker, Jackson and Allen single file four meters apart onto the paddy and moved quickly across to the tree line. As he started edging into the brush I waited for a signal, then headed out with my RTO when he gave the thumbs-up.

Fryer, Rushinski and Marvin followed me onto the sunbaked paddy and we began moving quickly across it. I pushed one foot ahead of the other onto the barren field and scanned the trees and brush with my eyes; we had taken fire in this area several times before and I felt like a magnet.

As I neared the brush line it seemed that the entire hillside to our north came alive with fire. In reality there were only two or three VC with weapons, but they were putting down enough fire to pin down all the men. I took a quick look back and saw that Marvin was lying facedown in front of a low dike while the others scrambled behind it. I hurried into the brush and grabbed the radio handset while my RTO poured a magazine into the offending tree line. I put my hand on the weapon and yelled at him to stop.

"Wait for a target. You can't see anything now, but you will draw fire. Hold up while I use the radio."

I saw Patterson and yelled, "Move up the hill, Pat. Get to the high ground and try to spot some targets. Take the heat off the guys out there."

He took his team slowly up a narrow trail along the low finger of a hill on the opposite side of the paddy from the snipers. A few minutes later I heard an explosion from the direction they had taken. I knew instantly they had hit a booby-trapped mine or grenade. A quick stab of helplessness and frustration came over me, but I knew I had to get hold of myself and handle the situation.

I grabbed the handset and began barking out orders, taking out my frustration on the radio and the men on the other end of the transmission. "2–6, get me a medic, a machine gun and reinforcements and get 'em here fast."

"Hold on 2–1. What's your situation there?"

Now I was enraged—why were they stalling? I screamed, "We've got at least three men down. I need some fucking help, and I need it right fucking now, dammit!"

I threw the handset to the RTO and made a quick decision to check on the lead element up on the low hill. At that instant Jackson came panting down the trail and gasped, "We hit a grenade. Patterson and Walker are wounded."

He turned to lead us up to them and I saw blood on his butt. "You're hit too, Jackson—are you OK?"

"I thought I felt something. It stings, but I'm all right."

As we neared the crest of the small hill, I stepped off the small trail to check on Patterson and my foot hit a wire—hard. Gawd—I tripped one and I'm a dead man, I thought. It must not have been my time because the wire didn't release on the grenade, so I gingerly pulled my foot back and made a mental note to remove the booby trap later. I saw Patterson lying against a tree with a bandage wrapped around his knee. He had tipped his steel pot back on his head and was holding on to his M-16, looking around wide-eyed. As I walked up he started to talk. "I did it this time, Pete. My knee is all fucked up. I hit that wire and—boom!"

"Take it easy, man. The medic's on his way; we'll get you out of here. I'll go check on Walker."

Walker was propped up a few feet away holding a bandage to his eye. He had some cuts on his hands and face, but when he spoke, he anxiously asked about one thing. "Look at my eye, Pete. Is it OK? Am I gonna lose that eye? I can't see out of it."

I glanced at it and saw a tiny piece of shrapnel sticking into the white near the pupil. It looked bad, but I said, "Just a little piece of shrapnel, Walker. The doc will take that out and you'll be fine."

I thought it was a lie, but what good would the truth do here? I put Jackson on guard for the two men, then headed back to the paddy where the shooting had picked up again. At the brush line I yelled at Fryer, down behind the low dike, to put some bloop rounds into the tree line while I called in Dustoff. He popped two rounds into the woods, then I heard a sound of metal hitting metal and he went down. After a few seconds he spoke in a strangulated voice. "I'm all right, I think! They hit my rifle and it bounced off and hit my shoulder. The gun's broke, but I'm all right."

I made another quick decision and gave it to them as it came into my mind. "You can lay out there and maybe get picked off slowly, or you can break for the brush while I cover you. Whaddya say?"

Rushinski and Fryer nodded, then Rushinski and I laid down fire while Fryer moved out safely into the woods. One of the snipers fired a burst that missed, then Rushinski came across while I covered. Now, Marvin remained alone, still not moving in front of the dike. Fryer spoke, "I heard him grunt when he was hit and moan a few more times. He's still alive, but I think he's hurt bad, Pete."

I saw Nuckols and the 3rd Squad with a machine gun come out of the bushes to the east and felt like running over and kissing them. Instead, I yelled into the handset, "Get the gun up to rake the woods to the north and put some bloop rounds in there."

I sent Fryer and Rushinski up the hill to safeguard Patterson and Walker, then I heard the comforting sound of Rich's gun pounding away at the woods and the bloop of the 3rd Squad's M-79. The snipers went silent and a few men from the 2nd Squad moved out into the paddy and picked up Marvin. I motioned them to take him up the hill to where Patterson was wounded; we could get a chopper in where we had received resupply last week. I filled Nuckols in about the situation up the hill, then left him in charge at the paddy and took a few more men up to secure the LZ and tend the wounded. I passed the men struggling along with Marvin lying on a poncho and remembered the Green Beret chewing us out as we carried a wounded man to the LZ a long, long time ago. I decided I wouldn't emulate him when I spoke to them.

"Be careful, take your time, guys. It's just a little farther."

When I got back to the LZ, the medic had set his bag on the ground and quickly began working on Patterson and Walker. After checking and rewrapping the bandages, he gave Pat a shot of morphine, then told Walker to sit back and take it easy.

The rest of the men, except for one gun crew and Lieutenant Nelson back at the perimeter, arrived with the four men carrying Marvin. He had taken a single round in the neck and was paralyzed, apparently, but still alive. I sent the men into the woods west and south of the LZ and told them Dustoff was coming, so the snipers would probably open up again. It was up to them to suppress the fire so we could get the wounded extracted. The chopper did arrive a few minutes later and the snipers did open up. One of the men inside the chopper lost his composure and started firing blindly into the woods with an M-16, so I rushed up and grabbed his leg and yelled as loudly as I could above the noise. "*No!* We've got men out there, you might hit them!"

He had a wild-eyed look, but he put the weapon down and began to help load the men. They struggled to get Marvin and Patterson aboard while Jackson limped over and sat on his good cheek. Somehow, Sergeant Nuckols had given the word to the pilot that three men needed evacuation, so when three men were on, the bird took off. I yelled at him, "They missed one. Walker is still here. Get him back down."

Nuckols took the handset from the RTO and spoke calmly, "Dustoff, this is Charlie 2–5, we've got one more Whiskey India Alpha here. Could you come back in?"

The chopper made a tight arc, came back in and hovered once more above the LZ as we got Walker, still holding the bandage to his eye, aboard. The pilot, sounding harried, but still professional, asked a little sarcastically if the evacuation was now complete. Nuckols was cool. "Affirmative, Dustoff, thanks much. Out."

Two more rounds snapped at the chopper as it lifted off with its cargo of damaged green-clad American bodies. The gun crew and some of the men opened up, spraying the hillside while Nuckols dialed up Spark Gap and gave the coordinates to the waiting gunships. Then I walked slowly into the brush and called the men back to the LZ where we formed a tight perimeter. A few minutes later the Cobras came in low, spewing out rockets, grenades and laying thousands of machine-gun rounds over the length, breadth and height of the offending hill.

As I lay behind a tree stump that had been shattered weeks before, watching the ships pound the hillside and trying to feel some sense of retribution, I was certain that Charlie was in a hole somewhere yet again, maybe laughing at us. I felt sad and despondent, like I had on the Cambodian border, as I listened to Nuckols thank the gunships. Then he tapped my helmet and said softly, "Come on, Pete, let's get the hell out of here. Those guys will be fine, now."

"Go ahead, lead the way. I've got to disarm this damned grenade booby trap before it gets somebody else. I'll keep Allen with me for security."

I pointed to the grenade and leaned over to examine it; there was another grenade on the back side of the small tree.

"They're fuckin' American grenades, Pete. How the hell do they get ahold of them?" Allen asked.

"GIs lose them or leave them. ARVNs or American supply sergeants sell them on the black market," I said matter-of-factly.

I waited as the remainder of the troops headed slowly down the trail, then branched away from the paddy toward the CP in the grove. Then I took a close look at the rusted wires and decided it was too risky to disarm, so I pulled the pin on one of my pineapple grenades and laid it under the others. I waited until Allen yelled his warning, "Grenade! Fire in the hole!" then released the handle and we beat a hasty retreat, diving behind a tree as the world exploded once more and shrapnel pounded the area. Another look told me the grenades were completely gone, so I buckled up my gear and moved down the trail away from the site of the day's carnage.

I had managed to keep my feelings under control while the one-sided battle took place, but as I moved along to the grove I felt like I was carrying the cross of Jesus and it got heavier at every step. When I got to the perimeter, it felt strange, like I'd never been there before. I sat down, leaned back against a tree and remained silent and motionless for a long while. The others, respecting my solitude, kept their distance while I let myself drift—what did it all mean? McCown, Belcher, Federline, Childers, Machado, the guy in the hooch, the troop grenaded in the foxhole, the stack of bodies on the border and so many others—all dead. The war went on.

Dozens, now including Marvin, had been wounded for life and the war went on. Maddox, Watson, Bennett, Scheffel, Mize and Vickers all went home alive, but undoubtedly scarred inside for life and the war went on. Westmoreland said we were winning and the war went on. People back home were burning their draft cards and marching in the streets in protest against the war, but it went on, and on. When would it swallow its last victim and be satisfied—when? A huge knot of frustration welled up into my chest and throat and I wanted to scream and break something, but I didn't move.

After thirty minutes or so I finally got up and walked slowly to the CP where Nuckols took one look at my face and said, "Pete, don't get mad at us. . . ."

I interrupted with a sigh, "I'm not mad at you, I'm mad at the circumstances. We should have had a machine gun, the medic and another bloop gun on the patrol. I knew they were out there—I *knew* it."

I put particular emphasis on the second "knew," in order to chastise myself for not insisting on more long-range firepower. I sat down again, feeling very old and tired and alone. I had lost Alexus and Patterson and most of my squad to injury or malaria. Lieutenant Nelson, remaining detached, said, "We're going in, Pete. Choppers will be here at 1700."

I nodded in acceptance and said: "I need a drink—a lot of drinks."

Back at camp I sent the last vestiges of my squad to round up some beer, then Lieutenant Nelson called me into the CP. "The colonel wants to see you. Come with me to this meeting, then you can talk to him later."

We went into the G-2 hooch, which had maps on the front wall and rows of chairs. I listened as a captain droned on about the upcoming days' events and points of concern. I felt the eyes of several junior officers poring over me as they wondered what the hell an EM was doing in Officer Land, but I adopted Lieutenant Nelson's "Don't fuck with me" attitude and ignored them. After the briefing, Lieutenant Nelson led me to Colonel Miller's Hill 54 "home." I thought I might get reamed out for some heavy-duty cursing that day on the radio, but he merely said, "Tough day today, Sergeant. Did the VC use any new tactics?"

"Nothing new, sir. But they did call the shots and we reacted as they knew we would."

I don't think he wanted to hear that, but he merely replied, "All right, son. Well, get some rest. Remember, you owe Charlie one. Dismissed."

I had wanted to say more, to question the entire American operation, but I realized how futile that would be. Instead, I told the lieutenant of my concerns after we were alone. "Why do we always react the same way? Why not ignore some of Charlie's shit and just probe around on our own? We shouldn't be so damned predictable."

"I've wondered about that myself. In the Army, it takes time to change things. I'll talk to the CO and see what happens. The trick is to make him think it's his idea."

I flipped him a half-hearted salute and made my way along the path back to the platoon tent, where I propped myself against the back step and tried to drink my blues away. I thought about the time, months and lifetimes ago, when I painfully realized how difficult it would be to win this war against a ragtag army. Now, after I had seen my fourteen-man patrol rendered helpless by two snipers, I realized that this was a war we could not win without a major shift in tactics and in national policy. We could not continue to dangle the youth of America as bait, hoping the enemy would come out and fight. We could not win a war of attrition against an army that has no moral compunctions about the number of men it must sacrifice. We could not win. . . . The words burned in my heart and mind and brought tears of frustration and sorrow to my eyes.

I tried to clear my head and think of Patterson. I would miss his companionship and humor, but I had to carry on. To do less would dishonor him and the many who had fallen while supposedly carrying their nation's banner. If the worth of a man can be measured in how he responds to adversity and challenges, then someone had certainly been measuring me a lot lately. I wondered to myself what I might have done to alleviate the situations presented today, but, aside from stopping the patrol in the bush and lying, nothing came to mind. I would take the blame for taking out a patrol with no heavy weapons or medic—the rest was karma.

Following orders the next morning, I took my three-man squad to have their sores lanced and cleaned. Once again I was bandaged from wrist to elbow on both arms because of the number of sores. After we left the dispensary, I headed to the company CP where the old Ranger sergeant grabbed me and pulled me off to the side.

"Here's my plan, Pete. We get a jeep, go for a ride and find some beer. We'll work out the details later."

"Not a bad plan, Ranger. Here's mine. Let's take a small truck, pick up my small squad and go see Patterson, then we'll get shit-faced drunk."

I knew Nuckols missed his old RTO also, so convincing him wasn't difficult. We procured a truck from Supply and headed to the MASH unit. Rules limited a patient to two visitors at a time, so Nuck and I commiserated with the lanky Patterson for a few minutes, then I stayed there as the others replaced him, one by one. I kidded him, "Pat, you shamming SOB, you kept tripping wires until you finally found one that would get you out of the field. Now you got a soft bed, nurses, rubdowns, good chow and all the trimmings."

"Yeah, man. I came in for the nurses and the good drugs. They've kept me pumped full of painkillers—it's great."

"Have you written to your folks so they won't worry when they get that damned telegram?"

"Yeah, the nurse wouldn't give me a back rub until I did."

The nurse came in to take his temperature and she smiled at the mention. She wasn't real pretty, but she was the first American female I'd seen since R&R, so she captured my full attention. I thought I'd see if she had a sense of humor.

"Ma'am, I'd like to stay here with Patterson. I'd sleep on the floor, I'm used to it, and we'd share his food. How does that sound to you?"

She sighed and gave me a small smile. "If you only knew how many times I've heard that one. He won't be with us long, anyway. He'll be going to Tokyo, probably, for surgery on his knee."

Patterson's eyes lit up at the mention of Tokyo. "Tokyo! Bike city! I love motorcycles."

"You won't be riding motorcycles for a few weeks. You've got a lot of rehab ahead of you, but you should come back in good shape." She looked at me, then continued, "He'll be going to sleep for a while now. Goodnight, soldier."

She poked a hypo into his arm, then patted his shoulder and left. I shook Kevin's hand, looked into his eyes and told him, "We gotta go, Pat. There's beer to be drunk. Write to me and keep me informed, guy. We were a damn good team out there until you turned into a minesweeper. Good luck, guy."

"I'll write, Pete. Keep your head down out there. So long."

As we took our leave, Nuckols informed me that Marvin was on the hospital ship off Da Nang in critical condition. I shook my head to clear the news, a quirk that I had been using a lot lately, but it hung there like some kind of fucking albatross. We drove the truck to the PX where we picked up some toiletries, then tooled down Highway 1 like it was Route 66 and we were Todd and Buzz. We stopped at an NCO club and the Korean club to find beer, then headed back to Hill 54, stopping at the wire to get some dirty ice from the urchins. We iced the beer down and left a man to guard it as we ate our evening chow and read our mail. Seeing Patterson had eased some of my gloom, but only a lot of beer could put a dent in my melancholy. I was alone, outnumbered and I felt as if I were only treading water.

I was given a mission the next morning: take the remains of your squad; one gun crew; Ralph and his radio; Potozoa, an FO and his RTO; the 2nd Squad minus its leader and chopper out to an island guarding a river inlet from the South China Sea. Our job was to stop and search any boats or sampans trying to enter the river. We were looking for weapons, military supplies or suspected VC. We landed and were replaced on the choppers by a unit from Bravo Company. I yelled a quick question at a sergeant as he headed out, "What's happening here, Sarge? What should I look for?"

"Nothin' much. We saw two boats in three days. Relax, swim and drink beer."

I placed the men in a relaxed half-perimeter with good sight lines in each direction and we lay back. Within a few minutes a group of Vietnamese youngsters came trudging down the wide road carrying Cokes and beer. This was my kind of war. I wondered if I could get a back rub.

Using our ponchos and some branches, we erected open sunshades and let the youngsters join us as we listened to Armed Forces Radio and relaxed. I tried to talk with the local citizens in their broken English and my fractured Vietnamese, but mostly we just "hung out" together. Some local militia troops stopped by and we offered them sodas. A boy about thirteen was with them, dressed as they were in light-green fatigues and pants. He carried a huge, for him, M-14, which I told him was a "number one" rifle. We sat on the shore and the boy, apparently in answer to a challenge from the men, fired the rifle at the far bank. The recoil nearly flattened the poor lad and the round fell short, so I borrowed the weapon and aimed high to allow for distance and drop. The weapon roared, kicked and a puff of dust arose on the other shore. The militia gave a cheer, so I offered them a trial with my M-16, but no one could hit the bank.

When the choppers came in with hot chow and mail, a larger

crowd of locals appeared. I wondered if they had a radio or had they been waiting in the brush? We shared some of our food with them and a few of the women cooked up some noodle soup. As it grew dark we shooed away the last of the youngsters, who were rapidly softening what was left of my heart, and set up a perimeter. A little girl, perhaps seven or eight years old, hugged my leg and wouldn't let go. I knelt down and hugged her tightly—regardless of her circumstances, I needed some compassion as much as she did. She left that night, but followed the patrol closely for the next two days.

Somehow, despite all the death and desolation I had seen lately, this urchin was melting a little bit of my gruff exterior. We spent three days there swimming, drinking beer and soda, and playing football with a rolled-up pair of socks. The saltwater was helping heal the sores on our arms and legs and we all felt relaxed and a little more human. When I saw the chopper coming after us on July 1, I felt a twinge of sadness; I would miss the trusting, friendly people, especially the children and most especially the little girl. I would definitely miss the relaxed feeling of safety. As I headed for the chopper, a sergeant asked me, "What's happenin' out here, Sarge? What should I look for?"

"Relax, enjoy yourselves. Treat the people nicely."

Back at Hill 54, we dropped our gear at the platoon tent, then lined up at the mess hall for pay. I paid part of my R&R debt to the poker player, then we loaded onto trucks and headed over to the battalion HQ where we attended classes on demolition and tactics. I had been in-country nine months, so I paid little attention to what was being said and my mind drifted—at first, back to the island, then to Japan, then across the ocean to home. It seemed a million years and another lifetime away.

"Wake up, Pete!" Sergeant Nuckols yelled as the class laughed. "Eighty-three days and a wake-up!"

I yelled back, setting off an outburst of DEROS chants. We left the outdoor classroom area, then stopped at the PX, where I picked up some cans of fruit. Back at the hill we drank beer through the night, singing songs while sitting on the ground outside the tent. Stach played a guitar and led our attempts at joyful sounds and we all joined in whenever we could remember the words. It was good therapy, brought us closer and helped bind a few wounds.

Incredibly, we arose at 0345, still wobbly and hungover, to load onto the APCs and head to a large ville a few klicks away. We unloaded and swept through it, with a few vomit breaks for those of us who were a little sick, then surrounded it as the ARVNs forced the villagers to pack what they could carry for movement to a more secure hamlet. It was another move that I didn't understand; this ville was close enough to the nearby ARVN compound to be considered friendly. After I felt better, I spoke with Lieutenant Nelson. "Sir, why can't the ARVNs just send a patrol out here every day or leave a platoon out here all night and let these villagers stay here and work like they always have? Why do we have to uproot people from the only home they know?"

I already knew the answer, but since I felt I had to complain, then I also felt I had to listen to his answer. "G-2 has received several reports that their villagers are supplying the VC with food and money. We have to take away their base of support, whatever that may entail. Higher says do it—we do it."

I felt that he, too, was tiring of the way we were conducting the war, so I continued talking. "I think we're turning people to the other side by tearing them from their homes. The VC don't have to recruit them; they just point at us."

I felt the by-now familiar bitterness rising into my throat. What we were doing didn't seem fair or just, at which we Americans were supposed to be the champions. Since my head ached, I didn't shake it, but shrugged my shoulders instead and moved back to my squad. A young man came walking up to us as we sat watching the people carrying their belongings out of their hooches. He was about seventeen, wore glasses and spoke excellent English. I soon learned that his name was Hin, he was a scholar in one of the coastal cities and he spoke very informatively about the United States. When he asked for reasons for the upheaval in the valley, I sent him to see Lieutenant Nelson. The two of them talked for an hour before he left to reenter the village. At 1600 the word came down—burn the village. I sat by the radio for a long time, staring at the people toting chests and cabinets as they moved through the brush. One of the men pulled out his lighter and flicked it a few times.

I spoke quickly and firmly: "No. My squad doesn't burn this village. These people did nothing to us and this squad isn't burning their homes."

I spat the words out bitterly, but my line was drawn. As we left the hooches, now in flames set by the rest of the platoon, Hin came over to us, a look of anguish on his face. "Why? Why do you burn our homes?"

I avoided his eyes and said slowly, sadly, "I don't know, Hin. I just don't know."

He looked around for Lieutenant Nelson, as if he could help. "Where's Bob? Bob!"

I spotted him a few APCs away and pointed him out. I suspected that, in our green jungle fatigues, with dirty faces and half-assed moustaches, we all looked alike to him. Hin called to the lieutenant and climbed onto the APC with him. I saw Nelson's shoulders shrug, then Hin left shortly afterward. When he was out of earshot, I yelled over to the lieutenant.

"We just created another VC, and a damn smart one at that."

He looked at me and spread his arms out to the side, palms up—the universal sign for *whaddaya want me to do?* or *Xin loi,* its Vietnamese counterpart.

I held on tightly to the APC all the way to Hill 54 and pondered our role here in Vietnam. I hoped other units were waging a different and more successful type of campaign in their areas of operation. I wanted to believe they were, although I feared they were butting their heads against the stupidity of higher command, just as we were. We were fighting the wrong kind of war and I was becoming more and more certain that we could not win, but I will not let the word "lose" enter my mind. As we entered the collection of hovels that made up the main street of our campside ville, I decided that while we would not lose the war, we might not win. Might not win.

Might . . . not . . . win. It was almost unfathomable.

We headed around to the other side of Hill 54 in the morning of July 3 to fire and check our weapons and observe the test firing of a beehive shell by the artillery crew. After it was fired at a huge board from about 100 feet away, I went down and took a look at the remains of the target. It had been torn and nearly shredded by hundreds of steel darts imbedded in the shell and which were loosened upon firing. It was an impressive display of weaponry and I was glad it was in our hands. Still, with weapons like these, we weren't doing what we should.

The platoon then lay around the rest of the day, cleaning rifles and writing letters. At 1800 we shouldered our packs, grabbed our weapons and headed to the main gate where we loaded once more onto the APCs. We moved about six klicks out into the boonies, again unloaded and broke into squad-sized ambushes. I had been given a couple of men on loan to bring my strength to six men and I carried my own radio. I set the squad up on a knoll overlooking a well-used trail and we spent the night peacefully.

"Golden Charlie 2–1, this is 2–6 Actual, over."

"This is 2–1. Goood moorrning, Vietnam. Over."

"2–1, be advised that the status of PFC Marvin, Joseph, has been changed from Whiskey India Alpha to deceased as a result of wounds suffered in combat. Over."

I paused and looked at my hands, which had begun shaking at some recent time. Marvin and I hadn't spoken three times in the nine months we spent in the same squad. He had made every attempt and taken every opportunity to stay in the rear, doing every menial task available and pretending to be sick. Sometimes his apparent cowardice had disgusted me, but look at what happened when he was sent back to the field. Did he deserve to die because he didn't want to fight and be shot at? If he had refused to fight, he would be alive today. Was refusing to fight the correct course of action? My traditional values were being shaken and twisted. I heard the handset crackle again, forcing me out of my absorption.

"2–1, did you copy? Acknowledge, over."

"Roger, copied. Marvin—Kool-Aid. *Xin loi.* 2–1, out."

Though I had never really known Marvin, I knew I would not ever forget his name. He died under my command.

I moved my shrunken squad down off the knoll and headed west about 200 meters where we set up in a daylight observation post between the stream and the trail. As the afternoon got hotter, and they always did, we took turns plunging into the refreshing waters of the small stream. At 1800, as we readied our move into a night ambush posture, I led the squad back to the stream bank where we dropped three grenades into the water, one at a time. After the ensuing *whumps,* I broke squelch on my radio by yelling, not too loudly,

"Happy birthday, America!" over the company net.

It was an almost insignificant effort, but I felt better. I had to lash out at something. I wanted to scream at the whole fucking world, "We're dying out here, and nobody gives a rat's ass! Look at me and tell me what it means, dammit. Before any more blood is shed, show me why!"

Since I couldn't safely do that, the grenading and the radio announcement would have to stand as my statements. I was now a protester, and it felt good. We ambushed the trail again overnight, but there was no activity.

We saddled up early the next morning, then moved two klicks to a new position along the same stream. During our intermittent dips, some of the troops had spotted a few good-sized fish in the stream.

Because we were closer to the enemy's lair, I decided against using grenades, so Fryer and Allen began carving hooks out of bamboo. They tied them onto some cord Allen found in his pack and baited them with C rations.

"You're not going to catch any fish using that crap. The only species on earth that eats C rats is Homo sapiens, and then only if he's in the Army."

I jested with them, but they were trying to make a connection with their youth, so they blithely, and correctly, ignored me. Several hours later, after the boys got tired of fishing with no action, I took a pineapple grenade from my belt, unscrewed the head, pulled the pin and tossed the blasting cap into the stream. After the small, muffled explosion, a few fish floated to the surface. We gathered and cleaned them, then fried them in the liquid from a can of ham and lima beans. They were terribly bony and tasted a lot like ham, but it was a veritable feast, a picnic, ambrosia from the gods, washed down with the nectar of a warm Coke one of the men had been humping for three days. Maybe life wasn't so bad, after all—yeah, it was. I could still see, smell and taste Vietnam.

On ambush, for maximum silence, which GIs don't do very well, the man with the radio kept the handset against his ear. I was monitoring the company net while on watch with one of my substitutes, Sandstrom, when the word came down that a chopper carrying troops from C Company had crashed at Hill 54. Three men were dead and several more injured, but it hardly made a dent in my hardening heart.

Early in the morning of July 6 we moved to the trail junction to join Lieutenant Nelson and get a ride back to base camp. We missed the lieutenant, but caught the second fleet of APCs and rode to the hill. Once there my spirits were lifted by the appearance of Martinez, Alexus and Rushinski. I had most of my squad back and it felt great. Also returning to the platoon were Alabama from R&R and Nuckols from a short illness. It called for a celebration so we pooled our funds, purchased a lot of beer and iced it down. Then we cleaned our gear and weapons and swapped stories and lies while it cooled.

Alexus had only a short-lived virus, Martinez had spent four weeks in school and Alabama had been thrown out of some of the best bars in Bangkok. It felt like old home week.

I showered and donned clean clothes and took some pictures with my camera, which Alabama had brought from rear base camp. After taking a few shots of the life on Hill 54, it got a little depressing, so I grabbed a can of semi-cool beer and sucked it slowly. Nuckols joined me.

"Well, I'm going to re-up. Another six years."

"Jeez, man. How can you sign away that many years?"

"Pete, I've already got nineteen in. It's the only life I know. What am I gonna do on the outside?"

"Anything but get shot at. You know they're gonna send you back here, if the war goes on. And it damn straight will go on, and on."

"I don't mind. I'll get another stripe if they do and I won't have to go out in the field. I'm used to the Army and this country by now, but I'll never get used to the death."

"Sometimes, Nuck, I think I've been here forever and I'll never go home again—and I know a part of me never will. This other crazy notion has been knocking around in my head—take a leave, then come back for the last five months of my hitch. I hate it here, but I'm a good soldier and the country appeals to me, it's a part of me. I guess I've lost my mind—*dinky-dau*."

"Naw, Pete, there's something that draws certain people to danger. I'm not very good with words, but I know what I mean."

"I guess there's certainly some intrigue and mystery in tempting the fates, but I believe that everything is preordained—that whatever happens, it's our karma. I believe that, at least most of the time. I think." I laughed, a short nervous, uncertain chuckle.

"I got a question, then, Pete. Is it our karma to get drunk today? I truly believe that's what we oughta do."

"I'll consider that an order, Sarge. Let's have at it."

I knew that there was one thing that I didn't need when I became depressed and that was another depressed person to talk to, so beer-pounding was a good idea at the time. As the night wore on, things got considerably better, or at least, less distinct.

31

On the morning of July 7 we were preparing our gear for an overnight ambush when I heard the platoon radio crackle out a message intended for my ears only.

"Charlie 2–1, report to Charlie Papa, ASAP. Out."

I checked in with Lieutenant Nelson, who was sitting on his bunk wearing an OD T-shirt and shorts, going through his mail.

"Sergeant Pete, were you considering reenlisting in the Army?"

My initial reaction was to laugh, but I had assimilated enough Army lore by this time to realize that he wasn't asking as an Army recruiting officer, so something must be afoot. I hedged a little. "Maybe. I haven't made that decision yet. I might."

A little lie couldn't hurt much, could it? He looked at me, then picked up a piece of paper and glanced at it.

"The brigade has authorized two temporary promotions to E-6 for their line companies because we're low on noncoms. Captain Gallegos asked me to recommend an E-5 that intends to stay in the Army."

I swallowed that and pondered it for a minute. "I'd like to be an E-6, but I'm not ready to re-up right at this time."

"Well, I'm putting your name up and if you decide later— good. If not, the Army's only out a few months' pay. After you think about it, I think you'll reenlist."

What have you been smoking, I thought, then said aloud, "As they say back home, 'we'll see.'"

"Got your men ready for the patrol and night ambush?"

"Now that I've got my team leaders back, I'm ready."

We moved out into AO Rabbit once again riding the backs of the trusty APCs. No one rode inside, it was too hot and too dangerous—hit a mine riding in there and it was body bag time. We dismounted at about eight klicks out and set up in the brush, then watched some Vietnamese women and children sifting through the ruins of a village that had been leveled several weeks ago. They had been evacuated but, like so many others, had made their way back to their ancestral home, now in pieces and ashes.

When we broke for chow I walked over to where Nuckols was scarfing down some beans and wieners. As we chowed down and talked, the radio came alive and was answered by Ralph, the RTO. As he listened, a grin came over his face. When the message was finished, he answered with the words, "Roger, I'll get 2–5 Actual. Wait one."

He put the handset down and began explaining to Nuckols, "Sarge, I asked the men in the rear to find me a job if they could. They have an opening, so I'm asking if I can go back there to work. It's up to you."

Nuckols gave him a stern gaze, then pondered it for a few minutes while finishing his beans. Finally he stopped chewing, picked up the handset and spoke. "This is Charlie 2–5. You can have this prick if I get a replacement. When we come back in, he's yours and you get me another RTO. Over."

Ralph jumped straight up in the air and wore a grin from ear to ear. He grabbed the handset from Nuckols' hand and yelled, "Isn't he the best damned E-6 in the whole damn Army?"

Nuckols grabbed the handset back and scolded McQueen for a few seconds before closing with proper radio procedure, as was his habit in the months I had known him. I felt good for Ralph, but I was a little bit jealous and offended; jobs in the rear should be a reward for good work in the field, I believed. It seemed if you did a good job in the field here in Vietnam, it only got you more time there.

At dusk we shifted positions and set up to ambush a trail across a paddy. Despite hearing numerous noises in the moonless night, there were no intrusions into our platoon kill zone. They were out there, probably in numbers, but it wasn't time yet.

I took my squad on patrol to a blocking position west of the village early in the morning before it got too hot. The 2nd Squad patrolled down to the village, where they spotted four Vietnamese heading toward my squad. They notified me and I put the men into a hasty line ambush, but the threat, and the suspected VC, vanished. We stayed in position throughout the steamy day. At 1500, I switched to the Armed Forces Net for a few minutes and heard the announcer report that it was 115 degrees in downtown Saigon. It seemed at least that hot in this part of Quang Ngai Province; you couldn't move without breaking into a sweat.

We rejoined the platoon and set up in a regular NDP between the village and the stream. The sniper fire that we had taken on previous trips to this area was missing, but I made sure the men dug in well and helped them put out plenty of trip wires and claymore mines. I had been given one of the most vulnerable points in the perimeter, so Nuckols sent his RTO to provide better communication in the event of an attack. Ralph joined Martinez and me on early watch and we held a bull session, complete with whispers and giggles. Ralph was still high in anticipation of becoming a member of the "queers in the rear." He spoke first, softly. "Pete, how many days you got left?"

"If we get the rumored ten-day drops, seventy-six and I'm gone. Seems like forever."

Martinez joined in with his countdown. "I'm at 139 and a wake-up."

"Didn't you hear, Martinez? You gotta make up the time you spent in NCO School. New policy, started in June."

"Fuck me. If I have to do that, I'll never smile again."

Ralph leaned back against a bamboo stand that covered us. "I'm at 255 and counting. I'll be here six months after you're gone, Pete. You know what I remember about my first day in the field? You guys had these great tans and you were having a ball—singing on patrol, swimming in that river."

"Yeah, that was like R&R compared to the real war. I'd love to go back there for the next two months."

I probably put too much emphasis on the "love," but I

trusted these guys enough to let a few emotions run freely. We talked until midnight, then I pulled the next watch alone with my thoughts. I could hear rustling in the nearby brush, but saw nothing during my stint. Martinez took over at 0130, but before I could doze off, the trip flare directly in front of our position, where the trail entered the river, popped off and the machine-gun position opened up. After a few seconds the firing stopped and I scanned the bushes by the flare's eerie light.

I figured that any enemy troops out there would be hiding inside the ditch about forty meters away. I decided that we should attempt to grenade them, so I pulled the pin on one of mine and yelled "Grenade!" I stood up and threw as hard as I could, then hit the dirt and listened to the explosion and the dirt and metal crashing into the brush.

I remembered that Martinez had been a quarterback in high school, so we put the grenades that we had in a little pile, then set up Ralph's air mattress just in front of him. Gus stepped back, then lunged forward and threw with all his might, then let his follow-through carry him onto the mattress. He put three or four grenades into the ditch, then we waited for further action, but the rest of the night was deathly quiet.

At first light, Martinez, Allen and I crawled along the edge of the paddy, hidden by the low brush, to the spot where the flare popped during the night. We scanned the area, but aside from seeing where the sand and weeds had been disturbed by several grenade blasts, we found no trace of the enemy. We moved quickly back to our position, wolfed down our C-ration breakfast, then filled in our hole and saddled up. Led by the 3rd Squad, we humped back about three klicks due east to where the coastal plains were covered by white sands. There we would meet the APCs for transport back to Hill 54.

The tracks weren't in the area yet, so we dropped our packs and lay around in the shade. I spotted a shell of a bombed out building, made of stone and mortar, with one wall standing. It had one window with bars on it, so Martinez and I clowned around by standing behind the bars and yelling for a lawyer. Alabama took a picture of the two of us, then Sergeant Cain took a turn in the "slammer." I told Martinez that as long as I was in the Army infantry and in 'Nam, I was a prisoner, a prisoner at war.

After we reached Hill 54 and our platoon tent, the word came down to get our gear cleaned and readied for a new operation in AO Dog—the one I called Sniper Valley. We set some beer on ice while we worked on our weapons and replenished our ammo. I looked around the tent as the men worked; no one said much. I felt a kinship to these young lads who were a slice out of middle- and lower-class America, victims of their upbringing. They never really had a chance to escape the draft or, at least, service to their country. They had been taught, by parents who had lived through the Depression and World War II, that they owed an obligation to their government; a debt to be paid in blood if necessary. The words of JFK, at his inauguration in 1961, cemented that bond, and his death spurred many of us to follow the long list of Americans who asked what they could do for their country. These brave men had a special place in my heart that would never be touched by anyone else. There was an unspoken bond, a love between us that made us all brothers and comrades, in arms.

Each time we went out on an extended operation, the platoon lost a few men. Going back to the boonies was like playing Russian roulette as we kept spinning the cylinder and pulling the trigger. Each of these young men probably had the same thought somewhere in their heads—is it my turn? To break this train of thought, I trudged up to the CP, picked up the mail, brought the sack back to the tent and watched as they eagerly tore open their letters and retreated into another world.

Because of the impending operation, feelings were a little more intense and passions for loved ones half a world away ran higher than normal. It was not unusual for a GI to profess his undying love to someone he barely knew or make a profound confession to his mate or parents.

Fear motivated and instigated, then twisted the mind. I wondered if the mind of a grunt would ever operate normally back in the World. I was thinking too much again. Alabama sat down beside me and started to ramble.

"I can't wait to get outta here, Pete. My mind is getting all bent outta shape from all the shit we've seen since I got here. What are you gonna do when you get out of the Army?"

"If I make it, Alabama, I'm goin' back to school—no doubt about it."

"Man, I got no idea of what I might do. Maybe be a cop?" He made it a question.

"Did you ever think about staying in the Army?"

Before he could answer, a ruckus arose inside the tent and we moseyed over to see what was happening. Our new man, Dibble, replacing Ralph as the RTO for Nuckols, was regaling the troops with a short story of how he managed to fall from grace and get traded for Ralph. The upshot was, he got a little drunk and didn't want to suck up anymore, so here he was. He then proceeded to show his new friends a series of gymnastic somersaults and tumbles. I laughed at his tale, admired his acrobatics and wished him luck.

Alabama brought out a bottle of Jack Daniel's and we toasted Patterson, Vickers, Bennett, Marvin and anybody else we could think of before he drained the bottle.

He then headed for his bunk, but turned back and said: "I don't feel sure about anything anymore, Pete. I just can't get this damn war straight in my mind. Maybe I'll figure it out someday. See ya, guy, I'm gonna go pass out."

"Don't think about it, redneck. Just keep that gun handy tomorrow. Here's to ya."

I toasted him. Then, remembering what was coming tomorrow, I lifted my beer can again in a silent toast to all grunts.

The 2nd Platoon unloaded from the Chinook in AO Dog, formed up and headed west. I led the troops over a slight rise, across a narrow paddy and into the brush. I sent the trusty Alexus and his team ahead to scout out the area where the platoon CP would encamp; we had last been here in May when Snow killed a VC in the night. Alexus returned twenty minutes later and gave an "all clear," so the 1st Squad led the platoon into the position.

After a rest and chow break, Nuckols sent the 1st Squad back into a daylight observation post where the trail crossed the paddy. I set up behind a bamboo stand where we staged a tremendous battle against the mosquitoes and leeches. Around 1500, as the mind was becoming groggy from the heat, I heard an explosion back near the CP—about 500 meters away. I looked at Alexus, who had his team about twenty meters away behind some brush. We nodded at each other without speaking—somebody had tripped a booby trap. I waited a few seconds for things to shape up, then lifted the handset slowly to my face and spoke three words: "Who bought it?"

I didn't really want to hear any names, but some vicarious demon raised his head inside me and demanded to know everything—names, numbers and the gory details. There was quite a long silence, during which I imagined that the entire CP had been obliterated, then Lee came on.

"Williams, La Roque and Salisbury—all Whiskey India Alpha."

I hesitated for a second, then grasped the news—Alabama had been wounded. The big redneck had somehow gotten into a position where the M-60 couldn't bail him out. I whispered the news to Martinez, who had become a good friend and wrestling buddy of Alabama. He crawled over to Alexus and gave him the word. Alabama had come in-country about the same time as Alexus and I had, so the old-timers list was now shortened to Betta, Alexus, Sawlski and me.

We returned to the CP to help anchor the LZ on the other side of the hill so the medevac chopper could extract the wounded. Alabama had been heading to the stream just down off the knoll from where the CP had located. The VC, knowing the Americans would come to the water, had set several traps on the stream bank. Alabama triggered one that sent shrapnel tearing into his thighs and hips, but missed his vital organs—not a mortal wound, but he wouldn't be coming back. Salisbury and La Roque had less severe wounds, but would be out of action for a while. Ironically, the water they were seeking was now undrinkable; the VC had poured kerosene in it.

Only the comforting presence of Martinez and Alexus kept me from falling even deeper into the well of despair I had spent so much time in lately. I sat near my foxhole that night and thought about the October day when I had joined the company—it seemed years ago now. There had been four of us assigned that day to the 2nd Platoon: Marvin, now dead; Hinzman, severely wounded in November; Doolittle, shamming somewhere, and me. I was the only one of those left; now Alabama was gone. Even though we had disagreed on several occasions, he was a soulmate. I felt again as if I had been here all my life and I would never leave. Alexus slid over from his position and whispered to me.

"It sounds like he's on his way home, Pete. It's a million-dollar wound."

"I envy that part, but he's in for a long road to recovery with wounds like that. Home, when I think of it now, Lexus, it seems like some hazy, distant memory or some unreachable goal."

"I know what you mean, guy. It's like I'm almost afraid to think about it, afraid I'll jinx myself."

"We've got those short-timer blues, man."

Alexus didn't know it, but the few words with him had helped me fend off a serious case of depression. As it was, I spent the night napping fitfully and feeling alone, tired and homesick, wondering and waiting.

In the morning I took the squad to another daylight OP about 200 meters from the CP and we set up in tree line where we could check the east-west trail. I was lost in dangerous, hazy rumination, contemplating my future in the real world, wondering how in the hell could I adjust to such amenities as a refrigerator with cold beer and a real bed with clean sheets.

I heard the pop of an M-16, a single round, and my mind snapped back to reality in an instant. I hissed "Down!" at the men, then hit the jungle floor and saw that they did the same. We waited for more action, but nothing happened for the next few minutes, so I picked up the PRC-25 handset, broke squelch and with a sigh, asked Lee, "2–6, 2–1. Can I have a sit-rep? Over."

"Roger, 2–1. 2–2 wounded himself in foot." He paused for a second.

"Reported as accidental, out."

The soldier had been sent back to the field and was running the 2nd Squad in the absence of Sergeant Cain, who was back at Chu Lai. I had no idea whether the wound was accidental or not, but I knew he had been trying to get out of the field. If, indeed, he had pulled the trigger intentionally, I wondered what terrible demons were pulling and twisting on his mind, forcing him into such action. I hoped they weren't related to mine.

We continued to move around AO Dog for the next two days, setting up daylight observation posts and platoon ambushes or perimeters each night. We had no contact and managed to avoid tripping booby traps, although we disarmed one and found several grenades and mines in a bunker. We blew the armaments in place with the blasting cap from a claymore mine and some C-4. On July 13 we doubled back to the LZ where we had landed three days earlier and took resupply. It began to rain and continued in a drizzle all afternoon. It was a welcome relief from the overpowering heat and sun, but man was not meant to live in a rain forest or a fishbowl for obvious reasons, so we dug in and put up poncho tents.

My pensiveness and feelings of impending doom continued to drag me down, and both were worsened by the fact that I hadn't received any mail for a week. I sat in our hooch as Martinez and Allen opened their letters and sang a popular tune about being lonely soldiers and never getting letters.

I received no sympathy from the guys, but the rain did let up for a minute, before coming back in force. Charlie didn't like the rain either, so it was a quiet night, which only intensified my anxieties. I realized that I had been merely going through the motions lately and if I continued in that manner, I would likely get myself and others hurt or killed. Part of my twisted mind was saying, "At least the worrying would be over," but I gave myself a mental tongue-lashing and vowed to pull myself together for the next two months and let the survival instincts guide me safely home.

We moved out early the next morning, slowly picking our way south and west, entering back into the big valley, which I had named VC Valley because of the infestation of enemy therein. We stopped near another abandoned ville for noon chow break and I continued my morning-long motivational monologue to myself until I opened a can of peaches. Peaches from Army C rations could almost make the entire tour of duty meaningful; they were both delicious and nourishing.

I looked around to find a place to sit down and savor the golden slices in their syrupy nectar when we began to receive sniper fire from the woods. Undaunted, I moved around behind a dying tree and began eating. I heard a couple of the rounds thud into the tree trunk, but I felt secure. Then a piece of a dead branch was clipped off and fell into my treasured fruit. I roared, "That does it! That fucking does it!"

I jumped up and grabbed Fryer's M-79 and a bandoleer of rounds and set off jogging toward the stream that separated us from the woods. I stopped and knelt at the edge of the stream and began pumping bloop rounds into the trees. After putting about six rounds into the thick canopy, I stood up and walked casually back to my tree, pulled the branch out of my peaches and finished eating.

I felt much better and the fruit seemed to taste better. Despite being a squad leader in a combat zone, or because of it, I had not fired a weapon in anger in almost two months. I hoped that I wouldn't have to fire one again, but you never know when the enemy will strike at your fruit.

The men looked askance at me but I shrugged and said, "Guys, they're messin' with the wrong man's peaches."

We continued to search the area, then moved back to the site of our noon break to set up a perimeter for the night. As we were digging, word came down of 320 VC massed to move into the valley. I strode up to the platoon CP and said, "Only 320? No sweat, GI, the 29 of us can handle them, OR we could *di di* back to Hill 54 and call in air strikes."

"Negative, Pete. This is my last trip to the field and I'm not running from anybody or anything. We get these reports all the time. I don't think there are 320 VC in this valley or we would have seen some of them."

"Well, sir, we have to treat the reports as authentic in order to be. . . ." I let my voice trail off, seeing no point in arguing with a man obviously bent on moving to his next job in a blaze of glory. I figured he was bothered by the fact that he had not received any medals and would welcome a chance to correct that situation. I hoped he could appreciate the fact that medals could be awarded posthumously.

Word of the perceived threat had spread around the perimeter like wildfire. A grim-faced Allen and Fryer had cut logs and branches and piled dirt on them in front of the large foxhole they had dug. I glanced around and noticed others doing the same. I dug into my rucksack and found a couple more trip flares that I strung up just inside the others near our position. I told Allen to place the claymore in front of a large tree, then camouflage it well. The man on watch would hold the wire to the firing device in his hand to detect any attempt to turn it around.

We dug a small pocket in the top forward wall of the foxhole and another in the floor at an angle down and forward. I gathered a few frag grenades and stored them in the top pocket to fling at any attackers, then added a flare to light up the area if needed. The bottom pocket was the receptacle for enemy grenades that might get thrown into the hole. In theory, we would kick the grenade into the pocket and it would contain the blast enough to save our lives and lessen injuries. Although I doubted I would sleep, I found my resting position behind a tree just to the right and two feet behind the hole. From there I could roll, slide or jump into the hole at a moment's notice. By dark we were as ready as we would be, and tensions were high.

I could hear movement in the brush near us throughout the night, and in my sleepless state I conjured up visions of hundreds of well-armed VC lying in wait to attack, laughing at our puny defenses. I wondered what they were waiting for. Then at about 0200 there was a crashing noise and a flare popped between our position and the gun crew. The M-60 and several 16s opened up as the phosphorescent glow flickered and illuminated the area. The bushes took on a sinister glow and seemed to grow and move. I peered around the tree, trying to spot the enemy, but no targets were available. I slid into the foxhole beside Allen and Gus.

"See anything?"

"No, I heard the flare pop, then the gun opened up and we both poured a magazine into the area."

The unearthly light from the flare was dying, so I fished into the top shelf and found the one I had stored there.

"I'm gonna throw another one. Hey, gun crew—flare out."

I pulled the pin, then tossed it near where the first one had been tripped and waited with pounding heart and bated breath as the flare once more painted the area with its flitting amber-hued light.

"It's a pig. There's a dead pig out there."

Allen had spotted it and spoken in awe. I breathed a sigh of relief and fumbled for the radio handset.

"2–6, 2–1. Be advised we have one enemy KIA. A VC pig."

"2–1, say again, over."

"2–6, I say again—one Victor Charlie Papa India Golf. Out."

The poor dumb wild pig had probably been searching for nuts or berries, smelled our refuse and come sniffing around.

Boy, did he pick the wrong night. Some of the tension was lifted by the action and I could hear several different snores coming from these nerve-worn and exhausted men. I decided I may as well stay awake for the rest of the night, so I leaned up against my tree and waited for the dawn or an attack. A few hours later, only the dawn came.

The 1st Squad took some ribbing in the morning, but it was good-natured and reflected the release of tension among the men. I mixed a canteen cup of double-strength coffee and headed to the platoon CP. Lieutenant Nelson looked up from his map and asked, "Were there any weapons or documents on the VC pig?"

"Just an ID tag. It said 'I'm a Pig' in Vietnamese."

"I wish you could have captured him. G-2 wanted to interrogate him."

"You mean they wanted to grill him—preferably with barbecue sauce, right?"

"Well, we know your squad was alert, anyway. Pete, I can get you an in-country R&R—China Beach or Vung Tau. Want it?"

"Does a snake have lips? Yeah, of course I want it."

"OK. Get on the resupply bird this evening."

After leaving the CP, I headed over to the 3rd Squad position where I confided to Sawlski that both his foxholes were guarded by sleeping men at dawn. I spoke quietly. "I don't know how you handle sleeping on guard, but that's what happened on last watch this morning."

He looked sharply at me and there was a cold, hard edge in his voice as he responded. "Do you think the guys in your squad never sleep on guard? Who the hell do you think you are? Fuck you, man. You take care of your squad, I'll take care of mine."

"Fine—just fuckin' kill the messenger, but they were asleep and somebody could have been killed because of it. I would expect you to tell me if you see that happen in my squad."

I moved back to my squad and we saddled up for patrol, then headed across the stream and swept through a village, taking four suspects into custody. The 3rd Platoon killed one VC and the entire company went without casualty despite sniper fire. We took the detainees with us to a hill about two klicks away, then set up in a perimeter for resupply. We put two de-tainees on the first bird, then I spoke to the squad. "I'm going on a three-day pass, in-country R&R to Vung Tau. Alexus has the squad—he'll take care of you and himself. I'll see you in a few days. Keep your heads down. I wanna see every damn one of you ugly assholes when I get back."

Alexus looked at me and winked without showing emotion. "They'll be here. Drink a few for me, Pete."

As the second chopper came in, I moved to the shoulder of the hill. The birds had been making a one-skid landing on the side of the hill below the crest to avoid snipers, so anyone ap-proaching had to duck low to avoid the deadly rotor blades that were still whirling. A guy from the 3rd Platoon, whom we called Alphabet because of his long unpronounceable name, and I were heading for the bird, heads down, with a female de-tainee. She didn't hear or couldn't comprehend the instructions to lower her head and walked into the revolving blade which opened the top of her scalp. It wasn't a mortal wound, but there was plenty of blood and she was frightened.

She looked at me with those imploring eyes that I had seen so many times before in my nightmares, then pointed to her head. The fear and pain in those eyes reached into my gut and began twisting. I grabbed for the towel around my neck, but Alphabet was ahead of me and wrapped his towel around the woman's head and we took turns putting pressure on the wound.

When we arrived at Hill 54 he took her to the dispensary for treatment and I reported in to the clerk's office. I looked down at my hands and saw blood—it was a fitting comment on the entire war and my experiences.

The clerk handed me a copy of my orders and produced a cold beer from a cooler. He told me I could bunk at the CP tonight, then he'd get me a ride to the airport in Chu Lai in the morning. I carried some water to the shower tank, then soaked off a layer or two of grime and gore and changed into clean fa-tigues. I drank a few more beers and slept on a real cot after fending off more inquiries about the platoon KIA, the now in-famous incident of the VC pig.

I slept well for the first time in weeks, it seemed, then took a leisurely shave. I didn't have any stripes on my sleeve, but I took my breakfast tray to the NCO table and ate alone. One of the perks of being an NCO is that you can leave your tray and some REMF has to clean it up. At first I didn't like doing that because of the training I had received as a child, then I remembered that these guys were getting out of field duty by doing these tasks, so I gladly left the tray after that.

On this particular morning I got up from the table and started leisurely out the door when I heard an angry yell directed at my back.

"Hey, asshole, pick up your tray!"

"Back off, shammer—that's your job."

"I'm gonna report your ass to the first sergeant."

"Fine, I'll go with you. We'll make sure we tell 1st Sergeant Wolfe it's Sergeant Peterson, 1st Squad leader, 2nd Platoon."

The guy froze in his tracks, then picked up the tray. I had made another enemy, but that was what the hell this war was all about, wasn't it? When I got back to the CP, the clerk said that Jack Betta was coming in on a chopper soon, then we could both go to the airport together. Jack was nearly blind without his glasses and he had broken yet another pair. I don't know how he ever got into the Army. Perhaps the draft board in his county was desperate, or the doctor on duty was pissed at somebody.

We got a ride to the airport at 1200, but after hanging around for a couple of long hours, the Spec 4 on duty suggested we head over to the Replacement Depot to hang out until tomorrow. He winked at us and said, "You guys aren't in any hurry to get to PKU, are you? Here, I'll change your orders to tomorrow's flight and you can check in at TFO and drink a few brews."

The Task Force Oregon headquarters was a huge complex consisting of large well-built wooden buildings with screened windows. Jack pointed out the air-conditioning units outside some of the buildings and laughed. "Must be officers. War is hell."

We managed to get assigned to a barracks for the night, then took a quick tour of the place and found a library where we could catch up on sports and entertainment news. We made a selection and sat down on the floor to read, since the newly furnished room had no chairs. Betta, who had no trouble seeing up close, was looking at a recent magazine.

"Pete, here's an article that says we're getting trapped into sending more and more men to fight this war because the ARVN don't have the guts or the ability to fight on their own. Quote: 300,000 ARVN regulars, 300,000 militia and 100,000 popular forces are led by incompetent officers. Many of them are more interested in looting peasant villages than going out on patrol, especially at night. American troops do most of the fighting and most of the dying while about fifty percent of the ARVN soldiers desert each year. End quote."

"Hey, somebody back there does know a little of what's going on over here. It's a fact, Jack, that the ARVN will never fight while we're in-country and we don't have the patience to train them properly. Does that article tell us how to change things?"

"Let's see. One suggestion is to integrate Vietnamese troops with the U.S. units."

"We're already trying that and they're not pulling their weight. They just can't cut it, man."

"Going on—'To retrain the South Vietnamese in the art of guerrilla warfare.' That would seem to be our best bet, Pete, but how do you teach morale?"

"You can't, man. That's why we have to fight this war, I guess. They're not capable and don't care. Read on, Betta. I want to see who wins."

"OK, let's see. Quote: After we save South Vietnam, end quote. It doesn't say how or when we do it. It certainly can't be the way we're fighting it now."

"After we save Vietnam? Well, if you know how a movie turns out, you can leave in the middle. It would be nice if war worked the same way. Personally, I wonder if we can win without saturation bombing of North Vietnam and the Cambodian sanctuaries and maybe invading the north, especially Hanoi. A second front would bring a lot of those VC and NVA home in a hurry."

"All this talk makes me hungry and thirsty, Pete. Let's try to find a mess hall, then an EM club."

As we headed down the neat gravel path toward the mess hall, we strolled past the milepost sign which you find in every Army overseas post. I saw a board that said "Chicago 11,000 miles" and figured that was as close as they would get to my home, so I saluted it. We eased past another building and behind it saw a PFC firing up an outdoor barbecue grill on a stone patio with lawn chairs strewn about. It was another incongruous sight in a wartorn country for us, but seemed to fit in around here. He took one look at our filthy, scuffed boots, wrinkled fatigues and the scabs and sores on our arms, then broke out in a huge grin that was the most sincere thing I had seen since I got to this place.

He spoke to us in a friendly manner. "Hey, Infantry. Come back in an hour for a barbecue. We'll have steaks, chicken, hamburgers and lots of cold beer." He reached into one of a half-dozen portable coolers, grabbed two cold ones and handed us each one. We nodded and took the beers back to our barracks, which we discovered was populated now by fuzzy-faced, slick-sleeved new guys, fresh from the States and ready to take their place behind their heavily armed desks. We did an about-face and went back outside to find some peace and shade in which to enjoy our beer.

At 1800 we went back to the barbecue pit, where we gazed upon a glorious spread of comestibles and elixirs. We got in line with the doctors, nurses, clerks and other rear personnel and loaded up. Later, as we sat on a low wall of sandbags, the music, from a tape player, began and the REMF party started in earnest. After about an hour of revelry for the party crew and silent drinking for us, I looked at Jack, who was squinting in the dusk.

"This sucks. There's about three lovely nurses that I would love to get to know, but they've only got eyes, and God knows what the hell else, for the doctors. Let's get some beer and *di di mau.*"

"I'm with you. These folks throw a fine party, but it's not the same. I don't know how to act around normal people anymore."

"Yeah, I couldn't think of a frickin' thing to say to anybody and I was afraid if I opened my mouth nothing but cuss words would come out. It just doesn't feel right."

We scavenged half a dozen beers from the PFC, then took them back to our assigned barracks and drank them while resting against an unused bunker. At about 2300 we went inside and picked up an Army blanket from our cots and spent the night on the ground. Old habits die hard, and they say old soldiers never die. I hope they're right, for I am a soldier and I feel very old.

In the morning we took a short hop to Duc Pho, then hopped on a different C-130 to finish the trip to Pleiku. We moved through the familiar terminal which seemed to be quite a bit busier than the other times I had been there; the 4th Infantry must be getting some reinforcements. Outside, we found a truck with 1st/14th on the door and jumped on the back. It was raining lightly and the temperature was about fifteen degrees cooler than in Quang Ngai Province, but it felt great. The truck took us to the new 4th Infantry base camp and dropped us off on a road that would lead to the company compound. We reported in to 1st Sergeant Wolfe, who pulled duty back here when the company was in the field at Chu Lai.

Betta and I found a bunk and took our footlockers out of storage. I found two decent pairs of fatigues, then asked 1st Sergeant Wolfe, who had returned a couple of days ago, if there was a place to get them pressed. He sent me toward the heart of the camp with directions while Betta headed for the brigade dispensary to get his glasses. I was looking for a combination barbershop, dry cleaning and seamstress establishment to press my fatigues and sew on my sergeant's stripes, name tag and patches. The paths all seemed to head at right angles through the whole damn place and everything was laid out in squares.

I stopped on the path and looked at the shop about thirty feet away across a patch of grass that some slick-sleeved REMF was working over. In order to get there I could follow the path and turn at the corner, walk about 150 feet and make two more right turns, or I could cut across the grass. As I climbed through the fence, I heard the guy yell, "Hey, asshole, get the hell out of that grass. Can't you follow the fuckin' path like everybody else?"

This was the second time in two days I had been called that particular part of the human anatomy by a REMF. I took a long deep breath, then decided not to lose my cool, or my rank, over something as ridiculous as a patch of grass. I said, "I'm going into this shop. I'll be out in fifteen minutes. If you want me for anything, anything at all, see me then."

I went on across the grass while he continued haranguing

me. The shop was practically empty, so I was able to get the patches sewn on and the uniforms pressed in short order. I put one of the shirts on, then walked out of the shop and across the grass toward the REMF, who was slightly larger than me, and had assumed a patronizing attitude and stance until his eyes took in my stripes, patches and combat infantryman's badge. I could almost hear his crest as it fell.

"Now, son, if you've got any problems you'd like to discuss with ol' Sergeant Peterson of Charlie Company, 1st of the 14th Infantry, with ten months of combat duty—this is the time and place."

He looked at me, then at my stripes, then spoke quietly. "Sarge, I've got orders to keep people off the grass or turn them in to HQ. Sorry, I didn't know you were a sergeant."

"That's infantry sergeant, to avoid confusion with any rear asshole. Now, you're gonna get your chance to turn in this line doggie, cause I'm walking back across the grass. Now, remember, that's Sergeant Peterson. I'll be in C Company."

I walked across the grass as slowly as if I was in a park on Sunday, then headed back to the new company compound. The entire camp had been ingested into the 4th Infantry base, which was probably a portent of things to come, and the brigade now occupied only a small segment of the huge perimeter.

The First Shirt explained the layout to Betta and me and showed us where to take mess. As we went through the line, the food, even by Army standards, was unappetizing, so I took some bread and ignored the undistinguishable gray mass in murky sauce. When I reported the situation to Top, he sent us to brigade mess, where he had a friend. After we mentioned Wolfe's name, the cook gladly gave us a ten-quart pail of fried chicken which we took back to the CP.

Wolfe ate a couple of pieces, the supply sergeant did likewise, then Betta and I polished off the rest of the container over the course of the evening and drank the supply sergeant's Ballantine beer to wash it down. Tomorrow I would fly to Saigon, heading toward another Oriental adventure, hopefully a quiet one.

32

The C-130 I boarded was not your run-of-the-mill commercial airliner. Along each side of the interior was a row of seating which consisted of long metal racks with seat belts every few feet. Two more rows of seats ran back-to-back down the middle. Cargo was hauled in the rear section and there was no wall between it and the passengers. Since the plane wasn't full, I was able to find a seat alone near the back. Despondency and paranoia were winning the war to control my mind, so I closed my eyes, hoping the drone of the plane would put me to sleep.

I lay across the metal rack trying to decide how best to fight my most recent enemies. Two hours later, as we began our descent into Tan Son Nhut Airport in Saigon, I had decided that the only way to fight the depression and apprehension was to confront them head-on. It was possible that, by leaving Vietnam when my tour was over, I would leave them behind, but it was more likely that they would take a brief hiatus, then return, perhaps even stronger. I wondered again if I should take a thirty-day leave, then return to the country to finish out my Army hitch of five more months. This might be the way to put my demons to rest. As the plane taxied to a halt, I put my thoughts aside and began to fantasize about something tall and curvaceous, with a long neck and beautiful brown skin—a bottle of cold beer.

I walked through the terminal and spotted a hand-lettered sign that said simply Vung Tau. The airman in charge checked my orders and pointed to where a truck would be pulling up soon.

As I sat on a row of sandbags in front of the building waiting, I saw a group of fresh-faced young men with no rank glancing around wide-eyed as they boarded a bus to Long Binh for processing. Some of them were looking at me and pointing me out to others, so I put on my hardest old-guy look, but a piece of my heart went out to them. I flashed back to my own processing days ten months, ten years, a millennium ago and I wanted to tell them so many things, but it would take a month, so I looked away and saw my truck pull up.

Vung Tau was a beautiful seaside resort community dotted with colonial mansions built by the French in their days of yore. White sandy beaches ran along the coast of the South China Sea and the streets were much cleaner than most city streets in Vietnam. It looked like one of those Oriental cities you see in movies, although I was sure there were tin shacks and cardboard lean-tos somewhere out of sight; the workers had to live somewhere. The truck pulled into the courtyard of a huge villa that had been converted into a hotel by the U.S. government for use by GIs on three-day in-country passes. When I entered the lobby with its ceiling fans and 40s decor, I thought I had stepped back in time—perhaps into an old Bogart flick.

The rooms were large, but I had to share one with three airmen, who dropped their bags and headed for the bar. I staked out my claim on a bunk, then threw off my clothes and took a long relaxing shower. Later, I dined on steak and potatoes, stopped in the bar for a cold fifteen-cent beer, then wandered onto the huge veranda to watch the sea in the distance. I saw several pedicabs (pedshaws) lined up at the courtyard gate, so I walked over and made a show out of haggling with several of them for the best price to ride downtown. I finally selected one, which angered the others, and rode in the open air into the market and business district.

It was still clean here, also, which was refreshing and made me wonder if the U.S. government paid Vietnamese workers to keep it that way. I walked leisurely down the street, mentally selecting a handful of small gifts from the various shops and open vendor stands to pick up later. I tried to pick out a clean bar to patronize, finally finding one with a Vietnamese name and a bevy of Saigon tea girls. My financial condition and mental deterioration prevented me from entertaining any romantic notions, so I drank a couple beers and sat in a corner booth alone.

Finally a sailor stationed nearby sat down with me and we

exchanged pleasantries and combat stories. At 2000, I returned to the hotel, slurped down a ton of fifteen-centers and assuaged my loneliness by engaging in a little flirtation with a beautiful Vietnamese waitress. Her name was Ly, but the hotel workers could serve only your desire for libation and caloric nourishment—fraternization was forbidden. I told her I was an American hero. She laughed and said the VC would get me. She had to leave with the other workers at 2200, so I sat on the veranda, drank alone and watched as some of the GIs on leave crossed the street to a government-operated brothel, complete with medically certified prostitutes. A few of them picked out their "dates" and returned to the veranda with them to listen to the Vietnamese band mangle American rock music.

I took a shower when I returned to the room, then showered again when I got up in the morning. My roomies, the airmen, were beginning to think I had a fetish for water, but I didn't think I had to explain anything to them. After all, they were fighting an entirely different war.

After a late breakfast, I took a walk—in my civilian clothes and without weapon, I felt naked and light. In the marketplace I picked up an orange and some gifts for my family, then took a pedshaw to the beach where I sat on the sand under a huge palm tree, watching the sea for hours. I thought about the incongruities in "the 'Nam": here was this beautiful city, complete with a government brothel and a spotless beach, yet only a few miles away men were dying in the jungle. I estimated that I was the only fighting man in the hotel at this time; I knew about the diversion of passes and R&R allotments to the REMFs who were suffering from the pressures of paperwork. In the field, GIs died or were maimed while waiting for their pass; the man in the rear went when he wanted to. It wasn't fair, but it was war, and war, by its nature, is never fair.

I thought about a way to raise morale—the Army and Marines could bring an entire company into Vung Tau for a day and night with free drinks, food and brothel services. Their spirits would be lifted and field operations would go more smoothly. It had been done in other wars, in better times, but I suppose we considered ourselves too civilized for that sort of behavior in 1967. Sure, the U.S. burns villages regularly, rips civilians from their homes and turns its head while South Vietnamese officials and some supply sergeants run a ridiculously profitable black market and slave trade. But, they can't supply U.S. troops with harlots—unless they pay, of course.

I spent the rest of my three-day pass drinking in the hotel bar until the sun went down, then moving to the veranda and watching the sea. I ate a couple more grilled steaks, showered a lot and watched and listened as the band murdered "Proud Mary" a dozen or more times. Some of the troops tried to dance with their partners, but it was quickly evident that dancing was not a strong suit of these particular girls. I told Ly I could protect her from the VC, but she just giggled and feigned horror—at least I hope she was feigning.

On July 21, I showered once more, donned my fatigues and loaded onto a truck for the ride back to Tan Son Nhut. The clerk on duty at the main desk looked at my CIB and stripes and whispered to me conspiratorially, "I'll leave your arrival date open in case you want to spend a night here or in Pleiku before reporting back."

I thanked him, then took my empty wallet and my duffel bag with a change of civilian clothing, and boarded the plane. I was finding that there were almost as many "good guys" in rear jobs as there were assholes. For every surly clerk or slick-sleeve doing menial tasks while trying to sound authoritative, there was an airport desk clerk willing to change your orders to be more convenient. It was a start.

I spent two nights in the new base camp before heading to Duc Pho and Chu Lai on the 23rd of July. From somewhere, Underhill appeared on the plane, looking completely exhausted and still disheveled from his R&R. He grinned and spoke in a tired voice.

"Stanley, my man. I'm back from R&R."

"Hill, you look like shit."

"I was in Bangkok for six days and I smoked myself— drinking and stompin' all day and night. I've been back for two days and I just stayed drunk 'cause I can't stand this place no more. I feel like goin' AWOL."

"Hey, we all go through that shit after R&R, but you're on the downhill side now, man. Hang on, you're a cinch for stripes, dude."

"Will they keep me alive? Don't want 'em if they don't."

"They won't keep you alive, but they'll pay you better while you are."

We both lay back on the rack and tried to sleep on the flight. I couldn't, but I soon heard Underhill snoring loudly. As we neared Chu Lai, the plane, flying at about 500 feet, began bouncing and bobbing, then dropped quickly about 100 feet. I was sitting near the open ramp, so I grabbed the mesh harness and hung on as my ears began popping. The pilot quickly righted the craft and we landed shortly afterward. As we unloaded, Underhill and I lurched, like John Wayne, to a truck with TFO painted on the door. The driver agreed to drop us at Hill 54, so we lay down in the back and began swallowing to ease the discomfort. When we got to base camp we were still dizzy and out of sorts, so we stopped at the dispensary and explained our problems.

The medic could offer no help for the situation, but he gave us each about twenty Darvon. "This'll help you sleep."

I took my pocketful of Darvon and shaky body to the platoon, where Nuckols grinned and greeted us with, "Pete and Underhill, just the guys I wanted to see. We're goin' on ambush at 1800. Welcome back."

We went out about three klicks, then set up along the main trail in a line ambush, platoon-sized. I was still experiencing some dizziness so I tried to sleep, but that made it worse. I popped a few of the pills, but nothing changed, so I popped a few more. I then pulled a double watch because I didn't feel sleepy. At 0200, I fell into a deep, dreamless slumber and didn't wake up until someone nudged me at 0700. My ears popped a couple of times on the trip back to Hill 54, then the problem was gone. I threw my gear down in the platoon tent, then relaxed.

After picking up the platoon mail at noon and disbursing it, I took my poncho liner to a shady spot near the bamboo thicket about ten feet from the tent and began to read mine. One of my brothers was a father again, another wanted some souvenirs. There were race riots in Detroit and Newark, with killing, burning and pillaging. I read a couple of clippings to Martinez, then began my added comments.

"This tour of duty will harden us up and prepare us for stateside duty. Riots, protests—the country is falling apart. That does it. I'm staying here."

"Medic! Medic! Pete's lost his mind. Dustoff!"

"Listen, ol' Breeze, I'm seriously considering filling out a 1049—take thirty days' leave and come back to finish my hitch. I could keep my rank and maybe get a job as an instructor, or supply sergeant. They always need those."

"They also need platoon sergeants in the field. That's where you'd probably end up, Pete. Forget it."

"I wish I could, but the closer I get to DEROS, the more it keeps pulling on me. At least I know where I stand here. I guess I'll wait until next month to decide."

I wrote a couple of short letters, then headed up to the CP to mail them. Danny Malarik, now a squad leader in the 1st Platoon with Sergeant Able, approached me. Danny had been involved with an ambush a few nights back and had taken some shrapnel in the face but was only superficially injured. He and his squad had killed three VC and he had been recommended for the Silver Star for his actions under hostile fire. I wondered if I had pegged him wrong. Maybe he wasn't just a glory grabber; maybe he was just a damn good soldier with a lust for rank.

He stopped and put his hand on my shoulder, then spoke. "Pete, I owe it all to you for teaching me so well. Thanks a lot, man. I hope I can repay you."

I hadn't expected that at all, but I answered sincerely. "Malarik, you're right. I did teach you well. But, you were on your own that night. You don't owe me a thing."

"Thanks, anyway. A guy told me you and Betta had some good fried chicken back at Pleiku. That right?"

"We acted like we'd never eaten before that night—good chicken. I also recommend Vung Tau if you get a chance for in-country leave. It's got everything you want, and it's cheap."

We continued a routine of sweep patrols by day and ambushes by night, mostly within a couple of klicks of our forward base camp. The rumor mill was working overtime due to our increased idle time and the proximity to brigade forward HQ. The men were bandying about such stories as: We're going to the DMZ; we're going to join the 25th Division at Cu Chi; they're going to form a new company, Delta, and take some of our officers and noncoms. Lieutenant Nelson will be the new CO and Pete will get a platoon.

I was intrigued by that one, but I didn't think anything

would come of it. If the ten-day drops came down, I only had about fifty-eight days left, so I didn't feel I could contribute much to a new outfit and didn't really want to leave Charlie Company. However, it was nice to feel wanted.

On July 25 we swept through a village in the morning, then piled back on the APCs at noon to head for another one to pull security for a medical check. As we pulled out, I took a quick count, came up one short, but decided he was on the other APC. We headed up about two klicks up Highway 1, then veered off to the east to surround the other hamlet and the medics began to give inoculations and treatments. As I checked my squad again, I got a cold chill in my heart and a knot in my stomach—I was a man short. I approached Sergeant Nuckols with a sinking feeling and great trepidation.

"Sergeant Nuckols, I need to take a patrol back to the other village. We left Gibbs there."

"Jesus, Pete. What the hell is going on? We can't go back now, we gotta stay here. Christ! How could you do this?"

I waited for him to cool down, but I knew we had to go back to the other ville and pray he was still there. He steamed in silence for a long while, then spoke more slowly, "All right. We've got to pull security here until they're done, but when we head back, I'll go with your squad and a couple of APCs to find him. Pete, what the hell are you gonna do next?"

I considered that to be a rhetorical question, so I rejoined my remaining squad members. At 1700 we headed back to Highway 1 and turned south. As we neared the turnoff to the first village, I realized that I would have to take the consequences if we couldn't find the guy, but I wasn't concerned about that, I just wanted him back. Just then I noticed a jeep pull up behind us. The grunt in the back was holding his M-16 on a young male Vietnamese. Nuckols yelled, "That your man?"

I had a big smile on my face and my heart felt like it had wings. "That's my man. Went all the way to Hanoi for a prisoner."

When we reached the main gate, Nuckols chewed Gibbs out for disappearing, then sent him with his prisoner to G-2. I escorted him to the CP, then pointed out the G-2 hooch, which was my second mistake. My man took the prisoner to Colonel

Miller's hooch by mistake, then took another terrible ass-chewing for bringing an unsecured prisoner to him. By the time he got to the platoon tent and presented himself to me, it was dark. He sighed and asked me, "I suppose you're really going to get on my ass?"

"Negatron. We both made mistakes today and we both learned some valuable lessons. Besides, you don't look like you've got much butt left. Get some rest."

Lying on the board floor in the corner of the tent with the flap raised, I wondered just how in the hell it had happened. How could I lose track of a man? From this moment on, I would keep a closer watch on all of the men. This would not happen again.

Mail call on the 26th brought letters from Kevin Patterson and Garland Walker. Kevin's letter told of his recuperation in the Philippines and how he was awaiting shipment home. He mentioned two operations on his knee already and said there would be some permanent damage, but the mood of his letter suggested that his spirits were high—or else he was getting some great drugs. Walker was getting ready to go home from a hospital ship, the USS *Sanctuary*. He thanked me for working with him, but he had lost the sight of his right eye and his mood was restrained. Jackson, the third man wounded on that fateful June day, was back on duty in the squad. I hoped that the Almighty was treating the soul of PFC Joseph Marvin kindly.

We had been taking short patrols in the coastal area near base camp and ambushing the main trails at night. I figured HQ was planning something major for the month of August for Charlie Company and was giving us the rest of July to replace personnel and equipment while securing the areas close to Hill 54.

On July 27 we moved out about four klicks and began sweeping through some abandoned villes. We ran across only a few stragglers and took no fire. We stayed one hill range away from real enemy territory and sent in a few detainees, but had no hostile action, saw no booby traps and suffered no casualties.

Like they said in the old western movies, "It's sure quiet out here, sir."

"Yeah, too quiet for me."

It was good training for the new 2nd Platoon leader and Sergeant Watley, who took over the Weapons Squad. Our new CO had been with us for several weeks, but had not worked with the 2nd Platoon, so we got to see what he was like in the field. After mail call on the 28th, Sergeant Nuckols came to talk with me. I could see he was agitated about something. He said, "Pete, I put my home return address on the film we used after Underhill and Sally shot up those dinks. My wife is really mad because I took pictures of dead people and sent them home where the kids could see them. What am I gonna do? She really chewed my ass in this letter."

"There's only one thing you can do, Nuck. Tell her the truth. You were captured by a company of NVA regulars and forced to take those pictures or die. Luckily, that night, you were able to escape and take the camera with you. While you were crawling those fifty miles back to American lines, you passed a mailbox and dropped the roll of film in. Since you didn't know where you would end up, you put your home address on the roll and that's how it got there."

"Thanks, Pete. I don't know what I'd do without you, but I'm willing to try."

We moved into Sniper Valley the next day, sweeping the big village where we had lost men and taken fire on each of our previous forays; this time it was quiet. At 1600 we made a big show of taking resupply and pretending like we were digging in next to the river where we had stayed in a night defensive position several times before. At dusk we moved out quietly to a nearby hill, which we had scouted out in the afternoon, and dug in quickly. At 2300 the position we had deserted took a barrage of rocket and rifle grenade fire that appeared to originate from the west side of the river. We couldn't tell if the VC also tried to attack the abandoned perimeter, but I didn't hear any small-arms fire after the original bombardment.

I had mixed emotions as I watched the fire and explosives rain down on their targets; it felt good to have completely fooled the VC, but their firepower frightened me. What if we hadn't moved? How many men would have been killed or wounded? I slept lightly the rest of the night, but the VC must have shot their wad and disappeared, as usual. To my surprise, we did not stay in the area the next day, partly because the source of the fire was out of our AO and also because we had to move a little more than three klicks to meet the APCs by 1100. We made the rendezvous, then rode back to Hill 54 for a couple days of rest. The next big operation was due to start on August 2.

On the night of July 31, Martinez, Fryer and I took an evening stroll, following the road down past the water tanks and makeshift showers, skirting the fly-covered crappers, on past the path that led to the dispensary on the right and the helipad on the left. It was near dark, we had the night off and we were heading to the barracks where rear personnel lived to visit Ralph McQueen. We passed the almost-darkened mess hall on our left where the shammers were cleaning the kitchen while listening to the Temptations, crossed over the road that ran down past the EM club and the barbershop to the main gate. On our right was the chapel and, finally, ahead of us were the barracks.

It was a narrow, unassuming wooden building with sandbags stacked halfway up the outside, then screen covering the rest of the sides to the metal roof. On the inside the men had most of the comforts of home, which I had decided wasn't worth getting upset over anymore. Ralph was standing by a portable grill, trying to fire up some charcoal briquettes. Fryer yelled at him, "Ralph, we can't leave you alone for a minute. Look at you, Bermuda shorts, barbecue grill—you've probably even got cold beer and steaks."

Ralph slapped hands with all of us, then gave us a cool one. "God, it's good to see you guys. Anything I can do for you?"

We talked for twenty minutes or so, but there was a gulf as wide as the DMZ between us even though he had been back here only about two weeks. The feelings were epitomized when one of the denizens of the furnished apartment brought out three huge steaks and handed them to our former platoon member.

"Here, McQueen. I want mine medium-rare, Jonesy wants his medium-well. Grill should be hot, so get 'em on there."

I looked at Ralph, searching out his eyes in the flickering light, but he averted my gaze and began grilling the raw meat. The men and I had saliva forming in our mouths as the meat sizzled, spat and began to throw off its delicious aroma. I stood up, shouldered my empty rifle and made ready to leave.

"Gotta go, man. Cold beer and hot steaks. This is no place for a grunt. I've gotta find a good place to throw my poncho liner on the ground before they all get taken. See ya, guy."

"See ya, Pete. You guys keep your heads down. I'll come over to the platoon tent soon."

He sounded almost apologetic and I knew he wouldn't ever come to the tent again, but it didn't matter. He had gone over—become a REMF. As we wandered back toward the platoon tent, Martinez found his voice. "I'd like to have a nice safe job in the rear, but no way could I handle that sucking up business. How can he take that?"

"I guess fear is the great motivator and we all handle it differently. In the field, we use it as a survival instinct, to build our respect for the enemy and stay alive. He lets fear use him, so he grovels for a rear job and sucks up to keep it. If he can live with it, more power to him. I couldn't."

I shrugged my shoulders and mentally closed another chapter in my life. *Xin loi,* Ralph.

July quietly turned into August and we took one more day-patrol, then got the night off. Our pay was burning a hole in our fatigue pockets, so we "cut a chogie" down to the Dragon's Lair and exchanged a good share of it for cold cans of beer. About fifty young and a few not so young men crowded around a few picnic tables and exercised their inalienable right to act stupid. One well-placed mortar round could really raise some hell here, but then the Vietnamese who work here might lose their jobs, so I figured we were safe. After about thirty minutes of the racket I got the attention of the manager of the place and notified him that I would like to purchase two cases of the stuff, and I wanted it cold.

He explained that he could only sell it cold over the bar and if I wanted it wholesale, it would be warm. I informed him that if he didn't sell me some cold beer I would have the 2nd Platoon, also known as the Savages, reduce the place to rubble in a matter of minutes. As is often the case, we were both bluffing, at least a little, so we managed to iron out a compromise. I purchased one case of cold beer at a slightly reduced price and he would consider selling another later.

Martinez and I returned to the platoon area and put the case down. Alexus and Betta joined us and we began telling lies and combat stories; after a while, no one could tell the difference or cared to. I saw Underhill and another black soldier come strolling down the path from the CP area. When they reached the area where the grunts stayed, the other black soldier stopped and said he had to go back to his hooch. He and Underhill spent the next five minutes or so exchanging handshakes and "daps," then ended with a fist salute.

"Hill, doesn't all that 'dapping' wear you black guys out? Your arms have to be tired after that. Whatever happened to just shaking hands?" I asked, with tongue firmly in cheek.

He flashed those white teeth of his in a broad grin. "Stanley, my main man, you oughta know us black folks never get tired. We're in good shape from all the shit you honkies been makin' us carry around for 300 years."

I wanted to throw some of the slang that the brothers used when they spoke, but I was woefully ignorant about it, which didn't stop me from trying anyway.

"What it is, bro. What it was, what it will be. Get down, Hill."

Underhill began to laugh, a deep rumbling laugh that sprawled him onto the tent floor. He continued for about five minutes in so engaging a manner that we all joined him. When he finally stopped, he staggered off to the water tank and splashed water on his face for a minute, then came back.

"Stanley, you made me really laugh for the first time in months."

"Am I a righteous dude, Hill, or what?"

"You're a righteous dude, bro. Can you handle some skin?"

We slapped fives in each direction and he showed me a couple of other daps of low degree. I offered him a beer and he helped us finish off the case, then we slept.

On the morning of August 2 word came down that the company would be heading out tomorrow for a long operation—at least several weeks. We were given the day off with orders to clean all gear and weapons and replenish ammunition and armament stocks. I had hoped, in a way, that we would somehow be put on guard duty at Hill 54 for the next seven weeks, but such was not my lot. I also knew that I had to confront all of my enemies at least once more, so let it be now. The ominous feeling crept over me again as I washed my weapon in kerosene and totally wiped it down.

Around noon I could take it no longer, so I formed a beer and ice patrol. We filled two barrels with beer and the dirtiest ice I had ever seen (I wondered where the water had come from), then finished our chores while it cooled. I picked up the mail and distributed it, then we took our noon meal. The mood was somber, resembling those movies about the final hours of a condemned man.

I went through the motions during the day, avoiding conversations and confrontations. As the skies began to darken and the beer began to flow, some of the rear personnel began to make their way to the tents. This pilgrimage, of sorts, was a salute, a farewell, and a means of communion for them with their brothers who were headed into harm's way. Some of them had been in the field before being shifted to a safer locale and this was their way to touch us with their spirit—to link hearts. I could feel the camaraderie in the air; it was like homecoming, New Year's and graduation all in one night. The feeling was magical, but heartbreaking.

I saw Sidney Lee, until recently an RTO with us, now in supply; Ray LaBarge began in the 2nd, now the clerk and everybody's favorite because he got the mail to us; Larry Vansworth, started with the 2nd, now also in supply. I felt no animosity or jealousy toward these men, for each had reached his position by the purest chance. It was as if the REMF angel had tapped them each on the shoulder and bade them to quickly "pick up your gear, son, you're going to the rear."

Our new platoon leader was holding court near a light at the tent doorway. He was chubby, bespectacled, of medium height and totally unimpressive. He was sweating profusely in the night air and I wondered what would happen in the heat tomorrow. Back in the World he had been running a golf course for the Army, now he would be at least partly responsible for thirty men on the verge of death. I listened for a minute and shuddered inside as he told how things would be now that he was in charge.

I walked away to the near darkness outside where I joined Martinez and LaBarge sitting on a piece of broken pallet,

singing along with a Simon and Garfunkel tune about a rock
feeling no pain. I guess I could remain a rock on the outside, as
long as I could keep my inner demons at bay.

I took the proffered bottle of Jim Beam whiskey and took a
long pull—there, that's one way to hold the bastards off. The
next time the bottle came around, I took a smaller sip, then
picked up my poncho liner, moved about thirty feet up the hill
and lay down across an empty bunker to wait for dawn.

33

As we walked through the morning haze toward the pickup
zone just outside the wire surrounding Hill 54, I took a quick
look at my surroundings. I made a mental note of everything in
the base camp for some reason as I hopped on the waiting
chopper, then tried to put on my war face as we lifted off in a
swirl of sandy dust. We were on our way again—back to the
jungle.

The choppers darted into the huge valley, hesitated just long
enough for us to be disgorged, then quickly *whap-whapped*
their way back out, taking only a few rounds of sniper fire as
they did. We quickly formed up, then headed out by platoons in
different directions, to rendezvous at 1800 near the burned-out
ville.

Alexus and I led the 2nd Platoon toward the northwest, then
stopped about 200 meters from the deserted village that we had
first swept through in May. We had checked back on it every
few weeks and always seemed to ferret out a few more VC. The
platoon remained in place while I took my squad on recon. I
sent Martinez and his team on a quick foray into the remains of
burned-out hooches, while Alexus and his team went with me
to look over the trail and river crossing.

It all checked out clean, so I called in the platoon and we set up a loose perimeter. The new lieutenant then sent the other two squads to search the rest of the ville thoroughly while my squad pulled CP security. At 1800 the company joined us and we set up our NDP, dug in and waited. It was the same position where we had taken sniper fire, perimeter probes and the VC had rocketed after we had left, but nothing happened on this night.

The company moved due south in the morning, then split up into platoons, which split further into squads. I took my squad on a patrol to double back near the south side of the same ville we had just left, where we hid in the bushes across the paddy from the ruins and waited for some sign of life. There was no moving air in the brush and the heat was intense throughout the day. At 1400, I sent Allen, Fryer and Galaviz to a well on the edge of the village, to fill our canteens. They circled to the west staying in the cover of the brush, then doubled back to the well where Fryer began filling the containers while the others guarded.

I was giving a radio sit-rep to the platoon when I heard a couple of yells, then a muffled explosion. The remainder of the squad went to full alert as we tried to find out what had happened. I saw the three soldiers milling around a bunker, then they picked up the canteens and headed to our position. When they reached us, I saw that Allen appeared dispirited and ashen-faced. Fryer gave me the story. "Allen heard these voices in the bunker, so he went up to check it, then yelled at them to come out. They didn't. Then he heard a click, like a safety being taken off, so he threw in a grenade. We checked it out—there were three dead bodies."

"Did they have weapons or anything like that?"

I wanted him to tell me that they all had weapons, so I was sure they were really VC, not civilians afraid to come out. Allen looked at me with his once-innocent blue eyes and grudgingly spat out his story. "I heard 'em laughing, so I walked over and took a quick look in. They were doin' it—havin' sex, in the bunker. Two men, one girl. One of the men had a light-green uniform on, the others wore black pajamas. I told them to come out. I thought they had a weapon, but I'm not sure. I threw the grenade in. Pete, I killed a woman."

He was in desperate need of reassurance, so I spoke calmly,

just so he could hear a voice. "You killed three VC, Allen. Some of their best troops are women and you probably removed some of the snipers from the area. The guy with the green uniform was probably cadre, the others were recruits. I don't know what kind of lessons he was giving with his pants down, but he won't do it again."

I made a mental note to keep an eye on Allen, then picked up the radio and made a report to the platoon. The new lieutenant, whose name I didn't care to learn because I had already decided I didn't like him, asked quickly, "Were there any weapons or gear? Over."

"Negative. Three VC, one dressed in fatigues." I thought he might send us back to check the bodies so I threw in a clincher. "Couldn't check them real close—bunker collapsed on them. Over."

"What were they doing in the bunker?"

"They were fornicating, 2–6. Caught with their pants down."

"2–1, say again, over."

"2–6, they were having Sierra Echo X-ray—some kind of ménage à trois. 2–1, out."

Our reputation was surely growing by leaps and bounds in the battalion. The same platoon that had killed the VC pig had now fragged an orgy. As I sat on the edge of my foxhole that night, I again questioned the type of war we were involved in. I still believe that we were right to be in 'Nam, but I was becoming more and more certain that we were waging the wrong kind of war. My heart went out to Allen, who had seen close-up the kind of carnage that had sent my mind reeling so many times. I hope he can pull himself together and not be overwhelmed by the event—those demons are waiting.

The 2nd Platoon humped down the valley the next day, then crossed the river and headed west over a low hill range into a larger valley—the one I knew as Death Valley. The new platoon leader continued to grate on my nerves as he insisted on making changes in platoon procedures without regard to safety or the time it took to implement them. I was certain that he was more concerned with putting his stamp on the troops and their actions than he was in improving them. If he had taken a little time and thought things through before issuing his petty orders, everyone would have been better off.

I continued to ignore him as much as possible, doing all my CP business through Sergeant Nuckols or one of the RTOs, but as we set up on a hill that overlooked a small ville and the major east-west trail, he made an inspection tour.

"Sergeant Peterson, your men have got to dig that hole deeper and fortify it better."

I had been digging holes for more than ten months, and it burned my butt to hear this from a fuzzy-faced, green officer whose only combat experience had been battling to keep the moles out of his golf course back in the World.

"We stopped when we hit rock. Can't go any further."

"I don't want to hear that. You're the squad leader. See that it gets done properly."

I turned slowly to face him, then loaded up my voice with as much sarcasm as I could muster and answered. "Yes, *sir!* Anything else, *sir?*"

I whipped a salute at him, something you didn't do in the boonies—a salute identifies the salutee as an officer to any enemy who might be watching. He was too green and full of himself to pick up on my deliberate indiscretion and I ducked down before he could answer back. In my paranoia I believed that Charlie was watching nearly every move we made and I didn't want him to think that I might be somebody important, somebody worth a bullet.

I decided to call him Lieutenant Prick, because of his overbearing attitude and his failure to draw on the experience of the men in the platoon, and because he acted like one. Later that night he came back to check on our hole in the dark. I had the men kneel down to make the hole look deeper—he glanced at us, then wheeled around and headed back to the CP hooch. Martinez held his laugh until he was gone, then let out as quiet a chortle as he could and added, "He'll never make it, Pete. If the enemy don't get him. . . ."

He left the remark hanging in the night air. Nobody wanted or needed to elaborate.

As we moved down off the low hill the next morning, the lieutenant called a halt to the column and ordered us to camouflage ourselves with branches and leaves. We complied, but not without a substantial amount of grumbling.

"Frickin' new lieutenant," Alexus said. "Like, the VC won't know we're here. We haven't camouflaged since the border, man."

I managed to snap off a couple of leafy branches and insert them into my elastic headband. "It might be a good idea, but why didn't he think of it earlier? We'll probably tip off the enemy to our presence by all this screwing around trying to make us less noticeable."

"Screw a bunch of new lieutenants, as Vickers would say," Martinez added.

"I hear ya, guy." Even after ten months, Alexus was still speaking Californian.

Because of the extreme heat we limited our daily movements to a few hundred meters. We found shade, then set up in a daylight ambush or observation post before heading to our preselected location for a NDP and/or an LZ. That night we set up on a large, two-tiered rice paddy next to the river we had crossed to get into the valley and joined the rest of the company to receive resupply.

About twenty minutes after the chopper lifted off, a sniper fired a burst of about ten rounds, waited a minute or two, then fired another. We scattered to the holes, then searched in vain for a target. After a few minutes of silence we climbed out and resumed our meals, and I picked up the squad's mail from the CP. I grabbed the copy of the *Stars and Stripes* and began reading, then I decided that Alexus should hear the news.

"Philip, my man, they're tearing things apart back in the World. Race riots, war protests and they're burning their draft cards in Berkeley—as if that'll make a difference. Maybe Tom Wolfe was right—you can't go home."

"The country is going to hell, Pete. I hope they let me take my 16 home with me."

At 2245 sniper fire ripped into our perimeter once more and Martinez and his fire team, on OP in front of our position, reported noise and movement in front of them. I took the rest of the squad out into the brush to reinforce them. As I lay there behind a log I could hear what sounded like something crawling between us and the river. My imagination, still on overtime in my eleventh month, estimated at least a battalion of VC were sneaking into the perimeter. I put the OP on 100 percent alert to listen for the source of the noise, but after an hour or so it stopped.

At 0230, I lowered the status to two men up, four down and I stayed awake, manning the radio and reporting sit-rep. At 0430 my head finally started to nod and I handed the receiver to one of the men on watch. An hour later I was awakened by a shout from the perimeter. I grabbed the handset from the dozing guard.

"This is 2–1. Sit-rep negative, over."

"Don't give that sit-rep negative shit. Where the hell have you been, 2–1? We've been trying to reach somebody out there for twenty minutes. Get your ass in here, we're gonna have a mad minute in 0–5. Out."

We hauled our embarrassed asses back to the perimeter and joined in on the mad minute, when the entire perimeter opens up—each troop fires a magazine or a few bloop rounds into their field of fire. Charlie had an amazing habit of sneaking in close to our perimeter to either snipe at us or go for our leftovers after we clear out. This random firing could put a crimp in his plans, if not his life, and also raised our morale. After all, we had guns, and guns were toys, weren't they? No matter what his age the male still likes to play with loud toys, create noise and be noticed; during our momentary madness, we did indeed make noise and ol' Charlie certainly must have noticed.

Luckily, Sergeant Nuckols was in charge of discipline for the platoon, so I presented myself before he asked for me.

"Sergeant Peterson, reporting for execution. We were asleep on guard duty. We had been awake until 0430, but that's no excuse. Could I have a last cigarette?"

"Get the hell outta here, Pete. I know you wouldn't sleep on guard. Send me the guys who did."

"It was my squad. I accept responsibility and punishment."

"Pete, you ain't helping these guys by covering for them. Send me the sleepers."

"All right, but remember they were awake all night until 0430. Be easy on them."

As I walked back toward my position I vowed that what had happened last night would not happen again. In my zeal I had overused my men and they had responded as long as they could, but—and I had to remember this—they were human. Humans get extremely tired in the jungle at night after working in the heat of the day, and when you're tired you make mistakes. Unless we were under direct attack, I would have at least one man resting at all times. I was still learning after ten months, and some lessons came hard.

As I passed near his position I heard Sawlski yell at me and whoever wanted to hear, "You boys took a nap on watch out there, Pete. I thought the great 1st Squad didn't do that."

"Never said that, man. We did it and we'll take our punishment like men."

I felt foolish snapping back at Sally and his flippant remark, but the honor of my squad, or what was left of it, was at stake. Nuckols sentenced the two men to shit-burning detail the next time we were in base camp as punishment and we saddled up to comb the hill to the north.

Allen asked, "What punishment does the squad leader give to the man on watch?"

"I didn't do a very good job planning the watch schedule, so I'm guilty, too. There'll be no added punishment, but it will not happen again. Ever," I said evenly.

As we moved out of the perimeter, the CO got word that a unit of the 196th was moving after a VC unit of undetermined strength in the mountains to the west. We were ordered to head in that direction to set up a blocking force at the base of the large mass of hills.

The CO quickly got on the horn and alerted all the platoons. The rear element then became the point and we set off in a southwesterly direction, following the main trail for about two klicks, then cutting across the rice paddies and crossing a small stream. By 1130 we were in a blocking position at the foot of the hills. We were extremely tired and sweaty, but we were ready to take on the VC unit, if it was really there. I set my squad along a hedgerow next to an abandoned hooch, where we had good shelter and a view of the hillside.

About forty minutes later the radio reported that the first element of troops from the 196th had spotted us and were coming forward. They straggled out of the tree line and made a beeline for a well next to the hooch at our position. They were tired, hungry and disheartened by another near-miss—in short, a lot like us. I spotted one of their old guys right away. He wore his tenure in his face; his eyes were sunken with heavy bags underneath and the lines on his countenance almost formed the map of Vietnam's I Corps. I moved over to talk with him and saw the look, the thousand-yard stare, that true veterans of this conflict always developed and wondered if I was looking in a mirror. He spoke out of a narrow slit that opened under a large nose and a dirty, bushy moustache. The words came out in a thick Texas drawl.

"Y'all chasin' ghosts down here, too?"

"Seems that way, Sarge. Hit and run, kill and hide—can't ever seem to pin 'em down."

"Shore takes a lot out of ya, don't it? My men are plumb tuckered out. Listen, Sergeant, could y'all spare some chow? We left our packs in the perimeter up yonder."

I made the rounds of the squad and came up with enough chow to feed them and we all took our chow break together. Afterward, they filled their canteens and began moving slowly back up the slopes of the hill mass. I felt better knowing there was another American unit close by, but we would have to maintain better fire discipline when we patrolled this end of our AO. Charlie Company then moved out to the north and resumed our search of the area. We moved slowly through the heat of the afternoon, then headed back to the same NDP we had maintained the previous night.

We re-dug the same holes, which was a lot easier than breaking new ground, then put out our flares and trip wires. For some reason the new lieutenant had steered clear of me for a day or so, which pleased me greatly. The 2nd Squad put out an OP just across the stream, where they hid in the brush near a branch of the main trail about thirty meters from my position. Just past midnight a trip flare popped there and they opened up. I rolled out of my sleeping trench into the foxhole and grabbed the handset in time to hear House yelling, "OP coming in, 2–6! We're comin' in, don't shoot!"

They came splashing across the water, then clambered up the steep bank like Olympic steeplechasers to the safety of the perimeter. House, once in my squad and now a team leader in the 2nd, was rattling on and on excitedly.

"I got one! I shot one! He was right there in front of me. I got one!"

We finally got him calmed down and into a fighting position. The perimeter remained alert for another hour or so, but the VC unit had apparently moved along or retreated. The OP-LP had done its job well, not only spotting a possible probing unit, but forcing them to flee in disarray. We did something right, I thought as I lay back in my trench. Hey, captains Federline and Childers, medics, Marvin—all of you ghosts—listen up. We did something right.

The 2nd Platoon crossed the river early on the morning of August 9, eager to find the bodies of the VC slain by House and his team. We found the broken wire and the shell of the expended flare and some spent cartridges, but no bodies and no blood trails. The Vietnamese jungle had swallowed all the evidence, if there had been any. House was quieter now, the adrenaline rush being replaced by a dose of daybreak and reality. He was mumbling softly, but still defiantly, "They came back for the body. I got one—right here."

"OK, Got One, let's move out," I said.

I could empathize with House, remembering the ambush we pulled back in February when Alabama's gun was surrounded and we opened up from the side. I thought for sure we would find several bodies in the morning, but only one was still there. House was a pretty good soldier who had volunteered for the LRRPs and left my squad. Later he changed his mind and came back to the platoon, but Nuckols put him in the 2nd Squad to give Cain another experienced hand. He talked and bragged a little too much for my tastes, but it wasn't a grievous sin and I would take him back in a Saigon minute.

The company headed south, then east back to Sniper Valley to check through the abandoned ville we had been through a few times before. We set up in a daylight observation, but there was nothing to observe, so we rested. That evening we moved into an old site we had used two months before and set up our perimeter. The new lieutenant inspected the perimeter at 1900, telling every position to dig deeper holes and fortify them. He had managed to enrage more men in the few days we had been on this operation than Lieutenant Nelson had in his six-month tour.

He didn't appear to have any favorites, but I felt like I was on the top of his shit list and he appeared to enjoy breaking my balls. Betta, Sawlski, Alexus and I had the most time in the field, all ten months or more, so he probably thought if he could show some authority over us, the others would fall in line. Logical in theory, but first he had to live through it. If one listened to the grumbling and attributed any validity to the scuttlebutt that went around our sector of the perimeter, one might believe that a terrible accident was looking for a place to happen.

I missed Lieutenant Nelson and his quirks. We had our differences and I thought he overused my squad and exposed the platoon to danger unnecessarily at times, but he never abused his authority with the men. He cared for the individual soldier and was quick to commiserate when a GI had something on his mind. Also, he was a good soldier. He had visited our tent as we prepared to leave last week and sat down to talk with Nuckols on the steps. He asked, "How was I, Nuck? Did I do all right as a platoon leader?"

"I've worked with worse. You did OK."

I could see he wanted more than an OK, so I told him he was one of the best platoon leaders I had seen in my ten months. That seemed to please him and I figured it wouldn't hurt my chances at getting a ten-day leave, if he had anything to say about it. As I thought about it now, I missed his leadership because it was genuine, not an affected manner. He was one of those men who wore the mantle of leadership as if he were born with it, while our new lieutenant looked like he was trying it on and it was the wrong size—too big for him.

We took no sniper fire or line probes that night, then headed out by platoons back into Death Valley in the morning. Because of the searing heat, my sweat-stained, salt-caked pants rubbed against my crotch, causing the heat rash to break out again in profusion. When we stopped in a small ville for noon chow, I stripped off my shorts and threw them into the bushes, then splashed water on my groin. After it dried I sprinkled a liberal dose of Army foot powder, which immediately cooled the area somewhat. I sighed and leaned back against a palm tree to munch crackers and cheese spread and it began to rain.

I glanced skyward. "You're testing me again, right?"

As we were finishing chow, Sergeant Nuckols' radio came

to life. After passing on some information on resupply, the familiar-sounding voice added some news for 2–5.

"2–5, be advised that you have a new Echo-6 in your platoon. Do you read? Over."

"Is that you, Ralph? Do you mean troop number 79? Over."

My ears perked up. The company used a numerical system to identify each troop on its roster and I thought 79 was my designation.

"Affirm and affirm. 2–1 is now an Echo-6. Congratulate him for me. Out."

"Well, Pete, did you hear that? You're now a damned E-6. Congratulations, staff sergeant. Beer's on you at base camp—again."

Staff Sergeant Cain was sitting on a dike near the trail and began shaking his head in disbelief at the news. "I've been in this man's Army eight years and I made E-6 in March. How long have you been in the Army, Pete?"

I was feeling a little giddy, but I tried to keep everything on a lighthearted basis. "Sixteen long, hard, damned months—count 'em. It seems like years, though, to me."

"Damn, man. You should still be a PFC. Oh, what the hell, congratulations, man. You're buying beer for sure."

I stepped over to the irrigation ditch to relieve myself, then announced to all who could hear, "Gentlemen, observe, if you will, how a staff sergeant takes a piss."

As we trudged along in the light rain, I thought of Sawlski, Betta and Alexus and how hurt and angry they must feel. They had not yet been awarded their buck sergeant's stripes, although I was certain that was in the works, and I had gotten another set. They had to harbor some bitterness and animosity toward me and the Army—they had worked as long and hard as I had, but had less to show for it. I decided I would do everything in my power to help them get their rank, beginning with my very next meeting with Nuckols. I knew they thought I had sucked up to get rank, but I really hadn't. I was, however, supremely confident of my abilities and I let my superiors know it.

We took some sniper fire as we came over a small hill between the valleys. I hit the wet ground alongside of the trail, searching for the source of the rounds that whizzed over our heads. Alexus held up his hand. "This time, Pete, just a flesh wound."

"You're getting too short for that, Lexus. You oughta. . . ."

I was interrupted by a yell from Underhill, who was behind me.

"You're an E-6, Stanley. Do something."

I laughed, rolled over and called for the bloop gun. I took a quick look at my map, which had little marks where I had spotted empty cartridges or other evidence of snipers. I picked out the closest landmark and familiarized myself with my surroundings. There was a large tree on the edge of the paddy below us, so I got up on one knee and took aim. I put two rounds dead into the tree, then handed the weapon back to Fryer. The sniper must have been near the target, as he stopped firing immediately.

After a few minutes, I yelled, "That good enough, Hill?" When in doubt, take action. It just might work.

We cut across the small paddy, then stopped at the edge of the brush. It was past 1800, so Sergeant Nuckols sent me out with a scouting party to check the top of a small brush-covered hill just to our north. I took a gun crew and Martinez' team and looked it over: it didn't have very good fields of fire and the ground was rocky, but the brush would provide good cover and the high ground should keep us safe until morning. I placed the gun near an open space to pull security until the rest of the platoon got into the perimeter. When I returned a few minutes later the gun crew was settling in and digging a hole. I spoke to Kentucky, who was head of the gun crew and as stubborn as they come.

"You've got to move the gun back ten meters to get into the perimeter with the rest of the platoon."

"Fuck it! We ain't movin'. You said put it here and we did and I ain't about to move it. What are ya gonna do, send me to 'Nam?"

I could think of several places I would liked to have sent him to right then, but I tried to remain calm. "This spot is in the field of fire from the 1st Squad positions. If you stay here you could get shot by our men. Once more, move the gun."

The other two men looked like they were ready to comply, but Kentucky was the spokesman, so they avoided eye contact as the gun carrier spoke again. "You said set up here and we ain't movin'."

I thought about hitting him, but I knew that wouldn't solve anything, especially if he prevailed in a fight. It seemed to me that there was little I could do at this moment. "You've been warned of the danger. I'm not wasting any more time or effort on you. We'll handle this back at base camp."

As I whirled around angrily, Martinez walked up to Kentucky. "Listen, asshole! If Pete said move the gun—move it!"

Apparently Kentucky had gone too far, in his mind, to retreat. He stood fast, so as to avoid a fight, I grabbed Martinez and threw the last gauntlet down. "Your position is back there. For the record, you've disobeyed orders. Think about it."

I felt frustrated by my lack of knowledge concerning the Army system of punitive action. I didn't know what I could or should have done there. I spoke to Gus at our foxhole.

"My first test as an E-6. I guess I should have issued a direct order, then had him arrested and court-martialed for failure to obey, but that seems a little extreme. We've all disobeyed orders at some time. Let's see what happens."

"Let me kick the shit out of him, Pete. He'll move the gun after that."

"Or shoot you—and me. There has to be a hammer, but you have to use it carefully in a combat zone. I'll talk with Sergeant Watley tomorrow and we'll straighten it out."

The night went quietly and we moved back down to the paddy for resupply in the morning. I had been hot and feverish during the night and was still slightly fatigued at daybreak, but I attributed it to the heat and my ubiquitous rash.

Just before we pushed off on patrol, I spoke with Sergeant Watley, whom I had grown to admire for his stability and quiet leadership. He said of his gunner, "He's one of the stubbornest crackers I've ever seen, but he can hump the gun. Let me talk to him. He won't try that again, I guarantee you. If he gives me any lip at all, we can both bust him. That's the way to handle guys like him, Pete. Take their money and stripes. Remember that."

I agreed with him that we should leave it at that, but I felt like I had been challenged and lost, so I decided that I would look for, but not push, another confrontation with Kentucky to regain my leadership status and redeem my bruised pride. We took resupply and our new addition, 1st Sergeant Wolfe, who was visiting the field for a few days, and headed down the valley, then north to the river. We stopped there to wash up and set up an LZ and NDP. The First Shirt quickly put up a regulation-type Army shelter half tent, neatly anchored by aluminum pegs. He then blew up his air mattress and lay down to write some letters.

"Top thinks he's on a field exercise at Fort Bragg. He'll probably police the area now. They should never let the rear echelon loose out here," Sergeant Watley said to me.

I replied with a grin. "I hope we can manage a little firefight while he's out here. Or, some sniper fire with nobody gettin' hit, just a couple of holes in his hooch."

I liked the first sergeant, thought he did a hell of a job keeping things flowing and wished him no harm, but we infantrymen felt a sense of pride in our abilities and accomplishments and in the degree of difficulty involved in performing our assigned missions. It bothered us when a member of the rear echelon passed through for a day or two, then returned to his haven to apply for his combat infantryman badge. Since Top already had his CIB from previous service, I had to give him the benefit of the doubt that he was just getting a taste of the field. Still, I thought to myself, some action would be nice. "Come on snipers, open up, but miss," I whispered.

We lay around all afternoon and evening, cleaning weapons and repairing gear. The new lieutenant, who had not yet acknowledged my promotion, checked the perimeter a couple of times, but could find nothing to get on my case about. That night the OP reported noise and movement, but nothing transpired—another pig or monkey alert.

In the morning we set out once more for Death Valley. We moved west along the stream, then north by west over the low hills and into the dreaded vale. It was late afternoon and extremely hot when we reached the LZ next to the river we had used three days before. We returned to our previous positions where we carefully and very slowly re-dug our fighting positions and holes.

The men were washing up and cooling off in the stream in groups of three or four while I found some shade behind a dike which bisected the perimeter on a northeast to southwest line and created a two-tier paddy. I was reading my mail when I heard one of the bathers yell, "Hey! VC! We got a VC in a hole here!"

I jumped up and headed for the stream bank, yelling, "Check him for weapons! Can you take him prisoner?"

"Yeah. No weapons. He's hurt—wounded."

"Search him, then take him to the CP."

I followed them as they helped the VC prisoner to the CP, then forced him to lie facedown. He had been shot in the upper right leg and left arm and the wounds were festering and ugly. House was talking excitedly to Sergeant Nuckols, "I told you I got one. I shot this guy. Pete, look, this is the VC I shot the other night."

House looked like he was going to swell up and burst, so I tried to deflate him a little by pointing to his wounds. "You shot him, you patch him up."

He shot me a vicious look but I was in a Robert E. Nelson don't-fuck-with-me mood, so when Doc Johnson arrived and took over, House helped clean and dress the wounds before tying the VC's hands and feet. The resupply chopper landed on the upper terrace as the CP huddled under the dike to avoid the swirling dust. As the rotors stilled and the air cleared, House put his prisoner on board and spoke to the door gunner who nodded and gave a thumbs-up. I wondered if the prisoner would make it back, but hell, I wondered also if I would. I slipped back to my position and pondered my remaining days. If all the rumors held up and the ten-day drops came about, I was looking at thirty-nine days and a wake-up. It scared the hell out of me to think about it.

34

The resupply chopper dropped off our C rations and other supplies, then lifted off in a swirling cloud of dust. I walked along the path that followed the stream bank, heading for the mailsack when the old Ranger, Sergeant Nuckols, who was lying back against the dike that bisected our latest LZ and perimeter, hailed me.

"Pete, I want you to take this new guy until Allen gets back from R&R, then we'll put him where's he's needed." In other words, take him off my hands. I looked at the new meat. He was a big dude, maybe six feet, probably 230, chubby and out of shape. The sweat was pouring down his dark brown face and his shirt was soaking wet. He took off his glasses, wiped them on his sleeve and announced, "I've got a case of VD, the clap. Got it down in Long Binh. I got a doctor's appointment on the day after tomorrow, but they sent me out anyway, so here I am."

I looked at Nuckols and shook my head. "Jeez, man, are we scraping the bottom of the barrel, or what?" Then I turned to leave and told the new guy, "Come on, Romeo, I'll show you the squad."

I found Alexus when I got back to our position and told him, "Break this dude in gently, Lexus. The guy's a lover."

"Welcome, lover. What's his name, Pete?"

"Don't know. Don't want to know. I'm too short to learn any more names. By the way, it's your turn for OP tonight. Take the new meat with you and show him the ropes."

I realized that I was treating the guy just like I had been treated by a few of the guys when I first reported to the field a hundred years ago. I didn't like it then, but in retrospect, the extra pressure of having to prove myself probably made me a better soldier. I was also being honest in what I told Alexus—I didn't want to know any more names. If they had a name, they were a person, an entity. If I didn't call them anything, they weren't anything and when they were blown up, I wouldn't be bothered.

After an uneventful night, the company broke camp in the morning. First Sergeant Wolfe ended his stay in the field by getting on the morning supply chopper and heading back to his refrigerator and comfortable bunk. The temperature was holding in the high 80s and the 2nd Platoon broke away from the company and moved out to the north along a branch of the east-west trail. Our mission was to check again one of the supposedly abandoned villages in the valley. As we humped along, one slow step after another, one of the omnipresent snipers opened up, scattering the troops into the brush.

The sniper was somewhere on the brush-covered hill above us. I took Martinez and his team and tried to cut our way through to the top, but the cover was so thick and strong we could make very little headway. I called back to the Aussie, Potozoa, who was our forward observer, to call in some artillery fire. He got permission from the new lieutenant, then brought in several rounds of HE and WP. The sniper ceased firing and the platoon continued on its weary way, eventually arriving in the targeted village.

The ville contained only a few buildings, but they were large and well constructed, signaling an elevated degree of prosperity peculiar to the poverty-stricken area. The ordinary farmer of this province (Quang Ngai) could barely raise enough rice or produce to provide his family with a living, let alone afford decent housing. Often they had to travel to the coast to catch fish to sell or eat. It wasn't hard to understand how the Viet Cong could persuade them that a new life could be theirs, especially after the Americans and the South Vietnamese uprooted them from their homes.

As I entered the largest hooch in the village, once more the chatter of an AK-47 rifle pierced the humid air and the rounds tore into the thatched roof. Martinez and I ducked quickly into the building, then I began searching the trees through the window. Potozoa called in a few more rounds onto the hillside and the sniper went quiet again. I had that old familiar feeling that again, he was in a hole, laughing at us. Martinez caught my eye from his spot near the door.

"That was just a reminder that he's watching everything we do, Pete. Everything."

"Could be. Or maybe he's afraid we'll find something in his house. Let's take a closer look."

Alexus came in with Fryer and the new guy and began checking the back room, a smaller lean-to off the main part. "Hey, Pete! Found some rice—a whole shitload of it."

In the corner of the room, a pile of firewood had been loosely stacked over an opening to a bunker. Inside the bunker were two large urns completely filled with rice. I reported the find to the platoon CP and the new lieutenant came hustling over. He inspected the find without a word, then called in a report to the company commander. While waiting for the Old

Man to get his instructions from battalion, we took our noon chow break. I leaned back on the wall of the hooch and felt the weight of the world on my shoulders. I was extremely fatigued, a little feverish, ached in body and spirit and had no appetite.

I glanced over at the new guy and saw that while his uniform was soaked through, he was eating, which seemed to be a good sign that he was adjusting to the conditions. Alexus was sitting a few feet away behind a large water cask. He took a dipper that was leaning against the vessel and dipped into it, then poured it on his head. I tossed him my neck-towel and told him to soak it, then laid it over my head and neck—it felt great. I slowly opened a can of crackers and munched on them, then washed them with tepid canteen water as I scanned the tree line once more. What was he waiting for? The lieutenant came out of the hooch.

"OK, Sergeant, burn it. When you get done, burn the hooch. We'll get the rest of the village."

He spun around and headed for the other end of the ville before I could open my mouth. I knew it was wrong to even joke about it, but I pointed my rifle at his back as he walked away and mocked a bang with my mouth. Alexus stood up and reached for his Zippo, then turned to me. "I'll burn it, Pete. It's VC rice and it should be destroyed."

My farm background flared up again, causing me to argue briefly. "It should be sacked up and taken to the people we've moved out of these villes. It's their rice. Dammit, it's a terrible waste." I made my protest, but now I had to keep my squad from jeopardy. "All right, do it before I do something crazy. But we're not burning hooches."

I had made my symbolic stand, but the rice was destroyed and the hooches were burned, the flames licking the dry walls and thatched roofs of the building with crackling glee as we saddled up and headed out. I kept expecting the sniper to open up as an act of revenge, but he was strangely silent as we headed west to a hilltop rendezvous with the rest of the company. I plodded along, putting one foot ahead of the other, trying not to think about how tired I was.

After settling into our night position, I consulted with Doc Johnson, our cherished platoon medic, about my deteriorating physical condition. My temperature was 101 degrees, but Doc couldn't find any real reason for my aching and fatigue. I wondered if it was a harbinger of malaria.

"No, Pete. If it was malaria, you would know it. It's much worse than what you've got. It's probably some bug, a virus you picked up from the water."

"You think it'll pass? That's a joke, Doc."

A man of few words, Doc also didn't waste his laughter. "Pete, your new guy is going in on the morning chopper. I don't think they'll send him back. He's got a real bad dose of the stuff."

"It's probably best. He's not much help to me the way he is. Hell, Doc, I'm not much help to me the way I am."

I dragged my weary body back to my sleeping trench and took a rest. Off to my right, at the gun position, I could hear Sergeant Watley arguing with my nemesis, Kentucky. I glanced over and saw that Watley was in the gunner's face and his finger was on Kentucky's chest. His voice was forceful as he told him in no uncertain terms, "Listen, you goddam cracker, you might be able to lip back at that fresh-assed lieutenant and get away with it, but I'll bust your ass for insubordination. Anything else you want, just say the word. Got that? Now, move your ass!"

I listened with bounding admiration for the good sergeant and memorized the words—that's how I'll handle my next problem. Probably.

We tromped slowly down to the rice paddy for resupply in the morning. My new guy got on the chopper and headed for his appointment with a needle and syringe filled with bicillin or something more potent. The platoon then headed due west to check out a few hooches on the other side of a small stream. I quickly soaked my sweat towel and filled a canteen in the clear but lukewarm water before we headed up the west bank.

As the 2nd Squad led us across a wide paddy, a sniper opened up from near a hooch less than a hundred meters away. The rounds ripped through the humid air just past our heads, humming their deadly songs. I hit the ground hard and tried to crawl to the nearest dike, but I had no strength. The firing continued, kicking up dust in the paddy inches to my left. I thought this was a hell of a way for it to end. Sweat poured off my face and I gasped for breath as the horizon tilted. As the troops ran or crawled by me on my right, they would look at me and ask, "You hit, Pete?"

"No, I just can't get up. Malaria, maybe," I would gasp.

Finally I reached down into that well for the last drops of competitive desire that athletes find when fatigue has drained them. I found something and began to half crawl and walk to the dike where I sat leaning against it. I didn't care if the sniper got me—I had to rest. Sawlski had taken the 3rd Squad after the sniper, but he had headed into the foothills to the west where our brothers in arms, the 196th Infantry, were located. Miraculously, no one was hit—the sniper must have been half-blind or terribly nervous. We couldn't call in artillery without clearing it with the task force HQ, because of the limits of our area of operations, so we searched the bushes and the hooches. Alexus led the squad through the now-familiar routines while I wiped the sweat off my face and rested. Doc gave me four all-purpose capsules and a couple of penicillin tablets and I persuaded myself that I felt better as the platoon finished noon chow and headed south.

We took more sniper fire as we headed across a small paddy near the river, but again his aim was faulty and we crossed over safely. We then immediately began a climb up the steep slopes of Hill 103. I struggled along, chanting "one more step, one more step" to myself all the away to the top. Once there, I found a tree, fell back against it and slid down. Doc Johnson came over to me and squatted down.

"I still don't think it's malaria. If you're feelin' this bad in the morning, I'll try to send you in. Hang in there."

"Yeah, Doc. Just leave a mess of those aspirin capsules and maybe some Darvon. I'll make it."

As I lay on that hillside that night I focused my feverish head and eyes on the evening stars and let my thoughts run freely. I was still upset about the burning of the rice and the general demeanor of the war effort. After nearly eleven months in-country I could see no discernible progress in the campaign against the North Vietnamese and the Viet Cong either at the local level or countrywide. We certainly weren't losing—we couldn't lose, but I could no longer say we were winning.

We weren't winning, the NVA and VC weren't winning, but the South Vietnamese civilians were losing. Smarter people than me would have to figure out why and how this was coming down, but I knew we couldn't wage a war the way we had been in Quang Ngai Province and hope to win. The mighty U.S. Army was shackled.

It was comparatively cool on the hill that night and in the early morning. I felt a little better after the rest and the penicillin had kicked in, so Doc and I decided to forgo the trip to the rear.

The resupply chopper disgorged its contents which included my big, brownskinned, bespectacled new guy who came limping toward me. I was surprised to see him back, but decided to forgo learning his name until after Allen came back to see if he was permanently mine. I loaded him down with C rations and sent him off toward Alexus while I got our marching orders.

My squad led the platoon down the south side of the steep hill, while the rest of the company went down the north slope. We would all then head west and converge on a small village near the low mountains to again wage our peculiar, dirty little war. At the bottom of the hill we left the trail and began cutting our way through to the river. I rotated the pointman on the machete every ten minutes to keep them fresh, but still the green lieutenant called me on the radio.

"2–1, speed up, we're getting behind the other platoons."

I grabbed the handset and snarled my reply. "2–6, this is 2–1. The other platoons are on a trail. Tell them to slow down. Out."

"2–1, I'm on my way to your position. Out."

A few minutes later I heard him thrashing his way up the column. He stumbled up toward me, then exploded. "Are you trying to make me look bad, Sergeant Peterson? That was damn near insubordination on the radio."

I wanted to say that I didn't have to make him look bad, he was doing a good job by himself. I wanted to say that he was an asshole of the first degree, but I had an obligation to my troops, so I tried to stay cool.

"Sir, I simply stated a fact. We're going through thick brush—they're not. We can't stay even with them."

"Sergeant, I told you to get these men moving faster. You're not doing your job."

I was starting to lose control and my voice rose in volume. "The welfare of my men is also my job, *sir!*"

"Don't push me, Sergeant."

He put a dripping emphasis on the *sergeant,* perhaps to remind me that he could take that rank from me easily enough. Before I could say anything else, which perhaps was best for both of us, he spun around and staggered back to the middle of the platoon. I stared at his back, then gave an order to the men of my squad in a whisper.

"Present arms."

I then led them in a middle-finger salute as he walked away. Alexus gave me a white man's soul-shake, which we managed without losing any fingers, then spoke, "The poor dumb son of a bitch doesn't know what he's doin'."

"What he's doing is gonna get some troops killed, unless. . . ."

I didn't finish, but Martinez looked up from his cutting and said: "Something bad happens to him."

The three of us exchanged an evil look, then said in unison, "Naaah!"

I wondered if we had been together too damned long.

After a couple hours of sweat and strain we made it through to the river, then crossed it slowly to maximize the cooling effect and to wet our towels and shirts with something besides sweat. We set up on the far side, broke for noon chow and rested. I began to feel weak and feverish again, but decided to say nothing. I merely gobbled down more capsules and penicillin.

As we finished our C rations, a call came in from battalion HQ about a possible major enemy troop movement. Charlie Company was ordered to move quickly into an intercept position at the base of the low mountains to the west once more.

Alexus and his fire team led the platoon due west across the dry and dusty rice paddies, through a ville and into position next to the 3rd Platoon where we stayed on alert for three hours. At 1600, HQ decided the threat was over, so we were ordered to search the village, then head back to the LZ with the two-tier rice paddy. We poked through a few of the hooches, but turned up only some black pajamas. Although they were the uniform of choice for the VC guerrilla, they were also worn by many of the peasants, so I didn't consider this much of a find.

At 1700 the word came down—be at the LZ in one hour for resupply. The 1st Platoon led off, then the 2nd, and the 3rd

Herd brought up the rear. My squad was at the rear of the 2nd as we headed up the trail to the northeast; we had four klicks to travel in less than sixty minutes. I kept my eye on the new guy just ahead of me: he was nearly awash with perspiration as we moved quickly along in the late afternoon. There was a hazy sky, but the temperature stayed around 100 and I wondered how fast we would try to travel in the hot, humid air.

The column slowed as we bunched at the small stream crossing, then sped up as we got on the east trail. I moved up next to the new guy and saw him wobbling a little and gasping for breath.

"How you doin', guy? Hang in there. We'll be in the LZ in a few minutes."

He nodded as if he understood, but his stare was vacant. When we reached the fork off the main trail that we would follow to the LZ, Alexus and I replaced two guys from the 1st Platoon on security to allow the rest of the company to move into their positions safely. Suddenly the new guy began thrashing wildly and tossed his M-16 rifle to the ground.

"Aaagh! I can't do it! I can't. . . !" He continued yelling but it was garbled, then he began swinging and flailing his arms uncontrollably.

A huge trooper from the 3rd Platoon wrapped his arms around him and tried to calm him with some reassuring words. "Easy, man, easy. Take it easy, bro. Just a few steps to the LZ and you can rest, man."

Then the huge troop turned his head and said to us, "Get some help—the man's gone."

I had already called for the medics on the radio, so I headed to help him but he was almost frenzied in his actions. One of the 3rd Herd troops stopped me.

"Let the brothers handle the guy, Pete. It might make a difference to him to see a bro, not a honky. You dig?"

I didn't dig, but I gave it my Vietnam shrug, then began directing traffic around the scene. I sent the rest of the troops in the company to their platoon positions on the perimeter, then pulled rear security as the black troops tried to mollify the frenzied new guy. I watched mesmerized as they soaked him with water from their canteens and wrestled him to the ground.

After a while he seemed to lose strength or desire and went

limp. The brothers then picked him up and carried him to the company CP. The medics looked him over, shook their heads and ordered them to carry him to the river.

I helped them slide him down the stream bank and into the water, then Doc Johnson and I began pouring water over his head. I caught Doc's eye and wrinkled my brow into a question. Doc just shook his head. I couldn't understand why the medevac wasn't on its way. I yelled to the CP, "Where the hell's Dustoff? Dammit, this guy's in real bad shape. Get 'im out here."

"It'll be a while. Just keep him cool—he'll be all right."

The company medic had determined that the guy wasn't in bad shape—just suffering from heat prostration. I left Doc as he was pouring water on the face of the now totally silent man, and went in search of Sergeant Nuckols. When I found him, I said, "The guy needs help, and he needs it now, Sarge. Can you do anything to get the medevac chopper in here?"

"I'll try, but I don't think it'll do any good. I think they're on another mission."

I sat on the bank and watched Doc Johnson check the guy for vital signs every few minutes. About thirty minutes later the word came down that the chopper was on the way. A few troops came over to help us get him back up the bank and over to the dike where the chopper came in, blowing sand and dust into our faces. We got the guy on, then turned our backs as the rotors picked up speed again and the bird lifted off. I was feeling extremely fatigued by now, but my troubles were nothing compared to his. I walked slowly to my position and collapsed in the sand.

A half hour later Doc came over. "He died on the way in, Pete. Never regained consciousness."

I was stunned. I could see he was in trouble, but I thought he would snap back after they got some fluids in him. "Jesus, Doc, how? What the hell, Doc, what the hell?"

"Probably broke a blood vessel in his brain. His general condition was poor and the VD and heat got to him."

"And the frickin' forced march. The damned Bataan death march got to him. Right?"

"That was part of it. Maybe it would have happened anyway. Hell, I'm only a medic, Pete."

He hung his head and appeared to be weeping silently. I put my hand on the shoulder of the soft-spoken man and said, "He had the best medic, Doc. The best in 'Nam."

After he left, something guided me over to the 1st Platoon sector where I found the position with the bloods who had carried him to the CP. I sat down in a ditch with a trail down the center of it, then slowly made my announcement to the all-black squad.

"He died on the chopper. He frickin' died from a broken blood vessel in his brain, Doc says. He had a bad case of the clap, but I think the heat and the fast march did it."

The big trooper who had tried to soothe the new guy first, sat down. "I think you're right, man. We moved way too fast in that heat. The brother's head couldn't take it no more."

"Screw it, man, it's always somethin'. They didn't bring in the dustoff sooner because they didn't think he was in bad shape. It's just not right, man."

I was bitter and searching for something to start making sense again, but all I could see was pain all around. The big guy grunted once, then spoke again bitterly.

"If he was white they would have hauled his ass out right away. Might be alive right now."

"Maybe they would have, I don't know. 2nd Platoon medic is black and the aides on the dustoff chopper were black."

"Don't mean nothin', Pete. They're tokens. Blacks just don't get equal treatment even in a motherfuckin' war."

"Right on, bro. Us bloods are expendable in this war," a little man with a scraggly goatee had joined in.

I let out a sigh, then slowly got to my feet and started back to my hole. Then I stopped and turned back to the men. "I don't know anymore. Just keep goin' is my motto. Keep your heads down, men."

I dragged my tired white butt back to my position and lay back on my pack. It really didn't make sense anymore. We busted our butts to get back to the LZ to meet the chopper, then it doesn't show up for more than an hour. A man collapses, the medevac bird takes an hour and the trooper dies, perhaps because of the delay. My aunt Ruth was right—we're all just cannon fodder. Nobody gives a damn.

Fuckin' new guy—I never had time to learn his name. Whoa, let's face it: I never took the time to learn his name.

What the hell is wrong with me? He was one of my men, I should've found out his name. I'll have to live with that, but who will live with causing the death of an unhealthy soldier? I wondered about the telegram that his loved ones would receive. What would be listed as the cause of death, apathy? Did racism play a giant part in his demise? No, not unless there is a code beside every trooper's name that could instantly be made known to all RTOs, medics and medevac units as they receive calls to pick up wounded. Since the name of a wounded man is never mentioned when the call is made, it is beyond the realm of possibility. There is, indeed, racism and bigotry in this man's Army, but when a soldier falls, he has no color.

Ah, Lord, Vickers was right—I'll never smile again.

35

Just before daylight on August 16, Charlie added insult to our injuries by emptying a magazine into the perimeter. No one was hit and I yelled at Fryer to put two bloop rounds into the big tree just north of the NDP, but I knew the sniper was already in a hole somewhere. The sporadic sniping, though highly ineffective in terms of inflicting physical casualties, was adding to our frustration and continuously lowering morale.

As we slowly went through our morning rituals in the already warm sun, the mood was subdued, almost somber. I had become totally benumbed by the magnitude and severity of the events of the last eleven months. I mourned the loss of life and devastation visited on all sides, but I mourned them silently for the most part. I now believed that, in total contrast to my views prior to my tour, this war would last a long time and was becoming unwinnable the way it was being fought. It left a bad taste in my mouth, a chip on my shoulder, guilt in my mind and a big pain in my heart. That was a lot of weight for one man to carry around.

The 2nd Platoon moved slowly to the north, then east to another old sniper site where we checked some abandoned hooches and took our noon break. I wanted to talk with somebody about yesterday, but to a man, the troops of the 2nd Platoon ignored the collapse and death of the new guy. I guess they really didn't have time to get to know him, so if they didn't think about it, then it hadn't happened and they didn't have to deal with it. They acted as if he never existed. I believed that a man has to leave a bigger mark than that, so I buried a can of beans in his honor.

The tomb of the unknown bean-eater will stand as a monument to him until the jungle claims it. I meant no disrespect for the dead, but I didn't know what else to do for a man whose real name I didn't have, or take time to learn.

I had felt a little better physically after a night's rest, but I could feel my strength fading once again as we rested in the shade. By the time the troops finished their chow, I was raging with fever, sweating profusely and barely able to stand. I asked Doc to check me once more and he got a reading of 104 degrees on his thermometer. He wrote out an evacuation slip, tied it to my shirt and went to the CP to see about an evacuation. I didn't want to go in, but I had no strength, so I leaned back against a tree and closed my feverish eyes for a few minutes. When I opened them, the grizzled platoon sergeant was staring down at me.

"There's nothing wrong with you, Pete. Get the hell up and get back to your squad. You haven't been doing your job lately."

He ripped off the tag and tore it to pieces. "See, Dr. Nuckols cures another one. Back to your squad."

"If I'm not doing my job, send me in and give the job to somebody who can do it better. 'Course, you won't find him in this war. I guess the only way out of here for me is in a fuckin' body bag. Screw it, screw you and this whole outfit."

I was filled with anger and a little shame. He was right in saying I hadn't been doing my job, but he was wrong in not recognizing the reason. He was also wrong in lumping me with other shammers; I only wanted to go in to discover what was wrong with me so I could get cured and get on with my tour and my life. If I had any strength I might have duked it out with him, but what the hell would it have proved, except that he was a helluva lot better fighter than I was.

I was getting too short for all this shit.

The platoon moved directly south on the east side of the river, heading for a night defensive position of the top of Hill 103. I pushed one foot ahead of the other, sucked water out of my canteen and splashed it on my face. We paused to fill our canteens before climbing the hill, so I soaked my towel and shirt and ducked my head in for a few seconds. I got a few more APCs (all-purpose capsules) from the medic and swallowed them, then we moved toward the hill.

The climb went slowly, but after the dip I managed to find enough strength to make it to the top. We moved back to our old 1st Squad position after checking for booby traps and I rested against the tree as the resupply chopper came in. It was disconcerting that Nuckols had reacted that way only one day after the fall of a trooper to heat and disease, but he apparently wanted to maintain the gruff exterior. If I'm tough and you're tough, we'll be all right. I hoped his hard-ass attitude wouldn't get any more troops killed—especially this troop.

I fell into a stupor that night—an image-filled dream state that left me covered with sweat. I awoke with a jerk, then slowly wiped the moisture off my face with my dirty towel and checked the guard. Martinez was cupping a cigarette and watching the perimeter. He whispered to me, "You were grunting and moaning in your sleep again, Pete."

"Yeah. Nightmares. It's a helluva deal, Gus. Can't sleep for days, then when you do, you have nightmares. I wonder if I'll ever get my mind straight."

Once again I felt better in the morning as we moved down off the north slope and descended into the vale of doom. We crossed the stream and I did my towel-dipping routine and filled my canteens. As we moved across the paddy, Victor Charlie tried again to draw the line by firing several bursts at us. Again we hit the parched, dusty ground and some returned fire wildly. I knew the sniper had a hidden hole and bunker that he could disappear into and was sitting there laughing at us again.

After the CO called in a few rounds of HE, we moved out again and entered a small collection of hooches built on the edge of the paddies. We searched them thoroughly for the second time this week and found evidence of recent activity and some black pajamas, but no supplies. I watched as the troops burned the clothing and kicked in the walls of the hooches. Fatigue was setting in again as we broke for noon chow on the edge of the ville.

I had begun to feel a pain in my stomach during the night, but ignored it all morning until I sat down. Suddenly it seemed to get sharper. I rubbed my abdomen, then began probing gingerly into my navel, where the pain was focused. I felt a tiny lump and quickly called the medic.

"Doc, I've got a tick or something in my navel."

Doc Johnson scanned it, pronounced it a tick and withdrew his tweezers from his medical pouch. He swabbed the area and the instrument with alcohol, grasped the insect and plucked it cleanly from my stomach with a flourish, then held the tiny tick up for scrutiny.

"That little bugger could be the cause of most of your troubles, Pete. I think you'll feel better by tomorrow if it was."

He gave me a few more all-purpose capsules and some penicillin, then we saddled up and headed east, setting up along the stream in a daylight observation posture. After a couple of hours my stomach stopped aching and I felt a flush of strength—it was hard to believe that a bug the size of a pinhead could bring down a combat-hardened troop, but that seemed to be the answer.

At 1700 we headed for rendezvous with the 3rd Herd on Hill 35 where we set up once again in an NDP. I sent Alexus and his team to an ambush OP overlooking the main trail, but the night was bright, calm and peaceful. My temperature had dipped to 101 and I was feeling a little stronger after a can of fruit cocktail—life was a little better.

Just after midnight the gun crew to our right heard something in front of their position. They opened up and lobbed a few grenades into the brush in front of and downhill from their foxhole. I directed the men to get into our hole while I lay in my sleeping trench and waited for further action. After a few minutes things quieted down, the gun crew went back to a normal security and we all got some rest. A quick morning patrol turned up nothing in the area of the suspected noise.

We took a morning resupply in the paddy near the NDP and Allen reported back from R&R. Someone had thrown a few camouflage covers for steel pots in with the supplies, so I grabbed one. On the front I put a staff sergeant's chevron. On one side I printed 2nd Platoon Savages, on the other Solitary Man, and on the back I wrote Eve of Destruction. After doing all that I found I still had some strength—I must be feeling better. The tick had apparently been the cause of my debilitating illness, but now it was over and I could prepare for my real enemy.

I found I had renewed strength as we moved back west to recheck the hooches. The new LT halted the platoon in some bushes when we reached the ville, then sent my squad to recon the area quietly in hopes of surprising any VC. We crept softly along the dike, then dashed towards the first hooch. A VC with a weapon went racing away from the dwelling as we reached it. He headed for the tree line as Allen, Fryer and Galaviz opened up. The black-clad young man knew he was in a race for his life as he sped on. He won and reached the woods. As he headed into the trees, I yelled at the three men, "Hold your fire. Drop your packs and go after him."

Martinez led them into the tree line and beyond to search for the soldier while I radioed the rest of the platoon to come into the area. They began to search the other hooches closely when one of them began shouting, "Over there—VC. A dink."

He whipped his grenade launcher around and fired wildly. The round hit into a hooch about 100 feet away and exploded, sending shrapnel flying. A member of the 2nd Squad who was standing near the shack took a few fragments in his arm and began to bleed profusely. Doc Johnson quickly applied a pressure bandage and held it to the wound to stem the flow, relaxing his grip every minute or so to minimize the damage.

The medevac chopper arrived about twenty minutes later and whisked another American male off to the meat-grinder. A female reporter got off the bird and asked a few questions, then decided to stay with us as we finished our search. We spent the rest of the day moving through and searching the area, then headed back east to the LZ by the river for resupply and a night defensive position.

The 2nd Platoon headed somberly into the LZ and took their now familiar spots on the perimeter. Charlie wasn't booby-trapping our old positions, perhaps because he liked and needed to sort through our garbage for leftover C rations. He didn't want us to get mad and maybe burn or booby-trap the trash, so he left the positions clear—one of those unspoken agreements between combatants that no one in the real world would be able to understand.

I stepped down from the higher level of the two-tier paddy and sat back against the dike. Sawlski was on top, heating up his C-ration meal over a flaming heat tab when the sniper gave us our evening greeting. One of the rounds clipped the can of Cs out of Sally's hand. He yelled, "Son of a bitch! He shot my beans!"

He then dove for cover behind the dike and unleashed a torrent of angry words and a magazine of ammunition. The north side of the perimeter also answered the volley, but you can't hit what you can't see—and you could see nothing on that brush-covered hill. The FO called in a few rounds of HE while the company finished their C rations. We were on alert most of the night as the OPs reported noises and movement several times, but there were no probes and no more sniping. It had almost developed into some kind of board game; whenever we moved to the west side of the smaller stream, we came under heavy fire. When we stayed along the river, we received only occasional sniping—our morning and evening ritual. Of course, if you thought you had Charlie figured out, you were always wrong. Even worse, you could be dead wrong.

On the morning of August 19, I was back to full strength, so

I took a quick dip in the river while waiting for orders, then began to shave. I used the water as a mirror, a trick I had mastered some months ago out of necessity. Martinez glanced at me as I was making the tentative strokes and said, "Here, Pete, use my mirror—get a good shave."

He tossed me a square of stainless steel that had become corroded and rusty in the humidity, but still could produce a likeness. I took a look at it and recoiled—there was a face of an old man in there. I was about to shave my father's face. I finished quickly, rinsed out my towel, then changed places with Martinez to pull security guard.

"Man, Pete, you're gettin' short. How many days?"

"If my leave comes through, I should be outta the field in less than two weeks. You guys can keep me alive that long, I think. Without the leave, DEROS is in thirty-two days. I'm too damn short to even talk about it."

"You still thinkin' about coming back to 'Nam after your leave to finish out your hitch?"

"I'm not sure now. The kind of fighting that we've had to do lately has me wavering. If I could be sure of being an adviser or instructor, I'd be on the next plane, but. . . ."

"When I get outta here, I'm heading back to California where the living is easy. I don't even want to hear about Vietnam again, man."

"You will, and for a long time if the war goes on like this. I know now why Bennett and Vickers and others were so frustrated when they left, and it's continuing. We haven't done diddly in my tour. Hard to believe that a country so powerful is sometimes so damn stupid."

Martinez had finished shaving his heavy dark whiskers and was climbing the bank when the call for the squad leaders came down. I grabbed Alexus and told him he should join me since he would be leading the squad if I got my ten-day leave and we journeyed along behind the protective dike to the CP. Our mission of the day, we learned, was to head slowly south along the west bank of the river, checking out a trail and looking for signs of a large enemy force believed to be moving into the area. As we headed into the bush, I put Martinez and his team on point with a few instructions.

"Go slow, be cool. G-2 thinks this is where some of the local

VC hang out when they're not snipin' at us. I'll be right behind your team."

I thought we would have to cut our way along the west bank, but we picked up a well-used trail that ran along the river and was totally hidden from view by the heavy brush and foliage. Allen led off, then Martinez and Fryer. I pulled in behind Fryer and the FO joined me with his radio. We found a couple of spider-holes that had been recently used as cover or for sleeping. I marked them on my map as a future target for artillery if we took some sniper fire from this direction. Through the morning we edged carefully along the trail, finding paper signs written in Vietnamese and rough arrows pointing north.

A branch of the trail headed northwest, which was well used and marked by two signs and arrows. We broke for noon chow at the intersection while the new lieutenant made reports to the Old Man, who once again was not with us. The men tore the signs down, so I scrounged around the squad for some playing cards and put up an ace of spades, which was rumored to be a bad-luck symbol to the Vietnamese. The presence of all the signs and the fact that the trail was well worn had the men and me nervous.

Fryer whispered a question while I munched my usual meal of crackers and water. "Pete, what do you think all the signs mean?"

"It sure looks like they're expecting company. Higher might be right once. There is an enemy force coming into the AO and they're being told where to go. They've got everything but stoplights and crosswalks here."

I didn't want to frighten anybody, but I had a tremendous sense of foreboding—something was coming up. The heat and humidity were especially oppressive since we were in an area that would be part of the riverbed during the monsoon season, about six feet below the rice paddies, surrounded by heavy undergrowth and a few large trees. I felt we were extremely vulnerable to ambush, although the 3rd Platoon was not far away to the northwest and the 1st was on the other side of the river.

I called the squad together and spoke with concern and as much confidence as I could muster just before we started back down the trail. "Guys, we could really run into something here, so be extra alert. Pointman, thumb on the safety and finger on the trigger guard. Go slowly and tread lightly. React to the situation, then listen for me if we hit the shit. Lead off, Gus."

Martinez took the point with his team once more and I fell into the fourth spot with the RTO-FO behind me. As we pushed along the sandy deposits, heading southwest, I reached silently behind me for the handset which the RTO slapped into my hand. I began whispering into it. "2–5, this is 2–1, give me your actual."

There was a delay of a few seconds while Dibble got the handset to Nuckols. "2–1, this is 2–5 actual, go ahead."

"2–5, be advised, I can smell Victor Charlie."

My nose had been the 2nd Platoon's early warning system since March and no one doubted its accuracy with the stakes so high.

"Roger, 2–1. I'm on my way to your position. Out."

As I gave the handset back to the RTO the point came under a vicious crossfire from automatic weapons. I quickly estimated three or four weapons, then heard the point element answer with a volley of their own. Nature had provided me with a pile of sand and dirt held in place by a sapling and carved into a pillar by past flood seasons. I leaned against it and waited for the firing to break for a few seconds. When it did, I yelled softly and calmly at the team. "Gus, you guys OK? What's the story?"

Martinez spoke rapidly in a voice pitched upward by strain, "Three or four VC in holes. They opened up, but nobody got hit. I think we hit 'em all. We're OK."

The new LT came bulling up the trail to my position and stopped. His face was flushed with excitement and he, too, began speaking quickly, almost babbling. "Let's go, let's rush 'em!"

I worked at speaking in a calm voice, keeping the butterflies under control and trying to bring him back to earth. "Sir, my men have it under control. No use putting any more men at risk on the trail. Alexus, take your team up the bank. We'll try to flank them. Go slow." I stopped for a minute, then aimed my voice at the point. "Gus, Alexus and I are coming up on top of the bank to your right. Don't fire in that direction. The lieutenant will be right behind you. Stay cool."

Alexus led his men up and over the bank and we moved slowly along the paddy edge, checking for any movement. I kept voice contact with Martinez and his team, and we converged at the ambush site a few minutes later. The faces of the team were tense and drawn by the fear and excitement and their eyes were darting about. I looked at the holes the VC had been hiding in a few minutes earlier and saw blood in three of them. Each of the point element held an abandoned weapon, but no bodies were found. I spoke quickly, "Good work, men. Now, let's get on the blood trails and see if we can find them."

I slapped Allen and Fryer on the back and grinned at Martinez as the lieutenant called in his report. We stood around like a bunch of kids who had won a game, waiting for the word to go play some more. Fryer was gushing a little as he spoke. "I did what you said, Pete. I flipped the lever and opened up—worked real good. We hit three of them, then they threw a grenade and *di died.*"

"Those VC could have been waiting for us or the 1st Platoon, but I think they were here to guide that large unit into the area. So, let's stay real alert, they could be coming anytime."

The lieutenant finally gave us the go-ahead, so we slowly followed the blood spatters across the rice paddy and into the heavy brush where they disappeared in the dark green foliage. I wondered how far I could make it if I was shot by an M-16—I had to admire their fortitude. I called Nuckols, "2–5, 2–1. Blood trail disappeared—no VC. I don't believe this one will live long. Lost too much. Over."

"Roger, 2–1. Same-same with the other trail. 2–2 lost it at the tree line. Bring your element back to the stream. Out."

We headed back slowly as the adrenaline rush was wearing down, leaving in its wake a squad of stress-weary troopers with an ever-deepening stare. I had appropriated one of the captured weapons as a squad trophy; Martinez and Allen toted the others. The river crossing was secured on the far side by the 1st Platoon who would lead us to the top of Hill 103 after we crossed. The 3rd Herd was closing from the north, so we were feeling more comfortable as we headed into the stream.

The crossing, which we had been using since we entered this AO seventeen days ago, was a walkway of smooth stones across the river where it widened and became more shallow. It was put in place by local indigenous personnel and allowed about three inches of water to flow over it, thus to prevent any damming. I wondered how it held up during the monsoon season flooding; it probably had to be rebuilt at the onset of dry weather. The worn paths leading to the bridge attested to its heavy usage by both the VC and Charlie Company.

We headed up the steep slope of Hill 103 and, for a change, I took it in stride. At the top we returned to our previous positions and began to re-dig our foxholes in slow motion. As we finished, the sun was falling, so Martinez and I sat back, opened our packs and rummaged for food. For the first time on this operation I was hungry. The original plans had been for a resupply during the day, but our ambush, firefight and pursuit of the enemy had thrown the plans awry. No choppers were available when we reached our NDP, so we would wait until morning to receive our resupply. Most of the time, the GI in the field carries enough spare C rations to tide him over times like these, but with the extreme heat and the daily forced marches, we had all tried to lighten our loads. I dug around in my pack and found one can, so I turned to Gus.

"Whaddya got, Gus?"

"I've got one fuckin' tin of grape jam, Pete."

"Well, I've been saving this damn can of pound cake for a special occasion, and this is it. We'll put your jam on my cake and split it."

Martinez' face lit up a little in the growing dusk as he realized a slight caloric gain, and we slowly nibbled away at our precious cake. After the repast, I headed for the CP to see if anybody had extra chow. The CO, the lieutenant and Sergeant Nuckols were scanning the darkened valley below. I followed their gaze and noticed four or five flickering dots of light moving slowly to the north in the proximity of the river. Nuckols turned to me. "We think this might be that large enemy force we've been hearing about, Pete. The FO is going to bracket them, then saturate the area with HE and WP. . . ."

"And we'll check it out tomorrow." I finished the statement resignedly. It never ends. This war never ends.

"Yeah, probably. But, maybe we'll kick their butts tonight and just mop up tomorrow."

I ambled back to my position as the shells began screaming through the night sky, wailing their bloody death chants and crashing into the valley below. I hoped it was the NVA force and that the shells would catch them in the open. But if the first shells were even slightly off target, a likely prospect in the dark, the enemy would scatter quickly before the next rounds landed, regroup later and continue on. I explained the situation to both squad positions as we listened to the shells exploding in the valley below us.

"This could be the force that those VC were waiting to escort today before you ruined their party. You guys did a helluva job and I'm recommending all three of you assholes for decorations for bravery."

"Pete, we just did what you told us to, and it worked," Fryer said.

"Well, of course it worked. Did you ever doubt it would? Your ol' squad leader wouldn't lead you wrong, would he?"

We joked back and forth, but I knew they were suffering the pangs of doubt and fear that follow a close brush with death. They wondered why they hadn't been hit and killed when the VC opened fire. Instead of rejoicing in their luck, most grunts believed that every time they escaped, it raised the odds of their eventual demise in a violent manner and they become almost resigned to the fate. I felt a little of it—I wondered why it happened when I was standing next to a mound. If it had not been there, would the rounds that missed the point element have torn into me? Fryer brought me out of my circle of thought with a query, "Who gets the weapons, Pete?"

"Chopper is coming in the morning. We'll tag these for the 2nd Platoon. If we could get one to Lieutenant Nelson, maybe he'll use his influence as XO to save the other two. Martinez gets one as pointman. Who gets the other one?"

The three men were silent for a minute, then Allen spoke, "I really don't want any, Pete. I'd like to take my M-14 with me when I go home."

"Well, I'll put my name on one, maybe a staff sergeant will have enough pull to get one through."

Fryer caught my eye and spoke fervently. "Pete, we were alert because of what you told us to do. That's why we made it through."

"You made it through because you're good soldiers, Fryer. I hope you're good soldiers because I did my job, but I can't be the judge of that. I do know that my squad is the best damn squad in Charlie Company and I'm proud of that."

The compliments were heartfelt, therapeutic and they made

both sides feel good. I considered the words of gratitude directed at me to be the highest award a man could receive. We continued to make small talk, still too charged up to sleep. When the talking finally died down, the demons of doubt once again took advantage of our battle-weary bodies and minds, planting their alternate scenarios of doom. What if that force had been waiting, instead of just four VC? What if. . . ? After wrestling with my personal fiends into the early hours, I finally fell asleep, content that my squad had and would continue to operate efficiently, even under extreme duress.

The resupply chopper flew in at 0730, bringing C rations, ammunition, mail and the executive officer of Charlie Company, one Lieutenant Robert E. Nelson. He came out to talk with the CO and platoon leaders about the company's future missions and day-to-day operations. He grinned and returned my salute, then handed me three tags for the captured weapons.

"Sergeant Peterson, there'll be some medals in this for you and your men, no doubt."

"Sir, the men on point did it all. I intend to write recommendations for all three of them when we get back to Hill 54."

"That won't be too long for you, Pete. Your leave papers have come through. You're leaving on September 2."

"That's the news I've been waiting to hear. You wouldn't want to come back to lead the platoon until I go in, would you, sir? This new guy's puttin' a lick on us. Somebody's gonna get killed if he doesn't straighten up."

"He'll come around, Pete. Give him time. I'll take those weapons back with me. Put your name and platoon on them and I'll try to get them to a safe place."

After his meeting, we loaded the weapons onto the chopper and I saluted him as he lifted off. I really missed his style of leadership. He wasn't perfect, but the longer he was away, the more I forgot his failings, the new lieutenant helping immensely in this regard. I handed out C rations to the squad, then headed to the platoon CP for orders.

"First Platoon will go north, cross the river, then sweep toward the area where we spotted the lights and movement last night. Third will cross here and sweep from the south. Second will block on this side of the river. The 2nd Squad will lead us out in exactly 2-0 minutes. That's all."

We followed Cain's squad and moved down the south slope and into our position along the east side of the river. If there was a force of NVA, we would cut off their retreat via the river crossing. After we settled in, Sergeant Nuckols came to my position, which was behind a clump of bamboo, and sat down.

"Pete, you guys kicked some butt yesterday, didn't ya? That was somethin'. You smelled 'em out and the boys shot the hell out of 'em."

"I thought ol' Lieutenant Prick was going to charge right into the middle of it, so I grabbed hold of him. I'm surprised the asshole didn't court-martial me."

"Your squad did a good job, Pete. There'll be some medals."

I grinned at him and decided it was time for a jab. "Sarge, I've always had the best damn squad, but we rarely get any credit."

"Yeah, I know, Pete, but I gotta keep 'em all happy. You'll be happy to hear that your orders for leave have come down. I'll send you in on the 29th or 30th."

"Well, I appreciate that. You know, if I get a ten-day drop, my DEROS would be around September 21. That ten-day leave from two to September 12. No way in hell I'm coming back to the field after that. So I've got to stay alive ten more days." I paused and pondered it for a minute, then continued. "But who's gonna keep you alive after I'm gone?"

He flashed his big grin and then turned serious, "Pete, you're a pretty good soldier. If you re-up, you'd do real good in the Army."

"I don't think so. I want to finish college, then maybe teach or write, or both."

The Ranger slapped my shoulder as he stood up. "I hope you get straight before you head home. This leave should help."

"You're an ornery cuss at times, Sarge, but you're the best damn NCO I've seen in this Army. Now, if we could just get that doofus lieutenant straightened out."

I waved as he walked away; at that moment I felt real close to him, like he was an older brother who looked out for me and kept me in line. He was a hard-case, but he was vulnerable, like all humans. His statements and offerings were as close as he would come to an apology for his previous actions—and I accepted them.

We spent the rest of the day blocking while the other platoons swept through the paddies. They converged at the pre-arranged site, then examined where the shells had landed last night. They found no bodies, blood or gear along the trail, so the artillery must have missed its target.

At 1600 the 2nd Platoon led the way back to the top of Hill 103 and we all resumed the positions we had occupied previously and took a long rest. That night as I was laying out my poncho and liner, Martinez approached me. I could see something was eating at him.

"Pete, I've been thinking," he started. "I'd like to get back to the gun squad again."

I hesitated for a second, then answered tentatively. "You know, Gus, this squad is yours when Alexus and I are gone—next month for sure."

"I know, but I don't think I want it right now. I'd like to be back on the gun. Let somebody else lead the squad."

"All right, let's think it over for a day or two. If you still feel that way then, we'll get it done—no sweat."

"Thanks, Pete. I hope you don't think I'm chicken, man."

"After all we've been through? You're one of the bravest men I've ever known, Martinez. The pressure just gets to all of us after a while. Get some rest, man."

As I lay on my back on Hill 103, I once more gazed at the panoramic night sky and tried to slip away. We were safe from all but artillery here, so I let my mind roam across the events of time, both recent and ancient, that had comprised my tour of duty on this foreign strand. The battles near the border had been the most deadly and dangerous for the entire battalion. We lost dozens of young men, with dozens more wounded, but we prevailed even though those who took up the sword and marched into the battles of those fateful days would be marked forever. We of the rank and file, who shouldered our muskets in combat, and lived, are pledged and condemned to remember the times, the battles and those who fought and fell.

The battles we have fought, the wars we have waged on this front are markedly different. While there is less loss of life, the threat is constant and more difficult to stamp out by its very nature. The enemy here has no choice but to hit and run, to snipe

and hide to fight another day. He is outnumbered and out-
gunned, so he must make up for it with his tactics, ingenuity
and spirit. We have not been able to defeat him and it is tearing
at my heart as the time to leave draws near. I want to leave, to
remove myself from harm's way, but my heart says, "It's not
over, come back."

I thought about the men I had served with over the past
eleven months and my heart swelled with pride and comrade-
ship. These men, who seemed so young (some would be forever so) and yet so old, were more dear to me than anything in
the world now and they would hold a special place in my heart
for as long as I live. These men are my brothers.

36

The sun was already pounding down on us, sending its bla-
tant blistering message of who do you think you are and how
dare you try me, as Charlie Company began its mission on August 21. The 1st and 3rd platoons would ease down the south
slope of Hill 103, head west, then sweep north. The 2nd Platoon moved down the north slope alone to patrol along the

stream, then swept west to link up with the others supposedly at the site of a downed chopper, near the base of the low mountains at the edge of our AO. I saw the lieutenant talking with Nuckols, who passed the word to me.

"Your squad's on point, Pete. Move out in 0-5."

"Who else would be on point? All right, you miserable beer-swilling lowlifes, saddle up. Gus, Alexus led off yesterday, so your team's on point."

Martinez shouldered his ruck, then mimicked my voice, "Who else would be on point?"

"You're the best I've got, after me, of course. When we get near the bottom of the hill, I'm putting Alexus and his team out on flanks. We'll be following along that trail where we hit the shit the other day, so be alert. Keep me posted if you see anything at all. Take 'em down, Gus."

We left our lofty sanctuary and entered the war once more. I didn't need my map as I knew the valley below me by heart; the terrain and its notable features were implanted in my brain, at least what was left of it. I felt as strong physically as I had in weeks and the success of recent days coupled with safer conditions at night had lifted my morale a few notches. Just to make sure I wasn't feeling too secure, after we had proceeded about halfway down the slope, the lieutenant sent word down the line.

"Camouflage your steel pots, rucks and web belts with leaves and branches."

"Sheeit, man! All right, hold up, guys. Break off some twigs and dress up like a bush. The enemy will never know we're here."

I couldn't believe the Mickey Mouse shit that was coming out of the platoon leader's head. Then I heard him crashing down the trail and the dulcet tones of his voice sang out, "What the hell is the holdup? Sergeant, get these men moving, now!"

"Sir, you can tell me to move them or tell me to have them put camouflage on, but I won't tell them to put the stuff on while they're moving. Too damned dangerous."

"Sergeant Peterson, you're not doing your job."

I half expected him to stomp his foot and pout. My personal temperature was headed toward boiling and I snapped. "Sir, my job is to carry out my mission while attending to the safety and well-being of my men. I can and will do that to the best of my ability."

"Move these men out now!"

"Yes, sir! We will move out!"

We abandoned the camouflage effort and headed down the hill. I could see it was going to be another long day.

After descending into the valley we headed north along the east bank of the river. I put Alexus out to the right with his men, then sent the point along the main trail. After a few cautious meters he stopped and signaled, pointing to his right at a narrow ditch. I moved slowly to the area and looked at a small hole under some heavy brush in a narrow gulch. You could see enough through the brush to determine that two or three VC had probably slept here as recently as last night. It was completely hidden from the air and visible only to sharp eyes on the ground. We tossed a few burning heat tabs into the dried branches and limbs and watched as it burned.

"I suppose we could put a few more branches in our pots and Charlie wouldn't know we burned that hideout," Alexus remarked in his laconic way, then continued, "That lieutenant's a real piece of work, isn't he?"

"He's a real piece of shit, if you ask me," Fryer added.

I congratulated myself on how perceptive, if in a primitive way, the men of my squad were, then we grudgingly left the fire and headed out once more. After we had moved another 500 meters, we turned west, crossed the river and picked up the main trail. I kept a flank up on the bank to improve our chances of spotting an ambush early and moved the men slowly for maximum safety. Even at that, we lost contact with the rest of the column when they stopped to check out a branch off the trail. I did a quick radio check, then we rested in place while they backtracked to the main trail, then caught up with us. I spoke to the Weapons Squad leader as the gun crew came into sight.

"Yo—Sergeant Watley and the gun crew. Good to see you guys again. What brings you to this part of the country?" A small, wry grin worked its way onto the face of the thin black man and he spoke quietly.

"Mostly my draft board. That green-assed lieutenant almost got us lost back there. We've been out here how long now?"

"Eighteen-nineteen days. Seems like a year."

"Eighteen days and he still don't know shit about the territory. If he was on point, we'd wind up in the Hanoi Hilton."

"And he's such a nice guy, too. I'm still waitin' for him to say something to Martinez and his team for their work the other day. I guess he hates me so much that he'll take it out on anybody in my squad."

The word came down to move out again, so I gave Watley a minor soul shake and took the squad forward. I liked Watley. He was quiet and sincere, quick-minded and tough. He was slender, almost reedy, but he wasn't the type you'd want to push around unless you were ready to visit the dispensary. He handled the gun crew sagely while minding his business and showed a healthy respect for the enemy. I wanted him by my side if we ever hit another battle like the one on the Cambodian border.

We headed up over the bank after we passed the August 19 ambush site, then crossed the paddy to the tree line where we broke for noon chow. The 1st and 3rd platoons, with the CO, were a few hundred meters south and ready to close. There was no sign of a breeze and the temperature again today was hovering around the century mark. Perspiration had soaked through our fatigue shirts that were already stained white with body salt from the last eighteen days.

We sought refuge among the palm trees just west of the paddy and munched on C rations while scanning the trees and bushes for enemy movement. I sat down beside Underhill. "Underdog, what's happenin', ol' Breeze?"

"Pete, I've been wearin' these fatigues for three weeks now and I'm really starting to smell. I'm tired of all this shit, man— the heat, the smells, the snipers, the war. Will any of it ever make sense?"

"Hill, when I'm humpin' in this heat, I take it one step at a time. Don't even think about the big picture, it'll just make you a zombie. Take it one step and one day at a time and then when somebody tells you it's time to DEROS, get on that big freedom bird and give Vietnam the finger."

I figured this was one of my more mangled speeches and Underhill took a sideways glance to see if I was drunk or out of my head again, but hell, I was almost 12,000 miles from home—what did he expect? He was silent for a minute.

"Pete, I really think sometimes I'm losin' it. I feel like blowin' up. I wonder if I'll ever be normal again."

"You gotta go back and play some ball again, man. Let that be your focus when things get bad."

"It's the only thing that keeps me goin' now. Man, I'd love to be squattin' down behind the plate, working with the pitchers, throwing out runners. Seems so far away, now."

"Everything back in the World seems like so far away, like I read about it in a book instead of living it, Hill. Stay focused and alert, man. We gotta get outta this place."

"You've only got a week or so until the big leave. You ain't comin' back after that, are you?"

"Don't plan to. I'll lay it out for the Top Kick. I'll tell him I've done more than my share and he can carry me for the last week or so as a rear echelon adviser. But, that's a couple of weeks away. I gotta avoid snipers and ambushes until then."

Word came down to saddle up and search the hooches again. We spent an hour or more looking through the empty dwellings, then the other platoons linked up with us. After the officers had talked for another hour or so, we moved out north along a trail between the rice paddy and the tree line to our left. I switched Alexus to the point and joined in behind Galaviz.

Martinez had his team on the right flank, in the paddy. I could see a hooch at the end of the narrow rice field, setting at the base of a small hill about 200 meters north. As we moved down the trail a sniper opened up on full automatic, spraying the area and sending the men scurrying for cover behind dikes and in the ditch along the trail.

After the magazine was spent, Nuckols put the men across the paddy behind dikes, then started a classic fire and maneuver drill. Half the men would lay down a base of fire while the other half raced for the next dike. The sniper stopped the advancing troops by unleashing another torrent of bullets that kicked up dirt around them, stripping them of their desire to move forward.

I had stepped down off the trail into a ditch alongside at the first firing, but something was stirring inside me and I was getting angry and restless. Something told me to get up and I suddenly found myself running along the trail toward the source of the fire, the hooch. The men in the point team began following me and the others stopped firing. I felt like I was watching a movie with me in it, yet I knew I was running and since I could hear somebody yelling, I figured that was me, too. I knew we were still taking fire, so I swerved and veered as I moved forward.

The sniper put a few more rounds down the trail at us, but since we kept running toward his hooch, he apparently thought that we were out of our heads and made a break for the woods. The troops in the paddy opened up again, but the sniper did another Viet Cong Olympic medal winner imitation, reaching the trees in record speed and disappearing. I led my squad to the hooch, where we stopped and began gasping for air. The running, heat and tension suddenly took a toll on us.

Alexus spoke between gasps, forcing the words to leave his mouth. "Pete, you been smokin' some of that funny weed?"

"I may be nuts, guy, but you followed me. Gotta take decisive action, it fools these damn snipers. Let's check the hooch out." I gasped the words out. I wiped the sweat that was running down my face and dripping off my nose, but I didn't feel tired, I was exhilarated after messing with Charlie's mind.

I yelled at Martinez to lead his team out of the paddy and after the sniper, then Alexus and I searched the hooch and the surrounding area. We found a small bag of rice, a pair of black pajama pants and some Ho Chi Minh sandals. We also found a small mound over a bunker that the sniper had used as his firing platform just outside of the hooch. There, we hit pay dirt, causing the reticent Alexus to whistle. "Hey, Pete, look at this. Three Chicom grenades, a couple dozen rounds of ammo and some kind of mine. That old dude was fixin' to set some booby traps and raise some hell."

The lieutenant and Nuckols took a quick look at the explosives, then called in the CO. He inspected the area, then called higher while I checked with Martinez to see if he had found anything. He gave me the same old story about leaving no trace, so I sent him back to where the VC had entered the woods while the rest of the platoon pulled security. After about twenty minutes or so Sergeant Nuckols came over to where I was sitting in the shade with Underhill.

"Pete, we're gonna move out and leave you and a couple of men behind to blow that pile of ordnance. Pick a couple of men and catch up with us."

Underhill spoke without hesitation. "I'll blow it." He stood up. "Get me some wire and a cap. I've got some C-4 in my pack."

"Hill can blow it while I stand guard. Alexus can wait for us up the trail."

While the company moved out to the northeast, Underhill readied his equipment and I found my spot in an irrigation ditch about fifty feet from the hooch. He began to carefully shape a piece of plastic explosive while I unrolled a wire from a claymore mine. I put the detonator switch in my pocket and headed for the ditch. From there, I kept my eyes on the tree line. I felt alone, naked, but confident that I could take care of any situation. Hill wrapped the charge around one of the grenades and set the other stuff on top, then placed the blasting cap into the C-4. Then he trotted toward me.

"Hook 'er up, Pete, and get ready."

He slid into the ditch as I hooked the end of the wire to the switch. I handed it to him to do the honors and watched as he grinned and turned the switch. Nothing happened. He checked the wires, then tried again, but still nothing. I unhooked the wires and put the detonator a few feet away for safety and volunteered to check the charge and reset it, but Underhill shook his head.

"You know the old rule—the man who sets it up takes it down. I know how I set it, so I'll take it apart and fix it."

He spent a few minutes rechecking the wire and cap, then ambled back while I rewired the switch for firing. "If it doesn't blow this time, we'll toss a grenade into it and run like hell."

"It'll blow, Pete. This time."

He turned the switch and the charge blew with a tremendous noise, dispatching shrapnel and dirt into the hooch and through the brush. We could hear pieces of metal hissing through the air over our heads, but we were safe in the ditch. Underhill and I slapped fives, then climbed out and, in the true fashion of boys of any age and any place on earth, checked the site of the blast. Finding nothing but a small crater and some blast marks, we moved out to rejoin the company, strutting a little as we walked. Alexus was waiting just around a small bend, sitting under a tree, looking like an ad for a cigarette company.

"Helluva blast, guys. Any problems?"

"Well, you know Hill. He wanted to make it interesting, so he fired it twice."

"The first one was practice, PJ. That was fun, though."

The three old guys walked up the trail, which had now widened enough for a truck to use, acting like schoolboys without a care in the world. We were working one another over pretty good until our banter was rudely interrupted by automatic weapons fire just ahead. We took a shortcut through the brush then emerged to find the entire company spread out in a ditch along the road. The 1st Platoon had stopped to fill their canteens in a stream near an old destroyed bridge. One metal beam was still spanning the gap and the platoon was strung out along the stream bank about ten feet below, taking cover from the fire. I caught up with Sergeant Nuckols near the company CP.

"Why isn't the 1st Platoon moving? Get up, rush him or try to flank him. Hell, don't just lay there."

"There's more than one, Pete. Able says they're pinned down and can't move."

I walked out onto the road, feeling like I had my Superman outfit on again. I had absolutely no fear, although the troops probably thought it was brains that I lacked. I was tired of these damned snipers immobilizing us.

"You mean they *won't* move. Can we get some HE on the hill?"

The CO had stood up by now and was looking around, probably to see who the asshole was in the middle of the road. The sniper put another few rounds through his AK-47, but I was convinced that we were too far away for him to be effective. The Old Man and the others hit the dirt and the other troops began returning fire, but I scowled at them and yelled, "Don't fire without a target, and *don't* fire from behind me like that! Save your ammo until you see something."

I had a quick flashback to the Green Beret saying almost those same words to me back in November—I had come a long ways since then. Now I was the wise old sage dispensing orders and advice. The CO stood back up tentatively and found his voice. "Hold your fire! Get me a target, FO."

I was pacing back and forth in front of the men in the ditch, then I turned to the sergeant. "Screw it. I'm taking my men across that beam and head for our NDP. Any problems with that?"

I pointed to the CO. Nuck gave him my plan and he grinned, "What are you waiting for, Sergeant?"

I yelled at my squad to get ready to move, then tightened down the shoulder straps of my ruck and began a trot down the road. I laughed out loud as I thought of crazy Bennett and how he would have loved this. I yelled to the troops lying along the road, "Hold your fire, then fall in behind us."

We loped toward the metal beam silhouetted against the green background. It couldn't have been more than four inches wide, but I decided I didn't even want to slow down to check it out. I trotted across the beam and grinned wildly at the 1st Platoon troops who were hiding ten feet below. My ruck was banging against my hips, but it felt like it was empty and I was flying; I was in one of those zones where I knew nothing could go wrong. The sniper opened up, but I figured if he couldn't hit me when I was standing still on the road, he damned sure couldn't hit a moving target. I hit the road on the other side of the beam and kept on running, while exhorting my men and laughing. I yelled back at them, "Come on, you assholes, there's ice cream in the LZ."

I slowed to a walk as the road entered an area that was out of the sniper's sightlines, then pulled my squad to the side and watched as the company followed along, a few at a time. I looked at Martinez, sighed and winked.

"Whooo! I'm way too short for this shit, Gus. Now I know why Bennett was the way he was."

"Does everybody get that crazy when they're short? You are a lot like him, Pete, but it was kinda fun."

"Wasn't it? I felt like I could do anything there for a minute. Shit, man. Sometimes I feel like nothing can ever kill me and sometimes I know I'm never gonna get out of here alive. My mind is definitely bent."

The company continued down the road another 500 meters, then forked off onto a smaller trail and climbed a low, brush-covered knoll we had used as an NDP a few nights ago. A couple of squads checked for booby traps, then we moved in and reclaimed our old perimeter positions and began digging in. By the time the new lieutenant made his rounds, we had only dug down to the rocks again, but he said nothing as he glanced at us. I gave him a shot as he walked away.

"I don't think he loves me anymore, guys. He didn't chew my ass like he usually does."

I was feeling tired, but in a good way. I thought about my actions during the day, and although they weren't always by the book, we did flush out a sniper, captured some of his weaponry and later made it across the stream while under fire. We were ensconced in our night wagon wheel and there had been no casualties: we must have done something right. Ah, Bennett, you would have been proud of me today.

At 2000, Nuckols sent his RTO to bring me to his tent, but when I arrived he was in a meeting at the company CP hooch. I stuck my head in to harass them, but the CO didn't recognize me and became angry at the interruption. I put on my best Lieutenant Nelson don't-fuck-with-me look then spun around and walked back to my position, muttering about lack of communication and sense of humor; the Old Man didn't even remember me as the hero of the afternoon. Such were the fates of this war. At our position, Martinez and Allen were joking with Fryer, so I sat down on the edge of the hole with them.

Overhead came the drone of an aircraft; Spooky, the gunship, was readying for a run on the next hill to the west. It was time to put a little excitement into the life of those miserable snipers. The big ship adjusted its sights, then unleashed a torrent of death from the mini-Gatling guns, the rotating barrels spewing out thousands of rounds per minute. It was like a sudden rainshower of hot metal covering every square foot of its field of fire. Every fifth round was a tracer, showing the line of fire to the gun crew and, combined with the flares dumped out of the plane, creating a bizarre lighting effect—an orange night light. I had seen it several times before, but it was still a powerful sight. Allen was moved enough to remark, "That Spooky can bring some pee, can't it? I almost feel sorry for Charlie."

"Charlie brought this on himself by scaring the Old Man. Besides, he's hiding in his hole, eating some rice and reading his Ho Chi Minh book."

As I finished speaking, Spooky pulled off from its first run and began a long, lazy circle to get into position for another. I could see a few tracer rounds coming back up from the hill towards Spooky and marveled at Charlie's nerve while questioning his intelligence. Spooky would pound him all night if he didn't wise up.

Something else jumped into my mind, so I said to Fryer,

"Remember when I put you out on flank alone because you had to carry all those dink grenades that were falling apart. I didn't want you to blow us up. Then that sniper fired at you and left the rest of us alone."

"Yeah, how can I ever thank you for that?"

"That was a real character-builder, Fryer. You're a better man for the experience."

I heard the ship making its second run and took a glance at it. Something looked different, but the ship burped again and the rounds came pouring down. Martinez was looking back at the show and now he said in an urgent tone, "It's too high! That's coming right at us!"

I could hear the sound of metal whacking into the dirt around us like hailstones. I tried to roll into the foxhole, but something hit me like a hot molten hammer in the back and threw me to the ground. I felt an immense burning pain in the middle of my back and the air seemed to leave my lungs. After the initial blow, the lower half of my body, from mid-chest down, turned numb. I lay on the side of the brush-covered hill just outside my foxhole, my legs twisted and useless, in tremendous pain and discomfort, but still conscious. I tried to grasp the situation and focus; I could hear Martinez groaning in obvious agony.

"I'm hit! I'm hit! Oh, God."

I tried to speak, to cry out, but could only gasp, "I'm . . . hit. . . . I'm . . ."

I heard yelling around the perimeter, then the firing stopped. Nothing happened for a few seconds, but I could hear excited voices and men scurrying around. Then I heard Allen yell in an anguished voice, "Medic! Martinez is hit. Medic! Pete's hit, too. Medic."

After another minute or so I decided to move whatever I could. The arms worked fine, but every move brought more pain. Then I saw the medic bending over me, looking concerned as he began cutting off my shirt. I tried to speak, but could only manage a whisper. "I'm a mess, Doc. Give me some morphine, I hurt bad."

He thought for a minute, then shook his head. "I don't think I should, Pete. One of your lungs is probably punctured and I don't want to slow down your respiration."

I looked into his dark face against the eerie backlighting of the flares now being shot up by the nearby firebase since the gunship had left the area.

"Doc, I really need it. The pain is terrible."

He reached down into his bag and found a syringe and an ampule. He turned toward the light to fill the syringe and I could see by the orange-yellow glow the fear in his face. I was then even more certain that my wound was deadly serious, perhaps even fatal, yet I was still able to think clearly. If I was dying, wouldn't I be going out of my head, I wondered. I thought about Marvin and Captain Federline, who had been taken alive from the field to die later and decided I would not let that happen to me. Doc gently poked the needle into my arm and emptied its contents. A few minutes later I felt a warm glow and the level of discomfort was lessened. The drug also loosened my tongue, so I tried to joke with my squad.

"Sorry, Alexus, I don't have any damned peaches in my pack."

His nearly-always placid face was drawn with concern as he knelt down beside me and spoke gently, "Shut up, asshole. You're still trying to make the other guy feel good, aren't you? Save your breath for those nurses."

"PJ, take care of my stuff. Make sure my wallet and other crap get sent home, OK?"

"No sweat, GI. Rest up, now."

He turned away quickly, then Underhill took my hand. "Pete, Pete, what the hell did you do? Dammit, man."

Underhill was shaking his head and seemed to be close to breaking up and I realized that these guys thought I might die, so I spoke up. "I'll be all right, big fella. I want you to help carry me to the chopper and see that I'm loaded on all right. Will you do that?"

He nodded. Sergeant Watley knelt down beside him. "Pete, what about me? Can I carry the other end of that stretcher? I'd really like to."

I touched his hand and Underhill clasped both of ours in his big paw and we shared a moment of silent communion. Doc Johnson came back from working on Martinez and leaned over.

"It'll be a while before we can get a medevac chopper in here, Pete. They're cutting an LZ, so hold on, man."

"I'm not goin' anywhere, Doc. How's Martinez?"

"He'll be OK. He took a round in his chest, came out his back near the kidney. Missed his heart, so he'll make it. Company medic's taking care of him."

"Couldn't hit his heart, Doc. He doesn't have one." I thought that was funny as hell, but nobody in the group was laughing.

Fryer sat down beside me and tried to sound cheerful, but he fell short by a mile or so. "Pete, you got a million dollar wound. You're goin' home."

"Not the way I wanted to go, Fryer. Doc, I feel awful. Can you turn me over?"

He hesitated, then enlisted Fryer and Allen to gently roll me onto my side. I heard Allen whisper as he saw my entry wound.

"God, look at that."

I felt even worse there, so I had them roll me back.

"Doc, a little more morphine if you can. Ooh, man."

He shook his head and wiped the sweat off my forehead. I closed my eyes briefly, then quickly opened them and again admonished myself—don't lose consciousness, don't go to sleep, you might not wake up. Don't give up . . . don't give up. The pain in my back and through into my chest was excruciating and my legs strangely felt like they were off to one side. Some nerve end was continuing to send the message that they were still hanging over the edge of my foxhole, even though I was now lying about six feet away. After nearly a lifetime, I finally heard the whapping of the rotor cutting into the night air. Doc Johnson, Underhill and a couple of other men lifted me gently onto the stretcher and waited for the bird to land. I whispered, "I sure hope that sniper is sleeping."

Underhill and Watley picked me up as gently as they could and began to carry me to the now idling chopper. Nuckols came up and grasped my hand and said in a rough voice, "Hang on, Pete. They'll have you in the hospital in a few minutes."

I saw Danny Malarik standing with a grave look on his face. "I'm sorry, Pete. Sorry, man."

My mind was now slightly altered by the morphine, so I figured that he was referring to his palm reading and the prediction that had come true. He probably felt responsible, I thought. "Not your fault, Malarik. Don't worry."

Underhill squeezed my hand after the stretcher was placed on the floor of the hovering bird. I was losing strength, so I curtailed my speech and waved my fingers at the gathering as the chopper lifted away from the Vietnamese jungle. I resisted the temptation to lift my head and take a last look at the perimeter below and instead, fixed my gaze on the roof of the bird. I heard the medics lifting Martinez and somebody else aboard, then the pilot headed straight for the coast and a few minutes later, we landed at a MASH unit near Chu Lai. Martinez and I were carried into triage, then quickly to an X-ray unit where they photographed us from all angles. As we waited for the photos to be developed, I looked around the room. There was only one nurse, or technician, so I asked her where Martinez was. She pointed to a table on the other side of the room. I mustered most of my remaining strength and called out, "How you doin', Gus?"

"Not so good, Pete. I'm hit pretty bad. How about you?"

"Kinda bad, too. I hope we can stay together. Nurse, can we stay together in the hospital? We've been buddies for a year. . . ."

My voice trailed off and the nurse looked at me with a quick glance that was both sympathetic and submissive. Even in my state of near-delirium, just for a second, I was sure that I saw the look, the thousand-yard stare in her eyes.

"You'll probably be on the same ward tonight."

The doors swung open and a doctor came in with the X rays in his hand and pointed to me. "Get him out to the hospital ship. We can't do anything for him here. Prep the other one for OR—move!"

My heart sank a little as I heard the words, indicating the wound was as severe as I had feared. I found some added strength and lectured myself once more—don't give up. The orderlies loaded me onto another chopper and one of them sat beside me as we headed out to sea. He talked to me, urging me to hold on as we crossed the coastline.

"Don't go to sleep, troop, it's just a few minutes more. Hang on."

He admonished me a couple more times as I was losing strength and wanted desperately to let go and sleep, to surrender to the blackness that encompassed me. After what seemed to be a long period of time, but was no more than a half hour, we touched down on the deck of the USS *Repose*.

I was lifted onto a gurney and wheeled through a door into a lighted passageway. I saw a sailor, then a male nurse who was getting blurry. I tried to blink, but the demons of darkness that had surrounded me now slipped their gentle veil over me.

37

There was a warm light ahead, pulling me toward it, gently but steadily. I felt as if I were crossing a river of some kind and the light was ahead of me, drawing me onward. The more I let myself go towards it, the better it felt—warm, peaceful, lovely. I felt, rather than saw, forms, perhaps beings, reaching for me, calling to me and I wanted to join them, but for some reason, I stopped and they faded away. I was hurt and angry and I suddenly felt the urge to wake up.

I glanced around as I awoke, unsure of my surroundings. I shook my head, trying to clear the cobwebs, then wondered who was supposed to be on watch and who was minding the radio. I tried to turn, but I was strapped onto a metal frame with tubes running into and/or out of my chest, stomach, arm and penis. As I became more alert, I felt intense pain in my back and chest and my legs were numb, but tingling, like fiery needles were being inserted into them by some giant vise. In the background I could hear a record or tape playing a refrain from a popular song, "Ding dong, the witch is dead." Then I heard a voice from beside the metal frame, "Are you back with us, Sergeant? You've been gone a while."

Even though the realization was creeping over me that I had been severely wounded and was now on a hospital ship, I didn't really want to confront all of that just yet. I shut my eyes tight and remained silent as the voice told me I was on the USS *Repose* in their intensive care ward, NC-4 (like the explosive, I thought). The voice continued to attack my reverie, "When you show improvement and regain some strength, they'll ship you to Japan or back to the States."

I opened one eye slightly and saw an arm checking my vitals, then the IVs, then a syringe appeared in the hand. My hopes arose when I heard the voice again, "I'm going to give you a little more morphine. I know you're in pain. Get some rest. I'll be right here."

I slipped back into the welcome darkness—maybe I can still find that river.

On the afternoon of August 23, at 5:00 P.M., a yellow taxi made its way down County Highway X in rural Crawford County in southwestern Wisconsin. My mother looked through the kitchen window of the converted schoolhouse that was now home to the Peterson family and wondered what would bring such a vehicle to their driveway. As she answered the door, she caught a glimpse of the face of the driver and knew something was wrong. He asked if this was the Stanley V. Peterson residence and when she nodded, he asked if she was Mrs. Peterson. After another nod, he produced a telegram and asked her to sign for it. With sinking heart and trembling hands, she signed, then opened and read:

The Sec. of the Army has asked me to express his deep regret that your son, Staff Sgt. Stanley R. Peterson, was placed on the seriously ill list in Vietnam on 21 Aug 67 as the result of gunshot wounds of back, with spine, chest and abdomen involvement and paraplegia. He was on combat operation when hit by friendly fire from gunships while engaged in firefight with hostile force. In the judgment of the attending physician, his condition is of such severity that there is cause for concern, but no immediate danger to life. Please be assured that the best medical facilities, doctors, have been made available and every measure is being taken to aid him. You will be kept informed of any significant changes in his condition. Address mail to him at USS *Repose* FPO San Francisco 96601.

S/ KENNETH G WICKHAM MAJOR GENERAL USA THE ADJUTANT GENERAL

As the yellow cab pulled away, my mother straightened up, dried her tears and sent my brother after my father, who was in the tobacco field. It was time to close the family ranks.

I felt a jerk on my body and a sudden overwhelming pain that forced a grunt from my lips. I opened my eyes and took a look around. I had been unceremoniously flipped over in my Stryker frame and was now lying uncomfortably on my chest and front, looking at the deck of the ship. A male orderly brought a toothbrush with paste and told me to open my mouth. I complied and he brushed my teeth while I lay there embarrassed and ashamed of my inabilities. I wanted to break free, rip the tubes out of my body and head back to the jungle. I quickly realized that this was impossible, so I decided to carry on with my new mission—to survive. I made eye contact with the kneeling orderly as he told me to rinse and spit. My aim was bad and I spat on his hand, so I found my voice for the first time.

"Sorry, man," I whispered huskily.

"It's OK, Sarge."

"How am I doin', Seaman?" I managed to rasp. "And what day is it?"

"I'm the wrong guy to ask. The doc will be around soon. But, you're still alive and it's the morning of August 24, Thursday."

I was alive, but barely, and paralyzed from mid-chest down—was it permanent? I had been unconscious or nearly so for over two days. It was time to take stock and figure out what I had to do to cope with the state of affairs that I found myself in, but first I needed to listen to somebody who knew about my state of affairs. Two hours later the corpsmen fastened the two parts of the frame together again and turned me belly-up to face the doctor on his rounds. I sized him up as a captain or the equivalent rank in the Navy, but I was certainly beyond saluting or acknowledging rank. I asked him, "Is this a permanent thing, or. . . ."

"It will take some time before we know—maybe months, a year. For now, we want to stabilize you and prevent infections so we can get you back to the States. I want you to dictate a letter to your parents so they won't be worried about how you are. The seaman will write it for you."

The seaman did write, in exquisite penmanship, the few words I could come up with, added a few of his own and helped me sign it. Then the nurse came back in with another syringe and I gladly took a nap. When I awoke, the tape player (I had deduced that it was somebody's tape of a radio broadcast from back home) was asking somebody to get me a ticket for an airplane. I shook the haziness from my head and looked up to see a Marine general standing at my bedside. He had a medal in his hand which he pinned to my pillow. He then stepped back and saluted me. "Son, as far as I'm concerned, this is the greatest honor you can receive. It signifies that you shed your blood and were willing to die for your country. Congratulations."

He saluted again and I nodded. It was all too much for me, so I asked for some more morphine after he left. It was time to check back out of the real world for a while.

"Wake up. Sergeant Peterson. Time to clean you up and turn you over."

I looked at the aide's watch and saw that it was 6:00. I didn't know if it was A.M. or P.M. and I didn't really care anymore. I did know I was in pain and some morphine would feel damn good, but there was no doctor or nurse in sight.

"We've got to get you to drink some water to flush your urinary tract. You've got a low-grade infection and we want to kill it with the antibiotics we're putting in your IV. We're going to change your colostomy, too."

My what? I glanced down as he removed a foul-smelling bloody bag from my lower abdomen and tossed it into the trash. He gently washed around an ugly-looking piece of intestine that had been formed into my new waste disposal unit, then placed another bag with an adhesive base around an opening over the aperture. Oh, man, my asshole doesn't even work now, I thought as I lay there wallowing in despair.

The orderly returned a little later with a piece of paper. "You received a message: Golden Charlie 2–1, this is an order. Get better A.S.A.P. I'll be out to see you soon. Signed, Golden Charlie 5, XO."

Lieutenant Robert E. Nelson had managed to reach across

the miles and raise my morale a few notches. I felt better, so I decided to nap without the morphine.

I awoke from a night of pain and wild, hallucinatory nightmares where I roamed the jungle all night, shooting and killing and running wild, then remembered that I had to be back in the hospital bed by morning—back into my shattered body. In the background I could hear yet another chorus of *Ding Dong*—if I had been in an enemy prison camp, I would have broken and given them all the information they wanted, then begged them to stop playing that demented melody. I twisted my head and neck back and forth to test my limits and to shake off the stiffness that had set in. When I stopped I saw a different doctor standing by my bed.

"Good morning. You know, you haven't been progressing as well as we had hoped. We're still feeding you through IV and your lung isn't clearing. We'd like to see you doing better." He said it in an accusatory tone, but I realized that he was probably trying to challenge me, to force an acceptance and test my desire. I avoided his eyes and lay wondering, since I've never been seriously injured, how the hell could I know how to react? Why was it my fault that I wasn't recuperating quickly enough? Military logic is following me even to my near-deathbed.

When he returned for his P.M. rounds, I decided to challenge him. "Doc, what the hell is my diagnosis and what's that other word for how I might do—prognosis?"

He flipped open a chart he was carrying. "OK, Sergeant. You have a fracture of the spine and your spinal cord was severed almost completely by the bullet that struck you. As you may have surmised, there is paraplegia from the T-6 level down with at least temporary loss of bladder and bowel control. The round splintered, with part of it entering and deflating the right lung; another part of it lacerated the diaphragm and liver and tore the intestine. We did a complete laminectomy of the sixth vertabra and a partial of the fifth and seventh. We have taken part of your intestine and brought it out through the stomach wall and created a colostomy which works well so far. You have a catheter for urine removal, a tube in your lower abdomen and one in your right lung for drainage. You have IVs for nourishment and administering medication and an irrigation bottle to flush your bladder. You've been through a lot already, but you should recover, barring complications."

I sucked in some air and asked the all-important question. "Is the paralysis permanent, Doctor? Will I use my legs again?"

He hesitated a second, then fudged an answer. "We can't tell for certain. It may take months before we know. But . . . the odds are against you. However, you can still lead an active life. I'll send you a nurse with a hypo. See you tomorrow."

He touched my shoulder, then left quietly and I closed my eyes and tried to think of something else. It was too much for my weary, pain-racked body and fried brain to contemplate. I had just spent eleven months battling the enemy, the jungle, the weather and the odds. Now, I was faced with the battle of my life, for my life and I wasn't prepared to deal with it. However, it was nearly time for some delicious, wonderful, dream-inducing morphine—my saving grace.

The blackness pulled me into it, sucking me downward and spinning me out of control. I went deeper and deeper into the dark, but it felt familiar, like I had been here before. I was gone . . . then I saw a light, shining softly, but warmly, pulling me back toward it. Something grabbed onto me and held me, then guided me as I rose slowly toward a surface. I broke through the barrier and became real again, awaking with a start. My face and chest were encased in sweat and my sheets had become wet from it. I knew that I had survived another battle and I knew there would be many more.

I heard, then saw, the shoes of the doctor, then felt pain as he examined the wound on my back. "It's looking a little better, Sergeant. No visible infection here. Let's get the orderlies to turn you over and I'll check your tubes."

One of the orderlies put the other part of the Stryker frame over me and began bolting it together at my feet. The other one bolted it at my head, then they each grabbed their end, counted to three and turned me over as smoothly as they could. I gave an audible gasp as the movement caused a wave of pain in my back and chest as far as I could feel. My legs and hips felt like they were encased in heavy cement and hot needles were still being pressed into them. I felt an enormous knot of pain in my groin pulsing into my lower abdomen and stomach and my right side ached in the lower lung area. Because of the nerve damage, these pains were not totally traceable, but could be caused by something real, according to the doctor.

"I'm going to remove your abdominal drain. You're starting to heal, soldier. We'll have you on your way home in a few days. How does that sound?"

Home—how could I go home like this? What would I do? I shook my head, then avoided thinking about it by changing the subject slightly. I asked the doctor, "What about the catheter? Will I be able to get along without it? I mean, will my penis work?"

"Perhaps. Some paras can train their bladder to drain at certain times by pressing on their lower abdomen."

"That's not what I meant, Doc."

"I know, but I can't tell you about other use. Each case is different. After you've healed more, they'll work on that in a hospital back in the States."

"Any idea where I might be headed, Doc?"

"I'm not familiar with Army hospitals, but I know there are some good ones. The orderly will clean you up and I'll see you later."

He left me pondering my future while the orderly bathed me with a sponge and a basin of water. "You should just get a hose and hose me down."

"Keep that sense of humor, Sarge, and you'll be all right."

Fax Washington DC 1220 EDT Mr and Mrs Stanley V. Peterson, Don't phone RR #2 Soldiers Grove Crawford Co Wis Additional information received states that your son, Staff S Stanley R. Peterson is making normal progress. However, he is still on the seriously ill list. Period of hospitalization is undetermined; evacuation to the United States is not contemplated at this time. You will be promptly advised as additional information is received. *KENNETH G WICKHAM MAJOR GENERAL USA C1480 THE ADJUTANT GENERAL. (29)1142P CDT AUG 27 67*

"Good morning, Sergeant Peterson. Good news—I think you've improved enough to be shipped to the States. Barring any unforeseen complications, you'll be medevacked to Da Nang tomorrow, the 28th, and on to a MAC flight the next day. How does that sound?"

"Scary as hell, Doc. I'd rather go back to the jungle. Tie me to a machine gun and put me on the perimeter. I hate going home like this."

"Sarge, I'm not going to b.s. you. You've got a long road ahead, but with the right attitude and a lot of rehabilitation, you can lead a long and useful life. I know that sounds like a cliché, but it's true. This is what you are now—take it from there." He paused, then added, "Use the same mental attitude and drive that got you through eleven months of combat and made you a sergeant. Don't give up."

I pondered this for a while after he left. He was right, but the pain and the overwhelming mental aspects of my debilitating injury were robbing me of my desire to carry on. I had given so much with nothing to show for it but a lousy Purple Heart and a few shreds of pride. The nation, my country, had, by virtue of improperly prosecuting the war effort, misused its warriors, thus breaking faith with a generation of its youth. Could that be possible? Was it all for nothing?

As I lay there, frustrated and hurting, I argued with myself—the reasons for waging a war in this tiny country so far from home were valid. We intended to protect them from Communism and to give them a chance for self-determination and the freedoms we enjoy. How could that be faulted? It had to be righteous, or my service and subsequent injury were, indeed, for nothing.

The country could still bail me out by changing their strategy, but it would require a change from the top down. Politicians and generals would have to admit mistakes and heads must roll. I was certain that pride and personal career aspirations would not allow this to happen, so the war would continue to be fought ville by bloody ville and paddy to deadly paddy. The blood of GIs, VC and NVA, and innocent civilians would continue to be shed the length and breadth of this ravaged land—South Vietnam.

On August 28th, I was carried from Ward C-4 to a waiting medevac chopper. As I was taken, headfirst, through the door, I saw a sailor looking down from his post on the next deck. He wore his youth like a badge, but he had a sad look on his face, so I waved and tried a grin. He waved back, then turned away; such was my last memory of the USS *Repose*. After arriving in

Da Nang, I was placed in a real hospital bed and immediately went to sleep. I woke up a few hours later to see a nurse reaching with a cool cloth to my face. She told me, "You've been thrashing around in your sleep, Sergeant. I brought you ten milligrams of Valium to calm you down." I jerked involuntarily as I heard muffled explosions a couple of klicks away, but she ignored them.

"Don't worry about that. The VC drop a few mortar rounds on Monkey Mountain every night, but they leave the hospital alone, maybe because we have a few prisoners in here."

"Sorry, ma'am. Just a reflex. If I was back in my platoon, we'd have to go check that out in the morning."

It was a good feeling to be close to the war again; I felt like I was back in my element. Home. Now I knew the feeling that those GIs in the war movies had when they ignored the doctors orders and returned to the front. Hmm, if the VC hit the hospital, I could be of some use. Then I remembered what kind of shape I was in and realized the only physical help I could give would be as an emergency sandbag. I felt a wave of self-pity and anger; I no longer had control of things because I couldn't control my body. A huge knot of frustration and anger formed in my throat and burned down to my heart. I pushed the call button and told the nurse when she came to my bed, "Ma'am, the pain is really bad tonight. Could I have some morphine so I can get back to sleep?"

"I'll ask the doctor. You know, when you get back to the World, you're going to have to get along without morphine. They'll cut you off when you get to a stateside Army hospital."

She left me pondering that cruel twist of fate: just when I thought I had figured out a way to survive in the World, she tells me that morphine won't be at my beck and call. I could see myself climbing the walls of an Army hospital, with my arms only, screaming for the drug.

"Morphine! Give me morphine! I gotta have it!"

The nurse returned with a syringe, eased it into my hip, then touched my hand gently. I looked at her face for the first time. She had blue eyes and her military-length hair was a deep auburn color, like you'd see sometimes in maple leaves in late September back home. She was pretty, but I was too tired to even follow her with my eyes.

"This will help you sleep. I'm sorry if I scared you. Once you get your strength back, you won't need this stuff anymore. Goodnight."

The next morning I was trucked to the airport at Da Nang where they loaded me and a dozen or so others on a huge C-130 cargo plane, which was fitting. Once you are dead or wounded, you become no more than cargo to the Military Machine. The inside was rigged for stretchers, so the medics strapped us along the sides of the plane, leaving room for an attendant to walk down the middle aisle. I glanced back at the rear of the plane as we waited to taxi down the runway and saw rows of shiny metal containers about the size of a casket. Then it hit me. Of course they were caskets. We were being shipped home with at least a dozen dead American soldiers. I thought of their families waiting back home, their dreams and hopes shattered, their lives in disarray.

As I lay there waiting for takeoff, the back ramp began to close. My last glimpse of Vietnam, framed by the caskets on the floor and by the top of the plane, was of a thick jungle scene outside the fence about 200 yards away. In the distance the mountains looked on serenely. Somewhere on the lower slopes of those mountains, men were fighting and dying as the war continued to take its terrible toll. The conflict had turned its back on the dead and the twisted and torn bodies of the wounded to continue its rapacious ways, hoping to devour the survivors.

The attendant brought me two small Darvons just before we taxied down the runway. He was about twenty-two, short and in need of a shave and, by the looks of the shirt with the sweaty half moons under the arms, probably a shower. He spoke quietly, "Should help you rest. Maybe you can sleep through the first leg. If you need anything, I'll be here."

We left the tarmac runway and I was certain I would see this beautiful but cursed land nevermore. Still, as I soared away on silver wings and Darvon, I felt the jungle and the conflict tugging at me, calling me back, saying, "We're not through with you yet. One way or another, you'll be back."

A few pain-filled hours later we touched down in Japan to add and subtract a few casualties, then lifted off once again with our cargo of the not-so-quick and the dead. We landed many hours later in Alaska, where more attendants and nurses checked our vital signs and bandages, wiped our faces, offered us lemonade and sent us on our way. I asked for and received more Darvon and made the last leg of the trip in a half-stupor. It wasn't as good as morphine, but it was a hell of a lot better than pain. We touched down in California on the afternoon of August 30, 1967, approximately twenty-four hours after leaving Vietnam. During that time, fifteen young Americans and dozens of Vietnamese from both sides died in combat back in the jungle, now thousands of miles and one very large mind-set away.

I was transported to the small Army hospital in Oakland, at the Army Replacement Depot where I had begun my odyssey eleven months before. The upper right side of my chest was hurting badly, so I informed the nurse and asked for some pain medication. She looked at me through steely eyes and said, "There's no doctor available. They keep sending our doctors to Vietnam or Japan. We've only got two or three on staff and they can't keep up. I'll call and try to get orders for something for you. Meanwhile, would you like some aspirin?"

She had spat the words at me like it was all my fault; the war was following me, licking at me. I was extremely fatigued, stiff, sore and slightly disoriented from the flight, so I closed my eyes for a few seconds, then heard a male voice call to me softly, hesitantly. "Sergeant, are you awake? I'd like to talk to you for a few minutes if I could."

Beside my bed stood a well-dressed handsome man in his late thirties with a microphone in his hand. Next to him was a blue-jeaned, long-haired kid in his early twenties with a television camera. The soft, syrupy voice spoke again. "I'm from Channel 3 in San Francisco. I'd like to interview you, as a returning serviceman from Vietnam, regarding the upcoming general elections in that country."

Part of me, a pain-racked, tired and wounded soldier, wanted to say no. The other part, the American from a generation who would do anything to be on TV, nodded yes. The kid set up the camera, turned on the world's brightest lights and we began talking about what we'd say. "I'll ask you if you have seen any Vietnamese politicians campaigning, and you'll say. . . ." He left it hanging.

"I did see some recently in the villages near the coast when we were doing a medical visit."

"How did you feel personally about the elections?"

"As an infantry soldier, I didn't have time to find out who was running or what they stood for. It was our job to insure their freedom so they could hold elections like these."

We rehearsed for another couple of minutes, then the camera rolled and we did the interview for real. I remember very little of the session as I was growing more tired and weaker by the second. The hippie cameraman told the newsman the sound wasn't very good and suggested we do it again. The newsman looked at me and shook his head.

"I don't think Sergeant Peterson has enough voice left to do another one, right, Sarge?" I tried a wan smile and nodded. He continued, "I think this will be on at six on Channel 3." They turned to leave, then the interviewer stopped, came back and shook my hand. "Welcome home, son."

God Almighty, I am back in the World and all I feel is tired as hell. I took a short nap, then the nurse shook my shoulder to wake me and handed me a phone on a long cord. "Give me your home number. It's time to talk to your family."

I managed to croak a few words to my mother in the farmhouse back in Bear Creek. I tried to reassure her that I was doing fine, just tired. She told me that Dad was working in the tobacco field and the Avon lady was there trying to sell her some perfume. I could tell that her voice was strained, like mine, probably from worrying about me. After we said our good-byes and I lay back on the pillow, a young aide came in with a portable TV set and hooked it up. She smiled, "You can watch yourself at six. You must be a hero or something, huh, Sergeant?"

"Or something, ma'am."

I then fell into a deep, dreamless sleep. I woke up at 9:00 P.M., looked around the room, saw the silent TV and realized I had slept through the newscast, but I didn't much care. An orderly passed by my bed, noticed I was awake and asked if I was hungry. I shook my head and asked for some water and a sleeping pill and upon receiving and swallowing it, I quickly reentered the world of somnolence.

The morning of August 31 found me being loaded into an ambulance and hauled, like a piece of meat, to the airport where I waited two hours for my flight to Denver. We landed in

the Mile High City at noon and I was unloaded and hauled to
Fitzsimmons Army Hospital, just a few blocks from the airport.
The hospital was a grand old brick-sided edifice standing five
stories above the plateau. The orderlies put my stretcher on a
gurney, handed my paperwork to the main desk and left. One
hour later, tired and hurting, I was taken to the third floor where
a nurse and two aides rolled me onto an addition called the
Neuro Porch, so named for its inhabitants, placed my stretcher
on the floor in an open spot next to the entryway and left me
alone.

By this time I was extremely sore, stiff, tired and upset that I
wasn't in a bed, but there was no one to complain to. After an
hour or so, my chest and back began to ache with every breath
and I began to moan—softly at first, then louder. I tried to stop,
but the pain was overwhelming. I hurt so badly, I thought it
would be easier to die and it would serve them right for not taking care of me. The other patients glanced, then glared at me as
the low moaning continued and you could see the words forming in their minds: "Shut up, you pussy!"

To their credit, no one spoke it aloud; it was as if I didn't exist. I stopped a nurse with a captain rank and begged for help in
the form of medication. She replied in a crisp military manner
that belied her sex. "We have no orders on you yet. The doctor
will talk to you and write orders, then you'll get something."

"You mean if I have no orders, I don't exist? I've been on the
floor for three hours and I'm really hurting."

"I'll send an aide with some water and aspirin."

The aspirin were as helpful as a Band-Aid on an amputa-
tion, but the water was nectar to my parched mouth and throat.
At 5 P.M. the doctor finally made his way to my torture chamber. He opened my file and looked at me. "Sergeant Peterson,
I'm going to examine you and ask some questions. But, first,
we're going to put you on a Circo-lectric bed frame."

He saw the relief on my face and smiled a tight smile.
"Sorry it took so long. I've been in surgery and consultations
all day."

A couple of aides lifted me onto a narrow bed situated on a
circular frame. It had a second mattress pad positioned above
the first, which could be clamped down on your body to make a

gimp sandwich. Then an electric motor would rotate the frame in a semi-circle, head to foot, placing you on your front to aid circulation and prevent bedsores. It was less painful than the Stryker frame, easier for the aides and could be adjusted to several positions. Once on the pad, I gave a deep sigh after the pain-filled hours on the floor. The doctor began his examination, physically and orally. After an hour or so, he finished, then ordered my medication. A little while later the P.M. nurse brought in a syringe filled with my salvation.

"Say goodnight, Sergeant."

"Goodnight, Sergeant. Thanks, ma'am."

The doctor stopped on his A.M. rounds September 1, shook his head at me and began speaking, "I've been reading your chart and I can't understand why you're still alive. The bullet that entered your back fractured the spine at the T5-6 vertebrae and lacerated most of your spinal cord. This caused the paralysis from the T-6 level. To answer the question in your mind—while we can't be absolutely certain that you won't have some return of sensation—the facts are that spinal cords do not regenerate. The paralysis will almost certainly be permanent and you should start from there to rehabilitate your body and your life."

He paused while I soaked in what I had suspected to be the truth since recovering consciousness on August 23. Then he began speaking slowly again. "We're going to slowly wean you off morphine. As your wounds heal the pain will moderate. You may experience ghost pains in your legs and hips, but we have no remedy for that. We're checking your urine for organisms. Your temp is 104, so you could have a problem and there could be some infection in your lung. Any questions?"

I had some, but it was too soon, so I shook my head.

"Now. I'm leaving military service after today, but I will be joining the staff as a civilian, so I'll still be around. Your doctor will be Captain Brad Billington, a good man."

He turned to leave, then flashed a thumbs-up, which I weakly returned. A good man—I had long ago learned that this was the common description and introduction when one officer spoke of another. It did not mean that the other officer was a good man, but if they did not use that tag line, you could be absolutely certain that he was not.

I began to settle in to the routines of an Army hospital. I got to know my fellow inmates: a motley group of injured military men and a couple of dependents who were happy to learn that I wasn't really a whiner. One had been involved in a jeep accident in Berlin which made him a quadriplegic; another had fallen from a telephone pole to become a para; an automobile wreck put a third in a Stryker frame to immobilize a neck fracture. One of the dependents was stricken with a cancer that was leaping around in his body, defying all medications and radiation treatments. I learned to jab and insult them as readily as they did me and each other, quickly.

The morale of the gimp squad, as we named ourselves, was propped up by our ability to laugh at ourselves. It was a razor-thin line we trod, but if we didn't laugh, we'd cry.

Over the next two weeks the antibiotics reduced my fever and killed the organisms in my urine. My lung was healing, although the capacity was reduced by sixty percent and I was slowly switched from morphine to Darvon and Valium—my new best friends. At night I popped two compound Darvons, a ten-milligram Valium and a beautiful red sleeping pill, then took my leave from this realm and into wild near-hallucinatory dreams, returning to my body just before it was time to wake up.

My parents and one of my brothers drove a thousand miles to make an emotion-filled visit, during which we choked back our tears and stifled our emotions, thus effectively reducing our conversations to small talk about family and friends—but that was plenty for me. The family only stayed for a day and a half, then hit the road back to Wisconsin. My father had always been ready to travel as far as anyone wanted, as long as he could be home before dark.

The visit raised my spirits immensely and the next day, I let a Red Cross volunteer take me outside in a rickety old wheelchair for a breath of mile high air. It felt good, but I began to get lightheaded after a few minutes and had to go in. I had been in the prone position for so long that the combination of exertion, excitement and thin air did me in.

A few days later I began to spike another high fever, in the 105 range, together with severe headaches and a stiff neck. I had become known, in fifteen days, for not complaining about pain, but this time it was so severe that I was reduced to begging for help. Blood was pulled out of every available vein in my arms, hands and feet in a search for answers to my complaints. The aides soaked my burning body in an ice bath on top of rubber sheets in my bed. I finally convinced the duty nurse to get some strong pain medication from the doctors, who were hesitant about giving me any for fear that I might lapse into a coma, by telling her to tell them, "I'd rather die than suffer like this. Give me something, I don't care what it does to me."

She finally got the orders and "bombed" me with a hypo of something powerful and I passed out for a few hours, then was "bombed" again when I woke up, as the pain and fever were still overwhelming me. The next day I was given a spinal tap and an X ray of the back. With the symptoms persisting, the doctor called to notify my parents, then I was wheeled into the operation room for exploratory surgery on my back wound. The surgeon drained a small abscess and two small arachnoid cysts the X rays had discovered along the spinal cord. He repaired the incisions, then irrigated and debrided the area with sterile saline.

When I woke up, the headache and pain had both eased, but I was sore and tired. Recovery was fairly fast and within a week I was back taking physical therapy. The therapist worked every useful muscle in my body and stretched those that had become useless. I was racked with pain again, but this time it was a good pain—the pain of overworked muscles. I was coming back. The antibiotics were discontinued and I was back exchanging insults with the boys on the porch. The young lad with cancer was experiencing some terrible side effects from the radiation treatments—nausea, vomiting, diarrhea. We tried to keep his spirits up but it was becoming difficult, for him and us.

In early October, I again spiked a high fever and suffered from neck and head pain. This time the doctors discovered I had developed bacterial meningitis. I was placed in a quarantine room and hovered on the brink for a few days, unable to keep food down and losing strength. My father and two of my brothers flew out to join me, and after a day or so I felt good enough to tell them to go back home, that I was going to make it.

A few days later my neck became stiff and I suffered extreme headaches and became weak. My parents received a telegram stating that I was seriously ill. While I was lying in my bed in the intensive care unit, my doctor received a call. I overheard him telling the callers, "Yes, it's very serious. You should come now to see him, because the prognosis is uncertain. I can tell you more when you arrive."

Even in my pain-filled state, I didn't think I was in danger of dying, so I figured he was talking about some other patient of his. Then he signed off the conversation with, "All right, I'll talk to you then, Mr. Peterson."

Then I began to feel bad. If the doctor was uncertain, what the hell was I supposed to think? As I lay there feeling sorry for myself, the nurse came in and asked if I was up to seeing a visitor. Although I wasn't, I told her yes; even on my near-deathbed, it was not in my nature to say no. When I looked up, I saw my cousin, Jim, walking up to my bed. He was passing through Denver on his way back to San Diego to resume his naval tour. He stayed for over two hours and I managed to make a couple of wisecracks. Although I was in pain and extremely weak and nauseous, we hashed over old times and I was glad he came. After he left I passed out or slept until the next day.

My father came into my room almost hesitantly. I could see the lines of worry on his face, but this time I could offer little in reassurance. That night I wavered between consciousness and the brink. My father sat next to my bed through it all—my pain became his. The only words spoken between us were questions of concern from him and grunts in answer from me. The doctors gave me a plasma transfusion, then started an intrathecol polymycin regimen.

I began to improve the following day. After my father saw I was doing a little better, he left to get some sleep and call home. When he returned he told me that my uncle had died of cancer during the night. I have always felt that there was a connection to these events; the night that I turned the corner, my uncle died. I was certain that our spirits met somewhere between Valhalla and purgatory—the quick and the dead separated by a heartbeat.

I began to feel better with each passing day throughout October. I watched with aching heart as nurses, aides and even doctors with whom I had formed close relationships were called to duty in Vietnam to serve the multiheaded monster. I surmised that the aides would spend six months or more as a combat medic and that some would not return. I pointed out to these men that, if they did their job, they would be revered by the troops of their unit. I also advised them: "Check your values at the departure depot; carry a weapon; firefights and ambushes are such fragmented battles that one or two people can easily get separated from the main unit. That's when Charlie will spot you and move in for the kill and you better be armed. Don't rush to the side of the wounded man in a firefight—wait till the shooting stops. As badly as he might be hurting, he doesn't want you to die trying to help him. Don't try to carry the burden of all that you do or see. It will only bring you down. Try to detach yourself and stay cool. Carry a journal or diary and write some of it down every day. None of what I say will mean much at first, but you'll see the wisdom of my words as time goes by. Keep your head down."

A nurse who had befriended and comforted me throughout the near-death meningitis episodes was called, as was an Army chaplain who had befriended and prayed over me often. I bade them godspeed and told them to write about their experiences, in letters if nothing else.

When the chaplain came to bid me farewell, I could see the pain and sadness of leaving his family in his eyes and face. I told him how much comfort he could bring to the men just by listening and talking as much as any other ministering. After talking for an hour or so, he left feeling a little better and I felt as if I had taken on part of his burden. If people of the cloth feel that way after each ministerial involvement, I could see how they would soon wind up carrying an impossibly heavy burden.

On November 3 an operation was performed to close my colostomy. I felt that I had regained control over a major part of my body—at long last, a victory. I continued physical therapy in the basement of the hospital and became strong enough to begin sitting in and using a wheelchair. Painstakingly, I also learned to balance and slide myself along on a bed or pad. Transferring into a wheelchair was the next logical step, but the hospital had no extra chairs with removable armrests. I continued to use an antique heavy wooden chair to get around the ward.

Going to the bathroom was another matter. After my colostomy was closed I was introduced to the hole-in-the-bed method. The lower frame had a foam mattress with a hole in the center, with sheets to match. Using springs that were part of the frame, a bedpan was attached to the underside of the mattress and the bed was placed into a sitting position. With a little help from a Silver Bullet suppository, the rest was up to Mother Nature. Therein lies a tale.

Fitzsimmons Army Hospital had a fine volunteer network that continually funneled entertainment to the various wards. On Thanksgiving night, three folksingers made their way to the Neuro Porch and began singing their mournful ballads. The inmate in the bed next to mine reached for his hand control so he could sit up and see the singers who had stopped next to him.

Once in the sitting position, he clapped his hands and sang a few protest verses along with them. At that moment nature took a hand and my roommate unloaded a perfect specimen through the hole, without suspecting a thing while I had an all too perfect view of it. The pan had been removed after his regular bowel program, so the defecation landed squarely on the floor under his bed and began radiating its normal, godawful odor.

I fought to stay under control, but I had to bury my head and gasp out my guffaws as the singers tried to locate the source of the smell while staying cool. It was my funniest moment in the Fitz—I will always remember the expressions on the faces of the folksingers and the incredulous look on my neighbor's face after I told him what he did. After the singers left, we giggled sporadically for hours and the story kept us smiling for the rest of the week.

In December I began the paperwork to facilitate my retirement from the Army. I also was informed that I would be moved to a VA Hospital before Christmas and was given a choice of either Cleveland or Memphis. Memphis was closest to western Wisconsin, so I requested it. On December 21, I was informed that I would be moving the following day, not to Memphis but to Milwaukee, which was only three hours from my home. They were opening a new spinal ward and I fit the profile. I didn't sleep much that night, but I let my mind wander as I lay there—I would not soon forget the friends I had made on the Neuro Porch and the kindnesses shown me by the staff. I was about to take another step in the long journey back to independence.

I was flown to a base in Illinois on December 22 and on to Milwaukee the next day. I was placed in a bed shortly after arriving at Wood VA Hospital and spent the afternoon watching the Packers win a playoff game, then several members of my family arrived. We celebrated for a while, then a reporter for the *Milwaukee Sentinel* asked if he could interview me for a feature on veterans in the VA Hospital at Christmas.

After he finished and my family left, the duty nurse told me I had a phone call. She and an orderly helped me onto a gurney and I was pushed to the phone—1st Sergeant Wolfe was calling from his home in California. He wished me well and sent me greetings from Martinez and some of the old gang from Charlie Company, now stationed at Fort Ord in California. I was delighted with the call and extremely happy that Martinez was doing well. A tremendous lump formed in my throat and my eyes began to swim as a kaleidoscope of images whirled around inside my head. I would have broken down if I had been alone—the memories and associations conjured up by that call were overwhelming to me.

I got into the routine at the VA Hospital right after New Year's Day and quickly learned that I was way behind. The rehabilitation was more intense in this newer hospital, with many more employees, but they had just begun accepting spinal cord–injured patients, so their procedures and equipment were based on old formulas. However, the hardworking therapists overcame this with their eagerness to teach, help and learn new methods. I responded well, after initial pain, to basic strengthening of arm, back, chest and trunk muscles and to balancing exercises. I learned to transfer in and out of the wheelchair quickly and from there worked on becoming independent.

I began lifting and resistance exercises to build my muscles up, spending an hour a day lifting weights. I also spent time in the vocational rehab and occupational therapy clinics as well as various medical clinics in the hospital. On January 30, 1968, I was given a Medical Discharge from the U.S. Army and received a 100 percent disability rating. I was free from the monster that had snatched me, and a million others, from civilian life, trained me to kill and destroy, then dropped me in a far-off jungle to fight a war for a people I knew very little about and who really didn't want me there. There, I had to learn to survive despite all my enemies—the VC and NVA, the heat and humidity, the terrain, monsoon rains, mosquitoes, leeches, snakes, diseases and friendly fire. I outlasted all but one. I had been a good soldier—nobody could say otherwise.

In late February, I began making weekend visits to my home, using tricks of transferring and maneuvering I had picked up in therapy and making up the rest. I left the VA Hospital on May 28 of the same year, driving a '68 Buick that I had purchased with my savings and back pay from August through January that arrived in one lump sum. I had learned to drive with hand controls and I headed up I-94, then took the Madison exit and followed Highway 14 to 61 to County X. I was home, but it wasn't my home, anymore.

I faced an uncertain future, a past that no one wanted to talk about and a huge chip on my shoulder. "OK, if you don't want to talk about it, you're an asshole" became my motto. I had some good friends who hung with me and a few who tried to feed off me, but I found my best friend was in a bottle. I became a near-alcoholic in order to ease the pain in my body and the torment in my mind.

The memories began to haunt me more unmercifully as I searched for a place and an identity. The places, the horrible, fear-filled moments and the long tedious hours, the friendships and the losses—oh, the losses. I would replay the firefights, the sniper fire, the explosions in my mind for hours on end. I could find no outlet for my torment, as the people of America turned their collective backs on a generation of its youth. I had a tremendous feeling of emptiness and I began to feel inadequate and impotent—like my country.

I tried to talk with other vets, those who hadn't been in 'Nam, to no avail. They dismissed it as a "pissant fight." Those who had been in-country weren't ready to talk—I soon became one of them. Over the years I grew more angry and resentful about the snubbing of my service to the country by the American public. I was also devastated by the shabby, inferior treatment by my government in its official mode (Veterans

Administration policies and benefits) and its refusal to acknowledge our efforts and sacrifices with a memorial, a parade or a day.

I tried to speak about the war with younger people from protesters to pacifists, patriots to hippies and pseudo-hippies. While I was slightly moved with the fervor that some of them believed and espoused, I was disappointed and amazed that they couldn't see that they were mostly just riding the wave in their opposition to the war. None of them seemed to look at the big picture or tried to see into their personal future when they would almost certainly reverse their beliefs in order to get on the proper career track. I also could not understand the ease with which they assumed that, because I was a soldier, I bore some guilt. Yeah, I was guilty—guilty of being poor, of caring enough for my country that I couldn't turn my back when I was called. Yes, I was guilty of being a little too innocent.

I sank into a morass with no bottom and no way out—and I did not know why. From my wounds I suffered physically, but I was devastated by the weight of my emotions; the burden of my perceived guilts and bitterness pervaded my soul, my heart and my life. My only salvation was my wife Joni, who tried to hold me together in the darkest times.

I believe that America, the military machine, America, the political animal, and America, the people, broke faith with me and my brothers. We were treated, by many, like pariahs when we were fighting, as the country wanted to believe the nasty little war that wasn't turning out right didn't really exist. Worse, we were treated as outcasts, by most, when we returned, as the nation wanted to forget the whole thing, especially any "leftover parts" such as hollow-eyed veterans with psyches scarred for life, or POW-MIAs. Because of this, I will no longer salute everything that is wrapped in the Stars and Stripes, and I will disagree with those who believe that America is always right. No man is more of a patriot than I—I love my country enough to want to point out when it is wrong, and it *is* wrong, on occasion.

When the U.S. pulled the pin on its military involvement in the war in 1973, I fell into a depression that lasted more than two years. As I watched the events of April 1975 unfold—the fall of Saigon and the demise of the Republic of South Vietnam—I wept unashamedly. I wept for my dead comrades and for the gentle Vietnamese people who were now prisoners, and for the terrible end of the arrogant dream that America had created. I cried alone and with my wife, for no one else wanted to know that someone might be hurting. All of America just wanted it to be over, so I hid my pain and buried my sorrow deep inside with my other burdens. No matter what the country believed, for those of us who fought and suffered, in body and spirit, it would never be over. For the families of the 58,000 names on the wall and the MIAs and the millions of Vietnamese dead, it would never be over.

As I watched the dedication of the Vietnam Veterans Memorial (The Wall) in 1982, I wept again. The tears rolled down my cheeks and I let loose with loud heartrending sobs as I watched and listened to interviews with Vietnam veterans tell of their problems with post-traumatic stress, Agent Orange and trying to live a normal life. I realized that these veterans were my brothers; they shared my feelings, my torment. I was no longer alone.

I have since met with some of my old comrades—Sgt. William E. Nuckols, Kevin Patterson, Donald "Alabama" Williams, Bob Sawlski, Fred Vickers, Garland Walker, Jack Betta, Arnold Martinez, Larry Vansworth, Ray Austin and Duane Duden (Bravo Company). I have talked with retired 1st Sergeant Wolfe a few times and I managed to spend a few minutes with Marshall Cain on the phone the week before he died of cancer believed to be caused by Agent Orange poisoning. We talk of our experiences, but only peripherally. We speak of people, places and events, but when the conversation turns to feelings, we back off. There is still too much pain. But we're all doing better. The reunions and meetings help our healing process, and we're turning into old veterans.

I have learned to adapt to life in a wheelchair and all it entails. I have adjusted my lifestyle to fit around my limitations and conducted myself through the years with as much energy and vigor as I could muster, including spending ten years as the president of my village. I still have not totally accepted my reversal from an active, healthy, strong young man to a wheelchair-using disabled veteran, but I am, above all else, a survivor. I will continue to adapt and I will prevail, for I am still a good soldier.

Epilogue

My generation went to war, not gladly, but confidently, filled with the enthusiasm of youthful naivete, certain that we would prevail—and damned quickly. Vietnam—the war took from us our youth, our innocence and our dreams and replaced them with a hardness that breached to the core of our souls. In our heart of hearts, surrounded by that hardened shell, were nestled our innermost feelings, our fears and cravings, our aches and desires, our primeval beasts. The layers of hardness that were added in the jungle, or tacked on by our fellow Americans once we were home, prevented their escape and kept all but our brothers from touching and entering.

We became hardened veterans; some called us zombies, or worse, and treated us as such, but we ached and wept inside. We were afraid to let it out for fear that the shell would collapse and take away the only protection in our lives. We began to act the way we were being treated—like second-class citizens, feeling that we were not good enough to belong anywhere. We were cast adrift by an ungrateful nation, our hearts and hopes shattered. We felt useless and in the way, much like the helicopters on the decks of aircraft carriers that were pushed overboard to make room for the survivors of the fall of Saigon. Would we be next?

When I think about the war, I think of the young men I served with—some of whom hadn't really lived yet. Those that survived lost their innocence and lost those important years when you raise your hell and make your life decisions, secure in your youthful confidence that it'll all work out. After 'Nam, those lads became like old men, robbed of that cocksureness, now certain of nothing. They were lost, crying out for help without saying a word, their faces frozen into the thousand-yard stare. The military-industrial complex that had devoured 58,800 of their comrades had stolen their youth, then moved onto another generation, ever-confident that someone, somewhere would start another conflagration, another feeding frenzy.

What America lost in this war was not national pride, an esoteric phenomenon at best. What America lost was not some geopolitical territory of slight importance; not the hardware that was abandoned; it was merely spent money that would have been piddled away somewhere else. What America lost was not its place among the world powers, for it was and still is the preeminent force on the planet. What America lost was so much more precious, so much more significant; the prosecution of the war cost the nation a generation of its youth, which is its future, thus putting the entire country into a malaise that lasted for the better part of two decades.

Was it all for nothing? At first I fought to convince others that my country was correct in its efforts because I needed to believe it myself in order to justify my devastating wounds. I suffered for my country. I didn't want to believe I was a relic—a part of an excellent army that won nearly every battle, but did not win a war. After a time I saw that the military efforts would not be successful without an overhaul of military tactics and strategy to include unconditional bombing throughout Vietnam, Laos and Cambodia. Since the government would never commit to this, or attempt an invasion of the North, the war was lost—not by the man in the field, but by the men behind the desks. America's young men never fought more valiantly with less support than the men who fought and died in Vietnam.

There have been many times over the years when I wrestled with the belief that dying would have been a hell of a lot easier than living with constant physical pain and the erratic, debilitating mental anguish. Since leaving the VA Hospital that first time, I have survived major surgery on my bladder and urinary tract and on my gallbladder. I have suffered seizures caused by an addiction to prescription drugs, decubiti ulcers (bedsores) that made me bedfast for eighteen months, migraine headaches, severe depression, insomnia, autonomic dysreflexia and a tremendous ache in my heart.

I am still learning to deal with the physical pain and the emotional aches though my nightmares have eased somewhat after twenty-six years. Still, in my darkest hours, I sometimes see the captain's eyes; the stacked-up bodies of the men of Alpha Company; the pleading faces of the dying women; the countenances of McCown, Marvin, Able and dozens of others. I can still hear the death cry of the soldier who knew he could not escape the grenade that landed on him, the explosions in the night, and the unmistakable, heart-stopping sound of enemy rockets whistling through a misty gray dawn. I can feel the heat, the rain, the mosquitoes and the pain from the wait-a-minute bushes tugging at my jungle fatigue shirt and ripping my flesh. And I feel the pain and sorrow that I know Fred Vickers, my old friend, fellow squad member and soulmate must have been feeling when he said, "I'll never smile again."

—*S. ROBERT PETERSON*
November 11, 1993

Glossary

As A rations, cooked
AIT Advanced Individual Training
AK-47 Soviet-made rifle carried by NVA and VC
Alpha Phonetic letter A
AO Area of operations
ARVN Army, Republic of Vietnam
ASAP As soon as possible
Beans and mothers C-ration ham and lima beans
Beaucoup French for many
Bird Helicopter
Boonie rat Infantryman
Bravo Phonetic letter B
Cs Combat rations, canned; also called C-rats
C-4 Powerful plastic explosive, also used to heat Cs
CA Combat assault
Caribou Small cargo plane, C-123
CH-47 Chinook helicopter, troop and cargo hauler, also called Shithook
CH-54 Flying Crane—largest helicopter
Charlie From Victor Charlie for Viet Cong; phonetic letter C
ChiCom Weaponry manufactured in China, usually grenades
Chieu Hoi Open arms; program to encourage surrender of NVA, VC
CIDG Civilian Irregular Defense Group; Montagnards commanded by Special Forces
Claymore Antipersonnel mines with hundreds of steel balls embedded in C-4
CO Commanding officer
Cobra Assault helicopter
CP Command Post
DefCons Defensive concentrations of artillery fire
Delta Phonetic D
DEROS Date Estimate Return from Overseas; everybody knew his
Di di pron. dee-dee; Vietnamese—to run; *di di mau* meant get the hell outta here to GIs
Dinks Slang for enemy or any Vietnamese you didn't like
Dustoff Medical evacuation
DX Direct exchange; also—to throw away
E-1 thru E-11 Army pay grades
Echo Phonetic E
EM Enlisted man
ETS Estimated Termination of Service; everybody knew his
FAC Forward air controller
Fast-mover F-4 Phantom jets
Firebase Artillery position, guarded by infantry

FNG Fuckin' new guy

FO Forward observer for artillery or air

Foxtrot Phonetic F

Frag Fragmentation grenade; also used to denote killing, sometimes of friendly officers or noncoms, by use of frag

Golf Phonetic G

Grease gun Submachine gun, .45-caliber

Grunt Infantryman, named after the sound made while humping a heavy pack, weapon, and gear in the hot jungle

Gunship A helicopter armed with rockets, mini-Gatling guns, and 40mm cannons which supported infantry

HE High explosives

Heat tabs Small, blue ignitable tablets used to heat C rations

H&I Harassment and interdiction—rounds and missions fired by artillery to disrupt enemy activity unexpectedly

Higher Commanders

Hooch Any building, tent, or hovel in Vietnam

Horn Radio

Hotel Phonetic H

Huey Helicopter of the UH-1 series; used as troop haulers and medevacs; also called Slicks for their landing gear

Hump Carrying your load while moving through the boonies

I Corps The military command area closest to North Vietnam

India Phonetic I

Juliet Phonetic J

KIA Killed in action; also called Koolaid in 1st/14th

Kilo Phonetic K

Klick Kilometer

LAW Light antitank weapon; 66mm rocket in a throwaway tube

Lima Phonetic L

LP Listening post, usually established fifty meters or more away from the main unit for early warning

LRRP Long-range reconnaissance patrol

LZ Landing zone

M-16 .223-caliber semiautomatic assault rifle, gas-operated and air-cooled; fired 650 rounds per minute on automatic; effective range 460 meters

M-60 .30-caliber machine gun, air-cooled and gas-operated; belt-fed automatic; made the difference in many battles

M-79 40mm grenade launcher; also called bloop gun

Mad minute Planned free fire to test weapons or harass Charlie

Mama-san Slang for older Vietnamese woman

MEDCAP Medical Civilian Assistance Program

Medevac Medical evacuation

MIA Missing in action

Mike Phonetic M

Montagnard Indigenous tribes living in hills

MOS Military Occupational Specialty; job code—infantry was 11B

MPC Military payment certificates; what we got instead of money

NCO Noncommissioned officer

NDP Night defensive position

November   Phonetic N
Numbah one   The greatest, best
Numbah ten   The lowest, worst
NVA   North Vietnamese Army, or one member
OD   Olive drab
OP   Observation post, established away from perimeter to observe enemy
Oscar   Phonetic O
P-38   Small can-opener for Cs
Papa   Phonetic P
Papa-san   Slang for older Vietnamese man
Piss-tube   Empty artillery shell container or similar tube buried in ground to piss in
Point   The lead man in patrol; also pointman
PRC-25   Prick-25; radio used by infantry and carried by RTO; backbreaker
Quebec   Phonetic Q
REMF   Rear echelon motherfucker
Rock 'n' roll   Firing a weapon on automatic
ROK   Republic of Korea
Romeo   Phonetic R
RPD   Soviet-made light machine gun
RPG   Rocket propelled grenade
R&R   Rest and relaxation
RTO   Radio telephone operator
Ruck   Backpack carried by infantry
RVN   Republic of Vietnam
Shammer   One who finds a way to get out of field duty by whatever means
Sierra   Phonetic S
Sit-rep   Situation report
Spooky   Large gunship with miniguns; can fire 6,000 rounds per minute; also
   called Puff, the Magic Dragon
Stand-down   Infantry unit returning to base camp for rest, training, replacement
   of personnel
Steel pot   Helmet
Tango   Phonetic T
Tee-tee   Very little
Tet   Lunar New Year in Vietnam
Top   First Sergeant; also called First Shirt
Tracer   Round with coating which leaves trail of fire
UH-1   Huey
Uniform   Phonetic U
VC   Viet Cong; enemy guerrilla and insurgent
Victor   Phonetic V
Ville   Village
Whiskey   Phonetic W
WIA   Wounded in action
Willy Peter   White phosphorous artillery round or grenade
World   Anyplace but 'Nam, especially the U.S.A.
XO   Executive officer
X-Ray   Phonetic X
Yankee   Phonetic Y
Zulu   Phonetic Z

Index

Experience the pain, the pride, and the
triumph of the Marine Corps

NOT GOING
HOME ALONE
A Marine's Story

by James J. Kirschke

All the members of 1st Lt. James J. Kirschke's mortar platoon and then rifle platoon knew what was expected of them: the Marines are America's military elite, required to train harder, fight longer, sacrifice more. Kirschke led by example in the hotly contested zone just south of the DMZ and in the dangerous An Hoa region southwest of DaNang. Sparing no one, he has written a powerful chronicle of the deadly war his Marines fought with valor.

Published by Ballantine Books.
Available at your local bookstore.

The only day-to-day account of this elite combat unit in Vietnam

DIARY OF AN AIRBORNE RANGER
A LRRP's Year in the Combat Zone

by Frank Johnson

When nineteen-year-old Frank Johnson arrived in Vietnam in 1969, he volunteered for the elite L Company Rangers of the 101st Airborne Division, a long range reconnaissance patrol (LRRP) unit. He kept a secret diary, a practice forbidden by the military to protect the security of LRRP operations. Now, more than three decades later, those hastily written pages offer a rare look at the daily operations of one of the most courageous units that waged war in Vietnam. Johnson's account is unique in the annals of Vietnam literature. It is a timeless testimony to the heroism of the LRRPs who dared to risk it all.

Published by Ballantine Books.
Available at your local bookstore.